The American Political Landscape Series

Encyclopedia of Minorities in American Politics

Titles in the American Political Landscape Series

Encyclopedia of Minorities in American Politics (2 volumes)
Encyclopedia of Religion in American Politics
Encyclopedia of Women in American Politics

The American Political Landscape Series

Encyclopedia of Minorities in American Politics

Volume 1
African Americans and Asian Americans

Edited by
Jeffrey D. Schultz, Kerry L. Haynie,
Anne M. McCulloch, and Andrew L. Aoki

Foreword by
Helen Thomas

Oryx Press
2000

The rare Arabian Oryx is believed to have inspired the myth of the unicorn. This desert antelope became virtually extinct in the early 1960s. At that time, several groups of international conservationists arranged to have nine animals sent to the Phoenix Zoo to be the nucleus of a captive breeding herd. Today, the Oryx population is over 1,000, and over 500 have been returned to the Middle East.

© 2000 by Jeffrey D. Schultz
Published by The Oryx Press
4041 North Central at Indian School Road
Phoenix, Arizona 85012-3397
http://www.oryxpress.com

Published simultaneously in Canada
Printed and bound in the United States of America

∞ The paper used in this publication meets the minimum requirements of American National Standard for Information Science—Permanence of Paper for Printed Library Materials, ANSI Z39.48, 1984.

Library of Congress Cataloging-in-Publication Data

Encyclopedia of minorities in American politics / edited by Jeffrey D. Schultz... [et al.].
    p. cm. — (The American political landscape series)
Includes bibliographical references and indexes.
ISBN 1-57356-129-0 (alk. paper)—ISBN 1-57356-148-7 (v. 1: alk. paper)—
ISBN 1-57356-149-5 (v. 2: alk. paper)
1. Minorities—United States—Political activity—Encyclopedias. 2. Afro-Americans—Politics and government—Encyclopedias. 3. Asian Americans—Politics and government—Encyclopedias. 4. Hispanic Americans—Politics and government—Encyclopedias. 5. Indians of North America—Politics and government—Encyclopedias. 6. United States—Politics and government—Encyclopedias. 7. United States—Ethnic relations—Encyclopedias. 8. United States—Race relations—Encyclopedias. I. Series. II. Schultz, Jeffrey D.
E184.A1 E574   2000
305.8'00973'03 21—dc21   99-043451
                                                               CIP

Contents

Contents

Contributors for Volume 1

Academic Advisory Board

Peter P. d'Errico
University of Massachusetts/Amherst

John A. Garcia
University of Arizona

Don Toshiaki Nakanishi
UCLA Asian American Studies Center

Raymond Winbush
Fisk University

Editors

Andrew L. Aoki
Augsburg College

Kerry L. Haynie
Rutgers University

Anne M. McCulloch
Columbia College

Contributors—African-American Section

[AAB] Abel A. Bartley
The University of Akron

[AD] Andy DeRoche
Community College of Aurora

[AJC] Akiba J. Covitz
Yale Law School

[CC] Corey Cook
University of Wisconsin

[CE] Caroline Emmons
Florida State University

[CEM] Charles E. Menifield
Mississippi State University

[CJM] Christopher J. Malone
Hunter College, The City University of New York

[DH] Dawn Herd
Florida State University

[EC] Eudora Chikwendu

[EP] Elizabeth Purdy

[FAS] Frank A. Salamone
Iona College

[FHJ] Frank H. Julian
Murray State University

[GAA] Gretchen A. Adams
University of New Hampshire

[ISM] Iain S. Maclean
James Madison University

[JCW] Jessamyn Charity West

[KC] Kareem Crayton
Stanford University

[KLH] Kerry L. Haynie
Rutgers University

[KR] Kristofer Ray

[LFW] Linda Faye Williams
University of Maryland, College Park

[LPM] Louise P. Maxwell

[LRW] Laura R. Woliver
University of South Carolina

[MRC] Mary R. Cross
Columbia College

[MWA] Mary Welek Atwell
Radford University

[PLF] Philip L. Fetzer
California Polytechnic State University

[RAM] Rachael Ann Murphey
University of North Carolina at Chapel Hill

[RLP] Richard L. Pacelle, Jr.
University of Missouri—St. Louis

[VDD] Veronica D. DiConti

[WPS] William Paul Simmons
Bethany College

[WWH] Walter W. Hill
St. Mary's College of Maryland

vii

Contributors—Asian-American Section

[AH] Arthur Hu

[ALA] Andrew L. Aoki
Augsburg College

[CGM] Cecilia G. Manrique
University of Wisconsin—La Crosse

[FHM] F.H. Min Min Lo
University of California, Berkeley

[JHT] Joan Hulse Thompson
Beaver College

[JK] Joan Kee
Harvard University

[KM] Ken Masugi
United States Air Force Academy

[MH] Michael Haas
University of Hawaii at Manoa

[MKT] Meta K. Townsend
Wagner College

[PL] Pei-te Lien
University of Utah

[RLP] Richard L. Pacelle, Jr.
University of Missouri—St. Louis

Foreword

by Helen Thomas

I have always felt greatly privileged to have a ringside seat to instant history at the White House. But I realized after a preview of the Oryx Press encyclopedias on women, religion, and minorities that there are big gaps in my education regarding the role these humanistic trends have played in American politics.

I believe the essays in these volumes are informative, objective, and in-depth, with a wealth of material for scholars, students, and researchers of all kinds. Of course, I was first drawn to the *Encyclopedia of Women in American Politics* for both personal and professional reasons. I am still outraged that women did not get the vote until 1920. Often when I am walking into the White House I look at the big black fence on Pennsylvania Avenue and I think of the suffragettes who chained themselves to it to gain the right to vote.

The strides women have made in the last half of this century are awesome, but not enough. World War II was the defining moment, but it has been a long struggle and women have miles to go to achieve true equality in the workplace.

I have often heard quoted the letter from that remarkable woman, Abigail Adams, who wrote to her husband, John Adams, on March 31, 1776, while he was attending the Continental Congress.

> I desire you would remember the ladies and be more generous and favorable to them than your ancestors. Do not put such unlimited power in the hands of the husbands.

I was covering the White House in 1961 when John F. Kennedy created the President's Commission on the Status of Women by executive order. It was considered a great leap forward in those days and the panel included the most prominent women leaders of the times, those who had reached the top in their fields. Eleanor Roosevelt, who had worked for so many years on behalf of women, was chosen as the chair.

Two years later, the Commission wrote a report that documented "pervasive discrimination against women in state and national laws in work and at schools." State commissions later pursued the goals of equal opportunity for women and followed up on complaints of sex-based employment discrimination.

Women then began to focus their efforts on ratification of the Equal Rights Amendment, but they failed to achieve the necessary two-thirds of the states. I thought it was a very sad day for the Republic. Women began to venture forth afterward more strongly into the path of political acceptance, and, by the 1970s, the women's movement to empower females had gained great momentum. But the movement hit a plateau when President Ronald Reagan moved into the White House in 1981 and the country became more conservative.

So women have had their hills and valleys, which are vividly illustrated in the biographies and the other entries in the *Encyclopedia of Women in American Politics*.

Every student of American history has some insight into the role that religion has played in the founding of the United States and into the profound impact of religious groups on the politics of different eras, dating back to colonial times. School children learn of the flight of the Pilgrims from religious persecution in England. The *Encyclopedia of Religion in American Politics* is a gold mine of information. As its introductory essay explains,

> The story of religion in American politics is largely an account of the quest to harness the moral idealism of religion for political purposes while attempting to restrain the potential of religion for bigotry. The overwhelming success of that quest for a civic-minded religion can be seen in the thriving diversity of religious groups in the United States today.

Fortunately, the *Encyclopedia* shows that religions fostered in the United States have not been all-consuming, domineering, or fanatical, so as to nurture the kind of age-old religious-cultural hatreds that have torn apart Northern Ireland, Bosnia, and the Middle East. Every day, the United States is involved in seeking to bring peace to these lands, where religion is a tinder box.

Ministers in the colonial era used their tracts and sermons to lay the groundwork for the American Revolution. The founding fathers were mostly religious, but they also devoutly believed in religious freedom.

Almost from its beginning, the United States has had a multiplicity of religions and therefore an admirable tolerance. The First Amendment stipulated that "Congress shall make no law respecting an establishment of religion or prohibiting the free exercise thereof." The founding fathers, while trying to reconcile the influences of reason and revelation on moral law, believed strongly in the separation of church and state.

Foreword

Politics in the new Republic depended on a shared morality rather than on a shared theology. The ministers of the post-colonial era fought the removal of the Cherokees from Georgia to the West, an infamous episode in American history known as the "Trail of Tears." The churches in the North were also leaders in the movement to abolish slavery, while religious institutions in the South played an equally important role on the other side of the controversy.

In this century, the best known minister in the struggle for civil rights was Martin Luther King, Jr., who first came to national attention when he spearheaded the boycott of segregated buses in Montgomery, Alabama, in 1955–56. Later, many religions banded together in support of the civil rights movement and it took a southern president, Lyndon B. Johnson, to push through Congress the Civil Rights Act of 1964 and the Voting Rights Act of 1965.

But the influence of religion in American politics during the twentieth century has swung from left to right. During the late 1970s and 1980s, the Moral Majority gained a foothold and, after its demise, was replaced by the Christian Coalition. The domestic agenda of the political conservatives includes restoring prayer in public schools and promoting family and pro-life values. Despite the strict wall that the Supreme Court has interposed between church and state in the past, recent years have seen a chipping away at that barrier with rulings permitting religious groups to gather and use schoolrooms and public facilities for their meetings.

Equally fascinating is the documentation in the *Encyclopedia of Minorities in American Politics* of the struggle for political rights of minorities, who have been historically un-der-represented in the American political system and who have had to fight to attain their rightful place as citizens. The discrimination against racial and ethnic groups is vividly chronicled in the *Encyclopedia's* biographies and historical references to past eras that were dominated by white males. Included among those discriminated against were blacks, Latinos, Asian Americans, and Native Americans. I can remember how often President John F. Kennedy was appalled to see signs at Boston job sites that read, "No Irish allowed." A sea change is occurring in the nation, and once-deprived groups are becoming increasingly involved in shaping the political dialogue in this country and in winning public office. Witness the number of big city black mayors currently holding office in the United States. Furthermore, no politician would dare to ignore the Cubans in Florida or the Hispanics in the Southwest and expect to get elected.

All this is to the good. It makes real the unity and validity of the melting pot and there is no question that these groups will have an even bigger voice in the future. My only hope and prayer is that they do not divide along ethnic and racial lines and forget that we are one people.

The three volumes in Oryx's American Political Landscape Series are a treasure trove for scholars and students, and provide the key to the significant historic trends that have made the United States great.

Helen Thomas is White House Bureau Chief for United Press International.

Preface

The last 30 years of American political history have seen dramatic strides in the impact that minorities play in U.S. politics. This two-volume set, *The Encyclopedia of Minorities in American Politics*, addresses the historical and contemporary impact of four of the largest minority groups in the United States. Divided into four sections, the *Encyclopedia* addresses the political struggles of African Americans, Asian Americans, Hispanic Americans, and Native Americans. The work draws attention to those events, people, and ideas that have shaped and will continue to shape the political dialogue of a diverse America. The last 30 years have seen civil rights movements for all four of these groups, as well as an increase in both political participation and political officeholding. These trends are likely to continue as the number of minorities continues to grow.

In selecting entries for the volume, the emphasis was placed upon being as comprehensive as limitations would allow. The work consists of nearly 2,000 alphabetically arranged entries divided into four sections. The work is the collaborative effort of more than 100 scholars. The entries cover people, events, court cases, movements, and organizations that have shaped the political struggles of African Americans, Asian Americans, Latinos, and Native Americans. Longer entries address some of the key issues that face minorities in American politics today. These "issue entries," such as those on affirmative action, immigration, bilingual education, and political participation (to name just a few), were written to give context to current politics and to show how these issues might be resolved.

Being a reference work, the *Encyclopedia* gives accurate information in manageable doses. And because a good reference work must be able to lead the reader to more information, *every entry* in the *Encyclopedia* has a bibliography that can serve as the next step for further research by the user of the volumes. In addition to bibliographies, entries are cross-referenced in two ways to aid the reader in successfully using the resources of the work. First, the work is internally cross-referenced through the use of **bold-faced** type. Bold-faced word(s) indicate to the reader that there is a separate entry on that person, event, concept, or issue. Second, many articles have **See also** listings at the end of the entry to offer other areas the reader may want to investigate. These two features, in addition to the index, will facilitate the user's ability to navigate the volumes.

The *Encyclopedia* also has appendixes. Each section offers reprints of selected important documents and speeches. Also, a directory of organizations that are directly or indirectly involved in politics is provided for each minority group. Each directory contains brief descriptions of the organization as well as contact information including Web sites (wherever possible). In addition, one general appendix for the entire *Encyclopedia* is a four-column timeline of minorities in American politics. It appears at the ends of both volumes of this *Encyclopedia*. Starting with the adoption of the Constitution and running to the present day, the timeline draws attention to the diverse history of the United States in a comparative context.

A comprehensive index covering both volumes is included in each volume. *The Encyclopedia of Minorities in American Politics* is the most comprehensive single source of its kind. It will prove an invaluable information resource for college and secondary students in political science, social science, and minority studies programs and classes, and it will answer the questions of public library patrons interested in American history or politics or in minority issues.

Acknowledgments

Every encyclopedia is the work of many people who share in the volume's success, and *The Encyclopedia of Minorities in American Politics* is no different. Kerry Haynie of Rutgers University, Anne McCulloch of Columbia College, and Andrew Aoki of Augsburg College, my coeditors, have contributed to the volume in numerous ways including editing entries, writing last-minute additions or supplying entries that were no-shows, shaping the table of contents, suggesting documents, and simply lending an ear to a swamped series editor.

The volumes' contributors also share in any praise that this work may find. All of them should take heart to know that they have helped to write a worthwhile and timely reference work. A few deserve special mention. Peter D'Errico has contributed so much to the success of this work. At the last minute, he helped fill in some holes in the text that could only be filled by a scholar of Peter's quality, graciousness, and perseverance. The same can be said of Christopher Malone, who wrote the introductory essay for the African-American section with little advance warning. It is an excellent piece and deserves the reader's attention.

Barry Katzen, a freelance editor based in White Plains, New York, deserves mention for the yeoman work he has done to clean up the text and generally improve the quality of the volume. It is undoubtedly a much better work because of his skill as an editor. George and Annie Kurian have encouraged me throughout the time it has taken to produce these volumes. They are both dear friends and constant supporters.

Jessamyn West, Bill Baron, Jeff Coburn, Sarah Hadley, Nancy Schultz, and Anne DeStefano all contributed in many ways to the successful completion of this two-volume set. Without all of these people, the work would still be sitting on my desk, far from ready to go out the door. All of them stepped up when I needed them, and they should be recognized for their efforts.

At Oryx Press, I would like to thank Martha Wilke, the person charged with author relations in the home office. Martha has always been honest and helpful to me, even when I was a difficult author. I am thankful for her help and apologize for all the trouble I have caused her along the way.

And finally, to my wife Elena and our son Sasha who are always there for me.

Part 1
African Americans

Introduction
African Americans and American Politics

by Christopher J. Malone

"The problem of the twentieth century is the problem of the color-line."

W.E.B. Du Bois, *The Souls of Black Folk*

Introduction: Race Relations at the Century's End

In February 1903, **W.E.B. Du Bois** beseeched his readers to listen as he described in detail "the strange meaning of being black here in the dawning of the Twentieth Century." Du Bois revealed in vivid and powerful terms how blacks in the United States lived in a state of "double-consciousness," behind a veil, forever striving to be "both a Negro and an American, without being cursed and spit upon by his fellows, without having the doors of Opportunity closed roughly in his face." Great works, such as Du Bois's *The Souls of Black Folk,* contain a vision large enough for all—they grant us the freedom to take from them what individually we deem vital. Yet if there was one underlying message Du Bois sought to make clear in *Souls,* it was that "the Negro Problem" in the United States had a profound effect on all Americans. "This meaning is not without interest to you, Gentle Reader," Du Bois admonished. The problem of the "color-line" was an American problem, and the history of the "raising and unveiling of that bowed human heart" of the Negro was (and is) American history.

At the dusk of the twentieth century, Du Bois's declaration still rings loudly in Americans' collective ears. It continues to force Americans to assess the state of U.S. race relations once again and to wonder aloud whether or not the problem of the twenty-first century shall also be the problem of the color-line. The twentieth century has witnessed great advances as well as unfulfilled promises, raising veils on the one hand and lowering them on the other. Americans as a nation have gone from poll taxes to political equality, from lynchings to landmark civil rights legislation, and from a segregated military to having an African American in the highest position in the armed services. Yet we have also seen civil rights leaders

gunned down for nothing more than standing on the principle of justice, race riots in every decade of the century, the rise of urban ghettos that look like demilitarized zones, and the creation of what sociologists call a permanent black underclass that shadows a vibrant black middle class—two nations within one African-American community, two souls within one body politic.

Equality under the eyes of the law has been attained in the United States. No longer are blacks assigned to the back of the bus or required to drink from a separate water fountain. No longer are blacks forced to live up to a different standard when it comes to the most basic elements of democracy. No longer is a black man told, for instance, that he must first answer the question "How many bubbles are in a bar of soap?" before he is allowed to register to vote (as he was as recently as the 1960s in Mississippi). No longer must a black woman explain all or parts of the Constitution or a state statute to register to vote—or pay a significant fee for the same right. We as a nation should take comfort in these simple strides, however obvious or small they might appear. But equality has several meanings, and while political equality has been granted, much work remains to be done toward attaining social or economic equality, which is just as vital to a nation that calls itself a democracy. For what good is freedom or political equality if there is no bread on the table?

In the United States at the end of the twentieth century, one out of every two black children lives beneath the poverty line (compared to one out of seven for whites). One-third of all African Americans live in **poverty** (compared to 11 percent for whites). The median income for a black family in 1997 was 56 percent of that for a white family. This statistic is alarming in and of itself, but when we consider that in 1967 a black family earned 59 percent of the average white family's income, we begin to question whether or not we are moving in the right direction. The average black family has secured just 8 percent of the wealth of the average white family and garners just 7 percent of the aggregate family income for the nation as a whole. Christopher Edley, professor of law at

Harvard University and special advisor to President Bill Clinton on Clinton's race initiative in America, has noted that most black families are but two paychecks away from poverty.

Infant mortality for black childbirths in the 1990s is still more than two times that for white childbirths (17 deaths per 1,000 births for blacks compared to 8 deaths per 1,000 births for whites). Six out of ten black children live in households headed by their mothers, compared to one out of six for whites. Life expectancy for blacks is 70 years, compared to 77 for whites. One out of three black males between the ages of 18 and 25 is in some part of the criminal justice system—in jail, on probation, or on parole. The leading cause of death for black males in the same age category is homicide, and, overall, blacks are nearly seven times more likely to be the victim of homicide than whites. The daily realities of life in black communities all across the United States have given rise to what Cornel West argues is a growing sense of nihilism—the belief that traditional values and principles are unfounded and that existence is senseless and useless. This belief in part explains youth violence in inner cities; despair and disillusionment overshadow the lives of many black Americans in the closing years of the twentieth century.

On yet another level, we must question where race relations stand in the United States in the late 1990s. To be sure, the days of legal segregation are a thing of the past. But if the United States is not segregated by law, isn't it nonetheless possible that Americans are segregated by heart? Is the ideal of integration, so prominent in the vision of Dr. **Martin Luther King, Jr**. and other civil rights leaders during the 1960s, also a thing of the past? In 1997, President Bill Clinton best summed up this sentiment on the fortieth anniversary of the desegregation of Central High School in Little Rock, Arkansas, when he said the following:

> Today children of every race walk through the same door, but then they often walk down different halls. Not only in this school, but across America, they sit in different classrooms, they eat at different tables. They even sit in different parts of the bleachers at the football game. Far too many communities are all white, all black, all Latino, all Asian. . . . Segregation is no longer the law, but too often it is the rule.

> The view one thus gets of race relations in the United States and the place of African Americans within the current political framework is opaque at best. Progress has occurred; but if there was progress over the course of the twentieth century, it was uneven, occurring in fits and starts. In the political climate at the end of the 1990s—where race-based affirmative action policies in employment and education were rolled back or done away with altogether, where congressional districts drawn to increase minority representation in our national government were later declared unconstitutional by the Supreme Court, and where black unemployment remained at twice the national average in a period of unprecedented economic expansion—it should behoove Americans to rededicate and commit themselves to the meaning of equality in all its various shades. Equality of opportunity is an honorable goal, but lucidity demands that we also pay keen attention to outcomes, consequences, and results. For neither equal opportunity nor democracy mean anything if we remain two nations, black and white, separate, hostile, and, for the most part, unequal.

At the start of the twentieth century, Du Bois's question of 1903—"How does it feel to be a problem?"—has perhaps been superseded by Rodney King's question of 1992—"Please, can't we all just get along?" At the least, these two questions frame the twentieth century—they are its bookends. All Americans must share collectively how "getting along" might best be attained if we are to prevent the problem of the color-line from persisting and tearing asunder the fabric of the country.

This *Encyclopedia of Minorities in American Politics*, while not necessarily providing answers to these questions, seeks at least to bring about a lucidity of the mind and a clearness of thought, such that the questions broached here can be addressed in a reasonable manner. Before we know where to proceed in American politics, we need to know what stands immediately before us, we need a comprehensive look at the current state of American politics and the place of African Americans within it. This topic is not without interest to any reader who, as Du Bois put it, is "seeking the grain of truth hidden here."

What follows is an overview of the place of African Americans within American political life on several levels. First, we look at the place of race and racism in American political culture. Next, we turn to a brief historical survey of the way race has affected American political development and the struggle African Americans have undergone for inclusion in the system. Finally, we close with thoughts on the ideal of "color blindness" in a society that is, for all intents and purposes, overly color-conscious.

Race, Racism, and American Political Culture

Since its inception, the United States has been characterized by most political theorists as the quintessential "liberal" society. Although not a unified body of thought, **liberalism** can be defined as a set of social and political beliefs, values, and attitudes that assumes the universal and equal application of the law and the existence of basic human rights superior to those of state and community. Any liberal society therefore embodies a specific set of principles or values, albeit in varying levels: liberty, equality, democracy, individualism, and constitutionalism or rule of law. However, this characterization immediately raises a red flag when we consider the plight of African Americans and the sordid history of **slavery** and subsequent **discrimination** in the United States. The question is simply this: How can there be a history of slavery, discrimination, and persistent **racism** in a society that calls itself "liberal" and that embodies all the principles just listed? Is it possible to reconcile the tenets of a liberal society with the dogged tenacity of racism in the United States, both of which were already present at the nation's origin?

The question of racism in American society at this level is a problem of American political culture—that set of beliefs and values to which the larger society aspires, if not wholeheartedly subscribes. When race and racism in the United

States are approached in this manner, two avenues of inquiry, two ways of looking at the problem, are opened to us. Borrowing from Jennifer Hochschild's *The New American Dilemma: Liberal Democracy and School Segregation* (1984) we may call these avenues of inquiry the Anomaly Thesis and the Symbiosis Thesis.

The Anomaly Thesis

When asked to reconcile racism with American political culture, our first response might be to say that the two are incompatible. Racism is anomalous to the principles of American liberal democracy; it never was or never should be part of our liberal American creed. We call this notion the Anomaly Thesis. It holds that racism is akin to weeds in a garden, and it is only through eradicating this pesky entity that the garden of American democracy can grow to its full potential. Although institutionalized racism existed in the United States for most of the country's history, it is not part of American liberalism because the principles of liberty, equality, and democracy cannot be squared with it.

The Anomaly Thesis has its origins in the Enlightenment thought that deeply influenced Americans and Europeans during the eighteenth century. In our context, it finds its clearest articulation in the principles set forth by Thomas Jefferson in the Declaration of Independence: "We hold these truths to be self-evident: that all men are created equal; that they are endowed by the Creator with certain unalienable rights; that among these are life, liberty, and the pursuit of happiness." Enlightenment thinkers such as John Locke asserted that human beings lived in a mythical state of nature before the formation of society and government. Perfect freedom and equality existed in this state of nature. In *Two Treatises of Government*, Locke argued that individuals were reasonable creatures capable of improving their social existence. Human nature was malleable because individuals could alter their circumstances. Furthermore, individuals were self-interested, concerned with their own well-being. Human beings formed a contract among themselves to protect in society what they had been endowed with by their Creator in the state of nature: life, liberty, and property. The freedom and equality found in the state of nature was not only approximated but also protected in political or civil society.

Locke and other Enlightenment theorists deeply influenced the men of the Revolutionary Era, most notably Jefferson himself. Yet these men were also troubled by the apparent contradictions between the belief that all were given, on the one hand, the gift of reason and what Jean Jacques Rousseau called "perfectibility" and, on the other hand, the practice of chattel slavery that denied the natural equality of all persons. How could one stand for the unalienable rights of life, liberty, and pursuit of happiness, only to turn around and deny slaves the opportunity for mental and moral improvement?

No one manifested more clearly the contradiction between the ideals of the Declaration of Independence and the ugly realities of slavery than Thomas Jefferson himself. Jefferson certainly abhorred slavery as a matter of principle, so much so that strong language of his on the issue was removed from an earlier draft of the Declaration by pro-slavery southerners for fear that it went too far. Jefferson wrote that King George III was waging "cruel war against human nature itself, violating its most sacred rights of life and liberty in the persons of a distant people who never offended him, captivating and carrying them into slavery. . . . [H]e is now exciting those very people to rise in arms among us, and to purchase that liberty of which he has deprived them, by murdering the people on whom he also obtruded them." Even though the rhetoric of the Revolutionary Era used the language of "slavery" to describe the treatment of the colonists by the English crown, this language could not be carried so far as to call into question completely the actual practice of chattel slavery—at least not by the large landowners of the South who had a vested interest in overthrowing the British monarchy on the one hand, but also maintaining slavery on the other.

In *Notes on the State of Virginia*, written in the decade after the Declaration of Independence, Jefferson was still afflicted with moral ambivalence over slavery, writing of its continued practice, "Indeed, I tremble for my country when I reflect that God is just." However, the same Jefferson apparently resolved the dilemma when he reached the following conclusion in the same work:

> I advance it therefore as a suspicion only, that blacks, whether originally a distinct race, or made distinct by time and circumstances, are inferior to whites in the endowments both of body and mind. It is not against experience to suppose, that different species of the same genus, or varieties of the same species, may possess different qualifications. . . . This unfortunate difference of colour, and perhaps of faculty, is a powerful obstacle to the emancipation of these people.

At the least, this passage explains how the writer of the Declaration of Independence, the ardent defender of the unalienable rights of life, liberty, and the pursuit of happiness, could keep nearly 200 slaves at Monticello until his death on July 4, 1826—50 years to the day after he penned the words of the Declaration of Independence.

With Jefferson, the Anomaly Thesis—the contradiction between racism and American political culture—made its appearance for the first time in full force. Later writers also touched upon the contradictions between the liberal democratic values of American society and the persistence of slavery and racism. In the 1830s, the French political philosopher Alexis de Tocqueville traveled across the United States and observed that the "basic fact" of American life was its "equality of conditions." Egalitarianism defined American political culture for Tocqueville. However, the eye of a visitor is always more perceptive than that of one who lives daily in his or her environs, and, in the 1830s, a full generation before the **Civil War**, Tocqueville saw clearly what was on the horizon for the United States, and what future Americans would experience to their horror.

> The most formidable of all ills that threaten the future of the Union arises from the presence of a black population upon its territory. The whites and blacks are placed in the situation of two foreign communities. These two races are fastened to each other without intermingling; and they are unable to separate entirely or to combine.

Tocqueville also predicted conditions of segregation for blacks in the United States once slavery ended.

> If I were called upon to predict the future, I should say that the abolition of slavery will, in the common course of things, increase the repugnance of the white population for the blacks. The danger of a conflict between the white and the black inhabitants *perpetually haunts the imagination of the Americans, like a painful dream* (emphasis added).

Part of this assessment rested on what Tocqueville saw in those parts of the country where slavery had been abolished. Concerning the conditions of blacks in the antebellum North, Tocqueville asserted the following:

> The prejudice of race appears to be stronger in the states that have abolished slavery than in those where it still exists; and nowhere is it so intolerant as in those states where servitude has never been known. . . . Thus the Negro is free, but he can share neither the rights, nor the pleasures, nor the labor, nor the afflictions, nor the tomb of him whose equal he has been declared to be; and he cannot meet him upon fair terms in life or death.

Tocqueville brought to light, not only for Americans of his generation, but also for succeeding generations of Americans, the character of the Anomaly Thesis. Tocqueville forcefully indicated the fundamental break that exists between the ideals, principles, and values of American democracy and its practices. Yet, perhaps nowhere was this sentiment articulated more powerfully than on July 4, 1852, in Rochester, New York, by **Frederick Douglass** to an all-white audience. In the decade before the Civil War, when the slavery issue was tearing both the political party system and the country apart, Douglass admonished his audience as follows:

> Americans! Your republican politics, not less than your republican religion, are flagrantly inconsistent. You boast of your love of liberty, your superior civilization, and your pure Christianity, while the whole political power of the nation, as embodied in the two great political parties, is solemnly pledged to support and perpetuate the enslavement of three millions of your countrymen. . . . You discourse eloquently on the dignity of labor; yet, you sustain a system which, in its very essence, casts a stigma upon labor. . . . [Y]ou notoriously hate (and glory in your hatred) all men whose skins are not colored like your own. You declare before the world . . . that you "hold these truths to be self-evident, that all men are created equal" . . . and yet, you hold securely in bondage . . . a seventh part of the inhabitants of your country.

Much the way Martin Luther King, Jr. would do over a century later, Douglass called upon Americans to live up to the principles they cherished by articulating the differences between those principles and the practices at the time.

The Symbiosis Thesis

A second response to the problem of racism in American political culture is to say that racism is every bit an ingredient of American liberalism as those lofty ideals of the American creed. Racism is not only part of the American creed, it is also part of the larger thought of the Enlightenment from which the American creed was born. For the notion of universal equality—the ideal that formed the foundation of Enlightenment political thought—actually rested on the idea that innate differences existed between races and cultures. Universal equality existed only *among* those of a certain race or stock of people, not *between* those of a certain race or stock of people. Thus, the Symbiosis Thesis asserts that the tenets of a liberal society can only be maintained if there is one group or class that maintains its superiority over another group or class.

The Symbiosis Thesis in the United States has its origins in a long line of thought traced back to a mythical past and to a mythical people, the Anglo-Saxons. In *Race and Manifest Destiny: The Origins of American Racial Anglo-Saxonism* (1981), Reginald Horsman traces the history of this thinking from its beginnings in sixteenth-century England to its culmination in the United States in the mid- to late nineteenth century. Horseman explains that the Englishmen who settled in America at the beginning of the seventeenth century brought with them "a clearly delineated religious myth of a pure English Anglo-Saxon Church, and in the seventeenth and eighteenth centuries they shared with their fellow Englishmen an elaborately developed secular myth of the free nature of Anglo-Saxon political institutions." Anglo-Saxon England before the Norman Conquest of 1066 had enjoyed freedoms embedded in the political institutions of the time unknown to date. Originally, defenders of Anglo-Saxonism glorified the character of the political institutions erected before the eighth and ninth centuries. Over time, however, the emphasis on political institutions turned to an emphasis on the innate quality of race, where only those of certain (Anglo-Saxon) bloodlines carried with them the capacity to sustain free and democratic political institutions. Horsman's point is that colonial thought of the seventeenth and eighteenth centuries came to focus more on the founders and protectors of free political institutions (i.e., those of Anglo-Saxon descent) than on the actual political institutions themselves. Innate qualities had become more important than nurturing a good and virtuous citizenry.

Not surprisingly, then, the men of the Revolutionary Era were influenced by the rhetoric of Anglo-Saxon racial superiority—perhaps just as influenced by this line of thinking as by the rhetoric of universal equality. And here we have to turn again to Thomas Jefferson, for Jefferson also stands at the center of Anglo-Saxon thought in the United States. A month after writing the Declaration of Independence, Jefferson asked: "Has not every restitution of the antient [sic] Saxon laws had happy effects? Is it not better now that we return at once into that happy system of our ancestors, the wisest and most perfect ever devised by the wit of man, as it stood before the 8th century?" Jefferson's interest in Anglo-Saxon England was to stay with him throughout his life. In the Revolutionary period, he wrote a simplified grammar of the Anglo-Saxon language in the hope of making it more accessible to all Americans; later, he made Anglo-Saxon part of the curriculum at the University of Virginia; and a year before his death, he commented that the study of Anglo-Saxon "is a hobby which too often runs away with me."

It is important here to understand the nature of the influence that Anglo-Saxonism had on the men of the Revolutionary Era, Jefferson included. As resentment grew among the elite in the colonies over British policies, the argument was made that the "People of the Colonies" were no longer English but a "distinct People," a people charged in fact with bringing about the divine mission of Anglo-Saxonism—a Protestant millennium designed to overcome Papist tyranny. The "golden age of Anglo-Saxon purity and freedom" (in Edmund Morgan's words) was upon the men of the Revolutionary era; they had to act, for they had a distinct aptness for liberty that was biologically definitive of their race. Indeed, God had ordained it. In 1765, John Adams remarked that "the settlement of America [is] the opening of a grand scene and design in Providence for the illumination of the ignorant and the emancipation of the slavish part of mankind all over the earth."

To borrow a phrase from Gordon Wood's *The Creation of the American Republic 1776–1787* (1998), Americans had become "more English than the English." Jefferson himself made it clear that the "golden age" was upon the men of his generation; in his pamphlet "A Summary View of the Rights of British Americans," written in 1774, Jefferson argued that the colonists got from their "Saxon ancestors" the right to free government and trade. However, nowhere is the notion of the "Chosen People" made more clear than in Tom Paine's "Common Sense," written two years later. Paine argued that Americans, and not the British, were the proud heirs of the constitutional republics of the Israelites of the Old Testament. The American Revolution was the crowning achievement for the "Chosen Ones": "The sun never shone on a cause of greater worth," Paine argued. "Tis not the affair of a city, a county, a province, or a kingdom; but of a continent." The Revolution marked the beginning of a new civilization and the apex of world history. For Paine, as for Adams and Jefferson, a new figure had appeared on the stage of history; in Hector St. John Crevecoeur's phrase, this "new man, the American," was to be a beacon of freedom for the rest of the world.

Yet, at the same time, this "new man" was of a certain breed or stock, and it is no coincidence that the Anglo-Saxon-centered view of a civilized nation left out peoples of darker skins (or women of any color, for that matter). Given this background, it no longer strikes us as a coincidence that Jefferson could write in his *Notes on the State of Virginia* that "This unfortunate difference of colour, and perhaps of faculty, is a powerful obstacle to the emancipation of these people." For Jefferson, like many men of the Revolutionary Era, simulta-

neously held to the principle of the unalienable rights of all and to the belief that only a certain few were destined to enjoy the fruits of these rights—to be part of the "Chosen."

Thus, the belief that Americans were the distinguished descendants of the Anglo-Saxons grew in the period after the Revolution. This argument was used increasingly by the defenders of slavery in the South in the antebellum period as the northern abolitionist movement became more visible and influential. Southern thinkers in the antebellum period actually made the case that slavery played a "nurturing" role. Thinkers such as John C. Calhoun and George Fitzhugh tried passionately to justify slavery's existence. Calhoun argued on the floor of the Senate in 1837 that slavery "is, instead of an evil, a good—a positive good." Slaves, according to Calhoun, were treated better in slavery than the poorest of the poor were treated in freedom in the North and in Europe. Calhoun concluded by "fearlessly" asserting that "the existing relation between the two races in the South. . . forms the most solid and durable foundation on which to rear *free and stable political institutions*" (emphasis added).

In several ways, Calhoun exemplified and drew out in detail white supremacist thinking in the antebellum period. First, rather than toiling in misery, slaves were actually treated well—much better than free laborers in the North. Slaves were content in slavery, and any effort to undermine that contentment would disrupt the natural order of things. Second, any sound society, such as the South, with its "free and stable political institutions," was founded upon "the peculiar institution" of slavery, and, at least for Calhoun and other defenders of slavery, there had never existed in history "a wealthy and civilized community in which one portion did not live on the labor of another; and . . . the form in which slavery exists in the South is not but one modification of this universal condition." Such reasoning prompted Richard Hofstadter to call Calhoun "the Marx of the Master Class." On the eve of the Civil War, George Fitzhugh would add a third component to white supremacist thinking as it related to American democracy by arguing in *Cannibals All! Or, Slaves without Masters* that slavery actually fit seamlessly within the notion of a Christian ethic.

> [T]he interests of all the members of a natural family, slaves included, are identical. Selfishness finds no place, because nature, common feelings and self-interest dictate to all that it is their true interest "to love their neighbor as themselves," and "to do as they would be done by,"—at least within the precincts of the family. To throw off into the world wife, children, and slaves, would injure, not benefit them. . . . Christian morality is neither difficult nor unnatural where dependent, family, and slave relations exist, and Christian morality was preached and only intended for such.

For Fitzhugh, slavery was an integral part of the Golden Rule of Christianity.

In the antebellum period, white supremacist thinking, and the racism it engendered, was a direct outgrowth of a line of thought that had its origins in the Anglo-Saxonism of the colonial period. By the middle decades of the nineteenth century the case could be made (however erroneously) that (1) blacks were happy and treated well under slavery, (2) that a sound political order rested on the belief that one race of people necessarily existed in servitude at the leisure of a dominant class, and (3) that slavery was "naturally" part of "Christian morality." This thinking defines the Symbiosis Thesis at its core, thus exposing the dark side of our American political culture. Several decades before Frederick Douglass brought to light the contradictions between slavery and the ideals embedded in the Declaration of Independence, David Walker, in his *Appeal to the Colored Citizens of the World* (1829), indicated the nature and extent to which racism was embedded in American political culture.

> The Christians, and enlightened of Europe, and some of Asia, seeing the ignorance and consequent degradation of our fathers, instead of trying to enlighten them . . . have plunged them into wretchedness, and to add to their miseries . . . tell them that they are an inferior and distinct race of beings. . . .
> For coloured people to acquire learning in this country, makes tyrants quake and tremble on their sandy foundation. Why, what is the matter? Why, they know their infernal deeds will be made known to the world. . . . The bare name of educating the coloured people, scares our cruel oppressors almost to death.

To both Douglass and Walker, American political culture in all its ambiguities, contradictions, and inconsistencies was nonetheless crystal clear. Throughout its history, the United States has struggled with the Janus-faced nature of that political culture: On the one side, attempting to live up to the self-professed ideals of equality and liberty for all; on the other, struggling to overcome the demons of white supremacy and what Du Bois called the "psychological wage of whiteness" that is so deeply embedded in the minds of many Americans. The United States is one nation forever struggling with two warring ideals.

Institutionalization of Race: The Constitution and American Political Development

From the moment a slave ship reached North American shores in 1619 with approximately two dozen indentured servants from the west coast of Africa, race became a significant part of the landscape of American politics. By the mid-seventeenth century, hereditary lifetime African slavery was instituted through several of the colonies; by the end of the century, most of colonial America had hereditary lifetime African slavery, replacing the earlier practice of bond servitude that held individuals of both African and European descent in forced labor for a certain amount of time. Gary Nash has demonstrated that the fight for independence during the Revolutionary period and the democratizing forces unleashed at that time led many Americans to question the entire practice of slavery. However, with the drafting of the Constitution in 1787, race was institutionalized and seared into the fabric of the new nation—and with it the indubitable problem of the color-line.

The Constitution is curious for the way it addresses the issue of race—or perhaps more accurately, the way it does not address the issue. On the one hand, the Framers sought to fashion a series of compromises on the issue of slavery; on the other, these compromises aspired to defer the problems slavery might create between North and South into the future. The word "slavery" does not appear in the original document and would not appear until 1865 with the adoption of the **Thirteenth Amendment** at the end of the Civil War. To be sure, the absence of the term lent more ambiguity to the issue, for both proponents and opponents of slavery argued that the Constitution firmly supported their position. The problem here, of course, is that both sides were correct to an extent. On one side, the system of slavery was protected, as we shall see; on the other, nowhere in the document does it expressly state that slavery is constitutionally the law of the land. The period of American political development from the drafting of the Constitution to the Civil War is testament to this legacy of ambiguity, compromise, and deferment: the **Fugitive Slave Act of 1793**, the **Missouri Compromise** of 1820, the **Compromise of 1850**, the **Kansas-Nebraska Act** of 1854, and even the case of ***Dred Scott v. Sandford*** (1857) are all attempts by the federal government to appease each side on the question of slavery—all of which really had the effect of appeasing no one. After the Civil War and into the twentieth century, race has been a major factor—if not the most important factor—in the political development of the nation.

Realizing that drafting a new Constitution would be impossible if a compromise over slavery was not crafted, the framers went to work to appease both northern and southern delegates to the Constitutional Convention in Philadelphia in the spring and summer of 1787. Article I, section 2 states that "Representatives and direct Taxes shall be apportioned among the several States which may be included within this Union, according to their respective Numbers, which shall be determined by adding the whole Number of free Persons, including those bound to Service for a Term of Years, and excluding Indians not taxed, three fifths of all other Persons." Known as the **three-fifths clause**, this compromise provision allowed states and the federal government to count every five slaves as three persons for taxation and representation purposes. The reason is clear: 90 percent of all blacks lived in the South in 1790, the year of the first census. Blacks made up 30 percent of the population of the six southern states—North and South Carolina, Maryland, Delaware, Virginia, and Georgia. If the slave population was not counted at all, the South would only receive 41 percent of the original 65 seats apportioned in the House of Representatives; if slaves were to be counted as "whole" persons for representational purposes, the South would receive roughly 50 percent of the seats in the House. Thus, the three-fifths compromise gave the South 47 percent of the seats, a compromise both northern and southern framers could live with.

Article I, section 9 of the Constitution contains another compromise set forth by the framers. It states that "The Migration or Importation of such Persons as any of the States now existing shall think proper to admit, shall not be prohibited by the Congress prior to the Year one thousand eight hundred and eight , but a Tax or duty may be imposed on such Importation, not exceeding ten dollars for each Person." This clause referred to the African slave trade, and it banned Congress from even touching the issue through statute for 20 years after the Constitution was drafted. Importation of new slaves from the West African coast caused heated debate between each side of the slavery issue. However, by 1807, Congress had passed a law banning the further importation of slaves, although some 250,000 were still imported after its passage.

Article IV of the Constitution contains a compromise over slavery that constitutional scholars have argued is implicitly contradictory. Section 2 of Article IV reads: "The Citizens of Each State shall be entitled to all Privileges and Immunities of Citizens in the several States." However, it continues: "No Person held to Service or Labour in One State, under the Laws thereof, escaping into another, shall, in Consequence of any Law or Regulation therein, be discharged from such Service or Labour; but shall be delivered up on Claim of the Party whom Such Service or Labour may be due." Fugitive slaves seeking freedom in northern states could make the claim that, as a resident of that state, they were entitled to the rights that any other resident was entitled to. On the other hand, southern slaveholders could make the case that the "Fugitive Slave Clause" compelled northern states to return fugitive slaves to their rightful owners. The ostensible contradiction between these two clauses in the Constitution formed the basis of the famous *Dred Scott v. Sandford* case of 1857.

The legacy of the Constitution was such that race became woven into the fabric of the new nation at the outset. Writing 200 years later to commemorate the bicentennial anniversary of the Constitution, Justice **Thurgood Marshall** reflected on race and the Constitution and how the founders dealt with the issue, but also what that meant for the United States in 1987. "For a sense of the evolving nature of the Constitution," stated Marshall, "we need look no further than the first three words of the document's preamble: 'We the People.' When the Founding Fathers used this phrase in 1787, they did not have in mind the majority of America's citizens." Marshall pointed out that the framers' words did not coincide with their deeds, and that this was intentional. Through a series of compromises, southern and northern elites were able to accede to one another on significant issues just as long as each got what they wanted. For the South, the continuance of the slave trade and the three-fifths clause (which gave the South more representation in the House of Representatives) were the main issues. The North wanted a more powerful central government to regulate commerce—in Alexander Hamilton's words, a federal government that had "energy." Marshall explained that "the economic interests of the regions coalesced: New Englanders engaged in the 'carrying trade' would profit from transporting slaves from Africa as well as goods produced in America by slave labor. The perpetuation of slavery ensured the primary source of wealth in the Southern states."

Soon after the ratification of the Constitution, Congress dealt with a growing problem southern planters were facing—runaway slaves. Thus, in 1793 they sought to strengthen the Fugitive Slave Clause of the Constitution by passing the Fugitive Slave Act, which required the federal government to assist in returning runaway slaves. Clearly this fortified the South's position on the issue of slavery; more important, however, it signaled the federal government's willingness to intervene on behalf of the slaveholding South.

Thomas Jefferson's purchase of Louisiana from the French in 1803 immediately doubled the size of the country. However, with new territories opening up, a new question arose: How would slavery be regulated in these territories while they awaited statehood? The only precedent in this matter was the Northwest Ordinance of 1787, written by the old Congress under the Articles of Confederation, which applied to the territory north of the Ohio River. One of the more significant provisions of the ordinance read: "There shall be neither slavery nor involuntary servitude in the territory, otherwise than in the punishment of crimes, whereof the party shall have been duly convicted." In the wake of the Louisiana Purchase, states were admitted both in the North and the South. However, in 1820, Congress once again stepped in to try to fashion a compromise between the proponents and opponents of slavery by forging the Missouri Compromise. The Missouri Compromise set up a boundary line to govern whether newly admitted states would enter as free or slave—to the north of the line only free states were to be admitted, to the south of the line only slave states were to be admitted. Once again, the Missouri Compromise only deferred the problem of slavery for a few decades as an imbalance in power between North and South became more evident.

The issue of slavery in the territories became more pressing with the commencement of the Mexican-American War in 1846. Immediately, Pennsylvania Democratic Congressmen David Wilmot introduced legislation (known as the Wilmot Proviso) designed to ban slavery in any new territories the war might produce. Southerners feared passage of the proviso would permanently tilt the balance of power between slave and free states. When California applied for admission as a free state in 1849, talk of secession first began to surface. In 1850, Henry Clay introduced a complex compromise that provided for admission of California as a free state; the organization of other territories acquired in the war (New Mexico and Arizona) without reference to slavery; the abolition of the slave trade (but not slavery) in the District of Columbia; and the toughening of the Fugitive Slave Laws (with the **Fugitive Slave Act of 1850**).

Of all the provisions of the Compromise of 1850, the one regarding fugitive slaves proved the most troublesome. The law created federal commissioners who had the exclusive right to decide fugitive cases. Yet the federal commissioners had to accept claims of slaveholders from state courts in slave states as "unimpeachable evidence." Marshals were then appointed to recover runaway slaves; yet these marshals received twice as much money for returning fugitive slaves than for finding on behalf of the black person. Further, fugitives could not testify in their own cause. In many instances, blacks who had enjoyed freedom in the North were dragged into slavery in the South for no justifiable reason. The Compromise of 1850 thus placed the federal government squarely on the side of the slave states in this rising conflict.

The next important development over slavery came in 1854, when Democratic Senator Stephen Douglas of Illinois drafted the Kansas-Nebraska Act. The act provided for the formation of territorial governments in Kansas and Nebraska, stipulating that each could decide the issue of slavery for themselves. This element of the argument for "popular sovereignty" essentially repealed the line drawn by the Missouri Compromise of 1820. Northern opposition intensified as the country headed for a showdown on the issue of slavery. Three short years later, Chief Justice Roger Taney delivered his decision in the Dred Scott case (1857), where he argued that slaves were not citizens and therefore had no recourse in the American judicial system. Taney further reasoned that the federal government had no authority to regulate slavery in the territories, and he intimated that states could not do away with slavery either, for doing so would violate the property rights of individuals. With the election of Abraham Lincoln in the presidential election of 1860, the country was already torn apart by the issue of slavery when southern states began to secede.

In the wake of the Civil War, the federal government moved vigorously to defend the rights of free blacks. The passage of the Thirteenth (1865), **Fourteenth** (1868), and **Fifteenth** (1870) **Amendments,** respectively, banned slavery, gave blacks the rights of citizenship and equal protection of the laws, and extended the right to vote regardless of race, color, or previous condition of servitude. Yet with the presidential election of 1876 and the Tilden-Hayes Compromise, **Reconstruction** came to a formal end, thus initiating what southerners termed "Redemption" and the dark period in American history known as Jim Crow—legal segregation.

Southern states immediately set out to deny blacks their constitutional rights on two fronts. On the one hand, they took away political rights such as voting by initiating a series of restrictions on voting that made it impossible for blacks to participate in the electoral process. Poll taxes were introduced, designed to deny poor blacks (and poor whites to an extent) the franchise. **Grandfather clauses** were put in place, which made it legal to vote only if one's grandfather could vote. Clearly, few if any freed slaves fell into this category. Literacy tests and later "understanding clauses" were instituted, both of which challenged the educational level of blacks. All these restrictions chased blacks out of the electorate, so that by the end of the nineteenth century only 1 to 2 percent of all blacks in the South could vote.

On the other hand, southern states took away the legal rights of blacks by instituting **Jim Crow laws**—statutes designed to separate the races in all public spaces. Separate bathrooms, water fountains, train cars, and accommodations in restaurants, theaters, movie houses, and hotels were all put in place so that the two worlds of black and white in the South—once intertwined so intimately under the "peculiar institution" of slavery—would forever remain separate from one another.

The Supreme Court verified the legality of segregation in the infamous *Plessy v. Ferguson* case of 1896. The Court ruled that segregation on public spaces such as trains was constitutional because "**separate but equal**" did not violate the Equal Protection Clause of the Fourteenth Amendment. The Court reasoned that political equality could be attained through statutory law, but social equality or a "commingling of the races" was something the law had no place in. In his lone dissent, Justice John Marshall Harlan rebuked this argument, saying that "our Constitution is color-blind."

The opening decades of the twentieth century saw repression in the South reach new heights. Lynchings increased tremendously during this time, and the federal government was reluctant to get involved in matters of civil rights. In the 1910s, blacks began moving to northern urban centers in considerable numbers, a "migration" that lasted through the 1960s. Several factors facilitated the move: southern white supremacist repression, the mechanization of the southern agricultural economy that pushed blacks off the farms, and the brutal effects of the Great Depression. As blacks streamed northward into cities such as Newark, New York, Chicago, Philadelphia, Detroit, and Washington, D.C., they became part of a burgeoning Democratic coalition that controlled these urban centers. However, they were faced with de facto **segregation** in housing and schooling. In the 1930s and 1940s, white Democratic leaders were reluctant to fully champion the cause of blacks, even though they had become a significant electoral base in the North. President Franklin D. Roosevelt refused to sign **anti-lynching legislation** in this period. The reason was clear: the odd and unstable New Deal coalition he constructed consisted of southern whites who favored segregation, northern blacks who opposed it, and white ethnics (South European Catholics and East European Jews) also residing in the North who were not wholly sympathetic to the cause of blacks. As long as civil rights stayed on the back burner, this coalition could hold. But only if civil rights remained in the shadows.

President Harry Truman took the positive step of desegregating the military in 1948 with **Executive Order 9981**. This move immediately sent shock waves through the white South, thus generating opposition to Truman in the presidential election of 1948 in the form of the southern Dixiecrats. Truman survived the election, but it signaled the beginning of the end of the Democratic coalition, an end that would be finalized in the mid to late 1960s.

Through the 1950s, the federal government took strides for the cause of civil rights, most notably in the landmark Supreme Court decision in ***Brown v. Board of Education*** (1954) which was argued by Thurgood Marshall and the Legal Defense Fund of the **National Association for the Advancement of Colored People (NAACP).** The Court, under the guidance of Chief Justice Earl Warren, overturned the decision in *Plessy* by arguing that "separate but equal" has no place in education. Separate schools are inherently unequal, the Court reasoned. In a second companion case (*Brown II*), the Court ordered schools to desegregate "with all deliberate speed." The decision in *Brown* energized African-American communities all over the country. Yet, while the importance of both *Brown* cases, in particular, and the overall legal strategy of civil rights leaders such as Marshall and **Charles Houston,** in general, cannot be overstated, it must also be pointed out that little happened in the cause of civil rights in their wake: the South dragged its feet on desegregation, and other institutions of the federal government moved slowly to end the abuses of white supremacy.

So what happened to tip the scales for the cause of civil rights that reached its culmination in the 1960s? One factor has to be singled out: the grassroots involvement of blacks themselves and their willingness to endure violence and even the threat of death for their cause. The **Montgomery bus boycotts** in the 1950s gave initial fuel to the movement immediately after *Brown*, with the 26-year-old Martin Luther King, Jr. at its helm. Soon boycotts turned to another successful tactic: **sit-ins.** On February 1, 1960, four black men sat down at a whites-only counter at Woolworth's in Greensborough, North Carolina, and demanded to be served. They were denied. The next day, 30 blacks returned; they too were denied, ridiculed, and spat upon. The third day, 50 blacks and four whites showed up at the same Woolworth's. Thus began another integral part of the effective strategy of the **civil rights movement.**

By the early 1960s, sit-ins, boycotts, and civil rights marches had made national news. In the comfort of their homes and through the growing medium of television, Americans watched with horror as peaceful demonstrators all over the South were sprayed down with firehoses, attacked with police dogs, beaten and dragged through the streets, and arrested by white police. The **March on Washington** in the summer of 1963 further brought the problem of civil rights to most American households, as King gave his eloquent **"I Have a Dream"** Speech. It was clear that the federal government could no longer drag its feet. The next year, President Lyndon Johnson signed the landmark **Civil Rights Act of 1964** and one year later he signed the **Voting Rights Act of 1965.** Both struck final blows to the two-pronged attack by whites on blacks in the era of Jim Crow—the former in abolishing legal segregation and discrimination, the latter in abolishing political disenfranchisement.

In the wake of these pieces of legislation, political equality was attained. Yet stubborn economic inequalities between white and black America persisted and were so deep rooted that black frustration soon reached new heights. Between 1962 and 1968, 164 ghetto revolts occurred, including the famous Watts outbreak in California in 1965. In this cauldron of discontent, the **black nationalism** movement was born, and its message of **black power**, **black separatism,** and black self-reliance came to rival the traditional civil rights movement's message of integration. In 1966, the **Black Panther Party** emerged to defend black communities from racist violence. Black nationalist leaders such as **Malcolm X**, **Huey Newton,** and **Stokely Carmichael** were of the mind that racism and white supremacist thought were so ingrained that no laws could overcome them. The message of "nonviolent resistance" now had to compete with "by any means necessary." And the only solution was to separate and build wholly black political and economic institutions.

By the late 1960s, the images white Americans were receiving in their living rooms changed dramatically: rather than seeing young black men in coat and tie and black women in dresses being hosed down and dragged through the streets for no other reason than marching peacefully, they were now witnessing black men and women attired in black leather jackets and black berets, standing at attention in military formation. They witnessed black athletes at the 1968 Summer Olympic Games in Mexico win track events and stand on the victor's platform with a black-gloved fist raised high in the air—the black-power salute. Blacks everywhere found a new sense of pride and power in the simple notion of "blackness," in the belief that for the first time in American history they had lifted the "veil." No longer were they viewed through someone else's eyes or culture; no longer were they "invisible," in Ralph Ellison's words. Yet, at least in the mind of much of white America, the civil rights movement of the 1950s and early 1960s had been replaced by nothing less than an armed resistance. And the federal government, with J. Edgar Hoover at the helm of the FBI, set out to destroy this new phase of the civil rights movement.

Black militancy gave whites the excuse to abandon the civil rights movement. By the early to mid-1970s, with Martin Luther King, Jr., Malcolm X, and **Medgar Evers** dead from gunshot wounds, with numerous members of the Black Panther Party in jail or in hiding, with southern whites fleeing the **Democratic Party** for the **Republican Party**, and with whites all over the country fleeing urban centers for the suburbs, the civil rights movement was but a mere shell of itself. By 1980, the conservative Ronald Reagan was elected to the presidency, and he followed through on his promise to cease the enforcement of most affirmative action policies. Within two decades of the peak of the civil rights movement, the hope that two worlds may become one, that black and white Americans could live peaceably among one another, was gone. As Andrew Hacker put it, the United States in the 1990s was still two nations, black and white, separate, hostile, unequal.

Contemporary American Society and the Ideal of "Color Blindness"

At the close of the nineteenth century, Justice John Marshall Harlan issued his famous dissent in *Plessy v. Ferguson*. Harlan wrote that "There is in this country no superior, dominant ruling class of citizens. There is no caste here. Our Constitution is color-blind." At the time, Harlan was railing against the Court's decision that authorized legal segregation in the South. For most of the twentieth century, defenders of civil rights for African Americans vigorously adopted Harlan's ideal of "color blindness" in our Constitution. "Separate but equal" was an insidious thought to a Thurgood Marshall or a Martin Luther King, Jr. They did everything they could to see to it that blacks were not treated separately, that they were treated just as anyone else under the privileges and immunities granted in the Constitution. Hence, the ideal of "color blindness" was the underpinning to the decision in the *Brown* case and to the goals of both the Civil Rights Act of 1964 and the Voting Rights Act of 1965. These actions on the part of the federal government guaranteed that our Constitution as such knew no dominant class or caste system. They guaranteed, in other words, an equality under the eyes of the law that had been denied to blacks for over 175 years.

But we are back to where we began these reflections on African Americans in the American political system. We noted at the outset that equality has several meanings, and for the past generation in American politics the struggle for equality for African Americans has shifted to other fronts that call into question the very ideal of a color-blind Constitution. It is often said that to get past race in America one has to talk about race in America. Similarly, we might ask whether to get to a color-blind society we need to have a color-conscious Constitution. To get to a point where race no longer matters in the United States, we need to be aware of race until relative equality exists between white and black Americans.

Persistent inequalities remain in various aspects of American economic and political life. The federal government in the late 1960s and early 1970s took steps to remedy these inequalities in the form of **affirmative action** policies in employment and education. In the 1980s and early 1990s, the government took steps in the way of **racial gerrymandering** in redistricting to boost minority representation in Congress by directing states to draw what is called "majority-minority" districts. In general, racial preferences were meant to remedy past discrimination. The Supreme Court in the Warren Court era upheld most of these government policies. Under the intellectual leadership of Justices Brennan and Marshall, the Court reasoned that contemporary society demanded a color-conscious reading of the Constitution. However, as the Court became more conservative, a color-conscious reading of the Constitution became suspect, so that by the late 1970s the Court ruled in *Regents of the University of California v. Bakke*

(1978) that quotas could not be used to achieve "diversity," and that race could only be one of many factors in admissions programs. Justice William Rehnquist went further and argued that he was not sure race could ever be used in admissions practices. In their dissent, Justices Marshall, Brennan, White, and Blackmun stated, "The position that our Constitution is color-blind has never been adopted by this Court as the proper meaning of the Equal Protection Clause."

Yet the ideal of color blindness had become the guiding judicial philosophy of the Court with regard to race in the United States. By the mid-1990s, the Court declared in *Adarand Constructors v. Pena* (1995) that "strict scrutiny" required a compelling state interest in racial classification and minority set-asides in government contracting work. In the same period, the Court decided in two important cases (**Shaw v. Reno** and *Miller v. Johnson*) that redistricting was unconstitutional when lines for congressional districts were drawn solely on the basis of race. In the wake of the 1990 census, numerous majority-minority districts were created in accordance with the **Voting Rights Act Amendments of 1982.** Black representation in Congress nearly doubled, so that in the 105th Congress 39 African Americans were serving (38 in the House, one in the Senate). However, in *Shaw*, Justice Sandra Day O'Connor wrote the following:

> Racial classifications with respect to voting carry particular dangers. Racial gerrymandering, even for remedial purposes, may Balkanize us into competing racial factions; it threatens to carry us further from the goal of a political system in which race no longer matters—a goal that the Fourteenth and Fifteenth Amendments embody, and to which the Nation continues to aspire. It is for these reasons that race-based districting by our state legislatures demands close judicial scrutiny.

Justice O'Connor touched upon an age-old idea in American politics: "the goal of a political system in which race no longer matters." Or in Du Bois's words, a system where the problem of the color-line is no longer a problem. At the close of the twentieth century, it is safe to say that nearly every American cherishes the thought of living in such a political system. Perhaps the dawning of the twenty-first century should begin with this question: How do we get there? **See also** Political Leadership; Political Participation; Racial Set-Asides; Relations with Other Minority Groups; Religion and African-American Politics; War on Poverty, and the various documents and speeches reproduced in Appendix 1 to this part.

Bibliography

Allen, Theodore William. *The Invention of the White Race.* New York: Verso Press, 1994.

———. "Slavery, Racism, and Democracy." *Monthly Review* 29, no. 10 (1975).

Andreano, Ralph L. *The Economic Impact of the American Civil War.* New York: Schenkman Press, 1967.

Appiah, Kwame Anthony. *Color Conscious: The Political Morality of Race.* Princeton, NJ: Princeton University Press, 1996.

———. *In My Father's House: Africa and the Philosophy of Culture.* New York: Oxford University Press, 1992.

Aptheker, Herbert. *Documentary History of the Negro People in the United States.* New York: Citadel Press, 1968.

———. *Racism, Imperialism, and Peace: Selected Essays.* Minneapolis: MEP Publications, 1989.

Asante, Molefi Kete. *Contemporary Black Thought: Alternative Analyses in Social and Behavioral Sciences.* Beverly Hills, CA: Sage Publications, 1980.

———. *The Historical and Cultural Atlas of African Americans.* New York: Macmillan, 1991.

———. *Malcolm X as Cultural Hero and Other Afrocentric Essays.* Trenton, NJ: Africa World Press, 1993.

Bartlett, Irving. *The American Mind in the Mid-nineteenth Century.* Arlington Heights, IL: Harlan Davidson, 1982.

———. *The New South, 1945–1980.* Baton Rouge: Louisiana State University Press, 1995.

———. *The Rise of Massive Resistance: Race and Politics in the South During the 1950s.* Baton Rouge: Louisiana State University Press, 1969.

———. *Southern Elections: County and Precinct Data, 1950–1972.* Baton Rouge: Louisiana State University Press, 1978.

Bartley, Numan. *Southern Politics and the Second Reconstruction.* Baltimore: Johns Hopkins University Press, 1975.

Bell, Derrick. *Faces at the Bottom of the Well: The Permanence of Racism.* New York: Basic Books, 1992.

Bennett, Lerone. *The Shaping of Black America.* Chicago: Johnson Publishing Co., 1975.

Bensel, Richard. *Sectionalism and American Political Development.* Madison: University of Wisconsin Press, 1987.

———. *Yankee Leviathan: The Origin of Central State Authority in America, 1859–1877.* New York: Cambridge University Press, 1990.

Berlin, Ira. *Slaves without Masters: The Free Negro in the Antebellum South.* New York: Pantheon, 1974.

Berman, William C. *The Politics of Civil Rights in the Truman Administration.* Columbus: Ohio State University Press, 1970.

Bilotta, James D. *Race and the Rise of the Republican Party, 1848–1865.* New York: Peter Lang, 1992.

———. *Politics and Society in the South.* Cambridge, MA: Harvard University Press, 1987.

———. *Southern Governors and Civil Rights: Racial Segregation as a Campaign Issue in the Second Reconstruction.* Cambridge, MA: Harvard University Press, 1976.

Black, Earl and Merle Black. *Politics and Society in the South.* Cambridge, MA: Harvard University Press, 1987.

———. *The Vital South: How Presidents Are Elected.* Cambridge, MA: Harvard University Press, 1992.

———. *Southern Governors and Civil Rights: Racial Segregation as a Campaign Issue in the Second Reconstruction.* Cambridge, MA: Harvard University Press, 1976.

Bloom, Jack. *Class, Race, and the Civil Rights Movement.* Bloomington: University of Indiana Press, 1987.

Boorstin, Daniel. *The Americans.* New York: Vintage Books, 1958.

Borden, Morton. *Parties and Politics in the Early Republic, 1789–1815.* Arlington Heights, IL: Harlan Davidson, 1967.

Branch, Taylor. *Parting the Waters: America in the King Years 1954–1963.* New York: Simon and Schuster, 1988.

Broadus, Mitchell and George Mitchell. *The Industrial Revolution in the South.* Baltimore: Johns Hopkins University Press, 1930.

Bruchey, Stuart Weems. *Cotton and the Growth of the American Economy, 1790–1860.* New York: Harcourt, Brace and World, 1967.

Burman, Stephen. *The Black Progress Question: Explaining the African American Predicament.* Thousand Oaks, CA: Sage Publications, 1995.

Carmines, Edward. *Prejudice, Politics, and the American Dilemma.* Stanford, CA: Stanford University Press, 1993.

Carmines, Edward and James Stimson. *Issue Evolution: Race and the Transformation of American Politics.* Princeton, NJ: Princeton University Press, 1989.

Carter, Dan. *The Politics of Rage: George Wallace, The Origins of the New Conservatism, and the Transformation of American Politics.* New York: Simon and Schuster, 1995.

Congressional Quarterly. *Presidential Elections, 1789–1992.* Washington, DC: Congressional Quarterly, 1997.

Cowley, Malcolm and Daniel Pratt Mannix. *Black Cargoes: A History of the Atlantic Slave Trade, 1518–1865.* New York: Penguin Books, 1962.

Cox, Oliver. *Caste, Class, and Race.* New York: Modern Reader, 1948.

Crew, Spencer. "The Great Migration of Afro-Americans, 1915–1940." *Monthly Labor Review* 110, no. 3 (March 1987): 34–36.

Daniel, Pete. *The Shadow of Slavery: Peonage in the South, 1901–1969.* Chicago: University of Illinois Press, 1972.

Davis, David Brion. *The Problem of Slavery in the Age of Revolution, 1770–1823.* Ithaca, NY: Cornell University Press, 1966.

———. *The Problem of Slavery in Western Culture.* Ithaca, NY: Cornell University Press, 1966.

Dawson, Michael C. *Behind the Mule: Race and Class in African-American Politics.* Princeton, NJ: Princeton University Press, 1994.

Dees, Jesse Walter and James Hadley. *Jim Crow.* Westport, CT: Negro Universities Press, 1970.

Delgado, Richard. *The Coming Race War? And Other Apocalyptic Tales of America After Affirmative Action and Welfare.* New York: New York University Press, 1996.

Douglass, Frederick. *The Life and Writings of Frederick Douglass.* Edited by Philip Foner. 5 vols. New York: International Publishers, 1955–1975.

Du Bois, W.E.B. *Against Racism: Unpublished Essays, Papers, Addresses, 1887–1961.* Amherst: University of Masachusetts, 1988.

———. *Black Folk, Then and Now: An Essay in the History and Sociology of the Negro Race.* New York: Holt and Company, 1939.

———. *The Black North: A Social Study.* New York: Arno Press, 1969.

———. *Black Reconstruction.* New York: Harcourt Press, 1935.

———. *Contributions by W.E.B. Du Bois in Government Publications and Proceedings.* Millwood, NY: Kraus-Thomson Organization, 1980.

———. *Dusk of Dawn.* Millwood, NY: Kraus-Thomson Organization, 1975.

———. *The Gift of Black Folk: The Negroes in the Making of America.* New York: Johnson Reprint, 1968.

———. *On Sociology and the Black Community.* Chicago: University Press, 1987.

———. *The Souls of Black Folk.* New York: New American Library, 1969.

———. *The Suppression of the African Slave Trade to the United States of America, 1638–1870.* New York: Russell & Russell, 1965.

Dyson, Michael Eric. *Race Rules: Navigating the Color Line.* Reading, MA: Addison-Wesley, 1996.

———. *Reflecting Black: African American Cultural Criticism.* Minneapolis: University of Minnesota Press, 1993.

Edsal, Thomas Byrne. *Chain Reaction: The Impact of Race, Rights and Taxes on American Politics.* New York: W.W. Norton, 1991.

Ezorsky, Gertrude. *Racism and Justice: The Case for Affirmative Action.* Ithaca, NY: Cornell University Press, 1991.

Ferguson, Thomas and Joel Rogers. *Right Turn: The Decline of the Democrats and the Future of American Politics.* New York: Hill and Wang, 1986.

Ferrand, Max. *United States Constitutional Convention (1787).* New Haven, CT: Yale University Press, 1911.

Fields, Barbara. "Slavery, Race, and Ideology in the United States of America." *New Left Review* (May/June 1990): 181.

Filler, Louis. *Crusade Against Slavery: Friends, Foes, Reforms, 1820–1860.* Algonac, MI: Reference Publications, 1986.

Fink, Gary M. and Merle Reed, eds. *Race, Class, and Community in Southern Labor History: Selected Papers, Seventh Southern Labor Studies.* Tuscaloosa: University of Alabama Press, 1991.

Fite, Gilbert. *Cotton Fields No More: Southern Agriculture, 1865–1980.* Lexington: University Press of Kentucky, 1984.

Foner, Eric. *Free Soil, Free Labor, Free Men.* London: Oxford University Press, 1970.

———. *Reconstruction.* New York: Harper and Row, 1988.

Fortune, Timothy Thomas. *Black and White; Land, Labor and Politics in the South.* New York: Arno Press, 1968.

Frady, Marshall. *Southerners: A Journalist's Odyssey.* New York: New American Library, 1980.

———. *Wallace.* New York: World Publishing, 1968.

Franklin, John Hope. *African Americans and the Living Constitution.* Washington, DC: Smithsonian Institute Press, 1995.

———. *Black Leaders of the Twentieth Century.* Urbana: University of Illinois Press, 1982.

———. *Color and Race.* Boston: Houghton Mifflin, 1968.

———. *The Color Line: Legacy for the Twenty First Century.* Columbia: University of Missouri Press, 1993.

———. *The Emancipation Proclamation.* Garden City, NY: Doubleday, 1963.

———. *From Slavery to Freedom.* New York: Alfred Knopf, 1987.

———. *The Militant South, 1800–1861.* Cambridge, MA: Belknap Press, 1970.

———. *The Negro in Twentieth Century America: A Reader on the Struggle for Civil Rights.* New York: Vintage Books, 1976.

———. *Race and History: Selected Essays, 1938–1988.* Baton Rouge: Louisiana State University Press, 1989.

———. *Racial Equality in America.* Chicago: University of Chicago Press, 1976.

———. *Reconstruction After the Civil War.* Chicago: University of Chicago Press, 1961.

Gaines, Stanley and Edward Reed. "Prejudice: From Allport to Du Bois." *American Psychologist* 50, no. 2 (1995): 96–103.

Gates, Henry Louis. *The Future of the Race.* New York: Alfred Knopf, 1996.

Glaberman, Martin. "Black Workers and the Labor Movement." *New Politics* 1, no. 4 (1988): 115–23.

Glaser, James. *Race, Campaign Politics, and the Realignment in the South.* New Haven, CT: Yale University Press, 1996.

Goldfield, Michael. "Class Race and Politics in the U.S.: White Supremacy as the Main Explanation." *Research in Political Economy* 12 (1990): 83–127.

Graham, Hugh Davis. *Civil Rights and the Presidency: Race and Gender in American Politics, 1960–1972.* New York: Oxford University Press, 1992.

———. *The Civil Rights Era: Origins and Development of National Policy, 1960–1972.* New York: Oxford University Press, 1989.

Greenberg, Jack. *Blacks and the Law.* Philadelphia: American Academy of Political and Social Science, 1973.

———. *Race Relations and American Law.* New York: Columbia University Press, 1959.

Hagen, Michael G. "References to Racial Issues." *Political Behavior* (Spring 1995): 49–88.

Hamby, Alonzo. *Beyond The New Deal: Harry S. Truman and American Liberalism.* New York: Columbia University Press, 1973.

Havard, William, ed. *The Changing Politics of the South.* Baton Rouge: Louisiana State University Press, 1972.

Haywood, Harry. *Negro Liberation.* New York: International Publishers, 1948.

Higginbotham, A. Leon. *Shades of Freedom: Racial Politics and Presumptions of the American Legal Process*. New York: Oxford University Press, 1996.

Hill, Herbert. *Citizen's Guide to Desegregation: A Study of Social and Legal Change in American Life*. Boston: Beacon Press, 1955.

Hochschild, Jennifer. *The New American Dilemma: Liberal Democracy and School Desegregation*. New Haven, CT: Yale University Press, 1984.

Horsman, Reginald. *Race and Manifest Destiny: The Origins of American Racial Anglo-Saxonism*. Cambridge, MA: Harvard University Press, 1981.

Huckfeldt, Robert. *Race and the Decline of Class in American Politics*. Urbana: University of Illinois Press, 1989.

Katz, Irwin. "Gordon Allport's 'The Nature of Prejudice'." *Political Psychology* 12, no. 1 (1991): 125–57.

Katznelson, Ira. *Black Men, White Cities, Race, Politics, and Migration in the United States, 1900–1930, and Britain, 1948–1968*. New York: Pantheon, 1976.

———. *City Trenches*. New York: Pantheon, 1981.

Katznelson, Ira and Bruce Pietrykowski. "Limiting Liberalism: The Southern Veto in Congress, 1933–1950." *Political Science Quarterly* 108, no. 2 (Summer 1993): 283–306.

Keech, William. *The Impact of Negro Voting: The Role of the Vote in the Quest for Equality*. Chicago: Rand McNally, 1968.

Key, V.O. *Southern Politics in State and Nation*. Knoxville: University of Tennessee Press, 1949.

Kinder, Donald. *Divided by Color: Racial Politics and Democratic Ideals*. Chicago: University of Chicago Press, 1996.

Kirby, Jack Temple. *Black Americans in the Roosevelt Era: Liberalism and Race*. Knoxville: University of Tennessee Press, 1980.

———. "Black and White in the Rural South, 1915–1954." *Agricultural History* 58, no. 3 (July 1984): 411–22.

———. "The Southern Exodus, 1910–1960: A Primer for Historians." *The Journal of Southern History* 49 (February 1983): 585–601.

Klarman, Michael J. "How *Brown* Changed Race Relations: The Backlash Thesis." *The Journal of American History* 81, no. 1 (June 1994): 81–118.

Kolchin, Peter. *American Slavery: 1619–1877*. New York: Hill and Wang, 1993.

Kousser, J. Morgan. *The Shaping of Southern Politics: Suffrage Restriction and the Establishment of the One-Party South, 1880–1910*. New Haven, CT: Yale University Press, 1974.

Ladd, Everett Carl. *Negro Political Leadership in the South*. Ithaca, NY: Cornell University Press, 1966.

Leuchtenberg, William Edward. *Franklin Roosevelt and the New Deal, 1932–1940*. New York: Harper and Row, 1963.

Levine, Bruce. *Half Slave, Half Free: The Roots of the Civil War*. New York: Hill and Wang, 1992.

Link, Arthur. *Progressivism*. Arlington Heights, IL: Harlan Davidson, 1983.

Litwack, Leon. *North of Slavery: The Negro in the Free States, 1790–1860*. Chicago: University of Chicago Press, 1961.

Logan, Rayford. *The Betrayal of the Negro from Rutherford B. Hayes to Woodrow Wilson*. London: Collier, 1965.

———. *The Negro and the Postwar: A Primer*. Washington, DC: Minorities Publishers, 1945.

———. *The Negro in the United States: A Brief History*. Princeton, NJ: Van Nostrand, 1987.

———. *What the Negro Wants*. Chapel Hill: University of North Carolina Press, 1944.

Maddox, William. "Changing Electoral Coalitions from 1952 to 1976." *Social Science Quarterly* 60, no. 2 (1979): 309–13.

———. *Speaking Truth to Power: Essays on Race, Resistance, and Radicalism*. Boulder, CO: Westview Press, 1996.

Marable, Manning. *Beyond Black and White: Transforming African-American Politics*. New York: Verso, 1995.

———. *Black American Politics from the Washington Marches to Jesse Jackson*. New York: Verso, 1985.

———. *How Capitalism Underdeveloped Black America: Problems in Race, Political Economy and Society*. Boston: South End Press, 1983.

———. *Race, Reform, and Rebellion: The Second Reconstruction in Black America, 1945–1982*. Jackson: University Press of Mississippi, 1984.

———. *W.E.B. Du Bois, Black Radical Democrat*. Boston: Twayne Press, 1986.

Marable, Manning and Leith Mullings. "The Divided Mind of Black America: Race, Ideology and Politics in the Post Civil Rights Era." *Race and Class* 36, no. 1 (1994): 61–72.

Mathews, Donald R. and James W. Prothro. *Negroes and the New Southern Politics*. New York: Harcourt Brace, 1966.

Meir, August and Elliot Rudwick. *Black Nationalism in America*. Indianapolis: Bobbs-Merrill, 1970.

Miller, William Lee. *Arguing About Slavery: The Great Battle in the United States Congress*. New York: Alfred Knopf, 1996.

Moton, Robert Russa. *What the Negro Thinks*. Garden City, NY: Doubleday, 1929. (Precursor to Myrdal's work).

Myrdal, Gunnar. *An American Dilemma: The Negro Problem and Modern Democracy*. New York: Harper and Brothers, 1944.

Nash, Gary B. *Class and Society in Early America*. Englewood Cliffs, NJ: Prentice-Hall, 1970.

———. *Race and Revolution*. Madison: Madison House, 1990.

———. *Race, Class, and Politics: Essays on American Colonial and Revolutionary Society*. Urbana: University of Illinois Press, 1986.

———. *Red, White, and Black: The Peoples of Early America*. Englewood Cliffs, NJ: Prentice Hall, 1974.

Nash, Gary B., and Richard Weiss, eds. *The Great Fear: Race in the Mind of America.* New York: Holt, Rinehart, and Winston, 1970.

Nieman, Donald. *Promises to Keep.* New York: Oxford University Press, 1991.

———, ed. *African American Life in the Post-Emancipation South.* 12 vols. New York: Garland, 1994.

Obie, Clayton, ed. *An American Dilemma Revisited: Race Relations in a Changing World.* New York: Russell Sage Foundation, 1996.

Ofari, Earl. *Blacks and Reds: Race and Class Conflict, 1919–1990.* East Lansing: Michigan State University Press, 1995.

Orfield, Gary. *The Reconstruction of Southern Education: The Schools and the 1964 Civil Rights Act.* New York: Wiley-Interscience, 1969.

Ottley, Roi. *Black Odyssey: The Story of the Negro in America.* New York: Scribners, 1948.

———. *New World A-Coming.* New York: Arno Press, 1968.

Patterson, Orlando. *Freedom.* New York: Basic Books, 1991.

Perman, Michael. *Emancipation and Reconstruction, 1862–1879.* Arlington Heights, IL: Harlan Davidson, 1987.

Pettigrew, Thomas F. "The Nature of Modern Racism in the United States." *Revue-Internationale-de-Psychologie-Sociale* 2, no. 3 (1989): 291–303.

Pickens, Ernestine Williams. *Charles W. Chesnutt and the Progressive Movement.* New York: Pace University Press, 1994.

Piven, Frances Fox. "The Case Against Urban Desegregation." In *The Politics of Turmoil: Essays on Poverty, Race and the Urban Crisis.* New York: Pantheon, 1972.

Powell, Thomas. *The Persistence of Racism in America.* Lanham, MD: University Press of America, 1992.

Quadragno, Jill. *The Color of Welfare.* New York: Oxford University Press, 1994.

Rabinowitz, Howard. *The First New South, 1865–1920.* Arlington Heights, IL: Harlan Davidson, 1992.

Rae, Nicol. *The Decline and Fall of the Liberal Republicans from 1952 to the Present.* New York: Oxford University Press, 1989.

Robinson, Donald. *Slavery in the Structure of American Politics, 1765–1820.* New York: W.W. Norton, 1979.

Roediger, David. *Wages of Whiteness: Race and the Making of the American Working Class.* London: Verso Press, 1991.

Rose, Peter Isaac. *Through Different Eyes: Black and White Perspectives on American Race Relations.* New York: Oxford University Press, 1973.

Rovere, Richard. *The Goldwater Caper.* New York: Harcourt, Brace and World, 1965.

Rowan, Carl. *The Coming Race War in America: A Wake-up Call.* Boston: Little Brown, 1996.

———. *South of Freedom.* New York: Alfred Knopf, 1952.

Simone, Timothy Maliqalim. *About Face: Race in Postmodern America.* New York: Atonomedia, 1989.

Sitkoff, Harvard. *A New Deal for Blacks: The Emergence of Civil Rights as a National Issue.* New York: Oxford University Press, 1978.

Sleeper, Jim. *The Closest of Strangers: Liberalism and the Politics of Race in New York.* New York: W.W. Norton, 1990.

Smith, Douglas. *The New Deal in the Urban South.* Baton Rouge: Louisiana State University Press, 1988.

Sniderman, Paul. *Race and Inequality: A Study in American Values.* Chatham, NJ: Chatham House Press, 1985.

Sosna, Morton. *In Search of the Silent South: Southern Liberals and the Race Issue.* New York: Columbia University Press, 1977.

Stampp, Kenneth. *The Peculiar Institution.* New York: Vintage Books, 1989.

Stewart, James Brewer. Holy Warriors: *The Abolitionists and American Slavery.* New York: Hill and Wang, 1996.

Swain, Carol. "The Future of Black Representation." *American Prospect* 23 (1995): 78–83.

Sydnor, Charles A. *The Development of Southern Sectionalism, 1819–1848.* Baton Rouge: Louisiana State University Press, 1948.

Takaki, Ronald. *Iron Cages: Race and Culture in Nineteenth Century America.* New York: Alfred Knopf, 1979.

Terkel, Studs. *How Blacks and Whites Feel About the American Obsession.* New York: New Press, 1992.

Thernstrom, Abigail. *Whose Votes Count: Affirmative Action and Minority Voting Rights.* Cambridge, MA: Harvard University Press, 1987.

Tindall, George. *The Emergence of the New South, 1913–1945.* Baton Rouge: Louisiana State University Press, 1967.

Washington, Booker T. *The Negro in the South: His Economic Progress in Relation to His Moral and Religious Development.* Philadelphia: G.W. Jacobs, 1907.

Wasserman, Ira. "A Reanalysis of the Wallace Movement." *Journal of Political and Military Sociology* 7, no. 2 (1979): 243–56.

Webster, Yehudi. *The Racialization of America.* New York: St. Martin's Press, 1992.

West, Cornel. *Encyclopedia of African-American Culture and History.* New York: Macmillan, 1995.

Wharton, Vernon Lane. *The Negro in Mississippi, 1865–1890.* Chapel Hill: University of North Carolina Press, 1947.

White, John. *Black Leadership in America: From Booker T. Washington to Jesse Jackson.* New York: Longman Press, 1990.

Williams, Patricia. *The Rooster's Egg.* Cambridge, MA: Harvard University Press, 1995.

Williamson, Joel. *The Crucible of Race: Black–White Relations in the American South Since Emancipation.* New York: Oxford University Press, 1984.

Wilson, William Julius. *The Declining Significance of Race: Blacks and Changing American Institutions.* Chicago: Chicago University Press, 1978.

———. *When Work Disappears: The World of the New Urban Poor.* New York: Alfred Knopf, 1996.

Wood, Gordon. *The Creation of the American Republic 1776–1786*. Chapel Hill: University of North Carolina Press, 1998.

Woodward, C. Vann. *The Burden of Southern History*. Baton Rouge: Louisiana State University Press, 1968.

———. *The Future of the Past*. New York: Oxford University Press, 1989.

———. *Origins of the New South: 1877–1913*. Baton Rouge: Louisiana State University Press, 1951.

———. *Reunion and Reaction: The Compromise of 1877 and the End of Reconstruction*. Garden City, NY: Doubleday, 1956.

———. *The Strange Career of Jim Crow*. New York: Oxford University Press, 1955.

Wright, Donald. *African Americans in the Colonial Era: From African Origins Through the American Revolution*. Arlington Heights, IL: Harlan Davidson, 1990.

Wright, Gavin. *Old South, New South: Revolutions in the Southern Economy Since the Civil War*. New York: Basic Books, 1986.

———. *The Political Economy of the Cotton South*. New York: W.W. Norton, 1977.

Ralph David Abernathy (1926–1990)

Ralph David Abernathy, a co-founder of the **Southern Christian Leadership Conference**, was a Baptist minister and close friend of **Dr. Martin Luther King, Jr**. Born in Linden, Alabama on March 11, 1926, and educated at Alabama State College and Atlanta University, he became pastor of the First Baptist Church, Montgomery, Alabama, in 1951. Instrumental in electing Martin Luther King as president of the Montgomery Improvement Association, he coordinated support for the **Montgomery bus boycott** in 1955, co-founded (with King and others) the Southern Christian Leadership Conference in 1957, and became the conference's full-time vice-president in 1961. He organized the 1960–61 sit-ins and Freedom Rides designed to desegregate public facilities, and led, with King, the 1963 Good Friday March in Birmingham, Alabama. He was with King at his assassination in Memphis in 1968 and subsequently delivered the eulogy. He succeeded King as president of the Southern Christian Leadership conference and served until 1977, when he ran unsuccessfully for the House of Representatives. He estranged many civil rights leaders by his 1980 endorsement of Ronald Reagan for the presidency. Abernathy died on April 17, 1990. (ISM)

BIBLIOGRAPHY

Abernathy, Ralph D. *And the Walls Came Tumbling Down: An Autobiography*. New York: Harper and Row, 1989.

Abortion

Abortion scholars believe that abortion in some form or another has been practiced for thousands of years. Opponents often argue that it is a result of the avarice and moral deprivation of the twentieth century—particularly of the women's movement. Documentation does exist for earlier abortions that were either self- or herbal-induced. **Angela Davis** (1986) argued that black women aborted themselves from the early days of slavery. The abortion debate since *Roe v. Wade* has been particularly poignant for minority women for three reasons: (1) the significance of controlling their bodies to women who were historically without control, (2) the disproportionate number of minority women who are poor, and (3) the differing beliefs in the black and white community over abortion.

Marian Faux stated (1988) that an effort was made to include black women in the preparation for *Roe*, but Davis suggested that women of color were absent from this debate because of the racist premise of the birth control movement, which lacked an accurate historical perspective. Slave women were not allowed to choose their own sexual partners and, as mothers, frequently saw their own children sold away and lost to them.

Minority women are likely to be poorer than their white counterparts. The Labor Department reported that in 1997 the median weekly wage for white women was $427, for black women $372, and for Hispanic women $315. Reports reveal that 66 percent of single mothers with at least one child under 6 lives in poverty, and minority women are twice as likely to be single mothers as are white women. Minority women are, therefore, more vulnerable to the economic dilemmas of additional children in the household. In 1976, Congress passed the Hyde Amendment, which banned Medicaid funding for abortions, effectively cutting out abortion access for many women of color. However, government funding for sterilization continued.

Studies reveal a significant difference in abortion opinions among the black and white communities. Barbara Hinkson Craig and David M. O'Brien (1993) reported that, even though blacks are less likely to approve of abortions, the proportional occurrence of abortions is twice as high among black women as among white women. The differences in opinion remained even when degrees of religiosity and socioeconomic status were controlled. (EP)

BIBLIOGRAPHY

Craig, Barbara Hinkson and David M. O'Brien. *Abortion and American Politics*. Chatham, NJ: Chatham House Publishers, 1993.

Davis, Angela. "Racism, Birth Control and Reproductive Rights." In Johnetta B. Cole, ed. *All American Women: Lines That Divide, Ties That Bind*. New York: The Free Press, 1986, pp. 239–55.

Faux, Marian. *Roe v. Wade: The Untold Story of the Landmark Supreme Court Decision That Made Abortion Legal*. New York: New American Library, 1988.

Abrams v. Johnson (1977)

Some Georgia citizens wanted the legislature to adopt a redistricting plan that would create two or three congressional districts in which African-American voters would predominate, even if the resulting districts were oddly shaped and barely geographically contiguous. In *Abrams v. Johnson*, 117

Sup. Ct. 1925 (1977), the Supreme Court ruled that the racial gerrymandering sought by the Georgia citizens was not authorized by the **Voting Rights Act of 1965 (VRA).** The Court also ruled that the creation of only one minority-majority district in Georgia did not violate the VRA because the impact of African-American voters was not impermissibly diluted. (FHJ)

BIBLIOGRAPHY

Carelli, Richard. "Court Upholds Diluted Remap Plan in Georgia." *Chicago Daily Law Bulletin* 143, no.120 (June 19, 1997): 1–3.

Act to Abolish the Slave Trade in the District of Columbia (1850)

The act was originally part of an omnibus bill introduced by Senator Henry Clay of Kentucky that was intended to calm the sectional crisis over slavery following acquisition of new territory won in the Mexican-American War. The passage of the act banning the sale of slaves in the nation's capital was finally secured through the efforts of Senator Stephen A. Douglas of Illinois as one of a group of bills known as the **Compromise of 1850.** (GAA)

BIBLIOGRAPHY

Foner, Philip S. *History of Black Americans: From Africa to the Emergence of the Cotton Kingdom.* New York: Greenwood Press, 1975.

Franklin, John Hope and Alfred A. Moss, Jr. *From Slavery to Freedom: A History of Negro Americans.* 7th ed. New York: McGraw-Hill, 1994.

Act to Prohibit the Importation of Slaves (1807)

Despite the British movement toward the restriction of the slave trade in the early 1800s, the American abolitionist efforts were declining in influence. Fear generated by slave uprisings in the Caribbean and the establishment of a free black republic of Haiti, however, lead to the passage of an act banning the trade. Passed in March 1807, the bill signed by President Thomas Jefferson banned importation of slaves into the United States after January 1, 1808. (GAA)

BIBLIOGRAPHY

Foner, Philip S. *History of Black Americans: From Africa to the Emergence of the Cotton Kingdom.* New York: Greenwood Press, 1975.

Franklin, John Hope and Alfred A. Moss, Jr. *From Slavery to Freedom: A History of Negro Americans.* 7th ed. New York: McGraw-Hill, 1994.

Affirmative Action

Affirmative action is a term that has been applied to many public and private initiatives designed to address problems of **discrimination** or exclusion in employment and education. In the area of employment, it goes beyond the pursuit of equal employment or anti-discrimination laws to ensure that candidates for employment are treated fairly. It is more appropriately applied to a wide range of strategies in which firms "act affirmatively" to include and increase the number of women and people of minority races and ethnic groups in the pool of candidates for positions through expansion of recruitment networks and review of qualifications to determine that they are necessary to perform the job. These activities range from the inclusion of the label "An Equal Employment Opportunity Employer" in job announcements to preferential hiring practices in the past and the establishment of general goals for the future. Programs that give preference to members of minority groups were rare and have generally been challenged successfully in the courts. Affirmative action is not synonymous with quotas.

The legal foundation on which affirmative action rests includes the Equal Protection Clause of the **Fourteenth Amendment** and **Executive Order 8802** issued by President Franklin D. Roosevelt on June 25, 1941. The executive order stated that "there shall be no discrimination in the employment of workers in defense industries or Government because of race, creed, color or national origin.... And it is the duty of employers and of labor organizations to provide for the full and equitable participation of all workers in defense industries, without discrimination because of race, creed, color, or national origin." **Title VI of the Civil Rights Act of 1964** prohibits discrimination on the grounds of race, color, or national origin in programs and activities receiving federal financial assistance. **Title VII of the Civil Rights Act of 1964,** as amended by the **Equal Employment Opportunity Act of 1972,** makes it unlawful to discriminate in employment practices on the basis of race, color, religion, sex, or national origin.

In 1965, President Lyndon Johnson issued **Executive Order 11246,** which, as amended by Executive Order 11375, prohibits employers doing business with the federal government from discriminating in employment because of race, color, religion, sex, or national origin. Employers must also take positive measures (affirmative action) to hire and promote qualified minorities and women. Typically, employers develop affirmative action programs in response to the activities of either the **Office of Federal Contract Compliance Programs (OFCCP)** or of the **Equal Employment Opportunity Commission (EEOC).** The OFCCP oversees the enforcement of executive orders issued by the president of the United States that prohibit federal contractors with 50 or more employees and contracts over $50,000 from discriminating on the basis of race, religion, national origin, or gender in employment decisions. The EEOC requires all companies with more than 15 employees to submit yearly reports on workplace diversity. The commission has the authority to investigate charges of discrimination, file suits in federal courts, and issue guidelines on employment discrimination.

An affirmative action program or plan is essentially a written commitment by an employer to engage in an affirmative search for qualified applicants for vacancies. The plan sets goals and timetables in hiring and promotion of representative numbers to be able to measure the outcomes of its efforts. A goal indicates a specific percentage or number of individuals that an employer or entity will attempt to achieve in its affirmative action plan. The timetable is the time period during which it is expected or hoped that the goal will be reached. An employer might wish to hire 20 percent minorities of entry-level firefighters and hope to achieve that in three years. The employer then makes special efforts to recruit qualified persons for those positions.

Affirmative action works only if it is strongly enforced, requiring companies and institutions doing business with the federal government not only to hire but also subsequently to promote minorities and women in approximate proportion to the number of available qualified candidates in their labor markets. Between 1974 and 1980, when enforcement was seriously pursued, federal contractors employed 19 percent more minorities and 15 percent more women. For non-contractors, the increases were 12 percent more minorities and 2 percent more women.

The early measures of voluntary affirmative action were not working as quickly as expected, so the Nixon administration introduced affirmative action numerical ratios, first in the hiring of construction workers in Philadelphia, where it was proven that both employers and unions conspired to prevent black workers from being hired. In situations where there has been long-standing discrimination, courts often imposed numerical hiring ratios between black and white applicants, such as one-to-one or one-to-three. Since 1969, numerous Supreme Court cases have been decided determining the legality of such race-conscious remedies. Some cases have dealt with affirmative action on behalf of women.

Plaintiffs have generally contested affirmative action on the principles of equal protection provided by the Fifth and Fourteenth Amendments of the Constitution. Race-conscious numerical remedies have been used to achieve school desegregation and even redistricting. Overall, the court has supported affirmative action based on numerical preferences on behalf of women, racial minorities, and the disabled if the action is narrowly tailored to compensate for past illegal exclusion of blacks or other protected class members, and to achieve a compelling government purpose. But in all cases, a qualification standard applies. The protected persons must be qualified to do the job.

Efforts to advance employers' affirmative recruitment efforts include visiting predominantly black or Latino schools, colleges, and universities and advertising in papers and on radio stations that serve the appropriate population. Organizations serving such groups can be contacted. These strategies are aimed to limit the exclusionary effects of word-of-mouth recruiting, whereby white workers who predominate in the work force are likely to recruit their friends to fill vacancies. Special training and scholarships for protected groups can also be provided. The overall intent of affirmative action was to make employers conscious of discriminatory practices and devise remedies to eliminate and overcome them.

Public opinion is largely opposed to discrimination; the general population favors full equality for blacks, women, and other minority groups. Americans believe that the remedies for discrimination should be special training programs and financial assistance for those who have been discriminated against to compensate them for past disadvantages. But the American populace opposes race-based remedies that force law schools, medical schools, employers, and others to take unqualified persons because of numbers. In fact, all race-based remedies have required that everyone selected be qualified.

After 1980, the validity of affirmative action was attacked by the Reagan administration, although the philosophical and formal base of affirmative action in employment remained intact. Reagan never rescinded Johnson's executive order. However, through the Justice Department, the Reagan administration tried to undermine and eliminate effective affirmative action. Initially, this took the form of urging courts to adopt positions opposed to race-based numerical remedies. Also, the Justice Department filed suits on behalf of white males, alleging "reverse discrimination."

Regarding the day-to-day enforcement of the rules and guidelines of affirmative action, there were severe budget cuts leading to significant OFCCP personnel reduction of more than 50 percent between 1979 and 1985. The number of back pay awards also showed a decline. Few contractors were barred from bidding on a federal contract, compared to the Carter administration years. Contractors were no longer required to commit to multi-year goals and timetables, but were left to write one-year goals. The EEOC shifted its focus to cases involving individuals rather than companies or industries, while many discrimination cases were dismissed as having "no cause."

The assault on affirmative action escalated from the Reagan administration years until it culminated in the California Civil Rights Initiative (CCRI), the ballot measure that succeeded in outlawing racial, ethnic, and gender preferences in state and local government in California in 1996.

The largely successful conservative assault on affirmative action was not countered by a decisive Democratic defense of the enterprise. Democrats were under pressure from working-class whites who refer to the issue as reverse discrimination. Sixty-three percent of white men voted for the Republican presidential candidate in 1992. Liberal intelligentsia have been forced to review the effects of affirmative action, especially on black Americans. The general consensus is that it has benefitted largely middle-class African Americans, who are most qualified for preferred positions with high salaries and better prepared for college admissions and job promotions. On the other hand, affirmative action does not address the problems of the truly disadvantaged, especially lower-class female-headed black families where most black children reside and where inferior education is common.

Liberals generally believe that a new direction is needed for affirmative action; it should be refocused, not discarded. It is important to improve education in the poor communities. The Head Start Program and financial aid for students should be emphasized. Teachers and successful schools should be given financial incentives. Apprenticeship programs should be expanded, using classroom instruction and on-the-job training. These programs should be race-blind and need-based. National youth service volunteers, who have inadequate education and skills, can be trained for positions that are in demand. Volunteers can help rebuild public infrastructures or deliver social services as their training regimen. Although experts believe that recruitment and training will not be adequate to address issues of discrimination in employment, the political climate in the 1990s, is antagonistic to any expanded application of affirmative action assistance to the poor. In May 1997, the Department of Justice published a plan to restructure the small, disadvantaged business program as part of the reforms to affirmative action in federal procurement. (EC)

BIBLIOGRAPHY

Blackwell, James E. *The Black Community: Diversity and Unity.* 3rd ed. New York: HarperCollins, 1991.

Greene, Kathanne W. *Affirmative Action and Principles of Justice.* New York: Greenwood Press, 1989.

Lipset, Seymour M. "Two Americas, Two Systems: Whites, Blacks and the Debate Over Affirmative Action." *The New Democrat* 7, no.3 (May-June 1995): 9–15.

Marable, Manning. *Beyond Black and White.* New York: Verso, 1996.

Simms, Margaret C. *Economic Perspectives on Affirmative Action.* Washington, DC: Joint Center for Political and Economic Studies, 1995.

African Blood Brotherhood

Founded in September 1919 by Cyril Valentine Briggs, the African Blood Brotherhood was formed in reaction to the Red Summer of 1919 (a period of great racial violence throughout the United States). The semi-secret communist organization spread racially motivated propaganda and claimed a membership of more than 50,000. The organization was largely disbanded after 1921 when it was accused of instigating race riots in Tulsa, Oklahoma.

BIBLIOGRAPHY

Draper, Theodore. *American Communism and Soviet Russia: The Formative Years.* New York: Vintage, 1986.

African Liberation Day Movement

The first conference of the independent African states was held in Accra, Ghana, on April 15, 1958. This historic day was celebrated as African Freedom Day. On May 25, 1963, 31 African heads of state met at the summit conference of the Independent African States in Addis Ababa, Ethiopia, to found the Organization of African Unity and sign the Charter of the Organization of African Unity. Thereafter, May 25 has been celebrated as African Liberation Day, a holiday celebrating the unity of all black people in their struggle against tyranny and oppression.

BIBLIOGRAPHY

Hutchings, Paul. "Report on the ALSC National Conference." *Black Scholar* 5, no. 10 (1974): 48–53.

Afrocentricism

Afrocentricism is an attempt to right the imbalance of history teaching. In the eyes of its advocates, it is a righting of old wrongs and an answer to black conservatives whom Afrocentric advocates believe have sold out the African-American cause. It is another example of "identity politics" at work in the African-American intellectual community. In simplest terms, Afrocentricism is a response to a pervading racism in American academic life. It is an attempt to promote pride in African-American students.

However, there is a serious issue of whether ethnic cheerleading can pass as scholarship. Those who oppose Afrocentricism view it as the wrong way to balance the scales. It is seen by these opponents as simply the obverse of white racism. It seeks to claim that blacks invented everything worth inventing and reminds people of some of the ridiculous claims of the old Soviet leaders.

Two books have emerged as central to the debate, offering different responses to the question "To what extent was classical Greek culture influenced by, or, in a more extreme formulation, derivative of, the cultures of ancient Africa, above all that of Egypt?" Normally, the popular press does not find itself involved in these types of academic squabbles. However, since Afrocentric scholars have claimed Egypt as a symbol of black culture, it has become an issue that goes beyond the academic. Therefore, calm discussion of the issue has become difficult because any attempt to prove or disprove Egypt's contribution to classical culture has become a test of racist inclinations. Moreover, any attempt to deny Egypt's black heritage has become tantamount to being labeled as even worse than racist.

Mary Lefkowitz's *Not Out of Africa* (1997), an attack on Afrocentrists, has led to a great deal of bitter attack on her motives. She attacks some of the more dubious claims about black history, including the one that Cleopatra, the last queen of Egypt, was black or that "Aristotle robbed the library of Alexandria," a library built after his death. As Lefkowitz notes, there is a tendency to confuse popularity with scholarship and a desire not to offend anyone. Any version of history is seen as equal to any other.

However, in Martin Bernal's *Black Athena* (1987), it is argued that the influence of Egyptian and Phoenician civilizations on Greece during the second millennium B.C. was in fact much greater than most scholars have allowed. Bernal employs a variety of evidence to support his conclusions. He argues that Egypt and Phoenicia had a great impact through their colonization of Greece on its vocabulary and culture. Bernal terms his theory the "Revised Ancient Model" and offers it as an alternative to the nineteenth-century model of splendid Greek isolation. Bernal argues that racism lay behind this isolationist theory because Europeans of the nineteenth century deemed Africans and Semites inferior to themselves. Thus, he names the isolationist model the "Aryan Model."

Nevertheless, Bernal himself rejects some of the extremes of Afrocentric theory. As one source has stated, "Extremists among Afrocentrists share unfortunate characteristics with Christian fundamentalists who want schools to teach 'creation science'" (*The New Republic,* May 19, 1997: 25). There is certainly a place to correct the historical errors of the past and to include more diverse views of the meaning of history. Schools have a place in promoting tolerance and respect and in incorporating the achievement of all Americans.

The author of *The New Republic* article argues that there can be an Afrocentric curriculum grounded in solid research that avoids the errors of some of the more radical advocates of Afrocentricism. "And, unlike 'creation science,' one can imagine an Afrocentric curriculum grounded in sound social research that nevertheless instills in black students both valid historical knowledge and a sense of racial pride."

BIBLIOGRAPHY

Bernal, Martin. *Black Athena.* New Brunswick, NJ: Rugers University Press, 1987.
Lefkowitz, Mary. *Not Out of Africa.* New York: Basic Books, 1997.

Alabama Democratic Conference

The Alabama Democratic Conference (ADC) was founded in 1960 as a vehicle through which African Americans could support the Kennedy–Johnson presidential ticket. Since that time, ADC, a membership organization, has worked on behalf of candidates (both black and white) who are responsive to the needs of Alabama's blacks and poor, helping to get these candidates elected to numerous national, state, and local offices. Over the years, ADC has had a significant role in redistricting and voting rights cases as well as in Alabama legislation. (VDD)

BIBLIOGRAPHY

Grossman, Lawrence. *The Democratic Party and the Negro.* Urbana: University of Illinois Press, 1976.

Jamil Abdullah Al-Amin. *See* H. "Rap" Brown

Albermarle Paper Co. v. Moody (1975)

This case was a class action suit brought against an employer. After the district court found that black employees had been locked into lower paying job classifications but were not entitled to back pay for losses sustained under a discriminatory system, the Supreme Court, in *Albermarle Paper Co. v. Moody*, 422 U.S. 405 (1975), held that given a finding of unlawful discrimination, back pay should be denied only for reasons which, if applied generally, would not frustrate the statutory purposes of eradicating discrimination throughout the economy and compensating persons for injuries suffered through past discrimination. (PLF)

BIBLIOGRAPHY

Belton, Robert. "Harnessing Discretionary Justice in the Employment Discrimination Cases: The Moody and Franks Standards." *Ohio State Law Journal* 44, no. 3 (Fall 1983): 571–610.

Fuller, Bradford A. "Title VII of the Civil Rights Act and Retroactive Relief." (Case note) *Pace Law Review* 4, no.2 (Winter 1984): 435–55.

Clifford L. Alexander, Jr. (1933–)

Clifford Alexander has had a long and distinguished career in law and public service. He served President Lyndon Johnson as a special counsel, associate special counsel, and member of the National Security Council from 1963 to 1967. Alexander chaired the **Equal Employment Opportunity Commission (EEOC)** from 1967 to 1969. He was Johnson's special ambassador to the independence ceremonies for Swaziland in 1968 and served on the Presidential Commission for Observation of Human Rights Year. An accomplished lawyer, Alexander was a partner in the powerful Arnold & Porter firm from 1969 to 1975; he was then a partner in Verner, Lipfert, Bernhard, McPherson & Alexander from 1975 to 1976. President Jimmy Carter appointed Alexander to be secretary of the army, a post he held from 1977 to 1980. Since 1981, he has headed the consulting firm, Alexander & Associates, Inc.

BIBLIOGRAPHY

Alexander, Clifford. "Colin Powell's Promotion: The Real Story." *New York Times* (December 23, 1997): A19.
United States Senate Committee on Armed Services. *Nominations of Clifford L. Alexander Jr., and W. Graham Clayton Jr.* Washington, DC: Government Printing Office, 1977.

Raymond Pace Alexander (1898–1974)

A 1923 graduate of Harvard Law School, Raymond Pace Alexander was a leading African-American lawyer in Philadelphia from the 1920s through the 1950s. Alexander defended some of the earliest school desegregation cases in the United States, successfully opening up a number of previously all-white schools and school districts to students of all races. Together with his wife, **Sadie Tanner Mossell Alexander,** with whom he formed one of the earliest husband-wife legal partnerships in the nation, he worked for and achieved victories in the desegregation of a wide variety of public accommodations in Philadelphia and across the state. Alexander also served as a counsel to the **NAACP Legal Defense and Educational Fund,** Inc. In this capacity, he replaced **Thurgood Marshall** in the famous case of the *Trenton Six* in 1951, defending two African-American men who were accused along with four others of murdering two white businesspeople in Trenton, New Jersey.

In 1951, Alexander, a Democrat, began a seven-year run as a member of the powerful Philadelphia City Council. His successful political career came to an end when he became the first African American to serve as a judge on the Court of Common Pleas of Philadelphia, eventually retiring in 1970 as President Judge of that court. (AJC)

BIBLIOGRAPHY

Potterfield, Thomas G., Miriam B. Spectre, and Terry Snyder. "A Guide to the Alexander Family Papers." Archives of the University of Pennsylvania, Philadelphia, PA, 1993.

"Raymond Pace Alexander." Obituary. *The Washington Post* (November 26, 1974): C6.

Sadie Tanner Mossell Alexander (1898–1989)

Not satisfied with such remarkable achievements as being one of the first African-American women to receive a Ph.D. in the United States (in 1921) and the first African-American woman to graduate from the University of Pennsylvania Law School (in 1927), Sadie Tanner Mossell Alexander spent her life struggling for the civil rights of African Americans in her city of Philadelphia and across the United States.

Alexander twice served as assistant city solicitor of Philadelphia. This appointment came on the heels of the victories that she and her husband and law partner, **Raymond Pace Alexander**, won in ending overt discrimination in the hotels, restaurants, and theaters of Philadelphia. She helped to draft the Pennsylvania public accommodations law in 1935, which served as a model for many states that later sought to make public accommodations truly public. Alexander and her husband pioneered techniques of nonviolent civil disobedience to support enforcement of the public accommodations law.

In 1946, Alexander was appointed by President Harry S. Truman to serve as a member of the Commission to Study the Civil Rights of All Races and Faiths, on which she served until 1948. The Commission's final report, "To Secure These Rights," called for the desegregation of all the armed services, a goal that was attained with the issuance of President Truman's **Executive Order 9981** in July 1948. She served two more presidents, as both a member of John F. Kennedy's Committee for Civil Rights under Law, and Jimmy Carter's White House Conference on Aging. (AJC)

BIBLIOGRAPHY

Franklin, Vincent P. *The Education of Black Philadelphia: The Societal and Educational History of a Minority Community, 1900–1950*. Philadelphia: University of Pennsylvania Press, 1979.

Polak, Maralyn Lois. "Sadie Alexander: At 83, a Woman for Any Age." *Philadelphia Inquirer Magazine* (March 29, 1981): 4–5.

Alexander v. Holmes County Board of Education (1969)

The issue before the Supreme Court in *Alexander v. Holmes County Board of Education*, 396 U.S. 19 (1969), was whether the Holmes County Board of Education and the state of Mississippi were in compliance with a previous court dictum that public schools should be desegregated with "all deliberate speed." The **National Association for the Advancement of Colored People (NAACP)** brought suit on behalf of 14 black school children, alleging that Mississippi was delaying integration in 33 school districts. The Supreme Court found that "all deliberate speed has turned out to be only a soft euphemism for delay" and that there was no justification for further delay. (EP)

BIBLIOGRAPHY

Davis, Michael B. and Hunter R. Clark. *Thurgood Marshall: Warrior at the Bar, Rebel on the Bench*. New York: Birch Lane Press, 1992.

"All Deliberate Speed"

This phrase comes from the majority opinion in ***Brown v. Board of Education, Topeka, Kansas*** (1954) in which the Supreme Court ruled that African Americans had to be admitted into desegregated public schools with "all deliberate speed." The Court chose this phrase, recognizing that the process of integration must balance the constitutional requirements and rights of the individual students with the practical political and social problems of school administrations and local communities. Most schools, however, by intentionally misinterpreting the phrase, used it as a method for delaying the process of desegregation.

BIBLIOGRAPHY

Berger, Morrow. *Equality by Statute: The Revolution in Civil Rights*. Garden City, NY: Doubleday, 1967.

Richard Allen (1760–1831)

Born a slave, Richard Allen was one of the founders of the **Free Africa Society.** In 1799, after being made a deacon, Allen organized the first African Methodist Episcopal church. Between 1799 and 1816, AME churches spread throughout the country; in 1816, the AME gained its independence from the American Methodist Church and became the first independent black denomination. **See also** Absalom Jones; Religion and African-American Politics. (AAB)

BIBLIOGRAPHY

Raboteau, Albert J. *A Fire in the Bones: Reflections on African-American Religious History*. Boston: Beacon Press, 1995.

William Barclay Allen (1944–)

Trained as a political scientist, William B. Allen has served in many capacities, including teacher, administrator, and appointed government official. From 1972 until 1993, Allen was a professor of political science at Harvey Mudd College in Claremont, California. From 1985 to 1987, he served on the California State Advisory Commission of the **United States Commission on Civil Rights.** During this time, he also served on the National Council for the Humanities. In 1987, President Ronald Reagan appointed the politically conservative Allen to chair the U.S. Civil Rights Commission. Allen was a controversial selection because of his vocal opposition to **affirmative action.** In 1989, President George Bush relieved Allen of his duties as chair in part because of a controversial speech he gave entitled "Blacks? Animals? Homosexuals? What Is a Minority?" The address, among other things, supported individual civil rights of homosexuals but argued that they could not be considered a minority group. Allen left the commission in 1992. In 1993, he became dean of James Madison College at Michigan State University, where he served until 1998, when outgoing Virginia governor George Allen selected William Allen to chair the State Council of Higher Education.

BIBLIOGRAPHY

Hsu, Spencer S. "Democrats Dislike Virginia Board's Choice." *The Washington Post* (June 6, 1998): B1.

Allen v. Board of Elections (1969)

In this case, the U.S. Supreme Court ruled that the Section 5 pre-clearance of the **Voting Rights Act of 1965** broadly applies to any law that directly or indirectly relates to voting. Black voters challenged new laws in Mississippi and Virginia that set special restrictions for third party candidates; none had been submitted to the federal Justice Department for pre-clearance. Although the states argued that these statutes were not VRA-covered voting laws, the Court concluded that the laws affected voting. In *Allen v. Board of Elections*, 393 U.S. 544 (1969), Chief Justice Earl Warren wrote that "the Voting Rights Act was aimed at the subtle, as well as the obvious, state regulations which have the effect of denying citizens their right to vote because of their race." (KC)

BIBLIOGRAPHY

Davis, Abraham L. and Barbara Luck Graham. *The Supreme Court, Race and Civil Rights*. Thousand Oaks, CA: Sage, 1995.

Alpha Suffrage Club (ASC)

Organized in 1913, the Alpha Suffrage Club (ASC) was co-founded by Ida B. Wells-Barnett and Belle Squire. The goal of the ASC was to register African-American female voters in Chicago's 2nd Ward, thus electing an African-American alderman to the Chicago City Council. The ASC reached its goal in 1915 when **Oscar DePriest**, a Republican elected from Chicago's 2nd Ward, became the first African-American alderman in Chicago. The success of the ASC led politicians, both black and white, to seek its endorsement. **See also** Ida B. Wells. (DH)

BIBLIOGRAPHY

Sterling, Dorothy. *Black Foremothers: Three Lives*. Old Westbury: The Feminist Press, 1979.

American Anti-Slavery Society

The American Anti-Slavery Society, led by William Lloyd Garrison, was the best known of the anti-slavery societies in existence before the Civil War. Gerda Lerner (1967) wrote

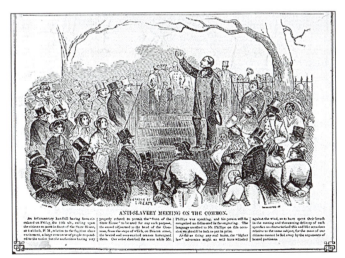

Founded by William Lloyd Garrison in the 1830s, the American Anti-Slavery Society sought to convince whites to end slavery through meetings such as the one depicted here. *Library of Congress.*

that the creation of this group marked a turning point in the anti-slavery movement, calling for immediate emancipation, greater access to education, and an end to racial prejudice. (EP)

BIBLIOGRAPHY

Lerner, Gerda. *The Grimke Sisters from South Carolina: Pioneers for Woman's Rights and Abolition*. New York: Schocken Books, 1967.

Locke, Marnie E. "From 3/5 to Zero: Implications of the 15th Amendment for African-American Women." In *Women and the Constitution: Symposium Papers Edited by the Carter Center of Emory University*. Atlanta: Carter Center of Emory University, 1990: 41–45.

American Colonization Society

The American Colonization Society was organized in 1817 to deport free Africans to a colony in Africa; white Americans were afraid that the presence of free Africans in the United States would make it difficult to discipline slaves. With funds from federal and state governments, agents of the society encouraged free Africans to emigrate to Liberia. Free Africans and later manumitted slaves were transported to Liberia. Up until 1831, whites from slave-holding states and some southern free Africans supported the scheme, but soon the divergent motives behind the program contributed to its failure. Most free Africans preferred to remain in the United States. Northern blacks were strongly opposed to the

Joseph Jenkins Roberts was the first president of Liberia, the African nation to which the American Colonization Society transported many freed American slaves. *Library of Congress.*

scheme because they believed that once free Africans left the United States, slaves would have no advocates to end the institution of slavery. Not more than 15,000 free Africans left the country on the colonization scheme. (EC)

BIBLIOGRAPHY

McCartney, John T. *Black Power Ideologues: An Essay in African American Political Thought*. Philadelphia: Temple University Press, 1992.

American Independent Party

The American Independent Party nominated George Wallace as a third-party candidate for United States president in 1968. Wallace, elected governor of Alabama for three terms, became nationally known for his racist positions and anti-integration activities. In the presidential election, Wallace received widespread and enthusiastic support from white lower-middle-class voters and won support from his home state, and from Mississippi, Arkansas, Louisiana, and Georgia. In 1969, Wallace supporters reorganized as the American Party but that party split up in 1976. (VDD)

BIBLIOGRAPHY

Abramson, Paul R., J.H. Aldrich, P. Paolino, and D.W. Rhode. "Third-party and Independent Candidates in American Politics: Wallace, Anderson and Perot." *Political Science Quarterly* 110, no. 3 (Fall 1995): 1–20.

American Missionary Association (AMA)

Arising from the 1841 *Amistad* case, which involved a Supreme Court trial of blacks who took control of a slave ship, and incorporated in 1846, the American Missionary Association (AMA) was an anti-**slavery**, Congregational mission that worked among American minorities. After the **Civil War,** the association focused on educating freed slaves, absorbing the **Freedmen's Bureau** and the Daniel Hand Educational Fund for Colored People. The AMA founded more than 500 schools and colleges (later universities) such as Hampton University, **Howard University**, Atlanta University, Dillard University, and Fisk University. The AMA also published the *American Missionary*. The association became part of the Division of Higher Education of the United Church Board for Homeland Ministries (United Churches of Christ). **See also** Religion and African-American Politics. (ISM)

BIBLIOGRAPHY

Richardson, Joe. *Christian Reconstruction: The American Missionary Association and southern Blacks, 1861–1890.* Athens: University of Georgia Press, 1986.
Stanley, A. Knighton. *The Children Is Crying: Congregationalism Among Black People.* New York: Pilgrim Press, 1979.

American Negro Academy

The American Negro Academy was founded in 1897, in part through the efforts of Reverend **Alex Crummell**. The purpose of the academy was to foster scholarship and promote literature, science, and art among African Americans to provide an educated elite that would help shape society. Founding members of the school included Paul Laurence Dunbar, William Sanders Scarborough, and **W. E. B. Du Bois**. Crummell served as the school's first president until his death in 1908. After Crummell's demise, Du Bois took up the school's presidency and helped involve the academy in publishing works by some of the era's leading activists and intellectuals. The academy went on to be headed in 1922 by Arthur Schomburg, who continued both Crummell's and Du Bois's administrative practices. In 1928, Schomburg ceased his activities with the school, and the American Negro Academy went out of existence.

BIBLIOGRAPHY

Moss, Alfred A. *The American Negro Academy.* Baton Rouge: Louisiana State University Press, 1981.

American Tobacco Company v. Patterson (1982)

The **Equal Employment Opportunity Commission (EEOC)** and a group of African-American employees of the American Tobacco Company sued American Tobacco over a seniority system the company had negotiated with the workers' union; the plaintiffs claimed that the plan had a discriminatory effect on the advancement opportunities of black employees. However, in *American Tobacco Company v. Patterson*, 456 U.S. 63 (1982), the Supreme Court ruled that the **Civil Rights Act of 1964** specifically permits bona fide seniority systems, including different wages, terms, conditions, and privileges of employment, as long as such systems are not intentionally discriminatory. **See also** Discrimination; Equal Employment Opportunity Act of 1972. (FHJ)

BIBLIOGRAPHY

Galub, Arthur L. *The Burger Court, 1968–1984.* Millwood, NY: Associated Faulty Press, 1984.

Reuben V. Anderson (1942–)

Reuben Anderson was born August 16, 1942, in Mississippi. In 1967, he became the first black graduate of the University of Mississippi School of Law. In 1975, he was appointed municipal court judge in Jackson, and in 1985, he became Mississippi's first black Supreme Court justice. He was elected president of the Mississippi Bar Association in June 1997.

BIBLIOGRAPHY

Donovan, Sharon. "Another First." *The National Law Journal* 13, no.19 (January 14, 1991): 2.

Anti-Lynching Legislation

The number of extralegal killings of black southerners by whites peaked in the 1890s, but continued to occur in the South into the 1950s. The **National Association for the Advancement of Colored People (NAACP)** led the fight for passage of anti-lynching legislation by the federal government. Although anti-lynching bills were almost passed on several occasions, Congress, manipulated by white southern politicians, never passed any meaningful legislation on the issue. Nevertheless, the tireless campaign waged by the NAACP brought national pressure on the South to end lynching. (CE)

BIBLIOGRAPHY

Zangrando, Robert. *The NAACP Campaign Against Lynching, 1909–1950.* Philadelphia: Temple University Press, 1980.

Dennis Archer (1941–)

Dennis Archer, a Democrat, was born in 1941 in Michigan. In 1970, he received his law degree from Detroit College of Law, where he later served as an associate professor. In 1986, he was appointed to the Michigan Supreme Court. He became mayor of Detroit on January 1, 1994 succeeding long-time Mayor **Coleman Young**.

BIBLIOGRAPHY

"A Man, A Plan: Detroit." *The Economist* 330, no. 7854 (March 12, 1994): A33.

"Atlanta Compromise Address"

The "Atlanta Compromise Address" was given by **Booker T. Washington** in September 1895 before the Cotton States and International Exposition at Atlanta. The address focused on the need for African Americans to work for and be allowed to earn equal citizenship privileges; the speech portrayed the equal rights cause as one of peace instead of destructive revolution. The speech also called for blacks to remain in the South despite the difficulties and to overcome their problems by acquiring property and improving themselves through self-help. Besides this, it illustrated the potential influence African Americans had in the South, given that they made up about one-third of the region's population.

Washington provided personal examples of how blacks could join society, discussing his experiences with the Tuskegee Institute where students produced lumber, baked bricks, and farmed land to gain needed skills and learn what he called "the dignity of labor." Whites were supportive of Washington's speech because it did not fully contradict white supremacy, even though it did imply eventual social equality. Blacks also initially supported the address, although some later felt that the compromise did not forcefully enough protect their rights, leaving them potentially in danger of gaining second-class citizenship. Whatever view was taken, the "Atlanta Compromise Address" helped Booker T. Washington become a leading figure of the time.

BIBLIOGRAPHY

Hawkins, Hugh. *Booker T. Washington and His Critics: The Problem of Negro Leadership.* Lexington, MA: Heath, 1974.

At-Large Districts

At-large districts are electoral districts that cover an entire political jurisdiction, such as a city or county. Forms of at-large districts can dilute the voting strength of minorities, particularly at-large districts with multiple representatives. White voters, representing a majority in the district, can cast ballots for a bloc of candidates, thereby preventing other candidates representing areas with even significant minority populations from obtaining office. With the *Baker v. Carr* decision in 1962, and the **Voting Rights Act of 1965**, some at-large districts were seen to violate the "one person, one vote" rule. A common remedy has been to draw district lines to give minorities a seat. The Supreme Court ruled in *Thornburg v. Gingles* that district lines could be drawn if the minority group is sufficiently large and compact, if it is politically cohesive, and if racially polarized voting has prevented minorities from obtaining office. (WWH)

BIBLIOGRAPHY

Davidson, Chandler, ed. *Minority Vote Delusion.* Washington, DC: Howard University Press, 1984.

Grofman, Bernard, Lisa Handley, and Richard G. Niemi. *Minority Representation and the Quest for Voting Equality.* New York: Cambridge University Press, 1992.

Crispus Attucks (ca. 1723–1770)

Crispus Attucks, an escaped Massachusetts slave and seaman, joined a street protest against the British in Boston on March 5, 1770. When the British fired on the crowd, Attucks became the first casualty of the American Revolution, a victim of what was later called the "Boston Massacre." (GAA)

BIBLIOGRAPHY

Franklin, John Hope and Alfred A. Moss, Jr. *From Slavery to Freedom: A History of Negro Americans.* 7th ed. New York: McGraw-Hill, 1994.

Quarles, Benjamin. *The Negro in the American Revolution.* New York: W. W. Norton and Co., Inc., 1973.

B

Baker v. Carr (1962)

Baker v. Carr, 369 U.S. 186 (1962), was a Supreme Court decision reinforcing the "one person, one vote" principle. Boundary lines for the Tennessee state assembly were drawn in 1901 and were unaltered for over 60 years. The transition of the population from rural areas to cities resulted in population ratios in both the state house and senate that greatly favored rural voters. In 1962, Charles Baker, a voter, brought suit against the state. Joe Carr was a state official in charge of elections. Baker argued that gross inequalities in constituency size violated both the Tennessee Constitution and the **Fourteenth Amendment.** In a previous case, *Colegrove v Green*, U.S. 549 (1946), the Supreme Court argued that it did not have jurisdiction over the Tennessee case and found that city dwellers had been underrepresented.

The decision in *Baker v. Carr* opened the way for legal challenges to state apportionment patterns based on the equal protection clause of the Fourteenth Amendment. The decision has been key in several cases related to the underrepresentation of racial minorities. (WWH)

BIBLIOGRAPHY

Grofman, Bernard N. *Voting Rights, Voting Wrongs.* New York: Twentieth Century Fund Press/Priority Press Publications, 1990.

Imamu Amiri Baraka (1934–)

Imamu Amiri Baraka was born Everett LeRoi Jones in Newark, New Jersey, on October 7, 1934. He is a poet, playwright, and community leader. Baraka is best known for his play *Dutchman*, written in 1964. The play typifies his body of work in its portrayal of blacks and whites in a startling metaphorical clash; the militant hostility towards whites for which Baraka is known is also evident. The play won a 1964 Obie Award. In 1965, he discarded his "slave" name, took the name Baraka, and headed his own Black Muslim group, Kawaida, an organization committed to bringing blacks into power in Newark. (FAS)

BIBLIOGRAPHY

Harris, W.J. *The Poetry and Politics of Amiri Baraka.* Columbia: University of Missouri Press, 1987.

Don H. Barden (1943–)

Don Barden was born in Detroit, Michigan. He was the first black city councilman elected in Lorain, Ohio, and the only African-American majority owner of a major casino in the U.S. He founded his own cable television company, Barden Communications, of which he has been president and chairman since 1981. (JCW)

BIBLIOGRAPHY

Smith, Eric. "Barden's Excellent Adventure." *Black Enterprise* 28, no. 10 (May 1, 1998).

Barrows v. Jackson (1953)

Barrows v. Jackson, 346 U.S. 249; 73 Sup. Ct. 1031 (1953), was an action brought by parties against a covenant that restricted the sale of real estate to non-Caucasians. The Supreme Court held that award by a state court of damages against a covenantor for breach of a restrictive covenant would constitute a state action depriving non-Caucasians of equal protection of the laws in violation of the **Fourteenth Amendment.** The Court had previously held in *Shelley v. Kraemer* that racially restrictive covenants could not be enforced in equity against African-American purchasers. (PLF)

BIBLIOGRAPHY

D'Amato, Anthony A., Rosemary Metrailer, and Stephen L. Wasby. *Desegregation from Brown to Alexander.* Carbondale, IL: Southern Illinois University Press, 1977.

Greenberg, Jack. *Race Relations and American Law.* New York: Columbia University Press, 1959.

Marion S. Barry, Jr. (1936–)

Born on a cotton plantation in Mississippi, Barry grew up in Memphis. In 1958, he earned a B.A. in chemistry at Fisk University in Nashville. He became involved in the **sit-in** movement, and in 1960 was chosen as a leader of the **Student Nonviolent Coordinating Committee (SNCC).** After receiving his master's degree, he taught chemistry until 1964, then began working full-time for the SNCC in New York.

In 1965, Barry moved to Washington, D.C., where he focused on helping black youths and stimulating economic growth. In 1971, he was elected to the school board, and in 1974 to the city council. A lifelong Democrat, he triumphed in the 1978 mayoral race and served as mayor until 1991. He succeeded to some extent in improving the city's public services and finances, but his tenure was plagued by charges of corruption and drug abuse. He was convicted of cocaine possession in 1990 and served a six-month prison sentence. Barry and his supporters charged that he had been entrapped, and in 1994 he again won election as Washington's mayor. (AD)

BIBLIOGRAPHY
Jonathan Agronsky. *Marion Barry: The Politics of Race.* Latham, NY: Bristole American Publishing. 1991

Ebenezer Don Carlos Bassett (1833–1908)

Ebenezer D. Bassett, born in Connecticut as the son of a mulatto and a Pequot Indian, was appointed consul general of the United States in Haiti in 1869 by President Ulysses S. Grant. Bassett shared the appointment with the famed anti-slave orator **Frederick Douglass.** These two men share the distinction of being the first African Americans to be appointed to a foreign diplomatic post. Bassett served in this capacity until 1877. He then returned to the United States, and in 1879 became consul general of Haiti in New York. Prior to his appointment to Haiti, Bassett was a teacher and school principal in Pennsylvania.

BIBLIOGRAPHY
"Celebrating Blacks in Foreign Affairs." *State Magazine* (February 1998): 1–2.

Batson v. Kentucky (1986)

In 1985, a state court in Kentucky, through the process of voir dire, excused blacks as potential jurors to serve on a case involving a black man because the court believed that the black jurors would not be impartial. Batson, the defendant in *Batson v. Kentucky*, 476 U.S. 79 (1986), was convicted, and he appealed his conviction, citing the exclusion of blacks from the jury. The Supreme Court ruled that "a state denies a black defendant equal protection when it puts him on trial before a jury from which members of his race have been purposely excluded." (CEM)

BIBLIOGRAPHY
Fried, Audrey M. "Fulfilling the Promise of Batson." *University of Chicago Law Review* 64, no. 4 (Fall 1997): 1311–36.

Bell v. Maryland (1963)

The case of *Bell v. Maryland*, 378 U.S. 226 (1963), involved a group of African Americans who were asked to leave a Baltimore restaurant because of their race. The group refused, and its members were charged with trespassing. At the trial, the group was convicted. While the case was on appeal, the state of Maryland enacted public accommodation laws making it illegal for restaurants in the state to deny service to customers on the basis of race. Because of this new legislation, the original trial findings were reversed, and the case was remanded for settlement.

BIBLIOGRAPHY
Barker, Lucius J. and Twiley W. Barker, Jr. *Civil Liberties and the Constitution.* Englewood Cliffs, NJ: Prentice Hall, 1994.

Sharon Sayles Belton (1951–)

Sharon Sayles Belton attended Macalester College. She worked as a parole officer and an assistant director of the Minnesota Program for Victims of Sexual Assault. She served on the Minneapolis City Council from 1983 to 1993, becoming council president in 1989. In 1997, Belton a Democrat, was elected mayor of Minneapolis. (JCW)

BIBLIOGRAPHY
Booker, Simon. "New VIP Faces in Black Politics." *Jet* (November 22, 1993): 4.

Berea College v. Commonwealth of Kentucky (1908)

In 1904, Kentucky passed the Day Law, which prohibited integrated classroom instruction. Berea College, which had conducted integrated college education for more than 50 years, was charged with and found in violation of the act. The college appealed the decision all the way to the U.S. Supreme Court. In *Berea College v. Commonwealth of Kentucky*, 211 U.S. 26 (1908), the Court upheld the Kentucky statute as constitutional. (CEM)

BIBLIOGRAPHY
Heckman, Richard Allen and Betty Jean Hall. "Berea College and the Day Law." *Register of Kentucky Historical Society* 66 (1968): 35–52.

Mary Frances Berry (1938–)

In 1977, President Jimmy Carter appointed Mary Frances Berry as the assistant secretary of education in the United States Department of Health, Education, and Welfare. In 1980, Berry was named a commissioner on the **United States Commission on Civil Rights,** where she has served as its chair. (DH)

BIBLIOGRAPHY
Franklin, John Hope and Alfred A. Moss, Jr. *From Slavery to Freedom: A History of African Americans.* New York: McGraw-Hill, Inc., 1994.

Mary McLeod Bethune (1875–1955)

Mary McLeod Bethune was the founder of the Dayton Educational and Industrial School for Negro Girls in 1904. She served as the school's first president from 1904 to 1942. The school eventually merged with the Cookman Institute and changed its name to Bethune–Cookman College. From 1936 to 1942, Bethune was director of the Negro Affairs National Youth Administration and served as a special advisor on minority affairs to President Franklin D. Roosevelt. Bethune served as president of several organizations, including the **National Association of Colored Women**, the U.S. branch of the United Peoples of Africa, the Florida State Federation of Colored Women's Clubs, and the Association for the Study of Negro Life and History. She also founded the **National Council of Negro Women** in 1935.

BIBLIOGRAPHY
Holt, Rackman. *Mary McLeod Bethune: A Biography.* Garden City, NY: Doubleday, 1964.

Peare, Owen. *Mary McLeod Bethune.* New York: Vanguard Press, 1951.

"Birmingham Manifesto"

The Birmingham-based Alabama Christian Movement for Human Rights (ACMHR), led by civil-rights activist Fred L. Shuttlesworth, issued the "Birmingham Manifesto" on April 2, 1963, to announce its resumption of sit-in demonstrations against the city's white-owned and operated retail establishments. The manifesto, which began, "the patience of an oppressed people cannot endure forever," spelled out the increasing frustration of Birmingham's black citizens with the city government's failure to institute promised reforms of its segregation laws. According to the manifesto's authors, in addition to the stonewalling of the city administration, the retreat by Birmingham's merchants on their prior pledge to abolish segregated facilities in their stores had pushed the ACMHR into launching a renewed assault on Birmingham's segregation ordinance. Citing the "absence of justice and progress" in Birmingham, the manifesto declared that the time had come for the city's black community to "make a moral witness."

Waiting until after the city had conducted its run-off elections for city commissioner on April 2, the ACMHR resumed its demonstrations the following day. This time, however, Birmingham's black citizens enjoyed the active support of the Reverend **Martin Luther King, Jr.** and his nationally recognized **Southern Christian Leadership Conference (SCLC)**. Although the campaign got off to a slow start, actions taken by Birmingham's Commissioner of Public Safety, Eugene "Bull" Connor, including the arrest and jailing of King and the sanctioning of brutal attacks on demonstrating schoolchildren, brought national attention to the situation in Birmingham. The resultant negative publicity finally forced the city's civic leaders to negotiate a compromise with Birmingham's black community. **See also** Sit-ins. (LPM)

BIBLIOGRAPHY

"'Birmingham Manifesto' Issued by ACMHR." *Birmingham World* (April 6, 1963): 12.

Branch, Taylor. *Parting the Waters: America in the King Years, 1954–1963.* New York: Simon and Schuster, 1988.

Birmingham Protests

Martin Luther King, Jr. and the **Southern Christian Leadership Conference (SCLC)** organized a nonviolent campaign against segregation in Birmingham, Alabama, in April 1963. Sheriff Eugene "Bull" Connor unleashed dogs and firehoses on the peaceful demonstrators, and arrested King.

In May, children participated extensively in the protests, going to jail by the hundreds. Dramatic footage from Birmingham, featured in media worldwide, convinced President John F. Kennedy to discuss civil rights on national television and to call for comprehensive legislation. This initiative eventually led to the **Civil Rights Act of 1964**. (AD)

BIBLIOGRAPHY

Fairclough, Adam. *To Redeem the Soul of America: The southern Christian Leadership and Martin Luther King, Jr.* Athens: University of Georgia Press, 1987.

Young, Andrew. *An Easy Burden: The Civil Rights Movement and the Transformation of America.* New York: HarperCollins, 1996.

The Birth of a Nation

From the moment of its public opening in 1915, *The Birth of a Nation* won both praise and condemnation—praise for its cinematic innovation, condemnation for its overtly racist reinterpretation of the pre- and post-Civil War period. After a White House viewing, President Woodrow Wilson remarked that the film was "like writing history with lightning."

Adapted from Thomas Dixon's *The Clansman*, the story centers on two white families, one from the North and the other from the South, and their plight during and after the Civil War. Yet, the most controversial aspects of the film address the "reign of carpet-baggers" and its effects on the South. Black state legislators are depicted as slovenly and barefoot, slouching on the floor of the legislature and eyeing white women in the gallery with lust. The climax comes when a band of whites is surrounded by a black militia, only to be saved by the Ku Klux Klan. At that point, a political awakening is initiated through the Klan's establishment of "justice." All blacks are deported to Africa, and the epilogue to this silent film states: "The establishment of the South in its rightful place is the birth of a new nation." (CJM)

BIBLIOGRAPHY

Griffith, D.W. *The Birth of a Nation.* New Brunswick, NJ: Rutgers University Press, 1993.

Sanford D. Bishop, Jr. (1947–)

Sanford Bishop, Jr. is an African-American Democratic member of the U.S. House of Representatives. He was first elected in 1992 from the second district in Georgia, which covers parts of Macon, Columbus, Albany, and Valdosta counties. He previously spent 16 years in the Georgia General Assembly and served as a civil rights lawyer. **See also** Congressional Black Caucus. (CEM)

BIBLIOGRAPHY

Guess, John F., Jr. "Featured Politico: Rep. Sanford Bishop." *Headway* 9, no. 1 (January 1997): 30–31.

Black Bourgeoise

Published in 1957, *Black Bourgeoise* is a book written by black sociologist E. Franklin Frazier that portrays middle-class blacks as "lacking intellectual culture and having no love for higher learning." Frazier also accused higher-class blacks of being status seekers. The book drew criticism but was also widely read in black circles and was an indicator for the rise of the black middle class as well as of the new spirit of critique and self-analysis within the black community.

BIBLIOGRAPHY

Quarles, Benjamin. *The Negro in the Making of America.* New York: Simon and Schuster, 1987.

Black Codes

After the abolition of slavery, a number of states instituted laws that were intended to prevent African Americans from gaining equal status with whites. Among the restrictions these "Black Codes" placed on blacks were Mississippi's requirement that African Americans under the age of 18 be "apprentices" of their former slave masters if the child was orphaned or if the child's parents were unable to support him or her. Black codes in other states denied blacks the opportunity to own property, forbade them from carrying firearms, and required them to carry permission passes to travel beyond certain boundaries.

BIBLIOGRAPHY

Stewart, Gary. "Black Codes and Broken Windows." *Yale Law Journal* 107, no. 7 (1998): 2249.

Black Nationalism

Black nationalism is a concept that views black America as constituting an oppressed "nation within a nation." Black nationalists criticize the domination of African Americans by the majority Euro-American majority population, and encourage African Americans to demand recognition of their full American citizenship rights. In the nineteenth century, black nationalism was manifested by African Americans working to invigorate and strengthen their communities through "Free African Societies" and other benevolent, fraternal, and religious organizations. In the twentieth century, **Marcus Garvey** and his followers sought to establish economic, political, educational, and cultural liberation of the African world.

In the 1960s, a black nationalist world view reemerged to criticize white-dominated U.S. institutional life as an impediment to African Americans' progress. To challenge and ultimately dissolve this oppressive monopoly, blacks had to mobilize, close ranks, and build group strength. This process involved all aspects of black life—political, economic, psychological, and cultural. Once unity had been achieved in these areas, blacks would form a significant power bloc and would be able to exercise true freedom of choice for the first time. They might choose to live in "liberated" urban enclaves, in a separate black-run nation-state, or simply in the realm of the psyche. Whatever the specific nationalist format, the black nationalist would be a self-actualized individual who is self-directed, assertive, and proud of his or her skin color and heritage. (EC)

BIBLIOGRAPHY

Moses, Wilson J. *Classical Black Nationalism: From the American Revolution to Marcus Garvey.* New York: New York University Press, 1996.

Van Deburg, William. *New Day in Babylon: The Black Power Movement and American Culture, 1965–1975.* Chicago: University of Chicago Press, 1992.

Black Panther Manifesto

The **Black Panther Party** was a revolutionary nationalist group founded in Oakland, California, in 1966. Although armed, Panthers noted that they did not use their guns to attack the white community, but only to defend themselves against unjust attack. The Black Panther Party saw itself as the revolutionary vanguard leading the urban masses in the destruction of the oppressive United States political machinery. The party manifesto demanded jobs for the unemployed, decent housing for the poor, quality education, exemption for black men from military service, an end to police brutality, release of black people from prisons, the trial of black people by a jury of their peers from the black community, and a greater voice for blacks in determining decisions affecting their communities. Black Panther chapters instituted free breakfast and health care programs, conducted classes in black history, and warned against the dangers of drug use. The Panthers sought to build racial pride in young black children and to instill confidence in their ability to reshape their lives. (EC)

BIBLIOGRAPHY

Van Deburg, William. *New Day in Babylon: The Black Power Movement and American Culture, 1965–1975.* Chicago: University of Chicago Press, 1992.

Black Panther Party

The Black Panther Party was organized in Lowndes County, Alabama, by **Stokely Carmichael** in 1966. It quickly spread to Oakland, California, where **Huey Newton** and **Bobby Seale**, two students working in California's poverty programs, organized chapters in October 1966. Using Mao Tse-tung's revolutionary theories, the organization stressed self-defense and self-determination, while preaching a radical form of **black nationalism** that denounced capitalism and promoted community organization. Panther members referred to themselves as "the children of **Malcolm X**." By 1967, **Eldridge Cleaver** and Bobby Hutton had joined the party, giving it a more effective means of voicing its programs. They sponsored such diverse programs as free breakfasts, free health clinics, educational enrichment courses, and slum clearance programs.

With nearly 4,000 members and a newspaper with a circulation of over 100,000, they stressed self-defense against the ongoing destruction of black communities. They condemned inadequate health care, malnutrition, diseases, drugs, and police brutality. Their work is shrouded in controversy because of the numerous violent clashes they had with the police, who they viewed as the military arm of the white oppressor. The Panthers, armed with cameras, followed the police, monitoring their actions during day-to-day dealings with black ghetto youth. Drug indictments and weapons charges radically reduced the organization's influence. Between 1968 and 1969, 28 Panthers were killed in clashes with the police. Arrests and deaths devastated the organization. Hutton was killed in a bloody shootout, Newton and Seale were jailed, and Eldridge Cleaver was exiled outside the country. (AAB)

BIBLIOGRAPHY

Hillard, David. *This Side of Glory.* Boston: Little, Brown and Co., 1991.

Black Power

Black Power was the title of a 1950s-era travel book written by **Richard Wright** detailing his experiences on the Gold Coast of Africa. In the book, he derides some of Kwame Nkrumah's (Nkrumah led Ghana to independence in 1957) policies while also denouncing British colonists and Protestants. The book sets the stage for the expansion of **Pan-Africanism.** The term "black power" was later advanced by radical wings of the **civil rights movement.** The term came into vogue in 1966, during a march in Mississippi, after **Stokely Carmichael** was arrested for putting up a tent on the grounds of a black high school. After his release, Carmichael delivered an angry speech in which he advocated black power. The term quickly became the slogan for all those who supported black militancy. Its meaning was as confusing as it was controversial. Each organization that used it employed the term differently.

For Carmichael and his friends at **Student Nonviolent Coordinating Committee (SNCC)**, it meant black economic self-determination and the exclusion of whites from policy-making decisions involving blacks. He advocated an economic program similar to that used by other ethnic groups to gain economic independence. Later Carmichael claimed the term as a logical growth of the unfulfilled promises of the civil rights movement and **Malcolm X**'s call for racial separation. Whatever the meaning, black power meant the end of the SNCC's racial cooperation. The group expelled whites, moved toward armed self-defense, and moved toward world revolution. For the **Black Panthers**, the meaning was black unity and resistance to the oppressive powers of the state. They added to this mix a call for increased cultural awareness by African Americans. Therefore, they would call for culturally relevant courses and expositions to display black achievements. After the election of **Richard Hatcher** in Gary, Indiana, and **Carl Stokes** in Cleveland, Ohio, in November 1967, black power took another form. For black leaders of the latter part of the era, who participated in the Black Power Conferences, it meant a unification of African-American political power to direct it at specific targets of reform. They advocated marshalling African-American voting strength to elect minority candidates to office. (AAB)

BIBLIOGRAPHY

Cone, James A. and Grayroud Wilmore, eds. *Black Theology.* Maryknoll, NY: Orbis, 1993.

McCartney, John T. *Black Power Ideologies.* Philadelphia: Temple University Press, 1992.

Black Separatism

During the 1960s, civil rights leaders fought for both equality and full inclusion in American society. At the same time that civil rights leaders were winning judicial and legislative victories, the idea of black separatism began to gain momentum in the African-American community. Black separatism followed in the wake of the **black power** movement when **Malcolm X**, a Muslim sect leader, won a large following on speaking tours that pressed for separatism. More recently, some African Americans have come to view racial separatism as the only solution to the problems in the black community. The institutions of the white community, they argue, continue to fail them. Therefore, black separatists call for the creation of separate but parallel black institutions. Black separatists, such as Conrad Worrill, of the National Black United Front, and **Louis Farrakhan,** of the **Nation of Islam,** the country's largest secular black nationalist group, push for separate schools, businesses, and celebrations for African Americans. **See also** Black Nationalism. (VDD)

BIBLIOGRAPHY

Bartholet, Elizabeth. "Race Separatism in the Family: More Transracial Adoption Debate." *Duke Journal of Gender Law & Policy* 2 (1995).

Beck, Joan. "Why Yearn for Africa When America Is Home." *Tampa Tribune* (February 24, 1997).

Black Star Steamship Line

The Black Star Line of steamships was founded in the early 1900s by **Marcus Garvey**, a noted Pan-Africanist, and founder of the **Universal Negro Improvement Association (UNIA).** The Black Star Line was part of Garvey's plan to provide economic, military, and political influence to blacks in the cause of equality. After negotiations between the UNIA and Liberia failed, and his financial and legal difficulties mounted, Garvey traveled abroad to raise backing for the steamship line. In 1925, Garvey was sentenced to a five-year prison term by the United States government for misusing the U.S. mail system to defraud investors of the Black Star Steamship Line. As a result, all plans for the steamship line were halted. **See also** Pan-Africanism.

BIBLIOGRAPHY

Clarke, John Henrik. *Marcus Garvey and the Vision of Africa.* New York: Vintage Books, 1974.

Black United Front

The Black United Front was first founded in 1968 by civil rights activists in Washington. They advocated community control over police and increased representation of blacks on the police force as a means to eliminate police brutality against African Americans. In 1980, the organization was revived by Reverend Daughtry of Brooklyn as a community action grassroots organization to address issues of unemployment, and to improve employment opportunity, education, and other social conditions of African Americans. (EC)

BIBLIOGRAPHY

Cole, Katherine, ed. *Minority Organizations: A National Directory.* Garnett Park: Garnett Park Press, 1992.

Black Women's Roundtable (BWR)

The Black Women's Roundtable (BWR) is a major program sponsored by the **National Coalition on Black Voter Participation**. BWR was founded in 1983 with the specific goals of emphasizing the importance of black women's votes; developing the leadership potential of black women and preparing them to run for public office; and ensuring the involvement of black women in policy discussions about gender issues and the importance of black women to the women's movement. The roundtable provides information on such women's issues as health care, child care, and literacy. **See also** Operation Big Vote.

BIBLIOGRAPHY

"The Black Women's Roundtable." National Coalition on Black Voter Participation Web site <http://www.bigvote.org>, 1998.

Lucien E. Blackwell (1931–)

Lucien Blackwell was born in Pennsylvania on August 1, 1931. He served four years in the Pennsylvania General Assembly and almost four full terms in Philadelphia City Council before being elected to the U.S. House of Representatives as a Democrat in 1991. He became a member of the **Congressional Black Caucus.**

BIBLIOGRAPHY

"Lucien E. Blackwell." *Congressional Quarterly Weekly Report* 49, no. 46 (November 16, 1991): 3406.

Bloc Voting

Bloc voting means that members of a particular group choose only their own preferred candidates in political contests and refuse to endorse candidates from other groups. Bloc voting occurs during elections where cleavages based on race, class, or partisanship have divided voters. As a result, a candidate's percentage of the vote will typically depend on his or her group's share of the electorate. For racial minorities, bloc voting is a barrier to office holding because a minority-preferred candidate cannot win if other racial groups will only vote for their own candidates. In a two-candidate race where only 35 percent of the voting population is black, no candidate preferred by blacks can win a majority of votes if whites vote as a bloc. According to the **Voting Rights Act Amendments of 1982,** racial bloc voting is one factor minorities may use to demonstrate racial discrimination in litigation. In cases like *Thornburg v. Gingles* (involving North Carolina's state legislature), the Supreme Court ruled that continued racial bloc voting warranted the creation of majority-black legislative districts. (KC)

BIBLIOGRAPHY

Grofman, Bernard, Lisa Handley, and Richard G. Niemi. *Minority Representation and the Quest for Voting Equality*. New York: Cambridge University Press, 1992.
Parker, Frank. *Black Votes Count*. Chapel Hill: University of North Carolina Press, 1990.

Daniel Terry Blue, Jr. (1949–)

Daniel Terry Blue, Jr., a Democrat from Wake County, North Carolina, was elected speaker of the North Carolina House of Representatives on January 30, 1991. Representative Blue is the first African American to hold this office in North Carolina, and the first this century to be speaker of a southern state legislature. First elected in 1980, Blue has been reelected to the house of representatives ever since. He has served as chair of the Appropriations Committee, the Judiciary Committee, and the legislative Black Caucus. (KLH)

BIBLIOGRAPHY

North Carolina Secretary of State. *Legislative Manual*. Raleigh: North Carolina Publication Division, 1989.

Board of Education of Oklahoma City v. Dowell (1991)

In *Board of Education of Oklahoma City v. Dowell*, 498 U.S. 237 (1991), the Supreme Court upheld Oklahoma City's Student Reassignment Plan, which essentially returned a number of public schools to segregated status and placed the school district under local control. In a scathing dissent, Supreme Court Justice **Thurgood Marshall** argued that the majority acted as if "13 years of desegregation was enough." Barker and Barker (1994) identified *Dowell* as only one example of Chief Justice Rehnquist Court's move away from judicial supervision of school desegregation. (EP)

BIBLIOGRAPHY

Barker, Lucius J. and Twiley W. Barker, Jr. *Civil Liberties and the Constitution: Cases and Commentaries*. Englewood Cliff, NJs: Prentice Hall, 1994.

Bob Jones University v. United States (1983)

Bob Jones University, a private, church-affiliated university in Greenville, South Carolina, had a policy denying admission to individuals engaged in or supportive of interracial marriage or dating. Because of this, the Internal Revenue Service (IRS) revoked the institution's tax-exempt status in 1975. The university responded by paying a portion of its taxes, but not the full sum. Moreover, the school filed for a refund of the taxes that it did pay. The IRS refused the refund request and filed a counterclaim asking for all unpaid taxes to be paid. The dispute eventually landed in U.S. district court. The university argued that the free exercise of religion clause of the First Amendment allowed it to maintain its alleged racially discriminatory admissions policies. The district court found for the university. However, on appeal, the district court's decision was reversed by the Supreme Court in *Bob Jones University v. United States,* 461 U.S. 574 (1983). **See also** the text of the **Fourteenth Amendment** in Appendix 1 to this part.

BIBLIOGRAPHY

Miller, R. Charles. "Rendering Unto Caesar: Religious Publishers and the Public Benefit Rule." *University of Pennsylvania Law Review* 134, no. 2 (January 1986): 433–56.
Pepper, Stephen. "A Brief for the Free Exercise Clause." *The Journal of Law and Religion* 7, no. 2 (Summer 1989): 323–62.

Bob-Lo Excursion Company v. People of State of Michigan (1948)

Bois Blanc Island was a Canadian recreational site near Detroit that could only be reached by private ferry supplied by

Bob-Lo Excursion Company. The company refused to carry African Americans to the island, and no other means of access existed. The Supreme Court, in *Bob-Lo Excursion Company v. People of State of Michigan*, 333 U.S. 28 (1948), ruled that Michigan's Civil Rights Act could be employed to require Bob-Lo to carry African Americans to the Canadian island because the island was a recreational adjunct of Detroit and a matter of local, as opposed to international, concern. (FHJ)

BIBLIOGRAPHY
Greenberg, Jack. *Race Relations and American Law*. New York: Columbia University Press, 1959.

Julian Bond (1940–)

Civil rights activist Julian Bond was born in Atlanta, Georgia, in 1940. Taught by **Martin Luther King, Jr.** in 1961 at Morehouse College, Bond was a student activist and a cofounder of the **Student Nonviolent Coordinating Committee** (**SNCC**). Bond participated in numerous **sit-ins** and voter registration drives. He became so well-respected that he was nominated for vice-president at the 1968 Democratic Convention in Chicago, an honor he had to decline because he was not old enough to serve. He served in the Georgia House of Representatives as a Democrat and in 1986 lost a congressional election for the United States House of Representatives. He has been successively teaching for the past seven years at the University of Virginia and American University. He is much in demand as a speaker and host of the *Black Forum* television program. (FAS)

BIBLIOGRAPHY
Bond, Julian. *Time to Speak, a Time to Act: The Movement in Politics*. New York: Simon and Schuster, 1972.

Bond v. Floyd (1966)

The black activist leader and Georgia state representative **Julian Bond** was excluded from his seat in the Georgia House of Representatives because of his stand against the Vietnam War and what he believed to be its deleterious effect on the African-American community. In the case he brought against Georgia, *Bond v. Floyd*, 385 U.S. 116 (1966), the U.S. Supreme Court ruled that while a state can require a legislator to take an oath swearing allegiance to the U.S. Constitution, it cannot restrict a legislator's right to speak freely on issues of common concern. (FHJ)

BIBLIOGRAPHY
Neary, John. *Julian Bond: Black Rebel*. New York: William Morrow, 1971.

Thomas Bradley (1917–1998)

Thomas Bradley was born in Calvert, Texas, on December 29, 1917. He attended the University of California, Los Angeles from 1937 to 1940. Upon graduation, he joined the Los Angeles Police Department. While a member of the department, he earned a law degree in 1956 from Southwestern University Law School. A Democrat, Bradley became the first African American on the City Council of Los Angeles in 1963. He became noted for his quiet manner and his patient movement for consensus. These political skills furthered his career and in 1973 he became the first African-American mayor of Los Angeles and one of the first two black mayors of cities over one million in the United States. (**Coleman Young** of Detroit was the other.)

Bradley was a popular mayor and served five terms during which he helped build Los Angeles into a more unified city instead of a series of suburban towns. He helped build a downtown center, complete with a skyline. In 1984, the Olympics came to Los Angeles, due partly to the city's newly unified identity, its reputation as a cultural center, and the political clout of Mayor Bradley. Bradley helped pass a series of major laws that included the construction of a mass transit system. In spite of his acknowledged political skills, Bradley twice lost gubernatorial elections to Republican opponents. The last years of his incumbency were marked by racial strife. The Rodney King beating by Los Angeles police officers and the riots that followed the not guilty verdict in the first trial of those officers resulted in a sour end to his fine career. (FAS)

BIBLIOGRAPHY
Payne, J. Gregory and Scott C. Ratzan. *Tom Bradley: The Impossible Dream*. Santa Monica, CA. Roundtable, 1986.

Breedlove v. Shuttles, Tax Collector (1938)

Breedlove v. Shuttles, Tax Collector, 392 U.S. 277 (1938), involved a Georgia statute that levied a poll tax of $1.00 per year on all inhabitants of the state (except those under 21 or over 50, and all females who did not register to vote), which had to be paid in full before an individual could register to vote. Breedlove, a white male citizen 28 years old at the time, argued that his **Fourteenth Amendment** rights were violated by the poll tax. The Court disagreed, finding that "voting is a privilege derived from the State" subject only to the limitations of the Fifteenth and Nineteenth Amendments. **See also** Fifteenth Amendment. (CJM)

Andrew F. Brimmer (1926–)

Andrew Brimmer was born in Louisiana in 1926. He received his Ph.D. in economics from Harvard in 1957. He was assistant secretary for economic affairs under President John F. Kennedy and was appointed by President Lyndon Johnson as the first black member of the Board of Governors of the Federal Reserve Bank. He served as chairman of the District of Columbia Financial Responsibility and Management Assistance Authority, a presidentially appointed panel that runs the government of Washington, D.C.; his term expired in June 1998. (JCW)

BIBLIOGRAPHY
"Congress Gives Noted Economist Andrew Brimmer Authority to Oversee D.C. Financial Recovery." *Jet* 92, no. 13 (August 18, 1997): 39–41.

Magnusson, Paul. "Putsch on the Potomac." *Business Week* (August 18, 1997): 48.

Edward W. Brooke III (1919–)

Edward W. Brooke III is a former U.S. Senator from Massachusetts. He won election in 1962 as attorney general of Massachusetts, gaining respect as a vigorous fighter of organized crime. Brooke was elected in 1966 as a Republican senator from Massachusetts, becoming the first African American in that body since Reconstruction. While in the Senate, he served on the President's Commission on Civil Disorders in 1967 and he played a major role in preventing the nomination of G. Harrold Carswell to the U.S. Supreme Court. He was defeated in his 1978 Senate race. (WWH)

Cutler, John Henry. *Ed Brooke: Biography of a Senator.* Indianapolis: Bobbs-Merrill, 1972.

Brotherhood of Sleeping Car Porters

The Brotherhood of Sleeping Car Porters was founded in 1925 by **A. Philip Randolph,** himself a former porter and railroad waiter. The original purpose of the organization was to assist African-American railway-car workers of the Pullman Palace Car Company, who were battling job-related discrimination, poor wages, and difficult working conditions. In 1935, Randolph and the Brotherhood of Sleeping Car Porters were successful in negotiating a union contract with the company that improved the working conditions for black workers. While the brotherhood continued to work for the rights of workers, it also later expanded its mission to include other civil rights issues. **See also** Edgar Daniel Nixon.

Brazeal, Brailsford Reese. *The Brotherhood of Sleeping Car Porters.* New York: Harper & Brothers, 1946.
Wright, Sarah E. A. *Philip Randolph.* Englewood Cliffs, NJ: Silver Burdett, 1990.

Corrine Brown (1946–)

Corrine Brown, a liberal Democrat who served in the Florida House of Assembly (1983–1993), was elected to Congress in 1992 to represent the largely poor 3rd Congressional District of northern Florida. She has worked to create opportunities for the poor at the numerous military bases in her district. (EC)

Sack, Kevin. "Victory of Five Redistricted Blacks Recasts Gerrymandering Dispute." *New York Times* 146 (November 23, 1996): N1, L1.

Elaine Brown (1943–)

Elaine Brown was born in Philadephia and moved to Los Angeles in 1965. She joined the **Black Panther Party** in 1968 and became its chairperson in 1974, the highest leadership role ever held by a woman in the party. She was a delegate to the Democratic National Convention in 1976 and is currently an activist, writer, and popular lecturer.

Brown, Elaine. *A Taste of Power: A Black Woman's Story.* New York: Anchor Books, 1994.

H. "Rap" Brown (1943–)

Activist H. Rap Brown, who later changed his name to Jamil Abdullah Al-Amin, was born in Baton Rouge, Louisiana. He worked on voter registration drives in the 1960s for the **Student Nonviolent Coordinating Committee (SNCC)** and later succeeded **Stokely Carmichael** as chair in 1967. A fiery orator, he emerged as one of the most militant of the "black power" advocates during the 1960s. Very popular with young African Americans, he was adept at gaining national media coverage. His book, *Die Nigger, Die!* was published in 1969. (PLF)

Al-Amin, Jamil. *Revolution by the Book: The Rap Is Live.* Boston: The Writer Inc., 1993.
"Ex-radical of the '60s, H. Rap Brown, Charged in Atlanta Shooting." *Jet* 88, no.16 (August 20, 1995): 46.

Jesse Brown (1944–)

Jesse Brown was born in Detroit, Michigan. He graduated from Chicago City College and served as a Marine in Vietnam where he was wounded and partially disabled by sniper fire. He worked at the Disabled American Veterans advocacy group and in 1988 became their first black executive director. He lobbied extensively for veteran causes. In 1993, he was appointed the first black secretary of veterans affairs under President Bill Clinton. He was re-appointed during Clinton's second term, but resigned in July 1997. (JCW)

Mcallister, Bill. "VA Secretary Submits Resignation." *Washington Post* (June 7, 1997): A8.

Ronald H. Brown (1941–1996)

Ron Brown was a lawyer and a politician. He became chair of the Democratic National Committee in 1989, the first African American to lead a major political party in the United States. He served as secretary of commerce in the Clinton administration from 1993 until 1996, when he died in a plane crash. After growing up in Harlem, graduating from Middlebury College, and serving in the army, Brown began working for the National Urban League in New York in 1967. He earned a law degree from St. John's University in 1970. In 1973, he accepted a position with the Washington, D.C. branch of the Urban League, and quickly rose to vice president of that branch.

From 1978 until 1981, Brown worked on the staff of Senator Edward Kennedy (D-MA). From 1982 to 1985, he held the post of deputy chairperson of the Democratic National Committee, then joined **Jesse Jackson's** campaign for president. At the 1988 Democratic Convention, he managed the floor for Jackson and demonstrated skill as a coalition builder. As chairperson for the Democratic National Committee from 1989 to 1992, he played a key role in Clinton's victory, helping to garner moderate support by stressing economic issues.

In 1993, Brown became the first black secretary of commerce. For the next three years, he worked to boost American trade overseas in hopes of creating more jobs at home. Brown remained an important presidential adviser until his death on April 3, 1996, in Croatia. (AD)

BIBLIOGRAPHY

Swarns, Rachel. "Harlem Remembers the Heart that Never Left." *New York Times* (April 5, 1996): A1, A13.

Willie L. Brown, Jr. (1934–)

The first African American to be elected mayor of San Francisco, Willie Brown has been called the most powerful black elected official in the United States. Leaving his family in the segregated town of Mineola in rural eastern Texas to attend college, Brown graduated from San Francisco State University and Hastings College of Law. He became a community activist, joining the **National Association for the Advancement of Colored People (NAACP)** and the National Urban League, and in 1964 was elected to serve San Francisco in the California State Assembly. Championing legislation benefitting minorities, elderly, and the poor, Brown rose to power within the Assembly Democratic Caucus. In 1980, after negotiating with Republicans, Brown mobilized a unique bipartisan coalition to elect him assembly speaker, becoming the first African American to hold the powerful post. Brown shrewdly wielded the formal and informal powers of the office by raising campaign contributions, assigning legislative staff, and largely directing the legislative process. Given his vast power, Brown called himself the "Ayatollah of the Assembly." After term limits forced Brown from office, he mobilized a multi-ethnic political coalition to score an overwhelming victory for mayor in 1995. Brown's exuberant public image energized the city. In addition to promoting regional economic growth, subsidizing affordable housing, and securing federal funds for San Francisco, Brown actively forges public-private partnerships to channel private resources to benefit poor, minority, and working-class residents. (CC)

BIBLIOGRAPHY

Beiler, David. "The Unsinkable Willie Brown: How One of America's Most Controversial Politicians Got Elected Mayor of San Francisco." *Campaigns & Elections* (February, 1996): 20–27.
Richardson, James. *Willie Brown: A Biography.* Berkeley: University of California Press, 1996.

Brown v. Board of Education, Topeka, Kansas (1954)

The doctrine of **"separate but equal"** established by the 1896 *Plessy v. Ferguson* decision was the target of the litigation sponsored by **National Association for the Advancement of Colored People (NAACP)** in *Brown v. Board of Education, Topeka, Kansas,* 347 U.S. 483 (1954), and throughout the first

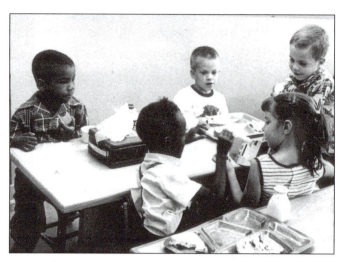

The goal of *Brown v. Board of Education* (1954) was to create integrated and equal education for all children. *National Archives.*

half of the twentieth century. The NAACP believed that pressure to provide equal physical facilities would in time prove too costly for states and would thereby cause states to abandon segregated education for practical reasons. The southern response was to appropriate more funds to maintain segregated schools. In 1950, NAACP Legal Defense Fund attorney **Thurgood Marshall** led the effort to directly confront the doctrine of "separate but equal" with a class action suit that concentrated not on physical facilities but on intangible factors that denied black children an equal educational experience.

Bringing together cases from Delaware, Virginia, and South Carolina with a suit against the Topeka, Kansas, Board of Education for appeal to the Supreme Court, Marshall and the NAACP argued that the plaintiffs' rights under the equal protection provision of the **Fourteenth Amendment** had been violated. Chief Justice Earl Warren, delivering the unanimous decision of the Court on May 17, 1954, said that elementary and secondary school education was "the very foundation of citizenship" and, as such, it "must be made available to all on equal terms." Warren held that education was not only affected by "tangible factors" such as facilities, but also by intangible factors such as the psychological impact of segregation. The court's decision in *Brown v. Board of Education* began the dismantling of the legal supports for segregation in the United States. **See also** NAACP Legal Defense and Education Fund. (GAA)

BIBLIOGRAPHY

Hall, Kermit, et al. *American Legal History: Cases and Materials.* 2nd ed. New York: Oxford University Press, 1996.
Tushnet, Mark V. *The NAACP's Legal Strategy against Segregated Education.* Chapel Hill: University of North Carolina Press, 1987.

Blanche K. Bruce (1841–1898)

Blanche Kelso Bruce, born into slavery in Virginia, became the first black person to serve a full term in the United States Senate, serving as a Republican from Mississippi (1875–1881).

He settled in Mississippi in 1869, where he became a prosperous landowner. He found success in local politics as registrar of voters in Tallahatchie County, and as tax assessor, sheriff, tax collector, and supervisor of education in Bolivar County. In the Senate, he supported government land grants in the West to black emigrants from the South; he opposed the Chinese exclusion bill of 1879, and called for a humane Native American policy. In 1889, he became re-

Blanche Kelso Bruce, born into slavery in Virginia, became the first African American to serve a full term in the United States Senate (1875-1881). *Library of Congress.*

corder of deeds for the District of Columbia and registrar of the treasury from 1897 until his death. (EC)

BIBLIOGRAPHY

Harris, William C. "Blanche K. Bruce of Mississippi: Conservative Assimilationist." In H.N. Rabinowitz, ed. *Southern Black Leaders of the Reconstruction Era.* Urbana: University of Illinois Press, 1982: 3–38.

Buchanan v. Warley (1917)

In *Buchanan v. Warley*, 245 U.S. 60 (1917), suit was brought by a white property owner, Buchanan who wanted to sell real estate to a black purchaser. Although the purchaser had agreed to the transaction, local ordinances restricted the sale of property to blacks. In finding the local ordinance in violation of the **Fourteenth Amendment,** the Supreme Court held that the racially restrictive covenant impaired the right of the plaintiff to sell his property because its effect was that the plaintiff could not sell the lot to a person of color who was willing and ready to buy the property and had obligated himself to take it. (PLF)

BIBLIOGRAPHY

D'Amato, Anthony A., Rosemary Metrailer, and Stephen L. Wasby. *Desegregation from Brown to Alexander.* Carbondale, IL: Southern Illinois University Press, 1977.
Greenberg, Jack. *Race Relations and American Law.* New York: Columbia University Press, 1959.

Ralph Bunche (1903–1971)

Ralph Bunche, scholar, activist, and diplomat, received widest acclaim for his part in the 1949 armistice agreement between Israel and the Arab states, garnering him the Nobel Peace Prize in 1950. Although Bunche is largely forgotten today, his socially progressive scholarship and civil service record is unsurpassed in the field of political science. Bunche was the first African American to earn a doctorate in political

science in the United States, and he served as the first African-American president of the American Political Science Association in 1953. Ralph Bunche was the only African American in the U.S. delegation charged with establishing the United Nations; he retired as Undersecretary-General of the UN. During the 1950s Bunche's individual career of "black firsts" was used against the African-American community's grievance of group **discrimination.** (RAM)

BIBLIOGRAPHY

Bunche, Ralph. *Ralph Bunche: Selected Speeches & Writings* In Charles P. Henry, ed. Ann Arbor: The University of Michigan Press, 1995.
Rivlin, Benjamin. *Ralph Bunche: The Man and His Times.* New York: Holmes and Meier, 1990.

Yvonne Brathwaite Burke (1932–)

Democrat Yvonne Brathwaite Burke made history when she became the first African-American woman from California elected to Congress. Winning her first political campaign in 1966, Burke became the first African-American female elected to the California State Assembly. Burke's success as an assemblywoman led her to run for and win a seat in the United States House of Representatives in 1972. Upon her resignation from Congress in 1978, Burke ran unsuccessfully for the position of attorney general of California. In 1992, Burke reemerged in politics by winning a seat as Los Angeles County supervisor. (DH)

BIBLIOGRAPHY

Potter, Joan, and Constance Claytor. *African-American Firsts: Famous, Little-Known and Unsung Triumphs of Blacks in America.* Elizabethtown, NY: Pinto Press, 1994.

Busing

Busing began as a way to remedy **de facto segregation,** which was more prevalent in the North than in the South. In the South, systems of **de jure segregation**, or segregation enforced by law, existed until they were challenged in the courts. In ***Brown v. Board of Education,*** for example, the U.S. Supreme Court found that separate school facilities were inherently unequal. Many northern school districts, however, had more trouble ending de facto segregation because the segregation was directly linked to housing patterns. Whites tended to live with whites and blacks tended to live with blacks. Because most schools educated students from the immediate neighborhood, this led to segregated schools. By the 1970s, schools in the North were more segregated than in the South.

Municipal governments, often under court order, began to initiate a variety of plans to integrate urban schools, but busing became one of the most common methods of desegregating schools. White students were bused to black schools and black students to white schools. Some school systems, such as Baltimore's districts, integrated successfully and peacefully; many, however, did not. For example, racial tension in South Boston skyrocketed when black students were bused to "all white" schools.

Busing failed to achieve racial integration in many cities as middle-class whites fled to the suburbs or enrolled their children in private schools. By the 1970s, integration was virtually impossible because children from racial and ethnic minorities formed a majority of the large-city school population. **See also** Education; Segregation/Integration/Separation; Separate But Equal. (VDD)

BIBLIOGRAPHY

DiConti, Veronica. *Interest Groups and Education Reform: The Latest Crusade to Restructure the Schools*. Lanham, MD: University Press of America, 1996.

Gitlin, Todd. *The Sixties, Years of Hope, Days of Rage*. New York: Bantam Books, 1987.

Williams, Juan. *Eyes on the Prize: America's Civil Rights Years 1954–1965*. New York: Penguin Books, 1998.

Richard H. Cain (1825–1887)

Richard H. Cain, a Republican from South Carolina, served two terms in the United States House of Representatives (1873–1875 and 1877–1879). He was the first African-American clergyman to serve in Congress. Born a free African American, Cain served as an Episcopal pastor in a Brooklyn, New York, parish from 1861 until 1865 when he moved to South Carolina. In 1868, he was elected as a delegate to the state constitutional convention. From 1868 to 1872, he served as a state senator. He left politics in 1880 when he was appointed bishop of the African Methodist Episcopal Church. Cain was also a founder and president of Paul Quinn College.

BIBLIOGRAPHY

Mann, Kenneth E. "Richard Harvey Cain: Congressman, Minister, and Champion of Civil Rights." *Negro History Bulletin* 35 (March 1972): 64–66.

John Calhoun (1899–1988)

John Calhoun was born in South Carolina and graduated from the Hampton Institute. He helped found the Atlanta Negro Voters League in 1948 and was the head of the Atlanta Chapter of the **National Association for the Advancement of Colored People (NAACP)**. He headed a community leadership group, Economic Opportunity Atlanta, from 1965 to 1972, when he was elected city councilman of Atlanta.

BIBLIOGRAPHY

Rabinowitz, Howard. *Southern Black Leaders of the Reconstruction Era.* Urbana: University of Illinois Press, 1982.

Stokely Carmichael (1941–1998)

Stokely Carmichael, known later in his life as Kwame Toure, was chairperson of the **Student Nonviolent Coordinating Committee (SNCC)** from 1966 to 1967. As chair, Carmichael focused on black voting issues, general political reform, and equal rights. Carmichael is often credited with first using the phrase "**black power**." This slogan was ultimately adopted by the SNCC and other African-American civil rights groups as a rallying cry and philosophy dedicated to proactively uniting African Americans to overcome oppression. Carmichael eventually joined the **Black Panther Party** in 1969 and accepted political asylum in Guinea. Carmichael had become such a radical voice that Congress discussed deporting him. Carmichael joined the Pan African Movement and helped establish worldwide chapters of the All-African Peoples Revolutionary Party. In 1979, he changed his name to Kwame Toure in honor of Kwame Nkrumah and Sedou Toure, his mentors. He died in Guinea in 1998. **See also** Pan-Africanism.

BIBLIOGRAPHY

Carmichael, Stokely. *Stokely Speaks.* New York: Random House, 1971.
Carmichael, Stokely and Charles V. Hamilton. *Black Power.* New York: Vintage Books, 1967.

Benjamin Chavis (1948–)

Although Benjamin Chavis is best known for his efforts in **civil rights**, he has been involved in many other events and organizations. He currently serves as national convener of the National African American Summit, which is made up of representatives of African-American organizations. For a brief period in the early 1990s he served as CEO of the **National Association for the Advancement of Colored People (NAACP).** However, he resigned under pressure because of growing financial and sexual scandals under his administration. He is also an ordained minister. (CEM)

BIBLIOGRAPHY

Chavis, Benjamin F. *Psalms from Prison.* New York: Pilgrim Press, 1983.
Thompson, Garland L. "A New Beginning as Chavis Takes the Helm." *The Crisis* (April/ May 1993): 24–26.

Henry P. Cheatham (1857–1935)

Henry Cheatham was born a slave on a plantation in North Carolina in 1857. After the **Civil War** and emancipation, Cheatham received his bachelor's degree from Shaw University. He was elected to the House of Representatives as a Republican in 1888, and reelected in 1890. He founded the Oxford Orphanage in Oxford, North Carolina, in 1901.

BIBLIOGRAPHY

Ragsdale, Bruce, and Joel Treese. *Black Americans in Congress, 1870–1989.* Washington, DC: U.S. Government Printing Office, 1990.

Shirley Chisholm (1926–)

In 1968, Shirley Chisholm became the first African-American woman to be elected to the United States Congress. In 1972, she became the first African American to make a serious bid to become president of the United States. Before serving in Congress, Chisholm was a representative in the New York State Assembly in Albany. A former nursery school teacher and day-care center director, Chisholm, who earned a master's degree in elementary education, introduced legislation in Albany to expand opportunities for college-level training, to extend unemployment insurance to domestic workers, and to publicly support day-care centers.

In Congress, Chisholm, who represented the majority-black and Puerto Rican 12th District in the Bedford Stuyvesant and Bushwick sections of Brooklyn, was a member of the all-important House Rules Committee and secretary of the House Democratic Caucus. Her legislative work focused on black colleges, compensatory education, minimum wage for domestics, immigration, and poverty policy.

In 1972, Chisholm entered the Democratic contest for president, the first African American to run for the nomination of one of the two major parties. Although her share of the popular vote never exceeded 7 percent and she won only 35 delegates in the 10 primaries she entered, Chisholm received 152 delegate votes on the first ballot at the Democratic Party's 1972 presidential nominating convention in Miami. Her candidacy, however, was not heavily supported by either black leaders or the black masses. Only roughly a quarter of the black delegates at the convention voted for her. Chisholm attributed her low support among blacks to gender, concluding in her book, *The Good Fight*, "If anyone thinks white men are sexist, let them check out black men."

After her presidential race, Chisholm continued to be reelected to her congressional seat by substantial margins, so it stunned many when she decided not to seek reelection in 1982. Conceding that her decision had been influenced by the growing conservatism in the nation, the defeat of many liberal lawmakers, and the election of Republican President Ronald Reagan in 1980, Chisholm announced that after seven terms in Congress she desired to return to "a more private life." Her retirement brought to an end a political career well known both in her home district and nationally. Chisholm remained active in politics, co-founding and heading the national Political Congress of Black Women in 1984 to encourage and assist more black women to enter politics as elected or appointed officials. In 1993, she was nominated by President Bill Clinton to serve as ambassador to Jamaica, an honor she declined. (LFW)

BIBLIOGRAPHY
Chisholm, Shirley. *The Good Fight*. New York: Harper and Row, 1973.
Haskins, James. *Fighting Shirley Chisholm*. New York: Dial Press, 1975.

City of Mobile, Alabama v. Bolden (1980)

City of Mobile, Alabama v. Bolden, 446 U.S. 55 (1980), was a class action suit by black citizens of Mobile challenging the city's at-large method of electing its commissioners. The Supreme Court held that the at-large electoral system in Mobile does not violate the rights of the city's black voters. The Court determined that racially discriminatory motivation is a necessary ingredient of **Fourteenth Amendment** equal protection and **Fifteenth Amendment** violations, that there is no right to guarantee the election of black candidates, and that equal protection does not protect any "political group" from electoral defeat. **See also** At-Large Districts. (PLF)

BIBLIOGRAPHY
Haddad, Mark E. "Getting Results Under Section 5 of the Voting Rights Act." (Case note) *Yale Law Journal* 94, no. 1 (November 1984): 139–62.
Soifer, Aviam. "Complacency and Constitutional Law." (Symposium: Judicial Review v. Democracy) *Ohio State Law Journal* 42, no. 1 (Winter 1981): 383–409.

City of Richmond v. Deans (1930)

J. B. Deans, an African American, challenged a Richmond, Virginia, ordinance that prohibited minorities from moving into neighborhoods or blocks that were mostly white. Additionally, the ordinance forbade interracial marriages. Deans sought an injunction against the city of Richmond after he bought a house in a majority white neighborhood. Deans was successful in his challenge of the ordinance at the lower court level. In the decision *City of Richmond v. Deans,* 281 U.S. 704 (1930), the city's appeal to the U.S. Supreme Court, the Court let stand the lower court's ruling, effectively striking down the city's ordinance.

BIBLIOGRAPHY
Bardolph, Richard. *The Civil Rights Record: Black Americans and the Law, 1849–1970*. New York: Crowell, 1970.

City of Richmond v. United States (1975)

The city of Richmond, Virginia, sought to annex an area adjacent to the city while maintaining the standards of the **Voting Rights Act of 1965**. The city proposed a new city council election system with nine members elected from nine geographically distinct districts to replace the current at-large system. A three-judge District Court, in *City of Richmond v. United States,* 422 U.S. 358 (1975), denied the application of the city because it believed that the new system would deny or abridge the right to vote based on race or color. On appeal, however, the U.S. Supreme Court disagreed with the lower court and remanded the case back for further study of the nine-member ward system. **See also** At-Large Districts. (CEM)

BIBLIOGRAPHY
Galub, Arthur L. *The Burger Court, 1969–1984*. Millwood, NY: AFP, 1984.

Civil Rights Act of 1866

The Civil Rights Act of 1866 was a measure proposed by Republican Senator Lyman Trumball of Illinois, chairman of the Senate Judicial Committee. The bill passed the 39th Congress and was then vetoed by President Andrew Johnson, precipitating an angry struggle between the executive and legislative branches of the government. The bill was designed to provide minimal protection of civil rights for former slaves. The bill gave to all persons, except Native Americans, national citizenship and spelled out their equal rights to bring suits, make contracts, and enjoy full and equal benefit of all laws and proceedings for the security of person and property. The bill authorized district attorneys, marshals, and Freedmen's Bureau officials to bring suit against violators in trials held in federal courts, and it provided for the fining or imprisonment of those found guilty. The measure was designed to provide meaning to the **Thirteenth Amendment** and set the parameters of the freed slave's new freedom. **See also** Reconstruction. (AAB)

BIBLIOGRAPHY

Cox, John and LaWanda Cox. *Politics, Principles, and Prejudices, 1865–1866*. New York: Free Press, 1963.

Civil Rights Act of 1870

Although the **Fifteenth Amendment** to the U.S. Constitution assured former slaves of the right to vote, many southern whites sought to prevent African Americans from registering and voting when the amendment took effect on March 30, 1870. Employers and landlords threatened blacks in the daytime, and the **Ku Klux Klan** sought to discourage blacks through terror at night.

On May 31, 1870, Congress passed the first voting rights act, establishing criminal penalties for anyone who used "force, bribery, threats, [and] intimidation . . . [to] hinder, delay, prevent, or obstruct" eligible voters from registering to vote, running for office, and voting. In addition, the law prohibited the following: the unequal application of any voting prerequisite on the basis of "race, color, or previous condition of servitude"; any deletion of the name of any office seeker from a ballot; any effort to prevent the winner of an election from taking office; registering dead persons or voting for dead persons or for persons more than once; harboring fugitives who committed these offenses; or obstructing federal marshals from enforcing provisions of the law. The president was authorized to use the armed forces if needed to enforce the law.

On February 28, 1871, the law was amended. The amendment, known as the Civil Rights Act of 1871, provided that residents of towns with a population over 20,000 could petition the nearest federal circuit court to provide two election supervisors to inspect registration and voting procedures.

As a result, African Americans were elected to Congress from the southern states. Blacks also held various offices in the local and state governments and served on juries in the South for the first time. These politcal gains for African Americans were lost with the end of **Reconstruction** in 1877. (MH)

BIBLIOGRAPHY

Coulter, E. Merton. *The South During Reconstruction, 1865–1877*. Baton Rouge: Louisiana State University Press, 1947.

Davis, William Watson. "The Federal Enforcement Act." In *Studies in Southern History and Politics*. New York: Columbia University Press, 1914.

Du Bois, W.E.B. *Black Reconstruction*. New York: Harcourt, Brace, 1935.

Franklin, John Hope. *Reconstruction after the Civil War*, 2nd ed. Chicago: University of Chicago Press, 1994.

Civil Rights Act of 1875

The Civil Rights Act of 1875 was originally proposed in 1870 by Republican Senator Charles Sumner of Massachusetts. It was the last piece of **Reconstruction** legislation passed by Congress to ensure fair treatment for African Americans. The bill was designed to provide "full and equal enjoyment" of all the amenities of society. The law outlawed racial discrimination in theaters, hotels, railroads, juries, and other public places. Aggrieved persons could be compensated with up to $500. It went beyond the rights guaranteed by the Reconstruction governments. The U.S. Supreme Court declared this act unconstitutional in 1883 after hearing several challenges. The Court argued that the Congress had overstepped its bounds and intentions as outlined in the **Fourteenth** and **Fifteenth Amendments**, which were designed to protect people from state sponsored **discrimination** rather than from private party discrimination, thus setting the stage for the segregation which spread throughout the South. **See also** Segregation/Integration/Separation. (AAB)

BIBLIOGRAPHY

Nieman, Donald G. *African Americans and the Emergence of Segregation, 1986–1900*. New York: Garland, 1994.

Civil Rights Act of 1957

This act provided limited means to guarantee African Americans the right to vote, which had been denied throughout the southern United States since about 1900. Vice President Richard Nixon championed the bill, after meeting with **Martin Luther King, Jr.** on June 13, 1957. Majority Leader Lyndon Johnson moved the bill through the Senate in August, but only after dropping the provision that would have allowed the attorney general to initiate suits against school segregation.

The act required that federal officials demonstrate that blacks were denied the right to vote solely because of race, and that a pattern of racial discrimination existed. The act required jury trials for state officials accused of violating blacks' voting rights. This provision virtually eliminated any assistance to black voters because few southern juries would find white officials guilty.

Indeed, the federal government won only a handful of cases brought under the Civil Rights Act of 1957. While it accomplished little itself, the act helped convince King and other black leaders to fight even harder for effective legislation. **See also** Civil Rights Act of 1960; Civil Rights Act of 1964; Voting Rights Act of 1965. (AD)

BIBLIOGRAPHY

Branch, Taylor. *Parting the Waters: America in the King Years, 1954–1963*. New York: Simon and Schuster, 1988.

Civil Rights Act of 1960

After months of debate and threats of a filibuster by southern senators, President Dwight Eisenhower, on May 6, 1960, signed Public Law 86–449, the Civil Rights Act of 1960. This act was an attempt to strengthen and extend the **Civil Rights Act of 1957**. In particular, its main focus was to halt the widespread southern resistance against blacks registering to vote. Among other things, the law raised the fines for obstruction of court orders, mandated that voting records be kept for 22 months, imposed a fine on anyone who damaged or concealed voting records, and held the governing area responsible if the registrar of voters resigned. Although more suits were brought under this act than under the Civil Rights Act of 1957, it offered little more than symbolic extension of civil rights. Few blacks were registered because of this law. (WPS)

BIBLIOGRAPHY

Berman, Daniel M. *A Bill Becomes a Law: The Civil Rights Act of 1960*. New York: Macmillan, 1962.

Perry, Huey L. "Pluralist Theory & National Black Politics in the United States." *Polity* 23, no. 4 (Summer 1991): 549–65.

Civil Rights Act of 1964

Several events during 1963 helped to advance the passage of comprehensive civil rights legislation onto the national agenda. **Martin Luther King, Jr.** and the **Southern Christian Leadership Conference** (**SCLC**) led demonstrations against segregation in Birmingham, Alabama. The brutal police tactics against peaceful demonstrators appeared nightly on national television news. Public reaction among blacks and whites to the beating of men, women, and children finally

President Lyndon Johnson signs the Civil Rights Act of 1964. *Library of Congress.*

provoked President John F. Kennedy to propose a major civil rights bill to Congress. The **March on Washington,** highlighted by King's **"I Have a Dream"** speech, brought further public attention to the issue. After Kennedy was assassinated in November 1963, President Lyndon B. Johnson made civil rights his top domestic priority.

The Civil Rights Act of 1964, passed over the threat of a filibuster by southern senators, provided for the banishment of segregation from many areas of American life by placing the authority of the federal government squarely behind integration in schools, public accommodations, and employment. The law banned **discrimination** based on race, sex, color, religion, or national origin. The U.S. Department of Justice was authorized to sue schools or other state or local agencies that discriminated, and to sue private businesses, such as restaurants, hotels, or theaters, if they refused service to members of the protected group. Public programs, such as educational institutions, that continued to discriminate, risked the loss of federal funding, a substantial part of their budgets. Title VII of the legislation prohibited employment discrimination, a goal of civil rights groups for decades. The act also established an enforcement mechanism through the **Equal Employment Opportunity Commission (EEOC),** which has the authority to investigate complaints and to recommend solutions.

The Supreme Court upheld the constitutionality of the Civil Rights Act of 1964 in two cases during that same year, *Heart of Atlanta Motel v. U.S.* and *Katzenbach v. McClung.* **See also** "Birmingham Manifesto"; Birmingham Protests. (MWA)

BIBLIOGRAPHY

Branch, Taylor. *Parting the Waters: America in the King Years, 1954–1963*. New York: Simon and Schuster, 1988.

———. *Pillar of Fire*. New York: Simon and Schuster, 1998.

Nieman, Donald G. *Promises to Keep: African Americans and the Constitutional Order, 1776 to the Present*. New York: Oxford University Press, 1991.

Civil Rights Act of 1991

The Civil Rights Act of 1991 was a response to four 5–4 decisions delivered in June 1989 by the Supreme Court; the cases included *Lorance v. AT&T Technologies, Inc., Martin v. Wilks, Patterson v. McLean Credit Union,* and *Wards Cove Packing Co. v. Antonio.* These cases narrowed the scope of **affirmative action.** Prior to these rulings, the burden of proof in job discrimination suits had been placed on employers, requiring businesses to prove that there was a legitimate business reason for alleged discriminatory practices. These cases shifted the burden of proof in Title VII employment **discrimination** cases from employers to employees.

Civil rights organizations lobbied the U.S. Congress to enact measures that would overturn the court rulings, arguing that the court had undermined the protection granted by federal civil rights and equal employment legislation. In October 1990, Congress approved a bill designed to reverse the court rulings, which strengthened provisions of the **1964 Civil**

Rights Act. But President George Bush vetoed the legislation, stating that it would encourage hiring quotas.

In 1991, following months of negotiation, Congress again passed the bill, which provided additional remedies to deter harassment and intentional discrimination in the work place. On November 21, 1991, President Bush signed the Civil Rights Act of 1991. (EC)

BIBLIOGRAPHY

Blackwell, James E. *The Black Community: Diversity and Unity.* New York: HarperCollins, 1991.

Perry, H.L. and W. Parent. *Blacks and the American Political System.* Gainesville: University Press of Florida, 1995.

Civil Rights Cases of 1883

In 1875, Congress passed a new Civil Rights Act which made it illegal for private operators to deny the use of public facilities on the basis of race. In 1883, five cases appeared before the Supreme Court that tested this act. Deciding all five cases together, the Court used a narrow interpretation of the **Fourteenth Amendment** to strike down the 1875 law. According to this amendment, the state cannot deprive anyone of their liberties because of race. The **Civil Rights Act of 1875**, however, made clear that no private individual can deny another individual access because of race. Thus, stated the Court, Congress misconstrued the meaning of the amendment. Although the state cannot deprive liberties, no federal authority can force a private citizen to alter personal preferences. With this ruling, the Court shifted responsibility for civil rights protection from federal to state governments. This, in turn, restored southern state power, helped bring about the **Jim Crow laws,** which prevented blacks from exercising equal freedom with whites, and indirectly established the doctrine of **"separate but equal."** (KR)

BIBLIOGRAPHY

Fairman, Charles. *Reconstruction and Reunion, 1864–1888.* New York: Macmillan, 1987.

Civil Rights Division of the Justice Department

The **Civil Rights Act of 1957** created the Civil Rights Division of the Justice Department. The idea, originally introduced by President Harry S. Truman, made the Civil Rights Division the primary agency in the federal government charged with enforcing specific federal civil rights laws that prohibit discrimination on the basis of race, color, religion, sex, national origin, and disability. These protections extend to activities such as voting, education, employment, housing, public accommodations, and health services. (VDD)

BIBLIOGRAPHY

Rowan, Carl T. *Breaking Barriers: A Memoir.* Boston: Little, Brown and Company, 1991.

Civil Rights Movement

As with many other great social movements, the movement for equal civil rights in the United States gathered momentum for many decades. Two events in the mid 1950s, the U.S. Supreme Court decision in **Brown v. Board of Education** and the **Montgomery bus boycott**, sparked the most activist phase of the struggle. As Dr. **Martin Luther King, Jr**. described it, the civil rights movement at that time became both a process of education and a process of legislation.

The Supreme Court ruled in the *Brown* case on May 17, 1954, that segregation in schools was inherently unequal and therefore a violation of the **Fourteenth Amendment** of the Constitution. The Court had established a legal principle, but years of struggle would be necessary before public schools actually stopped separating students on the basis of race. Opposition to the decision that schools must be desegregated led to white resistance across the South. Those who supported the black children who were attempting to enroll in white schools were subjected to economic penalties, bombings,

In 1965, the Rev. James Reeb, a Unitarian minister, was killed in Selma, Alabama, where he had gone to participate in demonstrations for African-American voting rights. *National Archives.*

cross burnings, and other intimidating tactics. State governments tried to avoid the Court's directive by coming up with schemes, such as "pupil placement," to maintain racial separation under another name. Neither Congress nor President Dwight D. Eisenhower intervened to support desegregation, and its accomplishment seemed to be left up to individual black families who sued in federal court, a slow and costly process. Meanwhile, the **National Association for the Advancement of Colored People** (**NAACP**) through its Legal Defense Fund (LDF) prodded the Supreme Court to prohibit segregation in other public facilities, such as parks, buses, golf courses, and beaches.

The issue of desegregation of public buses gave rise to the heroic refusal of seamstress **Rosa Parks** to give up her seat to a white person on December 1, 1955. After Parks was arrested for violating a Montgomery, Alabama, segregation ordinance, black citizens of the city organized the **Montgomery Improvement Association (MIA)** to boycott all city buses until the transit company addressed their grievances. A 36-year-old Baptist minister, Martin Luther King, Jr., was chosen as the MIA president. King advocated nonviolent protest that included a year-long refusal to ride the buses.

While the movement's leaders experienced white retaliation, such as arrests on trumped-up charges and bombings of their homes, they also filed suit in federal court challenging the segregation law. When the court found the Montgomery law unconstitutional, seating on the buses was finally integrated. The episode was the first of many, where, to break down segregation and carry out the law of the land, African Americans would use protests and direct action, and would then be met by violent white resistance. The publicity that resulted from these confrontations ultimately brought the issues of the civil rights struggle beyond the South into the consciousness of Americans across the country.

Congress first responded to matters of racial concern in recent decades by passing the weak **Civil Rights Act of 1957**. It included several mostly symbolic provisions. The Justice Department's efforts would be under the jurisdiction of an assistant attorney general for civil rights. A commission on civil rights would investigate voting discrimination; it would be a federal offense, prosecutable by the attorney general, to interfere with the right to vote. The **Civil Rights Act of 1960** was similarly moderate. It provided for federal investigation of fradulent voting practices, and criminal penalties for those who violated federal court orders (such as preventing integration) or who crossed state lines to engage in bombings or arson.

A new infusion of energy came into the civil rights movement in 1960 when a group of students from North Carolina Agricultural and Technical College in Greensboro demonstrated by "sitting in" at a lunch counter that catered to whites only. With impeccable manners, some of them dressed in ROTC uniforms, the students tried to order food and were refused. Each day they were reinforced by more students and by blacks from the community. They sat quietly while they were pushed and shoved and showered with insults and condiments. Students and adults in other cities modeled their protests on the Greensboro **sit-ins**, using the tactic of nonviolent resistance to challenge segregated restaurants, public facilities, hotels, and parks. The protesters followed a "jail, no bail" strategy when they were arrested for violating local ordinances. Filling jails across the South with peaceful demonstrators seeking legal access to public places further highlighted the intransigence of southern segregationists.

The sit-ins indicated the beginning of a more militant phase of the civil rights movement. Young African Americans founded the **Student Nonviolent Coordinating Committee (SNCC)**. The organization meant to push for the implementation of equal rights through direct action. They were joined by Martin Luther King's organization, the **Southern Christian Leadership Conference (SCLC)**, which also promoted civil disobedience.

The new administration of President John F. Kennedy, which took office in 1961, was a dubious ally to the civil rights movement. Although Kennedy opposed segregation, he also feared alienating the southern Democrats who had helped elect him and whose support he needed if Congress was going to back his foreign and domestic policy programs. In the spring of 1961, a group of young SNCC members, "freedom riders," travelled on interstate buses from Washington, D.C., into the South to test whether bus depots would respect a Supreme Court order to desegregate. When whites in Alabama attacked the freedom riders with bats and tire chains, and local police merely stood by without intervening, the Kennedy administration refused to use federal law enforcement to protect the demonstrators. In 1962, a federal court ordered the University of Mississippi to allow its first black student, James Meredith, to enroll. When a mob tried to force Meredith from campus, Kennedy sent federal troops and U.S. marshals to compel compliance with the court order.

In 1963, King turned the spotlight on Birmingham, Alabama, and forced the administration and the nation to take more decisive action in pursuing racial justice. King anticipated confrontation in Birmingham, a city that bitterly resisted integration and that relied on the ruthless police commissioner Eugene "Bull" Connor as its chief law enforcement officer. The SCLC organized sit-ins, boycotts, and marches on City Hall. The police responded with brutality and arrests. King escalated the confrontation by including children dressed in their Sunday clothes in the demonstrations. The peaceful "children's crusade" was greeted by the police with vicious dogs, high-pressure fire hoses, electric cattle prods, and swinging nightsticks. Four little girls died when a bomb went off in a black church just before Sunday school began. Americans across the country watched these scenes on the nightly television news with horror and outrage. The president used his authority to push for negotiations in Birmingham. He also moved to make a civil rights bill a high priority for his administration. During the summer of 1963, approximately 250,000 people marched on Washington, D.C., to demonstrate their support for the legislation. Some historians have viewed the **March on Washington** as the high point of the nonviolent phase of the civil rights movement.

When Kennedy was assassinated three months later and succeeded by Lyndon B. Johnson, the new president brought his own commitment to civil rights to the forefront. Urging Congress to pass the legislation, Johnson borrowed the words of the movement's anthem and stated "We shall overcome." The **Civil Rights Act of 1964** extended the role of the federal government in achieving the desegregation of schools, public accommodations, and employment. The law banned **discrimination** based on race, sex, color, religion, or national origin. If schools or other state and local agencies discriminated, or if private businesses refused service to members of the protected groups, the Department of Justice could sue them. If schools or other public agencies continued to discriminate, they risked the loss of federal funds, a sizeable portion of their budgets. The law also prohibited discrimination in hiring, salaries, and promotion, and created the **Equal Employment Opportunity Commission (EEOC)** to investigate complaints and propose solutions.

Even as the Civil Rights Act became law, other issues of racial injustice continued to surface. Demonstrators led by the SCLS and SNCC planned a march from Selma, Alabama, to Montgomery, the state capital, to support voter registration. Approximately 500 people began the march, although a permit had been denied. They were met by state police and a posse on horseback. Again the peaceful marchers, attempting to register to vote, were clubbed, shocked with cattle prods, and beaten with chains. The networks interrupted regularly scheduled television programs, and people around the country watched the events in Selma. Five months later, the Congress passed the **Voting Rights Act of 1965**. Ninety-five years after the Constitution had prohibited denial of the right to vote based on race, the power of the federal government would finally be used to ensure that prospective black voters would be registered and not hampered by such tactics as **literacy tests** or **poll taxes.** Under the Voting Rights Act, states and localities would be required to secure permission from the Justice Department before implementing any new voting restrictions.

In a series of decisions in 1965 and 1966, the Supreme Court upheld both the Civil Rights Act and the Voting Rights Act as constitutional. They also found that the federal government could prosecute anti-civil rights violence, a significant ruling because southern state courts seldom charged local whites who attacked or even murdered civil rights advocates.

By the late 1960s, some results of the civil rights movement were becoming clear. Most public accommodations—restaurants, hotels, theaters, ball parks—had been desegregated. Although in 1964, only 2 percent of black children in the South attended school with whites, by 1968, 18 percent did. Four years later, 46 percent of southern black children attended integrated schools. The process of desegregation was assisted both by the threat of losing federal funds and by a series of decisions in the federal courts that judged integration efforts not by their promises, but by their results. Voter registration in the South also showed impressive progress. By 1969, 67 percent of black adults were registered and 120 African Americans had won election to public office in the states of South Carolina, Georgia, Alabama, Mississippi, and Louisiana. Political participation by blacks also had the effect of forcing white politicians to consider them as constituents when campaigning and formulating policy.

On the other hand, the phase of the civil rights movement that removed legal barriers to full involvement in American life did not necessarily address other deep inequalities. Poverty, unemployment, inadequate educational opportunities, residential segregation, and abuses in the criminal justice system continued to be problems. These issues would move the focus of the civil rights movement from the South to the North, and would lead to a splintering of the movement between advocates of nonviolence and advocates of **"black power."**

Violent outbreaks, provoked by frustration and often touched off by an act of police brutality, occurred in Harlem in 1964 and in Watts in Los Angeles in 1965. There were 43 riots in 1966 and 164 in 1967. In 1968, while in Memphis to organize sanitation workers, Martin Luther King, Jr. was assassinated. Riots broke out in 130 American cities. Six days later, Congress passed fair housing legislation.

Most observers mark the end of the civil rights movement in 1968. Not only the death of King and subsequent divisions among the movement's leaders, but also the increased national preoccupation with the Vietnam War deprived the issue of public attention. The increasing political success of conservatives, especially the 1968 election of Richard Nixon as president, meant that the nation's leadership would be less receptive to programs that used the power of the federal government to promote social change. Although the Supreme Court delivered several employment decisions that were consistent with the objectives of the civil rights movement, such as *Griggs v. Duke Power Company*, the Court also moved to the right with the retirement of Chief Justice Earl Warren and his replacement by Warren Burger. **See also** Birmingham Protests; NAACP Legal Defense and Education Fund. (MWA)

BIBLIOGRAPHY

Blumberg, Rhoda Lois. *Civil Rights: The 1960s Freedom Struggle.* Boston: Twayne, 1984.

Branch, Taylor. *Parting the Waters: America in the King Years, 1954–1963.* New York: Simon and Schuster, 1988

———. *Pillar of Fire.* New York: Simon and Schuster, 1998.

Garrow, David G. *Bearing the Cross: Martin Luther King, Jr. and the Southern Christian Leadership Conference.* New York: Random House, 1986.

Graham, Hugh Davis. *Civil Rights and the Presidency: Race and Gender in American Politics, 1960–1972.* New York: Oxford University Press, 1992.

Nieman, Donald G. *Promises to Keep: African Americans and the Constitutional Order.* New York: Oxford University Press, 1991.

Sitkoff, Harvard. *The Struggle for Black Equality, 1954–1980.* New York: Hill and Wang, 1981.

Civil War (1861–1865)

The Civil War was a major domestic conflict in the United States between those Americans wishing to maintain the federal union and the secessionist Confederates. By the late 1700s, the southern region of British North America was dominated by a plantation economy dependent on slavery, while the northern economy was based on finance and industry. The extreme

Many African Americans enlisted to fight for the Union in the Civil War. Here soldiers stand as the Emancipation Proclamation is read aloud. *Library of Congress.*

northern region was to become Canada. The America colonialists became independent in 1783. Shortly thereafter they decided to phase out the slave trade, but they continued to permit slavery.

Westward expansion forced the question of the economy of the new territories. American territory increased with the Louisiana Purchase in 1803, victory in the Mexican War (1846–1848), and the accelerated of westward migration caused by the discovery of gold in California in 1848. The **Missouri Compromise** of 1820 permitted slavery south of 36 degrees 30 minutes north latitude. The **Compromise of 1850** had several provisions, one of which allowed California to enter the union as a free state while fugitive slave laws would be more strictly enforced. Regional hostility increased after the Supreme Court ruled against Dred Scott in 1857. Scott was a slave who left Missouri, traveling to Fort Snelling (now in Minnesota) in the Wisconsin territory. He therefore claimed to be free. On April 12, 1861, shots were fired on a federal base at Fort Sumter, South Carolina, and the Confederates captured the fort. The Confederate victory at the first Battle of Bull Run in July 1861 dashed federal hopes for a short war.

President Abraham Lincoln initially viewed the objective of the war as retaining the union rather than ending slavery. Initially, blacks tried to enlist in both the Union and the Confederate armies, but they were refused entry. In June 1862, Congress authorized the use of black troops. The Union army enlisted the services of slaves and free blacks under white military leaders in 1863. As the war continued, abolitionists, including **Frederick Douglass,** argued that the elimination of slavery would boost the Union cause. After the Union victory at Antietam in September 1862, Lincoln announced the **Emancipation Proclamation,** which became effective January 1, 1863. It freed slaves held in areas "in rebellion." It increased anti-war sentiment in the Union, but that was more than compensated for by the reduced motivation of European powers to enter the war. Draft riots in New York in 1863, partially against emancipation, resulted in perhaps 1,000 casualties. General Robert E. Lee's Confederate forces surrendered at Appomattox Courthouse in April 1865.

After the war, the **Thirteenth, Fourteenth,** and **Fifteenth Amendments** were added to the Constitution, prohibiting slavery, requiring due process, and extending voting rights to freed slaves. **See also** *Dred Scott v. Sanford.* (WWH)

BIBLIOGRAPHY

Freehling, William W. *The Road to Disunion.* New York: Oxford University Press, 1990.

McFeeley, William. *Civil War.* New York: Viking Penguin, 1999.

McPherson, James M. *Civil War and Reconstruction.* New York: St. Martin's Press, Inc., 1999.

William L. Clay (1931–)

William L. Clay, a Democrat from Missouri, was elected to the United States House of Representatives in 1968. From 1959 to 1964, Clay served on the St. Louis City Board of Aldermen. A firebrand civil rights activist known as "Wild Bill," Clay was an effective leader in the St. Louis area. Despite some ethical challenges in the 1970s that related to his billing the government for car trips back to his district (which he had not actually taken) and 328 overdrafts on the House Bank in 1992, Clay has consistently been reelected. A strong liberal voice, he is an active proponent of labor unions and worker's rights. He is the ranking minority member of the Education and the Workforce Committee.

BIBLIOGRAPHY

Clay, William L. *To Kill or Not to Kill.* San Bernardino, CA: Borgo Press, 1990.

——. *Just Permanent Interests.* New York: Amistad Press, 1992.

Eva Mcpherson Clayton (1934–)

In 1993, Eva Clayton became a member of the United States House of Representatives, representing the 1st Congressional District, North Carolina. She holds the dual distinction of being the first woman from North Carolina elected to serve a full term in Congress and the first African American elected to national office from North Carolina since Reconstruction. Clayton became the first of her race or gender to be elected president of a Democratic freshman class. Before running for office, Congresswoman Clayton spent many years promoting and producing economic development. To this end, she was the executive director of the Soul City Foundation from 1974 to 1976 and the CEO of Technical Resources International, Inc. (TRI), a consulting company specializing in economic development. (RAM)

BIBLIOGRAPHY

Gill, Laverne McCain. *African American Women in Congress: Forming and Transforming History.* New Brunswick, NJ: Rutgers University Press, 1997.

(Leroy) Eldridge Cleaver (1935–)

Eldridge Cleaver was born in Wabbaseka, Arkansas, in 1935. He was an influential black militant. His autobiography, *Soul on Ice* (1968), is a major statement on being black in America. Cleaver spent much of his early life in California prisons. His crimes ranged from minor theft to assault with intent to kill. In prison, Cleaver became a follower of the Black Muslims, especially **Malcolm X.** He also supplemented his high school education by reading a wide range of materials. He became the **Black Panthers'** Minister of Education. He fled the United States to escape an attempted murder charge, first to Cuba and then to Algeria, where he settled. For a time, he headed an international branch of the Panthers. In 1975, he posted bail for his attempted murder charge and pled guilty to a lesser crime of assault, receiving a sentence of five years probation with community service. (FAS)

BIBLIOGRAPHY

Rout, Kathleen. *Eldridge Cleaver.* Boston: Twayne, 1991.

Emanuel Cleaver (1944–)

Emanuel Cleaver was born in Texas in 1944, and received his divinity degree from Saint Paul School of Theology, Kansas City. He was elected mayor of Kansas City as a Democrat in 1991 and re-elected to a second term in 1995. He is also senior pastor of Saint James United Methodist Church.

BIBLIOGRAPHY

"A Rising Reverend." *The Economist* 318, no. 7700 (March 30, 1991): A24.

Cleveland Plan

The Cleveland Plan is a voucher program sponsored by the Ohio state legislature and implemented in 1996. It gives low income parents state-sponsored scholarships that can be used to send their children to either private or public schools. It was struck down by the Ohio appeals court in May 1997. The court claimed that the plan amounted to government aid to religious schools because most of the schools participating in the program are religious schools. Ohio Governor George V. Voinovich supported funding the plan for two additional years despite this ruling. (JCW)

BIBLIOGRAPHY

Walsh, Mark. "Voucher Plan in Cleveland Is Overturned." *Teacher Magazine* 16, no. 32 (May 7, 1997).

James E. Clyburn (1940–)

James Clyburn, a Democrat from South Carolina, was elected to the United States House of Representatives in 1992. Prior to his election to Congress, Clyburn served on the South Carolina State Human Affairs Commission; he has also been assistant to the governor for human resources development, executive director of the South Carolina Commission for Farm Workers, and director of the Neighborhood Youth Corps and New Careers.

BIBLIOGRAPHY

"Clyburn District Stands While NY Remaps Six." *Congressional Quarterly Weekly Report* 55, no. 32 (August 9, 1997): 1933.

Coalition Politics

Political coalitions are working relationships between groups designed to maximize political preferences. These coalitions involve communication, coordination, strategizing, and, typically, the creation of organizations to institutionalize these arrangements. Barbara Hinckley (1981) argued that coalition formation is based upon a calculation of whether an individual stands to gain more by cooperating than by working alone. Traditionally, three approaches to the study of political coalitions have persisted in American social science. The socio-psychological approaches popularized by William Gamson and Theodore Caplow use triads to determine when coalitions will emerge based on rationality. This approach has been applied significantly in international relations. Game theoretic models, developed by William Riker, John Von Neumann, and Oskar Morgenstern, assume perfect rational-

ity and information, and attempt to generate expectations regarding the likelihood of certain regime formations given relative power distribution. These studies have produced only a single hypothesis, the notion that only minimum winning coalitions would form, and this hypothesis has been influential in legislative studies literature.

Finally, there is a tradition of empirical research that considers the necessary preconditions for coalition formation. As ethnic studies scholars have recognized, multiracial political coalitions are complicated by differences in material interests between racial and ethnic groups as well as barriers engendered by racial ideologies. Scholars examining political coalitions, therefore, have attempted to discern whether interests or ideology matter more in determining the success of political coalitions—a debate characterized by Raphael Sonenshein (1993) as "goodwill versus practical political calculation." According to the so-called optimists, including Rufus Browning, David Tabb, and Dale Rogers Marshall (1984), political coalitions are based primarily upon shared ideology between ethnic minorities and white liberals. Conversely, the pessimists dispute this contention by maintaining that the interests of self-centered groups determine whether coalitions will form. In this "power approach," hostility is seen as the natural outcome of competition for scarce resources, and ethnic groups are merely the vehicles for the pursuit of self-interest.

Therefore, as **Stokely Carmichael** and Charles Hamilton concluded (1967), coalitions are unlikely to form across groups because white liberals are "unreliable allies when a conflict of interest arises." Raphael Sonenshein's work on the formation of political coalitions in urban settings synthesizes these diverse approaches, concluding that shared ideology, common interests, and creative political leadership are necessary components of stable political coalitions. (CC)

BIBLIOGRAPHY

Browning, Rufus, David Tabb, and Dale Rogers Marshall. *Protest Is Not Enough: The Struggle for Blacks and Hispanics for Equality in Urban Politics*. Berkeley: University of California Press, 1984.

Carmichael, Stokely and Charles V. Hamilton. *Black Power: The Politics of Liberation in America*. New York: Vintage Books, 1967.

Hinckley, Barbara. *Coalitions and Politics*. New York: Harcourt Brace Jovanovich, Inc., 1981.

Sonenshein, Raphael. *Politics in Black and White*. Princeton: Princeton University Press, 1993.

Barbara-Rose Collins (1939–)

Barbara-Rose Collins represented Michigan's 15th Congressional District from 1990 to 1996. A liberal Democrat, she opposed NAFTA and GATT, and parts of the crime bill which she considered unfair to minorities. She advocated the "save the black male" campaign and the development of a national urban policy to address issues of urban decay. She served on the Detroit School Board (1971–1973); in the Michigan House (1975–1981); and on the Detroit City Council (1982–1991). (EC)

BIBLIOGRAPHY
Wines, Michael. "Detroit Law Maker Ousted in Primary." *New York Times* 145 (August 8, 1996): PA12, PB10.

Cardiss Collins (1931–)

Cardiss Collins served in the U.S. House of Representatives for 23 years, making her the African-American woman with the longest service in Congress. She entered the House in 1973, replacing her husband who was killed in a plane crash. Collins was the first woman and first black to hold a Democratic leadership position in the House. Strongly supported by constituents in the 7th district of Illinois, Collins maintained a strong voice for minorities, women, children, the poor, health care reform, and the right to privacy. (EP)

BIBLIOGRAPHY
Ries, Paula, and Anne J. Stone, eds. *The American Woman, 1992–93: A Status Report*. New York: W. W. Norton, 1992.

George W. Collins (1925–1972)

George W. Collins, a Democrat from Illinois, was elected to the United States House of Representatives in 1970. He served there until his death in 1972. Before entering Congress, Collins served as an alderman on the Chicago City Council from 1964 to 1970.

BIBLIOGRAPHY
Memorial Service [for George W. Collins] Held at the House of Representatives of the United States. Washington, DC: U.S. Government Printing Office, 1973.

Commerce Clause

The Commerce Clause in Article I of the U.S. Constitution has been enforced in a variety of ways. In general, it regulates interstate shipping. However, the **Civil Rights Act of 1964** also rests on a broad interpretation of the same clause. The 1964 act forbids **discrimination** at lunch counters and other public accommodations on the grounds that they are engaged in interstate commerce by serving food and using products imported from other states. (VDD)

BIBLIOGRAPHY
Cooke, Frederick H. *The Commerce Clause of the Federal Constitution*. Fred B. Rothman and Company, 1987.

Communist Party USA (CPUSA)

The Communist Party USA, historically the most prominent American Communist third party, was at the forefront of domestic liberation struggles in the 1930s. Although the party was not immune to the racism endemic in the United States, it often took up issues of concern to African Americans (for example, in the case of the Scottsboro boys, wherein nine young black men were wrongly convicted of raping two white women), which mainstream political organizations would not. With the onset of the Cold War in 1945, radicalism of any sort became suspect in the United States and communists in particular came under ferocious attack. Several black leaders identified with the party. For example, the celebrated American singer and actor Paul Robeson and the noted social scientist, author, and activist **W.E.B. Du Bois** were among those who found their careers derailed and their lives altered in the anti-communist hysteria of the 1950s.

Since the 1950s, pressure has been put on black organizations to exclude communists from their ranks. By the zenith of the **civil rights movement** in the 1960s, the CPUSA had lost any prominent leadership position in the African-American liberation struggle, and in the era of deepening conservatism in the 1970s and the 1980s, the party became nearly extinct. Today, the remnants of the CPUSA continue to envision building a movement based on working-class interracial unity and committed to the ultimate demise of capitalism and the establishment of a workers' republic. (LFW)

BIBLIOGRAPHY
Kelley, Robin. *Hammer and Hoe: Alabama Communists During the Great Depression*. Chapel Hill: University of North Carolina Press, 1990.
Record, Wilson. *The Negro and the Communist Party*. New York: Atheneum, 1971.

Compromise of 1850

The Compromise of 1850 was reached during the western expansion of the United States to quiet the debate over slave rights in these new territories. The compromise was proposed by Senator Henry Clay (Whig-KY), who saw the ongoing slave arguments between the North and South as a hindrance to national unity. The compromise declared that the California territory would be admitted as a free state and that the District of Columbia would likewise abolish slavery. It also stated that the new territories of New Mexico and Utah would be formally organized and more fugitive slave legislation would be enacted. At the time, the Compromise of 1850 was considered a great step toward healing animosity caused between the North and South over the **slavery**-abolition debate. **See also** Act to Abolish the Slave Trade in the District of Columbia; Fugitive Slave Act of 1850.

BIBLIOGRAPHY
Holt, Michael F. *The Political Crisis of the 1850s*. New York: Norton, 1983.

Congress of African People (1970)

The Congress of African People was the last of a number of national conferences conducted between 1966 and 1970. Previous meetings, called Black Power Conferences, occurred in a variety of the nation's largest cities with the intention of giving prominence to the **black power** philosophy. After the last conference was set to be held in 1970 in Atlanta, the planning committee decided to change the gathering's name from the Black Power Conference to the Congress of African People, hoping the new title would allow blacks from around the world to feel more at ease about attending. As a result, delegates from North America, Latin America, the Caribbean, and Africa gathered in Atlanta for the proceedings. The Congress of African People provided a number of events to educate blacks on self-improvement through the influence of black power.

The Congress also successfully proposed government reforms on civil rights and liberties.

BIBLIOGRAPHY
Van Deburg, William L., ed. *Modern Black Nationalism.* New York: New York University Press, 1997.

Congress of Racial Equality (CORE)

The Congress of Racial Equality (CORE) was founded in 1942 as a nonviolent, direct-action protest organization. It gained national recognition in the 1960s for its southern "freedom ride" campaign and for conducting demonstrations at the 1964 New York World's Fair. Beginning in 1965, it took on many community development projects, emphasizing the organization of inner city ghetto residents. It helped to form tenants' councils and conducted rent strikes. In its community centers, it offered tutoring, sports, and craft programs; job counseling; information on family planning; health care; and voter registration. During this period, its black membership increased significantly, as did its African-American representation on its leadership bodies. In 1968, CORE excluded whites from its membership, becoming a black nationalist organization. (EC)

BIBLIOGRAPHY
Meier, August, and Elliot Rudwick. *CORE: A Study in the Civil Rights Movement.* New York: Oxford University Press, 1973.

Congressional Black Caucus (CBC)

The Congressional Black Caucus (CBC), an organization of the black members of Congress, was formally launched in 1971 to represent the collective interests of the national black community. In its early years, the CBC held hearings and conferences to develop a post-civil rights era black agenda and engaged in protest activities, for example boycotting President Richard Nixon's 1971 State of the Union address in response to Nixon's refusal to meet with the CBC to discuss its agenda.

As the black members of Congress grew in both number and seniority, and individual members were selected to chair a growing number of subcommittees and committees in the House of Representatives, the CBC became a more typical legislative strategy organization (LSO). By the mid-1970s, the organization concentrated on the internal mechanics of the legislative process and acted as a symbolic voice for blacks in Congress, not blacks in the country. Its symbolic role includes such activities as developing and introducing alternative budgets, providing recommendations and testimony on presidential nominations, strategy meetings with the president, and its annual legislative weekend, which attracts tens of thousands of people to participate in workshops on a wide range of domestic and foreign policy issues. After Republicans regained control of Congress in 1994, the CBC lost its official status as an LSO, but was able to continue most of its functions as a congressional member organization (CBO). (LFW)

BIBLIOGRAPHY
Bositis, David. *The Congressional Black Caucus in the 103rd Congress.* Washington, DC: Joint Center for Political and Economic Studies, 1994.
Clay, William. *Just Permanent Interests: Black Americans in Congress 1870–1991.* New York: Amistad, 1992.

Congressional Black Caucus Foundation (CBCF)

A research arm of the **Congressional Black Caucus,** the Foundation is a non-profit institute of scholars and policy experts located in Washington, D.C. The CBCF was established in 1976 to advise Congressional Black Caucus members and to educate the public about political issues affecting African Americans. The Foundation regularly hosts issue forums and conferences, including its Annual Legislative Conference, where over 30,000 attendees discuss the congressional agenda. The Foundation also publishes a journal summarizing its analyses of important federal and state policy.

BIBLIOGRAPHY
"Black Caucus Weekend Focuses on Helping Today's Youth." *Jet* 86, no. 23 (October 10, 1994): 6.
Gordon, Mary France. "Collective Voices, Community Change Imperative for Congressional Black Caucus." *Nation's Cities Weekly* 20, no. 39 (September 29, 1997): 12.

Conservatism

Conservatism has periodically been an important theme in African-American political thought. For example, **Booker T. Washington**'s conservative accommodationist philosophy dominated black intellectual thought at the turn of the century. Then, after becoming nearly non-existent during the civil rights years, black conservatism has again made a much publicized comeback in the 1980s and 1990s.

Although not the first black conservative, Booker T. Washington is now viewed by many as the godfather of the black conservative movement. In his famous "Atlanta Exposition Address" of 1895, Washington urged blacks to "cast down your buckets where you are," to accommodate themselves to their circumstances—circumstances created, argued many opponents, by the white majority. He argued that agitation for civil rights was fruitless in the prevailing climate of **Jim Crow laws.** Instead, blacks should work to improve their lives economically and morally within the prescribed limited occupations offered to African Americans at the time. Only through success in business and living righteous lives would blacks gain civil rights and full acceptance into the white community.

George Schuyler (1966), a columnist for the *Pittsburgh Courier*, was one of the leading black conservatives from the 1930s to the 1950s. Driven by an impassioned anti-communism, Schuyler vehemently opposed many of the attempts to secure civil rights for blacks. He opposed the marches on Washington because of concern that they were organized by communists. Moreover, he was convinced that civil disobedience and marches would not improve the conditions of blacks, but would only create more enemies of the race. Schuyler also warned against an overemphasis on the plight of the black family and black community. He believed that by stressing such problems as poverty, unemployment, and crime, black leaders were creating a feeling of despair and victimization among blacks.

After Schuyler, black conservatism dwindled in importance and prestige. Some black leaders, such as the Reverend J. H. Jackson of the National Baptist Convention, spoke out against the civil rights movements of the 1950s and 1960s. Jackson argued that politics was not the way of salvation, that instead blacks should look for an otherworldly solution to their problems. However, by the late 1960s, aside from the National Baptist Convention, black conservatism appeared to be close to extinction.

The 1980s and 1990s witnessed a resurgence of black conservatism on the national political scene. With the confirmation hearing of **Clarence Thomas** in 1991, Americans were confronted and somewhat confused by an intellectually astute black conservative. His nomination drew a great deal of attention because of the allegations of sexual harassment by **Anita Hill** and Thomas's avowed conservatism. His more controversial conservative views included opposition to **busing,** a call for welfare reform, and opposition to **affirmative action.** Despite intense criticism from many black leaders, Thomas's nomination was supported by Americans, black and white, and he was eventually confirmed as the second black Supreme Court justice.

By the 1990s, many other prominent black conservatives appeared on the national political scene. **Gary Franks** of Connecticut and **J.C. Watts** of Oklahoma were both elected to Congress as black Republicans from majority white districts. In 1996, **Alan Keyes,** a conservative talk-show host ran a grassroots presidential campaign extolling a pro-life and pro-family position. The political resurgence of black conservatism was matched by a revival of outspoken black conservatives in many diverse academic fields. Thomas Sowell, a professor of economics, argued that blacks should look less to governmental aid for economic development, and should imitate other ethnic groups, such as the Koreans, who had successfully built vibrant business communities without government aid.

Shelby Steele, a professor of sociology, has looked at the psychological effects of affirmative action on both whites and blacks. Steele claimed that affirmative action programs stamp blacks with a mark of inferiority. According to Steele, because of affirmative action, any gains by blacks will be attributed by whites to the preference program and not to individual merit. Blacks, in turn, will come to expect these preferences, and will increasingly perceive themselves as victims. Stephen Carter (1991), a law professor, has argued that affirmative action exacerbates the "best black syndrome," whereby any black who achieves success is not perceived by whites as successful, but as a successful black. Therefore, the successful black is seen as less successful than a successful white. Likewise, this lowered standard creates lower expectations on the part of many blacks.

Finally, at the grassroots level, there has always been a strong adherence to traditionally conservative viewpoints in the black community. Surveys have shown that many blacks support the conservative position on such key issues as lower taxes, tougher crime laws, stronger families, smaller government, welfare reform, and an emphasis on personal initiatives. Perhaps the greatest example of grassroots conservatism was the **Million Man March** led by **Louis Farrakhan** in 1994. The marchers pledged to work toward community development and self-improvement ethically, socially, and economically.

This resurgence of black conservatism in the 1980s and 1990s was precipitated by several factors. First, blacks mirrored the nationwide trend toward more conservative views during the "Reagan Revolution." Second, since the **civil rights movement,** a significant number of blacks have moved into the middle and upper classes. Their conservatism may reflect a growing awareness of class interests at the expense of race interests. Finally, many blacks are alarmed at the chronic problems in their communities, such as drugs, crime, and unemployment, and have grown disillusioned by the inability of liberal, governmental solutions to meaningfully address these problems.

Black conservatism is such a diverse movement that it defies easy definition. In many ways, black conservatism is defined in relation to either black radicalism or black liberalism. For instance, Booker T. Washington, originally seen as radical, is conservative in relation to **W.E.B. Du Bois** and the **National Association for the Advancement of Colored People (NAACP).** Likewise, **Martin Luther King, Jr.,** originally radical, is conservative in relation to **Malcolm X** and **Stokely Carmichael.** In similar fashion, black neo-conservatism of the 1980s and 1990s can be defined by its opposition to black liberalism. Conservatives like Clarence Thomas and Thomas Sowell advocated self-help, individual responsibility, and race neutrality as opposed to massive governmental programs and race preferences for improving the plight of blacks.

Although vilified by mainstream black leaders, many black conservatives are, despite financial and political support, also uncomfortable with white conservatives and the **Republican Party.** Black conservatives have been shocked by such actions as Ronald Reagan's insistence on public funding for a segregated college, the failure of many Republicans to distance themselves from former Ku Klux Klan Grand Wizard David Duke, and the frequent reliance on the race card by conservatives such as Pat Buchanan, Jesse Helms, and Ronald Reagan.

In conclusion, the 1980s and 1990s have seen the phoenix of black conservatives. If nothing else, black conservatives have demonstrated that black thought is not as homogenous as it originally appeared; and they may serve as a warning to the **Democratic Party** to not neglect its black constituency. Despite much publicized attempts by the Republican Party to attract black voters, an overwhelming majority remain Democrats. It remains to be seen whether the growing black conservatism will lead to an increase in the number of black Republicans. (WPS)

BIBLIOGRAPHY

Carter, Stephen L. *Reflections of an Affirmative Action Baby*. New York: Basic Books, 1991.

Conti, Joseph G. and Brad Stetson. *Challenging the Civil Rights Establishment: Profiles of a New Black Vanguard*. Westport, CT: Praeger Publishers, 1993.

Faryna, Stan, Brad Stetson, and Joseph G. Conti. *Black and Right: The Bold New Voice of Black Conservatives in America*. Westport, CT: Praeger Publishers, 1997.

Randolph, Lewis A. "A Historical Analysis and Critique of Contemporary Black Conservatism." *Western Journal of Black Studies* 19, no. 3 (1995): 149–63.

Rees, Matthew R. *From the Deck to the Sea: Blacks and the Republican Party*. Wakefield, NH: Longwood Academic, 1991.

Rueter, Theodore. "The New Black Conservatives." Theodore Rueter, ed. *The Politics of Race: African Americans and the Political System*. New York: M.E. Sharpe, 1995.

Schuyler, George S. *Black and Conservative: The Autobiography of George S. Schuyler*. New Rochelle, NY: Arlington House, 1966.

Williams, Armstrong. *Beyond Blame: How We Can Succeed by Breaking the Dependency Barrier*. New York: Free Press, 1995.

Contractors Association of Eastern Pennsylvania v. Secretary of Labor (1971)

In 1970, President Richard M. Nixon issued Labor Department Order No. 4, which required building contractors on federal projects in the five-county area around Philadelphia to adopt **affirmative action** plans containing hiring goals for minority workers. The plan was referred to as the Philadelphia plan. The plan was challenged by nonminority contractors who claimed that the order exceeded the authority of the president because only Congress had the authority under the **Fourteenth Amendment** to order an affirmative action program. In *Contractors Association of Eastern Pennsylvania v. Secretary of Labor*, 442 F. 2d 159 (3d Cir. 1971), the Circuit Court of Appeals held that the president's order was valid and binding and was not prohibited by any congressional enactment. (FHJ)

BIBLIOGRAPHY

Jones, James E., Jr. "Twenty-one Years of Affirmative Action." *Chicago-Kent Law Review* 59 (1982): 67–122.

John Conyers, Jr. (1929–)

In 1964, Democratic lawyer John Conyers became the second African American elected to the U.S. House of Representatives from Michigan. Conyers strongly backed the **Voting Rights Act of 1965**. After the death of **Martin Luther King, Jr.** in 1968, Conyers began fighting for a national King holiday.

In the early 1970s, Conyers joined with his fellow Michigan representative **Charles Diggs** in founding the **Congressional Black Caucus**. He saw the group's power grow through the 1980s and 1990s, reaching a membership of 40 in

John Conyers (D-MI) is the most senior African American serving in Congress. *Courtesy of U.S. House of Representatives.*

1992. Conyers, a strong liberal voice in the House, still represents the citizens of Detroit. (AD)

BIBLIOGRAPHY

Clay, William. *Just Permanent Interests: Black Americans in Congress, 1870–1991*. New York: Amistad, 1991.

Mercer Cook (1903–1987)

Mercer Cook received his Ph.D. from Brown University in 1936. He was an assistant professor of languages at Howard University and a professor of French at Atlanta University. He was appointed ambassador to Nigeria by President Kennedy in 1961 and served until 1964 when he became the envoy to Senegal and Gambia. (JCW)

BIBLIOGRAPHY

"Will Mercer Cook, 85, Ambassador, Educator Dies." *Jet* (October 26, 1987) :25.

Cooper v. Aaron (1958)

Cooper v. Aaron, 358 U.S. 1 (1958), a case that was argued and won by **Thurgood Marshall** and the **NAACP Legal Defense and Educational Fund, Inc.,** was brought about because of attempts by the white citizens and community leaders of Little Rock, Arkansas, to maintain segregated public schools, even after the decision in ***Brown v. Board of Education of Topeka***. African-American students who attempted to enter Little Rock's Central High School were turned away by Arkansas National Guard troops who had been ordered to do so by Governor Orval Faubus. Following a preliminary court injunction that prohibited the governor from further interference, African-American students again attempted to enter Central High School. After a large crowd gathered and threatened the safety of the children, which prompted the students to be removed from the school, the mayor of Little Rock sought assistance from President Dwight D. Eisenhower.

Eisenhower nationalized the Arkansas National Guard and dispatched more than 1,000 United States Army soldiers to escort the African-American students through the hostile crowd. William G. Cooper, representing the Little Rock School Board, was granted a three-year delay in implementing desegregation plans by the Arkansas district court. John Aaron, representing the African-American children who were attempting to get into the high school, appealed, and the Arkansas district court decision was quickly overturned in the United

States Court of Appeals for the Eighth Circuit. A special session of the United States Supreme Court affirmed the Eighth Circuit decision, and the process of desegregating the public schools of Little Rock began. (AJC)

BIBLIOGRAPHY

Bates, Daisy. *The Long Shadow of Little Rock, a Memoir.* New York: David McKay, 1962.

Freyer, Tony A. *The Little Rock Crisis: A Constitutional Interpretation.* Westport, CT: Greenwood Press, 1984.

Huckaby, Elizabeth. *Crisis at Central High, Little Rock, 1957–58.* Baton Rouge: Louisiana State University Press, 1980.

Samuel Eli Cornish (1790–1859)

Samuel Cornish was an outstanding journalist who helped to shape social and economic philosophy for African Americans. In 1822, Cornish organized the first African American Presbyterian Congregation. Best known for working with **John Russwurm** in 1827 to found *Freedom's Journal,* the first African-American newspaper, Cornish also edited *Rights of All* (1829), *Weekly Advocate* (1836), and the *Colored American* (1837). (RAM)

BIBLIOGRAPHY

Bennett, LeRone, Jr. "Founders of the Black Press." *Ebony* (February 1987): 96–100.

Hutton, Frankie. *The Early Black Press in America, 1827–1860.* Westport, CT: Greenwood, 1993.

Ellis Jonathan Cose (1951–)

Ellis Cose first worked in journalism at the *Chicago Sun-Times* from 1970 to 1977. He was president of the Institute for Journalism Education at the University of California—Berkeley from 1983 to 1986 and became editorial page editor for the *New York Daily News* in 1993. He is a contributing editor to *Newsweek* and has written several books about media, class, race, and politics. (JCW)

BIBLIOGRAPHY

Cose, Ellis. *A Nation of Strangers.* New York: Morrow, 1992.

"Senior Black Editor Resigns from Daily News." *New York Times* (March 5, 1993): B6.

Cotton v. Scotland Neck City Board of Education (1972)

North Carolina passed a statute that authorized the creation of a new school district for the small town of Scotland Neck. Previously, the Scotland Neck students had attended a countywide district that was in the process of dismantling its historically segregated school system. A lawsuit was filed to block the new school district. In *Cotton v. Scotland Neck City Board of Education*, 407 U.S. 484 (1972), the Supreme Court struck down the creation of the new, mostly white school district because its creation would have a deleterious effect on desegregation efforts in the county. The fact that the school district was authorized by state statute was of no constitutional significance, concluded the Court. **See also** Education; Segregation/Integration/Separation. (FHJ)

BIBLIOGRAPHY

Galub, Arthur L. *The Burger Court, 1968–1984.* Millwood, NY: Associated Faculty Press, 1984.

Council of Federated Organizations (COFO)

The Council of Federated Organizations (COFO) was an organization of various civil rights groups, most notably the **Student Nonviolent Coordinating Committee (SNCC),** that worked to help African Americans exercise their civil rights in the South. To achieve their goal of voter registration in Mississippi, COFO launched the **Mississippi Freedom Democratic Party (MFDP)** in 1964, an alternative to the all-white **Democratic Party** in the South. Although not seated at the Democratic National Convention, the MFDP demonstrated that African Americans would vote if given the chance. (DH)

BIBLIOGRAPHY

Sitkoff, Harvard. *The Struggle for Black Equality.* New York: Hill and Wang, 1981.

Crime and Punishment

One of the major issues associated with criminal justice in the United States is the relationship between race and crime. One is immediately aware of the disparity between the numbers of African Americans and other minorities in the general population and their numbers among those incarcerated in jails and prisons. Although approximately 12 percent of the population of the United States is African American, blacks represent over half of those imprisoned. In the mid-1990s, blacks were incarcerated at a rate six times that of the white population. In addition, four in ten of those on death row are black, and young black men are far more likely than whites to be the victims of police brutality. Blacks are also disproportionately represented among victims of crime. African Americans are three time more likely than whites and others to be victims of robbery and more than twice as likely to be victims of aggravated assault. It is impossible to examine crime and punishment in the United States without addressing whether these disparities are the result of **discrimination,** and whether such discrimination is a feature of the criminal justice system or whether criminal justice simply mirrors the **racism** and inequality that exists in the larger society.

For many white Americans, "crime" means violent crime, the typical offender is young, black, and male, and the typical victim is white. In fact, based on arrest statistics for all crimes except murder and robbery, the typical offender is white. The majority of crimes are intraracial, involving offenders and victims of the same race. However, politicians and the mass media have used sensationalism and misinformation to intensify the public's fears and to lead to policies that promise to be "tough" on crime, but which tend to ensnare poor, minority youths in the criminal justice system. Popular policies such as "three strikes and you're out," which mandate life sentences for three-time offenders, the abolition of parole, and the mandatory sentences for relatively minor drug crimes, help to account for the disparities between the number of minorities in the population and their numbers behind bars. While such policies may not have overt racist intentions, they have the result of perpetuating inequality based on race.

Discussions of race and criminal justice often focus on confrontations between police and members of minority groups. Incidents such as the Rodney King beating in Los Angeles in 1992 and its aftermath, or the 1997 assault on Abner Louima in a New York police station seem to represent the embodiment of prejudice in the criminal justice system. There is no doubt that historically the poor and minorities were most commonly victims of "curbside justice" at the hands of law enforcement officers, and that until the 1980s, they were most likely to be shot by the police as "fleeing felons." Currently, African Americans and Hispanics consistently rate the police lower than white Americans. These negative perceptions are based not only on incidents of police brutality or misconduct, but on a belief that police departments will not discipline the officers who are guilty, but rather will form a wall of silence to protect them. Thus, for many minorities, misconduct goes beyond the actions of individual racist policemen and women and extends to the institutional policies that refuse to make such officers accountable.

Many citizens have adopted community policing strategies to address hostile relations between law enforcement officers and minority neighborhoods in particular. Such programs use foot patrols to get the police out with the citizens in non-confrontational situations. They work with community groups to deal with neighborhood problems and to reduce victimization. In some cases, minority police officers are assigned to minority neighborhoods.

Nationwide the number of minority police officers has increased since the early 1970s when federal law prohibited racial or gender employment discrimination by state or local governments. The 1990 census indicated that 10 percent of police in the United States were African Americans and 5.2 percent were Hispanic. The percentages are far higher in cities where aggressive efforts have been made to recruit minority officers.

In the second stage of the criminal justice system, the courts, the connection between race and bail decisions, charges, jury selection, legal representation, and juvenile processing is ambiguous. Partly because the Supreme Court in the 1960s repeatedly ruled that the constitutional rights of the accused must be respected by the state courts, overt racism is seldom seen in most American courtrooms in the late twentieth century. On the other hand, there are indisputable links between such things as economic status and the quality of legal representation. Research also demonstrates that factors such as unemployment, a prior criminal record, and pretrial detention (the inability to make bail) have an impact on the probability of conviction. Members of minority groups who are also more likely to be poor, suffer a double disadvantage in the court system.

Many observers of the American criminal justice system have claimed that racial discrimination is clearly observable in sentencing. They charge specifically that African Americans are likely to receive harsher sentences than whites who are convicted of similar crimes. Others argue that blacks receive heavier sentences because they commit more and graver crimes. Mandatory federal sentences that impose penalties that are 50 times heavier for distribution of crack cocaine (used mostly by African Americans) than for powdered cocaine (used mostly by whites) seem to symbolize the disparity.

Studies of sentencing discrepancies reveal a complex situation where blatant racism is seldom a factor, but where some judges do take race into account by imposing harsher sentences on African Americans who commit violent crimes against whites and more lenient sentences when blacks are victims. In some jurisdictions, in marginal cases, whites are more likely to get probation while blacks are more likely to be sent to prison. With respect to juvenile processing, white youths are more apt to be released to their parents, while a juvenile facility is a more probable destination for minority youths.

Examinations of the correlation of race with the death penalty show one consistent pattern: Those who murder whites are more likely to receive a capital sentence than those who murder African Americans. On several occasions, the Supreme Court has been asked to rule on the constitutionality of the death penalty given the racial disparity in its use. Although the Court acknowledged in *McCleskey v. Kemp* (1987) that there was statistical evidence of race as a factor in the application of capital punishment, the justices refused to find the discrimination unconstitutional.

The United States has one of the highest rates of incarceration in the world, and minorities are disproportionately included among those confined. During the 1990s, more African Americans were under the supervision of the correctional system (i.e., they were in jail or prison, on probation or parole) than were enrolled in college. It is impossible to ignore the implications for the future, if sizeable numbers of young people receive their higher education in a correctional institution rather than on a college campus. Although minorities have always been overrepresented in American prisons, the disparity has increased dramatically since the 1980s. Most observers attribute this growth to the war on drugs. Law enforcement agencies at both the federal and state level have focused their efforts on visible and open drug trafficking, the sort that occurs in poor, minority neighborhoods. They make more arrests in such communities than in affluent or suburban areas where drug use is likely to be less obvious. The numbers of arrests, coupled with mandatory sentences for drug offenses, help to account for the expanded minority populations in prisons.

In examining the issues of race and criminal justice, many scholars have concluded that the system is characterized less by overt racial discrimination than it was in the past. Changes in the legal status of minority groups, Supreme Court decisions protecting the rights of the accused, and political action by African-American, Hispanic, and other ethnic groups have helped to reduce some racism. But discrimination remains a factor in accounting for the disparate experiences of whites and minorities at all stages of the criminal justice system, from encounters with the police, to indictment, to sentencing. Coupled with the economic biases inherent in the system, race and color continue to influence Americans' experiences of crime and punishment. (MWA)

BIBLIOGRAPHY

Donziger, Steven R. *The Real War on Crime: The Report of the National Criminal Justice Commission.* New York: Harper and Row, 1996.
Hacker, Andrew. *Two Nations: Black and White, Separate, Hostile, Unequal.* New York: Ballantine, 1992.
Hawkins, Darnell F., ed. *Ethnicity, Race, and Crime.* Albany, NY: State University of New York, 1995.
Mann, Coramae Richey. *Unequal Justice: A Question of Color.* Bloomington, IN: Indiana University Press, 1988.
Miller, Jerome G. *Search and Destroy.* New York: Cambridge University Press, 1996.
Walker, Samuel, Cassia Spohn, and Miriam DeLone. *The Color of Justice: Race, Ethnicity, and Crime in America.* Belmont, CA: Wadsworth, 1996.
Wilbanks, William. *The Myth of a Racist Criminal Justice System.* Monterey, CA: Brooks/Cole, 1987.

The Crisis

The Crisis is the official publication of the **National Association for the Advancement of Colored People (NAACP).** The founders of the NAACP wanted to publicize both the accomplishments of African Americans and the **discrimination** they faced. They hoped that this would lead to greater pride and activism among black Americans and greater tolerance and understanding among white Americans. The first editor of the magazine was **W.E.B. Du Bois,** who established *The Crisis* as one of the century's most influential magazines for and about African Americans. (CE)

BIBLIOGRAPHY

Kellogg, Charles. *NAACP: A History of the National Association for the Advancement of Colored People. Vol 1: 1909–1920.* Baltimore: Johns Hopkins University Press, 1968.

George W. Crockett, Jr. (1909–1997)

George W. Crockett, a Democrat from Illinois, was elected to the United States House of Representatives in 1980 and served until his retirement in 1990. Crockett served as a judge in the Detroit Recorders Court from 1946 to 1966 and again from 1972 to 1978. In 1946, Crockett served as associate legal counsel for the International United Auto Workers–Congress of Industrial Organizations (UAW-CIO). From 1946 to 1947, he was the executive director of the UAW-CIO Fair Employment Practices Committee in Detroit. Crockett was the senior attorney in the U.S. Department of Labor from 1939 to 1943.

BIBLIOGRAPHY

"George William Crockett, Jr." *Jet* 92, no. 18 (September 22, 1997): 56–58.

Crossover Strategy

Crossover strategies refer to the practice of black politicians attempting to appeal to white voters by emphasizing issues of importance to them in an attempt to become politically viable in districts with a white majority. It is often seen in tandem with deracialization, which is the practice of blacks articulating their political demands in ways that are not racially specific so as to appeal to a wider segment of the population. Both strategies are useful in helping black politicians and their constituents consolidate advances for black concerns while still maintaining the power necessary to support those advances.

BIBLIOGRAPHY

Barker, Lucius and Mack Jones. *African Americans and the American Political System.* Englewood Cliffs, NJ: Prentice Hall, 1994.

Alexander Crummell (1819–1898)

Alexander Crummell laid the institutional and intellectual foundation for the African-American intelligentsia. He is best known for the 20 years he spent in Liberia and Sierra Leone as an Episcopal minister and educator and his cooperation with the emigration schemes of the **American Colonization Society.** Believing that the future of Africans in the United States necessitated moral elevation, self-help, and economic development, Crummell founded the **American Negro Academy,** the first national learned society among African Americans. (RAM)

BIBLIOGRAPHY

Franklin, V.P. *Living Our Stories Telling Our Truths: Autobiography and the Making of the African-American Intellectual Tradition.* New York: Scribner's, 1995.
Meier, August. *Negro Thought in America, 1880–1915.* Ann Arbor: The University of Michigan Press, 1963.

Cumming v. Richmond County Board of Education (1899)

After the Board of Education of Richmond County, Virginia, used funds to assist the maintenance of a whites-only high school, similar steps were requested for the black children's high school. When the request was denied, Cumming brought the situation to court by seeking an injunction against the maintenance of the white school. The state court denied the injunction, stating that the board's actions did not warrant a restraint against the white school. Furthermore, the court denied allegations that the Board of Education had acted in a discriminatory manner. The Supreme Court, in *Cumming v. Richmond County Board of Education*, 175 U.S. 528 (1899), stated that in all situations concerning the **Fourteenth Amendment** rights should be protected, and that the collection and use of public taxation must be shared by all citizens regardless of race. However, the Court also felt that no clear violation of rights could be held, because the maintenance of schools and taxation for such was a matter soley for state jurisdiction. As a result, the Supreme Court affirmed the lower court decision. **See also** Education.

Bibliography
Kull, Andrew. *The Color-Blind Constitution*. Cambridge, MA: Harvard University Press, 1992.

Elijah E. Cummings (1951–)

Elijah Cummings was born in Baltimore, Maryland. He received his B.S. from Howard University in 1973 and his J.D. from the University of Maryland in 1976. He was elected to the U.S. House of Representatives as a Democrat from Maryland in 1996. He serves on the Government Reform and Oversight Committee. (JCW)

Bibliography
"Elijah E. Cummings, D-Md." *Congressional Quarter Weekly Report* 54, no. 16 (April 20, 1996): 1070.
"New Faces of 1997." *Ebony* 52, no. 3 (January 1997): 64.

D

Angela Y. Davis (1944–)

Angela Y. Davis teaches philosophy, aesthetics, and women's studies at San Francisco State University and the San Francisco Art Institute. She was a central figure in an internationally known trial. Guns were smuggled into a Superior Court in San Rafael, California, in August 1970 in an effort to free three black defendants. Four lives were lost in the melee. Davis was accused of purchasing two of the guns, resulting in charges of murder, kidnapping, and criminal conspiracy. In June 1972 she was acquitted of all charges. She ran as the U.S. vice presidential candidate for the Communist Party, USA in 1980 and 1984. (WWH)

BIBLIOGRAPHY

Chappell, Kevin. "Where Are the Civil Rights Icons of the '60s?" *Ebony* 51, no. 10 (August 1996): 108.

Margoshes, Pamela. "Thank You, Angela." *Essence* 26, no. 4 (August 1995): 50.

Rouse, Deborah L. "Rediscovering Angela Davis." *Emerge* 8, no. 8 (June 1997): 88.

Benjamin Oliver Davis, Jr. (1912–)

Benjamin Davis, Jr. attended West Point from 1932 to 1936, becoming the first African American to graduate from the institution in 50 years. Davis was also one of the first black air cadets to graduate from Advanced Army Flying School. During World War II, Davis flew more than 60 missions while commanding the 99th Fighter Squadron and later the all-black 332nd Fighter Group (better known as the Tuskegee Airmen). On October 27, 1954, under the appointment of President Dwight Eisenhower, Davis was made chief of staff of the 12th Air Force. In 1957 Davis was made chief of staff of the U.S. Air Forces in Europe (USAFE); this was followed by appointments in 1961 as director of Manpower and Organization, and in 1965 as chief of staff for the United Nations Command and U.S. forces in Korea. Davis was made deputy commander-in-chief of U.S. Strike Command in 1968, and he served in this position until his retirement in 1970. **See also** Benjamin Oliver Davis, Sr.

BIBLIOGRAPHY

Davis, Benjamin O., Jr. *Benjamin O. Davis, Jr., American: An Autobiography.* New York: Plume, 1992.

Benjamin Oliver Davis, Sr. (1877–1970)

Born in segregated Washington, D.C., in 1877, Benjamin Oliver Davis, Sr. enlisted in the United States Army during the Spanish-American War in 1898. He rose quickly through the ranks, earning a commission in 1901. Davis became the first black full colonel in 1930 and the first black brigadier general in 1940. **See also** Benjamin Oliver Davis, Jr. (GAA)

BIBLIOGRAPHY

Davis, Benjamin O., Jr. *Benjamin O. Davis, Jr., American: An Autobiography.* New York: Plume, 1992.

Davis et al. v. Schnell et al. (1949)

Davis et al. v. Schnell et al., 336 U.S. 933 (1949), was a per curiam decision involving voting rights in Alabama. Davis et al. brought suit challenging an amendment to the Alabama state constitution requiring that any person registering to vote must "understand and explain" any article of the Federal Constitution. The District Court held that such an amendment violated the **Fifteenth Amendment**. The Supreme Court agreed. (CJM)

William L. Dawson (1886–1970)

In 1943 William L. Dawson was elected as a Democrat to the United States House of Representatives from Illinois, serving in that capacity until 1970, when he decided not to seek reelection. Dawson began his political career as a Republican, while practicing law in Chicago in the 1930s. As a Republican he was elected to serve on the Chicago City Council for five terms, before switching to the Democratic Party in the 1940s. While active as a Democrat, Dawson advanced to become the first African American to vice-chair the Democratic National Committee. (DH)

BIBLIOGRAPHY

Hornsby, Alton, Jr. *Milestones in 20th-Century African American History.* Detroit: Visible Ink Press, 1993.

Drew S. Days III (1941–)

Drew Days was the solicitor general of the United States during President Clinton's first term (1992–1996). Days served as an attorney for the **NAACP Legal Defense and Education Fund** before he became the first African American to head the Civil Rights Division of the Justice Department during the Carter Administration. During that time, he played an important role in formulating the government's position in the *Bakke* case, a suit that successfully challenged racial quotas in college admissions, and was widely considered a defeat for **affirmative action**. Days left the office of solicitor general in 1996 to return to the faculty of Yale University Law School. (RLP)

BIBLIOGRAPHY
Caplan, Lincoln. *The Tenth Justice*. New York: Vintage Books, 1987.

Dayton Board of Education v. Brinkman (1979)

Known as *Brinkman II*, the Supreme Court upheld a Court of Appeals decision in *Dayton Board of Education v. Brinkman*, 443 U.S. 526 (1979), stating that the Dayton School Board had continued to operate a "dual" school system since *Brown I* and therefore had to take "affirmative" action to ensure that this segregated system was disestablished. The case is noteworthy for its brief but firm dissent on the part of Justice Rehnquist, who railed against the convergence by the majority of what he calls **de facto segregation** and **de jure segregation**. (CJM)

BIBLIOGRAPHY
Ballance, Bernadine S. "The Impact of *Columbus Board of Education v. Brinkman* on Proving Segregative Intent School Desegregation Cases." (Case note) *North Carolina Central Law Journal* 12, no. 1 (Fall 1980): 219–33.
Gutermann, Paul Eric. "School Desegregation Doctrine: The Interaction Between Violation and Remedy." *Case Western Reserve Law Review* 30, no. 4 (Summer 1980): 780–815.

De Facto Segregation

De facto segregation refers to segregation that is inadvertent, and is not established in law or caused by state action. De facto looks beyond the formal law to see if segregation exists in effect. Residential patterns, income distributions, and other social patterns can lead to de facto segregation. To attack de facto segregation under the **Fourteenth Amendment**, the Supreme Court requires that the state demonstrate a clear intent to discriminate. Thus, it is very difficult to attack de facto segregation under the Constitution. (RLP)

BIBLIOGRAPHY
Pritchett, C. Herman. *Constitutional Civil Liberties*. Englewood Cliffs, NJ: Prentice Hall, 1984.

De Jure Segregation

De jure refers to segregation that is based on law or official governmental action. The Jim Crow laws in the South, which mandated the separation of the races, are examples of de jure segregation. The Supreme Court considers de jure segregation to be highly unconstitutional under the **Fourteenth Amendment**. The Court holds that race is a suspect classification, triggering strict scrutiny. Thus, such laws are considered inherently unjust and require the most exacting judicial examination. (RLP)

BIBLIOGRAPHY
Pritchett, C. Herman. *Constitutional Civil Liberties*. Englewood Cliffs, NJ: Prentice Hall, 1984.

Robert C. DeLarge (1842–1874)

Robert DeLarge was born a slave in Aiken, South Carolina, in 1842. He was chairman of the committee at the South Carolina Republican Convention where he supported racial reconciliation, universal public education, and universal male suffrage. He was elected to the South Carolina state legislature in 1868 as a Republican and was appointed land commissioner by the legislature in 1869. He was elected to Congress in 1870, defeating Christopher Bowen, his white opponent. Bowen challenged the outcome, claiming DeLarge's election was a result of voter fraud. Although DeLarge was sworn into the 42nd Congress in March 1871, the House Committee on Elections began an investigation into Bowen's charges in the following December. In January 1873, the Committee reported that the election of 1870 involved so many instances of voter fraud that the winner could not be determined. The House therefore declared DeLarge's seat vacant. Before his removal from office, DeLarge fought to maintain federal troops in the South and advocated strict enforcement of the **Fourteenth Amendment** to prevent the intimidation of blacks by white terrorist groups. After serving 22 months, he was removed from his congressional seat after being found guilty of electoral fraud.

BIBLIOGRAPHY
Ragsdale, Bruce and Joel Treese. *Black Americans in Congress 1870–1989*. Washington, DC: U.S. Government Printing Office, 1990.

Ronald V. Dellums (1935–)

Ronald V. Dellums, a Democrat, served in the United States House of Representatives from California from 1971 until his retirement in 1998. Prior to being elected to Congress in 1970,

With federal troops at the doors, Central High School in Little Rock, Arkansas, was desegregated by these African-American students in 1957. *Library of Congress.*

Dellums worked with the San Francisco Economic Opportunity Council and had a career as a psychiatric social worker. While in Congress, Dellums served on the influential Armed Services Committee, as well as the District of Columbia Committee. When Dellums arrived in Congress, he was a firebrand liberal who used his seat on the Armed Services Committee to criticize the military and intelligence communities and expenditures. However, over the years, Dellums moderated his views to the point of being a leading advocate for military spending during the Clinton administration. He unexpectedly announced his retirement in 1997, wishing to return to private life.

BIBLIOGRAPHY

Fitch, Bob. *Right on Dellums*. Mankato, MN: Creative Educational Society, 1971.

James, Victor V. "Cultural Pluralism and the Quest for Black Citizenship." Master's Thesis, University of California at Berkeley, 1975.

U.S. Congress. *Full Committee Consideration of Committee Resolution Honoring the Honorable Ronald V. Dellums*. Washington, DC: U.S. Government Printing Office, 1998.

Delta Sigma Theta

Delta Sigma Theta Sorority was founded on January 13, 1913, at Howard University by 22 undergraduate women. It has a membership of over 190,000 predominantly African-American women and over 870 chapters worldwide. It is a nonprofit organization whose purpose is to provide services and programs to promote human welfare. The sorority focuses specifically on areas of educational and economic development, physical and mental health, and political awareness and involvement. Notable Deltas include **Shirley Chisholm**, **Barbara Jordan** and Ruby Dee Davis.

BIBLIOGRAPHY

Malveaux, Julianne. "Scholarship, Sisterhood, Service (Black Women in African American Fraternities)." *Black Issues in Higher Education* 14, no 8 (June 12, 1997): 28.

Democratic Party

The Democratic Party, one of the two major political parties in the United States, has been known as the party of the "common man" since the presidency of Andrew Jackson in the 1830s. One group of common folks the Democratic party did not embrace for much of its history, however, was African Americans. It was roughly 100 years after Jackson's presidency, during Franklin Delano Roosevelt's (FDR) administration, that the Democratic party began to make any serious attempt to address the needs of African Americans. The economic benefits of FDR's New Deal encouraged a majority of the blacks who could vote in 1936 to support the Democratic Party. When Democratic President Lyndon Baines Johnson (LBJ) signed the **Civil Rights Act of 1964**, he converted a healthy majority of black voters into a nearly unanimous bloc for the Democrats. Since 1964, blacks, Latinos, and white women have become the Democratic Party's most loyal constituencies.

At nearly every major turning point in the nation's political history since the 1830s, the Democratic Party's fortunes have been heavily influenced by the issue of race. In the mid-nineteenth century, the issue of slavery split Democrats into two regional factions. In the South, Democrats, led by Jefferson Davis, insisted on the protection of slavery throughout the United States. In opposition, northern Democrats, led by Stephen Douglas, supported the doctrine of popular sovereignty which left it up to settlers in a territory to decide whether or not to ban slavery. At its presidential convention in 1860, the party was so split that northern Democrats nominated one candidate (Douglas) and southern Democrats another (John C. Breckinridge) as their presidential candidates. This factionalism enabled the newly formed antislavery party, the Republicans, to elect the party's first president, Abraham Lincoln, and set the stage for the **Civil War**.

In the aftermath of the Civil War, white southerners associated the Republican Party with the end of slavery and consequently remained firmly Democratic until almost midway into the twentieth century. A basically conservative and agrarian-oriented party, the Democrats came out of **Reconstruction** (the brief period after the Civil War) bent set on rebuilding white racial privilege in every domain of society. Throughout the one-party South, Democratic governors and state legislators introduced black codes, literacy tests, grandfather clauses, poll taxes, white primaries, and a host of other mechanisms designed to disenfranchise the newly freed African-American population. As a result, by the turn of the twentieth century, the vast majority of blacks could not vote. For more than 50 years after Reconstruction, only a relatively small proportion of the black population (mostly in northern cities) was enfranchised. In response to these developments, those few blacks who could vote in the post-Reconstruction and Jim Crow periods heavily supported the Republican party, known widely as the party that "freed the slaves."

It was 1912 before a Democratic presidential nominee made even a modest effort at altering black voting patterns. In that year, nominee Woodrow Wilson overtly appealed for black votes and won the endorsement of several prominent black civil rights activists such as **W.E.B. Du Bois** and **William Monroe Trotter**. For the first time in northern cities such as New York, 25 percent of the black vote went to the Democratic nominee. Once in office, however, Wilson approved of racial segregation and quietly introduced it throughout the federal bureaucracy, further disillusioning African Americans and blunting his party's appeal to them.

It took a crisis of major proportions and an appeal based more on economics than race to move blacks into the Democratic party. The Great Depression of the 1930s provided such a crisis. In the crucible of despair, blacks became Democrats in response to the economic benefits of FDR's social programs, and they joined Jews, Catholics, farmers, northern urban voting blocs, intellectuals, organized labor, and southern whites in the Democrats' New Deal coalition in spite of Roosevelt's lack of a substantive record on race. Yet, despite garnering strong black support, FDR refused to support anti-lynching legislation, black enfranchisement, or any of more than 150 civil rights bills introduced in Congress during his presidency. In addition, there was inequality in the distribution of the New Deal's programs, with blacks suffering more, but getting less. Roosevelt's constant response to black and white liberals alike was that he could not afford to alienate southerners who chaired 12 of the 17 major House Committees and nine of the 14 major Senate committees in Congress. On questions of race, the political economy of the South in the cotton plantation areas, southern dominance of the committee system in Congress, and the coalition needs of FDR and the Democratic party continued to shape the party's promise and performance through the 1930s.

At the same time, the shift of black voters to the Democratic party was part of a larger process of politicization that was changing the political habits of African Americans. The New Deal's agricultural policies had the effect of driving millions of sharecroppers from the rural South and into northern ghettos (causing an approximate doubling of the black population between 1920 and 1940 in the North). In this new setting, it became possible for blacks to articulate common political interests and promote leaders. The massing into concentrated areas also fostered the development of specialized interest groups with particular political objectives. It created an environment conducive to the emergence of black political leadership. It brought blacks under the sway of local Democratic political machines, and it made the black vote a sufficient force to warrant attention from the national parties. Two of the first results were Roosevelt's establishment of the Fair Employment Practices Commission (in response to the threat that blacks, led by **A. Philip Randolph**, would mount a march on Washington) and a Roosevelt-oriented Supreme Court that declared the white primary election unconstitutional in the early 1940s.

Even such minor concessions in Roosevelt's final years marked the beginning of a new posture by national Democratic leaders toward the cause of civil rights and engendered intense antagonism among white southern leaders, thus creating a deep strain between the northern and southern wings of the party. By the late 1940s it appeared that the party had developed a coalition composed both of southern whites and northern blacks, and that liberal whites could endure only so long as the issue of race was submerged. FDR succeeded in doing this during his lifetime, but Democratic party and congressional leaders found it an increasingly difficult issue to manage during the late 1940s and 1950s.

The diminution of the economic crisis and the increasing racial consciousness of African Americans as a consequence of World War II brought racial issues to the fore in the 1940s in ways that had not occurred during FDR's years. Democratic president Harry S. Truman looked to civil rights as a means to transform black Roosevelt supporters into black Democrats. As a result, in 1948, for the first time, Democrats had black delegates at their nomination convention and worked closely with civil rights activists to get the black vote. These actions, along with Truman's executive orders to desegregate the military and to create a Fair Employment Practices board within the Civil Service Commission, allied a majority of blacks not just with the party's nominee but with the party itself for the first time. In response, alienated southern whites began to leave the party in droves.

In the 1960s, Washington's efforts to expand American influence in the Third World where the British and French empires had recently disintegrated provided another reason for the Democrats to take up the cause of civil rights in the South, where they were seriously embarrassed by the system of racial segregation. As America's image became tarnished by scenes of segregation in the South, President John F. Kennedy proposed what became the landmark Civil Rights Act of 1964.

After Kennedy was assassinated, Democratic president Lyndon Baines Johnson not only signed the Civil Rights Act but followed by signing the **Voting Rights Act** into law in 1965, and the Department of Justice began to make good Johnson's promise of implementation. Now the vast majority of blacks could vote. In addition, Johnson's Great Society programs had a significant impact on the economic position of blacks—expanding aid to the poor and creating jobs for the middle class—further solidifying blacks' link with the party. As a result blacks moved more overwhelmingly into the Democratic party than ever before. While only 58 percent of blacks identified themselves as Democrats in 1960, approximately 80 percent or more have identified themselves as Democrats since 1964.

One concomitant was that racial differences in party preferences mushroomed. Between 1944 and 1960, differences in presidential voting choice by blacks and whites ranged from a low of 12 percentage points to a high of 40. Although black support for the Democrats jumped in 1964, racial voting was held to 36 points because a substantial majority of whites voted Democratic. But racial differences jumped to 56 points in 1968 and never fell back to the levels of the 1944 to 1960 period. A virtual sea change had occurred in the nation's party system: the historic party of slavery, the Democrats, emerged from the 1960s with the image of being not only a liberal party, but the party for civil rights. Conversely, Republicans turned their backs on 100 years of racial leadership and gained the image of being not only the conservative party, but the party for states' rights.

The Democrats remained the nation's majority party through the 1970s, usually controlling both Congress and the White House, but by the 1980s, the Democratic coalition faced serious problems. Even as the Democrats increased their strength among African-American, Latino, and white female voters, the once-solid South often voted for Republicans, along with many blue-collar northern white voters, especially white men. Although the party maintained a strong base in the bureaucracies of the federal government and the states, in labor unions, and in the not-for-profit sector of the economy, the

Democrats found it extremely difficult to win presidential elections in the 1980s. Instead two conservative Republicans, Ronald Reagan and George Bush, were the presidents of the 1980s.

Trying to regain the presidency, the Democratic party underwent serious internal strains over the issues of race and social policy, resulting in two sharply bifurcated wings. On one side, liberals and progressives (Traditional/Old Democrats) argued that Republicans had won most presidential contests since 1968 by consciously and aggressively spreading the politics of divisiveness. According to the Traditional Democrats, what the Democrats needed to do was not to desert social policies that worked or a strong defense of civil rights, but to speak more forcefully to the pocketbook issues that had once guaranteed the party success. On the other side, moderates and conservatives (New Democrats) countered that just such "liberal fundamentalism" was itself the real problem. According to the New Democrats, Democrats lost the White House because they became too identified with "special interests," thereby alienating the party's white working- and middle-class constituencies. To rebuild, New Democrats counseled, the party needed to deemphasize issues of racism, poverty, and civil rights (especially affirmative action) and instead focus on the concerns of the middle class in terms of lower taxes, opposition to quotas, and a tough approach to welfare and crime.

Jesse Jackson emerged as the most visible symbol and outspoken proponent of the Traditional Democratic wing. His attempts to create a "Rainbow Coalition" and influence the party in 1984 and 1988 were sharply turned back. Meanwhile, during the 1980s, conservative and moderate Democrats established the Democratic Leadership Council (DLC) to promote their views and candidates within the party. Members of the DLC were able to take control of the party nominating process, and they promoted a conservative agenda in an attempt to broaden middle-class white support for the Democrats. In 1992, one of the former chairs of the DLC, William Jefferson Clinton, was elected president. Clinton's support of international trade agreements—which generally were opposed by organized labor, his efforts to restrain the growth of spending on social programs, and his agreement to turn back 60 years of a social policy regime that had guaranteed every American at least a modicum of security not dependent on the market, signaled a shift toward a more conservative, business-oriented philosophy within the Democratic Party.

In 1994, Clinton's unpopularity (as measured by public opinion polls) was widely viewed as leading to the loss of Democrats' control of both houses of Congress for the first time since 1954. However, voters, demonstrating their volatility throughout the 1990s, reelected Clinton by solid margins in both the popular and electoral votes. Although a plurality of white men voted for Robert Dole, the Republican nominee, African Americans, Jews, Latinos, and white women continued to be the most loyal supporters of the Democratic Party. As the twentieth century drew to a close, the more moderate-to-conservative posture of the Democratic Party's most prominent leaders, the party's efforts to court moderate and conservative whites and to downplay its appeal to people of color, and its agreement on many issues with the Republicans appeared to be shaping a political picture in which there were nearly as many differences within each of the two major parties as between them. (LFW)

BIBLIOGRAPHY

Carmines, Edward G. and James Stinson. *Issue Evolution: Race and the Transformation of American Politics*. Princeton: Princeton University Press, 1989.

Edsall, Thomas and Mary Edsall. *Chain Reaction: The Impact of Race, Rights and Taxes on American Politics*. New York: W W Norton and Co Inc, 1991.

Grossman, Lawrence. *The Democratic Party and the Negro: northern and National Politics, 1868–92*. Urbana: University of Illinois Press, 1976.

Piven, Frances and Richard Cloward. *Poor People's Movements: Why They Succeed, How They Fail*. New York: Vintage Books, 1979: Chapter 4.

Pohlman, Marcus. *Black Politics in Conservative America*. New York: Longman, 1990.

Stanley, Harold. *Voter Mobilization and the Politics of Race: The South and Universal Suffrage, 1952–1984*. New York: Praeger, 1987.

Reed, Adolph. *The Jesse Jackson Phenomenon*. New Haven: Yale University Press, 1987.

Shafer, Bryon. *Quiet Revolution: The Struggle for the Democratic Party and the Shaping of Reform*. New York: Russell Sage, 1983.

Tate, Katherine. *From Protest to Politics: The New Black Voters in American Elections*. Cambridge: Harvard University Press, 1994.

Oscar De Priest (1871–1951)

Oscar De Priest, a Republican, represented Chicago in Congress from 1928–1934, becoming the first black congressman ever from outside the South. He introduced a bill providing a pension for ex-slave citizens, and he attempted to make states and counties responsible for the prevention of lynching. He served on the Cook County Board of Commissioners in 1904; he was a member of the Chicago City Council (1915–1917); and he was elected 3rd Ward committeeman in 1924. After his congressional career, he was again elected 3rd Ward alderman and he served once more on the Chicago City Council until his defeat in 1947. (EC)

BIBLIOGRAPHY

Mann, Kenneth Eugene. "Oscar Stanton De Priest: Persuasive Agent for the Black Masses." *Negro History Bulletin* 35 (October 1972): 134–37.

Deracialization

Deracialization is an electoral campaign strategy adopted by African-American politicians in which racial issues and themes are minimized, if not avoided, and a rigorous appeal is made for white voter support. Deracialization increases the number of African-American elected officials, but it does not threaten traditional black politics. Deracialized political campaigns require black candidates to run campaigns differently from traditional black candidates, in that they must appeal to whites, ethnic groups, and other racial minorities. Deracialization results in African-American candidates having to restrain their natural political impulses to openly advocate black causes in order to attract white electoral support; it also challenges white voters to be less race-bound in their voting preferences. (EC)

BIBLIOGRAPHY

Perry, Huey, L., ed. *Race, Politics and Governance in the United States.* Gainesville: University of Florida Press, 1996.

Derrickson v. City of Danville (1988)

Derrickson v. City of Danville, 845 F. 2d 715 (7th Circ. 1988), began as a suit under the **Voting Rights Act (VRA) of 1965,** seeking an injunction against an at-large system used by the City of Danville, Illinois, to elect its municipal government. The four elected commissioners of the city possessed both executive and legislative authority. The district court issued an injunction against state prosecution of the commissioners. On appeal, the circuit court held that proceedings leading to approval of a consent decree did not preclude criminal prosecution of commissioners for violating the VRA of 1965. (CJM)

BIBLIOGRAPHY

Karlan, Pamela S. "Law and the Political Process." *Stanford Law Review* 50 (February 1980): 731–63.

Charles C. Diggs, Jr. (1922–)

Charles C. Diggs won a seat in the U.S. House of Representatives as a Democrat in 1954, becoming the first African American elected to Congress from Michigan. Representative Diggs was a founding member of the **Congressional Black Caucus**. Diggs' legislative interests included civil rights and African issues. He was a member of the Foreign Affairs Committee and served as chair of its subcommittee on Africa from 1969 until 1979. He fought for sanctions against the white governments in southern Rhodesia (now Zimbabwe) and South Africa, and helped form TransAfrica in 1977. He resigned in 1980. (AD)

BIBLIOGRAPHY

Christopher, Maurine. *Black Americans in Congress.* New York: Thomas Crowell, 1976.
Schraeder, Peter. *United States Foreign Policy Towards Africa: Incrementalism, Crisis and Change.* Cambridge: Cambridge University Press, 1993.

David Norman Dinkins (1927–)

David Dinkins was mayor of New York City from 1989 to 1993. He is the first and, to date, the only African American to hold this position. Prior to his election to the mayor's office, Dinkins was Manhattan borough president from 1986 to 1989. From 1975 to 1985, he was city clerk and from 1972 to 1973, he was president of the New York City Board of Elec-

tions. Dinkins served in the New York Assembly from 1965 to 1966.

BIBLIOGRAPHY

Finch, Peter. "David Dinkins: How's He Doin'?" *Business Week* (June 18, 1990): 182–86.

Discrimination

Discrimination is the use of any unreasonable and unjust criterion for exclusion or unequal treatment of a person or persons based on group membership. It is closely related to prejudice (the tendency of an individual to think about other groups in negative ways and to attach negative emotions to other groups), but unlike prejudice, discrimination refers to actual behavior, not just thought or feelings. An example of discrimination would be an employer who refuses to hire an individual because she is a woman (or African American, Mexican American, Jewish, Korean, 70 years old, gay, and so forth). If the unequal treatment or unreasonable exclusion is based on the group membership of the individual, the act is discriminatory.

Discrimination always has a purpose. It generates or sustains advantages for the group doing the discriminating even as it produces or perpetuates disadvantages for the group(s) discriminated against. For instance, in the American experience, whites have discriminated against blacks to maintain their position of dominance and accrue and secure the majority of society's most coveted values (jobs, income, businesses, wealth, political power, and so forth).

Discrimination can be overt or covert, individual or institutionalized. For example, when African Americans were prevented from voting in the American South, discrimination was obvious, blatant, and widely understood by blacks and whites alike. It existed to disenfranchise the black community and keep it politically powerless. Similarly, when public schools use "aptitude" tests that are biased in favor of the white culture, decisions about who does and who does not take college preparatory courses may be made on discriminatory grounds even if everyone involved sincerely believes that objective criteria are being applied in a rational way. When employers use the "old boy" network to identify job applicants and make hires (for example, advertising only in places likely to attract white male applicants or filling the job from those—or the friends of those—already employed by the company), institutional discrimination is at work although the individuals involved may harbor few, if any, racist sentiments.

As these examples indicate, discrimination often occurs together with prejudice, but not always. For example, in settings regulated by strong civil rights protections, even people who are highly prejudiced in their feelings and thoughts (bigots) may abide by civil rights laws and not discriminate. Conversely, situations in which prejudice is strongly approved, supported, and even encouraged might evoke discrimination in otherwise nonprejudiced individuals. For example, regardless of a white person's actual level of prejudice, in the American South during the height of **segregation** it was usual and customary for whites to treat blacks in a discriminatory manner.

Discrimination against women of all races, people of color, and non-Protestant religious groups has a long history in the United States. For instance, in the colonial era women could not own property or vote, and those of African descent were enslaved and denied all democratic rights. As the nineteenth century drew to a close, immigration policy was one mode of discriminating against Chinese Americans, who for decades were excluded from citizenship by the Chinese Exclusion Act of 1882. In the early twentieth century, California's Alien Land Act of 1913 declared Japanese (and other Asians) to be aliens who were ineligible for citizenship; these groups remained politically disenfranchised and segregated from white schools and residential areas for decades. By the middle of the twentieth century, decades of discrimination against the Japanese conditioned whites to support imprisoning Japanese Americans in internment camps after Japan attacked the U.S. naval base at Pearl Harbor during World War II. Even the original native peoples of the American continent (Native Americans) were excluded from citizenship until 1924 and continue to be provided far fewer opportunities to develop themselves (opportunities for education and employment) and their capital (opportunities to develop and control their natural resources and businesses on reservations). In fact, discrimination in the United States has been so rampant that some white groups such as Jews and the Irish have spent large parts of their history being treated as "a race apart"—relegated to living in their own ethnic ghettos and forced to develop occupational niches to begin their move up the ladder of social mobility.

Despite the widespread existence of discrimination against many groups in the United States, however, some groups have suffered more grievously from discrimination than others. Blacks, the only group enslaved by whites, must assuredly rank among those suffering the severest and longest discrimination. It took the **Civil War** to end whites' enslavement of African Americans and begin the path toward eliminating racial discrimination. Even then, the battle against discrimination had only just begun.

After a short-lived period (**Reconstruction** after the Civil War) when the "equal protection" clause of the **Fourteenth Amendment** made civil rights for all—regardless of color—the law of the land, the Supreme Court turned conservative. According to the Court's interpretation in the late 1870s, the Fourteenth Amendment was only intended to protect individuals from discrimination by *public* officials of state and local governments. The court therefore declared the **Civil Rights Act of 1875** unconstitutional on the grounds that the act sought to protect blacks against discrimination by *private* businesses.

In 1896, the Supreme Court went still further in bolstering discrimination against blacks. In the infamous case *Plessy v. Ferguson*, the Court ruled that the Fourteenth Amendment's "equal protection of the law" clause was not violated by exclusion of blacks from any facilities as long as the facilities provided to blacks were equal, thus establishing the "**separate but equal**" doctrine that prevailed well into the mid-twentieth century. The reality was that segregated accommodations (schools, recreational centers, restaurants, and so on) were never equal. In effect, the Court mandated that the use of race as a criterion of exclusion and unequal treatment in public and private matters alike was not unreasonable.

In the 1940s, a burgeoning civil rights movement, revelation of Nazi racial/ethnic atrocities, and the shame of discrimination against African-American military personnel during World War II began to bring national attention to racial discrimination. Shortly before World War II, the Supreme Court began to change its position on discrimination. Then in 1946, President Harry Truman appointed a Commission on Civil Rights to study discrimination. In 1954, in the case ***Brown v. Board of Education*** the Supreme Court withdrew all constitutional authority to use race as a criterion of exclusion and unequal treatment. The *Brown* decision altered the course of discrimination in two fundamental ways. First, after *Brown*, the states no longer had the power to use race as a criterion of discrimination in law; second, the federal government from then on had the power (and indeed the obligation) to intervene with strict regulatory policies against discriminatory actions in the public and private sectors.

It soon became clear that *Brown* was little more than a small opening move, however. Particularly in the South there was massive white resistance to implementing *Brown*. Racial discrimination in schools, employment, public accommodations, juries, voting, and other areas of social and economic life remained the de facto (actual) pattern of the nation, even if it was no longer a de jure (legal) practice.

A decade after *Brown*, it became obvious that the goal of ending discrimination and guaranteeing "equal protection" required positive, or "affirmative," action. In response to economic modernization of the South, American embarrassment abroad in the context of the end of colonialism, and massive growth of the **civil rights movement** and the **black power** movement in the 1950s and 1960s, Congress and the presidential administrations of John F. Kennedy and Lyndon B. Johnson grew ready to act. The chief products of the mid-1960s (from Johnson's administration) were the **Civil Rights Act of 1964** (which outlawed discrimination on the basis of race, color, gender, religion, and national origin in the private sector and provided for the withholding of federal grants-in-aid to any local government, school, or private employer as a sanction to help enforce civil rights laws); the **Voting Rights Act of 1965** (which strengthened legislation protecting voting rights and required that the same standards be used registering *all* citizens in federal, state, and local elections); and the **Open Housing Act of 1968** (the Fair Housing Act, which prohibited discrimination in the sale or rental of most housing). On the heels of these acts, the Supreme Court handed down several decisions establishing rights for language minorities as well. For example, *Lau v. Nichols* (1974), a suit filed on behalf of Chinese students in San Francisco, ruled that school districts must provide education for students whose English is limited. Similarly, the concept of rights for the disabled began to emerge in the 1970s, culminating in 1990 with passage of the Americans with Disabilities Act (which guarantees equal employment opportunity and access to public businesses for the disabled). In 1996, the Supreme Court in *Romer v. Evans* also explicitly extended civil rights protection to gays and lesbians, declaring discrimination against gay people to be unconstitutional.

Not only have efforts to end discrimination spread to an increasing number of groups in American society since the 1960s, but the narrow goal of eliminating discriminatory barriers has also developed toward a broader goal of **affirmative action** (compensatory efforts to overcome the consequences of past discrimination). Affirmative action requires that race and/or gender be taken into consideration for compensatory action. According to the policy's proponents, the only way to guarantee an "equal playing field" and compensate for past discrimination is to give an advantage to the woman or minority who is essentially equal to the white male in skills, background, training, and education for positions in colleges and universities, employment, and business contracting. As President Johnson put the case in 1965: "You do not take a person who, for years, has been hobbled by chains and liberate him, bring him up to the starting line of a race and then say 'You are free to compete with all the others,' and still justly believe that you have been completely fair. Thus, it is not enough just to open the gates of opportunity. All our citizens must have the ability to walk through those gates." With these words, Johnson called for compensatory programs.

According to affirmative action's critics, however, the policy has instead created "reverse discrimination" (discrimination against white men, who had been historically advantaged as a result of discrimination, in favor of people of color and white women, who had been historically disadvantaged). Some opponents of affirmative action even claim that racial discrimination has declined so dramatically in significance that the large racial disparities in income, poverty, and occupational prestige that continue to be suffered especially by blacks, Latinos, and Native Americans have virtually nothing to do with racial discrimination.

Despite such claims, it is clear that the issue of discrimination against people of color and against women is by no means over. Settings for disputes can arise in places such as Denny's restaurant (a 1993 case where, faced with a pattern of systematic discrimination and numerous lawsuits, the chain paid $45 million in damages to plaintiffs in Maryland and California) or the Fleet Financial Group (a 1996 case that settled a discrimination claim in favor of blacks and Latinos who had been charged higher prices for home mortgage loans than had comparably qualified whites). In addition, there is considerable evidence in hiring- and housing-audit studies conducted by government departments (such as Justice or Housing and Urban Development) and private sector research organizations (such as the Urban Institute) showing that blacks, Latinos, and Asian Americans are denied opportunities strictly as a result of their race and/or ethnicity. Meanwhile, white men still hold nearly all of the most coveted positions in American society. As a 1995 Glass Ceiling Commission report found, white men had 97 percent of the top positions in the nation's most profitable corporations (the Fortune 500 companies), 97 percent of the seats in the United States Senate, 90 percent of the seats in the United States House of Representatives, and 89 percent of the seats on the Supreme Court.

In sum, the story of discrimination has not ended and is not likely to end in the foreseeable future. Discrimination remains a key (but ugly) factor in the American experience. **See also** De Facto Segregation; De Jure Segregation; Racism; Segregation/Integration/Separation. **See** "Civil War Amendments" in Appendix 1. (LFW)

BIBLIOGRAPHY

Baer, Judith A. *Equality under the Constitution: Reclaiming the Fourteenth Amendment*. Ithaca, NY: Cornell University Press, 1983.

Feagin, Joe R. and Clarice B. Feagin. *Discrimination American Style: Institutional Racism and Sexism*. Englewood Cliffs, NJ: Prentice Hall, 1978.

Hacker, Andrew. *Two Nations: Black and White, Separate, Hostile, Unequal*. New York: Scribner's, 1992.

Omi, Michael and Howard Winant. *Racial Formation in the United States from the 1960s to the 1980s*. New York: Routledge and Kegan Paul, 1986.

Portes, Alejandro and Robert L. Bach. *Latin Journey: Cuban and Mexican Immigrants in the United States*. Berkeley: University of California Press, 1985.

Takaki, Ronald T. *A Different Mirror: A History of Multicultural America*. Boston: Little Brown, 1993.

Wilson, William J. *The Declining Significance of Race*. Chicago: University of Chicago Press, 1980.

Zinn, Maxine Baca and Bonnie Thornton Dill. *Women of Color in U.S. Society*. Philadelphia: Temple University Press, 1994.

Julian C. Dixon (1934–)

Julian Dixon (D-CA), trained in law, was elected to the U.S. House of Representatives in 1978, where he continues to serve. As the ranking Democrat on the District of Columbia Committee, he has been very active in assisting the elected officials of the District of Columbia to handle the district's fiscal trouble. Furthermore, he has worked to serve his Los Angeles, California, constituents. He was instrumental in bringing relief funds for those people affected by the L.A. earthquakes of 1994; he has also dealt with problems surrounding illegal immigration and the Metro Rail Subway system of Washington, D.C. (CEM)

BIBLIOGRAPHY

"A Look at the 13 Cardinals." *CQWR* 52, no. 19 (May 14, 1994): 1182.

Frederick Douglass [Frederick Augustus Washington Bailey] (1817–1895)

Frederick Douglass was the most significant black advocate for the abolition of slavery in the nineteenth century. Born into slavery in Maryland in 1817, he was sent to Baltimore, where he learned to read and write. He escaped to New York and became an agent of the Massachusetts Anti-Slavery Society.

Former slave Frederick Douglass worked tirelessly for abolition before the Civil War and for equal rights afterwards. *National Archives.*

His abolitionist efforts were primarily accomplished through public speaking tours, publishing, and utilizing political connections. He toured the Northeastern U.S.A., Canada, and England before publishing his *Narrative of Frederick Douglass* (1845), one of the most influential abolitionist writings. In 1847 he founded a newspaper, The *North Star*, subsequently published as *Frederick Douglass's Paper*. In 1855 he published *My Bondage and My Freedom* and in 1858, *Douglass's Monthly*. At the outbreak of the **Civil War**, he met with President Abraham Lincoln and assisted him in the formation of the 54th and 55th Massachusetts Negro Regiments.

By 1871 he was serving in the territorial legislature for the District of Columbia, and in 1872 he was a presidential elector for New York. He held various posts in Washington, D.C., until he was appointed minister resident and U.S. Consul General to the Republic of Haiti in 1889. However, he resigned this post in 1891 to protest unscrupulous American business practices. He died on February 20, 1895, at Mount Cedar, Washington, D.C. (ISM)

BIBLIOGRAPHY

Rogers, William B. "We Are All Together Now." In *Frederick Douglass, William Lloyd Garrison, and the Prophetic Tradition.* New York: Garland Publishing, 1995.
Washington, Booker T. *Frederick A. Douglass.* Philadelphia: George W. Jacobs, 1906.

Dred Scott v. Sandford (1857)

Dred Scott, a slave, claimed that he was entitled to his freedom because he had spent time in territory where slavery was prohibited. In 1834 Scott accompanied his owner Dr. John Emerson, a surgeon in the army, to a military post at Rock Island, Illinois, and then in 1836–1838 to another posting at Fort Snelling, in the upper Louisiana Territory (part of Wisconsin today), north of the latitude of 36 degrees 30 minutes north—the free–slave line delineated in the **Missouri Compromise**. After this second post, Emerson returned to Missouri.

After Emerson died, Scott sued for his independence in Missouri courts in *Scott v. Emerson* (1846). Scott had reason to hope that his case would be decided in his favor. The Supreme Court of Missouri in *Rachel v. Walker* (1836) had granted freedom to a slave who had, like Scott, spent a number of years in free territory. However, by 1850 when Scott's case reached the Missouri high court, the justices were not inclined to follow the precedent of *Rachel*. Instead, they ruled that Scott remained the property of Emerson's widow.

Scott appealed the Missouri ruling to the federal courts. In the intervening time between the Missouri supreme court ruling and his appeal to federal courts, Mrs. Emerson had moved to Massachusetts and left Scott to her brother John A. Sanford (the name was misspelled in court records). Many historians have concluded that the continuation of the case was an attempt by abolitionists to win a decisive victory in the courts, rather than a true suit over Scott's freedom. In any case, the federal circuit court rejected Sanford's claim that Scott could not sue (because, as a slave, he was not a citizen of Missouri); however, the court did agree that Scott's status of slave returned when he reentered the slave state of Missouri.

Scott appealed to the U.S. Supreme Court, which heard the case as *Dred Scott v. Sandford,* 19 Howard 393 (1857). The Court concluded that no blacks, not even free ones, could be citizens of the United States; therefore, Scott lacked any constitutionally mandated protections—including the right to sue in federal courts. It would take the upheaval of the **Civil War** and the passage of the **Fourteenth Amendment** to undo this decision of the Court.

The Court also invalidated the free–slave boundary-line provision of the Missouri Compromise. But the Court's decision went further than merely striking down this provision. The majority opinion of the Court, written by Chief Justice Roger B. Taney, concluded that "free soil" federal laws, which held that a slave who entered into a free territory was no longer a slave, were unconstitutional because they deprived the slaveholder of just compensation. *Dred Scott v. Sandford* is considered by many scholars to be one of the most ill-conceived decisions in the history of the Supreme Court.

BIBLIOGRAPHY

Fehrenbacher, Don E. *The Dred Scott Case: Its Significance in American Law and Politics.* New York: Oxford University Press, 1978.
Stampp, Kenneth. *America in 1857: A Nation on the Brink.* New York: Oxford University Press, 1990.

W. E. B. Du Bois [William Edward Burghardt Du Bois] (1868–1963)

W. E. B. Du Bois was born on February 23, 1868, in Great Barrington, Massachusetts. After graduating from high school in 1884, he attended Fisk College. In 1888 he graduated from Fisk and joined the junior class at Harvard University. He graduated cum laude in 1890 and then received his M.A. in 1891. He spent two years at the University of Berlin, before completing his dissertation at Harvard and graduating with his Ph.D. After graduating he had a succession of teaching jobs, where he did ground-breaking research on African Americans, before being appointed director of publicity for the **National Association for the Advancement of Colored People (NAACP)** working for racial justice and editing their periodical, *The Crisis*. He made an early name for himself by delivering a masterful criticism of **Booker T. Washington**'s program of accommodation in his classic work, *The Souls of Black Folk* in 1903. This was just one of many books he would write in his lifetime. Du Bois was also very active in the Pan-African movement, a movement organizing several conferences and representing African causes at the Versailles Conference. During the 1930s he flirted with communism and in 1948 was dismissed from the NAACP. During the 1950s and early 1960s he worked to help developing African Republics avoid the traps of neocolonialism. However, his association with communism limited his appeal in the U.S., and he eventually left the country and denounced his American citizenship. He died in Ghana in 1963. (AAB)

BIBLIOGRAPHY

Byerman, Keith Elvon. *Seizing the Word: History, Art, and Self in the Work of W. E. B. Du Bois*. New York: Simon and Schuster, 1988.

Edward Richard Dudley (1911–)

While **Ebenezer D. Bassett** and **Frederick Douglass** share the honor of being the first African Americans appointed to head an overseas diplomatic post, Edward Richard Dudley was the first African American to hold the title of ambassador to a foreign country. Appointed by President Harry S. Truman, Dudley served as ambassador to Liberia from 1948 until 1953. After leaving his diplomatic post, Dudley served on the New York State Supreme Court from 1965 to 1985, where he continued to be a strong voice for minorities. Prior to his appointment as ambassador to Liberia, he served two terms (1943–1945 and 1947–1948) as assistant special counsel to **Thurgood Marshall** at the **National Association for the Advancement of Colored People.**

BIBLIOGRAPHY

Bracey, John H., Jr. and August Meier, eds. *Papers of the NAACP.* Bethesda, MD: University Publications of America, 1994.
"Celebrating Blacks in Foreign Affairs." *State Magazine* (February 1998): 1–3.

Dunn v. Blumstein (1972)

Dunn v. Blumstein, 405 U.S. 3303 (1972), was a challenge to state residence laws for voters. Tennessee closes its registration books 30 days before an election, but requires residence in the state for one year and in the county for three months. The Supreme Court held that such laws do not further any compelling state interest and violate the equal protection clause of the **Fourteenth Amendment** by burdening the right to travel, penalizing bona fide residents who have recently traveled from one jurisdiction to another. (PLF)

BIBLIOGRAPHY

Heck, Edward V. "Constitutional Interpretation and a Court in Transition: Strict Scrutiny from *Shapiro v. Thompson* to *Dunn v. Blumstein* and Beyond." *United States Air Force Academy Journal of Legal Studies* 3 (Annual 1992): 65–90.

Mervyn Malcolm Dymally (1926–)

Mervyn Dymally, a Democrat, represented California's 13th Congressional District (1980–1992). He served in the California assembly (1963–1966), was a member of the state senate (1967–1975), and lieutenant governor in 1974. In Congress he served on the House Foreign Affairs Committee, chairing its Sub-Committee on International Operations. (EC)

BIBLIOGRAPHY

Ragsdale, Bruce and Joel D. Treese. *Black Americans in Congress, 1870–1989*. Washington, DC: U.S. Government Printing Office, 1990.

E

Marian Wright Edelman (1939–)

Marian Wright Edelman, founder of the Children's Defense Fund (CDF), began her political activism while in college. In law school, Edelman became involved in the **Student Non-violent Coordinating Committee (SNCC)**, by attempting to register voters in Mississippi. As a young attorney, Edelman directed the **National Association for the Advancement of Colored People (NAACP)** Legal Defense Fund and Educational Fund in Mississippi. The poverty in Mississippi led Edelman to seek ways to help America's poor, especially children. Established in 1973, the CDF has lobbied for children's needs. (DH)

BIBLIOGRAPHY

Lanker, Brian. *I Dream A World: Portraits of Black Women Who Changed America*. New York: Stewart, Tabori, and Chang, 1989.

Education

Arguments about "how best to educate the Negro" have been carried on since before the **Civil War**. In the pre-civil War South, it was illegal for slaves to learn how to read and write. Even though illegal, a fair proportion of African Americans did become literate. The example of **Frederick Douglass** is instructive. As related in his *Autobiography*, he used every possible means to learn how to read, believing that the risk of being caught was worth the potential gains.

African Americans have always played a vigorous role in the argument for educating African Americans. The argument has vital implications beyond the African American community. Certainly, the basic premise to which most people agree is that in a democracy the educational system should equip individuals for successful participation in a society.

The commitment of the African American community to education is seen in the following statistic. In 1870, 80 percent of the black population over 10 years of age was illiterate. That number was significantly reduced to 50 percent by 1900. Critics note that too often, however, the educational system has been an instrument of social control: a means of imposing normative values and of classifying individuals according to dominant ideals. The argument has been that schools have a hidden curriculum that teaches conformity to the ideals and values of those in control. However, the very books assigned tend to neglect and denigrate the contributions of women and minorities, defining "American" in a white, middle-class context. James Turner, Head of the African American Studies Department at Cornell University is a strong supporter of this position.

Moreover, there has been a debate within the African-American community over whether to educate African Americans for gainful employment and self-help, a position espoused by **Booker T. Washington**, or to concentrate on the "talented tenth" who would raise their brethren up, a position held by **W.E.B. Du Bois**. Washington argued that black education's first priority should be to counteract the harmful effects of slavery. Blacks, he argued, had lost the sense of self-responsibility. He founded the **Tuskegee Institute**, a school that blended manual labor and life-management skills.

From the very ending of slavery in the 1860s, black leaders have emphasized the need for a good education to give African Americans a more equal opportunity. *Library of Congress.*

If students learned useful trades while in school, he suggested, they would feel confident that they had something to offer and could therefore lay claim to a position in the social structure. His position is summed up in his often quoted statement that "Friction between the races will pass away in proportion as the black man . . . can produce something that the white man wants or respects in the commercial world."

In contrast, W.E.B. Du Bois argued that it is insufficient simply to train blacks for economic usefulness. He felt that the message sent by training African Americans for manual labor without the benefit of education, culture, and ideas ridicules them and implies that they are inferior. Peace and equality in race relations, he argued, can only arise between two self-respecting, cultured, educated races. They can never be found between a dominant elite majority and a forcibly subjected, and, consequently, hostile minority.

A series of cases involving professional and graduate education paved the way for major breakthroughs in civil rights. The Supreme Court required admission of blacks to formerly all-white institutions when separate facilities for blacks were clearly not equal. The major legal progress came in 1954. In the case of **Brown v. Board of Education of Topeka, Kansas**, the Supreme Court held that separate facilities are, by their very nature, unequal. In spite of this decision, it took more than 10 years before meaningful school integration took place in the South. In the North, segregated schools resulted from segregated housing patterns and from control of school districts. Because of these factors, **de facto segregation** of races in public schools increased after 1954. The 1954 *Brown v. Board of Education of Topeka, Kansas,* decision, ending school segregation with all due speed appeared to be a victory for the Du Bois position. Court decisions against de facto segregation and for busing children to achieve integration appeared to uphold a commitment to racial equality. Subsequent **affirmative action** policy offered further hope that higher education and educational opportunity in general would be more available to African Americans and that greater equality, measured in economic and political terms, would be available.

Although strides have been made, there has been a concern with the failure of many black Americans to meet their educational potential. The African-American social psychologist Claude M. Steele suggests that the predominant reason for the failure of many African Americans to perform to their capability in school is a continuing stigmatization. In numerous subtle, and not-so-subtle, ways they are told that they really have no place in learning higher level skills. The argument of Du Bois is clearly taken up by Steele. Steele argues that the identification of this attitude as the root of poor school performance does "lead us to a heartening principle:" if blacks are made less racially vulnerable in school, they can overcome even substantial obstacles.

The issue of black nationalism or Afrocentricism has been seriously discussed for over two decades. For those people committed to integration there is a disturbing element in observing people wanting to separate themselves. The failure of the **"separate but equal"** policy in the past and the fear of dividing the country along racial/ethnic lines makes many wary of a separatist stance. Debates over Afrocentricity are often violent. However, they also provide opportunity for reasoned

discussion that can bring differences into the open and lead to positive changes. These discussions and changes could reduce racial conflict on college campuses.

However, affirmative action on campuses as well as off sparks the greatest controversy. It is a truism that even the most highly qualified African-American students and faculty alike are accused of being inferior and of having their positions only because of their color. White students frequently argue that programs that seek to bring in minority students weaken the overall program of the school and penalize qualified whites. However, educators such as James Turner argue that "education is pivotal to maintaining the racial hierarchy and perpetuating competition for status and opportunity." In order to overcome this link between racial hierarchy and education, African Americans have sought to shape education into a means for "self-determination and the redefinition of self." The dilemma has been that education offers both a means for liberation and an obstacle to it. It is, in sum, necessary, in the views of many Afrocentric leaders, to reshape education so that it provides opportunities without the racist detrita that have been attached to it.

However, it is unfortunate that African-American students who attend formerly all-white institutions often encounter hostility. The trend, moreover, has been toward a numerical loss of African-American students since the 1970s, especially of African-American men. Furthermore, the lack of African-American faculty in numbers sufficient to provide role models and mentors further works to marginalize students. As Turner notes, "Black faculty constitute less than 2 percent of the national total. Future prospects are not encouraging, as the pipeline from graduate schools producing new black Ph.D.s has narrowed significantly during the last decade." Unfortunately, students are further estranged by academic counselors who too often advise them not to matriculate in African-American studies classes because of their lack of "relevance."

Given these conditions, it is easy to see why for many students, black nationalism is not a militant uprising against the white power structure. Rather, they view it as a way of keeping their own ethnic identity and self-respect because their education is pushing them into the mainstream world dominated by members of the white middle class. It should be remembered that until 1948 most blacks seeking higher education attended private black colleges. Most of these colleges are located in the South; most were founded right after the **Civil War** as a joint effort of blacks, northern church groups, and the Freedmen's Bureau. Among these were Fisk University, Atlanta University, Morehouse College, and Spelman College.

After 1948, improvement began to be made for blacks in many state universities, and for the first time black students began to appear in colleges that had formerly been all white. In the 1970s the percentage of blacks attending college increased significantly. However, in the 1980s the number of blacks in colleges and universities declined. James Turner notes that the presence of black students on "white" campuses has always been problematic. From 1826, when the first African-American student graduated from college, "black students have encountered obstacles in their quest for meaningful lives through education." It is notable that in 1954 barely 1 percent of the students in white schools of higher education were African American. Within 25 years over half of all African-American students were enrolled in former "white" colleges. Unfortunately, the incidence of racial confrontation began to increase in the 1980s and the number of African-American students in higher education began to fall.

Turner argues that the problems facing African Americans in higher education will not end until the following steps are taken. "College and universities most likely to be successful in combating racism are those that (1) have well established African-American studies departments, (2) actively hire Black faculty, (3) appoint Black administrators to decision-making positions with real power, and (4) empower Black students by asserting the value of diversity to quality education and the principle of equal participation of all students in every aspect of campus affairs." He further argues that until black students take the lead in reform, as they did in the 1960s, there will be no real progress made in moving toward a lasting solution and racial harmony. (FAS)

BIBLIOGRAPHY
Eldridge, Deborah. "Diversity in Language Arts Classrooms." *Education Digest* 62, no. 4, 1996: 51–54.

Educational Amendments of 1972

Congress passed a sweeping set of mandates that came to be known as the Educational Amendments of 1972, in an effort to guarantee greater equal educational opportunity by barring sexual discrimination in "any program or activity receiving Federal financial assistance." School systems that receive federal funds are required to follow guidelines in all aspects of operation, including athletics, where equal participation opportunities for male and female athletes, through a formula of proportionality, must be provided. (VDD)

BIBLIOGRAPHY
Pitsch, Mark. "The Letter of the Law." *Education Week* (March 1995): 14, 39.

Joycelyn Elders (1933–)

Joycelyn Elders, a pediatric endocrinologist, was Surgeon General of the United States during the first Clinton administration, 1993–1994. Elders, one of eight children of Arkansas sharecroppers, learned early from personal experience about poverty and the lack of health care. She writes in her autobiography that the only health care her family had growing up was herbs and prayers. *Ebony* called her nomination one of the nastiest battles in recent history. Dr. Elders' outspoken views on abortion, legalization of marijuana, and sex education made her a visible target for conservative criticism and eventually cost her the support of President Clinton. She resigned her office in 1994. (EP)

BIBLIOGRAPHY
Elders, Joycelyn, et al. *Joycelyn Elders, M.D.: From Sharecropper's Daughter to Surgeon General of the United States of America.* New York: William Morrow, 1996.
Randolph, Laura B. "In the Eye of the Storm: Surgeon General Joycelyn Elders Challenges the Status Quo." *Ebony* (February 1993): 154–60.

Robert B. Elliot (1842–1884)

Robert Elliot was one of the African-American delegates to the South Carolina Constitutional Convention and was elected as a Republican to the state House of Representatives. He was elected to Congress in 1870 and 1872. He was known as a "racial militant" for his support of anti-discrimination laws. He was speaker of the state House of Representatives from 1874 to 1876.

BIBLIOGRAPHY
Ragsdale, Bruce and Joel Treese. *Black Americans in Congress 1870–1989.* Washington, DC: U.S. Government Printing Office, 1990.

Emancipation Proclamation (1863)

On January 1, 1863, the Emancipation Proclamation was issued by President Abraham Lincoln, making it the most significant civil rights legislation to date. The act freed all slaves dwelling in states that had seceded from the Union. However, the proclamation failed to assist the 800,000 slaves living in areas occupied by Union forces.

The Emancipation Proclamation also led to the establishment of black military regiments of the United States Army, many of which were commanded by Martin Delany. These regiments included the 54th and 55th Massachusetts Infantry, as well as the units later known as the United States Colored Troops. These regiments contributed greatly to the Union war effort and began a long history of African-American soldiers serving in the United States military service. **See also** Civil War.

BIBLIOGRAPHY
Henry, Christopher E. *Forever Free: From the Emancipation Proclamation to the Civil Rights Bill of 1875, 1863–1875.* New York: Chelsea, 1995.

Empowerment Zones (EZs)

Empowerment Zones (EZs) are part of the Clinton administration's plan to revitalize poverty-stricken areas in the United States. It is a small-scale effort to induce private capital to invest in six urban and three rural economically strapped communities and regions. The central objective of the EZs is to improve the plight of economically distressed communities in urban and rural America through the implementation of national policy that involves participation at all levels of government and builds a partnership between governments, businesses, and communities. When the program was first announced in 1993, the efforts by communities to become part of one of the empowerment zones awakened these communities to assess their own needs and create a vision for their future.

The EZs aim to create a process for the solution of the problems of the distressed communities by encouraging entrepreneurs and employees to enter or remain in areas that they would otherwise find unattractive. The EZs seek to include a comprehensive, coordinated, and integrated approach of mixing community-based initiatives plus private sector resources and federal and state support to yield economic revitalization in poor areas. EZs will be given direct grants for social services such as drug and alcohol rehabilitation, services to pregnant women and mothers and their children, job training, after-school care, job counseling, transportation services, business counseling, financial management, emergency shelters, and home ownership programs. (EC)

BIBLIOGRAPHY

Smith, Kimberly. "Investing in America's Third World: The Tri-State Delta Empowerment Zone Initiative." *Congressional Black Caucus Foundation Policy Review* 1, No. 2 (November-December 1994): 18–21.

Enterprise Zones

Enterprise Zones are economically distressed areas that have been designated as warranting government preferential assistance to promote investment and job creation by private industry. During the early 1980s bills to create enterprise zones were introduced in Congress by Jack Kemp (R-NY), and Robert Garcia (D-NY), which failed and again by Kemp and Charles Rangel (D-NY). The latter also failed. In spite of the federal government's failure to create enterprise zones, 37 states and the District of Columbia designated enterprise zones, each providing diverse benefits to businesses. States sometimes offered tax benefits, direct aid or loan guarantee and bonds for infrastructure improvement.

In the wake of the April/May 1992 riots in Los Angeles, national leaders of both parties again called for enterprise zones. New Jersey has operated enterprise zones successfully since it started the program in 1985. In Newark alone, 3,000 jobs were created and $800 million in private investments were made in the zone areas. Both businesses and consumers in the zone areas receive tax breaks, while businesses can also receive grants and low-interest loans to buy and rebuild abandoned property. Advocates also propose that the businesses in the economically depressed areas be owned by the members of the racial/ethnic communities where programs are located, and that there should also be intense social reform of depressed areas. (EC)

BIBLIOGRAPHY

Tidwell, B.J., ed. *The State of Black America, 1992.* New York: National Urban League, 1992.

Equal Educational Opportunity Act (EEOA) of 1974

The Equal Educational Opportunity Act (EEOA) of 1974 states, in part, that "no state shall deny equal educational op-portunity to an individual on account of his race, color, sex, or national origin, (or)...[fail] to overcome language barriers that impede equal participation by its students in its instructional program." At that time, education, which was limited to English-proficient students, became a public school concern. EEOA sought to guarantee equal educational opportunity through bilingual education programs. (VDD)

Cornell, Charles. "Reducing Failure of LEP Students in the Mainstream Classroom and Why It Is Important." *The Journal of Educational Issue of Language Minority Students* 15 (Winter 1995): 1–16.

Equal Employment Opportunity Act of 1972

The Equal Employment Opportunity Act of 1972 granted the **Equal Employment Opportunity Commission (EEOC)**, which is the agency established to administer Title VII of the **Civil Rights Act of 1964**, the enforcement power to bring civil action against employers and unions in federal courts. Title VII prohibits discrimination in employment because of race, color, religion, sex, or national origin. Previously, the EEOC was restricted to recommending that the Attorney General institute civil action suits where discrimination was established. (VDD)

BIBLIOGRAPHY

Haveman, Robert H., ed. *A Decade of Federal Antipoverty Programs: Achievements, Failures, and Lessons.* New York: Academic Press, 1977.

Equal Employment Opportunity Commission (EEOC)

The Equal Employment Opportunity Commission (EEOC) was created through Section 705 of the **Civil Rights Act of 1964** to implement the provisions of Title VII of that act. The commission comprises five bi-partisan members, appointed by the president to staggered five-year terms. Other laws that have since come under EEOC jurisdiction include the **Equal Employment Opportunity Act of 1972** which added educational institutions and government agencies to the commission's coverage. EEOC also enforces provisions of the Age Discrimination in Employment Act and Amendments (1974, 1978) and the Fair Labor Standards Act Amendments of 1974. The EEOC enforces nondiscrimination by private employers, unions, and employment agencies, by suing on behalf of complainants, and if EEOC is successful in its suit, the court can issue an injunction, order reinstatement with back pay, raises, and double damages, in compensation for denied wages, opportunities, and benefits to the complainant. The EEOC can also expand any individual complaint into a broad indictment of discrimination against entire groups of employees, then seek financial damages for each affected employee. (EC)

BIBLIOGRAPHY

Simms, Margaret C. *Economic Perspectives on Affirmative Action.* Washington, DC: Joint Center for Political and Economic Studies, 1995.

Michael (Mike) Espy (1953–)

Mike Espy, a Democrat from Mississippi, served in the Clinton administration from 1993 to 1994 as U.S. secretary of agriculture, the first African American to hold this post. Prior to this position, he was a four-term member of the United States House of Representatives from 1986 through 1993. From 1984 to 1986, Espy was the head of the Consumer Protection Division of the Mississippi State Attorney General's Office. Espy resigned as secretary of agriculture in 1994 amidst allegations of ethical improprieties. He was subsequently indicted on charges of accepting gifts from poultry producer Tyson Foods and other companies; in December 1998 a federal jury acquitted him of the charges.

BIBLIOGRAPHY

Behar, Richard and Michael Kramer. "Something Smells Fowl." *Time* 144, no. 16 (October 17, 1994): 42–45.

Grann, David. "Prosecutorial Indiscretion." *The New Republic* 218, no. 5 (February 2, 19998): 18–24.

Schultz, Jeffrey D. "Presidential Scandals." *Congressional Quarterly*, 1999.

Melvin H. Evans (1917–)

Melvin Evans received his M.D. from Howard University in 1944 and his master's degree in public health from the University of California—Berkeley in 1967. He was the first native-born black governor of the Virgin Islands territory and in 1971 became its first elected governor, serving until 1975 after which he became a member of Congress as a Democrat.

BIBLIOGRAPHY

Ragsdale, Bruce and Joel Treese. *Black Americans in Congress 1870–1989*. Washington, DC: U.S. Government Printing Office, 1990.

Evans v. Newton (1965)

Controversy began when a section of land was willed to the mayor and City Council of Macon, Georgia. According to the provision of the will, the land was to be used as a park exclusively for whites, with an all-white board of managers to maintain and oversee the project. The city eventually asked to be removed as a trustee, stating that it could not legally operate a segregated park. The park was established and desegregated, angering individuals who saw the action as a violation of the will's contract obligations, and who brought suit in *Evans v. Newton,* 382 U.S. 296 (1965). The case eventually landed in the Supreme Court, which allowed the City of Macon to give its trust rights to a private board of managers. However, the park was not allowed to become segregated as the Court affirmed that the passing of land from municipal ownership to a private board did not omit the jurisdiction of the **Fourteenth Amendment**'s equal protection requirements over the property.

BIBLIOGRAPHY

D'Amato, Anthony A., Rosemary Metrailer, and Stephen L. Wasby. *Desegregation from Brown to Alexander*. Carbondale, IL: Southern Illinois University Press, 1977.

Charles Evers (1922–)

Brother of African-American civil rights leader **Medgar Evers,** Charles served as mayor of Fayetteville, Mississippi, from 1973 until 1981. In addition he ran for the governor's office in 1971 as an independent and received 22 percent of the vote. In 1978 he ran for a seat in the U.S. Senate as an independent where he received 20 percent of the popular vote. He returned to Mississippi after the assassination of his brother to head the field office of the **National Association for the Advancement of Colored People (NAACP)**. (CEM)

BIBLIOGRAPHY

Evers, Charles. *Have No Fear: The Charles Evers Story*. New York: John Wiley and Sons, 1997.

Medgar Wiley Evers (1925–1963)

Medgar Evers was Mississippi field director of the **National Association for the Advancement of Colored People (NAACP)** from 1954 until his death in 1963. Activities associated with his position at the NAACP subjected Evers and his family to constant threats of physical harm and violence. Evers was responsible for organizing a number of boycotts and the Jackson movement, a coalition of black organizations that fought against segregation. In 1963 Evers was murdered at his home; his death made him a national martyr and highlighted the need for far-reaching civil rights legislation.

BIBLIOGRAPHY

Read, Frank and Lucy McGough. *Let Them Be Judged*. Metuchen, NJ: Scarecrow, 1978.

Executive Order 8802

On July 25, 1941, President Franklin D. Roosevelt issued Executive Order 8802, which was intended to assist African Americans in overcoming discrimination. Roosevelt's actions were, in part, a response to a proposed protest march organized by **A. Philip Randolph**. The order banned discrimination in the defense industry and led to the creation of the **Fair Employment Practices Committee**. This action was considered by civil rights activists to be a moral victory as well as a step closer to the equality they sought.

BIBLIOGRAPHY

Anderson, Jervis B. *A. Phillip Randolph: A Biographical Portrait*. Berkeley: University of California Press, 1986.

Estell, Kenneth. *African America: Portrait of a People*. Washington: Visible Ink Press, 1994.

Executive Order 9981

Executive Order 9981, issued by President Harry S. Truman on July 26, 1948, resulted from a mixture of pressure, pragmatism, and politics. Despite some small gains by blacks in the military during World War II, equality of opportunity and conditions were still not secure. Following the war, black leaders and veterans reasserted their claims and demanded that the armed forces end its **Jim Crow** system. In the 1948 presidential campaign Truman faced New York governor Thomas

Executive Order 9981, issued by President Harry S. Truman on July 26, 1948, ended the segregation in the U.S. military that these African-American soldiers from World War II had known. *Library of Congress.*

E. Dewey, a candidate with a strong civil rights record. Truman responded by challenging Congress to enact a comprehensive civil rights program and by issuing Executive Order 9981, which declared that there would hereafter be "equality of treatment and opportunity for all persons in the armed services." The order formally ended segregation in the armed forces. **See also** Lester B. Granger; **see** "Executive Order 9981" in Appendix 1. (GAA)

BIBLIOGRAPHY

McCoy, Donald R. and Richard T. Ruetten. *Quest and Response: Minority Rights and the Truman Administration.* Lawrence: University Press of Kansas, 1973.

Quarles, Benjamin. *The Negro in the Making of America.* New York: Simon & Schuster, 1996.

Executive Order 10730

President Dwight Eisenhower issued Executive Order 10730 in 1957 in response to the growing conflicts involved in school desegregation. The order gave authority to the secretary of defense to use the military in order to force individual schools and school districts to comply with the constitutional mandate to desegregate their schools.

BIBLIOGRAPHY

Blaustein, Albert P. and Robert L. Zangrando, eds. *Civil Rights and the American Negro.* New York: Washington Square Press, 1968.

Executive Order 10925

Executive Order 10925 was issued by President John F. Kennedy on March 6, 1961. The order established the **Equal Employment Opportunity Commission (EEOC)**, which was originally charged with eliminating obstacles to government employment based upon race, creed, color, or national origin. The order also called for affirmative action in government hiring to help rectify what the administration saw as a practice of discrimination.

BIBLIOGRAPHY

Sedmak, Nancy J. *Primer of Equal Employment Opportunity.* Washington, DC: Bureau of National Affairs, 1991.

Executive Order 11053

Executive Order 11053, entitled "Providing Assistance For The Removal of Unlawful Obstructions of Justice In The State of Mississippi" was enacted by President John F. Kennedy to authorize the use of federal troops to restore order after riots erupted on the University of Mississippi campus on September 30, 1962. The catalyst to these riots was Governor Ross Barnett's attempt to block the court-ordered admission of James Meredith, the first African-American student accepted by the University of Mississippi. Meredith was escorted to class by U.S. marshals on October 2, 1962. (JCW)

BIBLIOGRAPHY

Brauer, Carl. *John F. Kennedy and the Second Reconstruction.* New York: Columbia University Press, 1979.

Executive Order 11246

An executive order issued by President Lyndon B. Johnson in 1965, E.O. 11246 prohibited employment discrimination based on race, color, religion, sex, or national origin by any federal government contractor with 50 or more employees and contracts worth more than $50,000. The order was administered by the Office of Federal Contract Compliance. The purpose of the order was to ensure that protected groups were treated fairly in hiring, training, and promotion practices. The specific goals were to eliminate barriers to employment encountered by protected group members and to improve employment opportunities available to specific underutilized groups. (CEM)

BIBLIOGRAPHY

Seymour, Richard T. "A Point of View: Why Executive Order 11246 Should Be Preserved." *Employee Relations Law Journal* 11, no. 4 (Spring 1986): 568–84.

Fair Employment Practices Committee (FEPC)

President Franklin D. Roosevelt issued **Executive Order 8802** on July 25, 1941, which banned discrimination in the defense industry. He also created the Fair Employment Practices Committee (FEPC) to investigate and publicize cases of discrimination in defense-related employment, which relied on publicity and persuasion rather than coercion to expose and alter biased practices. During World War II the president did not want to offend white segregationists and threaten national unity. The FEPC achieved only mixed success: it could not stand up against railroad brotherhoods and southern railway lines who discriminated against African Americans, but it forced a Philadelphia union to accept the upgrading of black jobs on streetcars. In spite of its lukewarm record, southern members of Congress succeeded in cutting off funding for the FEPC in 1946. (EC)

BIBLIOGRAPHY

Sitkoff, Harvard. *A New Deal for Blacks: The Emergence of Civil Rights as a National Issue.* New York: Oxford University Press 1978.

Fair Labor Standards Act of 1938

The Wage and Hour Division of the U.S. Department of Labor enforces the Fair Labor Standards Act of 1938 (FLSA), the federal law which sets minimum wage, overtime, employer record keeping, and child labor standards. Over 80 million American workers are protected by the FLSA. For example, child labor regulations prohibit persons younger than 18 years old from working in certain jobs and set rules concerning the hours and times employees under 16 may work. (VDD)

BIBLIOGRAPHY

Fair Labor Standards Act Explained. Chicago: CCH, Inc., 1997.
Foster, G. W. Jr. *Jurisdiction, Rights, and Remedies for Group Wrongs under the Fair Labor Standards Act.* Chicago: American Bar Foundation, 1975.

Wallace D. Fard

Wallace D. Fard appeared in Detroit, Michigan, in 1930 as a silk salesman preaching Islam as "the religion of the black man." He founded Temple of Islam Number One in Detroit and disappeared in 1934, leaving his chief lieutenant, **Elijah Muhammad** as the Black Muslim movement's leader. (JCW)

BIBLIOGRAPHY

Clegg, Claude Andrew. *An Original Man: The Life and Times of Elijah Muhammad.* New York: St. Martin's Press, 1997.

James Farmer (1920–)

James Farmer was a civil rights leader, pacifist, and educator. In 1941, he was race-relations secretary for the pacifist group Fellowship of Reconciliation. In 1942 he founded and became the executive director of the Chicago-based **Congress of Racial Equality (CORE)**, a Gandhian movement. From 1946 to 1960 Farmer worked as a labor organizer for trade unions and a civil rights advocate for the **National Association for the Advancement of Colored People (NAACP)**. He again became executive director of CORE (1960–1966), during its greatest influence. In spring 1961 he organized the first freedom rides, and he led CORE contingents in strikes, sit-ins, voter education programs, and demonstrations. He served briefly as assistant secretary of Health, Education and Welfare in Nixon's administration. In the 1970s and 1980s he advocated black economic advancement, but was unable to secure sufficient funding for his projects. He taught at Mary Washington College in Fredericksburg, Virginia from 1982 to the early 1990s. (EC)

BIBLIOGRAPHY

Farmer, James. *Lay Bare the Heart: An Autobiography of the Civil Rights Movement.* New York: Arbor House, 1985.
Meire, August and Elliot Rudwick. *CORE: A Study in the Civil Rights Movement.* New York: Oxford University Press, 1975.

Louis Farrakhan (1933–)

Louis Farrakhan, head of the **Nation of Islam**, emerged as a national figure while supporting **Jesse Jackson**'s 1984 presidential campaign. His anti-Semitic, anti-Catholic, and anti-gay reputation has made him one of the most controversial figures in America. His successes include arranging the **Million Man March** in 1995.

In 1955 **Malcolm X** recruited Louis Walcott for the Nation of Islam. He quickly rose to a position of leadership, and in 1965 received the name Farrakhan. In 1975 he left the original organization and founded a new Nation of Islam in 1978. Upon learning in 1983 that Jesse Jackson intended to run for president, Farrakhan opted to audibly support him. His backing of Jackson helped rally Muslims and young blacks to the campaign. However, his threatening criticism of a *Washington Post* reporter, who leaked Jackson's off-the-record characterization of New York as "Hymietown," started a feud between Farrakhan and the Jewish community.

In the 1988 presidential campaign, Jackson refused any overt support from Farrakhan because of Farrakhan's anti-Semitic reputation. Lecturing at colleges, Farrakhan has received fierce criticism from Jewish students and their supporters. Nonetheless, he has resurrected the Nation of Islam into a powerful organization that battles gangs, drugs, and AIDS in urban areas. He succeeded in gathering over 800,000 black men together in Washington on October 16, 1995, for the Million Man March, urging them to take responsibility for their families; his presence, however, made the event very controversial. (AD)

BIBLIOGRAPHY

Haskins, James. *Louis Farrakhan and the Nation of Islam.* New York: Walker and Col, 1996.

Marshall, A. *Louis Farrakhan: Made in America.* BSB Publishing, 1996.

Chaka Fattah (1956–)

Chaka Fattah (born Arthur Davenport) was elected to the United States House of Representatives as a Democrat in 1995, winning his seat by the widest margin of victory of any incoming first-term member, even in that Republican-dominated year. He had previously served as both a Pennsylvania state representative (from 1982 to 1988) and state senator (from 1988 to 1994). Fattah holds degrees from the University of Pennsylvania, where he studied government and political science.

Throughout his public life, Fattah has focused his energies on the complex issues facing America's minority communities in its inner cities. His initiatives have included the convening of a national conference on America's cities and their revival, and the relocation of families from large, crumbling public housing towers into single-family homes in neighborhoods. (AJC)

BIBLIOGRAPHY

Janofsky, Michael. "For Some, a Threat to Fragile Stability." *New York Times* (August 5, 1996): A12.

Walter Fauntroy (1933–)

Walter Fauntroy became the District of Columbia's first elected representative in the United States Congress (1971–1990). With a Bachelor of Divinity degree from Yale University in 1958, he became minister of Washington's New Bethel Baptist Church. In 1960 Dr. **Martin Luther King, Jr.** appointed him director of the Washington Bureau of the **Southern Christian Leadership Council (SCLC)**, and he was the D.C. coordinator of the 1963 March on Washington. He was also national coordinator of the 1968 Poor People's Campaign. In Congress Fauntroy advocated and won limited self-rule for the District, supported legislation for affordable housing, and was chairman of the **Congressional Black Caucus** from 1981–1983. (EC)

BIBLIOGRAPHY

Ragsdale, Bruce A. and Joel D. Treese. *Black Americans in Congress, 1870–1989.* Washington, DC: U.S. Government Printing Office. 1990: 53–54.

Clarence Clyde Ferguson, Jr. (1924–)

Clarence Ferguson was born in Wilmington, North Carolina. He graduated from Ohio State University and received his LL.B. from Harvard University. He taught at Rutgers as a law professor until he became general counsel to the **United States Commission on Civil Rights** in 1961. He became dean of **Howard University** in 1963 and was appointed U.S. ambassador to Ghana in 1970. (JCW)

BIBLIOGRAPHY

Logan, Rayford. *Howard University: the First Hundred Years, 1867–1967.* New York: New York University Press: 1969.

Cleo Fields (1962–)

Cleo Fields was elected to the U.S. House of Representatives as a Democrat in 1992 and was subsequently reelected in 1994. Representative Fields' political career began in 1987 when he was elected to the Louisiana State Senate. In 1995, Fields surprised political pundits by securing a slot in the runoff election for governor of Louisiana. In 1996, Fields retired from Congress after the 4th Congressional District in Louisiana was redrawn. (CJM)

BIBLIOGRAPHY

Jones, Joyce. "The Shape of Things to Come: Cleo Fields is the First to Fall as Redistricting Changes the Political Map." *Black Enterprise* 27, no. 3 (October 1996): 19.

"Rep. Cleo Fields Battles for Louisiana's Governorship After Primary Victory." *Jet* 89, no. 1 (November 13, 1995): 5.

"Rep. Fields Leads Fight to Keep Blacks in Congress." *Jet* 85, no. 19 (March 14, 1994): 5.

Fifteenth Amendment

The Fifteenth Amendment, which was ratified on February 3, 1870, prohibits both the federal and state governments from denying or abridging a citizen's right to vote on account of his race, color, or previous condition of servitude. Section 2 of the last of the **Civil War** Amendments allowed Congress to pass any appropriate legislation to enforce the amendment. The amendment formed the basis of the congressional passage of the **Voting Rights Act of 1965** and its subsequent amendments.

BIBLIOGRAPHY

Banfield, Susan. *The 15th Amendment.* Hillside, NJ: Enslow Publishers, Inc., 1998.

Gillette, William. *The Right to Vote.* Baltimore: Johns Hopkins Press, 1969.

Mathews, John M. *Legislative and Judicial History of the 15th Amendment.* New York: AMS Press, Inc.

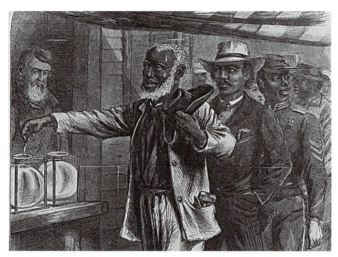

The Fifteenth Amendment, ratified in 1870, guaranteed African Americans the right to vote. This drawing shows a former slave casting his first ballot. *Library of Congress.*

Firefighters Union No. 1784 v. Stotts (1984)

Firefighters Union No. 1784 v. Stotts, 467 U.S. 561 (1984), was an affirmative action case. As a result of a consent decree with the city of Memphis, at least 50 percent of the firefighters hired had to be African Americans. When budgetary deficits forced layoffs, the city followed a "last hired, first fired" policy based strictly on seniority. The result was disproportionate layoffs of African-American firefighters. The Supreme Court upheld the "last hired, first fired" policy, narrowing the interpretation of Title VII of the **Civil Rights Act of 1964**. (RLP)

BIBLIOGRAPHY

Robinson, William L. and Stephan L. Spritz. "Did the Stotts Decision Really Spell the End of Race-Conscious Affirmative Action?" *New York Law School Human Rights Annual* 2, no. 1 (Fall 1984): 1–17.

First Reconstruction Act

The First Reconstruction Act was passed in 1867 to provide the general principles for congressional reconstruction of southern states after the American **Civil War**. The act separated southern states into military districts, each headed by a high ranking military official, to best establish gradual changes in the designated areas. It also provided states with the ability to establish military tribunals, as well as the authority to suppress insurrection and violence to protect the people and property of the district. The First Reconstruction Act also included restrictions against cruel and unusual punishment against offenders in the South, such as clauses that mandated presidential approval of all court-ordered executions. Moreover, the act created a delegation to draft laws in accordance with the Constitution of the United States. This action was seen as the last step in reuniting the North and the South under one government.

BIBLIOGRAPHY

Johannsen, Robert W. *Reconstruction, 1865–1877.* New York: Free Press, 1970.
Rozwenc, Edwin C., ed. *Reconstruction in the South.* Lexington, MA: Heath, 1972.

Floyd Harold Flake (1945–)

Democrat Floyd Flake represented the 6th Congressional District in New York (1986–1997). As pastor of the Allen A.M.E. Church in Jamaica, New York, from 1976 to 1986, Flake spearheaded numerous community development projects including construction of a senior citizens' complex, creation of a housing rehabilitation corporation, and establishment of a home health care service. He advocates for minorities and the poor, working to promote the interests of New York's big banking and financial interests which provide jobs in his district. (EC)

BIBLIOGRAPHY

Ragsdale, Bruce A. and Joel D. Treese. *Black Americans in Congress, 1870–1989.* U.S. Government Printing Office. Washington, DC, 1990: 55–56.
Traub, James. "Floyd Flake's Middle America." *New York Times Magazine* (October 19, 1997): 60–65, 102–04.

Flemming v. South Carolina Electric and Gas (1956)

Sarah Mae Flemming took a second row seat on a public bus after the seat had been vacated by a white woman. She was berated by the driver, sent to the back of the bus, and berated again when she attempted to leave by the front door. The Federal Court, in *Flemming v. South Carolina Electric and Gas*, 239 F. 2D. 277 (4th Cir. 1956), noted that following the Supreme Court's decisions in the desegregation cases, "separate but equal" was no longer acceptable policy. Consequently, a state could no longer segregate members of the public by race on public transportation. (FHJ)

BIBLIOGRAPHY

Greenberg, Jack. *Race Relations and American Law.* New York: Columbia University Press, 1959.

Arthur Allan Fletcher (1924–)

Arthur Allan Fletcher was born in Phoenix, Arizona, and received his B.A. from Washburn University. He served as assistant secretary of labor, appointed by President Nixon in 1969. He authored the **Philadelphia Plan** to desegregate the construction industry under Nixon and wrote the book *The Silent Sellout,* which addressed employment discrimination by the federal government in the craft unions.

BIBLIOGRAPHY

Walton, Hanes. *African American Power and Politics.* New York: Columbia University Press, 1997.

Henry O. Flipper (1858–1940)

After graduating from the United States Military Academy in 1877, Henry Flipper was made a second lieutenant in the all-black 10th Cavalry. He served with the military until 1881, when he became involved in a controversial legal proceeding that resulted in his court martial. Despite being upset over the apparent injustice done against him, Flipper continued to be active in government-related projects; he worked on the American western frontier as a prominent mining engineer and consultant (as well as a translator of Spanish land grants), and he served as an assistant to former Senator A. B. Fall when Fall was appointed secretary of the interior.

Nearly a century after he left West Point, Flipper's records underwent a routine review. As a result of this review, the military found that Flipper's court martial was indeed unjust, and, in fact, he had been framed by other cadets. As a result, Flipper was posthumously granted an honorable discharge from the military and, in 1981, was honored by having a bust of his likeness displayed in the Cadet Library of the Military Academy.

In 1877, Henry O. Flipper became the first black man to graduate from West Point. *National Archives.*

BIBLIOGRAPHY
Pfeifer, Kathryn B. *Henry O. Flipper.* New York: Twenty-First Century Books, 1993.

Harold Eugene Ford (1945–)

Harold Ford became Tennessee's first black congressman, serving from 1974 to 1996. He was the ranking Democrat on the Ways and Means Subcommittee on Human Resources, overseeing much of the welfare reform proposals. He authored the landmark Family Support Act of 1988, which aimed to increase opportunities for work, training, and education among welfare recipients. He proposed that welfare recipients and other poor people not on welfare should receive at least $9 per hour for public or private sector jobs, not the $4.25-per-hour minimum wage. Ford first won election to the Tennessee House in 1970 at age 25. In his first term, he was majority whip and chaired a committee that investigated the rates and practices of utilities in the state. (EC)

BIBLIOGRAPHY
New York Times 145 (April 12, 1996): A11, A24.

James Forten (1766–1842)

James Forten was born free in Philadelphia in 1766. After learning the sailmaking trade, he took over a sailmaking company in 1798 and amassed a fortune. He donated heavily to support such causes as abolitionism, education, equal rights, peace, and temperance. Forten died in 1842 at the age of 76. (AAB)

BIBLIOGRAPHY
Johnston, Brenda A. *Between the Devil and the Sea: The Life of James Forten.* New York: Harcourt Brace Jovanovich, 1974.

T. Thomas Fortune (1856–1928)

T. Thomas Fortune, editor of the *New York Age,* became one of the most militant journalists who actively encouraged African Americans to protest for their rights in the late nineteenth and early twentieth centuries. Fortune believed that it was im-

portant for African Americans to have political rights if changes were to occur in America. To get his message across, Fortune used his newspaper and helped to establish and serve as temporary chair of the National Afro-American League, which opposed lynchings, the convict lease system, and discrimination. Although the organization was never as successful as Fortune had envisioned, it foreshadowed civil rights organizations that preceded it including the National Afro-American Council, the leading area of African American thought at the time, and the **Niagara Movement**, which led to the formation of the **National Association for the Advancement of Colored People (NAACP)**. (DH)

BIBLIOGRAPHY
Thornbrough, Emma Lou. *T. Thomas Fortune: Militant Journalist.* Chicago: University of Chicago Press, 1972.

Fourteenth Amendment

Ratified on July 9, 1868, the Fourteenth Amendment was the major resolution of the slavery controversy that led to the **Civil War**. The amendment redefined American federalism by prohibiting state power to deprive any person of "life, liberty or property" without due process. Although these prohibitions had always applied to the federal government through the Bill of Rights, the Fourteenth Amendment extended them to state governments. It also established the terms and conditions under which states that joined the Confederacy could be reinstated as members of the Union.

By empowering Congress to adopt necessary legislation for enforcement, the amendment placed the federal government as the ultimate guarantor of individual rights. All citizens, regardless of color, are assured equal protection under the law. Early in the twentieth century, the Supreme Court used the amendment to prohibit state discrimination against minorities in the education, housing, and employment sectors. More recently, though, the Court's concern about the rights of white citizens led to a limitation on the efforts states may use to remedy discrimination against minorities.

BIBLIOGRAPHY
Berger, Raoul. *Government by Judiciary.* Indianapolis: Liberty Fund, Inc., 1997.
Curtis, Michael K. *No State Shall Abridge.* Durham, NC: Duke University Press, 1990.
Flack, Horace. *The Adoption of the 14th Amendment.* New York: AMS Press, Inc., 1999.
Gerard, Jules B. *One Hundred Years of the 14th Amendment.* New York: William S. Hein and Co., Inc., 1973.
Meyer, Hermine H. *The History and Meaning of the 14th Amendment.* New York: Vantage Press, Inc., 1977.
Nelson, William E. *The 14th Amendment.* Cambridge, MA: Harvard University Press, 1995.

Frank McNiel et al. v. Springfield Park District (1988)

In *Frank McNiel et al. v. Springfield Park District,* 851 F. 2nd 937 (1988), the Court of Appeals for the Seventh Circuit ruled that an at-large (or multimember district) system for electing members to the party district board and the school board of

Gary A. Franks

Springfield, Illinois, did not constitute a case of "vote dilution" and thus did not violate the rights of black voters as established by section 2 of the **Voting Rights Act of 1965**. McNiel et al. appealed the court of appeals decision to the U.S. Supreme Court, but the writ of certiorari was denied. (CJM)

BIBLIOGRAPHY
Piene-Louis, Stanley. "The Politics of Influence." *University of Chicago Law Review* 62 (Summer 1995): 1215–41.

Gary A. Franks (1953–)

Gary Franks, a Republican from Connecticut, was elected to the United States House of Representatives in 1990. Upon his election, Franks became the first African American ever elected to Congress from Connecticut and the first African American to serve in the House since 1935. Prior to serving in Congress, Franks was active in local politics. After serving three terms in Congress, he lost his bid for a fourth term in 1996.

BIBLIOGRAPHY
Franks, Gary. *Searching for the Promised Land.* New York: Regan Books, 1996.

Frazier v. North Carolina (1972)

Johnnie Frazier, an African American, was tried and convicted of the murder of Carla Jean Underwood and the armed robbery and kidnapping of Rose Collins. On April 13, 1971, Frazier was sentenced to death. Frazier appealed his sentence all the way to the U.S. Supreme Court, claiming that the death penalty was imposed because he was black. In *Frazier v. North Carolina* (1972), the Supreme Court ruled that, in light of its *Stewart v. Massachusetts* (1972) decision outlawing the death penalty as then administered, the state of North Carolina should reconsider the case. The North Carolina court did so and changed Frazier's sentence to life imprisonment. The North Carolina court found that the imposition of the death sentence on African-American defendants was unduly harsh in comparison with white defendants tried for similar cases. (FAS)

BIBLIOGRAPHY
Aguirre, Adalberto and David V. Baker. *Race, Racism, and the Death Penalty in the United States.* Berrien Spring, MI: Vande Vere, 1991.
Jackson, Jesse and Jesse Jackson, Jr. *Legal Lynching: Racism, Injustice, and the Death Penalty.* New York: Marlowe & Co., 1996.

Free Africa Society

The Free Africa Society was founded in 1787 by Absalom Jones and Richard Allen when a black congregation left St. George's Church in Philadelphia because of discrimination and other mistreatment. The Free Africa Society began as an "nondenominational" church but later joined the African Methodist Episcopalian denomination. It pioneered mutual aid movements and in 1789 its Rhode Island branch supported an early Back to Africa movement. The movement spread throughout the United States, and there were branches in many areas of the east coast. (FAS)

BIBLIOGRAPHY
Amistad Research Center. *Author and Added Entry Catalog of the American Missionary Association Archives, with References to Schools and Mission Stations.* 3 vols. Introduction by Clifton H. Johnson. Westport, CT: Greenwood Publishing, 1970.

Freedmen's Aid Society

The New England Freedmen's Aid Society, established in Boston in 1862, worked in the South during and after the **Civil War** to ease the transition of African Americans from slaves to free citizens. Although moderately successful early on, the shift away from Radical **Reconstruction** under President Ulysses Grant caused the society to decline in importance; by 1874 it no longer existed. This had a negative impact on the lives of African Americans after 1876, as segregation and discrimination became accepted aspects of American life. (KR)

BIBLIOGRAPHY
Du Bois, W.E.B. *Black Reconstruction in America, 1860–1880.* New York: Simon and Schuster, 1962.

Freedmen's Bureau

The Bureau of Refugees, Freedmen, and Abandoned Lands, better known as the Freedmen's Bureau, was created on March 3, 1865. The newly created bureau provided former slaves with basic health and educational services while also administering and redistributing land that had been abandoned during the **Civil War.** The Freedmen's Bureau quickly drew a number of the country's most prominent figures into service, including **John Mercer Langston,** who acted as the bureau's inspector general, and Oliver Otis Howard, who went on to become the organization's commissioner general. Under this leadership, the bureau continued to provide food, clothing, and medical supplies to needy African Americans while also establishing and maintaining close to 4,000 schools open to blacks in conjunction with other organizations. The Freedmen's Bureau went on to support the 1866 **Civil Rights Act** and the 1867 Reconstruction Act, both of which helped to alleviate pressures brought against both the organization and the nation's African American population.

BIBLIOGRAPHY
Bentley, George R. *A History of the Freedman's Bureau.* New York: Octagon Books, 1970.
Estell, Kenneth. *African America: Portrait of a People.* Washington: Visible Ink Press, 1994.

Freedom's Journal

Freedom's Journal, the first African-American newspaper, was established in New York City by a group of African Americans as a means of countering an 1826 smear campaign in the press which claimed blacks were a menace to the peace and safety of white New Yorkers. **John B. Russwurm,** the publisher, began publication in 1827. *Freedom's Journal* would go on to provide a literary voice for black authors who were denied publication in mainstream America because of color. (VDD)

BIBLIOGRAPHY

Jackson, Blyden. *A History of African-American Literature. Vol. I. The Long Beginning: 1746–1895.* Baton Rouge: Louisiana State University Press, 1989.

Freeman v. Pitts (1992)

Following a 1969 desegregation suit in DeKalb County, Georgia, that had placed the school district under federal jurisdiction, *Freeman v. Pitts*, 503 U.S. 467 (1992), concerned the school district's desire to remain independent after consistent attempts to end segregation. The court agreed that, even though the standard of **Green v. School Board of New Kent County, Virginia,** had not been fully met, compliance could continue in incremental stages. The *New York Times*, identifying *Freeman* as the most significant desegregation case since **Brown v. Board of Education,** called the decision wrong and potentially destructive. (EP)

BIBLIOGRAPHY

"Loss of Zeal for School Desegregation." *New York Times* (April 3, 1992): 1.

Stewart, Lisa A. "Another Skirmish in the Equal Education Battle." (Case note) *Harvard Civil Rights-Civil Liberties Law Review* 28, no. 1 (Winter 1993): 217–36.

Henry E. Frye (1932–)

Henry E. Frye is the first African American to serve on the North Carolina Supreme Court. He was appointed associate justice in 1983 and was subsequently elected to the position in 1984 and reelected in 1992. Justice Frye has served in both the North Carolina House (1969–1980) and Senate (1981–1982). Upon his election to the House of Representatives in 1969, Justice Frye became the first African American elected to that body during this century. (KLH)

BIBLIOGRAPHY

Swofter, Stan. "Remember Ethnics' Role." *News & Record* (October 5, 1995): B1.

Fugitive Slave Act (1793)

The rhetoric of "liberty" during the American Revolution produced an atmosphere conducive to the abolition of slavery in northern states although the new federal constitution allowed the institution to continue. Concerned with recapturing slaves who escaped to free states and territories, southern congressmen promoted a bill that allowed any black to be returned to slavery on the testimony of the purported owner. Harboring a fugitive slave or interfering with recapture was punishable by a $500 fine. (GAA)

BIBLIOGRAPHY

Foner, Philip S. *History of Black Americans: From Africa to the Emergence of the Cotton Kingdom.* New York: Greenwood Press, 1975.

Franklin, John Hope and Alfred A. Moss, Jr. *From Slavery to Freedom: A History of Negro Americans.* 7th ed. New York: McGraw-Hill, 1994.

Fugitive Slave Act (1850)

The Fugitive Slave Act of 1850 denied runaway slaves the right to a trial by jury and removed their cases to a court-appointed special commissioner; it also paid the commissioner 10 dollars for every fugitive returned to the South, but only five dollars for every person set free. Further, the act circumvented state authority by empowering federal marshals to summon citizens to aid in capturing fugitives. To many in the North this not only invited cases of corruption and mistaken identity, but also forced Americans to perform the distasteful function of man-hunter. The open opposition of northerners swelled the ranks of the anti-slavery movement, and this combined with the **Kansas-Nebraska Act** of 1854 to irrevocably renew sectional hostility. (KR)

BIBLIOGRAPHY

Potter, David. *The Impending Crisis, 1848–1861.* New York: Harper and Row, 1976.

Lenora Fulani (1950–)

Lenora Fulani earned her Ph.D. in developmental psychology at the City University of New York. She ran for lieutenant governor of New York in 1984. She became chair of the New Alliance Party in 1988 as well as its first presidential candidate. In 1988 and 1992, she became the first African-American woman to be placed on the ballot in all 50 states and the District of Columbia. She is currently chair of the Committee for a Unified Independent Party.

BIBLIOGRAPHY

Pleasant, William, ed. *Independent Black Leadership in America.* New York: Castillo International, 1990.

Fullilove v. Klutznick (1980)

At issue in *Fullilove v. Klutznick*, 448 U.S. 448 (1980), was the "minority business enterprise," or MBE, provision of the Public Works Act of 1977, which "set aside" 10 percent of government public works contracts for minority-owned businesses, including African Americans, Hispanics, Asian-Americans, Native Americans, American Eskimos, and Aleuts. Although the Court upheld the provision, Melvin I. Urofsky suggests that the justices reached agreement from differing viewpoints. Some, he writes, believed that Congress had the power to develop programs aimed at ending past discrimination, while others maintained that establishing quotas was a reasonable government objective. (EP)

BIBLIOGRAPHY

Urofsky, Melvin I. *A March of Liberty: A Constitutional History of the United States. Vol. II: Since 1865.* New York: Alfred A. Knopf, 1988.

Furman v. Georgia (1972)

In *Furman v. Georgia*, 408 U.S. 238 (1972), the death penalty was declared to constitute cruel and unusual punishment as dictated by the Eighth Amendment to the United States Constitution. Attorneys for the American Civil Liberties Union, the Synagogue Council of America and the **National Association for the Advancement of Colored People (NAACP)** argued that the discretion of judges and juries in imposing the death penalty was too selectively applied, allowing for economic, political, social, and ethnic characteristics to unjustly play a part. The Supreme Court agreed with these sentiments but found that state legislatures could create laws that provided more structure and guidelines in capital punishment cases. After such procedures were established, death penalty cases could again be subject to review and possible utilization.

BIBLIOGRAPHY

Shatz, Steven F. and Nina Rivkind. "The California Death Penalty Scheme: Requiem for Furman?" (*Furman v. Georgia*) *New York University Law Review* 72, no. 6 (December 1997): 1283–1343.

Steiker, Carol S. and Jordan M. Steiker. "Sober Second Thoughts: Reflections on Two Decades of Constitutional Regulation of Capital Punishment." *Harvard Law Review* 109, no. 2 (December 1995): 355–438.

Harvey Gantt (1943–)

Harvey Gantt was the first black student at Clemson University in South Carolina and the first black mayor of Charlotte, North Carolina. Gantt is best known for his two attempts in 1990 and 1996 at unseating conservative North Carolina's Republican Senator Jesse Helms. Political commentators claim that Gantt lost both races because of his ineffective responses to Helms' racially inflammatory television advertisements. The most noteworthy example is the now famous "pink slip" ad. In this advertisement a pair of white hands crumpled a rejection slip and blamed affirmative action for the loss of white jobs. Gantt remains a successful architect in Charlotte, North Carolina. (RAM)

"Harvey Gantt Named to Head Planning Agency for D.C." *Jet* 88, no. 2 (May 22, 1995): 38.

"Harvey Gantt Wins North Carolina Primary, Earns Rematch with Senator Jesse Helms." *Jet* 90, no. 2 (May 27, 1996): 25.

Wells, Robert Marshall. "Special Report: Presidential, Congressional Candidates Plot Separate Courses on Way to 1996 Elections." *Congressional Quarterly Weekly Report* 54, no. 26 (June 29, 1996): 1844.

Wells, Robert Marshall and Jonathan D. Salant. "1990 Nominee Gantt Pursues Rematch with Helms." *Congressional Quarterly Weekly Report* 54, no. 6 (February 10, 1996): 368.

Henry Highland Garnet (1815–1882)

Henry Garnet was one of the most militant African-American intellectual leaders of the nineteenth century, and a prominent preacher and abolitionist. Garnet's "An Address to the Slaves of the United States," delivered at the Free Colored People Convention in Buffalo, New York, in 1843, called upon enslaved African Americans to violently resist their oppressors through a general strike and armed rebellion. So electrifying was the effect of the speech on Garnet's audience, **Frederick Douglass** recessed the convention to allow passions to cool. Born a slave in Maryland, Garnet escaped to Pennsylvania with his parents when he was nine. In 1840, he graduated from the Oneida Institute in Whitesboro, New York. Interested in emigration but opposed to the racism of the **American Colonization Society**, Garnet formed the African Civilization Society in 1858. Garnet served as president of Avery College in Pittsburgh, Pennsylvania, from 1864 to 1870, and in 1881, he was appointed U.S. minister to Liberia by President James Garfield. **See also** Negro Convention Movement. (RAM)

BIBLIOGRAPHY

Ofari, Earl. *Let Your Motto Be Resistance: The Life and Thought of Henry Highland Garnet.* Boston: Little, Brown and Co., 1972.

Pasternak, Martia B. *Rise Now and Fly to Arms.* New York: Garland, 1994.

Schor, Joel. *Henry Highland Garnet: A Voice of Radicalism in the 19th Century.* Westport, CT: Greenwood, 1977.

Marcus Garvey (1887–1940)

Marcus Garvey was born in St. Ann's Bay, Jamaica on August 17, 1887. At the age of 14 he left school and was apprenticed as a printer. Garvey complained about the British use of tokenism to control blacks in Jamaica. In 1912 he went to London, where he first met Africans and read **Booker T. Washington**'s *Up From Slavery*. This book inspired Garvey, who returned to Jamaica and founded the Universal Negro Improvement and Conservation Association and African Communities League. Its goal was to bring people of color together. Garvey attempted to open a trade school modeled after the **Tuskegee Institute.**

In 1916, after Washington's death, he went to New York where he traveled widely, speaking and drumming up support for his **Universal Negro Improvement Association (UNIA),** an American version of his Jamaican organization. He eventually headquartered his UNIA in Harlem and began to recruit members. In 1918 he began publishing a newspaper, *The Negro World*. By 1919 Garvey had opened a number of businesses including a steamship line called the **Black Star Line**. Garvey sent agents to Liberia where he planned to prepare the area for his Back to Africa program. In 1923, with information supplied by J. Edgar Hoover, he was tried and convicted of fraud. In 1925 he went to prison, but in 1927 he was released and deported. He moved back to Jamaica before going to England, where he died in 1940. (AAB)

BIBLIOGRAPHY

Archer, Jules. *They Had a Dream: The Civil Rights Struggle, from Frederick Douglass to Marcus Garvey to Martin Luther King, Jr., and Malcolm X.* New York: Viking, 1993.

Gaston County, North Carolina v. United States (1969)

North Carolina sought to reinstate its literacy test as a condition for voting in the state. The state had used the literacy test for years as a barrier to granting voting rights to many African-American citizens. The Supreme Court, in *Gaston County, North Carolina v. United States*, 395 U.S. 285 (1969), held that a federal court has the right to question whether or not such a test would unduly burden the right to vote of minority citizens, especially in view of the state's historic separate and unequal school systems which left many African Americans with a substandard education. (FHJ)

BIBLIOGRAPHY
D'Amato, Anthony A., Rosemary Metrailer, and Stephen L. Wasby. *Desegregation from Brown to Alexander*. Carbondale, IL: Southern Illinois University Press, 1977.

Gayle v. Browder (1956)

Following on the heels of **Brown I** and **Brown II**, the Supreme Court, in *Gayle v. Browder*, 352 U.S. 903 (1956), a per curiam (a decision handed up by the entire Court without opinion) decision, affirmed the lower court's ruling that the practices of the Montgomery City Lines bus company to segregate on the basis of race was a clear violation of the **Fourteenth Amendment.** The lower court argued that it could not in good conscience "perform our duty as judges by blindly following the precedent of **Plessy v. Ferguson**. . . ." (CJM)

BIBLIOGRAPHY
D'Amato, Anthony A., Rosemary Metrailer, and Stephen L. Wasby. *Desegregation from Brown to Alexander*. Carbondale, IL: Southern Illinois University Press, 1977.
Greenberg, Jack. *Race Relations and American Law*. New York: Columbia University Press, 1959.

Georgia v. United States (1973)

In *Georgia v. United States*, 411 U.S. 526 (1973), the Supreme Court addressed Georgia's 1971 reapportionment plan. Section Five of the **Voting Rights Act** requires that any state with a record of past discrimination receive a federal declaratory judgment before changing its electoral process. The Supreme Court agreed that Georgia was bound by Section Five and that black voting power could be adversely affected by the plan in question. Consequently, Georgia was forced to redistrict. (EP)

BIBLIOGRAPHY
Barker, Lucius J. and Twiley W. Barker, Jr. *Civil Liberties and the Constitution: Cases and Commentaries*. Englewood Cliffs, NJ: Prentice Hall, 1994.

Kenneth Allen Gibson (1932–)

Kenneth Gibson was born in Alabama and moved to New Jersey when he was eight. He received his B.A. from Newark College of Engineering and served as chief engineer of housing projects for the Newark Housing Authority. In 1970 Gibson, a Democrat, became the first black mayor of Newark where he served four terms during which he helped revitalize the city through public works programs. Defeated for reelection in 1986 he founded his own consulting firm.

BIBLIOGRAPHY
Groh, George W. *The Black Migration*. New York: Weybright and Talley, 1972.

William F. Gibson (1941–)

William F. Gibson received his D.D.S. from Meharry Medical College's School of Dentistry. He practiced as a dentist and was active in his local **National Association for the Advancement of Colored People (NAACP)** chapter. In 1985 he was elected chairman of NAACP where he served until 1995 when he was removed over disputes regarding allocations of finances.

BIBLIOGRAPHY
Holmes, Steven. "Gibson Is Ousted as NAACP Head." *New York Times* (February 19, 1995): 1.

Gladstone Realtors v. Village of Bellwood (1979)

The village of Bellwood, a Chicago suburb, and some residents of the village brought an action under the Fair Housing Act and the **Civil Rights Act of 1866** against real estate brokers who were accused of "steering" African-American potential home buyers toward a "target" neighborhood and white buyers away from the same neighborhood, in *Gladston Realtors v. Village of Bellwood*, 441 U.S. 91 (1979). The Supreme Court ruled that the village and residents had reasonable cause to sue because they were being damaged by the loss of racial balance and stability. (FHJ)

BIBLIOGRAPHY
Huber, Gary M. "*Gladstone Realtors v. Village of Bellwood*: Expanding Standing Under the Fair Housing Act." *Boston College Environmental Affairs Law Review* 8, no. 4 (Fall 1980): 783–819.
Wesolowski, Ted. "Standing: Nuance or Necessity." (Case note) *University of Pittsburgh Law Review* 41, no. 4 (Summer 1980): 821–39.

W. Wilson Goode (1939–)

W. Wilson Goode, mayor of Philadelphia from 1984 to 1992, was noted for his efforts to aid children and teenagers. Goode is currently deputy assistant secretary, U.S. Department of Education. He continues to be actively involved in outreach programs with parents, schools, businesses, religious organizations, and other community-based organizations, especially Good Cause (which he founded). Additionally, Goode is associate professor of political science and urban policy at Eastern College in St. David's, and adjunct professor of urban ministry at Lutheran Theological Seminary. During his career he has taught at a number of colleges and has also found time to be a lay minister. Prior to becoming mayor of Philadelphia, Goode was managing director of Philadelphia, putting him second only to the mayor. He received a B.A. from Morgan College and an M.A. from the University of Pennsylvania. (FAS)

BIBLIOGRAPHY

Bowser, Charles W. *Let the Bunker Burn*. Philadelphia: Camino Books, 1989.
Goode, W. Wilson. *In Goode Faith*. Valley Forge, PA : Judson Press, 1992.

Grandfather Clause

The Grandfather Clause was part of a systematic plan throughout the South to disenfranchise black Americans in the post-**Reconstruction** period. The Grandfather Clause, first introduced in Louisiana in 1898, stipulated that in order to vote, a man's grandfather had to be a qualified voter as of January 1, 1867. This eliminated virtually all black voters in the South (and some poor whites). Other southern states quickly adopted similar clauses. The Grandfather Clause was declared unconstitutional in 1915 in *Guinn v. U.S*.

BIBLIOGRAPHY

Franklin, John Hope. *From Slavery to Freedom: A History of African Americans*. New York: McGraw-Hill, 1994.

Lester B. Granger (1896–1976)

Lester B. Granger was executive director of the **National Urban League (NUL)** from 1941 to 1961. Prior to taking this position, he served as NUL's assistant executive secretary. Granger served as chairman of the Federal Advisory Council on Employment Security and as a special advisor to James Forrestal, secretary of the navy, during World War II. Granger was the architect of the policy established by the U.S. Navy for ending racial segregation. In 1947 he received the President's Medal for Merit. **See also** Executive Order 9981.

BIBLIOGRAPHY

Brown, Annie Woodley. "A Social Work Leader in the Struggle for Racial Equality." *The Social Service Review* 65, no. 2 (June 1992): 266.

William H. Gray III (1941–)

Born in Louisiana, Gray received a B.A. from Franklin and Marshall College in Pennsylvania in 1963. While serving as a pastor in New Jersey, he earned a master's degree from Drew Theological Seminary and another from Princeton Theological Seminary. During this period he also began working to improve low-income housing. In 1972 he became pastor of Bright Hope Baptist Church in Philadelphia, and he continued his activism on housing and other issues.

In 1978 he won a seat as a Democrat in the U.S. House of Representatives, and he quickly became a powerful and respected member of the **Congressional Black Caucus**. In 1985 he became the chair of the crucial House Budget Committee. He worked hard to influence U.S. policy towards southern Africa, and in 1986 he helped enact powerful sanctions against South Africa over President Reagan's veto. In 1989 he was chosen majority whip, making him the most powerful African American in Congress, ever. In 1991 Gray left Congress to assume leadership of the United Negro College Fund. (AD)

BIBLIOGRAPHY

Salley, Columbus. *The Black 100*. New York: Citadel, 1994.

Gray et al. v. Board of Trustees of the University of Tennessee et al. (1952)

The appellants in the case *Gray et al. v. Board of Trustees of the University of Tennessee et al.*, 342 U.S. 517 (1952), sued in District Court to enjoin the University of Tennessee from a **Fourteenth Amendment** violation in refusing to admit blacks. A three-judge panel held that the case was not within their jurisdiction, and ordered that the case proceed before a single district judge. Gray et al. appealed. The Court held that the case was moot, since the University of Tennessee had indicated that the appellants and all those "similarly situated" (i.e., African Americans) would be admitted. (CJM)

BIBLIOGRAPHY

Barker, Lucius and Twiley W. Barker, Jr. *Civil Liberties and the Constitution: Cases and Commentaries*. Upper Saddle River, NJ: Prentice-Hall, 1999.
———. *Freedom, Courts, Politics: Studies in Civil Liberties*. Englewood Cliffs, NJ: Prentice-Hall, 1972.

Green v. County School Board of New Kent County, Virginia (1968)

As part of its desegregation plan, New Kent County, Virginia, adopted a "freedom of choice" plan under which students could decide which school they wished to attend. The Supreme Court, in ruling on *Green v. County School Board of New Kent County, Virginia*, 391 U.S. 430 (1968), noted that no white student had transferred from previously all-white schools and only 15 percent of black students had chosen to attend the traditionally white schools, and it struck down the "freedom of choice" plan and ordered the school district to take affirmative steps to desegregate its school system quickly and efficiently. (FHJ)

BIBLIOGRAPHY

Bunch, Kenyon D. and Grant B. Mindle. "Testing the Limits of Precedent: The Application of *Green* to the Desegregation of Higher Education." (Unequal Protection: Constitutionally Sanctioned Discrimination) *Seton Hall Constitutional Law Journal* 2, no. 2 (Spring 1992): 541–92.

Dick Gregory (1932–)

Although Dick Gregory may currently be best known for his nutritional business, Gregory is also a comedian, author, and civil rights activist. Born in St. Louis, Missouri, he began his career as a comedian. By 1962 he was entertaining audiences at Carnegie Hall. Active in the **civil rights movement** of the 1960s, he participated in nonviolent protests and incorporated his views into his act. He was also active in the anti-war movement during Vietnam. In 1968 he ran for president. (CEM)

BIBLIOGRAPHY

Gregory, Dick. *From the Back of the Bus*. New York: Dutton, 1962.

Griffin v. Prince Edward County School Board (1964)

The case of *Griffin v. Prince Edward County School Board*, 375 U.S. 91 (1964), revisited many of the issues in **Brown v. Board of Education** (1954). Because the mandated issues of *Brown* had never been implemented, a number of mishandled procedures occurred in the Prince Edward County School System. Not only had the Board of Supervisors decided against providing funding for integrated schools, state-supported white schools flourished in the region. In fact, it was pointed out that no African-American student had attended a Prince Edward County school from 1959 to 1963. After long delays in deliberating the matter due to complicated state and national jurisdiction issues, the school system's segregation practices were found to be discriminatory. In doing so, the Supreme Court ruled that the creation and use of whites-only private schools with public funding denied blacks protection under the **Fourteenth Amendment.**

BIBLIOGRAPHY

D'Amato, Anthony A., Rosemary Metrailer, and Stephen L. Wasby. *Desegregation from Brown to Alexander.* Carbondale, IL: Southern Illinois University Press, 1977.

Franklin, John Hope and Genna R. McNeil, eds. *African Americans and the Living Constitution.* Washington, DC: Smithsonian Institution Press, 1995.

Griggs v. Duke Power Company (1971)

The Supreme Court, in *Griggs v. Duke Power Company*, 401 U.S. 424 (1971), ruled that Duke Power Company's hiring and promotion practices were racially discriminatory in violation of **Title VII of the Civil Rights Act of 1964.** After a long history of job segregation, Duke Power established aptitude tests as a requirement for promotion into the formerly all-white job categories. Griggs, a black employee, sued because the test prevented him from qualifying for a promotion. The Court said that all barriers that perpetuated past discrimination must be removed, and that even though the tests appeared racially neutral, they had the effect of maintaining black workers in a disadvantaged position. In the future, tests required for employment or promotion must be job-related and approved by the **Equal Employment Opportunity Commission (EEOC).** According to the Court, any employment practice—regardless of the employer's intent—was illegal if it had a "disparate impact" on a group protected by the Civil Rights Act. (MWA)

BIBLIOGRAPHY

Nieman, Donald G. *Promises to Keep: African-Americans and the Constitutional Order, 1776 to the Present.* New York: Oxford University Press, Inc., 1991.

Archibald H. Grimke (1849–1930)

Archibald H. Grimke, a former slave and the nephew of abolitionists Angelina and Sarah Grimke, became noted for his political activism for the rights of blacks in the late nineteenth and early twentieth centuries. Initially a Republican, Grimke became an Independent Democrat and was named the American Consul to Santo Domingo in 1894. (DH)

BIBLIOGRAPHY

Bruce, Dickson D., Jr. *Archibald Grimke: Portrait of a Black Independent.* Baton Rouge: Louisiana State University Press, 1993.

Lani Guinier (1950–)

Lani Guinier received her law degree at Yale Law School and taught law at the University of Pennsylvania. She was nominated by President Clinton to be assistant attorney general in the Justice Department's Civil Rights Division in 1993. Clinton later retracted this nomination because of pressure from conservatives who felt her opinions were too controversial. (JCW)

BIBLIOGRAPHY

Walton, Hanes. *African American Power and Politics.* New York: Columbia University Press, 1997.

Guinn v. U.S. (1915)

Guinn v. U.S., 238 U.S. 347 (1915), was the case in which the U.S. Supreme Court ruled that the use of **Grandfather Clauses**, which stipulated that in order for a man to vote his grandfather had to be a qualified voter as of January 1, 1867, and which worked to eliminate blacks from voting in the South, was unconstitutional. It was also the first major case brought by the **National Association for the Advancement of Colored People (NAACP)** to the U.S. Supreme Court. The Grandfather Clauses in Oklahoma and Maryland were found to be incompatible with the **Fifteenth Amendment.** Although the decision was an important moral victory for black Americans, it actually had little practical effect. (CE)

BIBLIOGRAPHY

Kellogg, Charles. *NAACP: A History of the National Association for the Advancement of Colored People. Vol 1: 1909–1920.* Baltimore: Johns Hopkins University Press, 1968.

Gulf Oil Company v. Bernard et al. (1980)

This case grew out of a class-action lawsuit over racially discriminatory practices in hiring and employment on the part of the Gulf Oil Company; the case that reached the U.S. Supreme Court was over the federal rules governing class-action lawsuits. In the midst of the class-action suit, a Texas district court ordered a limit on communications between the plaintiffs (Bernard et al.) and their lawyers. In *Gulf Oil Company v. Bernard et al.*, 452 U.S. 89 (1980), the Supreme Court held unanimously that such limitations were not in accord with the federal rules of civil procedure. (CJM)

BIBLIOGRAPHY

Johnson, Vincent R. "The Ethics of Communicating with Putative Class Members." *The Review of Litigation* 17 (Summer 1998): 497–524.

Hadnot et al. v. Amos (1968)

The appellants in this case, members and candidates of the National Democratic Party of Alabama (NDPA), brought suit against Alabama state officials; NDPA claimed that certain state laws were unconstitutional because they had been used in a discriminatory manner to keep the names of NDPA candidates from ballots in the 1968 elections. In *Hadnot et al. v. Amos,* 394 U.S. 358 (1968), the U.S. Supreme Court reversed the district court ruling and held that application of state laws violated both the **Fourteenth Amendment** and section 5 of the **Voting Rights Act of 1965. See** the text of the Fourteenth Amendment in "Civil War Amendments" in Appendix 1. (CJM)

BIBLIOGRAPHY

McDonald, Laughlin. "The 1982 Extension of Section 5 of the Voting Rights Act of 1965." *Tennessee Law Review* 51 (Fall 1983): 1–82.

Hale v. Commonwealth of Kentucky (1938)

In 1936, Joe Hale, an African American, was convicted of murder and sentenced to death in McCracken County, Kentucky. Hale sought to have his indictment set aside on the grounds that African Americans were unfairly and systematically excluded from the jury. Hale's conviction and sentence were upheld by the Court of Appeals of Kentucky. Both, however, were overturned by the U.S. Supreme Court in *Hale v. Commonwealth of Kentucky*, 303 U.S. 616 (1938); the Court ruled that such racially influenced exclusions were in violation of the **Fourteenth Amendment. See also** Crime and Punishment. **See** the text of the Fourteenth Amendment in "Civil War Amendments" in Appendix 1.

BIBLIOGRAPHY

Brand, Jeffrey S. "The Supreme Court, Equal Protection, and Jury Selection." *Wisconsin Law Review* (March/April 1994): 511–631.

Fannie Lou Hamer (1917–1977)

The daughter of a sharecropper and granddaughter of a slave, Fannie Lou Hamer became a **civil rights movement** leader, directing **Southern Christian Leadership Council (SCLC)** and **Student Nonviolent Coordinating Committee (SNCC)** voter registration drives. In 1964, Hamer founded the **Mississippi Freedom Democratic Party** to challenge the systematic disenfranchisement of black voters by the state Democratic Party. (CC)

BIBLIOGRAPHY

Mills, Kay. *This Little Light of Mine: The Life of Fannie Lou Hamer*. New York: Dutton, 1993.

Joseph "Big Lester" Hankerson (ca. 1920s–1988)

Joseph Hankerson was a former seaport gangster in Atlanta, Georgia, who was converted to a nonviolent approach to conflict resolution through listening to a sermon by **Hosea Williams.** He became a close associate of **Martin Luther King, Jr**. (JCW)

BIBLIOGRAPHY

Branch, Taylor. *Pillar of Fire: America in the King Years, 1963–1965*. New York: Simon and Schuster, 1998.

Jeremiah Haralson (1846–1916)

Jeremiah Haralson, a former slave, served in the United States House of Representatives as a Republican from Alabama from 1874 to 1876. He was defeated for reelection in 1876 and ran again unsuccessfully in 1884. He served in the Alabama House of Representatives from 1870 through 1872.

BIBLIOGRAPHY

Biographical Directory of the United States Congress, 1774–1989. Washington, DC: U.S. Government Printing Office, 1989.

Harmon v. Tyler (1926)

In *Harmon v. Tyler*, 273 U.S. 668 (1926), a per curiam decision, the Court reversed a Louisiana State Supreme Court decision, determining that a New Orleans ordinance providing for residential segregation did not violate the **Fourteenth Amendment** rights of blacks. In doing so, the Court cited an earlier decision involving a similar situation in Kentucky, in *Buchanan v. Warley*, 245 U.S. 60 (1917). (CJM)

BIBLIOGRAPHY

D'Amato, Anthony A., Rosemary Metrailer, and Stephen L. Wasby. *Desegregation from Brown to Alexander*. Carbondale, IL: Southern Illinois University Press, 1977.

Harper v. Virginia State Board of Elections (1966)

The Twenty-fourth Amendment to the Constitution bans the use of the poll tax in federal elections. The Amendment sought to end discrimination of African Americans and poor citizens at the polls during presidential and congressional elections. The tax, however, continued in five states, including Virginia, during state elections. The U.S. Supreme Court stopped the practice when it declared the tax unconstitutional in *Harper v. Virginia State Board of Elections*, 383 U.S. 663 (1966), because it violated the **Fourteenth Amendment's** equal protection guarantee. (VDD)

BIBLIOGRAPHY

Grofman, Bernard, Lisa Handley, and Richard G. Niemi. *Minority Representation and the Quest for Voting Equality*. New York: Cambridge University Press, 1992.

Alice Harris (1934–)

Community activist "Sweet" Alice Harris founded a nonprofit organization called Parents of Watts in 1979. The community organization serves as a crisis center that also provides an adult learning center, an emergency shelter and a social service referral system. She is also vice-chair of the Rent Adjustment Commission of the City of Los Angeles. (JCW)

BIBLIOGRAPHY

Hendrix, Kathleen. "Sweet Alice's Chariot Ride." *Los Angeles Times* (October 19, 1992): E1.

Patricia Roberts Harris (1924–1985)

Patricia Roberts Harris was noted for becoming the first African-American female ambassador and cabinet member. Harris began her political activities during the **civil rights movement** by participating in student sit-ins. In 1965 President Lyndon Johnson appointed Harris as the American Ambassador to Luxembourg. During President Jimmy Carter's administration Harris was named the secretary of Housing and Urban Development. In 1979 President Jimmy Carter also appointed Harris secretary of Health, Education, and Welfare, a position she held until 1982. (DH)

BIBLIOGRAPHY

Potter, Joan and Constance Claytor. *African-American Firsts: Famous, Little-Known and Unsung Triumphs of Blacks in America*. Elizabethtown, NY: Pinto Press, 1994.

Beverly Baily Harvard (1950–)

Beverly Harvard became chief of police in Atlanta, Georgia, in 1994, making her the first African-American woman to lead the police department of a large American city. Prior to becoming chief, Harvard served as deputy chief, affirmative action specialist, and patrol officer in Atlanta's Department of Public Safety.

BIBLIOGRAPHY

White, Paula M. "Wonder Woman." *Black Enterprise* 27, no. 9 (April 1997): 114–16.

William Henry Hastie (1904–1976)

An accomplished graduate of Washington, D.C.'s Dunbar High School, Amherst College, and Harvard Law School, William Henry Hastie's most lasting contribution to the life of minorities in the United States is, perhaps, his role as a mentor to generations of students at Howard Law School. At Howard he was instructor, professor, and dean, and he helped to guide and shape generations of lawyers, **Thurgood Marshall** most prominently. Hastie, together with his cousin, **Charles Houston,** helped to chart the course that the **National Association for the Advancement of Colored People (NAACP)** would take in attacking racial segregation, especially in schools.

After serving in a number of important positions in the federal government during the New Deal, for which he was recruited by Harold L. Ickes, Hastie became the first African American to serve as a federal judge in 1937. He left this post soon after, returning to Howard Law School, eventually becoming its dean. During World War II, Hastie served as a civilian aide who was charged with working towards reducing segregation in the armed services. He was able to accomplish little against centuries of entrenched segregation and racism and he resigned after a two-year struggle. In 1946, Hastie became the first African-American governor of the Virgin Islands, a position that he held for three years before returning to the federal bench, and eventually retiring in 1971 as senior judge of the United States Court of Appeals for the 3rd Circuit. **See also** Howard University. (AJC)

BIBLIOGRAPHY

McGuire, Phillip. *He, Too, Spoke for Democracy: Judge Hastie, World War II, and the Black Soldier*. New York: Greenwood Press, 1988.
Ware, Gilbert. *William Hastie: Grace under Pressure*. New York: Oxford University Press, 1984.

Alcee Hastings (1936–)

Alcee Hastings is a U.S. congressman representing Florida's 23rd Congressional District, which includes Dade County and much of south Florida. He was born in Altamonte Springs, Florida, and graduated from Fisk University, then went on to attend law school at Howard University School of Law and Florida A&M University. Representative Hastings is a Democrat and is currently serving on the International Relations Committee and the Science Committee. He is also a member of the Democratic Steering Committee and **Congressional Black Caucus**. Representative Hastings was elected to Congress in 1992, three years after being impeached from the federal bench on charges of perjury. The impeachment was overturned on a technicality. Rep. Hastings had been one of the South's first black judges. (CE)

BIBLIOGRAPHY

Volcansek, Mary. *Judicial Impeachment: None Called for Justice*. Urbana: University of Illinois Press, 1993.

Richard Gordon Hatcher (1933–)

Richard Hatcher was one of the first African Americans to become mayor of a major city when he was elected to that position in Gary, Indiana, in 1967. Hatcher held the post of mayor for two decades until he was defeated for reelection in 1987. A combative personality, Hatcher oversaw the city as it struggled to address race relations and a declining economic base. In the 1960s, 1970s, and 1980s, the city lost major employers and nearly one-third of its population, and many critics linked the city's decline to Hatcher's aggressive personality. He often feuded with neighboring towns over joint projects and scared many whites with his talk of **black power.** He attempted a political comeback in 1991 but was once again defeated.

BIBLIOGRAPHY

Terry, Don. "Hatcher Begins Battle to Regain Spotlight in Gary." *New York Times* (May 6, 1991): A12.

Walters, Ron. "Time for a Third Party? Black Democrats." *Nation* 241 (November 2, 1985): 440–43.

Augustus "Gus" Freeman Hawkins (1907–)

Augustus Hawkins, a Democrat, was elected to Congress in 1962, after serving in the California Assembly (1935–1963), where he introduced fair housing and fair employment practices acts, low-cost housing and disability insurance legislation, and workmen's compensation provisions for domestic workers. In Congress he served on the Education and Labor Committee and sponsored job creation and civil rights legislation. He helped establish the **Equal Employment Opportunity Commission (EEOC)** in **Title VII of the Civil Rights Act of 1964.** He authored the Full Employment and Balanced Growth Act of 1978. (EC)

BIBLIOGRAPHY

Ragsdale, Bruce A. and Joel Treese. *Black Americans in Congress, 1870–1990.* Washington DC, U.S. Government Printing Office, 1990: 65–66.

Hawkins v. Board of Control of Florida (1954)

Hawkins v. Board of Control of Florida, 47 So. 2nd 608 FL, was the court case involving Virgil Hawkins' long and ultimately unsuccessful attempt to integrate the University of Florida Law School. In 1949, he applied for admission to the law school and was refused on the basis of his color. He applied again in 1954 after the *Brown* decision. However, although the case eventually went to the U.S. Supreme Court (347 US 971 [1954a]), it was remanded back to the Florida Supreme Court, which eventually refused again to admit him. (CE)

BIBLIOGRAPHY

Cooper, Algia R. "*Brown v. The Board of Education* and Virgil Darnell Hawkins: Twenty-Eight Years and Six Petitions to Justice." *Journal of Negro History* 64 (Winter 1979): 1–20.

Charles Arthur Hayes (1918–)

Charles Hayes, a Democrat from Illinois, was elected to the U.S. House of Representatives in 1982 and served until 1993. Prior to entering Congress, Hayes was vice president of the United Food and Commercial Workers Union. He is a co-founder of **Operation PUSH,** an organization founded in Chicago to assist in educational and economic opportunities for African Americans, and has served as a trustee of the Martin Luther King Center for Social Change.

BIBLIOGRAPHY

"Washington Report." *National Minority Politics* 3, no. 10 (March 1992): 9.

James C. Hayes (1946–)

James Hayes was born in Sacramento, California. He received his B.A. from the University of Alaska in 1970. He was an attorney-investigator for the Office of Consumer Protection in Fairbanks from 1972 to 1990 and served on city council from 1987 to 1992. He was elected mayor of Fairbanks in 1992. (JCW)

BIBLIOGRAPHY

"James C. Hayes: Alaska's First Black Mayor." *Ebony* (October 1, 1993). 64.

George Edmund Haynes (1880–1960)

In 1910, George Haynes co-founded the National League on Urban Conditions Among Negroes (now the **National Urban League**) and served as its director until 1918. From 1918 to 1920 he was a special assistant to the U.S. secretary of labor, whom he advised on the economic problems of African Americans and on child labor conditions. From 1920 to 1921, Haynes was a member of the President's Unemployment Conference. He also served as deputy secretary for race relations for the Federal Federation of Churches of Christ in America from 1922 through 1946.

BIBLIOGRAPHY

Haynes, George E. *Trend of the Races.* Stratford, NH: Ayer, 1977.

Parris, Guichard. *Blacks in the City: A History of the National Urban League.* Boston: Little, Brown and Co., 1971.

Hazelwood School District v. United States (1977)

In *Hazelwood School District v. United States,* 433 U.S. 299 (1977), a suburb of St. Louis, Missouri, was brought to court after racist hiring practices were cited in the school district. These charges were based on the school district's history of alleged racially discriminatory practices, statistical discrepancies in hiring, and primarily subjective hiring practices devoid of set procedures. In addition, 55 separate cases of unsuccessful employment applications by black teachers were introduced, adding weight to the alleged racist hiring procedures. All of these actions were declared as a violation of **Title VII of the Civil Rights Act of 1964.** The school district countered that such allegations were incorrect because they sought to hire African-American teachers based on the number of black students. The Supreme Court decided that the number of black teachers hired should instead be equal to the amount in other school districts, not reflective of internal student ratios. As a result, the hiring practices of the Hazelwood School District were found to be illegal.

BIBLIOGRAPHY

Meler, Paul, Jerome Sacks, and Sandy L. Zabell. "What Happened in Hazelwood: Statistics, Employment Discrimination, and the 80% Rule." *American Bar Foundation Research Journal* no. 1 (Winter 1984): 139–86.

Sugreve, Thomas J. and William B. Fairley. "A Case of Unexamined Assumptions: The Use and Misuse of the Statistical Analysis of Castaneda-Hazelwood in Discrimination Litigation." *Boston College Law Review* 24, no. 4 (July 1983): 925–60.

Healthy Start

The Healthy Start program seeks to decrease infant mortality in certain targeted urban and rural communities that have infant mortality rates 1.5 to 2.5 times greater than the national average. Begun in 1991 with an original five-year mandate, Healthy Start targeted 15 locations across the United States with the expressed intention of cutting infant mortality by 50 percent. The preliminary report issued by the General Accounting Office in 1998 found no conclusive evidence that the program was having its intended effect. (CJM)

BIBLIOGRAPHY

Williams, C. L., et al. "Healthy Start." *Preventive Medicine* 27, no. 2 (1998): 216.

GAO. *Healthy Start: Preliminary Results from National Evaluation Are Not Conclusive.* Washington, DC: GAO, 1998.

Heart of Atlanta Motel v. United States (1964)

The *Heart of Atlanta Motel v. United States*, 379 U.S. 241 (1964), case was an early test of the constitutionality of the **Civil Rights Act of 1964.** The Heart of Atlanta Motel refused accommodations to African-American travelers. The motel challenged the public accommodations provisions of the Civil Rights Act of 1964, which forbade discrimination by hotels, motels, and restaurants. The motel claimed that the accommodations provision was beyond the scope of Congress.

The Supreme Court unanimously upheld the Civil Rights Act, ruling that Congress had the authority to pass the Civil Rights Act under the interstate commerce clause of the Constitution. The Court ruled that travelers were part of interstate commerce and by refusing accommodations, the motel was interfering with interstate commerce. The Civil Rights Act and the decision in this case represented broad extensions of the commerce clause. The decision gave Congress sweeping authority to use the commerce clause as a source of federal police power to protect civil rights. (RLP)

BIBLIOGRAPHY

Pritchett, C. Herman. *Constitutional Law of the Federal System.* Englewood Cliffs, NJ: Prentice Hall, 1984.

Dorothy Height (1912–)

Dorothy Height, activist and reformer, is dedicated to working through women's organizations for the advancement of African-American civil rights and equality. With a master's degree in educational psychology from New York University, Height worked for the Brownsville Community center in Brooklyn, was a caseworker for the New York City Department of Welfare, and was also assistant director of the Emma Ransome House of the Harlem YWCA. She has been on the national board of the YWCA since 1944. Height served as president of **Delta Sigma Theta** (1947–1956) and in 1957 she became president of the **National Council of Negro Women (NCNW),** leading the wide variety of women's organizations under the NCNW in civil rights struggles and in articulating the needs and interests of Diaspora African women. (EC)

BIBLIOGRAPHY

Giddings, Paula. *In Search of Sisterhood: Delta Sigma Theta & the Challenge of the Black Sorority Movement.* New York:William Morrow, 1988.

A. Leon Higginbotham, Jr. (1928–1998)

After graduating from Yale Law School in 1952, A. Leon Higginbotham, Jr., despite strong support from some of the nation's most respected professors, was unable to secure a position in the segregated law firms of Philadelphia. After serving as a law clerk and an assistant district attorney in Philadelphia, he co-founded an African-American law firm that took on many civil rights cases. By 1964, Higginbotham had begun to achieve national prominence, in part through his membership on the Pennsylvania Human Relations Commission. In that year, President Lyndon Johnson nominated Higginbotham as a United States district judge. At only 35, Higginbotham became the youngest federal judge since the early 1930s, and the only African-American judge sitting on a federal district court. President Jimmy Carter, in 1977, nominated Higginbotham to the United States Court of Appeals for the 3rd Circuit, and he became chief justice of that court in 1989.

Higginbotham produced an enormous number of articles in a wide variety of publications, including a controversial open letter to Justice Clarence Thomas, in which Higginbotham takes Thomas to task for Thomas' opposition to affirmative action programs. The first volume of Higginbotham's trilogy, *In the Matter of Color: Race and the American Legal Process* (1978), is considered a seminal work in the history of law and in its interaction with minority life in the United States. He was a member of the faculties at the University of Pennsylvania and Harvard University, and was the first African American to serve as a trustee of Yale University. President Clinton presented Higginbotham with the Presidential Medal of Freedom in 1995. (AJC)

BIBLIOGRAPHY

Feeney, Mark. "Off the Bench, But Still in the Arena: A Retired Federal Judge Continues His Pursuit of 'a Mighty Cause'." *Boston Globe* (May 21, 1995): F47.

Higginbotham, A. Leon Jr. "Why I Didn't March." *Washington Post* (October 17, 1995): A17.

Anita Hill (1956–)

Anita Hill, an attorney and former employee of the **Equal Employment Opportunity Commission (EEOC)** and Department of Education, gained notoriety in 1991 when she brought sexual harassment charges against the United States Supreme Court nominee and her former EEOC supervisor, Clarence Thomas. The United States Senate hearings on the charges resulted in a heightened awareness and sensitivity to gender issues in the workplace. Thomas was eventually confirmed as a Supreme Court Justice, and Hill went on to a career as a professor of law.

BIBLIOGRAPHY
Brock, David. *The Real Anita Hill*. New York: Free Press, 1994.
Mayu, Jane. *Strange Justice*. Boston: Houghton Mifflin, 1994.

Earl F. Hillard (1942–)

Earl Hillard represents the 7th Congressional District of Alabama (1992), the first African American from Alabama to serve in Congress since **Reconstruction.** He served in the Alabama House (1975–1981), and in the Alabama Senate (1981–1993). In Congress Hillard, a Democrat, supports social and economic policies, although he opposed the North American Free Trade Agreement (NAFTA) and gun control. He serves on the Small Business and Agriculture Committees. He also serves on the Congressional Rural Caucus and on the Forestry 2000 Task Force. (EC)

BIBLIOGRAPHY
Duncan, Phillip D. and Christine C. Lawrence. *Politics in America 1998. The 105th Congress*. Washington, DC: Congressional Quarterly Press, 1997: 24–26.

Eric H. Holder, Jr. (1951–)

Eric Holder Jr. received his J.D. from Columbia College. He worked as an associate judge for the Superior Court of Washington from 1988 to 1993. He was the first African American to hold the post of U.S. Attorney in Washington, D.C., which he held until he was appointed deputy attorney general for the Justice Department in 1997. (JCW)

BIBLIOGRAPHY
Locy, Toni. "D.C. Politics Beckons, Repels Holder." *Washington Post* (December 21, 1996): A1.

Jerome H. Holland (1916–1985)

Jerome Holland was U.S. ambassador to Holland from 1970 to 1975. In 1972, he became the first African American elected to the board of directors of the New York Stock Exchange. Holland also served on the board of directors of the United Negro College Fund (1976–1985) and was chairperson of the board of governors of the American Red Cross (1979–1985). From 1953 to 1960, Holland was president of Delaware State College. He served as president of Hampton Institute from 1960 to 1970.

BIBLIOGRAPHY
Link, Ruth. "Ambassador Holland and the Swedes." *Crisis* 78, no. 2 (1971): 43–48.

Hollins v. Oklahoma (1935)

The petitioner in *Hollins v. Oklahoma*, 295 U.S. 394 (1935), was an African American convicted of rape in Okmulgee County, Oklahoma. Hollins challenged the jury panel on the grounds that blacks were excluded from jury service solely on the basis of race or color, thus depriving him of his **Fourteenth Amendment** rights. The Court reversed the Criminal Court of Appeals decision and remanded for further proceeding. (CJM)

BIBLIOGRAPHY
Frankel, Marvin E. *The Grand Jury*. New York: Hill and Wang, 1977.

M. Carl Holman (1919–1988)

M. Carl Holman was born in Miner City, Mississippi. He graduated from Lincoln University and received his M.A. from University of Chicago and his M.F.A. from Yale. He taught English at Clark College and became active in the **civil rights movement**, co-founding the Atlanta Committee for Cooperative Association and the *Atlanta Enquirer*, an all black newspaper that had extended coverage of civil rights. In 1962, Holman joined the **United States Commission on Civil Rights** and in 1968 he joined the National Urban Coalition and eventually became its first black president in 1971 and was a major voice for the poor and urban renewal. (JCW)

BIBLIOGRAPHY
Krebs, Albin. "Carl Holman, 69, A Major Figure in Civil Rights Movement Is Dead." *New York Times* (August 11, 1988): D20.

Holmes v. City of Atlanta (1955)

After the decision of ***Brown v. Board of Education*** in 1954, the **National Association for the Advancement of Colored People (NAACP)** launched a campaign to end segregation in public places. At issue in *Holmes v. City of Atlanta*, 350 U.S. 876 (1955), were municipal golf courses that were segregated under a local law banning people of color from parks maintained for the use of whites. Melvin I. Urofsky maintains that the strategy in a number of these cases was for a district judge to cite *Brown* as a precedent, ending segregation in public places, then have the Supreme Court uphold in an unwritten decision. (EP)

BIBLIOGRAPHY
Urofsky, Melvin I. *A March for Liberty: A Constitutional History of the United States. Vol. II: Since 1865*. New York: Alfred A. Knopf, 1988.

Benjamin Lawrence Hooks (1925–)

Benjamin Hooks played a pioneering role for African Americans in the legal profession. After receiving a Bachelor of Arts degree from Howard University in 1944 and a Juris Doctor degree from De Paul University in 1948, Hooks returned to his hometown of Memphis to practice law. Hooks quickly became active in the **civil rights movement**, serving on the board of directors of the **Southern Christian Leadership Conference (SCLC)** from its founding in 1957 to 1977. Hooks continued to practice law and was appointed assistant public defender of Shelby County, Tennessee, in 1961. Four years later, he was appointed to fill a vacancy in the county's Criminal Court, becoming the first black criminal court judge in the state. In 1972, Hooks was nominated by President Richard Nixon to serve on the Federal Communications Commission, becoming the first African American to do so.

Hooks became executive director of the **National Association for the Advancement of Colored People (NAACP)** in 1972, at a difficult time in the organization's history. As executive director, Hooks attempted to improve the NAACP's financial position and to revitalize its image. Hooks stepped down as executive director in 1992 amid disputes over the leadership and direction of the organization. After his departure from the NAACP, Hooks continued to serve as chairman of the **Leadership Conference on Civil Rights,** a coalition of organizations concerned with civil rights issues which he had led since the 1980s. (LPM)

BIBLIOGRAPHY

Delaney, P. "Struggle to Rally Black America." *New York Times Magazine* (July 15, 1979): 20.

"New Voice of the NAACP." Interview. *Newsweek* (November 22, 1976): 46.

Housing Act of 1937

The Housing Act of 1937, created by Congress, established the United States Housing Authority. In 1942 the agency was renamed the Federal Public Housing Administration and then in 1947, the Public Housing Administration. The Act began the first attempt by the federal government to help provide low-income families with some form of housing assistance. Through grants to states, the federal government was able to subsidize the building of low-rent public housing by local authorities. (VDD)

BIBLIOGRAPHY

Haveman, Robert H., ed. *A Decade of Federal Antipoverty Programs: Achievements, Failures, and Lessons.* New York: Academic Press, 1977.

Charles Houston (1895–1950)

Charles Houston was the dean of the Howard Law School, who trained black lawyers in constitutional law. Later, he ran the **National Association for the Advancement of Colored People's (NAACP)** legal department using a strategy he called "social engineering" which emphasized using the law to fight segregation. (AAB)

BIBLIOGRAPHY

McNeil, Genna Rae. *Groundwork: Charles Hamilton Houston and the Struggle for Civil Rights.* Philadelphia: University of Pennsylvania, 1983.

White, Vibert L. "Charles Houston and Black Leadership of the 1930s and 1940s." *National Black Law Journal* 11, no. 3 (Fall 1990): 331–47.

Howard University

An accredited coeducational institution located in Washington, D.C., Howard University was chartered by an act of Congress. Although privately owned, it receives substantial federal funds. It is named after Major General Otis Howard, a **Civil War** veteran. It was founded in 1867 to promote the welfare of recently freed slaves and other free blacks. The university has more than 2,000 faculty members and approximately 12,000 students. It contains numerous facilities including a teaching hospital. Its television station is the only black-owned and operated public station. (WWH)

BIBLIOGRAPHY

"Howard University Tops in Producing Black Graduates." *Jet* 90, no. 8 (July 8, 1996): 23.

Logan, Rayford W. *Howard University.* New York: New York University Press, 1969.

Mercer, Joye. "New President Outlines Ambitious Agenda to Rejuvenate Howard University: Plans Include Reorganizing Academic Programs and More Alumni Fund Raising." *The Chronicle of Higher Education* 42, no. 46 (July 26, 1996): A39.

Humphrey-Hawkins Full Employment and Balanced Growth Act of 1978

The Humphrey-Hawkins bill was originally devised to eliminate widespread unemployment plaguing depressed communities. As introduced, the bill called for a Job Corps, a Job Guarantee Office, and automatic federal spending to curb unemployment. After much debate, a watered-down bill was signed into law. The Humphrey-Hawkins Act mandated that the federal government devise a plan and work toward granting the right to work for all those willing and able. However, these goals have been largely ignored in favor of other economic priorities. (WPS)

BIBLIOGRAPHY

American Enterprise Institute for Public Research. *Reducing Unemployment: The Humphrey-Hawkins and Kemp-McClure Bills.* Washington, DC, 1976.

Smith, Robert C. *We Have No Leaders: African Americans in the Post-Civil Rights Era.* New York: State University of New York Press, 1996.

Hurd et al. v. Hodge et al. (1948)

The case *Hurd et al. v. Hodge et. al.*, 334 U.S. 68 (1948), a companion case to **Shelley v. Kraemer** (1948), involved the private conveyances of real estate in the District of Columbia. A set of 1906 "covenants" forebade any person from selling certain lots to "any Negro or colored person" under threat of a $2,000 fine. The Court held that the covenants were valid, but their enforcement by the Courts of the District of Columbia was prohibited by a federal statute which guaranteed to all citizens of the U.S. equal rights to inherit, purchase, lease, sell, hold, and convey real estate and personal property. (CJM)

John A. Hyman (1840–1891)

John Adams Hyman was born a slave in North Carolina. He was elected as a Republican to state senate in 1868 and became North Carolina's first black congressman in 1874. He left politics in 1877 after failing to win reelection and moved to Washington, D.C., where he attempted to form coalitions between black Republicans and white Democrats.

BIBLIOGRAPHY

Ragsdale, Bruce and Joel Treese. *Black Americans in Congress 1870–1989*. Washington, DC: U.S. Government Printing Office, 1990.

I

"I Have a Dream"

Martin Luther King, Jr. gave his most famous speech at the apex of the **March on Washington** on August 28, 1963. King wanted to unite those in favor of peaceful change in civil rights. Therefore, at the end of the Birmingham campaign, one marked by terrible police violence, King helped to organize the March on Washington which united a number of civil rights leaders and organizations. On August 28, 1963, these leaders assembled an interracial gathering of over 200,000 people, who stood peaceably in the shadow of the Lincoln Memorial. These people clamored for equal justice for all citizens under the law.

At the height of the gathering, King delivered his famous "I Have a Dream" speech. The emotional and prophetic quality of the speech was enhanced by King's use of biblical passages and cadences. He stated his belief that all people would eventually be brothers. His hope that blacks and whites would be joined together in a common destiny with black children and white children joining hands struck deep emotional chords in the American public.

The emotional high produced by the speech and the peaceful march helped stir up support for civil rights legislation. The favorable opinion polls helped push legislation through Congress in 1964. The **Civil Rights Act of 1964** gave the federal government authority to enforce desegregation of public accommodations. It also outlawed discrimination in publicly owned facilities and employment. King received the Nobel Peace Prize in 1964.

BIBLIOGRAPHY

Lischer, Richard. *The Preacher King*. New York: Oxford University Press, 1995.

Ida B. Wells Club

Founded in Chicago, in 1893, the Ida B. Wells Club was one of many black women's clubs created in response to the anti-lynching crusade of **Ida B. Wells.** This club not only lobbied against lynchings and police brutality, but it was also very active in the community, setting up a kindergarten and performing other charity work. In 1896, the club joined with scores of other groups to form the **National Association of**

Colored Women (NACW). See also Anti-Lynching Legislation. (WPS)

BIBLIOGRAPHY

Knupfer, Anne Meis. *Toward a Tenderer Humanity and a Nobler Womanhood: African-American Women's Clubs in Turn-of-the-Century Chicago*. New York: New York University Press, 1996.

Wells-Barnett, Ida B. *Crusade for Justice: The Autobiography of Ida B. Wells-Barnett*. Alfreda E. Duster, ed. Chicago: University of Chicago Press, 1970.

Roy Emile Alfredo Innis (1934–)

Born in St. Croix, Virgin Islands, Innis attended the City University in New York City following his return from military service in Korea. After several years of involvement in the Harlem Branch of the **Congress of Racial Equality (CORE)**, he was appointed CORE's national director in 1968. Under Innis' leadership, CORE has grown to be the third largest civil rights organization in the country. Innis is also on the Board of Advisors for the Foundation for the Advancement of Monetary Education (FAME). (VDD)

BIBLIOGRAPHY

"Civil Rights Leader Roy Innis to Run for Governor of New York." *Jet* 85, no. 19 (March 14, 1994): 8.

Millner, Denene. "CORE More Than $2 Million In Debt, Records Show." *Knight-Rider/Tribune News Service* (February 26, 1994).

International Brotherhood of Teamsters v. United States et al. (1976)

In *International Brotherhood of Teamsters v. United States et al.*, 431 U.S. 324 (1976), the United States government instituted litigation under **Title VII of the Civil Rights Act of 1964**, charging that the International Brotherhood of Teamsters had engaged in a pattern of discriminating against blacks and "Spanish-surnamed persons." The Court held that the Teamsters had engaged in discriminatory practices, but retroactive seniority for minorities was awarded as relief for post-Act discriminatees. The latter drew a partial dissent from both **Thurgood Marshall** and William Brennan. (CJM)

BIBLIOGRAPHY

Schell, George K.H. "Bonafide Seniority Systems: Guidelines for the Use of Disparate Impact in the Teamsters Analysis." (Case note) *UCLA Law Review* 31, no. 4 (April 1984): 886–920.

Tisdale, John A. "Deterred Nonapplicants in Title VII Class Actions: Examining the Limits of Equal Employment Opportunity." *Boston University Law Review* 64, no. 1 (January 1984): 151–97.

International League of Darker Peoples

The International League of Darker Peoples was an organization formed by Madame C.J. Walker and Adam Clayton Powell in 1919. The organization was concerned with international issues pertaining to people of African descent. Walker attempted to attend the Versailles Conference as a delegate of the **National Equal Rights League** to ensure inclusion of blacks in the treaty. She and other members of the delegation were unable to obtain passports. The organization was a precursor to **Marcus Garvey**'s **Universal Negro Improvement Association.**

BIBLIOGRAPHY
Hine, Darlene Clark. *Speak Truth to Power: Black Professional Class in United States History.* New York: Carlson Publishing, 1996.

International Migration Society

The International Migration Society was founded by black nationalist Bishop Henry McNeal Turner in 1894 with the purpose of recolonizing blacks in Africa. It received support from the **American Colonization Society.** Its first major act was to send of a steamship with 200 emigrants to Liberia in March of 1894; a second ship sailed two years later with an additional 321 passengers. The emigrants met with extreme hardship in Liberia, prompting a reverse exodus in 1896 and fomenting existing dissent in the United States. The society ceased to exist in December 1899.

BIBLIOGRAPHY
Fierce, Milfred. *The Pan-African Idea in the United States 1900–1919.* New York: Garland Publishing, 1993.

J

Jesse L. Jackson (1941–)

A political progressive, human rights advocate, and Baptist minister, Jesse Jackson emerged as a **civil rights movement** leader by directing demonstrations while a student at North Carolina A&T College. Jackson participated in voting rights protests and later became the national director of Operation Breadbasket, which organized economic boycotts and promoted open housing policies as part of **Southern Christian Leadership Council's (SCLC)** Chicago Freedom Movement. In 1971, Jackson founded **Operation PUSH** to promote urban education, further economic justice, register voters, and address problems of drug abuse and teenage pregnancy. Jackson concluded each meeting by reciting the powerful chant "I am somebody, I may be poor, but I am somebody. I may be uneducated, I may be unskilled, but I am somebody. I may be on welfare, I may be prematurely pregnant, I may be on drugs, I may be victimized by racism, but I am somebody. Respect me. Protect me. Never neglect me. I am God's Child."

Jackson sought the **Democratic Party** nomination in 1984, founding a national **Rainbow Coalition** to unite those "locked out" of society including racial and ethnic minorities, family farmers, the elderly, and the poor. Emphasizing an agenda of jobs, peace, justice, and the redistribution of power, Jackson added a spiritual and ethical dimension to national party politics and scored an impressive 21 percent of the primary vote. Four years later, Jackson reentered the presidential race, becoming the frontrunner for the Democratic Party nomination after one of his seven primary election victories, and secured over six million voters. (CC)

BIBLIOGRAPHY

Jackson, Jesse L. *Legal Lynchings: Racism, Injustice, and the Death Penalty*. New York: Marlowe and Company, 1996.

Jackson, Jesse L. *Straight from the Heart*. Roger D. Hatch and Frank E. Watkins, eds. Philadelphia: Fortress Press, 1987.

Jesse L. Jackson, Jr. (1965–)

Jesse Jackson, Jr., a Democrat from Illinois, was first elected to the United States House of Representatives in a special election in 1995 and subsequently reelected in 1996 and 1998. He is the oldest son of the Reverend **Jesse L. Jackson**, the civil rights activist. Prior to his election to Congress, the younger Jackson was national field director for the national **Rainbow Coalition**, president of the "Keep Hope Alive" Political Action Committee, and vice president at large for **Operation PUSH.**

BIBLIOGRAPHY

"Generation Next." *People* 46, no. 1 (November 18, 1996): 50–54.

"Jesse Jackson, Jr." *Jet* 89, no. 8 (January 8, 1996): 6.

Wagner, Betty. "Jesse Jackson, Member of Congress." *U.S. News & World Report* 119, no. 23 (December 11, 1995): 32.

Maynard H. Jackson, Jr. (1938–)

Jackson grew up in Atlanta and graduated from Morehouse College in 1956. He earned a law degree in 1964 from North Carolina College and began practicing in Atlanta. He established a reputation as a civil rights activist, and in 1970 won election as a Democrat as the city's first black vice-mayor.

He triumphed in the 1973 mayoral race, becoming Atlanta's first black mayor and its youngest ever, at 34 . During his first two terms, from 1974 to 1982, he worked to improve the job prospects for women and minorities. After leaving office he became an investment banker, then again became Atlanta's mayor in 1989. Jackson joined in attracting the 1996 Olympics to Atlanta, then returned to banking. (AD)

BIBLIOGRAPHY

Manning, Marable. *Race, Reform, and Rebellion: The Second Reconstruction in Black America, 1945–1990*. Jackson: University of Mississippi Press, 1991.

John E. Jacob (1934–)

John Jacob was born in Louisiana in 1934. He received bachelor's and master's degrees from Howard University in social work. He worked for the Baltimore Department of Public Welfare in the early 1960s and then joined the Washington Urban League as education director. He served as their executive director from 1968 until 1970 when he left to temporarily become executive director of the San Diego Urban League. He returned to Washington in 1975 and became president of the Washington Urban League in 1982, replacing **Vernon E. Jordan, Jr.**

BIBLIOGRAPHY

Parris, Guichard. *Blacks in the City: A History of the National Urban League*. Boston: Little, Brown, 1971.

Daniel "Chappie" James (1920–1978)

One of the famed Tuskegee Airmen, Daniel "Chappie" James was commissioned in the Army Air Corps in 1943. Following service during World War II and the wars in Korea and Vietnam, he became the first African-American four star general in the history of the U.S. Armed Forces. In 1975 he was appointed to command the North American Air Defense Command in Colorado Springs, Colorado. **See also** Vietnam War. (GAA)

BIBLIOGRAPHY

Phelps, J. Alfred. *Chappie, America's First Black Four-Star General: The Life and Times of Daniel James, Jr.* Los Angeles: Presidio Press, 1992.

Sharpe James (1936–)

Sharpe James, a Democrat, was elected mayor of Newark, New Jersey, in 1986. Prior to becoming mayor, James served 17 years (1970–1986) on the Newark City Council. He is a member of the United States Conference of Mayors and has served as a board member of the National League of Cities.

BIBLIOGRAPHY

Balar, Denise. "NLC President Will Outline Legislation Action Agenda." *Nation's Cities Weekly* 17, no. 10 (March 7, 1994): 1–3.
Moody, John. "The Rumor Stumbles." *Time* 146, no. 2 (July 10, 1995): 34.

James v. Valtierra (1971)

California voters amended the state constitution requiring community approval before any low-income housing project could be undertaken. When two local referenda were defeated, low-income individuals sought a judicial declaration that the amendment violated the federal Constitution. The Supreme Court, in *James v. Valtierra*, 402 U.S. 137 (1971), noted that California had a long history of using popular referenda; such referenda were permissible as long as they were not used for unconstitutional purposes, and the housing referendum was not "constitutionally suspect" because it was not racially motivated. (FHJ)

BIBLIOGRAPHY

D'Amato, Anthony A., Rosemary Metrailer, and Stephen L. Wasby. *Desegregation from Brown to Alexander.* Carbondale, IL: Southern Illinois University Press, 1977.

William J. Jefferson (1947–)

William Jefferson graduated from Harvard Law School in 1972. He was a member of the Louisiana State Senate from 1980 to 1990 and was chosen twice to be Louisiana Legislator of the Year. He was elected to the House of Representatives as a Democrat in 1990 and has served three consecutive terms. (JCW)

BIBLIOGRAPHY

Jones, Joyce. "Capital Ideas for Small Businesses: Tax Strategies Could Help Provide Needed Resources for Minority Firms." *Black Enterprise* 27, no. 10 (May 1997): 20.

Jim Crow Laws

Jim Crow is a phrase used to encompass a broad variety of discriminatory measures passed against black southerners in the post-**Reconstruction** period. These measures created almost complete segregation between the races in the South in places of public accommodation and included laws which discriminated against African Americans in the judicial system, employment, education, medical care, and virtually every other area of society. The origins of the term "Jim Crow" are still debated but may refer to a minstrel character of that name. (CE)

BIBLIOGRAPHY

Woodward, C. Vann. *The Strange Career of Jim Crow.* New York: Oxford University Press, 1974.

Eddie Bernice Johnson (1935–)

Eddie Bernice Johnson, a Democrat from Texas, was elected to the United States House of Representatives in 1992 and subsequently reelected in 1994, 1996 and 1998. Before entering Congress, Johnson was a member of the Texas State House of Representatives (1972–1977) and the Texas Senate (1986–1992). Johnson is also a former president of the **National Council of Negro Women.**

BIBLIOGRAPHY

"Texas: Eddie Bernice Johnson." *Congressional Quarterly Weekly Report* 50, no. 44 (November 7, 1992): 52.

James Weldon Johnson (1871–1938)

James Weldon Johnson was a poet, educator, writer, and social reformer. After serving as principal of a high school in Jacksonville, Florida, Johnson left the city with his brother and traveled the country selling songs which they had written. He later was appointed U.S. Consul to Venezuela but was replaced by Woodrow Wilson. He joined the **National Association for the Advancement of Colored People (NAACP)** and eventually rose to executive secretary where he led an unsuccessful struggle to get an anti-lynching bill passed. He is the author of several books, poems, plays and songs including the national Negro anthem "Lift Every Voice and Sing." (AAB)

BIBLIOGRAPHY

Johnson, James Weldon. *Along this Way: The Autobiography of James Weldon Johnson.* New York: Penguin, 1990.

Johnson v. Transportation Agency, Santa Clara County (1987)

The Santa Clara County Transportation Agency voluntarily adopted an affirmative action plan. The Supreme Court held in *Johnson v. Transportation Agency, Santa Clara County*, 480 U.S. 616; 107 Sup. Ct. 1442 (1987), that the agency appropriately took into account as one factor the sex of the female employee in determining that she should be promoted over her male counterpart because (1) an employer seeking to justify the adoption of an affirmative action plan need not point to its own prior discriminatory practices but rather it need point only to a conspicuous imbalance in traditionally segregated job categories, (2) the plan did not unnecessarily trammel the rights of male employees. (PLF)

BIBLIOGRAPHY

Beltun, Robert. "Reflections on Affirmative Action after Paradise and Johnson." (Symposium on Civil Rights and Civil Liberties in the Workplace) *Harvard Civil Rights-Civil Liberties Law Review* 23, no. 1 (Winter 1988): 115–37.

Eskridge, William N., Jr. "Overruling Statutory Precedents." *Georgetown Law Journal* 76, no. 4 (April 1988): 1361–1439.

Joint Center for Political and Economic Studies

The Joint Center for Political and Economic Studies is a Washington D.C.-based nonprofit institution that conducts research on public policy issues of special concerns to African Americans. Founded in 1970 (as the Joint Center for Political Studies) with funding from the Ford Foundation and through the sponsorship of **Howard University** and the Metropolitan Applied Research Center of New York City, the center also promotes the involvement of African Americans in the governmental process. The Joint Center produces numerous publications; it also collects and publishes data on the number of government positions held by African Americans on local, state, and national levels. **See also** Eddie N. Williams.

BIBLIOGRAPHY

Jones, Joyce. "The Silent Force." *Black Enterprise* 25, no. 9 (April 1995): 96–101.

Absalom Jones (1747–1818)

An Episcopal minister born into slavery in Delaware, Absalom Jones bought his freedom and became a leader of the free black community in Philadelphia. He was a founder of the **Free African Society** (1787) and the African Church of Philadelphia (1793).(GGA)

BIBLIOGRAPHY

Nash, Gary B. *Forging Freedom: The Formation of Philadelphia's Black Community, 1720–1840*. Cambridge, MA: Harvard University Press, 1988.

Quarles, Benjamin. *The Negro in the Making of America*. 3rd ed. New York: Touchstone Books, 1996.

Elaine R. Jones (1944–)

Elaine Jones was the first black woman to receive a law degree from the University of Virginia. She joined the **National Association for the Advancement of Colored People (NAACP)** Legal Defense and Education Fund (LDF) in 1970 and worked temporarily as special assistant to the secretary of transportation from 1975 to 1977. She returned to the LDF and became the head of the organization in 1993 where she has fought to steer the anti-affirmative action trend. (JCW)

BIBLIOGRAPHY

"NAACP Rights Fund to Expand Role." *Washington Post* (March 11, 1993): A10.

Eugene Kinckle Jones (1885–1954)

Eugene Jones received a M.A. from Columbia in 1908. He worked for the **National Urban League,** becoming its executive secretary in 1917 where he supported greater rights for black workers. He was also responsible for the formation of the Schonsbury Collection of black artifacts at the New York Public Library. With Charles S. Johnson, he co-founded *Opportunity: A Journal of Negro Life* which was published from 1923–1948. He served as an advisor to the U.S. Department of Commerce on African-American concerns.

BIBLIOGRAPHY

Parris, Guichard. *Blacks in the City: A History of the National Urban League*. Boston: Little, Brown, 1971.

Nathaniel R. Jones (1926–)

Nathaniel Jones served as executive director of the Youngstown, Ohio, Fair Employment Practices Commission from 1966 to 1969, as well as an assistant United States Attorney for the northern District of Ohio and a judge in the U.S. Court of Appeals. Jones was made general counsel for President Lyndon Johnson's Commission on Civil Disorders, also known as the Kerner Commission, in 1967. In 1969 he became general counsel of the **National Association for the Advancement of Colored People (NAACP)**, where he worked for reform in the United States military justice system. He remained with the NAACP until 1979.

BIBLIOGRAPHY

Harris, Fred R. and Roger W. Wilkins, eds. *Quiet Riots*. New York: Pantheon Books, 1988.

Harris, Jacqueline L. *History and Achievements of the NAACP*. New York: Watts, 1992.

Jones v. Alfred H. Mayer Co. (1968)

Jones v. Alfred H. Mayer Co., 392 U.S. 409 (1968), was an action to recover damages, due to the refusal of defendants Alfred H. Mayer Co., to sell a home in a private subdivision to plaintiffs solely because of race. The Supreme Court held that all citizens of the United States shall have the same rights, in every state and territory, as those enjoyed by white citizens thereof to inherit, purchase, lease, sell, hold, and convey real estate and personal property, barring all racial discrimination, private as well as public in the sale or rental of property. (PLF)

BIBLIOGRAPHY

Aleinikoff, T. Alexander. "Updating Statutory Interpretation." (Symposium: *Patterson v. McLean*) *Michigan Law Review*, 87 no. 1 (October 1988): 20–66.

Colbert, Douglas L. "Liberating the 13th Amendment." *Harvard Civil Rights-Civil Liberties Law Review* 30, no. 1 (Winter 1995): 1–55.

Barbara Charline Jordan (1936–1996)

Barbara C. Jordan was born in Houston, Texas, in the 5th Ward, an African-American neighborhood characterized by poverty, strong families, and many churches. Her father was a Baptist minister, her mother a domestic worker. She graduated ma-

gna cum laude in 1956 from Texas Southern University. She
went to Boston University law school, graduating in 1959,
and soon became involved in politics. She achieved many
"firsts": in 1966 she was elected to the Texas State Senate, the
first African American elected to the Texas Senate since 1883,
and she was the first African American to chair a major committee in the Texas Senate. In 1972 she was elected from the
18th U.S. Congressional District of Texas, the first woman
and the first black elected to Congress from Texas.

Congresswoman Jordan made a memorable stance for the
rule of law and the sanctity of the United States Constitution
as a member of the House Judiciary Committee during the
1974 hearings and votes on the Articles of Impeachment
against President Nixon before the Judiciary Committee. She
explained when casting her "yes" vote for the Impeachment
Articles, "My faith in the Constitution is whole, it is complete, it is total, and I am not going to sit here and be an idle
spectator to the diminution, the subversion, the destruction of
the Constitution." Jordan's page one obituary in The *New York
Times* noted how her resonant voice had mesmerized and
"stirred the nation with her Churchillian denunciations of the
Watergate abuses of President Richard M. Nixon."

In political office she resisted being categorized as a
woman or as an African American, and she often insisted that
she was in office as a citizen, like everyone else. As both a
state and national elected official she worked to ease the burdens of poverty for people. She sponsored legislation to extend
provisions of the 1965 **Voting Rights Act** to Mexican Americans. Health problems linked to multiple sclerosis pushed her
to retire from the House of Representatives in 1978. She went
on to a long and distinguished second career as a visiting professor at the University of Texas in Austin's Lyndon B. Johnson
School of Public Affairs. Jordan was a keynote speaker at the
1976 and 1992 Democratic conventions. In addition to her
devotion to the state of Texas, she was a loyal and proud Democrat. She received 15 honorary doctorate degrees and many
national awards and honors. (LRW)

BIBLIOGRAPHY
Clines, Francis X. "Barbara Jordan, A Lawmaker of Resonant Voice,
Dies at 59." *New York Times* (January 18, 1996): 1.
Jordan, Barbara and Shely Hearn. *Barbara Jordan: Self Portrait.*
Garden City, NJ: Doubleday, 1979.
Pitre, Merline. "Jordan, Barbara Charline." Darlene Clark Hine, Elsa
Barkley Brown, Rosalyn Terborg-Penn, eds. *Black Women in
America: An Historical Encyclopedia. Vol. 1.* Bloomington, IN:
Indiana University Press, 1993.

Vernon E. Jordan (1935–)

Vernon E. Jordan, a veteran of the **civil rights movement**, is
an influential informal advisor to President Bill Clinton. Born
in Atlanta, Jordan earned a law degree from **Howard University** in 1960. After working for the **National Association for
the Advancement of Colored People (NAACP)**, he took over
the southern Regional Council's Voter Registration Program
in 1965, helping to sign up some 2 million black voters. He
participated in President Lyndon Johnson's 1966 White House
conference on civil rights. From 1972 until the end of 1981,
Jordan directed the **National Urban League,** increasing the
budget and expanding operations.

In 1982 Jordan joined the law firm of Akin Gump, whose
clients included giants like American Airlines, AT&T, and
Archer Daniels Midland. Jordan is a long-time Democratic
Party activist. In 1988, he advised Democratic presidential
candidate Michael Dukakis on a speech to a black Baptist
convention, and he co-chaired President-elect Clinton's transition team in 1992–1993. (AD)

BIBLIOGRAPHY
Cottle, Michelle. "Mr. Smooth Comes to Washington." *Washington
Monthly* (June 1997): 20–25.
Williams, Marjorie. "Clinton's Mr. Inside." *Vanity Fair* (March 1993):
172–75, 207–13.

Kaiser Aluminum and Chemical Corporation v. Weber (1979)

Kaiser Aluminum and Chemical Corporation v. Weber, 443 U.S. 198 (1979), was one of three voluntary affirmative action cases heard by the Supreme Court concerning a program put into effect by Kaiser Aluminum in cooperation with The United Steelworkers of America. The fact that Kaiser Aluminum's skilled workforce was mainly white while its unskilled workforce remained mostly black was due, in part, to the exclusion of blacks from craft unions. Barker and Barker point out that the Court determined that **Title VII** of the **Civil Rights Act of 1964** should be used as a catalyst for remedying past discrimination. (EP)

BIBLIOGRAPHY

Barker, Lucius J. and Twiley W. Barker, Jr. *Civil Liberties and the Constitution: Cases and Commentaries.* 7th ed. Englewood Cliffs, NJ: Prentice Hall, 1994.

Shapiro, Linda. "Financial Weakness Is Relevant but Inconclusive as Defense to Clayton Act Violations." (Case note) *Washington University Law Quarterly*, 60, no. 2 (Summer 1982): 631–44.

Kansas-Nebraska Act

The Kansas-Nebraska Act of 1854 effectively destroyed the stability of the Union by repealing the **Missouri Compromise** of 1820. Originally written by Stephen Douglas as a means of approving a trans-continental railroad, the bill contained the dubious concept of popular sovereignty. This idea, which called for citizens of the territories to determine the status of slavery for themselves, was despised by northern Free-Soilers and southern slaveholders alike. Thus, the passage of the act in 1854 destroyed the uneasy sectional truce which had existed since the **Compromise of 1850**. (KR)

BIBLIOGRAPHY

Nevins, Allan. *Ordeal of the Union, Vol. II: A House Dividing, 1852–1857.* New York: Charles Scribner's Sons, 1947.

Potter, David M. *The Impending Crisis, 1848–1861.* New York: Harper and Row, 1976.

Katzenbach v. McClung (1964)

Katzenbach v. McClung, 379 U.S. 294 (1964), was a companion case to *Heart of Atlanta Motel v. United States*. Ollie's Barbecue, a restaurant in Birmingham, Alabama, refused to serve African Americans. Unlike the Heart of Atlanta Motel, Ollie's did not serve interstate travelers. But the Supreme Court's decision was consistent with the *Heart of Atlanta Motel* decision: the public accommodations provision of the **Civil Rights Act of 1964** was constitutional and the restaurant violated the Civil Rights Act by refusing to serve African Americans. The Court held that because almost half the food the restaurant served came from outside Alabama, Ollie's was involved in interstate commerce. As a consequence, Congress had power under the Commerce Clause to prohibit restaurants from discrimination. The decision was significant because it represented one of the broadest extensions of Congressional power under the Commerce Clause. The Civil Rights Act was a critical weapon in the fight against racial discrimination. (RLP)

BIBLIOGRAPHY

Pritchett, C. Herman. *Constitutional Law of the Federal System.* Englewood Cliffs, NJ: Prentice Hall, 1984.

Katzenbach v. Morgan (1966)

Article II, Section I of the New York Constitution contained within it a provision that limited the right to vote to those who could "read and write English." However, Section 4(e) of the federal **Voting Rights Act of 1965** provided that no person who had completed the sixth grade in a school in Puerto Rico, even if the language of instruction was in Spanish, shall be denied the right to vote because of his or her inability to read or write English. This section was included in the Voting Rights Act because, in many places in the United States, literacy tests had long been used to discriminate against people on the basis of color or race. *Katzenbach v. Morgan*, 384 U.S. 641 (1966), pitted Nicholas deBelleville Katzenbach as attorney general of the United States against John and Christine Morgan, citizens of New York, who had argued that the U.S. Congress had overstepped its bounds and usurped powers reserved to the states in the Tenth Amendment, in seeking to void a section of the New York Constitution.

A district court agreed with the Morgans. Justice William J. Brennan, referring to Section Five of the **Fourteenth Amendment** and the so-called Supremacy clause of Article VI of the United States Constitution, reversed the district court ruling in his opinion for the United States Supreme Court.

The Court upheld the constitutionality of the Voting Rights Act of 1965, as well as the broader right of Congress to enforce the equal protection clause of the Fourteenth Amendment by means of appropriate legislation. (AJC)

BIBLIOGRAPHY

Carter, Stephen L. "The Morgan 'Power' and the Forced Reconsideration of Constitutional Decisions." *University of Chicago Law Review* 53 (Summer 1986): 819–63.

Neary, Jonathan. "Poker-faced Lawman on the Spot." *Life* 60 (May 6, 1966): 49–50.

Sharon Pratt Dixon Kelly (1944–)

In 1990, Attorney Sharon Pratt Kelly (then Dixon) became the first black woman elected mayor of the nation's capital and the first black female mayor of any major city in the United States. National **Democratic Party** treasurer and the District of Columbia's woman representative to the Democratic National Committee, Kelly was better known nationally than locally when she launched her bid for mayor. She was elected by a coalition of upscale blacks and whites in an atmosphere of dissatisfaction over years of rising taxes, declining services, a municipal budget deficit of more than $200 million, and the conviction of former Mayor **Marion Barry** on a drug charge. Her chief campaign promise was to "clean house" and bring the District's finances under control, and although she eliminated the jobs of nearly 2,000 city employees through attrition and layoffs, the changes proved to be neither broad nor deep enough to close the gap between the District's revenues and its expenditures. Facing a rising crescendo of complaints from Congress and growing disaffection among all class and race segments of the city, Kelly was defeated by Barry in 1994. She bequeathed Barry a deficit twice the size she had inherited, setting the stage for imperiling the District's home rule. (LFW)

BIBLIOGRAPHY

Harden, Blaine. "Chapter Seven: 1990–1994." *Washington Post* (June 18, 1995): 1.

Alan L. Keyes (1950–)

Alan L. Keyes served in government as a Reagan administration appointee. He has been ambassador to the U.N. Economic and Social Council. Keyes was defeated when he ran on the Republican ticket against the incumbent Paul Sarbanes for a Senate seat in Maryland in 1988. He unsuccessfully ran against the other Maryland senator, Barbara Mikulski, in 1992. He received 38 and 29 percent of the vote in the respective general elections.

In 1996 Keyes ran to obtain the Republican nomination for president, the only African American attempting to lead a major party that year. He was recognized as an eloquent speaker, but he failed to win any significant support in the primaries. He is currently a talk show host. (WWH)

BIBLIOGRAPHY

Ireland, Doug. "Alan Keyes Does the Hustle." *The Nation* 261, no. 14 (October 30, 1995): 500.

Lewis, Michael. "The Messenger: Campaign Journal." *New Republic* 214, no. 9 (February 26, 1996): 24.

Merida, Kevin. "The Serious Non-Contender: Look for Keyes' Return at the GOP Convention." *Emerge* 7, no. 8 (June 1996): 18.

Stengel, Richard. "Moralist on the March: The Silver-tongued Alan Keyes Has Surprised the GOP by Mounting a Vigorous Presidential Campaign." *Time* 146, no. 10 (September 4, 1995): 33.

Keyes v. School District No. 1, Denver, Colorado (1973)

In *Keyes v. School District No. 1, Denver, Colorado*, 413 U.S. 189 (1973), a ruling that for the first time acknowledged the problem of racial segregation in public schools in the North, the Supreme Court held that a finding of intentionally segregative school board actions in a significant portion of school systems created a prima facie case of unlawful segregated design on the part of school authorities, and shifted to those authorities the burden of proving that other segregated schools within the system were not the result of intentionally segregative actions. (PLF)

BIBLIOGRAPHY

Baker, Keith. "Selecting Students for Bilingual Education under the Keyes Agreement." *La Raza Law Journal* 1, no. 3 (Fall 1986): 330–41.

Fishman, James J. and Lawrence Strauss. "Endless Journey: Integration and the Provision of Equal Educational Opportunity in Denver's Public Schools: A Study of *Keyes v. School District No. 1*." *Howard Law Journal* 32, no. 3 (Fall 1989): 627–728.

Carolyn Cheeks Kilpatrick (1945–)

Carolyn Kilpatrick was born in Detroit and received her M.S. from the University of Michigan. She was a teacher in the Detroit school system until she was elected to the Michigan House of Representatives as a Democrat in 1978 where she chaired the Black Caucus from 1983 to 1984 and is currently a member of the appropriations committee. Reelected to Congress since first serving in 1978, Kilpatrick has become a leading voice for African Americans on Capitol Hill. (JCW)

BIBLIOGRAPHY

"Black Caucus Members Keep Their Strength in House in 1996 Election." *Jet* (November 25, 1996): 4.

Coretta Scott King (1927–)

Coretta Scott King has fought for peace and racial equality through five decades, carrying on the legacy of her late husband **Martin Luther King, Jr.** She led the fight for a national holiday in his honor, and has promoted education in nonviolence for young people.

Born in rural Alabama, Coretta Scott attended the New England Conservatory of Music, where she met Martin King in 1951. They married in 1953. While raising four children, Coretta King played a strong supporting role as her husband became a civil rights leader. She participated in marches and fundraising concerts over the years, helping to achieve victories such as the **Voting Rights Act of 1965**.

After her husband's death in 1968, she founded the Martin Luther King, Jr. Center for Nonviolent Social Change in

Atlanta, where she has kept alive his legacy through educational programs. Though relatively uninvolved in campaign politics, she supported Jimmy Carter's presidential campaign in 1976. She took part in his inauguration and served as a delegate to the United Nations. In 1984, she refrained from endorsing **Jesse Jackson's** campaign, contending that Walter Mondale had a better chance of beating Ronald Reagan.

Coretta King helped establish Martin Luther King Day in 1986 and coordinated the annual national celebration each year thereafter. Although she passed control of the King Center on to her children in the 1990s, she has remained a powerful figure in the ongoing struggle for peace and justice. (AD)

BIBLIOGRAPHY

Coretta Scott King. *My Life with Martin Luther King, Jr.* rev. ed. New York: Henry Holt, 1993.

Lynn Norment, "The Woman Behind the King Anniversary." *Ebony* (January 1990): 116–22.

Martin Luther King, Jr. (1929–1968)

Born the son of his namesake, who was the pastor of Atlanta, Georgia's Ebenezer Baptist Church, Martin Luther King, Jr. went on to become the single most influential and eloquent voice for the civil rights of people of color and for all Americans, and a figure recognized throughout the world for his courageous leadership of many organizations and movements.

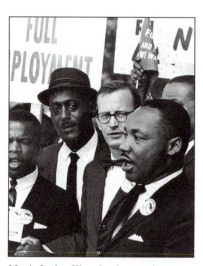

Admitted to Morehouse College when he was 15, King went on to studies at Crozer Theological Seminary, and Boston University, where he received his Ph.D. in 1955. In the preceding year, King and his new wife, Coretta Scott King, returned to Coretta's native Alabama, where King took the position of pastor of Montgomery's Dexter Avenue Baptist Church.

Martin Luther King, Jr., the most important figure in the Civil Rights Movement, advocated peaceful methods to obtain change. *National Archives.*

King was chosen to lead the newly founded **Montgomery Improvement Association** in the wake of the bus boycott begun by Rosa Parks' refusal to yield her seat to a white passenger in December of 1955. Within a year, a federal court had ordered that the buses in Montgomery be desegregated. This important victory led to similar protests using King's tactics in a number of cities, from Birmingham, to Tallahassee, to New Orleans. King and others, including **Ralph D. Abernathy, Joseph E. Lowery,** and Fred L. Shuttlesworth, successfully combined elements of slain Indian leader Mohandas K. Gandhi's method of satyagraha, or active but entirely non-violent resistance and civil disobedience, with notions taken from Christian teachings, and tactics based on a practical, savvy understanding of politics as driven by the media. King soon began to take his position as a leader in the growing civil rights movement in the United States, helping to found the **Southern Christian Leadership Conference (SCLC)** in 1959 in Atlanta, where King had moved, and becoming co-pastor in his father's influential church.

Initial setbacks to his efforts at combating segregation through carefully planned, passive sit-ins in Albany, Georgia, led to a more active but still nonviolent approach used in Birmingham, Alabama, in the early months of 1963. The local authorities, led by Theophilus Eugene "Bull" Connor, responded with cruelty and brutality. These shocking scenes were broadcast on television and covered by all forms of media around the country and the world. This elevated the question of segregation—and King's stature and influence—even further. King's arrest and his subsequent "Letter from a Birmingham Jail" in April clarified to all the level of racism and degree of injustice that people of color had been forced to endure in the South, and why direct and immediate action was necessary.

In August of 1963, the SCLC helped to organize the **March on Washington.** His **"I Have a Dream"** speech during the massive Washington march is often considered among the most important and memorable orations given in American history. The **Civil Rights Act of 1964** soon followed (the passage of which also benefitted from President John F. Kennedy's support). That same year, King was awarded the Nobel Peace Prize. King and his SCLC then targeted Selma, Alabama, but this time drawing attention to the many barriers to voting registration and voting itself that Selma's African Americans faced. The local authorities acted with similar brutality to that shown by their counterparts in Birmingham. Soon after, the **Voting Rights Act of 1965** was passed.

With the growing racial tensions and then race riots in northern cities, King's efforts in subsequent years were centered largely on such cities as Chicago, Cleveland, and Louisville. This was part of a larger campaign to begin to shift the focus in his work away from purely racial issues to the burden of poverty afflicting Americans—and people everywhere—of all colors. In this period, King began to oppose the Vietnam War, leading to ever-closer scrutiny and infiltration of his organizations by federal authorities. While King was planning his "Poor People's March on Washington" to highlight his new approach, he was assassinated on April 4, 1968, in Memphis, Tennessee, where he had gone to support striking sanitation workers.

Even in death, King's legacy continues to be one that shapes American politics. As an example, a national holiday named in King's honor and first observed in 1986 has often become the source of political posturing by those who wish to identify themselves with—or oppose themselves to—the civil rights and liberties of people of color and other minorities. (AJC)

BIBLIOGRAPHY

Garrow, David J. *Bearing the Cross: The Southern Christian Leadership Conference and Martin Luther King, Jr.* New York: William Morrow, 1986.

Lewis, David L. *King: A Critical Biography.* New York: Praeger, 1970.

Oates, Stephen B. *Let the Trumpet Sound: The Life of Martin Luther King, Jr.* New York: Harper and Row, 1982.

Ron Kirk (1954–)

Ron Kirk was born in Austin, Texas, and received his J.D. from the University of Texas in 1979. He worked as legislative assistant to Senator Lloyd Bentsen from 1981 to 1983 and was the assistant city attorney and chief lobbyist for the city of Dallas from 1983 to 1989. He was elected mayor of Dallas, as a Democrat, in 1995. (JCW)

BIBLIOGRAPHY

Verhovek, Sam. "Dallas Is First Big City to Elect a Black to Be Mayor." *New York Times* (May 8, 1995): A11.

Ku Klux Klan (KKK)

Formed originally in 1871 by a group of six young Confederate veterans of the **Civil War,** The Ku Klux Klan was established in the small town of Pulaski, Tennessee, on December 15, 1865. The founders included Captain John C. Lester, Major James R. Crowe, John B. Kennedy, Calvin Jones, Richard R. Reed, and Frank O. McCord. The name derives from the Greek word *kuklos,* which means circle or band. At the time of its establishment, the word was part of the title of a popular fraternity, Kuklos Adelphon.

The Ku Klux Klan (KKK) has been well known as an advocate of white power and segregation. Klan members, who wear uniforms or costumes made from white sheets, and pointed hats, have been involved in numerous violent acts against African Americans including cross burnings, hang-

The Ku Klux Klan's membership was strongest immediately after the Civil War, but also increased during the 1920s. Pictured here is an initiation ceremony held in Mississippi in 1923. *Library of Congress.*

ings, shootings, church bombings, and beatings since the KKK's beginning in the deep South following the Civil War. Although African Americans are the primary target of the KKK, the organization also preaches intolerance of Jews, Catholics, and almost any other racial or religious minority. Its revival in 1915, following a wave of European immigration, spread into a national movement that still exists in the 1990s. (VDD)

BIBLIOGRAPHY

Fredrickson, Kari. *The Ku Klux Klan of the 1920s.* Armouk, NJ: M.E. Sharpe Inc., 1998.

MacLean, Nancy K. *Behind the Mask of Chivalry.* New York: Oxford University Press, Inc., 1995.

Nelson, Jack. *Terror in the Night.* Jackson: University Press of Mississippi, 1996.

Ku Klux Klan Act (1871)

The **Ku Klux Klan's** ostensible purpose was to protect white Protestant southern society and culture from black "pollution," although other racial, ethnic, and religious minority groups were targeted as well. It committed numerous acts of violence, and no degree of romanticization can begin to excuse its brutality. Faced with inability to control the violence of the Klan, **Reconstruction** governments looked to the federal government for help.

Congress passed a series of laws to face the problem. Adopted in 1870 and 1871, a series of Enforcement Acts, including the Ku Klux Klan Act of 1871 were passed by Congress in hopes of ending the savagery. The first act, a criminal code of elections, forbade state officials from discriminating among voters on the basis of race and authorized the president to appoint election supervisors with the power to bring corruption or violence cases to the federal courts. The second act strengthened enforcement powers in large cities. The failure of these acts to end Klan violence led Congress to enact a more radical measure—the Ku Klux Klan Act of April 1871, declaring that the combined acts of unlawful harassment or terrorism committed by the Klan constituted a rebellion against the U.S. Government, and that in areas where such workings were occurring, the president could suspend the privilege of the writ of habeas corpus and proclaim martial law.

The first Klan was effectively ended. Some Klan leaders were even punished. However, the general situation in the country had changed, and soon an alliance of southern Democrats and conservative Republicans ended Reconstruction and its promise, leaving southern African Americans without a political voice and generally without any economic power and with very little hope for social equality and justice for wrongs committed against them by the KKK. (FAS)

BIBLIOGRAPHY

Haas, Ben. *KKK.* Evanston: Regency Books, 1963.

Ridgeway, James. *Blood in the Face.* New York: Thunder's Mouth Press, 1995.

Tyler, Charles Waller. *The K.K.K.* Freeport, NY: Books for Libraries Press, 1972.

L

Lane v. Wilson et al. (1939)

Lane v. Wilson et al., 307 U.S. 268 (1939), is a case which originated in Oklahoma concerning voter registration. In the wake of *Guinn v. United States* (1915), in which the Court invalidated the "**grandfather clause**," Oklahoma passed a statute requiring that anyone eligible to vote in 1916 must register within a three-week period or face perpetual disenfranchisement. Whites were "grandfathered" in, since their ancestors were on voting lists in 1914. In 1934, I.W. Lane, a black, was denied registration based upon the state statute. The Court held that the Oklahoma statute violated the **Fifteenth Amendment.** (CJM)

BIBLIOGRAPHY

Barker, Lucius and Twiley W. Barker, Jr. *Civil Liberties and the Constitution: Cases and Commentaries.* Upper Saddle River, NJ: Prentice-Hall, 1999.
——. *Freedom, Courts, Politics: Studies in Civil Liberties.* Englewood Cliffs, NJ: Prentice-Hall, 1972.

John Mercer Langston (1829–1897)

An emancipated slave, Republican John Mercer Langston became one of the first African Americans elected to public office in 1855. During the **Civil War**, Langston spoke on behalf of African Americans who were attempting to enlist in the United States Army. In 1877 Langston was sent to Haiti as an official representative of the United States, where he investigated the political and economic conditions of the island. After a contested election in 1888, Langston was seated in the United States House of Representatives in 1890. (DH)

BIBLIOGRAPHY

Cheek, William and Aimee Lee Cheek. *John Mercer Langston and the Fight for Black Freedom.* Urbana: University of Illinois Press, 1989.

Lassiter v. Northampton County Board of Electors (1959)

In *Lassiter v. Northampton Board of Electors*, 369 U.S. 45 (1959), the U.S. Supreme Court upheld state literacy tests as a qualification for voting. Lassiter, a black North Carolinian who refused to submit to a test, argued that the qualification was an unconstitutional limitation on a fundamental right. Writing for the majority, Justice William O. Douglas concluded that states must ensure that their standards are not discriminatory and do not contravene any restriction that Congress has imposed. Without evidence of racial bias, the literacy test was allowable under the Constitution. "Certainly," Douglas concluded, "we cannot condemn it on its face as a device unrelated to the desire of North Carolina to raise the standards for people of all races who cast the ballot." (KC)

BIBLIOGRAPHY

Grofman, Bernard, Lisa Handley, and Richard G. Niemi. *Minority Representation and the Quest for Voting Equality.* New York: Cambridge University Press, 1992.
Kousser, J. Morgan. *The Shaping of Southern Politics.* New Haven, CT: Yale University Press, 1974.

Leadership Conference on Civil Rights

The Leadership Conference on Civil Rights was organized in 1950 by **A. Philip Randolph, Roy Wilkins**, and Arnold Aronson to implement the recommendations of President Harry S. Truman's **Presidential Committee on Civil Rights**. The Committee had published a report entitled "To Secure These Rights," which urged greater federal involvement in promoting racial equality, endorsed the removal of the poll tax and other discriminatory obstacles to voting, recommended the creation of a Civil Rights Division in the Department of Justice, and encouraged desegregation in the armed forces, interstate transportation, and government employment. Black leaders used the Leadership Conference to demand presidential leadership and commitment to civil rights to counteract the intense pressure on President Truman from southern white politicians to move slowly on racial matters. The Conference has been responsible for coordinating the campaigns for the successful passage of the **Civil Rights Acts of 1957**, **1960, and 1964; the Voting Rights Act of 1965; and the Open Housing Act of 1968** (the Fair Housing Act). Presently the Leadership Conference on Civil Rights includes approximately 157 organizations representing ethnic and racial minorities (e.g., Latinos, Asian Americans, and Jews, as well as African Americans) women, major religious groups, the disabled, the aged, labor unions, and minority businesses and professions. (EC)

BIBLIOGRAPHY

Stanfield, Rochelle L. "In Person." *National Journal* 28, no. 46 (1996): 2501.

Watson, Denton. *Lion in the Lobby: Clarence Mitchell, Jr.'s Struggle for the Passage of CR Laws.* New York: Morrow 1990.

Sheila Jackson Lee (1950–)

In 1994, Sheila Jackson Lee, a Democrat from Texas, was elected to the United States House of Representatives, serving the district that includes central Houston. Prior to being elected to Congress, Lee was a member of the Houston City Council from 1990 to 1994 and served as a municipal judge from 1987 to 1990. Lee also served on the United States House Select Committee on Assassinations as staff counsel from 1977 to 1978. In the House, she currently serves on the Judiciary Committee and the Science Committee. **See also** Congressional Black Caucus.

BIBLIOGRAPHY

Gill, LaVerne McCain. *African American Women in Congress.* New Brunswick, NJ: Rutgers University Press, 1997.

Lee v. Macon County Board of Education (1967)

In *Lee v. Macon County Board of Education*, 389 U.S. 25 (1967), the Supreme Court struck down one of the earliest uses of the voucher principle when parents used state school grants to send their children to private institutions in an effort to avoid desegregation. The Supreme Court affirmed a lower court decision ordering the desegregation of Alabama's school districts and declared state school grants to white students attending segregated private schools unconstitutional. (VDD)

BIBLIOGRAPHY

D'Amato, Anthony A., Rosemary Metrailer, and Stephen L. Wasby. *Desegregation from Brown to Alexander.* Carbondale, IL: Southern Illinois University Press, 1977.

McGough, Lucy S. and Frank T. Read. *Let Them Be Judged: The Judicial Integration of the Deep South.* Metuchen, NJ: The Scarecrow Press, Inc., 1978.

Mickey Leland (1944–1989)

A six-term Congressional Representative, Democrat Mickey Leland worked tirelessly to eliminate global and domestic hunger and malnutrition. After graduating from Texas southern University with a degree in pharmacy, he provided free medical screenings to poor communities in Texas. In Congress, Leland sponsored legislation creating the National Commission on Infant Mortality and providing public services to the homeless as chairman of the Select Committee on Hunger, and he headed numerous congressional delegations to Africa. Leland died in a plane crash in Ethiopia while bringing relief to a UN refugee camp. (CC)

BIBLIOGRAPHY

Leland, Mickey. *The Politics of Hunger among Blacks.* Self-published. 1990.

USIA. Special Report: Mickey Leland. Washington, DC: USIA, 1989.

John Robert Lewis (1940–)

John Robert Lewis was born on February 21, 1940, in Troy, Alabama, the son of a sharecropper. Lewis received his first B.A. degree in 1961 from American Baptist Theological Seminary in Nashville, Tennessee. While at the seminary, Lewis met and befriended student activist Diane Nash and joined the rapidly expanding **civil rights movement**. The two formed the Nashville Student Movement, which organized sit-ins and demonstrations to protest segregation. In 1960 he became a founding member of **Student Nonviolent Coordinating Committee (SNCC)** and served as chairman of the organization from 1963 to 1966. During that period he participated in the Freedom Rides and the Mississippi Freedom Summer Project. In 1965 he was a visible leader of the Selma to Montgomery march. In 1966, Lewis left SNCC and began working on voter registration projects with the **Southern Regional Council and the Voter Educational Project.** In 1967, he received his second B.A. from Fisk University, and by 1970 he was actively involved in politics. Jimmy Carter appointed him to a federal agency in 1977. Then, in 1982 he was elected at-large to the Atlanta City Council. In 1986 he won a seat in the House of Representatives as a Democrat, a position he continues to hold. (AAB)

BIBLIOGRAPHY

Branch, Taylor. *Parting the Waters: America in the King Years 1954–1963.* New York: Simon and Schuster, 1988.

Liberalism

Liberalism represents a tradition of political thought that is difficult to define precisely, for the term contains within it a set of diverse philosophical and ideological positions. However, when viewed historically liberalism can be traced with some coherence as a movement of ideas developing within the discourse of modern and contemporary western politics. In short, we might say that in liberalism we find "unity in diversity." The primary concern here is with understanding how liberalism in its American context affects minority groups in the American political system.

Liberalism as a set of political ideas has its origins in the seventeenth century. We can identify two basic concepts around which the liberal political tradition revolves. The first centers on the idea of liberty. Liberalism has always expressed a singular commitment to the significance and value of individual freedom. In other words, the basic political unit under liberalism is the individual, and the goals of society are thereby defined in terms of individual interest. Thus, the diverse strands of liberal political thinking approach the problem of organizing state and society in a way that is capable of maximizing freedom for all its citizens.

A second principle of liberalism concerns some basic notion of equality. Liberalism holds fast to the belief that all individuals in society should be equal under the eyes of the law, i.e., that politically the state is impartial in its treatment of individuals. Law must be accepted and applied universally. At the same time, it should not be administered arbitrarily.

For this reason, constitutionalism and the rule of law have become fundamental precepts of liberalism, since it is through the creation of universally accepted and applied laws that at least a rudimentary level of equality is ensured.

Notions of liberty and equality have formed the backbone of the liberal ethos for over three centuries. However, questions arise at this point: Which liberty? What type of equality? Liberty and equality have meant different things to different people at different points of history. It is for this reason that liberalism is characterized by internal tensions, ideological splits, and political deviations over the course of the last three centuries. Briefly, we shall look at the major strands of liberal thought before coming back to the American context and the position of minorities within it.

We can divide liberalism into two categories: classical liberalism and contemporary liberalism. John Locke (1632–1704) defined the classical liberal position most succinctly. In his *Second Treatise of Government* (1690), Locke argued that governments were formed by consent to protect "natural rights" given to individuals by God. These were: life, liberty, and property. To this degree, individuals in political society were equal. Beyond that basic function, government played little if any role in the private lives of individuals. For Locke, society should be characterized by limited government because the state was seen more as an impediment to individual liberty than as a facilitator. Thus, he held to what we would call a "negative" view of the state.

Locke's work defined liberalism as a set of political ideas for a century after his death, and it served as a springboard for the economic doctrine of laissez-faire capitalism which found its most forceful articulation in Adam Smith's *Wealth of Nations* (1776). Yet, as England underwent the social and economic changes wrought by the industrial revolution, liberal thinkers began to question whether Locke's "negative" state was adequate for meeting the challenges of the day. Social and economic inequalities forced liberals to rethink the relationship between liberty and equality and the state's role in ensuring both.

At this point, the classical liberal position begins to move in the direction of what we have identified as contemporary liberalism. Jeremy Bentham (1748–1832) argued for a more "positive" state that focused on government's role in the promotion of equality as well as liberty. Bentham advocated for an active government which pursued several policies, including: (1) maintaining an ordered and rational legal system; (2) securing wealth and prosperity of its citizens by ensuring that they receive the rewards of their labor; (3) moderating the extreme forms of economic, political, intellectual and moral inequality whenever possible through the principle of utility (the greatest happiness for the greatest number); and (4) cultivating the spirit of benevolence among its citizens.

With Bentham in the late eighteenth and early nineteenth centuries, liberalism took on a more interventionist view of the state. Later thinkers would further carry liberalism in the direction of a positive state. In *On Liberty* (1859), John Stuart Mill (1806–1873) revised Bentham's utilitarian theories by arguing that human happiness was grounded in intellectual development as well as physical notions of pleasure and pain. In turn, intellectual development led to social progress. Real social and cultural progress presupposed that individuals would be allowed to challenge most elements of public opinion. This could only be accomplished through a state which not only tolerated but actually promoted and protected the practice of individual criticism and dissent. Mill's version of liberalism therefore called for a common good cultivated by state and based upon individual freedom of speech and thought.

Late nineteenth and early twentieth century liberal thinkers such as T.H. Green (1836–1882) and Thomas Dewey (1859–1952) embraced contemporary liberalism and the positive state theorized in the earlier works of Bentham and Mills. In effect, these thinkers continued to move liberalism toward the view that state power is a trustee of individual liberty and equality rather than a potential intrusion into them, as classical liberal theory held.

The two versions of liberalism discussed here have essentially divided over the role of the state in the preservation of the fundamental tenets of liberalism: liberty and equality. Contemporary liberalism generally views state power in a benign or positive light when it comes to ensuring the basic values of liberty and equality. On the other side, classical liberalism holds that state power is a threat to liberty (and by extension equality) and should therefore be minimalized. Given this context, where does one place the United States in the tradition of liberalism? Further, what impact does "American liberalism" have on the place and role of minority groups in the American political system?

It has been said that America, through the creation of the Constitution, is the quintessential Lockeian liberal society. The creation of checks and balances which limit government power, the guaranteed protection of private property, and the creation of a Bill of Rights which enumerates basic individual liberties are all examples of Locke's influence on the framers of the Constitution. Questions concerning the development of American liberalism and the commitment to the precepts of liberty and equality do, however, arise.

The case of African Americans serves as the most prominent example. In this quintessential Lockeian liberal society, slavery was constitutionally protected for nearly a century, as blacks were denied both liberty and equality. After liberty was granted, blacks in most of the South were denied the barest requisites of equality, as legal segregation and political disenfranchisement were imposed for almost another century. In a society governed by a constitution which was intended to "secure the Blessings of Liberty," blacks have found American liberalism lacking, the trustee of neither liberty nor equality for much of American history. A history of struggle has left blacks wondering whether they are "of the world" of American liberalism, repeatedly seeking an answer to the famous question asked by W.E.B. Du Bois in *The Souls of Black Folk*: "How does it feel to be a problem?"

Only through strong state intervention have blacks in the United States enjoyed the fundamental tenets of the liberal ethos. The **Thirteenth, Fourteenth,** and **Fifteenth Amendments** were passed in the wake of the **Civil War** which constitutionally protected liberty and equality by, respectively, ending involuntary servitude, ensuring equal protection of the law, and guaranteeing the right to vote. In the period of **Reconstruction** (1865–1877), the federal government safeguarded the protection of fundamental liberties in the post-war South as blacks were elected to state and national political office for the first time. Yet, when the last federal troops pulled out of the South signaling the end of Reconstruction, the political and civil liberties of blacks were violated as most southern states came under **Jim Crow** laws and legal segregation.

Not until the 1960s, a period many thinkers have termed "the Second Reconstruction," did blacks in the South regain the basic political and civil liberties that were afforded to all other Americans. Once again, strong federal intervention was necessary to effect such social changes. Images of federal troops protecting black children as they attended newly integrated southern schools in the wake of ***Brown v. Board of Education*** (1954) inhabit American minds. The passage of the **Civil Rights Act of 1964** and the **Voting Rights Act of 1965** reinforced the Fourteenth and Fifteenth Amendments by targeting specific practices of discrimination and providing remedies for them, thus ensuring that the political and civil liberties of blacks would be protected under the watchful eye of the federal government.

In short, throughout the history of the United States, blacks have found that the basic principles of liberalism outlined here—liberty and equality—are only secured when strong state intervention is present. Thus, it is no coincidence that as a group blacks tend to favor a contemporary liberal perspective as opposed to the classical liberal perspective. Attitudes toward affirmative action are but one example of this. African Americans view the national government as a guarantor of liberty and equality because history has shown that a positive, interventionist state was the only thing that stood between them and servitude or second-class citizenry.

To be sure, African-American history is quite distinct and exceptional in the pages of the American narrative. Nonetheless, this is a significant finding as we attempt to assess the overall impact of American liberalism on the position of minority groups as they struggle for liberty and equality in the American political system. Given a current political climate in which many of the "positive," welfare state policies enacted over the previous 60 years face termination, prospects for the return to a more classical liberal perspective—laissez-faire style government— are very real. President Bill Clinton affirmed as much in his 1995 "State of the Union Address" when he stated that "the era of the government is over." This is nothing new in the American version of liberalism. Yet, in the minds of minority groups in the United States, questions concerning the protection of the basic principles of the liberal ethos—liberty and equality—may also resurface. (CJM)

BIBLIOGRAPHY

Bentham, Jeremy. *Fragment on Government and an Introduction to the Principles of Morals and Legislation.* Wilfred Harrison, ed. Oxford: Basil Blackwell, 1967.

Dewey, John. *The Public and Its Problem.* New York: Henry Holt, 1927.

Du Bois, W.E.B. *The Souls of Black Folk.* New York: New American Library, 1969.

Locke, John. *Two Treatises of Government.* New York: New American Library, 1965.

Marable, Manning. *Race, Reform and Rebellion: The Second Reconstruction in Black America, 1945–1982.* Jackson: University Press of Mississippi, 1984.

McClelland, J.S. *A History of Western Political Thought.* New York: Routledge Press, 1996.

Mill, John Stuart. *On Liberty.* Stefan Collini, ed. New York: Cambridge University Press, 1989.

Wiser, James L. *Political Philosophy: A History of the Search for Order.* Englewood Cliffs, NJ: Prentice Hall, 1983.

The Liberator

The Liberator was a radical anti-slavery newspaper first published by William Lloyd Garrison in 1831. Invoking the rhetoric contained within the Declaration of Independence, Garrison demanded immediate and unconditional emancipation for all southern slaves. Southern slaveholders blamed the incendiary remarks within the *Liberator* for causing the unsuccessful insurrection led by **Nat Turner** in Virginia. As a result, slaveholders increasingly demanded government protection for their peculiar institution, and anti-slavery became an issue which dominated America until the outbreak of the **Civil War.** (KR)

BIBLIOGRAPHY

Tyler, Alice. *Freedom's Ferment: Phases of American Social History from the Colonial Period to the Outbreak of the Civil War.* New York: Harper and Row, 1962.

Walters, Ronald G. *American Reformers, 1815–1860.* New York: Hill and Wang, 1978.

Literacy Tests

As a result of the qualification that voters be required to demonstrate an ability to "read, write and understand" the English language, some states created literacy tests specifically to counteract the **Reconstruction** enfranchisement of blacks. The tests easily disqualified former slaves because of forced illiteracy, but illiterate whites were often unaffected due to "grandather clauses" exempting from such tests those whose grandfathers could vote in previous elections. After literacy rates rose in the black community, some registrars devised special, complicated exams designed to disqualify would-be black voters. Literacy tests were suspended by the **Voting Rights Act of 1965.** (KC)

BIBLIOGRAPHY

Grofman, Bernard, Lisa Handley, and Richard G. Niemi. *Minority Representation and the Quest for Voting Equality.* New York: Cambridge University Press, 1992.

Woodward, C. Vann. *Origins of the New South, 1877–1913.* Baton Rouge: Louisiana State University Press, 1971.

Local Number 93, International Association of Firefighters v. City of Cleveland (1986)

In *Local Number 93, International Association of Firefighters v. City of Cleveland*, 478 U.S. 501 (1986), African-American and Hispanic firefighters filed a class action against the City of Cleveland claiming discrimination in hiring, assigning, and promoting firefighters. The firefighters' union intervened as a party plaintiff, and the union objected when the city agreed to a consent decree which employed a race-conscious solution to the grievance. The Supreme Court held that Congress intended for employers to comply voluntarily to correct discriminatory practices, and that it does not matter if some of the firefighters who were helped by the consent decree were not victims of discrimination. (FHJ)

BIBLIOGRAPHY

Fischer, Louis. "Voluntary Race-Conscious Affirmative Action Plans: The Significance of Two Recent Supreme Court Decisions." (*International Association of Firefighters v. City of Cleveland; Wygant v. Jackson Board of Education*) *Equity & Excellence* 23, no. 1–2 (Spring 1987): 81.

Jefferson Franklin Long (1836–1901)

Jefferson Franklin Long, a former slave, served in the United States House of Representatives (R-GA) from 1869 to 1871. He was one of the founders of Georgia's state Republican Party and worked to register African Americans to vote. He is the only African American to serve in Congress from Georgia in the nineteenth century. Disappointed with his own treatment in Congress by white Republicans, he encouraged blacks to support candidates from either party who served their interests.

BIBLIOGRAPHY

Rees, Matthew. *From the Deck to the Sea.* Wakefield, NH: Longwood Academic, 1991.

Walton, Hanes. *Black Republicans.* Metuchen, NJ: Scarecrow, 1975.

Louisiana et al. v. United States (1964)

Decided just months before President Lyndon Johnson signed the **Voting Rights Act of 1965**, *Louisiana et al. v. United States*, 380 U.S. 145 (1964), focused on a voter registration practice that sought to unlawfully deprive African Americans of their voting rights. The practice in question was known as the interpretation test, instituted in the state constitution of 1921 to replace the "grandfather clause" which had been declared unconstitutional by the Supreme Court in 1915. Citizens registering to vote were required to give a reasonable interpretation of any section of the state or federal Constitution. The Supreme Court found the test a violation of the **Fourteenth** and **Fifteenth Amendments**. (CJM)

BIBLIOGRAPHY

D'Amato, Anthony A., Rosemary Metrailer, and Stephen L. Wasby. *Desegregation from Brown to Alexander.* Carbondale, IL: Southern Illinois University Press, 1977.

Loving v. Virginia (1967)

Loving v. Virginia, 388 U.S. 1 (1967) involved a challenge to Virginia's anti-miscegenation statute. The Court had dodged the issue for a decade after **Brown v. Board of Education**, reasoning that it was better to move cautiously on the issue. In this case, Mildred Jeter, a black woman, and Richard Loving, a white male, were married in Washington, D.C., and moved to Virginia, where they were arrested and charged with violating the law. The Loving couple pleaded guilty and were sentenced to a year in jail, but the sentence was suspended on the condition that the couple leave the state of Virginia and not return for 25 years.

The Supreme Court unanimously declared the law unconstitutional as a violation of the Due Process and Equal Protection clauses of the **Fourteenth Amendment.** The Court ruled that marriage was a fundamental right, triggering strict scrutiny of the anti-miscegenation law, and that the state had no legitimate reason for the law. The decision continued the incremental process of dismantling de jure racial discrimination that began with *Brown*. (RLP)

BIBLIOGRAPHY

Pritchett, C. Herman. *Constitutional Civil Liberties.* Englewood Cliffs, NJ: Prentice Hall, 1984.

Joseph E. Lowery (1921–)

Joseph E. Lowery was president of the **Southern Christian Leadership Conference (SCLC)** from 1977 to 1997. He is a retired Methodist clergyman. In 1957, Lowery cofounded SCLC with **Martin Luther King, Jr.** Lowery remains a firm believer in integration and opposes separatists of any race. Lowery battled the Reagan administration's attempt to curtail civil rights legislation. He also led SCLC in opposition to Reagan's Central American policy, leading the Federal Bureau of Investigation to put the organization under careful watch. Lowery worked to end apartheid in South Africa. His last great campaign as head of the SCLC was to challenge law enforcement officials to do more to solve the 1995 bombings of black churches. (FAS)

BIBLIOGRAPHY

Peake, Thomas R. *Keeping the Dream Alive: A History of the southern Christian Leadership Conference from King to the Nineteen-Eighties.* New York: Peter Lang, 1987.

Lucy v. Adams (1955)

In 1952 Autherine Lucy and Polly Anne Myers sought admission to the University of Alabama, but were denied due to their race and were referred to all-black institutions in Alabama's racially segregated higher education system. In *Lucy v. Adams*, 350 U.S. 1 (1955), the Supreme Court permanently enjoined university officials from denying the qualified students admission based on their race. To deny students equal access to higher education merely because of their race is unconstitutional, concluded the High Court. (FHJ)

BIBLIOGRAPHY

D'Amato, Anthony A., Rosemary Metrailer, and Stephen L. Wasby. *Desegregation from Brown to Alexander.* Carbondale, IL: Southern Illinois University Press, 1977.

Greenberg, Jack. *Race Relations and American Law.* New York: Columbia University Press, 1959.

John R. Lynch (1847–1939)

A former slave, Republican John R. Lynch served as Speaker of the House during his second term in the Mississippi House of Representatives. During his three terms in the United States House of Representatives, Lynch actively promoted civil rights, education, and protective tariffs. (DH)

BIBLIOGRAPHY

Franklin, John Hope, ed. *The Autobiography of John Roy Lynch.* Chicago: University of Chicago Press, 1970.

M

Charles H. Mahoney (1886–1966)

Charles H. Mahoney was appointed as the first African-American permanent delegate to the United Nations (UN) on August 7, 1954, by President Dwight D. Eisenhower. Mahoney served the United States at the UN until he retired from public life in 1959. Prior to his appointment to the UN, he was a commissioner of the Department of Labor and Industry in Michigan (1922–1954).

BIBLIOGRAPHY

"This Week in Black History" *Jet* (June 1, 1998): 19.

Malcolm X (1925–1965)

Malcolm X was born Malcolm Little on May 19, 1925, in Omaha, Nebraska. Malcolm dropped out of school in the eighth grade and embarked on a life of crime. Malcolm made a name for himself as a street hustler until going to jail from 1946 to 1952. He converted to Islam and discovered the **Nation of Islam.** The group's leader, **Elijah Muhammad,** taught Malcolm the organization's message of black pride, self-help, and racial separation.

In 1952, Malcolm moved to Detroit and then Harlem where he organized 40 mosques for the group, rising to national spokesman for the organization. By the early 1960s relations between him and Elijah Muhammad had become strained. In March 1964, Malcolm left the nation and went to Mecca. Upon his return, he moderated his views and began to give tacit support to the **civil rights movement.** He formed two organizations: the Muslim Mosque, Inc., and the **Organization of Afro-American Unity.** Malcolm used these organizations to preach his new form of Islam and spread his ideas about black nationalism and racial pride. On February 21, 1965, he was murdered by members of the Nation of Islam as he delivered a speech in New York City. (AAB)

BIBLIOGRAPHY

Malcolm X. *The Autobiography of Malcolm X.* New York: Ballantine Books, 1992.

Weisbrot, Robert. "Marching Toward Freedom, 1957–1965: *From the Founding of the Southern Christian Leadership Conference to the Assassination of Malcolm X.* 1994: New York: Chelsa House, 1994.

Manpower Development and Training Act of 1962

The Manpower Development and Training Act of 1962 was the second New Frontier/Great Society anti-unemployment program. The program provided training in several job areas that the Kennedy and Johnson administration believed held widespread job vacancies. The program's goals were to raise the number of African Americans in the workplace by providing them with the necessary job skills.

BIBLIOGRAPHY

Mangum, Garth L. *MDTA, Foundation of Federal Manpower Policy.* Baltimore: Johns Hopkins Press, 1968.

March on Washington

When most conjure up images of the August 28, 1963, March on Washington, they have in their mind's eye the more than 250,000 people scattered at the feet of **Martin Luther King, Jr.,** his hands and voice raised on the steps of the Lincoln Memorial, while he spoke of his great dream for America. However, it must be remembered that the road to those steps was long and hard, and those who built it and walked upon it were many and varied.

The immediate groundwork for the march had been laid in Birmingham, Alabama, in the spring and early summer of 1963, where America and the world had watched as a collection of civil rights groups led by King had faced down racists and segregationists in that city. The carnage and viciousness of the scenes played out in Birmingham had led President John F. Kennedy finally to deliver a powerful and wide-ranging civil rights bill to Congress on June 19, 1963.

In order to see that road leading to the steps of the Lincoln Memorial for all its true complexity, one must look much further than King and the recent victory of beginning the process of integration in Birmingham. That road began at least in 1941, when **A. Philip Randolph** and his colleagues both inside and outside of the then powerful **Brotherhood of Sleeping Car Porters and Maids** had first conceived of a mass march on Washington to bring about federal government action on civil rights. Randolph successfully used the threat of a march to convince President Franklin D. Roosevelt to begin the process that led to the formation of the **Fair Em-**

ployment Practice Committee. The committee attempted to deny federal funds to those organizations that had openly used discriminatory hiring practices. But this initiative had begun to lose ground to segregationists by the early 1950s, despite

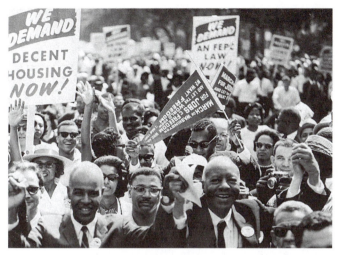

In August 1963, hundreds of thousands of people converged on the Mall in Washington, D.C., for a giant civil rights rally. *National Archives.*

the first Freedom Rides undertaken by Randolph and such pioneers as **Bayard Rustin** and **James Farmer** in the **Congress of Racial Equality (CORE).**

With the victories of the **civil rights movement** of the early 1960s mounting, Randolph and Rustin returned to the idea of a massive march through the streets of Washington. As the scale of the endeavor began to grow, President Kennedy expressed his opposition to such a march, which he feared would lead to violence. Kennedy was soon convinced by a delegation led by Randolph and King to lend his support to the march and its organizers.

Randolph was the first to address the crowd that stretched from the Lincoln Memorial to the Washington Monument and beyond, and it was Randolph who introduced the throng to King, **John L. Lewis, Roy Wilkins,** and the other speakers that day. In the views of some of those who organized the demonstration, what made it such a success was its broad base of support and its overlapping themes, which included racial harmony, fuller employment, economic equality, and the passage of President Kennedy's civil rights bill. While some major labor organizations (including the AFL-CIO) decided not to support the march, dozens of other groups (including the Congress of Racial Equality, the **Southern Christian Leadership Conference (SCLC),** the **Student Nonviolent Coordinating Committee (SNCC),** the **National Association of the Advancement of Colored People (NAACP),** many unions, and numerous Jewish, Catholic, and Protestant groups) combined their organizational strengths with those of Randolph and Rustin to produce the political success that was the March on Washington. Various anniversaries of the 1963 march have been celebrated with large demonstrations in

Washington and elsewhere, and each has drawn on the power of Randolph's vision for its own success and influence. (AJC)

BIBLIOGRAPHY

Anderson, Jervis. *A. Philip Randolph: A Biographical Portrait.* New York: Harcourt Brace Jovanovich Inc, 1973.

Lewis, David L. *King: A Critical Biography.* New York: Simon & Schuster, 1979.

Viorst, Milton. *Fire in the Streets: America in the 1960s.* New York: Penguin Books, 1987.

Williams, Juan. *Eyes on the Prize: America's Civil Rights Years, 1954–1965.* New York: Penguin Books, 1987.

Thurgood Marshall (1908–1993)

Thurgood Marshall was the first African American appointed solicitor general of the United States, and the first African American to serve on the U.S. Supreme Court. As director of the **National Association for the Advancement of Colored People (NAACP) Legal Defense and Education Fund,** Marshall helped design a legal strategy directed at ending discrimination in education, voting, housing, and public accommodations. He won 29 cases in the Supreme Court including landmark precedents like *Smith v Allwright* and *Brown v. Board of Education* (1954).

After two decades with the Legal Defense Fund, Marshall was appointed to the Court of Appeals for the Second Circuit by President John Kennedy. President Lyndon Johnson appointed Marshall to be solicitor general of the United States. In 1967, Johnson appointed Marshall to the Supreme Court to take the seat vacated by Justice Tom Clark. As with his court of appeals nomination, southern senators delayed his confirmation hoping to prevent him from being confirmed. As a Justice, Marshall was one of the most consistently liberal members of the Court. During the Warren Court, he helped expand many of the precedents he created as a litigant. During the more conservative Burger and Rehnquist Courts, he often dissented in cases that weakened or reversed the precedents he had worked for as an attorney and justice. Due to failing health, Marshall retired from the Court in 1991.

BIBLIOGRAPHY

Davis, Michael B. and Hunter R. Clark. *Thurgood Marshall: Warrior at the Bar, Rebel on the Bench.* New York: Birch Lane Press, 1992.

Tushnet, Mark V. *Making Civil Rights Law: Thurgood Marshall and the Supreme Court.* New York: Oxford University Press, 1994.

Martin v. Wilks (1989)

The city fire department of Birmingham, Alabama, had been under a consent decree that mandated the hiring and promoting of black firefighters for 25 years when a group of white firefighters sued the city for reverse discrimination. The U.S. Supreme Court heard the case, *Martin v. Wilkes,* 490 U.S. 755 (1989), and found that the affirmative action practices of the city's fire department were discriminatory against white applicants for both new hires and promotion. This case became another one of the cases decided by the Supreme Court in the late 1980s and early 1990s that led to the paring back of affirmative action programs. (EP)

BIBLIOGRAPHY

Barker, Lucius J. and Twiley W. Barker, Jr. *Civil Liberties and the Constitution.* Englewood Cliffs, NJ: Prentice Hall, 1994.

Mayor and City Council of Baltimore v. Dawson (1955)

A group of African Americans were denied access to public beach facilities in the city of Baltimore, Maryland, solely because of their race. The peoples in the group sued, alleging that their constitutional rights were violated and that the denial of access violated those rights guaranteed by the **Fourteenth Amendment**. The U.S. District Court agreed with the plaintiffs that the enforcement of racially segregated public beaches and bathhouses was unconstitutional. The U.S. Supreme Court affirmed this decision in *Mayor and City Council of Baltimore v. Dawson*, 3350 U.S. 377 (1955), highlighting the discriminatory practices inherent to such segregation. **See** the text of the Fourteenth Amendment in "Civil War Amendments" in Appendix 1.

BIBLIOGRAPHY

Barker, Lucius J. and Twiley W. Barker, Jr. *Civil Liberties and the Constitution.* Englewood Cliffs, NJ: Prentice Hall, 1994.

McCleskey v. Kemp (1987)

The Supreme Court upheld the conviction and death sentence of Warren McCleskey, a black man convicted of killing a white police officer. Using statistical analysis, McCleskey's attorneys argued that capital punishment was being inflicted in a racially discriminatory way and that it was unconstitutional under the Eighth Amendment as cruel and unusual punishment, and under the **Fourteenth Amendment** as a violation of the equal protection of the law. In *McCleskey v. Kemp* 481, U.S. 279 (1987), the Court held that although the statistics indicated a pattern of **discrimination,** McCleskey had not demonstrated bias in his particular case. Therefore they rejected his claim to unconstitutional treatment. The four dissenting justices believed that McCleskey had shown significant risk of discrimination and that this was sufficient to overturn his sentence. (MWA)

BIBLIOGRAPHY

Walker, Samuel, Cassia Spohn, and Miriam DeLone. *The Color of Justice: Race, Ethnicity and Crime in America.* Belmont, CA: Wadsworth, Inc., 1996.

Frederick D. McClure (1954–)

Frederick McClure received his bachelors degree from Texas A&M University and his J.D. degree from Baylor University School of Law. He began working for the law firm of Reynolds, Allen and Cook in 1981 and joined Senator John Tower's staff in 1983. He was the U.S. associate deputy attorney general from 1984 to 1985 when he was appointed to serve as presidential special assistant for legislative affairs by President Ronald Reagan. He served as government affairs staff vice president of Texas Air Corporation until he was appointed by President George Bush to serve as presidential special assistant for legislative affairs. (JCW)

BIBLIOGRAPHY

Boyd, Gerald. "Two Named to Fill White House Jobs." *New York Times* (December 22, 1988) :D22.

Floyd McCree (1923–)

Floyd McCree was born in Missouri in 1923. He is a register of deeds in Gennessee County, Michigan. He served on the city council of Flint, Michigan from 1958 to 1970 and was elected mayor of Flint as a Democrat in 1966. (JCW)

BIBLIOGRAPHY

Narvaez, Alfonso. "F.J. McCree, Early Black Mayor." *New York Times* (June 18, 1988): 32.

Wade McCree (1920–1987)

Wade McCree was solicitor general of the United States during the Carter administration. McCree, the first African American to be elected to the Detroit city bench, was the second African American to be selected as a federal district court judge, and was a Court of Appeals judge for the Sixth Circuit when President Carter tabbed him to be the solicitor general. He was also the second African American, after **Thurgood Marshall**, to serve as solicitor general.

BIBLIOGRAPHY

Salokar, Rebecca. *The Solicitor General: The Politics of Law.* Philadelphia: Temple University Press, 1992.

McDonnel Douglas Corporation v. Green (1973)

Percy Green participated in an illegal action of blocking access to his ex-employer's plant, alleging discriminatory rehiring practices of laid-off employees. In *McDonnel Douglas Corporation v. Green*, 411 U.S. 792 (1973), the Supreme Court held that a plaintiff can make a prima facie case against an employer by showing racial preference in hiring. An employer must then demonstrate a valid reason for not hiring the plaintiff. If the employer does so, the burden then passes to the plaintiff to prove that the company's reasons for not hiring constitute a discriminatory policy, or that there was past discriminatory treatment while the plaintiff was an employee. (FHJ)

BIBLIOGRAPHY

Corbin, Peter Reed and John E. Duvall. "Employment Discrimination." *Mercer Law Review* 44 (1993): 1165–86.

Donald F. McHenry (1932–)

Donald McHenry was appointed U.S. ambassador to the United Nations in 1979 by President Jimmy Carter after the resignation of **Andrew Young**. A career diplomat, McHenry began working for the State Department in 1963. At the State Department he held a variety of positions including chief officer of the Areas Section of the Office of United Nations

Political Affairs. From 1973 to 1977, McHenry was the director of humanitarian policy studies at the Carnegie Endowment for International Peace.

BIBLIOGRAPHY

McHenry, Donald F. *Interview with Donald F. McHenry.* Braamfontein, South Africa: South African Institute of International Affairs, 1984.

Cynthia Ann McKinney (1955–)

Cynthia A. McKinney, a Democrat, was elected to the U.S. House of Representatives in 1992 as the first black female representative from Georgia. She became a national symbol of the newly extended power of women and minorities. During a bitter 1993 battle over renewal of the Hyde Amendment, a law that forbids the use of federal funds for abortions, McKinney informed her colleagues that she was fed up with those members who consistently voted against the poor, people of color, and women. Former Congresswoman Marjorie Margolies-Mezivinsky contends that McKinney's weapon against oppression is her eloquence when speaking and writing.

In addition to struggling for women, minorities, the poor, and government accountability, McKinney spent extensive time fighting for the survival of her 11th District, created to strengthen the black vote in Georgia. In 1995, the Supreme Court overturned the district, agreeing that it was "bizarrely" drawn; and McKinney was forced to build a new base of support in the 4th District, which was only one-third black. She then won the 1996 election with 57.8 percent of the vote. (EP)

BIBLIOGRAPHY

Bingham, Clara. *Women on the Hill: Challenging the Culture of Congress.* New York: Time Books, 1997.

Margolies-Mezivinsky, Marjorie. *A Woman's Place...: The Freshmen Women Who Changed the Face of Congress.* New York: Crow Publishers, Inc., 1994.

Floyd B. McKissick (1922–1991)

Floyd McKissick was born in North Carolina in 1922. He was the first African American to earn an LL.B. degree from the law school at the University of North Carolina at Chapel Hill. He became the national director of the **Congress of Racial Equality (CORE)** in 1966, taking a positive stance on the **black power** movement and speaking against **Martin Luther King, Jr.**'s call for nonviolent civil disobedience in the northern cities. He resigned from the congress in 1968 and began work on a project to start a self-sufficient community of 50,000 people in North Carolina called Soul City. He received a $14 million bond issue from the U.S. Department of Housing and Urban Development and a loan from First Pennsylvania Bank. The plan was not successful and the government assumed control of the project in 1980. McKissick died in 1991 and is buried in Soul City.

BIBLIOGRAPHY

Fowler, Glenn. "Floyd McKissick." *The New York Times* (April 30, 1991): D19.

Omang, Joanne. "Fighting Still." *Washington Post* (July 2, 1979): A1.

McLaurin v. Oklahoma State Regents (1950)

In *McLaurin v. Oklahoma State Regents,* 339, U.S. 637 (1950), a 58–year-old black student working toward a doctorate in education was forced to sit in special sections marked "Reserved for Coloreds" in the classroom, library, and dining room. The Supreme Court held that this separation had denied McLaurin's right to equal protection and inhibited his ability to study, to engage in discussions, to exchange views, and to learn his profession. (EP)

BIBLIOGRAPHY

Davis, Michael B. and Hunter R. Clark. *Thurgood Marshall: Warrior at the Bar, Rebel on the Bench.* New York: Birch Lane Press, 1992.

Carrie P. Meek (1926–)

Carrie P. Meek, a Democrat from Florida, was elected to the United States House of Representatives in 1992 and reelected in 1994, 1996, and 1998. Prior to being elected to Congress, Meek was a member of the Florida State House of Representatives from 1979 to 1982 and the Florida State Senate from 1982 to 1992. Meek is a founder and former president of the Afro-American Democratic Club. In the House, she serves on the Appropriations Committee, becoming the first freshman congressperson to do so. A committed liberal, she has been a vocal critic of former speaker Newt Gingrich and the Republican majority. **See also** Congressional Black Caucus.

BIBLIOGRAPHY

Gill, LaVerne McCain. *African American Women in Congress.* New Brunswick, NJ: Rutgers University Press, 1997.

"GOP's Strike Carrie Meek's Comments on Gingrich from U.S. House Record." *Jet* 87, no. 14 (February 13, 1995): 40.

Ralph Harold Metcalfe (1910–1978)

Ralph Metcalfe was born in Chicago, Illinois. Metcalfe is best remembered as an American sprinter who was a member of the famous U.S. Olympic team that starred at the 1936 Olympic Games in Berlin. This was the team that defeated Adolf Hitler's propaganda of Aryan superiority by featuring African Americans who excelled in numerous events. Metcalfe was a prominent member of the 400-meter relay team that won a gold medal. Metcalfe was once known as "the world's fastest human." In both 1932 and 1936 he won Olympic silver medals in the 100-meter dash. Metcalfe also had a distinguished political career. Upon leaving the world of track and field, he received a master's degree from the University of Southern California. Metcalfe was an alderman and ward leader in Chicago before serving in Congress from 1971 through 1978. In Congress, Metcalfe broke away from the political machine of Chicago mayor Richard Daley and distinguished himself as an independent politician. Metcalfe was a founding member of the **Congressional Black Caucus**.

BIBLIOGRAPHY

"[Obituary:] Ralph Harold Metcalfe." *Washington Post* (October 14, 1978): A16.

Metro Broadcasting, Inc. v. Federal Communications Commission (1990)

In 1977 the Federal Communications Commission adopted an **affirmative action** policy aimed at encouraging minority ownership in the broadcast industry. The plan used minority status as one of many factors in granting new licenses. Over a decade later, Metro Broadcasting challenged this plan when it sought to construct stations in Orlando, Florida. In *Metro Broadcasting, Inc. v. Federal Communications Commission,* 110 S. Ct. 2997 (1990), the U.S. Supreme Court narrowly sustained the use of preferential treatment. Writing for the majority, Justice William Brennan argued that Congress has the power to employ race-based measures even if such measures are not remedies for past discrimination. **See also** Racial Set-Asides. (CJM)

BIBLIOGRAPHY

"Forty Megahertz and a Mule: Ensuring Minority Ownership of the Electromagnetic Spectrum." *Harvard Law Review* 108, no. 5 (March 1995): 1145–62.

Rogers, Edward D. "When Logic and Reality Collide: The Supreme Court and Minority Business Set-Asides." *Columbia Journal of Law and Social Problems* 24, no. 1 (Winter 1990): 117–68.

Kweisi Mfume (1948–)

Kweisi Mfume is the president of the **National Association for the Advancement of Colored People (NAACP).**

He was elected to the U.S. House of Representatives for the 7th district of Maryland as a Democrat in 1986. A substantial portion of this district represents the city of Baltimore. He gained a reputation as a stern critic of drug use and destructive behavior. Mfume was appointed head of the Black Caucus Task Force to preserve affirmative action. In 1992 he was elected chairman of the **Congressional Black Caucus** by a 27–9 vote. While there he was able to keep a separate Africa Subcommittee on International Relations by having Democratic leaders ease a subcommittee limitation rule. He did not seek reelection in 1996, opting to become the president of the NAACP. As president he has repudiated the burning of African-American churches, and violence in the African-American community. (WWH)

BIBLIOGRAPHY

Boyer, Peter J. "The Rise of Kweisi Mfume." *The New Yorker* 70, no. 23 (August 1, 1994): 26.

"Business Group Salutes Mfume." *Jet* 91, no. 16 (March 10, 1997): 25.

Cose, Ellis. "The Last Best Hope." *Newsweek* 127, no. 7 (February 12, 1996): 71.

Haywood, Richette. "Can Kweisi Mfume Turn the NAACP Around?" *Ebony* 52, no. 3 (January 1997): 94.

Kalb, Deborah. "Mfume to Focus NAACP on Voters." *Congressional Quarterly Weekly Report* 54, no. 16 (April 20, 1996): 1066.

"NACCP President Mfume Says He Thinks That It Is Time To Stop Bashing Justice Clarence Thomas." *Jet* 91, no. 15 (March 3, 1997): 6.

White, Paula M. "NAACP Back in the Black: Perennial Civil Rights Group Retires $3.2 Million Debt." *Black Enterprise* 27, no. 7 (February 1997): 28.

"Why Kweisi Mfume Leaves Congress to Head NAACP." *Jet* 89, no. 10 (January 22, 1996): 4.

Juanita Millender-McDonald (1938–)

Juanita Millender-McDonald received her M.Ed. from California State University. She was elected to the Carson City council in 1990. She served on the California State Assembly from 1993 to 1996 and was elected to the U.S. House of Representatives as a Democrat in 1996. She was also the founder of the League of African American Women. (JCW)

BIBLIOGRAPHY

"Black Caucus Members Keep Their Strength in House in 1996 Election." *Jet* 25 (November 1996): 4.

Thomas E. Miller (1849–1938)

Thomas Miller, a self-taught lawyer from South Carolina, was elected to Congress in 1888 after the Democratic candidate named the winner was found to have used fraudulent techniques. He returned to private practice in 1891 and was elected to South Carolina's House of Representatives, where he served from 1894 to 1896. He also helped found State Negro College and was its first president.

BIBLIOGRAPHY

Ragsdale, Bruce and Joel Treese. *Black Americans in Congress 1870–1989*. Washington DC: U.S. Government Printing Office, 1990.

Milliken v. Bradley (1974)

Milliken v. Bradley, 418, U.S. 717 (1974), was a second generation, northern desegregation case. A federal district court ordered a desegregation plan to encompass the city of Detroit and 53 suburban school districts. Because the city schools were almost exclusively composed of African-American students and the suburban schools primarily consisted of white students, the district court argued that an interdistrict remedy was needed and busing across school districts was the solution. The Supreme Court, in a 5–4 decision, ruled that the district court exceeded its authority by imposing an interdistrict remedy on school districts that had no proven history of constitutional violations. The majority ruled that the Equal Protection Clause of the **Fourteenth Amendment** does not reach **de facto segregation** that results from residential patterns caused by "white flight" to the suburbs. The Supreme Court ruled that under de facto discrimination, federal courts cannot order busing as a solution in the absence of proof that the school board demonstrated a clear intent to discriminate. The decision marked a major retreat from school desegregation and busing as a resolution to the matter. (RLP)

BIBLIOGRAPHY

Jackson, Donald W. *Even the Children of Strangers: Equality Under the U.S. Constitution.* Lawrence, KS: University of Kansas Press, 1992.

Million Man March

On October 16,1995, the largest public demonstration of African Americans in United States history occurred at the Million Man March in Washington, D.C. According to park police, about 875,000 black men marched from the U.S. Capitol to the Lincoln Memorial on the Federal Mall at the request of its organizer and keynote speaker, the **Nation of Islam's** Minister **Louis Farrakhan.** Farrakhan, along with other leaders from the black community, addressed the crowd on topics including economic development, continued support of black businesses, and a commitment to black unity. (VDD)

BIBLIOGRAPHY

Cose, Ellis. "Watch What They Do: A Year after the Million Man March, The Glow Lingers and Small Deeds Add Up." *Newsweek* 128, no. 15 (October 7, 1996): 62.
"Farrakhan Urges Marchers to Return Home and Make a Positive Difference." *Jet.* 88, no. 25 (October 30, 1995): 10.
Madhubuti, Haki R. "The Strong Men Keep Coming: It's Been a Year Since The Million Man March and Day of Atonement, But the Victories Continue." *Essence* 27, no. 7 (November 1996): 50.
Murray, Barbara. "Interpreting the Atonement: Race." *U.S. News & World Report* 23, no. 16 (October 27, 1997): 44.
Pinckney, Darryl. "Slouching Toward Washington." *The New York Review of Books* 42, no. 20 (December 21, 1995): 73.
Wall, James M. "Message and Messenger: The Million Man March." *The Christian Century* 112, no. 31 (November 1, 1995): 1003.
Warren, Kenneth. "Marching In Place." *The Nation* 261, no. 15 (November 6, 1995): 524.

Minority Business Development Administration (MBDA)

The Minority Business Development Administration (MBDA), formerly known as the Office of Minority Business Enterprise, was created by executive order in 1971 to help the Department of Commerce promote the development of minority-owned businesses and also to demonstrate how to secure government contracts. Additionally, the MBDA provides funds for Minority Business Development Centers and American Indian Development Centers. In 1996, the MBDA was able to survive an attempt by the 104th Congress to eliminate the department in a round of budget cuts. (VDD)

BIBLIOGRAPHY

Cobb, Joe. *How to Close Down the Department of Congress.* Washington, DC: The Heritage Foundation, Backgrounder Number 1049, August 21, 1995.

Mississippi Freedom Democratic Party (MFDP)

The Democratic Party in Mississippi essentially prevented African Americans from voting by blocking their registration. When segregated precinct meetings chose delegates to the national convention, no black delegates were selected. To protest this exclusion and reverse decades of political segregation, the Mississippi Freedom Democratic Party (MFDP), founded by **Fannie Lou Hamer** in 1964, held their own state convention and selected 68 delegates to the 1964 Democratic Convention, including four whites, who endeavored to unseat the all-white Mississippi delegation. Although a "compromise" prevented them from unseating the party regulars, Hamer's testimony before the credentials committee gained considerable national attention, and the MFDP successfully registered over 80,000 African Americans in Mississippi. (CC)

BIBLIOGRAPHY

Holt, Len. *The Summer that Didn't End.* New York: Da Capo Press, 1992.
McLemore, Leslie Burl. PhD Dissertation University of Massachusetts, Amhurst. The Mississippi Freedom Democratic Party: A Case Study of Grass-Roots Politics. 1971.

Missouri Compromise

The increasing number of settlers migrating west in the early nineteenth century led many Americans to question the necessity of extending the institution of slavery. In Missouri its existence caused a dangerously heated sectional debate that necessitated a unique and ultimately unsuccessful compromise.

In 1817 the territory of Missouri petitioned Congress for statehood. Two years later Congress officially debated the issue, at which time Representative James Tallmadge, Jr. proposed an amendment requiring Missouri to abolish slavery as a condition for its admission. This proposal touched off a sectional firestorm, and although the House narrowly passed the amended bill, the Senate destroyed it in March 1819. Finally, in March 1820, Congress negotiated a compromise entailing two major provisions. First, they sanctioned slavery in Missouri but admitted Maine so as to keep the proper ratio of free to slave states. Second, they abolished the "peculiar institution" north of 36° 30'. Although suitable to put the controversy to rest in 1820, this compromise re-emerged as a primary issue in the sectional debates of 1850–1861. (KR)

BIBLIOGRAPHY

Sellers, Charles. *The Market Revolution: Jacksonian America, 1815–1846.* New York: Oxford University Press, 1991.

Missouri ex rel. Gaines v. Canada, Registrar of the University of Missouri (1938)

Shortly after the decision in *Donald Murray v. the University of Maryland*—in which the university law college's segregated enrollment practices were found discriminatory—a similar case was brought against the University of Missouri. While the university did offer a separate school for black students, Lincoln College, this college failed to offer a law degree. After Lloyd Gaines tried to gain entrance to the university's law program and was denied, he went to court claiming a violation of his **Fourteenth Amendment** rights. The state court denied Gaines' pleas, but in *Missouri ex rel. Gaines v. Canada, Registrar of the University of Missouri,* 305 U.S. 337 (1938), the court of appeals reversed the decision, stating equal services were not offered at both schools. While the case did not directly affect the school's segregation of colleges, it did help provide equal educational opportunities to African-American students. **See also** Education; *Sweatt v. Painter* (1950). **See** the text of the Fourteenth Amendment in "Civil War Amendments" in Appendix 1.

BIBLIOGRAPHY

Owsley, Brian. "Black Ivy: An African-American Perspective on Law School." 28 (Spring 1997): 501–49.

Missouri v. Jenkins (1995)

The Supreme Court overturned a federal district court's ruling that had ordered across-the-board salary increases and state funded education enrichment programs for the Kansas City, Missouri, school district. The district court had reasoned that the higher salaries for teachers and other school personnel and massive expenditures for facilities such as art galleries, swimming pools, and movie screening rooms were necessary to increase the district's "desegregative attractiveness." The district court held that because Kansas City student achievement scores were at or below the national average, although the scores had shown improvement, the remedies were necessary to remove the effects of past discrimination which had occurred when the schools were segregated.

The Supreme Court ruled that the district court had exceeded its authority in mandating the salary increases and the other expenditures, and that it could only order remedies that addressed specific violations. "Desegregative attractiveness" seemed to the Court a vague and inappropriate goal. The majority of the Court also reminded the district court that their ultimate goal was to return the governance of schools to the local districts.

Justice **Clarence Thomas**, the only African-American member of the Supreme Court, agreed with the majority opinion of the court, but wrote a stronger criticism of the district court's ruling. He charged that they were experimenting with the education of black youth, and that the action in Kansas City violated the principles of federalism and the separation of powers.

Another concurring opinion from Justice Sandra Day O'Connor also found that the lower court had overstepped its authority. The courts could not, in her view, remedy all social ills and they should confine themselves to narrowly tailored remedies to specific constitutional violations.

The Supreme Court decision in *Missouri v. Jenkins* is considered part of a trend away from affirmative action and race-conscious efforts to remedy past discrimination. (MWA)

BIBLIOGRAPHY

Joundeph, Bradley W. "Missouri v. Jenkins and the De Facto Abandonment of Court-Enforced Desegregation." *Washington Law Review* 71, no. 3 (July 1996): 597–681.

Arthur W. Mitchell (1883–1968)

Arthur Mitchell (D-IL) served in the United States House of Representatives from 1934 to 1942. His election to Congress is especially noteworthy because he was the first African-American Democrat to serve in Congress. In winning his seat, Mitchell defeated another African American, Republican incumbent **Oscar S. De Priest,** who was the first African American in the twentieth century to serve in Congress from either party. While in Congress, Mitchell was a strong supporter of Franklin Roosevelt's New Deal Programs. He declined to seek reelection in 1942.

BIBLIOGRAPHY

Nordin, Dennis S. *The New Deal's Black Congressman.* Columbia: University of Missouri Press, 1997.

Parren J. Mitchell (1922–)

Parren J. Mitchell represented the 7th U.S. Congressional District of Maryland from 1971 to 1986, becoming the first black congressman from Maryland with his election in 1970. The district covers inner-city Baltimore. He had a successful lawsuit in the early 1950s to integrate the University of Maryland graduate school. (WWH)

BIBLIOGRAPHY

Thomas, Arthur E. *Like It Is: Arthur E. Thomas Interviews Leaders on Black America.* New York: Dutton, 1981.

Montgomery Bus Boycott

On December 1, 1955, **Rosa Parks** was asked to give up her seat on a Montgomery, Alabama, bus to a white man. She was not the first to defy Alabama law in refusing to give up her seat. There had been numerous earlier refusals that paved the way for what followed. When Parks was arrested in front of the Empire Theater by two police officers, however, a boycott of the buses by 50,000 Montgomery blacks followed. Edgar Daniel Nixon, a Pullman Porter, bailed Parks out of jail. On December 6, 26–year-old **Martin Luther King, Jr.** was elected president of the **Montgomery Improvement Association** and led a boycott of city buses. The boycott lasted for more than a year and demonstrated the leadership qualities of King and the willingness of African Americans to stick together. It also demonstrated the effectiveness of black economic power. Those involved in the boycott stayed off buses for 381 days, risking their jobs and sometimes their lives. These unsung heroes made up 75 percent of the ridership of buses. Simply, without their patronage, the buses could not afford to operate. The boycott is often seen as the beginning of the modern **civil rights** movement.

BIBLIOGRAPHY

Celsi, Teresa Noel. *Rosa Parks and the Montgomery Bus Boycott.* Brookfield, CT: Millbrook Press, 1991.

Hughes Wright, Roberta. *The Birth of the Montgomery Bus Boycott.* Southfield, MI: Charro Press, 1991.

Montgomery Improvement Association

The Montgomery Improvement Association was formed on December 5, 1955, as part of the **Montgomery bus boycott.** Dr. **Martin Luther King, Jr.** was the president of the association, which provided free transportation for tens of thousands of African Americans who were boycotting the Montgomery, Alabama, bus system because of its racially discriminatory practices. The association also challenged the constitutionality of the city's policies by filing suit against the city on February 1, 1956. The case eventually reached the U.S. Supreme Court; on November 13, 1956, the Court upheld the ruling of the lower courts that struck down the discriminatory practices of the Montgomery bus system, *NAACP v. Alabama ex. Rel. Flowers,* 377 U.S. 288 (1964).

BIBLIOGRAPHY

Branch, Taylor. *Parting the Waters: America in the King Years, 1954–1963.* New York: Simon & Schuster, 1988.

Robinson, Jo Ann Gibson. *The Montgomery Bus Boycott and the Women Who Started It.* Knoxville: University of Tennessee Press, 1987.

Moore v. Dempsey (1923)

The case of *Moore v. Dempsey,* 261, U.S. 86 (1923), began in 1919 after an incident where a meeting of black sharecroppers was interrupted by an armed mob and several deaths resulted. The black farmers were quickly sentenced to death but the case attracted national attention when the **National Association for the Advancement of Colored People (NAACP)** stepped in to try to save the men. The case was eventually carried to the U.S. Supreme Court, which in 1923 reversed the convictions because the men did not receive due process of law. (CE)

BIBLIOGRAPHY

Franklin, John Hope. *From Slavery to Freedom: A History of African Americans.* New York: McGraw-Hill, 1994.

Morgan v. Commonwealth of Virginia (1946)

Morgan v. Commonwealth of Virginia 328, U.S. 373 (1946), involved the constitutionality of Virginia laws which required the segregation of the races in both intrastate and interstate motor carriers. Irene Morgan, a black, had refused to sit in the back of a Greyhound bus and was convicted for violating the Virginia statute. The Court held that the laws were invalid because they "burden[ed] interstate commerce contrary to Article I, sec. 8, cl. 3 of the Constitution." The case is also noteworthy because the Court ruled that the Tenth Amendment does not validate state statutes that unlawfully burden interstate commerce. (CJM)

BIBLIOGRAPHY

D'Amato, Anthony A., Rosemary Metrailer, and Stephen L. Wasby. *Desegregation from Brown to Alexander.* Illinios: Southern Illinois University Press, 1977.

Greenberg, Jack. *Race Relations and American Law.* New York: Columbia University Press, 1959.

Ernest Nathan "Dutch" Morial (1929–1989)

Ernest "Dutch" Morial made a career of being first in Louisiana politics. Born in New Orleans on October 9, 1929, Morial, a Democrat, rose to become the city's most influential black politician. His "career of firsts" include first black graduate of Louisiana State University Law School (1954); first black assistant U.S. Attorney in Louisiana (1966); first black legislator in Louisiana since **Reconstruction** (1968); and first black mayor of New Orleans (1978–1986). As mayor he organized relief during the floods of 1978, used the National Guard to break up a police strike in 1979, and hosted the 1984 World's Exposition. (CJM)

BIBLIOGRAPHY

Laborde, Errol. "Dutch's Big Announcement." *New Orleans Magazine* 32, no. 4 (January 1998): 128.

John Howard Morrow (1910–)

On June 18, 1959, John H. Morrow was appointed by President Dwight D. Eisenhower as the first American ambassador to Guinea. Morrow served until March 3, 1961. Prior to his appointment as ambassador, Morrow was chair of the Department of Foreign Languages at North Carolina College. His appointment drew both praise and criticism. Those who praised his appointment recognized the extensive knowledge of the region that Morrow brought to the post. Those that criticized him believed that a more experienced diplomat was needed in the unstable region.

BIBLIOGRAPHY

Morrow, John H. *First American Ambassador to Guinea.* New Brunswick, NJ: Rutgers University Press, 1967.

Carol Moseley-Braun (1947–)

The first African-American woman elected to serve in the United States Senate, Carol Moseley-Braun was elected to an Illinois Senate seat as a Democrat in 1992. A civil rights activist at the University of Illinois—Chicago, Moseley-Braun marched with **Martin Luther King, Jr.**, participated in student sit-ins, and campaigned on behalf of **Harold Washington** for mayor of Chicago. While serving a multiracial Chicago district in the Illinois House of Representatives, promoting health care reform and gun control, Moseley-Braun won election in 1987 as Cook County Recorder of Deeds. After expressing outrage over the **Clarence Thomas** Supreme Court confirmation hearings, the little-known Moseley-Braun challenged conservative incumbent Alan Dixon in the primary election and achieved national acclaim with her stunning upset victory. Moseley-Braun scored a comfortable victory in the general election, crafting an electoral coalition crossing both geographic and demographic lines which particularly energized suburban women voters. Moseley-Braun was defeated in her bid for reelection in 1998. She was appointed ambassador to New Zealand in 1999. (CC)

BIBLIOGRAPHY

Jelen, Ted. "Carol Moseley-Braun: The Insider as Insurgent." Elizabeth Adell Cook, Sue Thomas, and Clyde Wilcox, eds. *The Year of the Woman: Myths and Realities.* Boulder: Westview Press, 1994.

Robert Parris Moses (1935–)

Robert Moses's political activism is guided by the Christian idea of a beloved community, nonhierarchical leadership, grassroots struggle, local initiative, and pacifism. In 1960 Moses joined the **Student Nonviolent Coordinating Committee (SNCC)** and engaged in full-time voter registration. In 1964 he helped organize the **Mississippi Freedom Demo-**

cratic Party (MFDP). Opposed to the Vietnam War, Moses moved to Canada and then to Tanzania, where he taught mathematics. He returned to the U.S. in 1976 and in 1980 founded the Algebra Project, which helps underprivileged children get an early grounding in mathematics. In 1992 he launched the Delta Algebra project to help the children of the impoverished Mississippi region. (EC)

BIBLIOGRAPHY

Sitkoff, Harvard. *The Struggle for Black Equality. Revised Edition.* New York: Hill and Wang, 1993.

Constance Baker Motley (1921–)

Constance Baker Motley was appointed to the United States District Court for southern New York by President Lyndon Johnson in 1966, making her the first African-American woman appointed to a federal judgeship. In 1982, she was named chief judge of the federal district court that covers Manhattan, the Bronx, and six counties north of New York City. She was named senior judge in 1986. In 1964 Motley had become the first African-American woman elected to the New York State Senate. She was also Manhattan borough president from 1965 to 1966, the first woman to be a borough president in New York City.

BIBLIOGRAPHY

Motley, Constance Baker. *Equal Justice under Law.* New York: Farrar, Straus and Giroux, 1988.

Moynihan Report on the Negro Family

In 1965, Daniel Patrick Moynihan, who was assistant secretary of labor, issued a report on the Negro family that cited census data and other developments indicating that the family structure of blacks was seriously deteriorating. The report documented that teenage pregnancies were on the rise, single-parent households were becoming more numerous, out-of-wedlock births were increasing, and young black males were experiencing consistently high unemployment rates that made it difficult for them to support a family. The report also included statistics on rising school dropout rates among African Americans and the increase in the number of black recipients of Aid to Families with Dependent Children (AFDC) benefits. Moynihan emphasized that these devastating conditions had their roots in **slavery** and were exacerbated by subsequent segregation and discrimination. Moreover, Moynihan suggested that these circumstances had led to pathological conditions in black ghettos that made it difficult for African Americans to begin to take advantage of the opportunities that were being won in the civil rights struggle. Immediately after its content and conclusions became public, the report became embroiled in controversy and fierce political and academic debates. **See also** Poverty.

BIBLIOGRAPHY

Ginsburg, Carl. *Race and Media: The Enduring Life of the Moynihan Report.* New York: Institute for Media Analysis, 1989.
Zollar, Ann C. *A Member of the Family.* Chicago: Nelson-Hall, 1985.

Mrs. Murphy Exemption to Open Housing Act of 1968

The **Civil Rights Act of 1968** banned discrimination in housing on the basis of race, color, religion, and national origin in the sale, rental and financing in federally assisted units and most of the private housing market. One exemption, commonly known as the Mrs. Murphy exemption, referred to dwellings of up to four separate living units in which the owner maintained a residence. This type of housing was often referred to as Mrs. Murphy Housing. (VDD)

BIBLIOGRAPHY

1968 Act Including the Open Housing Requirement. HR. 2516 Public Law - 90–284.

Elijah Muhammad (1897–1975)

Born Elijah Poole in Sandersville, Georgia, in 1897, Elijah Muhammad met **Wallace D. Fard**, the founder of the Temple of Islam (the forerunner of the **Nation of Islam**), in Detroit in 1932. After Fard's disappearance in 1934, Muhammad took over the organization. Imprisoned in 1942 for urging African Americans to avoid military service, he was released in 1946. Under his leadership, the Nation of Islam became an active and growing voice for African Americans. His teachings included a call for racial separation, self-help, and self-defense in what he saw as an oppressive white society. **See also** Religion and African-American Politics. **See** Excerpts from the Writings of Elijah Muhammad in Appendix 1. (AAB)

BIBLIOGRAPHY

Lincoln, C. Eric. *The Black Muslims in America.* Westport, CT: Greenwood Press, 1982.

Muir v. Lousiville Park Theatrical Association (1954)

A private theatrical association leased part of a city park for its performances. African Americans were not permitted to attend, although they could use all city-run facilities. Lower federal courts held the private organization could discriminate if it wished, and the city was not a party to the discrimination because it merely leased its facilities to the private organization. In *Muir v. Lousiville Park Theatrical Association* 202 F.2D 275 (6th CIR.1953), 347, U.S. 971, the Supreme Court overturned the decision, noting that it conflicted with the Court's then-new school desegregation ruling. (FHJ)

BIBLIOGRAPHY

D'Amato, Anthony A., Rosemary Metrailer, and Stephen L. Wasby. *Desegregation from Brown to Alexander.* Illinois: Southern Illinois University Press, 1977.
Greenberg, Jack. *Race Relations and American Law.* New York: Columbia University Press, 1959.

George Washington Murray (1853–1926)

George Washington Murray was born a slave in South Carolina. He was elected as a Republican to Congress in 1892, serving only a single term. He was also a delegate to guard Republican National Conventions. He was a working farmer with several farming patents in his name. He wrote two books on the subject of race: *Race Ideals* and *Light in Dark Places*.

BIBLIOGRAPHY

Gaboury, William J. "George Washington Murray and the Fight for Political Democracy in South Carolina." *Journal of Negro History* 61 (July 1977): 258–69.

Ragsdale, Bruce and Joel Treese. *Black Americans in Congress 1870–1989.* Washington DC: U.S. Government Printing Office, 1990.

NAACP Legal Defense and Education Fund, Inc. (LDF)

In 1939, the **National Association for the Advancement of Colored People (NAACP)** determined that it was losing the contributions of many past and potential donors because it did not qualify for tax-exempt status, due to its various political and lobbying activities. It resolved to organize an independent organization that was tax exempt, and that would focus exclusively on bringing about social change through the courts and the schools. The NAACP Legal Defense and Education Fund, Inc. (most often called the "Inc. Fund" or the "LDF") was created in March 1940, with a charter written by **Thurgood Marshall**. The legal strategy of the LDF, focusing on the inequality of schools segregated by race, was originally devised by **Charles Houston** and Marshall, his **Howard University** Law School student. This strategy has been carried out by generations of its attorneys, board members, advisors, and interns. Many other organizations have used the LDF as a model, including the Children's Defense Fund, which was founded by former LDF assistant counsel **Marian Wright Edelman.** Among this distinguished group of LDF staff members and supporters since its founding are Jack Greenberg (who took over for Marshall in 1961 and led the group as director-counsel until 1984), Derrick A. Bell, Charles L. Black, Jr., Paul Brest, Haywood Burns, Julius L. Chambers, Drew S. Days III, Marian Wright Edelman, John Hope Franklin, **Lani Guinier, William H. Hastie, Elaine R. Jones,** Milton R. Konvitz, **Constance Baker Motley,** Louis H. Pollak, and Spottswood Robinson III. The LDF has sought to desegregate America's schools, and to protect and expand the rights and privileges of America's voters, bus boycotters, Freedom Riders, and death row inmates, in front of courts, supreme and otherwise, and in places such as Topeka, Selma, Little Rock, and throughout the United States. (AJC)

BIBLIOGRAPHY

Greenberg, Jack. *Crusaders in the Courts: How a Dedicated Band of Lawyers Fought for the Civil Rights Revolution.* New York: Basic Books, 1994.

Kluger, Richard. *Simple Justice: The History of Brown v. Board of Education and Black America's Struggle for Equality.* New York: Alfred A. Knopf, 1975.

Tushnet, Mark V. *The NAACP's Legal Strategy against Segregated Education, 1925–1950.* Chapel Hill, NC: University of North Carolina Press, 1987.

NAACP v. Allen (1974)

In *NAACP v. Allen,* 493 F. 2d 614 (1974), the Second District Court of Appeals rendered a decision on a class-action suit charging that the state of Alabama was racially discriminatory in its hiring practices for police personnel. The court ruled that the state exhibited a long history of intentional discrimination in the recruitment and hiring of minority personnel. The court held that quota relief was essential to redress the state police's 37–year record as an all-white organization. (CEM)

BIBLIOGRAPHY

Harvey, James C., Elizabeth A. Semko, and Janace H. Goree. "Affirmative Action and Promotions: The Alabama and California Cases." *Howard Law Journal* 31 (1988): 17–32.

James Madison Nabrit, Jr. (1910–)

Lawyer, educator, and civil rights advocate, James Madison Nabrit, Jr. was born in Atlanta, Georgia. He graduated from Morehouse College in 1923 and received his J.D. from Northwestern University in 1927. In 1936 he joined the staff at **Howard University** Law School and became its president in 1960. As a member of the legal staff of the **National Association for the Advancement of Colored People (NAACP)** he argued or participated in many of the most important civil rights cases, including *Sweatt v. Painter* and *Bolling v. Sharpe.* (PLF)

BIBLIOGRAPHY

"James Nabrit, Jr., Civil Rights Lawyer and Former President of Howard University Dies at 77." *Jet* 93, no. 8 (January 19, 1998): 18.

Nation of Islam

Nation of Islam, sometimes called the Black Muslims, is a small religious sect founded in 1930 by **Wallace D. Fard** Muhammad, a door-to-door peddler in Detroit. In 1934 after Fard mysteriously disappeared, the organization was taken over by **Elijah Muhammad,** who remained in this position until his death on February 25, 1971. The Black Muslims believe in Allah and the Koran. They look upon Elijah Muhammad and W. D. Fard as prophets sent to teach them the truth and call for the complete separation of blacks from whites. Their economic and social programs are modified versions of

Marcus Garvey's **Universal Negro Improvement Association (UNIA)** ideas of black nationalism and self-reliance. Black Muslims are known for developing a group of disciplined men and women who believe in their philosophy of economic self-sufficiency, moral discipline, and intellectual development. The Nation of Islam has had success developing numerous businesses and its official organ, The Final Call, has the largest circulation of any black periodical in the nation. The organization has a paramilitary wing called the Fruit of Islam (FOI), a Muslim girls training corps class, and a University of Islam. Estimates of membership vary from around 50,000 to well over 100,000. They have been successful recruiting athletes and stars who have lent credibility to their movement. Today **Louis Farrakhan** heads the largest section of followers of Elijah Muhammad and the numerous organizations he founded. (AAB)

BIBLIOGRAPHY
Banks, William. *The Black Muslims*. Philadelphia: Chelsea, 1997.

National Association for the Advancement of Colored People (NAACP)

The National Association for the Advancement of Colored People (NAACP), an interracial civil rights organization, was founded in 1909 with the merging of the **Niagara Movement,** a black protest group led by **W.E.B. Du Bois,** and a group of concerned whites including activists such as Mary White Ovington. Created to struggle for the abolition of segregation and discrimination in American society and to ensure democratic rights for all, regardless of race, the NAACP is a membership organization with more than 1,800 local branches. Formal decision-making authority rests with the annual national convention, and in the interim, with the 64–member national board of directors. Although in practice, most decisions are made by the executive director, his staff, and increasingly the chairman of the board; in principle at least, the NAACP is guided by a popular mass base—a clearly identified constituency that is empowered to pass and execute judgement on its leaders' action. This feature (governance by an individually based membership) separates the NAACP from most political entities rooted in black America and helps account for the organization's century-long survival while other black organizations waxed and waned.

Throughout its history the NAACP has used a wide variety of political means to advance racial equality and progressive social policy, including public education campaigns, direct action/protest, and voter registration drives, but its most successful efforts have been in the areas of expanding constitutional rights through legal redress and securing enactment of laws through highly successful lobbying campaigns. In addition, the NAACP has increasingly sought to become more directly involved in the economic development of black communities, negotiating a number of what it calls "Fair Share" agreements with public and private sector entities in order to encourage hiring black workers and contracting black businesses. Long headquartered in New York, the organization moved its national office to Baltimore, Maryland, in 1986. (LFW)

BIBLIOGRAPHY
Kellogg, Charles. *NAACP: A History of the National Association for the Advancement of Colored People.* Baltimore: Johns Hopkins University Press, 1967.
Ovington, Mary. *Black and White Sat Down Together: The Reminiscences of a NAACP Founder.* New York: Feminist Press at the City University of New York, 1995.

National Association of Colored Women (NACW)

The National Association of Colored Women (NACW) was formed in 1896, with **Mary Church Terrell** as its first president. By 1916 NACW represented 50,000 women in 28 federations and over 1,000 clubs. It was led and directed by black women, without support from whites. It was the first national black organization, existing before the **National Association for the Advancement of Colored People (NAACP)** and the **National Urban League,** to deal with racial issues. Members provided scholarship loans for women to attend college; aided thousands of southern black women who migrated north to find jobs; protected young girls from unscrupulous labor agents; and provided job placement and training facilities in New York City. The emergence of the **National Council of Negro Women** in 1934 eclipsed the NACW. Newer civil rights and welfare organizations began to accomplish a good deal of the work NACW had done in the past more efficiently and with financial support of whites. (EC)

BIBLIOGRAPHY
Salem, Dorothy. *To Better Our World: Black Women in Organized Reform, 1890–1920.* Brooklyn, NY: Carlson, 1990.

National Black Election Study (NBES)

The 1984 and 1988 elections offered a special opportunity for scholars to shed light on a long history of African-American politics by going directly to African Americans in a broadscale national telephone survey. The National Black Election Study, conducted by the Institute for Social Research at the University of Michigan, examined the attitudes and political preferences of the black electorate during the 1984 and 1988 presidential campaigns. The 1984–1988 NBES is, in many respects, unique. Unlike past studies, the sample size is large enough to accommodate systematic and robust methodological techniques, and continuity within the African-American electorate over a critical four-year period. (VDD)

BIBLIOGRAPHY
Tate, Katherine. *From Protest to Politics: The New Black Voters in American Elections.* Cambridge: Harvard University Press, 1993.

National Coalition on Black Voter Participation, Inc.

The National Coalition on Black Voter Participation, Inc. is a nonprofit, nonpartisan membership organization based in Washington, D.C., consisting of 88 groups. Founded in 1976, the coalition is a leader in the nationwide effort to increase black voter registration and turnout and to eradicate the barriers to full political participation for blacks and other minorities. Operation Big Vote, the coalition's largest and most successful grassroots national voter participation program, conducts registration, education, and Get-Out-the-Vote activities. (VDD)

BIBLIOGRAPHY
Joint Center for Political Studies. *How to Organize and Implement a Successful Nonpartisan Voter Participation Campaign.* Washington, DC: Joint Center for Political Studies, 1996.

National Council of Negro Women (NCNW)

Founded in 1935 by **Mary McLeod Bethune,** the National Council of Negro Women (NCNW) was established to unite the talents and resources of all female African-American organizations. The NCNW was founded during the Great Depression, when President Franklin Roosevelt's New Deal legislative measures often discriminated against African Americans. Through the NCNW's journals and newsletters, members were and are urged to speak out on behalf of child welfare, education, voter registration, and economic self-help programs. (DH)

BIBLIOGRAPHY
Blackwell, Barbara Grant. "The Advocacies and Ideological Commitments of a Black Educator: Mary McLeod Bethune 1875–1955." Ph.D. dissertation, University of Connecticut, 1978.
Ross, Joyce. "Mary McLeod Bethune and the National Youth Administration: A Case Study of Power Relationships in the Black Cabinet of Franklin D. Roosevelt." In John Hope Franklin and August Meier, eds. *Black Leaders of the Twentieth Century.* Urbana: University of Illinois Press, 1982.

National Emigration Convention

The National Emigration Convention arose out of the black sovereignty movement of the early 1800s which advocated American blacks emigrating to countries such as Liberia or Haiti. The National Emigration Convention first met in 1856 under its president Martin Delany and succeeded in securing a $20,000 pledge from the Haitian secretary of state to assist emigrationists. The convention met again in 1858 with Delany being replaced by William H. Day. Delany became foreign secretary and travelled to Liberia in 1859 where some convention members eventually settled. The convention disbanded about the time of the **Civil War.**

BIBLIOGRAPHY
Robinson, Cedric. *Black Movements in America.* New York: Routledge, 1997.

National Equal Rights League

There were two distinct incarnations of the National Equal Rights League. The first was in the 1860s under the leadership of **John Mercer Langston.** The league was the outgrowth of a series of conventions held between 1830 and 1864 to address the conditions of African Americans in America. The

second incarnation of the National Equal Rights League was in 1908. The group was formed under the leadership of **William Monroe Trotter** of Boston who wanted to challenge **Booker T. Washington's** accommodationist position. Specifically, the group sought to prevent the election of William Howard Taft. However, the group failed in its goal to prevent Taft's election and soon after dissolved because of the growing power of the **National Association for the Advancement of Colored People (NAACP).**

BIBLIOGRAPHY
Bell, Howard H., ed. *Minutes of the Proceedings of the National Negro Conventions, 1830–1864.* New York: Arno Press, 1969.
Harding, Vincent. *There Is a River: The Black Struggle for Freedom in America.* New York: Harcourt Brace Jovanovich, 1981.

National Federation of Afro-American Women

Founded in Boston in 1895 as an outgrowth of the first National Conference of Colored Women of America, the National Federation of Afro-American Women was the first national organization representing African-American women. The group sought to improve the image of African-American women by instilling traditional middle class values. The organization merged with the National League of Colored Women in 1896 to form the **National Association of Colored Women (NACW).**

BIBLIOGRAPHY
Harly, Sharon and Rosalyn Terborg-Penn, eds. *The Afro-American Woman: Struggles and Images.* Port Washington, NY: Kennikat Press, 1978.

National Negro Business League (NNBL)

The National Negro Business League (NNBL), founded in 1900 by **Booker T. Washington,** was organized to help with the development of African-American owned businesses. The NNBL members hoped to set a positive example for the African-American masses and prove to white Americans how successful they could be once given the chance. Until his death in 1915, Booker T. Washington served as the sole president of the NNBL. (DH)

BIBLIOGRAPHY
Harlan, Louis R. "Booker T. Washington and the Politics of Accommodation." In John Hope Franklin and August Meier, eds. *Black Leaders of the Twentieth Century.* Urbana: University of Illinois Press, 1982.
Hornsby, Alton, Jr. *Milestones in 20th-Century African American History.* Detroit: Visible Ink Press, 1993.

National Negro Committee

In 1908, following race riots in Springfield, Illinois, an interracial group composed mainly of whites and a few prominent African Americans, including **W.E.B. Du Bois,** met and formed an organization called the National Negro Committee which soon changed its name to the **National Association for the Advancement of Colored People (NAACP).** Its goals were to end segregation, discrimination, disenfranchisement, and racial violence, particularly lynching. They were particularly concerned with the educational opportunities of black children and attaining the right for blacks to vote. They held their first conference May 31, 1909.

BIBLIOGRAPHY

Library of Congress. "The Booker T. Washington Era" <http://lcweb2.loc.gov/ammem/aaohtml/aopart6.html> in The African American Odyssey Web page <http://lcweb2.loc.gov/ammem/aaohtml/aohome.html>, 1998.

National Negro Congress

The National Negro Congress (NNC) was founded in 1935 at **Howard University** to seek improvement in the economic conditions of African Americans. The congress included labor, civic, religious, and fraternal organizations. NNC's first meeting was held in Chicago; at this meeting, **A. Philip Randolph** was selected to be president. The congress adopted three main goals at this first meeting: opposing discrimination against foreign-born blacks, encouraging unity among native and foreign-born blacks, and addressing the conditions of black people on an international basis.

BIBLIOGRAPHY

Papers of the National Negro Congress. Frederick, MD: University Publications of America, 1988.

National Urban League

Founded in 1910, the National Urban League is a social service and civil rights organization. The league is a nonprofit, community-based organization headquartered in New York City, with 114 affiliates in 34 states and the District of Columbia. The organization's mission is to assist African Americans in the achievement of social and economic equality. In the 1990s, the league, under the leadership of Hugh B. Price, emphasizes greater reliance on the resources and strengths of the black community. (VDD)

BIBLIOGRAPHY

Ayers-Williams, Roz. "The New Rights Agenda." *Black Enterprise* 28, no. 1 (August 1997): 85.
"Cities: The Soul of America: Make America Work For All Americans." *Vital Speeches* 62, no. 10 (March 1, 1996): 293.
Coleman, Trevor W. "Change at the Top." *Emerge* 6, no. 1 (October 1994): 44.
Ryder, Julianne Ryan. "Urban League President Says Local Officials Must Work for the Children." *Nation's Cities Weekly* 17, no. 49 (December 12, 1994): 12.
"Urban League Releases 'State of America Report:' Calls for Urban Jobs Policy." *Jet* 91, no. 4 (December 9, 1996): 6.
Weiss, Nancy. *National Urban League, 1910–1940.* New York: Oxford University Press, 1974.

National Welfare Rights Organization

The National Welfare Rights Organization was an organization of poor African-American women founded in 1966. Active in the 1960s and early 1970s, the group lobbied for changes in the welfare programs through the use of protests and sit-ins. Among the goals of the group's agenda were increased cash payments and more government caseworkers who were sympathetic to their situations.

BIBLIOGRAPHY

Pope, Jacqueline. *Biting the Hand that Feeds Them.* New York: Praeger, 1989.
West, Guida. *The National Welfare Rights Organization: The Social Protest of Poor Women.* New York: Praeger, 1981.

Negro Convention Movement

The Negro Convention Movement, which began in 1830 as a means of achieving broad leadership among northern blacks, continued until the onset of the **Civil War**. The group provided a forum for debating the issues of the time such as **slavery** and **discrimination;** the movement also held national conventions. The organization represented a peaceful movement, preferring to rely on moral persuasion rather than violence. Despite this, at the 1843 convention in Buffalo, New York, a motion was made by **Henry Highland Garnet** to "declare violence an acceptable tool in the destruction of slavery." The motion was subsequently voted down 19–15.

BIBLIOGRAPHY

Bell, Howard H. *Survey of the Negro Convention Movement.* Stratford, NH: Ayer, 1970.

The New Black Politics

The new black politics was a movement which began in the late 1960s representing a change from black politics as a struggle for rights to black politics being a quest for power. After the civil rights gains of the 1960s and 1970s, black politicians had access to resources and a voting constituency that could place them in positions to assist their communities and further work for economic and social equality. The aim of the new black politics was to use the authority of elected positions to unify the black community to create social change for themselves. The movement ran into problems when black elected officials found themselves without the broad-based support they felt their elections had implied, or without a coherent sense of mission within their constituency. Mayor of Cleveland **Carl Stokes,** who was elected in 1967, was felt to be an example of the rise and fall of new black politics.

BIBLIOGRAPHY

Preston, Michael, ed. *The New Black Politics: The Search for Political Power.* New York: Longman, 1982.

The New South

In 1866 *Atlanta Constitution* editor Henry Grady expressed a boosterism dear to the hearts of middle-class businessmen in both the North and the South when he told the New England Society that "There was a South of slavery and secession—that South is dead." Grady's comments were meant to facilitate sectional reconciliation and secure financing for industrial projects; his aim was to ease northern fears about "unreconstructed rebels" while reminding wealthy northerners of the South's low taxes and nonunionized workforce. Grady's claim of a "new" South in the postbellum years was but the first of several such claims made between the late 1860s and the 1970s. For African Americans, however, the era brought **Jim Crow**

laws that formalized **segregation** and **discrimination** in the South, thus removing political, social, and economic opportunity. (GAA)

BIBLIOGRAPHY

Gaston, Paul. *The New South Creed: A Study in Southern Mythmaking*. New York: Alfred Knopf, 1970.
Woodward, C. Vann. *The Origins of the New South, 1877–1913*. Baton Rouge: Louisiana State University Press, 1971.

New York State Club Association v. City of New York (1988)

Local law in New York prohibited **discrimination** on the basis of race, creed, color, national origin, or sex by any place of public accommodation while exempting, as "distinctly private," benevolent orders and religious corporations. In *New York State Club Association v. City of New York,* 487, U.S. 1 (1988), the Supreme Court held that the First Amendment was not facially violated by the law nor by the provision that some clubs within the reach of the law were exempted as "distinctly private." The **Fourteenth Amendment** challenge under the equal protection clause was also denied. (PLF)

BIBLIOGRAPHY

Finlay, Paula J. "Prying Open the Clubhouse Door: Defining the 'Distinctly Private' Club after New York State Club Association v City of New York." *Washington University Law Quarterly* 68, no. 2 (Summer 1990): 371–97.

Huey P. Newton (1942–1989)

Huey Percy Newton was born on February 17, 1942, in New Orleans, Louisiana. Newton was a black militant activist and a co-founder with **Bobby Seale** of the **Black Panther Party** (originally called Black Panther Party for Self-Defense).

Newton was an illiterate high school graduate who taught himself to read. He met Bobby Seale at the San Francisco School of Law. Seale and Newton founded the Black Panther Party in response to their feeling that such a party was required to stop police brutality and defend the black community. The party never had much more than 2,000 members.

In 1967 Newton was convicted and imprisoned on charges of voluntary manslaughter of a police officer. Less than two years later Newton was freed when his conviction was reversed. In 1971 he turned to nonviolence, stating that the Panthers would focus on community service and nonviolence.

In 1974 Newton was charged with another murder. After fleeing the country for three years, he returned to face trial. Two trials led to hung juries. Newton held a Ph.D. in social philosophy from the University of California at Santa Cruz (1980); his dissertation, "War Against the Panthers," was subtitled "A Study of Repression in America."

The Panthers disbanded in 1982. The party was torn by dissension. In 1982 Newton was given a six-month jail term for using funds intended for a Panther-founded school. In August 1989, Newton was shot dead during a drug deal in Oakland, California.

BIBLIOGRAPHY

Pearson, Hugh. *The Shadow of the Panther: Huey Newton and the Price of Black Power in America*. Reading, MA: Addison-Wesley, 1994.

Niagara Conference

In 1905, a group of 29 highly educated black men, led by **W.E.B. Du Bois**, met in Canada near Niagara Falls to organize a protest movement against the widespread **civil rights** abuses suffered by blacks. This meeting was also a reaction against the accomodationist philosophy of **Booker T. Washington**. From this conference came the **Niagara Manifesto** with its call for agitation and protest to achieve civil rights. Subsequent conferences were held annually until 1909, when the organization was dissolved, only to be reborn as part of the **National Association for the Advancement of Colored People (NAACP)**. (WPS)

BIBLIOGRAPHY

Du Bois, W.E.B. *Dusk of Dawn: An Essay Toward an Autobiography of a Race Concept*. New York: Schocken Books, 1968.
Marable, Manning. *W.E.B. Du Bois: Black Radical Democrat*. Boston: Twayne, 1986.

Niagara Manifesto

Written mainly by **W.E.B. Du Bois** and **William Monroe Trotter,** the Niagara Manifesto was the official platform of the 1905 **Niagara Conference**. This "Declaration of Principles" called for manhood suffrage, civil rights, and educational reform. Agitation and protest were advocated to achieve these ends. "We claim for ourselves every single right that belongs to free born Americans, political, civil, and social; and until we get these rights we will never cease to protest and assail the ears of America." (WPS)

BIBLIOGRAPHY

Lester, Julius, ed. *The Seventh Son: The Thoughts and Writings of W.E.B. Du Bois*. New York: Random House, 1971.
Lewis, David Levering. *W.E.B. Du Bois: Biography of a Race, 1868–1919*. New York: Henry Holt, 1993.

Niagara Movement

Founded in 1905 under the leadership of **W.E.B. Du Bois** and **William Monroe Trotter,** the Niagara movement challenged the philosophy of **Booker T. Washington**. The Niagara movement was the impetus for blacks drifting away from the Republican Party, and contributed to the formation of the **National Association for the Advancement of Colored People (NAACP)**.

Du Bois decided to form an alternative organization after attempting to work with Washington's supporters. Du Bois became discouraged because they rejected his suggestions, and also because Washington prevented newspapers from printing any criticism of his methods. In June 1905, Du Bois invited black leaders to gather in Buffalo, New York, to pursue black freedom and protest Washington's tactics.

Unwelcome in Buffalo's hotels, the group of 29 instead convened in Fort Erie, Ontario, on July 10, 1905. The meeting produced a "Declaration of Principles" calling for justice for America's 10 million blacks, and a group known as the Niagara Movement. They met again in August 1906 in Harper's Ferry, Virginia. In a rousing final statement, Du Bois advocated quality education and suffrage for blacks. He questioned why America could absorb 10 million immigrants into citizenship, but not 10 million blacks.

During the third and largest meeting of the Niagara Movement, in Boston during August 1907, a split between Du Bois and Trotter became evident. Lack of funds and dissension among his colleagues was beginning to overwhelm Du Bois. In 1908 Trotter left the organization. In 1909 Du Bois and others began laying the groundwork for a new civil rights group, which became the NAACP in 1911. That summer Du Bois canceled the Niagara convention and urged its members to join the NAACP. Most did and the Niagara Movement was no more; however, its goals were kept alive by the NAACP. (AD)

BIBLIOGRAPHY

Lewis, David Levering. *W.E.B. Du Bois: Biography of a Race, 1868–1919*. New York: Henry Holt, 1993.

Robert C. Nix (1928–1987)

Robert Nix earned his law degree from the University of Pennsylvania. He was first elected to Congress in a special election in 1958 and was Pennsylvania's first black congressman. A Democrat, Nix served on the Veteran's Affairs Committee and the Foreign Affairs Committee. In 1977 he became chairman of the Committee on the Post Office and Civil Service. He was not renominated in 1978 and retired from political life.

BIBLIOGRAPHY

Ragsdale, Bruce and Joel Treese. *Black Americans in Congress 1870–1989*. Washington DC: U.S. Government Printing Office, 1990.

Edgar Daniel Nixon (1899–1987)

Edgar Daniel Nixon was born in Alabama and worked as a Pullman car porter from 1923 until 1964. In 1938 he became the president of the newly unionized Brotherhood of Sleeping Car Porters. He worked actively for voter registration rights and became president of the Alabama chapter of the **National Association for the Advancement of Colored People (NAACP)** in 1947.

BIBLIOGRAPHY

McKissack, Pat. *A Long Hard Journey: The Story of the Pullman Porter*. New York: Walker.

Nixon v. Condon (1932)

Many southern states instituted use of a white primary to exclude African Americans from voting in the post-**Reconstruction** period. Denying African Americans partici-

pation in the Democratic primaries, in an overwhelmingly Democratic region, effectively eliminated them from voting. The **National Association for the Advancement of Colored People (NAACP)** spearheaded the fight against the white primary and this case was one of its first victories. In *Nixon v. Condon,* 286, U.S. 73 (1932), the U.S. Supreme Court ruled the Democratic Party in Texas was, in effect, a state agency bound by federal election laws that prohibited excluding members on the basis of race. (CE)

BIBLIOGRAPHY

Hine, Darlene Clark. *Black Victory: The Rise and Fall of the White Primary in Texas*. Millwood, New York: KTO Press, 1979.

The North Star

On December 3, 1847, a newspaper appeared in Rochester, New York called *The North Star*. Its editor and guiding spirit was **Frederick Douglass,** and its staff was composed partly of former slaves like Douglass. The North Star's motto, written boldly under its title, was "Right is of No Sex—Truth is of No Color—God is the Father of Us All, and All We are Brethren." The name "North Star" was chosen to recall the star that shines brightest when all else is dark. As that first issue explains, the North Star pointed the way to the free, northern states and Canada. This star was "to millions in our boasted land of liberty . . . the Star of Hope."

Two years earlier, in 1845, Douglass had become a leading voice in the anti-slavery movement with the publication of his "Narrative of the Life of Frederick Douglass." Douglass spent nearly all of the next two years overseas, fearing that his former owner in Baltimore would attempt to recapture him. It was only after some of his British supporters purchased his freedom that Douglass returned to the United States and started publishing *The North Star*.

In 1851, Douglass joined his successful newspaper with the *Liberty Party Paper*, and the new publication was then called, simply, *Frederick Douglass' Paper*. This paper continued its run until the eve of the **Civil War** in 1860. Using his powerful voice amplified even further by his newspapers, Douglass showed the way to many—in part via the Underground Railroad, on which his house in Rochester was a station—on the road to freedom. (AJC)

BIBLIOGRAPHY

Douglass, Frederick. *The Life and Writings of Frederick Douglass. 4 vols.* Philip S. Foner, ed. New York: International Publishers, 1950–1955.
Fuller, Edmund. *A Star Pointed North*. London: Harper, 1946.
Levine, Robert S. *Martin Delaney, Frederick Douglass, and the Politics of Representative Identity*. Chapel Hill, NC: University of North Carolina Press, 1997.

Eleanor Holmes Norton (1938–)

Eleanor Holmes Norton, a Democrat, is currently a member of the U.S. House of Representatives. First elected in 1990, she represents the District of Columbia as a nonvoting delegate. While in Congress, she has served as the vice-chairperson of the Congressional Caucus for Women's Issues. From 1977 to 1981, Norton chaired the United States **Equal Employment Opportunity Commission (EEOC).** She was chair of the New York Commission on Human Rights from 1970 to 1976. Norton has also served as assistant legal director for the American Civil Liberties Union.

BIBLIOGRAPHY

Diamonstein, Barbaralee. *Open Secrets: Ninety-Four Women in Touch with Our Time.* New York: Viking, 1972.

Leeman, Richard W., ed. *African-American Orators: A Bio-Critical Sourcebook.* Westport, CT: Greenwood, 1996.

Office of Federal Contract Compliance (OFCC)

Under the guidance of President Lyndon B. Johnson, the Office of Federal Contract Compliance (OFCC) was issued the task of implementing **Executive Order No. 11246** and imposing any relative sanctions. This order, which forced all federal contractors to assure the government of nondiscriminatory hiring practices, also held as one of the first pieces of legislation set to take **affirmative action** toward equal opportunity and protection. These affirmative action plans made contractors regularly evaluate the hiring of minority personnel in regards to promotions, transfers, and other employment practices; it also helped regulate the 100,000 or so federal contract firms which at the time hired about one-third of the country's labor force. In 1968 and 1970, the OFCC clarified their contractor guidelines for affirmative-action programs. These new guidelines allowed for more monitoring and guidance by the OFCC, while having contractors analyze their use of minority workers, create goals to cover any incorrect practices, and document periodically the movement toward these goals.

BIBLIOGRAPHY

Corpus, David A. and Linda Rosenwerg, eds. *The OFCC and Federal Contract Compliance.* New York: Practicing Law Institute, 1981.

James E. O'Hara (1841–1905)

James O'Hara studied law at **Howard University** and was admitted to the North Carolina bar in 1873. After serving as a delegate to the state constitutional convention in 1875, he was elected to the House of Representatives as a Republican in 1882 where he actively campaigned for civil rights. He served two terms, being defeated for reelection in 1886. He returned to the practice of law.

BIBLIOGRAPHY

Ragsdale, Bruce and Joel Treese. *Black Americans in Congress 1870–1989.* Washington DC: U.S. Government Printing Office, 1990.

Reid, George W. "Four in Black: North Carolina's Black Congressman 1874–1901" *Journal of Negro History* 64 (Summer 1979): 229–43.

Hazel O'Leary (1937–)

During President Gerald Ford's administration, Hazel O'Leary was appointed to her first national political position as director of the Office of Consumer Affairs for the Federal Energy Administration. In 1977 O'Leary became deputy director and later director of the Economic Regulatory Administration for President Jimmy Carter. In this role she enforced price controls on the oil, natural gas, and electric utility industries in an attempt to deal with the energy crisis.

In 1981 she left public office and took a position in private industry. A major donor to the Democratic Party and to Bill Clinton's 1992 presidential campaign, O'Leary was appointed Secretary of Energy in 1993, becoming the first African American to hold that post. She left office after Clinton's first term in 1997. However, O'Leary continued to be controversial because she was part of an ongoing investigation of influence peddling in the Clinton administration.

BIBLIOGRAPHY

Glick, Daniel. "Hazel O'Leary Had Better Be Tough." *Working Woman* 19 (December 1994): 42–47.

Open Housing Act of 1968

The Fair Housing Act of the Civil Rights Act of 1968, the first open housing law in the United States, prohibits discrimination based on race, sex, national origin, color, religion, handicap, and familial status and also in the sale, rental, financing, and advertising of housing. The act further provides significant penalties for violators, awards the Department of Housing and Urban Development the authority to initiate complaints, and awards the Department of Justice litigation authority. (VDD)

BIBLIOGRAPHY

Bartley, Numan V. and Hugh D. Graham. *Southern Politics & the Second Reconstruction.* Baltimore: The Johns Hopkins University Press, 1975.

Operation Big Vote (OBV)

Operation Big Vote (OBV) is one of the largest programs sponsored by the **National Coalition on Black Voter Participation**. It is a nationwide, nonpartisan, grassroots organization committed to intensive voter registration and education as well as get-out-the-vote campaigns in black communities. There are 35 OBV chapters across the United States. **See also** Black Women's Roundtable.

BIBLIOGRAPHY

Fletcher, Michael A. and Hamil R. Harns. "Farrakhan Announces Voter Drive." *Washington Post* (October 19, 1995): A3.

Overbea, Luix. "OBV Moves to Register Minority Voters." *Christian Science Monitor* (July 19, 1983): 7.

Operation PUSH (People United to Serve Humanity)

In 1971, the Reverend **Jesse L. Jackson**, one of America's foremost civil rights leaders for over 30 years, and **Charles Author Hayes,** a member of Congress from 1983–1993, co-founded the Chicago-based Operation PUSH (People United to Serve Humanity) with a dedicated core group of associates and clergymen. The organization's expressed mission is to expand the educational and economic opportunities for the disadvantaged and minority communities. Under Jackson's direction, Operation PUSH has become one of the most influential self-help human rights organizations in the world. (VDD)

BIBLIOGRAPHY

"Operation PUSH Maps Strategy to Stop Inner-city Violence During Its 23rd Annual Convention in Atlanta." *Jet* 86, no. 17 (August 29, 1994): 12.

"Rev. Jackson to Lead Operation PUSH Again in Chicago." *Jet* 89, no. 6 (December 18, 1995): 4.

"Rev. Jessie Jackson Celebrates 25th Anniversary of Operation PUSH." *Jet* 90, no. 21 (October 7, 1996): 8.

Oregon v. Mitchell (1970)

Oregon and several other states challenged three provisions in the Voting Rights Amendments of 1970, claiming that they were unconstitutional. The states argued that Congress did not have the power to: (1) lower the minimum age for voting from 21 to 18 in state and federal elections; (2) bar the use of literacy tests; and (3) forbid states from disqualifying persons from voting in federal elections because they did not meet state residency requirements. In *Oregon v. Mitchell* 400, U.S. 112 (1970), the Court ruled that the minimum age of 18 was valid for federal elections but that states could determine minimum age for their elections; that the literacy test could be banned; and that state residency was not a requirement for voting in federal elections. (AD)

BIBLIOGRAPHY

Bybee, Keith J. *Mistaken Identity*. Princeton, NJ: Princeton University Press, 1998.

Celada, Raymond J. *Voting Rights Act Amendments of 1970*. Washington, DC: Congressional Research Service, 1971.

Organization of Afro-American Unity

Founded in 1965 by the leader of the **Nation of Islam, Malcolm X**, the Organization of Afro-American Unity sought to link together Black Muslims from around the world. This universal brotherhood of Islam would then address common concerns. The organization, however, ceased to exist after the assassination of Malcolm X in 1965.

BIBLIOGRAPHY

Bracey, John H. *Black Nationalism in America*. Indianapolis: Bobbs-Merrill, 1970.

Malcolm X and Alex Haley. The Autobiography of Malcolm X. New York: Chelsea House, 1996.

Major Owens (1936–)

Elected to the New York Senate in 1975, Owens served for eight years before he was elected to the U.S. House of Representatives in 1982 from the Central Brooklyn, Flatbush areas. He currently serves as the ranking Democrat on the Workforce Protections Committee. (CEM)

BIBLIOGRAPHY

Duncan, Philip D. and Christine C. Lawrence. *Politics in America: 1996 The 104th Congress*. Washington, DC: Congressional Quarterly Press, 1995.

Wiley, Ed III. "Owens Calls for 'Marshall Plan' for Inner Cities." *Black Issues in Higher Education* 6, no. 23 (February 15, 1990): 10.

P

Alan Page (1945–)

Alan Page played professional football with the Minnesota Vikings from 1967 to 1978 and for the Chicago Bears from 1978 to 1981. He completed his law degree in 1978 and became a corporate lawyer in 1981. He practiced in the office of the state attorney general and was elected to the Minnesota Supreme Court in 1993. (JCW)

BIBLIOGRAPHY

Margolick, David. "From Football Glory, a Step Up to Bench." *New York Times* 1, (January 1993): A1.

Pan-Africanism

Pan-Africanism is the term used to describe the movement to create a link between all peoples with African ancestral antecedents. Pan meaning all and Africanism referring to the continent of Africa and the peoples living there, Pan-Africanism incorporates several aspects of this movement. The American antecedents go back to Paul Cuffe, **Frederick Douglass**, and Martin Delaney, who all tried to turn the African-American struggle into an international struggle. Pan-Africanism influenced **Richard Allen** and **Absalom Jones** who developed the independent black church. Pan-Africanism came into popular use in 1900 after several conferences were organized by Benito Sylvain and Henry Williams, a Haitian and a Trinidadian, respectively. **W.E.B. Du Bois** dominated the first Pan-African conference. Between 1900 and 1915 Joseph Casely-Hayford, an Ethiopian kept the movement going. Pan-Africanism got a boost from **Marcus Garvey** and his **Universal Negro Improvement Association (UNIA).** They successfully pushed the world towards an emphasis on African unity. After World War I interest in Africans increased as the Europeans divided up Africa among its victors. By the 1950s, African nations were slowly throwing off their colonial chains and moving towards independence. In the 1960s, Pan-Africanism got another boost from the work of Kwame Nkrumah, **Malcolm X** and W.E.B. Du Bois who all emphasized African unity and economic development. In 1963 the rival groups associated with the Pan-African movement met in Addis Ababa, Ethiopia, where they wrote the charter for the Organization of African Unity, the official Pan-African organization. (AAB)

BIBLIOGRAPHY

Geiss, Immanuel. *The Pan-African Movement.* London: Methuen, 1974

Moses, Wilson J., ed. *Classical Black Nationalism.* New York: New York University Press, 1996.

Rosa Parks (1913–)

Rosa Parks is credited with starting the **Montgomery Bus Boycott** in Alabama on December 1, 1955, when she refused to give up her seat and move to the back of the bus. Parks, contrary to myth, was a member of the **National Association for the Advancement of Colored People (NAACP)** who had challenged segregated busing many times before her arrest. Parks has become a symbol of dignified defiance to inequality. In 1996, President Bill Clinton gave her the Medal of Freedom. She moved to Detroit and worked for many years for Congressman **John Conyers** (D-MI) and founded the Rosa and Raymond Parks Institute for Self-Development to foster leadership among black youth. (FAS)

BIBLIOGRAPHY

Gray, Fred D. *Bus Ride to Justice.* Montgomery, AL: Black Belt Press.

Parks, Rosa. *Rosa Parks: My Story 1995.* New York: Dial Books, 1992.

Patton v. Mississippi (1948)

Patton, who was black, was convicted of the murder of a white man and sentenced to death. He appealed on the grounds that African Americans had been systematically, intentionally, and deliberately excluded from jury service in the county where his trial took place, and therefore his Equal Protection rights under the **Fourteenth Amendment** had been violated. In *Patton v. Mississippi*, 332, U.S. 463 (1948), the Supreme Court agreed, noting that no blacks had served on a jury in that county for over 30 years, although one-third of the population was African American.

BIBLIOGRAPHY

Fukurui, Hiroshi. *Race and the Jury.* New York: Plenum Press, 1993.

McDonald, Laughlin. *The Rights of Racial Minorities.* Carbondale: Southern Illinois University Press, 1993.

Donald M. Payne (1934–)

In 1994, Payne was selected as chair of the Democratic **Congressional Black Caucus,** which brought him national notoriety. Payne was first elected to the U.S. House of Representatives in 1988 in the 10th district of Newark and Jersey City, New Jersey, becoming the states's first black elected to Congress. He has been very active in international affairs, especially with regard to Haiti, Africa, and human rights in general. (CEM)

BIBLIOGRAPHY

Cheers, D. Michael. "Donald Payne: New Jersey's First Black Congressman." *Ebony* 44, no. 7 (May 1989): 92–94.

Duncan, Philip D. and Christine C. Lawrence. *Politics in America: 1996 The 104th Congress.* Washington, DC: Congressional Quarterly Press, 1995.

Clarence Pendleton (1930–1988)

Born in Louisville, Kentucky, Clarence Pendleton became the first African-American chairman of the U.S. Commission on Civil Rights. Appointed by President Ronald Reagan in 1981, Pendleton frequently made headlines during his years on the commission. He was an outspoken critic of **affirmative action,** calling such programs "the new racism." A **Howard University** graduate, Pendleton served as president of the Urban League of San Diego from 1975 to 1981. In 1988, while still chairman of the Commission on Civil Rights, Pendleton died of a heart attack. (VDD)

BIBLIOGRAPHY

Devroy, Ann. "Longtime Bush Ally to Head Rights Unit; President Aims to Make Commission 'Respectable Again,' Aides Say." *The Washington Post* (March 22, 1989): A9.

Miller, Jeffrey. "Claremont Professor Takes Helm of Civil Rights Panel." *The Los Angeles Times* (September 25, 1988): 10.

"Reagan Praises Civil Rights Chief as Apostle of Justice." *The Associated Press* (June 6, 1988).

Anna Perez (1951–)

Anna Perez began her career in journalism running a community newspaper in Tacoma, Washington. She was a congressional press aide to Senator Slade Gorton (R-WA). In 1989 she was appointed to be Barbara Bush's press secretary, the first African American ever to hold that position. She is an executive at Creative Artists Agency.

BIBLIOGRAPHY

"Anna Perez Boards Bush Administration as First Lady's Press Secretary." *Jet,* February 6, 1989.

Edward S. Perkins (1928–)

Edward S. Perkins, career diplomat, became the first African-American ambassador to South Africa in 1986. During his four-year tenure, he routinely criticized the apartheid regime. From May 1992 until January 1993, he was the first African-American U.S. ambassador to the United Nations appointed by a Republican. (AD)

BIBLIOGRAPHY

Baker, Pauline. *The United States and South Africa: The Reagan Years.* New York: Ford Foundation, 1989.

Philadelphia Plan

The Philadelphia Plan was an **affirmative action** program instituted by the Department of Labor under the leadership of Secretary George Shultz. The plan required that companies bidding on contracts of $500,000 or more must submit an acceptable affirmative action program for the work to be done. To avoid problems of quotas, bids had to express the target ranges of their plans in percentages. Congress attempted to ban the plan in 1969, however, the Nixon administration successfully prevented it. A challenge to the plan in the federal courts reached the Third Circuit Court of Appeals in 1971. The court held that the plan was constitutional.

BIBLIOGRAPHY

Graham, Hugh Davis. *The Civil Rights Era.* New York: Oxford University Press, 1992.

Samuel Riley Pierce, Jr. (1922–)

Samuel Pierce, Jr. served as secretary of the U.S. Department of Housing and Urban Development (HUD) during the Reagan administration. While in this position, Pierce was accused of political corruption in his handling of HUD's rehabilitation program contracts, though never charged with a crime. Earlier, from 1970 to 1973, during the second Nixon administration, he was general counsel for the U.S. Treasury Department. From 1956 to 1957, Pierce served as associate counsel and counsel for the House Judiciary Antitrust Subcommittee. From 1953 to 1955, he was assistant to the undersecretary of labor. Pierce also served as a judge in the New York Court of General Sessions in 1959 and as an assistant U.S. attorney for the southern District of New York from 1953 to 1955.

BIBLIOGRAPHY

DeLeon, Peter. *Thinking about Political Corruption.* Armonk, NY: M.E. Sharpe, 1993.

"Former HUD Secretary Samuel Pierce Will Not Be Charged." *Jet* 87, no. 12 (Jan 30 1995): 39.

Schultz, Jeffrey D. *Presidential Scandals.* Washington, DC: Congressional Quarterly. 1999.

Pinckney Benton Stewart Pinchback (1837–1921)

P.B.S. Pinchback was among the founders of the Republican Party in Louisiana and was elected to the state's 1867 constitutional convention. He became lieutenant governor of Louisiana in 1871 and was acting governor for six weeks in 1872 and 1873, following the impeachment of Governor Warmoth. He advocated for universal suffrage, civil rights, tax-supported education, and opposition to legal discrimination. He won election to the United States House of Representatives in 1872 and to the U.S. Senate in 1873, but was denied his seat. He continued to be prominent in Louisiana politics until he moved to New York City in 1897, and continued his political activism. (EC)

BIBLIOGRAPHY
Haskind, James. *Pinckney Benton Stewart Pinchback.* New York: Macmillan, 1973.

Plessy v. Ferguson (1896)

In 1896, Homer Plessy, a mixed race man, deliberately defied Louisiana's 1890 law segregating public transportation by boarding a "white" railway car in order to provide a test case challenge. Plessy and his supporters asserted that segregated facilities were a violation of his **Thirteenth** and **Fourteenth Amendment** rights under the U.S. Constitution and sought a ruling barring New Orleans Parish Judge John H. Ferguson from proceeding with the prosecution of the case. Rejected by the state courts, Plessy appealed to the Supreme Court of the United States. In *Plessy v. Ferguson,* 163, U.S. 537 (1896), the Supreme Court denied his suit ruling that although the Fourteenth Amendment provided political equality, it did not provide social equality.

Justice Henry Brown, for the majority, held that Louisiana's statute providing for "equal but separate accommodations" existed for the "promotion of the public good" and not the specific "oppression of a particular class." Therefore, according to Justice Brown, it was a reasonable part of the state's regulatory interest. Brown's decision further cited the example of segregated schools "even where the political rights of the colored race have been longest and most earnestly enforced." Justice John Marshall Harlan, in a dissenting opinion, called the law " a thin disguise" for exclusion of blacks for the convenience of whites and, that as such, it did constitute a symbolic "badge of servitude" in violation of the Thirteenth Amendment. Following the decision, "separate but equal" would be accepted as the criterion for evaluating segregation law cases until the 1954 decision in *Brown v. Topeka, Kansas Board of Education,* 347, U.S. 483 (1954). (GAA)

BIBLIOGRAPHY
Lofgren, Charles A. *The Plessy Case: A Legal-Historical Interpretation.* New York: Oxford University Press, 1987.
Tushnet, Mark V. *The NAACP's Legal Strategy against Segregated Education.* Chapel Hill: University of North Carolina Press, 1987.

Political Leadership

The study of leadership is as old as mankind and absolutely central to the study of politics and political theory. It is difficult to precisely define the concept of political leadership when variables such as political behavior and institutional structures must be taken into consideration. These different variables account for a plethora of different explanations and definitions of political leadership. One common definition of political leadership asserts that qualities of an effective leader include those that sustain individuals, groups, or peoples during times of tribulations and acute crisis, enabling them not only to endure the existing situations—often of hardship—but to challenge them sufficiently to transcend them.

Political leaders in minority communities often have two very different sets of relationships with at least two communities. Leaders in minority communities must have at least a working relationship with the "majority" community and at least a positive, representative working relationship with their own or the minority community that they represent. Historically the interests of these two communities are portrayed as being in direct opposition to each other. For example, much of the competitiveness, rivalry, and opportunism of African-American political leadership emanates from the need to satisfy—or not exceed—the demands of white supporters, while remaining responsive to the desires of black constituents. As a result many political leaders that are members of a minority group refer to their craft as a "politics of limited options."

Frederick Douglass, the preeminent African-American abolitionist of the nineteenth Century, is an excellent example of this dilemma. In his relationship to the white majority of society he often had to deal with paternalism and hostility. Whites controlled the abolition movement. When blacks began to function within its ranks, there was often a tendency by whites to assume a paternal posture. Many white abolitionist leaders expected to set policy and make decisions. When blacks challenged this paternalism, the reaction of formerly sympathetic white allies could be severe. Douglass not only had to deal with the expectations of sympathetic whites, but also with the actions of hostile ones. African American political leadership in slave societies and post-**Reconstruction** America was met with discouragement and most often violence. The pro-**slavery** forces did not hesitate to utilize physical violence to intimidate or silence contrary voices.

Another example of this struggle is the battle between the accommodationist educator **Booker T. Washington** and the political and legal activist **W.E.B. Du Bois**. Washington's **Tuskegee Institute** was financed through wealthy white businessmen such as Andrew Carnegie. Many historians suggest that as a result of the influence and support of the white elite Washington did not advocate for the natural legal rights guaranteed to all citizens of the United States focusing instead on economic development. Du Bois, whose relationship to the majority white community was significantly different from Washington's, advocated for immediate legal, economic, and social equality.

Both Washington and Du Bois, as well as many other historical and contemporary minority leaders, dealt with jealousy, rumors, and the charge that they "lost their roots." Sometimes the elevation to prominence and recognition of political leadership will produce in itself an alienation of that individual from the drive and urgency that first propelled them to public notoriety. There is also a danger inherent in leadership that the leaders become so far removed from the roots of their own experience that they lose contact with those roots. The alienation of black leadership from the roots of the black experience is an especially pertinent problem in the contemporary black community.

Contemporary research conducted by **Lani Guinier** suggests that fundamental institutional processes encumber leadership in minority communities more so than political leadership. Guinier contends that as a matter of broad democratic theory, political leadership should begin to worry more about the fundamental fairness of a permanent majority hegemony in a political system whose legitimacy is based solely on the consent of a simple, racially homogenous majority. Guinier also tries to refocus the analysis upon the problems affecting marginalized groups within the legislative decision-making process. Other examples of institutional processes that hinder minority political leadership include lack of public financing of campaigns; lack of a national referenda; the incremental nature of how decisions are made within state, local, and federal bureaucracies that favor the status quo; and the structure and role of interest groups. Her main point argues that political leadership should be more concerned with having minority political preferences satisfied than mere physical representation.

Since 1965 minorities have made measurable progress in stimulating voter registration and electing candidates to public office, especially from electoral units in which they are in the majority. Relatively few minority office holders, however, have been elected from majority white electoral districts. Neither the election of minority office holders nor being the swing vote on determining which majority candidate will be elected constitutes prima facie evidence that the minority vote has transformed into minority political power. The real test of political power and political leadership is the extent to which those who are elected with minority support are able to secure passage of public policies supportive of minority interests.

Carol Swain sets out to examine political leadership in minority communities by asking what is distinctive about black representation of blacks, how white members of Congress fit into the picture, and how black representation can be increased. If the minority group is a majority in the electoral district, it can elect a representative of its own choosing. If not, its members must forge coalitions with others to elect candidates and pursue its interests.

Swain examines racial gerrymandering, the manipulation of district lines to enhance or reduce the representation of particular racial groups, and the subsequent creation of majority black single member districts. She concludes that they are not the answer to the crisis in black political leadership. Swain argues that future growth in the political leadership of African Americans in Congress cannot come from creating newly black districts and that increased black representation from majority-white districts is possible. She further argues that packing black voters into one district diminishes the overall representation of blacks and that whites can represent the interests of members of minority communities. Swain reports that the black community as well as other minority communities are beset with problems that cannot be adequately addressed by minority members of Congress alone. Not only must minorities in Congress make alliances with like-minded

representatives from other races and ethnic backgrounds, but they must also rethink their own priorities and the relationship of those priorities to their respective community's needs.

Central to any theory of democracy is the idea that liberty depends on sharing in self government. In the deliberative democracy of the United States, unfortunately, race and gender questions have always been fundamental antagonisms. Substantial factions from each community are inclined to view an unfavorable outcome as a threat to its way of life. In *Democracy's Conversation*, Lani Guinier suggests that "Visible sores of a poisoned, winner-take-all electoral political system" have greatly damaged civic culture. According to Guinier, a "discourse of blame" has taken over democratic citizenship and politics as a zero sum game has resulted in an alarming political reality; people don't think about issues, they simply choose sides. Under such circumstances, majority rule decisions are often met with defiance by one side or the other. Such tensions are inherent when there is a commitment to both majority rule and minority rights.

The issue of political leadership in minority communities is complex and difficult to measure. Institutional changes as radical as the **Fifteenth** and Nineteenth Amendments to the Constitution, and the **Civil Rights Act of 1964,** as well as institutional changes as incremental as gerrymandering and campaign finance reform, effect the available options for minority political leadership. Political leadership in minority communities must build effective coalitions and partnerships in order to attain significant political power that ensures passage of policy preferences. (RAM)

BIBLIOGRAPHY

Blondel, Jean. *Political Leadership.* London: Sage Press, 1987.
Gardner, John. *On Leadership.* New York: The Free Press, 1990.
Guinier, Lani. *Tyranny of the Majority, Fundamental Fairness in Representative Democracy.* New York: The Free Press, 1994.
Jones, Bryan., ed. *Leadership and Politics.* University Press of Kansas, 1989.
Williams, Lea. *Servants of the People, the 1960's Legacy of African American Leadership.* New York: St. Martin's Press, 1996.

Political Participation

As the end of the twentieth century draws near, there is widespread fear of counteracting the progress of African Americans toward becoming equal participants in the political systems. These concerns are neither irrational nor unfounded. The courts, for example, have limited the creation of majority black legislative districts for fear that they racially segregate voters. Congressional Republicans have bitterly opposed attempts to use statistical sampling to correct for the well-documented undercount of urban minorities in the upcoming census. Public misconceptions about the **Voting Rights Act of 1965 (VRA)** have prompted the **National Association for the Advancement of Colored People (NAACP)** to issue press releases advising that voting is a constitutional right that will not change even without the VRA.

Scholars like J. Morgan Kousser, who characterize the civil rights era as America's Second Reconstruction, acknowledge that any advancement made in political participation is subject to later revision. As it did in the first **Reconstruction,** a retrogressive period can seriously reverse the enhancement of three particular aspects of black political power: voting, office-holding, and policy-making. Thus, viewing present challenges to the Second Reconstruction in light of its predecessor should provide some insight to identifying issues and strategies for black participation in coming decades.

The status of African Americans at the start of the 1900s can only be described in the bleakest terms. Politically, economically, and socially, blacks had been relegated to the periphery of the American Dream. This stark reality was nowhere more apparent than in the southern states, where the Reconstruction had made the largest improvements in the lot of black citizens. "By 1868," for example, "more than 700,000 blacks had been registered to vote under supervision of federal troops" (Grofman, et al., 84). In addition, blacks were elected to 15 percent of southern governmental positions from lieutenant governor to U.S. senator. The extent of black political success was most apparent in South Carolina's legislature, where blacks "occupied a majority of seats in the lower house" (Davidson, 27).

The end of Reconstruction in 1877 invoked gradual efforts to remove virtually every vestige of black political success. Works like C. Vann Woodward's *Strange Career of Jim Crow* offer a thorough accounting of the processes that led to the whites-only political system. During state constitutional conventions, southerners imposed literacy tests and poll taxes that in effect excluded illiterate and poor blacks from the electoral process (Grofman et al., 14). For those blacks who could still vote, legislatures manipulated electoral rules to minimize black voting strength. Both with at-large or multi-member districts, southern whites made sure that black citizens could not elect a candidate of their choice (Grofman, 32). When manipulating institutions was ineffective, organized mobs like the **Ku Klux Klan** used intimidation and violence against blacks who attempted to vote and to run for office.

As a result of these legal and extralegal maneuvers, the percentage of black eligible voters plummeted throughout the South. The number of registrants in Mississippi fell to 6 percent in 1890, while no more than 2 percent of its black citizens registered in the state of Alabama by 1906 (Davidson, 32). The slow disappearance of the black voter from southern politics, in turn, reduced the number of black elected officials. Nationwide, the total number of black congressmen and state legislators dropped from 324 in 1872 to only five by 1900. U.S. Representative George White was the last black to leave Congress in the following year, but not before making a prophetic farewell speech about the future of black participation:

> . . . This, Mr. Chairman, is perhaps the negroes' temporary farewell to the American Congress; but let me say, Phoenix-like he will rise up some day and come again. These parting words are in behalf of an outraged, heart-broken, bruised, and bleeding, but God-fearing people, faithful, industrious, loyal people—rising people, full of potential force (Higginbotham et al., 1953).

From the 1920s until the 1950s, black political participation was concentrated mainly in the northern urban areas, where black local officials sometimes provided votes for successful presidential candidates. Franklin Roosevelt and Harry Truman were among the earliest beneficiaries of black support in cities like Chicago, but their northern urban coalition with southern Democrats was at best tenuous concerning the issue of minority participation (Kleppner, 31). Nonetheless, the New Deal brought blacks "direct economic aid for the first time," and "the right to vote during the war" for veterans (Lawson 28). These were significant advances, but Congress and the president avoided any coherent strategy for protecting black civil rights. In the absence of support from the other federal branches, civil rights organizations like the **National Association for the Advancement of Colored People (NAACP)** used the judiciary to challenge discriminatory laws and practices. Until 1944, however, the Supreme Court remained deferential toward states' rights (Grofman et al., 77). The first notable success came in *Smith v. Allwright,* where the Court ruled that all-white primaries were unconstitutional because they excluded blacks from an essential part of the electoral process (Kluger 362).

The beginning of the so-called Second Reconstruction did not start until Republicans regained the White House. Hoping to please northern black voters, President Dwight Eisenhower pushed for the adoption of the 1957 Civil Rights Bill (Davidson, 46). Though strongly opposed by southern congressmen in districts with large black populations, the Act proved less than effective at increasing registration. During the law's enforcement, not one unregistered black voter qualified to vote in the South. Congress later passed two other civil rights bills—in 1960 and in 1964—to correct the flaws in the initial legislation, but both were unable to break the South's exclusive political system. The average rate of black voter registration in the deep South (Alabama, Georgia, Mississippi, Louisiana, and South Carolina) averaged 22.5 percent—still less than a quarter of those eligible (Lawson, 61). Mississippi, with the largest black population, trailed every state in the nation with fewer than one in every 10 eligible blacks registered to vote.

The presidential election of 1964 was pivotal in the development of black participation. While the contest led to important legislation regarding voting rights, it also began what Edsall and Edsall describe as a "chain reaction" within the Democratic South. The incumbent, Democrat Lyndon Johnson, decisively won reelection against Arizona Senator Barry Goldwater, a conservative Republican. But for the first time since the Reconstruction, the Republican candidate carried states within the solid Democratic South. Many scholars attribute this political rift to differences between the candidates concerning civil rights. Goldwater had sided with southern Democrats by opposing the proposed 1964 Civil Rights Bill. Inheriting John F. Kennedy's agenda of moderate civil rights enforcement, Johnson spoke in favor of the legislation. Not long after his inaugural, though, Johnson also faced political violence in Selma, Alabama, where law officers attacked marchers calling for fair voter registration. For perhaps both reasons, Johnson moved quickly during his first full term to enact the **Voting Rights Act of 1965 (VRA)**. The original VRA, along with its amendments, caused very immediate and enduring improvements in participation for blacks both in the South and throughout the entire nation. Moreover, it provided federal protections for blacks and other minorities against state actions that threatened equal political opportunity.

Among other results of the act, the number of blacks registered in southern states increased dramatically over a relatively short period. In only four years following passage of the act, no state in the deep South had registered less than half its black population, which raised the nationwide rate for blacks to 66 percent. During the last two decades, this upward trend in black voter registration continued with "the greatest gains occurring in Alabama (37 percent), North Carolina (28 percent), and Mississippi (20 percent)" (Lawson 220). The larger number of blacks in the electorate, in turn, created opportunities for more diverse representation on all levels. Along with promoting more moderate white candidates for office, the act made black campaigners for office much more likely than before. Within the first three years of the VRA, approximately 3,000 black candidates took offices from the local to the federal level; that number more than doubled by 1988 to 6,829 (Lawson 260). In some cases, the law has even brought about the philosophic conversion of those who opposed black enfranchisement. Southern politicians like Strom Thurmond and George Wallace both adjusted some of their political positions to add black voters to their electoral coalitions.

Mobilizing blacks to join the political system stands as the first major challenge for greater participation. The Constitution explicitly protects the right to vote, but more individuals must exercise that right to avoid a revision and reversal of black political gains. The Census Bureau reports that fewer than 40 percent of blacks voted in the 1994 elections, compared to almost half of whites. People are not likely to go to the polls absent specific regard for the act of voting. Community-oriented activism and the development of civic associations in areas with low-participation may serve as an avenue to encourage greater participation. One existing organization with proven success with mobilization is the church. With its wealth of resources and extensive social networks, black churches can serve as an important component to register blacks to vote.

Even if more blacks go to the polls, their ability to affect who is elected matters just as much to continued participation. An important lesson of the first Reconstruction is that the level of black voting and office-holding have both significantly changed when the political process itself has changed. For example, Congress has eased the qualification process by passing the National Voter Registration Act, which allows citizens to register when they apply for other state services. A more controversial change came in 1982, when the Voting Rights Act was amended to (among other things) allow blacks to challenge district-drawing that was less than representative of their voting strength. While some states sought to create districts with black majorities, citizens have filed lawsuits challenging the propriety of using race as a consideration for redistricting. Just as institutions and processes worked to undermine black participation before, adjustments may also have a positive effect on black participation. Thus, the challenge in the next century is to advocate innovations in the political process that expand opportunities for blacks to participate.

Perhaps the most complex challenge is coalition-building with groups across lines of race and party. Unlike the previous Reconstruction, though, America's politics today are more diverse than black and white. One undeniable demographic trend is that blacks are becoming an increasingly smaller portion of the American citizenry; indeed, African Americans will be outnumbered by Latinos early in the next century. Multiracial coalitions, while vital, should not be viewed too simplistically. In city populations where Latinos and blacks comprise the majority, cooperation sometimes gives way to competition over scarce resources. Given the reality of America's changing population, though, blacks must find shared policy agendas with other racial groups to make their presence effectual in decision making.

Promoting relationships within both political parties may also prove helpful. One of the more difficult issues about majority-black districts is that the elected legislators (almost always Democrats) often enter a political environment that is increasingly hostile to their policy interests. While scholars disagree about whether creating these districts makes Republicans viable elsewhere, the underlying problem has to do with the commitment of blacks to a single party. Unalterable alliances with Democrats may not only cause the GOP to marginalize black interests but can also encourage Democrats to take the allegiance of blacks for granted. As Missouri Representative William Clay has argued, to remain a competitive force in politics, blacks should have "no permanent friends and no permanent enemies, only permanent interests." (KC)

BIBLIOGRAPHY

Applebom, Peter. "Race Politics in South's Contests: Hot Wind of Hate or Last Gasp?" *New York Times* (November 5, 1990).

Barrett, Laurence. "Race Baiting Wins Again." *Time* (November 19, 1990): 43.

Bensel, Richard F. and M. Elizabeth Sanders. "The Impact of the Voting Rights Act on Southern Welfare Systems." In Benjamin Ginsberg and Alan Stone, eds. *Do Elections Matter?* New York: M.E. Sharp, 1986.

Davidson, Chandler. "The Voting Rights Act: A Brief History." In Bernard Grofman and Chandler Davidson, eds. *Controversies in Minority Voting*. Washington, DC: The Brookings Institute, 1992.

Donovan, Beth. "New 'Majority Minority Districts' May Mean Lower Black Turnout," *Congressional Quarterly* (March 7, 1992): 563–64.

Duncan, Phil. "Creating Black Districts May Segregate Voters." *Congressional Quarterly* (July 28, 1990): 2463.

Edsall, Thomas B. and Mary Edsall. *Chain Reaction: The Impact of Race, Rights, and Taxes on American Politics*. New York: W.W. Norton & Company, 1992.

Fineman, Howard and John McCormick. "The New Politics of Race." *Newsweek* (May 6, 1991): 22–26.

GAO Report on Voter Turnout. *Congressional Digest* (March 1993).

Grofman, Bernard, Lisa Handley, and Richard Niemi. *Minority Representation and the Quest for Voting Equality.* Victoria, Melbourne, UK: Cambridge University Press, 1992.

Higginbotham, A.L., Gregory Clarick, and Marcella David. "Shaw v. Reno: A Mirage of Good Intentions with Devastating Racial Consequences." *Fordham Law Review* 62 (1994): 1593–1659.

Kaplan, Dave. "Constitutional Doubt Is Thrown on Bizarre-Shaped Districts." *Congressional Quarterly* (July 3, 1993): 1761–63.

Kleppner, Paul. *Chicago Divided.* De Kalb, IL: Northern Illinois University Press, 1985.

———. "Louisiana Ruling May Offer Guidelines for Other Cases." *Congressional Quarterly* (January 8, 1994): 29–31.

Lawson, Steven. *Running for Freedom.* Philadelphia: Temple University Press, 1991.

Powledge, Fred. "George Bush Is Whistling 'Dixie.'" *The Nation* (October 14, 1991). 446–47.

Swain, Carol. *Black Faces, Black Interests.* Cambridge, MA: Harvard University Press, 1993.

Thernstrom, Abigail. *Whose Votes Count?* Cambridge, MA: Harvard University Press, 1987.

White, Jack. "The Limits of Black Power." *Time* (May 11, 1992): 38–40.

Poll Tax

A poll tax was a common requirement for voters that was created in many southern states at the turn of the century. Along with literacy tests, the tax was a means of minimizing black participation after **Reconstruction.** To qualify for an upcoming election, a voter had to pay the poll tax with other state and county taxes. The financial payment was a particular burden for blacks, many who worked as farm laborers. The Twenty-fourth Constitutional Amendment banned poll taxes. (KC)

BIBLIOGRAPHY

Grofman, Bernard, Lisa Handley, and Richard G. Niemi. *Minority Representation and the Quest for Voting Equality.* New York: Cambridge University Press, 1992.

Woodward, C. Vann. *Origins of the New South, 1877–1913.* Baton Rouge: Louisiana State University Press, 1971.

Salem Poor

Salem Poor, who had been born a free black man, was a member of the Massachusetts Militia at Bunker Hill in 1775 and was commended by 14 officers for bravery in that battle in their petition to the legislature. He also served with distinction at Valley Forge and White Plains. (GAA)

BIBLIOGRAPHY

Franklin, John Hope and Alfred A. Moss, Jr. *From Slavery to Freedom: A History of Negro Americans,* 7th ed. New York: McGraw Hill, 1994.

Quarles, Benjamin. *The Negro in the American Revolution.* New York: W.W. Norton, 1973.

Poor People's Campaign

The **National Welfare Rights Organization (NWRO)** sought ways in which to broaden its base of legislative support. In the spring of 1968, the **Southern Christian Leadership Conference's (SCLC)** Poor People's Campaign provided the NWRO with just such an opportunity. Originally planned by **Martin Luther King, Jr.** to focus on hunger conditions, the Mother's March on May 12 (Mother's Day) was led by **Coretta Scott King** and George King. Some 5,000 demonstrators marched through areas of Washington, D.C., that had been damaged by rioting after the assassination of Dr. King in Memphis. **Ralph Abernathy,** who presided at the christening of Resurrection City on May 13, was able to report that many goals had been reached during the march. Food was to be provided to the neediest counties, low-income housing was to be increased, and the U.S. Office of Economic Opportunity had plans for expanding programs. (MRC)

BIBLIOGRAPHY

Piven, Frances Fox. *Poor People's Movements: Why They Succeed, How They Fail.* New York: Vintage, 1979.

"Poor People's Campaign Marches on Washington, D.C." *DISCovering Multicultural America.* Detroit: Gale, 1998.

"A Poor People's March on Washington Focuses on U.S. Hunger Problems." *DISCovering Multicultural America.* Detroit: Gale, 1998.

Poverty

Even though the United States is one of the richest and most highly developed nations in the world, poverty has always existed. As the country was settled, many people cultivated their own food. Since land was readily available, whole families often relocated in hopes of greater prosperity. According to Sara Evans, by the latter half of the nineteenth century, hunger and homelessness accompanied industrialization as recent immigrants moved into impoverished and disease-ridden communities. In Chicago in 1889, Jane Addams and Ellen Gates Starr opened Hull-House, an early settlement house, to deal with the problems of the poor. In 1893 a major depression left thousands of people without homes and jobs; and, by the turn of the century, there were approximately 100 settle-

Most African Americans remained in the South after the Civil War and worked as tenant farmers. This photo of a share-cropping couple from Anniston, Alabama, was taken around 1900. *Library of Congress.*

ment houses. In 1929, the Great Depression resulted in widespread poverty, and thousands of people with lost incomes stood in line at soup kitchens to feed themselves and their families. Others traveled around the country seeking prosperity.

Families, churches, and private individuals and organizations have always played an important role in dealing with overt problems of the poor. However, it was not until 1932 that the United States government became an active participant. Franklin Roosevelt, promising to use the power of the national government to deal with the Great Depression, turned the United States into a social welfare state. World War II marked the end of the Great Depression as the country geared up to help supply embattled nations with weapons of war. Despite prosperity after the war, poverty continued. Large numbers of blacks left the rural areas of the South and moved northward. In response, whites left cities and began the move to the suburbs, leaving minorities in northern ghettos. By the 1960s, these ghettoes were filled with large numbers of unemployed black women supporting their children alone. Evans notes that between 1940 and 1967, the illegitimacy rate grew from 17 to 29 percent, and the proportion of black women in the labor market rose to 58 percent. In 1964, Lyndon Johnson declared **War on Poverty,** establishing Medicare, a health program for the elderly, and creating anti-poverty programs that included public housing, job training, and food subsidies.

Despite the War on Poverty, the economic status of minorities remained below that of white Americans. By 1978, for example, 30.6 percent of all poor families were black, as opposed to 8.7 percent of all white families. That number rose to 41 percent for black female-headed households and 11 percent for white female-headed households. Since minorities were more likely to be recipients of entitlement programs, whites frequently tried to limit access to programs to reduce burdens on taxpayers. In Alabama, for instance, the legislature denied Aid to Families with Dependent Children (AFDC) benefits to any mother who "cohabited" with any able-bodied male inside or outside of her home. Some states established one-year residency requirements for receiving welfare benefits and for receiving nonemergency medical care; others cut off benefits for mothers with illegitimate children. The Supreme Court struck down these state laws and another that denied a hearing to recipients whose benefits had terminated. The large number of cases that placed the poor in a separate class led to a demand for poverty to be declared a "suspect" class, along with race and national origin. Yet, in *San Antonio Independent School District v. Rodriquez* (1973), the Supreme Court held that poverty was not suspect, thus, not worthy of the "strict scrutiny" requirement. The Court admitted that poverty sometimes led to denial of rights, and this was made clear with *Gideon v. Wainwright* (1963), whereby states were required to furnish lawyers for those who could not afford them. Lucius and Twiley Barker assert that everyday life for the poor is filled with a lack of adequate food, shelter, jobs, clothing, and health care, and that inferior education and high crime rates place them in a world of their own.

The election of Ronald Reagan in 1980 led to a new war—not on poverty—but on the poor. The Reagan administration slashed social programs to the bone, and the hardest hit of the victims were women and children, resulting in what became known as the "feminization of poverty." Census reports indicate that in 1980 the poverty rate for black female-headed families was 53.1 percent and 52.5 percent for Hispanic female-headed families. Two years later the poverty rate increased to 57.4 percent for both black and Hispanic female-headed families. Since the 1980s, the stereotype of the unemployed black mother with several illegitimate children, living high off government subsidies has received a lot of attention. In actual fact, the average monthly AFDC benefit in 1995 ranged from a low of $119.09 in Mississippi to a high of $719.81 in Alaska. Government reports indicate that 73 percent of families receiving public assistance have no more than two children, and that more white families receive benefits than do black families. Poverty among black women cannot be solely attributed to those who do not work. The 1994 median yearly income for black women was $5,310, and the 1995 poverty level for a family of three was $12,158. This is attributable to the difference in wages of men and women, as well as to the difference in white and minority wages. The Women's Action Coalition reports that black women with a college degree working full-time make less than the white male high-school dropouts. Another reason for the large number of black women who live in poverty is the number of absent fathers who fail to pay child support. Jo Freeman notes that black women are also less likely to remarry than white women. Many elderly women are also faced with poverty. For example, in 1992, 33 percent of elderly black women and 22 percent of elderly Hispanic women were poor.

Due to the number of children who now live in female-headed households, poverty among children is extensive. Studies reveal that one out of every five children below the age of six lives in poverty, and most of these belong to minority mothers. At the lowest point of Reagan's war on the poor, the infant mortality rate, based on the number of deaths per 1,000 live births, was 19.2 for black children and 15.2 for Native Americans and Native Alaskans—figures more comparable to the rate of developing countries than to the 9.3 for white children and the 9.5 for Hispanic children. The rise in infant mortality was directly related to cuts in prenatal care for pregnant mothers and well-baby care for existing babies. Public outcry caused the rates to drop to 16.6 and 11.3 for black and Native American children respectively in 1991. In the summer of 1991, a special edition of *Newsweek* devoted to America's children stated that 13 percent of black children were born underweight, potential causes of deafness, blindness, and mental retardation. The report cited a 1988 study that revealed that more than half of black children were likely to suffer from lead poisoning. A number of studies have also shown that minority children are less likely to be immunized, making them more susceptible to childhood diseases and resulting complications.

Throughout the history of the United States, black men have held a unique position in society. Physically and mentally exploited in the days of slavery, they became victims of the myth that black men lust after white women establishing a pattern that continues today. As **affirmative action** became the norm and the **civil rights movement** brought sweeping changes to American society, black men sometimes lost jobs to black women who satisfied the requirement of hiring two protected classes and who were seen as less threatening than black men. Jo Freeman notes that the number of black men out of the labor market has tripled since 1960. Wage differentials continue through the present day. In 1997, the median weekly wage is $426 for black men and $369 for Hispanic men. This compares to a $599 median weekly wage for white men. Black men also suffer increased health risks: lower life expectancy and higher rates of death from stroke and cancer. Freeman argues that it is the economic plight of black men that has led to the large number of female-headed black families living in poverty. The high incidence of crime in the United States has been well documented. Crime rates have particular poignancy for black men. The Department of Justice suggests that the lifetime chance of going to prison for black men is almost eight times—and for Hispanic men almost four times—the chance of white men going to prison. Reports also show that in 1991, 65 percent of all prison inmates were minorities. On the other hand, the number of blacks who received a high-school degree has been more promising. The number of black dropouts declined to 12.6 percent in 1994, almost half of what it was in 1975. For Hispanics, the rate of 30 percent in 1994 changed little from 1975.

It has been argued that Reagan's war on the poor reached its culmination in 1996 when the Republican Congress negotiated a complete overhaul of the welfare system. The Personal Responsibility and Work Opportunity Reconciliation Act ended cash entitlements, created block grants giving states control over access to social programs—including programs aimed at fostering two-parent families, revised commodity distribution programs, cut benefits for mothers who would not help to establish paternity, suggested community service for recipients who did not find work within two years, and capped eligibility for welfare at five years.

Scholars often disagree on how to deal with poverty and what it means to those who are poor. William Ryan argues that poverty in the United States is generally dealt with by blaming the victim. He maintains that the stereotype of the black matriarchal family with pervasive illegitimacy makes it easy for society to opt out of its share of the blame. Kurt Finsterbusch and George McKenna believe that the real problem of poverty stems from its persistence among generations, leading to what some call the "culture of poverty," the norms of which are lack of self-discipline and an unwillingness to

work. Thomas and Mary Edsall contend that acceptance of poverty has led to segregating the poor in high crime areas, allowing the growing underclass to reinforce racial stereotypes, which then validates racist attitudes. Class position is significant, of course, even in the United States which prides itself on being a classless society. As Gregory Mantsios points out, one's position in the class structure determines the chances one has in life. Thus, the implications of poverty involve not only income; they also control general health, infant mortality, life expectancy, educational achievement, employability, social status, sense of well being, and the right to pursue happiness promised to all Americans in the Declaration of Independence. (EP)

BIBLIOGRAPHY

Barker, Lucius, J. and Twiley W. Barker, Jr. *Civil Liberties and the Constitution: Cases and Commentaries,* 7th ed. Englewood Cliffs, NJ: Prentice Hall, 1994.

Cowley, Geoffrey. "Children in Peril." *Newsweek* (Summer 1991): 18–21.

Edsall, Thomas Byrne and Mary D. Edsall. *Chain Reaction: The Impact of Race, Rights, and Taxes on American Politics.* New York and London: W.W. Norton, 1992.

Evans, Sara M. *Born for Liberty: A History of Women in America.* New York: The Free Press, 1989.

Finsterbusch, Kurt and George M. McKenna. *Taking Sides: Clashing Views on Controversial Social Issues,* 7th ed. Guilford, CT: Dushin, 1992.

Freeman, Jo. *Women: A Feminist Perspective,* 4th ed. Mountain View, CA: Mayfield, 1989.

Mantsios, Gregory. "Rewards and Opportunities: The Politics and Economics of Class in the United States." In Paula S. Rothenberg, ed. *Race, Class, and Gender in the United States: An Integrated Study.* New York: St. Martin's, 1992, 96–110.

Ryan, William. "Blaming the Victim." In Kurt Finsterbusch and George M. McKenna, eds. *Taking Sides: Clashing Views on Controversial Social Issues,* 7th ed. Guilford, CT: Dushkin, 1992, 155–62.

Urofsky, Melvin I. *A March of Liberty: A Constitutional History of the United States. Vol. II: Since 1865.* New York: Alfred A. Knopf, 1988.

Women's Action Coalition. *WAC Stats: The Facts about Women.* New York: The New Press, 1993.

Adam Clayton Powell, Jr. (1908–1972)

Adam Clayton Powell, Jr. was born in Harlem on November 28, 1908. He descended from free Virginia blacks, and was the son of a celebrated minister. Both father and son believed in economic self-reliance. For 35 years, Powell was pastor of the Abyssinian Baptist Church on 138th Street. During the Great Depression, Powell used the Abyssinian Baptist Church to promote various social programs to aid his congregation, including training and employment services. In many ways Powell anticipated the modern civil rights movement, leading nonviolent protests, for example, against white stores in Harlem that refused to hire African Americans.

In 1944, Powell was elected to Congress as a Democrat from New York. He was the first African American to be elected from the Northeast. In Congress, Powell became a leader in the **civil rights movement,** integrating the Congressional Dining Hall and the press gallery. He opposed the system of segregation, gaining great popularity and consistently being reelected to Congress without campaigning. Powell's seniority earned him chairmanship of the House Committee on Education and Labor in 1961. He guided President Lyndon Johnson's Great Society programs through Congress. This legislation includes federal aid to higher education and training for the unemployed and the handicapped. It also included the **Civil Rights Act of 1964** that eliminated legal bars to black progress. His committee churned out the remarkable number of 60 major bills in five years. Even more remarkably, they were all passed into laws by the Congress.

Unfortunately, Powell's skills were mixed with an arrogance some attributed to his aristocratic background. He lived a luxurious lifestyle that led to numerous questions about his finances. He lost a libel case and refused to pay. He moved to Bimini to escape prosecution. His obvious attraction to women led many to question his morals.

In 1967, the House of Representatives voted to exclude him from Congress, an action the Supreme Court later ruled unconstitutional. Powell died of cancer in 1972. In spite of his problems, the public held him in their affections and more than 100,000 filed past his body at Abyssinian Baptist Church for his funeral. (FAS)

BIBLIOGRAPHY

Robinson, Frederick. *King of the Cats: The Life and Times of Adam Clayton Powell, Jr*. Earl G. Graves Publishing Company, Inc., 1993.

Colin Luther Powell (1937–)

Colin L. Powell, a four-star general, was chairman of the Joint Chiefs of Staff—the nation's highest uniformed military position—from 1989 to 1992. From 1987 to 1989, he served as the assistant to the president (under George Bush) for national security affairs. Powell is the first, and to date, the only African American to hold these positions.

Powell served two tours of duty in the Vietnam War, during which he was decorated 11 times. Upon his return to the United States in 1972, he worked as a White House Fellow in the Office of Management and Budget. In 1973 he was appointed battalion commander in Korea. Among his other appointments and positions are commanding general of the 5th Army Corps in Germany (1986), senior military assistant to the secretary of defense (1983–1986), and commander of the 4th Infantry Division (1981–1982). General Powell also oversaw the successful U.S. military effort in Operation Desert Storm from 1990 to 1991.

BIBLIOGRAPHY

Banta, Melissa. *Colin Powell.* New York: Chelsea House, 1995.
Powell, Colin L. *My American Journey.* New York: Random House, 1995.

Powell v. McCormack (1969)

This case pitted **Adam Clayton Powell, Jr.,** a powerful member of the United States House of Representatives, and a number of his constituents in the 18th Congressional District of New York, against John W. McCormack, the influential Speaker of the House, and the remainder of the members and officers of the House in the 90th Congress. Powell had risen to prominence as pastor of Harlem's large Abyssinian Baptist Church, succeeding his father as pastor in 1937. He then went on to election to New York's city council before starting his first term in the House of Representatives in 1946.

Powell was duly elected to his 10th term in 1966. In January 1967, however, Powell was not permitted to take the oath of office with the rest of the members-elect and was then not permitted to take his seat. This came about because of the results of an investigation that took place during the previous congressional term. This investigation found that there was strong evidence that Powell, as chairperson of the Committee on Education and Labor, had "deceived" the House about certain travel expenses, and that "certain illegal salary payments had been made to Powell's wife."

A select committee was appointed after Powell was refused his seat. Powell appeared before this committee but refused to answer questions about anything other than the qualifications for taking a seat in the House of Representatives as set out in Article I, Section 2, of the United States Constitution. In his view, this was the only relevant and legitimate matter in the investigation. The committee sought to extend the scope of the investigation to Powell's activities in previous congresses, as well as to Powell's attempts to avoid prosecution in a matter pending in the New York courts. Powell refused to appear at a number of the select committee hearings. In the view of some, racist undertones were evident in the work of the committee and in some members of Congress.

When the select committee's findings were presented, the seated members of the House of Representatives voted 307 to 116 to exclude Powell from the House and declare his seat vacant, despite the recommendation by the select committee simply to censure Powell, fine him, and deprive him of his seniority. Powell and a number of his constituents filed suit. In the meantime, in a special election, Powell was again elected by his constituents. The lower courts sided with McCormack and dismissed the suit, but the United States Supreme Court agreed to hear the case.

In *Powell v. McCormack,* 395, U.S. 486 (1969), the opinion of Chief Justice Earl Warren concludes that, under the terms of Sections 3 and 5 of the Constitution, neither the House of Representatives nor the Senate has the authority to exclude a person who meets all the requirements for membership that are expressly prescribed in Article I of the Constitution, and who has been duly elected by his or her constituents. After his victory, Powell went on to complete his term in the House. He was defeated in his bid for reelection in 1970, and died soon after, in April of 1972. (AJC)

BIBLIOGRAPHY

Dionisopoulos, P. Alan. *Rebellion, Racism, and Representation: The Adam Clayton Powell Case and Its Antecedents*. De Kalb, IL: Northern Illinois University Press, 1970.

Hamilton, Charles V. *Adam Clayton Powell, Jr.: The Political Biography of an American Dilemma*. New York: Atheneum, 1991.

Weeks, Kent M. *Adam Clayton Powell and the Supreme Court*. New York: Dunellen, 1971.

Presidential Committee on Civil Rights

After World War II, returning African-American veterans were met with violence and lynching in the South. In 1946, civil rights organizations such as the **National Association for the Advancement of Colored People (NAACP)** met with President Harry Truman to discuss the protection of their **civil rights.** Truman appointed a commission to investigate and recommend a program of corrective action. The President's Committee on Civil Rights, as it was called, was a bi-racial body that issued its report in 1947, To Secure these Rights. (VDD)

BIBLIOGRAPHY

Goldfield, David R. *Black, White, and Southern: Race Relations and Southern Culture, 1940 to the Present*. Baton Rouge: Louisiana State University Press, 1990.

Presley v. Etowah County Commission (1992)

In *Presley v. Etowah County Commission*, 502 U.S. 491 (1992), the U.S. Supreme Court ruled that changes reducing the governing authority of newly elected minority public officials are not covered by the **Voting Rights Act of 1965**. The case concerned an Alabama county in which blacks had recently been elected to formerly all-white city commissions; the county board then removed most spending authority from those commissions and gave it instead to a county engineer who was appointed by the county commission. (JCW)

BIBLIOGRAPHY

Evans, Carol A. "Limitations of the Voting Rights Act of 1965." *Harvard Journal of Law and Public Policy* 15, no. 3 (Summer 1992): 1031–40.

Karpiak, Jim R. "Voting Rights and the Role of the Federal Government: The Rehnquist Court's Mixed Messages in Minority Vote Delution Cases." *University of San Francisco Law Review* 27, no. 3 (Spring 1993): 627–52.

Proportional Representation

Proportional representation is a system of representation whereby a group's share of policymaking power in the political arena is directly dependent on its share of support in the population. Each elected official serves as a direct representative of a single group or interest within the larger population. For example, in a campaign featuring strict proportional representation, a group receiving 30 percent of the votes in the election will control a third of the seats in a representative body. Often, proportional systems allow many smaller groups to win seats in representative bodies. Additionally, PR systems where no one party controls a majority vote can necessitate coalition-building among minority groups.

PR is distinct from majoritarian systems, where a majority vote wins a group total representation. Groups with at least 50 percent support often get over-represented in these systems. In many U.S. majoritarian elections, groups that finish in second or third place win no official power. Although Section 2 of the **Voting Rights Act of 1965** explicitly avoids proportional representation, its provisions have sometimes led courts to approve representation for minorities.

BIBLIOGRAPHY

Guinier, Lani. *The Tyranny of the Majority*. New York: The Free Press, 1994.

Hart, Jenifer. *Proportional Representation*. New York: Oxford University Press, 1992.

Ryden, David K. *Representation in Crisis*. New York: State University of New York Press, 1996.

Public Works and Economic Development Act of 1965

The Public Works and Economic Development Act of 1965 (42 USC 3121) established the Economic Development Administration (EDA) to generate new jobs, help retain existing jobs, and stimulate industrial and commercial growth in economically distressed areas of the United States. To increase aid to distressed cities, Congress reoriented the focus of EDA in 1974 from a largely rural development agency to one that gave greater attention to urban areas, particularly those with the most unemployment. (VDD)

BIBLIOGRAPHY

Tanner, Michael. *The End of Welfare: Fighting Poverty in the Civil Society*. Washington, DC: Cato Institute, 1996.

Quarles v. Philip Morris, Inc. (1968)

In Quarles v. Philip Morris, 279 F. Supp. 505 (1968), the court held that Philip Morris was in violation of the **Civil Rights Act of 1964** by continuing to have discriminatory advancement practices that unfairly kept blacks from being promoted within the company. The court held that "a departmental seniority system that has its genesis in racial discrimination is not a bona fide seniority system." Philip Morris was also found to have discriminated against their black employees with regard to pay scale. See also Discrimination. (JCW)

BIBLIOGRAPHY

Schell, Beorge K. H. "BonaFide Seniority Systems: Guidelines for the Use of Disparate Impact in the Teamsters Analysis." *UCLA Law Review* 31, no. 4 (April 1984): 886–920.

R

Racial Gerrymandering

To gerrymander is to draw political districts that unfairly exaggerate the power of a group. Such districts are often highly irregular in shape. The term originated in 1812 when Governor Elbridge Gerry of Massachusetts rearranged election districts into a shape that recalled a salamander to help the Jeffersonians retain control of the state.

Racial gerrymandering occurs when districts are drawn to unduly influence the voting power of a racial group. Historically, this was done to dilute the minority vote. A typical strategy was to split the minority population into several districts so that their influence in any given district was small. At the national and state level, gerrymandering contributed to the exclusion of African Americans from office in many states with significant black populations from **Reconstruction** to the **civil rights movement.**

The *Baker v. Carr,* 369, U.S. 186 (1962), decision, and the **Voting Rights Acts** have been interpreted to mean that political district lines should not be drawn to dilute the minority vote. A subsequent ruling in *Thornburg v. Gingles* (1986) involving state legislative districts in North Carolina was interpreted to mean that district lines should be drawn in favor of minority populations whenever possible. The specific criteria included racial bloc voting in areas with a large and geographically compact population.

However, in Mobile, Alabama, district lines had excluded blacks from office. The Supreme Court permitted those district lines, ruling that there was no intent to discriminate. In *Shaw v. Reno* (1996), the Supreme Court ruled that "bizarre" shaped congressional districts in North Carolina should not be drawn solely to favor minorities. (WWH)

BIBLIOGRAPHY

Eddings, Jerelyn. "An Old War, A New Fight: Can Gerrymandering by Race Be Right?" *U.S. News & World Report* 117, no. 12 (September 26, 1994): 52.

Gruenwald, Juliana. "Florida Black-Majority District Is Ruled Unconstitutional." *Congressional Quarterly Weekly Report* 54, no. 16 (April 20, 1996): 1071.

———. "Revised Challenge Filed in Louisiana Case." *Congressional Quarterly Weekly Report* 53, no. 28 (July 15, 1995): 2097.

O'Connor, Sandra Day and David H. Souter. "Did North Carolina Go too Far in Drawing Congressional Districts that Favor the Election of Minority Candidates?" *CQ Researcher* 4, no. 30 (August 12, 1994): 713.

Swain, Carol M. "Limiting Racial Gerrymandering: The Future of Black Representation." *Current* no. 379 (January 1996): 3.

Racial Quotas

The idea of racial quotas reflected a shift in the civil rights debate that centered on the question of equality of opportunity versus equality of results. Although equality of opportunity had been legislated since the **Civil Rights Act of 1957**, the actual number of minority workers employed or in higher level positions was not in proportion to the surrounding population, making the actual existence of equal opportunity suspect. As a result of this discrepancy, **Title VII of the Civil Rights Act of 1964** instituted new **affirmative action** programs, such as quota systems and set-aside programs, which would encourage minorities and women to apply for positions.

Quotas met several legal challenges. In 1978, the Supreme Court ruled in *Regents of the University of California v. Bakke* (1978) that the use of strict quotas, in this case for medical school admissions, was inappropriate. The Court stated, however, that the medical school was free to "take race into account" in its admission policies.

The use of affirmative action programs in general and the use of quotas in particular came under further attack during the Reagan presidency when a conservative Supreme Court overruled earlier liberal interpretations of anti-discrimination laws. In a three-month period in 1989, the Supreme Court handed down five decisions limiting affirmative action programs, forcing Congress to enact the **Civil Rights Act of 1991**. The new legislation overruled the earlier Supreme Court rulings but specifically prohibited the use of quotas to avoid any further legal challenges. (VDD)

BIBLIOGRAPHY

Brody, Carl E., Jr. "A Historical Review of Affirmative Action and The Interpretation of its Legislative Intent by the Supreme Court." *Akron Law Review* 29 (1996): 291–334.

Kaufman, Nancy, Gary Miller, and Kevin Ivey. "Affirmative Action and the White Male in America." *Labor Law Journal* 46 (November 1995): 692–98.

Oh, Reggie and Frank Wu. "The Evolution of Race in the Law: The Supreme Court Moves from Approving Interment of Japanese Americans to Disapproving Affirmative Action for African Americans." *Michigan Journal of Race and Law* (1996): 165–203.

Racial Set-Asides

In *City of Richmond v. J.A. Croson* (1975), racial set-aside programs were at issue. J.A. Croson, a company owned by whites, contested a 1983 decision by the Richmond City Council of a 30 percent set-aside for minority contractors in the construction industry. The U.S. Supreme Court ruled that a racial preference plan must pass a "strict scrutiny" test consisting of statistical evidence showing (1) the plan intends to break down historic patterns of racial discrimination; (2) the plan does not unnecessarily diminish the rights of whites; and (3) it is a temporary measure intended to eliminate racial imbalance. Following the *Richmond* ruling, several other set-asides were dismantled, making it particularly difficult for local and state governments to justify minority set-aside programs. (EC)

BIBLIOGRAPHY

Blackwell, James E. *The Black Community: Diversity and Unity.* New York: HarperCollins, 1991.

Racism

Racism is a system of ideas, beliefs, attitudes, and practices that asserts that a particular racial group (defined on the basis of physical appearance, especially skin color, but symbolizing social conflicts over scarce societal resources) is inferior to one's own group. Racism denies the supposedly inferior group the dignity, opportunities, freedoms, and rewards that it offers the supposedly superior group. Thus, racism arises in order to rationalize and legitimize systematic inequalities along racial lines. It becomes incorporated into the culture of a society, separate from the individuals who may inhabit the society at a specific point in time, and is passed from generation to generation like any other part of the cultural heritage.

Arguably, in the United States it has been the white man's relationship with African Americans that has led to the most powerful expressions of racism, but other groups (Native Americans, Latinos, and Asian Americans in particular) have also been victimized by racism. More often than not, these groups, often victimized on the basis of nationality, culture, and language, are rendered additionally vulnerable by their skin color and other physical features. Nationality then combines with a "nonwhite (although not black) physical appearance to subject Native Americans, Latinos, and Asian Americans to an oppression that is a form of racism. These groups' social conditions (especially in the case of Latinos and Native Americans) affirm the negative outcomes of a combination of national, cultural, and racial oppression.

Systems of racism have evolved over time. In the United States, the first racial system was religiously based. Blacks and the native peoples of the Americas were designated as "heathens" because they were non-Christian. Ignorance about the white man's God was taken as sufficient proof of the separate and permanent inferiority of the Native American and the African, and their oppression was justified on just that basis. In the mid-nineteenth century this idea received scientific legitimacy from the biological sciences: the new science of craniometry held that brain size was correlated with intelligence. The idea that black subordination was related to the configuration of the black skull was seized upon by southern whites who saw it as providing scientific validation for **slavery.** And what craniometry was for the nineteenth century, intelligence testing became for the twentieth.

By the 1930s, systematic clinical refutation had effectively stripped racism of any claim to scientific validity, and a new consensus arose that there are no inborn or innate racial differences in intelligence. At that point, however, scientific racism was replaced by cultural racism, which purported that it cultural differences generate racial inequality and justify the inferior status of some races. For example, in the system of cultural racism as practiced against blacks, racists pointed to dissimilarities in family structure, supposedly disparate attitudes toward the Protestant work ethic, and other presumed cultural differences as the reason for systematic racial inequalities—rather than the structure of unequal opportunity that had been instituted.

Through these evolving systems of racism, racist acts have played (and continue to play) a strong role in world history. Such racist acts have ranged from overt genocide and murder, to subtle gestures of social exclusion, to passive acquiescence in the racist acts of others. Thus, racism can be both overt and covert, both individual and institutionalized.

Individual racism consists of overt acts by individuals to assert the superiority of one's own group over another. For example, when white terrorists in the United States set fires to black churches simply because the parishioners are black, that is an act of individual overt racism. Similarly, a store clerk who suspects that black youths in his store are there to steal a shirt (but that white youths are there to purchase a shirt), and who treats the youths differently—the blacks as probable delinquents and the whites as probable customers—also illustrates individual racism. Unlike the church fire terrorists, the store clerk may not be a bigot and may not even consider himself prejudiced, but his behavior is shaped by racial stereotypes that have been part of his subconscious over a lifetime.

By contrast, institutionalized racism, embedded in society's major institutions, tends to be less overt, far more subtle, and less identifiable in terms of specific individuals committing the acts. It includes practices that are not necessarily motivated by racial animus but that nevertheless reinforce or perpetuate racial inequities. For example, when a government agency such as the Federal Housing Administration (FHA) refuses to provide mortgages to families moving into integrating neighborhoods on the rationalization that integration will cause property values to decline, that is an act of institutional racism. Similarly, when a university provides entrance only to students who have high test scores, but those tests are designed primarily for white suburban high schools, this admissions policy necessarily excludes black and other low-income students educated in different economic and cultural milieu. The university's admission criteria may not be intended to be racist, but the university is pursuing a course that perpetuates institutional racism. In short, institutional racism, deeply embedded in societies such as the United States, denies people of color access to valued goods and opportunities. It provides the essential sustenance, reinforcement, and means of reproduction for the unequal positions of racial and ethnic groups in the social and economic stratification system. In turn, people who live in societies characterized by institutional racism are likely to acquire high levels of personal prejudice and to routinely practice acts of **discrimination.** Thus, the relative advantage of the dominant racial group is maintained from day to day by mutually reinforcing patterns of prejudice, discrimination, and individual and institutional racism.

Some argue that this characterization of racism is no longer applicable in the United States. Indeed, in the 1980s, the concept of the "declining significance of race" became fashionable. Many influential commentators, politicians, and scholars argued or implied that the civil rights revolution of the 1950s and 1960s was a watershed that more or less resolved the issue of "race." According to this view, white racism in particular is no longer a serious, entrenched national problem, and people of color (especially African Americans) must take total responsibility for their own individual and community problems. From this perspective, widespread discrimination in most institutional arenas is seen as a thing of the past. In particular it has been posited that the black middle class no longer faces significant discrimination and is thriving economically—indeed more so than the white middle class. Problems of the black poor, dubbed the "underclass," have come to be seen as the central issue for black America, and the argument is that that class's condition has little to do with racism. The solution is that lower-class people of color must acquire the education and skills that are a prerequisite for social mobility.

Other commentators, politicians, and scholars reject the idea that racism has declined and argue that it has simply changed forms. They point to substantial empirical evidence and research showing that people of color still face extensive racial discrimination in all arenas of daily life. The growth in white supremacy group membership since the 1970s; the hundreds of acts of vandalism and intimidation directed at people of color; continuing discrimination in the workplace, business, colleges, public accommodations, and in historically white neighborhoods; and major, persisting economic inequalities between people of color and white Americans as demonstrated in wide gaps in unemployment rates, family income, wealth, and a racially stratified occupational structure are all cited as proof of the ongoing significance of racism. These commentators maintain that many people fail to understand the continuing significance of race even in the context of an increasing significance of class, due to their failure to understand modern racism, which is more subtle, complex, and indirect.

In the view of those who contend that racism continues to have a starkly negative effect, modern racism incorporates several assumptions. First, it denies the continuing importance of racism and discrimination in American society. Second, it posits that any continuing racial inequality is the fault of members of the minority group. Third, it insists that government efforts at overcoming racial inequality are unjustified; the responsibility for change, improvements, and racial progress rest instead on people of color, not on the larger society. Thus, modern racism deflects attention away from centuries of oppression and continuing patterns of inequality and discrimination in modern societies without invoking the traditional image of innate inferiority. Moreover, modern racism has a dramatic public policy effect. Researchers have consistently found that those who hold views consistent with modern racism are substantially more likely to oppose policies and programs intended to reduce racial *and* class inequalities. **See** also De Facto Segregation; De Jure Segregation; Discrimination; Segregation/Integration/Separation. (LFW)

BIBLIOGRAPHY

Carmichael, Stokely and Charles V. Hamilton. *Black Power: The Politics of Liberation in America.* New York: Vintage Books, 1967.

Dovidio, John E. and Samuel Gartner, eds. *Prejudice, Discrimination and Racism.* Orlando: Academic Press, 1986.

Feagin, Joe R. and Hernan Vera. *White Racism.* New York: Routledge, 1995.

Katz, Phyllis and Dalmas Taylor, eds. *Eliminating Racism: Profiles in Controversy.* New York: Plenum Press, 1988

Roediger, David R. *The Wages of Whiteness: Race and the Making of the American Working Class.* New York: Verso, 1993.

Wilson, William J. *The Declining Significance of Race.* Chicago: University of Chicago Press, 1980.

Rainbow Coalition

Emerging in the 1984 presidential campaign of **Jesse Jackson**, the Rainbow Coalition included African Americans, gays, Hispanics, Native Americans, small farmers, and youths, among others. By 1988 the Coalition was a national organization that succeeded in registering millions of voters, criticizing Republican ideology, and conducting traditional interest-group politics.

Jackson recognized people's desire for a movement that would challenge the political structure. Deciding to run for president, he appealed to diverse groups who felt left out of Ronald Reagan's America and identified them as the Rainbow Coalition. In the 1984 Democratic primary, over 3 million voters supported Jackson's new Coalition.

In April 1986, delegates from 43 states attended the Rainbow Coalition's first national convention. By the 1988 Democratic primaries, the organization had succeeded in rallying 7 million voters behind Jackson, advocating causes such as environmentalism, job training, increased access to health care, welfare reform, and affirmative action. While unsuccessful in electing Jackson as president, the Rainbow Coalition forged unprecedented alliances across the lines of race, ethnicity, age, class, and sexual orientation. (AD)

BIBLIOGRAPHY

Collins, Sheila. *The Rainbow Challenge: The Jackson Campaign and the Future of U.S. Politics.* New York: Monthly Review Press, 1986.

Joseph Rainey (1832–1887)

Joseph Rainey was born a slave in Georgetown, South Carolina. His father, a barber, purchased freedom for the entire family between the years of 1840 and 1850. Rainey received some private schooling and also became a barber. Although free, during the **Civil War** he was forced to work on the fortifications to Charleston harbor. However, he escaped to the West Indies and returned to the United States after the Union's victory. After the war he became the first African American to serve in the U.S. House of Representatives (1870–1879). Earlier, he had served as a delegate to the South Carolina constitutional convention and a member of the state senate. Rainey, a Republican, established a reputation as a strong advocate for civil rights for all minorities, being an active advocate for the rights of Chinese Americans and Native Americans as well as African Americans. He became a U.S. internal revenue agent for South Carolina from 1879 to 1881 and then worked in banking and brokerage enterprises in Washington, D.C.

BIBLIOGRAPHY

Packwood, Cyril O. *Detour Bermuda, Destination U.S. House of Representatives.* Hamilton, Bermuda: Baxter's, 1977.

A. Philip Randolph (1889–1979)

A(sa) Philip Randolph was born in 1889 in Crescent City, Florida. At the age of 19, he came to New York City to attend City College of New York. During college he began his union activity, organizing the elevator operators. He also organized the Brotherhood of Sleeping Car Porters in 1925, bringing them into the American Federation of Labor as the first black union. It took Randolph more than 10 years to gain recognition by the Pullman Company, the manufacturer of sleeping cars for trains, as an official bargaining agent for the Brotherhood of Sleeping Car Porters. During World War II, Randolph had threatened to lead a march on Washington to convince President Franklin D. Roosevelt to put the **Fair Employment Practices** Committee into operation. Although he was persuaded to postpone the march in the name of national unity during the war, he later became one of the organizers of the **March on Washington** in 1963. His importance to the labor movement was recognized in 1955 when he became vice president of the AFL-CIO, a post he held until 1960. (FAS)

BIBLIOGRAPHY

Anderson, Jervis. *A. Philip Randolph: A Biographical Portrait.* New York: Harcourt, 1973.

Charles Bernard Rangel (1930–)

Charles Bernard Rangel was born on June 11, 1930, in Harlem. A Democrat, he was elected to Congress in 1970 and has served on the House Ways and Means Committee, and the subcommittee on Select Revenue Measures. He has been an active member in the **Congressional Black Caucus,** and is a consistent liberal voice for minorities. Prior to becoming a member of Congress, Rangel was a member of the New York State Legislature, an assistant U.S. attorney for the South District of New York, and had a distinguished war record in Korea. (FAS)

BIBLIOGRAPHY

"Musical Chairs on the Hill." *Black Enterprise* 27, no. 4 (1996): 121–23.

Alonzo Jacob Ransier (1834–1882)

Alonzo Ransier was the U.S. Internal Revenue collector for South Carolina from 1875 to 1876. A Republican, Ransier was elected to the U.S. House of Representatives from South Carolina in 1873 and served until 1875. He served as lieutenant governor of South Carolina in 1870 and was president of the southern States Convention held in the city of Columbia in 1871. Ransier also participated in South Carolina's 1868 and 1869 constitutional conventions.

BIBLIOGRAPHY

Franklin, John Hope. *Reconstruction—After the Civil War.* Chicago: University of Chicago Press, 1994.

James Thomas Rapier (1837–1883)

James Rapier was born in Alabama, and educated in Ontario, Canada. In 1864 he moved to Nashville, Tennessee, and later to Alabama, where he became a prosperous cotton planter. In 1867 he was elected a delegate to Alabama's constitutional convention. In 1872 he was elected to Congress and served as a Republican on the House Committee on Education and Labor. He wanted federal funding for southern public schools to educate blacks. He strongly advocated for black emigration to the West, using the profits from his cotton lands to help blacks settle in Kansas. (EC)

BIBLIOGRAPHY

Schweningre, Loren. "James T. Rapier of Alabama and the Noble Cause of Reconstruction." In H.N. Rabinowitz, ed., *Southern Black Leaders of the Reconstruction Era.* Chicago: University of Illinois Press, 1982, 79–99.

Reconstruction (1863–1877)

On December 8, 1863, Abraham Lincoln presented his "10 percent" plan for Reconstruction. The plan stated that when 10 percent of a state's population swore allegiance to the federal government, that state would be reinstated to the Union and be able to govern itself. There are indications that this plan was essentially a wartime strategy and that Lincoln was moving to a more comprehensive peacetime scheme of Reconstruction. However, any plans Lincoln may have had were destroyed with his assassination in 1865.

Andrew Johnson, Lincoln's successor, ignored protests that a 10 percent plan was too lenient on the South and ignored the needs of the freedmen. Johnson did state that high Confederate officials and those who owned $20,000 worth of property would need a presidential pardon to vote. However, Johnson was quite lenient with his pardons. His refusal to take steps against the Black Codes, which southerners passed to prevent freedmen from exercising their rights, enraged northerners.

Johnson's actions helped move Union policy to aide in the abolition of slavery, as provided in the **Thirteenth Amendment** (1865) and equal rights for blacks as stated in the **Fourteenth Amendment** (1868) and **Fifteenth Amendment** (1870). Johnson's veto of the Civil Rights Act of 1866 and the Freedmen's Bureau Bill of the same year moved moderate Republicans to unite with their radical colleagues and override his vetoes.

While the Republican Party wished to maintain political control in the former Confederacy, Radical Reconstruction was also motivated by a genuine desire to improve the condition of freedmen and for social justice. Senator Charles Sumner of Massachusetts and Representative Thaddeus Stevens of Pennsylvania were genuinely committed to their cause and felt the South should be punished for its actions.

A series of laws set up Congressional Reconstruction in 1867. These laws strengthened the **Freedmen's Bureau,** providing assistance to freed slaves. Before any state could be readmitted to the Union, it had to accept the Thirteenth and Fourteenth Amendments, and later the Fifteenth Amendment as well. Except for Tennessee, all former Confederate States became part of one of five military districts and an army of occupation moved into these districts. These former Confederate states had to accept the principle of black suffrage.

President Johnson continued to oppose Reconstruction on the grounds that it gave the federal government too much power. His southern background and anti-black sympathies did not aid his national popularity. His firing of Secretary of War Edwin Stanton led to his impeachment for violating the Tenure in Office Act and his near conviction. He was saved that dishonor because his opponents failed to reach a two-third majority in the Senate by one vote.

African Americans actively participated in all aspects of public life during Reconstruction. They eagerly took advantage of their right to vote, participated in the conventions that formulated new state constitutions in the South, and held political office at the local, state, and federal levels. Fourteen African Americans were elected to the U.S. House of Representatives, and two were elected to the U.S. Senate. As Reconstruction progressed, African Americans began to increase their participation in politics. They began to wield power commensurate with their numbers in states such as South Carolina, Mississippi, and Louisiana.

African Americans set up systems of public education and also established private schools and colleges. The Freedmen's Bureau, along with northern church groups, aided in these efforts. Public accommodations legislation was also passed that required businesses to serve blacks. Hopes for the "40 acres and a mule" promised in Republican oratory were kept alive but very few freedmen purchased land. These hopes were further dashed by the establishment of the **Ku Klux Klan** and other forms of violence that helped lessened voter participation by blacks and white Republicans.

However, the restoration of the vote to ex-Confederates and the slowing of the reform movement among northern Republicans led to the Compromise of 1877. Democrats in Florida, South Carolina, and Louisiana agreed to let the Republican presidential candidate, Rutherford B. Hayes, win the election of 1876 in return for the removal of federal troops from these states and election victories in these states' elections.

Reconstruction left many African Americans in virtual slavery and the hopes of the Civil War era unfulfilled. It took another hundred years to begin to restore rights that had once been safeguarded. (FAS)

BIBLIOGRAPHY

Foner, Eric. *Reconstruction: America's Unfinished Revolution, 1863–1877.* New York: Harper & Row, 1988.

Nieman, Donald G. *To Set the Law in Motion: The Freedmen's Bureau and the Legal Rights of Blacks, 1865–1868.* Millwood, NY: KTO Press, 1979.

Regents of the University of California v. Bakke (1978)

Allan Bakke was denied admission to the medical school at the University of California at Davis despite grades and scores that were as good as or better than the median students admitted, and much better than the so-called special admittees. Bakke challenged the special admissions program that reserved 16 seats for disadvantaged students. Because no white person had ever been admitted under the special program, Bakke argued that it was a quota system that violated the Equal Protection Clause of the **Fourteenth Amendment** and the **Civil Rights Act of 1964**.

Both the California state trial court and appeals court ruled in favor of Bakke, stating that the special admissions program did indeed violate federal law and the Fourteenth Amendment. Consequently, the medical school was ordered to admit Bakke. Then in *Regents of the University of California v. Bakke,* 438 U.S. 265 (1978), the U.S. Supreme Court, in a complex and fragmented 5–4 decision, upheld the California appeals court decision to admit Bakke as well as the appeals court's invalidation of the medical school's affirmative action program. However, the Supreme Court also ruled that race or minority status *may* be used as a consideration in admissions decisions, but it cannot be the only consideration. **See** the text of the Fourteenth Amendment in "Civil War Amendments" in Appendix 1.

BIBLIOGRAPHY

Domino, John C. *Affirmative Action and the Supreme Court.* New York: HarperCollins Publishers, 1996.

Halon, William. *Landmark Supreme Court Decisions.* New York: HarperCollins Publishers, 1996.

Landsberg, Brian K. "Balanced Scholarship and Racial Balance." *Wake Forest Law Review* 30, no. 4 (Winter 1995): 819–29.

Natapoff, Alexandra. "Trouble in Paradise: Equal Protection and the Dilemma of Interminority Group Conflict." *Stanford Law Review* 47, no. 5 (May 1995): 1059–96.

Reitman v. Mulkey (1967)

An amendment to the California Constitution passed by the electorate in a referendum overturned anti-discrimination statutes and granted private citizens the right to discriminate against potential buyers or lessees without state interference. Lincoln Mulkey, a black man, filed suit against property owners in Orye county to challenge the validity of the measure. In *Reitman v. Mulkey,* 387, U.S. 369 (1967), the Supreme Court ruled that the constitutional provision violated the federal Constitution, because it put the state in the position of authorizing private discrimination as a matter of state policy. Such close involvement of the state in private discrimination crosses the constitutional line established by the **Fourteenth Amendment.** (FHJ)

BIBLIOGRAPHY

Weiser, Philip J. "Ackerman's Proposal for Popular Constitutional Lawmaking: Can It Realize His Aspirations for Dualist Democracy?" (Bruce Ackerman) *New York University Law Review* 68, no. 4 (October 1993): 907–59.

Relations with Other Minority Groups

Urban areas have changed dramatically in the past 25 years. Beginning in the 1970s, American producers have faced increasing global competition due to the penetration of the American market with international products and capital. Because of relatively low labor wages abroad, as well as a series of economic shocks, labor-intensive businesses have become increasingly noncompetitive. A revolution in transportation and communication technology magnifies this trend by increasing the tempo of both domestic and international transactions, enabling the sudden movement of goods and capital globally, and increasing capital mobility.

American cities have borne the brunt of these changes as manufacturing employment has declined precipitously since 1973. This structural industrial decline, marked by both downsizing and the closing of plants, coupled with the growth of the "informational economy" or corporate, public, and nonprofit service sector in urban areas has transformed urban areas from industrial to informational centers. At the same time that urban areas experienced a sudden decline in their industrial structure, cities became increasingly ethnically diverse. Combined with the worsening economic prospects of inner-city residents, the widespread immigration of poor nonwhite minorities into American cities has profoundly shaped the appearance of urban America. This growing socio-economic inequality is reflected in the emergence of socially and spatially polarized "dual cities" which Matthew Drennan terms the development of "two cities in one space"—one white and wealthy, holding both economic and political power, the other of color and poor, and essentially powerless. This demographic transformation of urban America provides the potential for both explosive relations between minority groups, as well as the possible realization of multi-ethnic and multi-racial coalitions.

In his book *Blacks, Latinos, and Asians in Urban America,* James Jennings explains that, "it is important to ask what kinds of political relationships will emerge between these groups" because of the potential for destabilizing social interactions over issues such as employment, political incorporation, culture, and immigration. Examples of this type of racial hostility abound in both the popular culture and accounts of relationships between blacks and Koreans in Los Angeles and New York City. Conversely, Jennings offers some optimism that, "in many American cities, blacks, Latinos, and Asians have an opportunity to develop a political foundation that could support new and innovative policy strategies and human service approaches to these kinds of challenges."

In ethnic studies literature, various theories of intergroup conflict have been offered to explain how racial groups respond to the socio-economic opportunity structure of their communities. Jennings groups these diverse explanations into five distinctive categories of intergroup conflict. The ethnic succession model argues that while ethnic groups gradually and naturally assimilate into the socio-political system, they effectively gain economic and social mobility. Conflict between racial and ethnic groups, then, merely reflects competition among them as they seek economic advantages, and it disappears naturally once groups are effectively assimilated. This perspective assumes that African Americans, like white ethnic minorities before them, will gradually share in the benefits of society and that racial and ethnic demarcations will disappear.

Conversely, the resentment model asserts that ethnic tension results from resentment between long-term residents of a community and those newly arriving groups which might achieve certain political or economic gains. For example, some scholars have suggested that conflict between African Americans and Koreans reflects the fear among African Americans that Koreans will gain socio-economic advances more rapidly than they will, in spite of their greater longevity in the community. The job competition model suggests that the competition for employment exacerbates tensions between groups, and that newly arriving groups might be taking jobs once held by another racial or ethnic group. Political rhetoric and media accounts provide frequent examples of this process while discussing immigration.

The social and economic status model maintains that relations between groups are inversely correlated with the relative similarity of the objective social characteristics of groups. In other words, groups experiencing similar economic conditions are less likely to exhibit contentious behaviors than groups living under widely varying material conditions. Numerous scholars implicitly invoke this model when asserting that blacks and Latinos are more likely to form political coalitions than blacks and Asians or blacks and Anglos. The racial hierarchy model argues that racial themes, images, and conflicts are continually mobilized and exploited by the dominant group to maintain their own position of privilege. In contrast to the previous models, the racial hierarchy perspective suggests that racial and ethnic groups are pitted against one another in order to insulate advantaged groups from the systematic destruction of this caste-like system.

Although examples of each of these models abound in the literature, none has gained ascendancy. Not surprisingly, anecdotal evidence for each of these theories has been found in communities undergoing urban reconstruction. For instance, Karen Umemoto finds that increased conflict between blacks and Koreans exists because of competition between their respective socio-political institutions which resulted when Koreans replaced Jews in black communities. Similarly, Alan Saltzstein and Raphael Sonenshein predict that "interethnic conflict may increase as Latinos move into Black neighborhoods." Still, the emergence of ethnically diverse communities has the potential for cooperative arrangements to emerge. In the influential book *Protest is Not Enough*, Rufus Browning, David Tabb, and Dale Rogers Marshall provide a somewhat optimistic framework outlining the potential for political coalitions to emerge between communities of color. In this study of multi-racial political coalitions, the authors focus both on the factors producing these coalitions—demographic strength, past protest activity, electoral mobilization, and the presence of white liberals in elected office—and their effectiveness.

Writing almost a generation after the height of the civil rights movement, Browning, Tabb, and Marshall are concerned with governmental responsiveness to black and Latino interests in American cities. By examining 10 northern California cities, the authors discovered impressive gains in minority representation in local governments along with some meaningful public policy achievements. Based on the evidence they uncovered, Browning, Tabb, and Marshall argue that while mere representation of people of color in public positions is substantively meaningless, political incorporation, defined as the inclusion of these public officials in the dominant majority coalition on the city council, is necessary for black and Latino interests to be served.

In cities that have achieved political incorporation, of the majority of those considered by the authors, blacks and Latinos achieve certain tangible benefits such as the increased diversity of municipal employment, the creation of police review boards, the increased appointment of minorities to city boards and commissions, the implementation of effective **affirmative action** policies, enhanced contracting with minority-owned businesses, and greater responsiveness to minorities in both the delivery of services and in economic development policies. According to this study, then, contentious relations between groups can be effectively managed through coalition formation. Although considerable controversy remains over which of these models most accurately captures the reality of urban America, the experience of the coming 25 years should provide a wealth of examples of interaction between African Americans and other racial groups in American cities. (CC)

BIBLIOGRAPHY

Browning, Rufus, Dale Rogers Marshall, and David Tabb. *Protest Is Not Enough: The Struggle of Blacks and Hispanics for Equality in Urban Politics*. Berkeley: University of California Press, 1984.

———. eds. *Racial Politics in American Cities*. New York: Longman Press, 1990.

Drennan, Matthew. "The Decline and Rise of the New York Economy." In Mollenkopf and Castells, eds. *Dual City: Restructuring New York*. New York: Russell Sage Foundation, 1991.

Eisinger, Peter. *Patterns of Interracial Politics: Conflict and Cooperation in the City*. New York: Academic Press, 1976.

Jennings, James. *Blacks, Latinos, and Asians in Urban America: Status and Prospects for Politics and Activism*. London: Praeger Publishers, 1994.

Saltzstein, Alan and Raphael Sonenshein. "Los Angeles: Transformation of a Governing Coalition." In Savitch and Thomas, eds. *Big City Politics in Transition*. London: Sage Publications, 1991.

Tedin, Kent L. and Richard W. Murray. "Support for Biracial Political Coalitions among Blacks and Hispanics." *Social Science Quarterly* 75, no. 4 (1994).

Umemoto, Karen. "Blacks and Koreans in Los Angeles." In James Jennings, ed. *Blacks, Latinos, and Asians in Urban America*. Westport, CT: Praeger Press, 1994.

Religion and African-American Politics

African-American religion, while today not exclusively Christian, was primarily the consequence of a synthesis of African religious beliefs and rituals brought to the United States by enslaved Africans, and the predominantly evangelistic Christianity of the eighteenth and nineteenth centuries. African-American religion was fundamentally marked by the slavery experience and the accompanying racism which continued after Emancipation. It was the racial discrimination within the then dominant Baptist, Episcopal, Methodist, and Presbyterian Churches that led to the founding of independent African-American churches, both in the antebellum and particularly, in the postbellum periods. The most well-known of these is the African Methodist Episcopal Church (AME), which was formed by the withdrawal of **Richard Allen** and **Absalom Jones** from St. George's Episcopal Methodist Church in Philadelphia, and it was incorporated in 1816. Similar withdrawals of African Americans from dominantly white denominations

Religion and politics have always been linked in the African-American experience. Pictured is the Rev. J.W. Washington praying at a reception for President William Howard Taft (immediately behind Washington) in about 1910. *Library of Congress.*

led to the founding in 1821 of the African Methodist Episcopal Zion Church. After the **Civil War,** African Americans from the southern Methodist Episcopal Church seceded to form the Christian Methodist Church, and many emancipated ex-slaves gathered to form independent Black Baptist congregations. By 1895 separate Baptist groups joined to form the National Baptist Convention.

African-American religion was molded by its practitioners as a means of survival under the devastating impact of slavery, and as almost the only institution controlled by African Americans, it performed diverse functions and sought thereby to preserve the whole person. **W.E.B. Du Bois** stated that these churches served not just narrow spiritual ends, but they also functioned as a center for black social life, as a lending bank, a mutual-aid society and additionally , as a hospitality network for black travelers excluded by racial segregation from public facilities such as hotels and restaurants. Thus in African-American churches the spiritual, economic, political, and the social were never sharply demarcated as they were in the larger society, and this has remained a defining characteristic of African American religion. Thus, as early as the 1830s, ministers of existing African-American denominations had organized the National Negro Convention Movement to agitate for social and political reform, and in particular to abolish **slavery.**

In its Christian forms, African-American religion has often been misunderstood as a "haven for the masses," or as a "refuge in a hostile white world." The implication is that such religion was individualistic, pietistic, and without a wider social impact. However, modern scholarship, beginning with the seminal work of W.E.B. Du Bois, challenged this negative, passive view of the African-American Church and has devoted much attention to the issue of slave religion, exposing it as a complex dialectic of accommodation and opposition. On the one hand African-American religion did serve as a source of individual meaning and as an otherworldly refuge, a religious attitude certainly encouraged by slave owners. On the other hand, however, African-American Christianity, which adapted the Exodus story and the judgment themes of Revelation to its own doctrine, encouraged opposition to the dominant cultural norms and institutions, most obviously those of **racism** and slavery.

As religious participation by slaves was, if not proscribed, subject to various limits and constraints due to slave-owners' fears of revolt, it has been aptly described as the "invisible institution." This paradoxically named institution did in fact foster hopes of rebellion, which intensified after the successful slave revolt against the French of Santo Domingo (Haiti) from 1791–1802. This encouraged similar revolts in the southern states, under Gabriel Prosser at Richmond (1800), **Denmark Vesey** in South Carolina (1822) and **Nat Turner** (1830) in northern Virginia. Significantly, each rebel justified his role in terms of biblical imagery.

African-American religion, then, served both as the preserver of black identity and as the source of resistance to slavery and white racism. Thus, even prior to the **Civil War,** African-American ministers and congregations in the North championed abolitionism. During **Reconstruction,** black ministers filled numerous federal and state political positions, including those of state representatives and senator. However, all these gains were reversed in the late nineteenth century through the failure of state and federal agencies to enforce the U.S. Constitution and through the enactment of **Jim Crow** laws. The most prominent reaction against such legally sanctioned racial prejudice was an upsurge in **black nationalism.** This movement had its origins in religious Ethiopianism (derived from Psalm 68:31 "Ethiopia shall soon stretch forth her arms to God."), a nineteenth century-movement which claimed a messianic and millenial role for all black people, who would soon be Christianized, and especially for American blacks, who would be liberated from slavery.

Apart from providing the basis for a distinctive destiny for blacks, such beliefs also fostered black nationalism and **Pan-Africanism.** Such themes were in print as early as 1829 in Robert Alexander's "The Ethiopian Manifesto" and **David Walker's** "Appeal . . . to the Colored Citizens of the World." Bishop **Henry McNeal Turner** of the AME, perceiving that the Civil War and Reconstruction had not guaranteed black civil rights, advocated separatism and a return to Africa. Such views were developed by Edward Blyden and **Alexander Crummell,** pioneer missionaries and colonists in Liberia, and reformulated philosophically by W.E.B. Du Bois at the end of the nineteenth century. Such beliefs were related either to plans for independent black states in the South, or to an exodus back to Africa. While the former plan never gained much impetus, the latter belief did gain popularity for a brief time under the charismatic leadership of **Marcus Garvey** in the 1920s. Yet the social role of religion endured, and in 1934 most African-American churches participated in the first black ecumenical organization, the Fraternal Council of Negro Churches, which in its social agenda, prefigured much of the later **civil rights movement.**

Martin Luther King, Jr., arguably the most influential twentieth-century American figure and leader of the civil rights movement until his assassination in 1968, was himself a third-generation Baptist minister and the founder and president of the **Southern Christian Leadership Conference (SCLC)** which organized much of the protest activity in the South during the 1950s. King, through his creative synthesis of Christian teachings on love, American Civil Religion, and Ghandian nonviolent opposition to evil, led the movement to abolish segregation and to assert and establish the equality of African Americans. Out of the civil rights movement came the National Conference of Black Christians which was instrumental in the development of African-American liberation theology, and numerous black caucuses in the predominantly white mainline denominations and the National Council of Churches. The Conference's most radical political moment was its support for James Forman's presentation of the "Black Manifesto" on April 26, 1969, in New York. However, by the mid-1970s, these organizations had lost much of their political force as African-American unity fragmented before the evidence that integrationism and nonviolence as goals and tactics had failed.

The civil rights movement, after the loss of Martin Luther King, Jr. was overshadowed by more radical successors in the **black power** and black theology movements which sought not so much reform as revolution. **Stokely Carmichael,** the originator of the black power slogan, understood it primarily as an assertion of black self-determination, rather than as an exclusive or defensive statement. This was the central theme for the black theology movement, developed by Albert B. Cleage and James H. Cone, who were earlier involved in the civil rights and black power movements. Black theology understood Jesus as one who struggled against all forms of oppression, thus justifying the black political struggle against racism. It absorbed elements of Latin American liberation theology during the 1970s but it remained abstract and never permeated down to the congregational level.

However, as groups as disparate as white liberals and black power activists realized the common structural determinants of poverty, a realization shared earlier by Martin Luther King, Jr. and **Malcolm X**, coalitions between these groups, their constituents and other racial minorities (Native Americans, Mexican Americans, and white working classes) began to form, only to be fragmented by the impact of the intensifying Vietnam War in the late 1960s. Two clergymen prominent in subsequent political movements were the Reverend **Benjamin Chavis** (United Church of Christ) and the Reverend **Jesse Jackson** (Baptist). Chavis, a church civil rights organizer and one of the "Wilmington 10," went on to eventually become a controversial director of the **National Association for the Advancement of Colored People (NAACP)** from 1993–1994 and then founder of the National African American Leadership Summit. Jackson, one of King's assistants in the Southern Christian Leadership Conference's Chicago projects in 1966, used Operation Breadbasket to initiate **Operation PUSH** (People United to Save Humanity) in 1971. His continued civil rights activity led to his running for Democratic contender for the presidency in 1984 and 1988. He galvanized much African-American support for the presidential elections largely though the Black Church and through coalition building.

African-American religion has typically been described as synonymous with the "Black Church." However, this obscures not only the great diversity among the churches, but the differing religious expressions such as Black Judaism and the even more prominent and varied Black Muslim movements, the most politically active being the **Nation of Islam,** known for its sharp critique of white racism and of Christianity as complicit therein. The first Black Muslim movement emerged in Detroit when **W.D. Fard** founded the heterodox Nation of Islam in 1930 from Timothy Drew's (Noble Drew Ali) Moorish Science Temple. He was succeeded in 1933 by **Elijah Muhammad** (Poole), who led the movement until his death in 1975. While not orthodox Islam, Black Muslims were per-

haps proto-Islam, geared toward reaching the black underclasses and building self-awareness, respect, and economic independence. They drew national attention during the 1960s and 1970s, and through the influence of the teachings of Malcolm X and the conversion of world heavy-weight champion boxer Muhammad Ali (Cassius Clay). Malcolm X (Malcolm Little) broke with the Nation of Islam in 1964, in part over differences over Black Muslim political participation. The next year saw his pilgrimage to Mecca; conversion to orthodox, non-racialistic Islam; and the founding of the Organization for Afro-American Unity to re-establish black nationalism and to criticize the civil rights movement for its commitment to nonviolence and its failure to address economic and class issues. Malcolm X thus anticipated much of the black power movement.

In 1975, under Warith Deen Muhammed, the Nation of Islam, now renamed The American Muslim Mission, adopted an orthodox Sunni position, prompting a schism under **Louis Farrakhan** in 1978, who continued to lead the Nation of Islam. Farrakhan's emphasis on Fard's original teachings have led in recent years to charges of racism and to sharp antagonism between the Nation of Islam and the Jewish community. On October 16, 1996, together with Benjamin Chavis, Farrakhan organized and led the controversial **Million Man March** in Washington, D.C.

An African-American religious movement overlooked until recently is that of Pentecostalism. Emerging out of nineteenth-century Holiness movements, it was initiated by an African-American pastor, William Seymour, and it led to the formation of numerous Pentecostal-Holiness groups, the largest being the Church of God in Christ (the fastest growing black denomination). Earlier scholarly treatments overlooked Seymour's role and that of African Americans, and the interracial make-up of the early Pentecostal movement. Belatedly entering the social and political arenas, Pentecostals made news when in 1994 the white Pentecostal Fellowship of North America voted itself out of existence and merged with its African-American counterparts. (ISM)

BIBLIOGRAPHY

Baer, Hans A. and Merrill Singer. *African-American Religion in the Twentieth Century: Varieties of Protest and Accommodation.* Knoxville, TN: University of Tennessee Press, 1992.

Burkett, Randall. *Garveyism as a Religious Movement: The Institutionalization of a Black Civil Religion.* Metuchen, NJ: Scarecrow, 1978.

Cox, Harvey. *Fire from Heaven: The Rise of Pentecostal Spirituality and the Reshaping of Religion in the Twenty-First Century.* Reading, MA: Addison-Wesley, 1995.

Du Bois, W.E.B. *The Negro Church.* Atlanta, GA: Atlanta University Press, 1903.

Frazier, E. Franklin. *The Negro Church in America.* New York: Schocken, 1974.

Genovese, Eugene D. *Roll, Jordan Roll: The World the Slave Made.* New York: Vintage, 1974.

Lincoln, C. Eric. *The Black Muslims in America.* Grand Rapids, MI: Eerdmans, 1994.

Paris, Peter J. *The Social Teaching of the Black Churches.* Philadelphia: Fortress, 1985.

Raboteau, Albert J. *Slave Religion: The "Invisible Institution" in the Antebellum South*. New York: Oxford University Press, 1978.

Wilmore, Gayraud. *Black Religion and Black Radicalism*. Maryknoll, NY: Orbis Press, 1983.

Reparations

In the African-American community there has been a consistent and long-term effort to receive reparations or monetary awards from the United States Government as a way to compensate blacks for the suffering of their ancestors and as a means to amend the injustices of **slavery.** The issue of economic reparations is not unprecedented. Advocates of black reparations point to other groups which received monetary awards in an effort to solidify their case against the government. For example, Japanese Americans incarcerated in detention camps in several western states during World War II received an official national apology and payment of $20,000 per victim for their wrongful interment. Additionally, numerous Native-American nation states received court settlements for prior seizure of their land. In Europe, the German government has paid almost $50 billion in reparations to Holocaust survivors. More recently, in 1988, Daimler-Benz, a German automobile manufacturing company, agreed to pay almost $12 million to victims of Nazi forced labor policies and to their families.

What form should reparations take in the United States? Historically, there have been several types of reparations sought as a means to redress injustices against African Americans. One form, many times with racist overtones, was a call for a repatriation effort. For example, the nineteenth-century American Colonization Society called for government support of its program to provide free transportation and land in Liberia for any blacks willing to settle there. Then in 1892, in the British colony of Natal (part of present day South Africa), white British missionary Joseph Booth created an "African Christian Union." In order to fund its activities, the organization requested that the United States Government pay 100 pounds for every African American who volunteered to emigrate.

In addition to calls for repatriation efforts, reparations advocates also advanced proposals for the creation of a black state in the South. In 1928 the Communist Party of the United States argued that African Americans, especially in the South, were a distinct people and had a national identity. As such, the party argued that blacks were entitled to a homeland and had the right to carve out an independent African-American polity in the "black belt" states of the South. Further north, in 1934 the Chicago-based National Movement for the Establishment of a 49th State also called for a new state to be created in the American South. A new state would give blacks "the opportunity to work out their own destiny, unbridled and unhampered by artificial barriers."

In the 1950s, the **Nation of Islam** called for the establishment of a separate black state. Under the Nation of Islam's plan, the United States would supply and maintain the population of the proposed black state for at least 20 to 25 years until it had reached some level of economic and political autonomy.

One group located in Harlem, called the "Provide the Government of the African-American Capital," advocated the creation of a state, supported and aided by the American government, south of the Mason-Dixon Line. A similar program advocated by the separatist group the Republic of New Africa, a nationalist organization, demanded an independent black nation that would encompass the states of Louisiana, Mississippi, Alabama, Georgia, and South Carolina, in 1993.

Following the **Civil War,** economic restitution as a form of reparation came to the forefront of the reparations debate when "forty acres and a mule" became the historic rallying cry for reparations after an abortive experiment on the Sea Islands off the coasts of Georgia and South Carolina. In that location General William T. Sherman granted forty acres of land and the loan of a government mule to some African Americans near the end of the war. However, in mid-1865, under a proclamation of amnesty, President Andrew Jackson returned most of the donated property to its antebellum white owners. Another proposal during the same period sought to provide African Americans with free transportation to the American West, where, under the Homestead Act, they could obtain free land.

Pensions were also proposed as a form of reparations. In 1890, white Congressman William J. Connell (R-NE), prompted by a wealthy and influential constituent, introduced a bill that would grant government pensions to blacks in partial recompense for the suffering of slavery. Various bills would propose pensions for African Americans in Congress, always unsuccessfully. Then in 1955 "Queen Mother" Audley Moore, a Communist, began her campaign to press for reparations, especially in a pamphlet entitled "Why Reparations? Money for Negroes." At one point in 1962, she even met with President John F. Kennedy to air her views. On the 100th anniversary of the **Emancipation Proclamation**, Moore formed the Reparations Committee for the Descendants of American Slaves. By 1966, the **Black Panther Party** also called for economic restitution from the white community as part of its party's political platform.

More recently, economic reparations have included claims filed by some African Americans with the Internal Revenue Service (IRS). In 1996, the IRS received and denied thousands of tax claims for slavery reparations. In Texas, con artists were telling taxpayers that they could file Form 2439, Notice to Shareholders of Undistributed Long-term Capital Gains, to collect up to approximately $40,000 in reparations, and the IRS was receiving thousands of requests daily for Form 2439.

Variations of the "black-tax" story have been floating around the country since at least 1993, when an article in *Essence* Magazine, a periodical aimed at black women, urged readers to seek reparations from the Internal Revenue Service on their tax forms and gave instructions on how to do so. More than 20,000 people followed *Essence* author L.G. Sherrod's advice in 1994 and claimed they had already paid $43,000 in "black taxes"—the amount Sherrod said the government owed each black household. An IRS spokesperson stated that the basis of the claims dated back to the 1860s when Congress voted to provide each former slave with 40 acres and a mule as redress for their years in slavery. Economists have estimated the current value of 40 acres and a mule at $40,000.

The calls for economic restitution have caused a schism in the reparations debate. The division stems from whether or not economic reparations should be distributed to blacks as individuals and families, or to community-based organizations. Numerous ideas for some form of collective reparations were advanced. For example, during the 1960s, James Forman, a former executive secretary of the **Student Nonviolent Coordinating Committee (SNCC)** from 1961 until 1966, who created the Black Economic Developed Conference (and of which Forman was a leader), did not request direct payments to African Americans, but requested instead that the first $500 million installment would go toward forming, among other things, television stations owned and run by blacks, publishing houses, employment training centers for individuals and communities, and a southern Land Bank that would provide for those who wanted land. The bank and an African-American university proposed by the manifesto would receive over $300 million of the total.

Another argument for collective reparations came from the academic community. Arguing in 1992 that the nation owes a singular debt to African Americans beyond normal **affirmative action** programs, sociologist Paul Starr called for the establishment of a privately funded National Endowment for Black America, which would foster the economic growth of the black community. Other forms of reparation would create institutions in the black community. For example, Detroit real estate agent Ray Jenkins supports a form of reparation wherein the United States Government would create "an unlimited educational fund to establish free scholarships for African Americans to attend any college or university in this country." For the past 30 years, Jenkins, dubbed "Reparations Ray," has travelled extensively across the United States and become the leading voice in a national campaign to force the United States government to compensate African Americans for enslavement of their ancestors.

Reparations efforts in the 1990s also include "The Reparations Study Bill" or H.R. 40, which has been introduced six times in Congress since 1989, by U.S. Congressman **John Conyers** (D-MI). The new legislation is intended to elevate the discussion and public awareness of the issue through a Study Commission that would hold a series of public meetings. The bill, with 21 co-sponsors, has, however, remained in the House Judiciary Committee, despite support from prominent organizations like the the **National Association for the Advancement of Colored People (NAACP)**. But in 1997, Congressman Tony Hall, (D-OH), introduced legislation in Congress to have the federal government apologize to African Americans for the enslavement of their ancestors. Both Jenkins and Conyers received the support of the National Coalition of Blacks for Reparations in America (N'COBRA), a major umbrella organization formed in 1987 and based in Maryland. But an apology seems more likely, at least from the Clinton administration, than any form of economic reparation. In June 1997 President Clinton told members of the press that he would consider making an apology similar to the one he made in May to black men who were the subjects 50 years ago of the government's Tuskegee Syphilis Study. But, Clinton added, he would not support reparations. (VDD)

BIBLIOGRAPHY

America, Richard F. *Paying the Social Debt: What White America Owes Black America*. Westport, CT: Greenwood Press, 1993.

Bell, Derrick. *And We Are Not Saved: The Elusive Quest for Racial Justice*. New York: Basic Books, 1987.

American Institute of Certified Public Accountants. "IRS Receives Thousands of Claims for Slavery Reparation." *Journal of Accountancy* (October 1996): 182, 34.

Republican Party

The Republican Party, also known as the Grand Old Party (GOP), arose out of the mid-nineteenth century conflict over **slavery**, and it remains one of the two major political parties in the United States. Opposed to slavery at its birth, the party (whose first president was Abraham Lincoln) emerged from the **Civil War** with the image of being the party in favor of civil rights for all, regardless of race. For almost 75 years after the North's victory in the Civil War, the Republicans were the nation's dominant political party. During these years (1860–1932) the Republicans became less and less the party associated with racial equality and more and more the party associated with big business. The party of Lincoln became the party of Wall Street, a development that began to break the party's hold on black voters during the Great Depression of the 1930s. The 1936 election was the first time that a majority of black voters cast their ballot for the other major party,

For the first 75 years after the Civil War, most African Americans were members of the Republican Party, the party of Lincoln. Shown here are the first black members of the U.S. Senate and House of Representatives. *Library of Congress.*

the Democrats. When Democratic President Lyndon Johnson signed the **Civil Rights Act of 1964** and Republican presidential nominee Barry Goldwater campaigned against it, a healthy bloc of black voters for the Democrats grew to become a nearly universal one. Since 1964, only small minorities of black and Latino voters have supported the Republicans in national elections. In 1980, white women also began to be less supportive of the party. Meanwhile, by the closing decades of the twentieth century, the Republicans gained strength with white male voters in particular, and southern whites and religious fundamentalists in general. Along with the business and elite interests that had long supported the party, these new groups were enough to produce a majority coalition for the party in presidential elections throughout the 1980s and a majority in Congress in 1994 and 1996.

The party's origins and evolution demonstrate how substantially a political organization's image and coalition of support can change over time. When the 1854 **Kansas–Nebraska Act** overturned two compromises (the **Missouri Compromise of 1820** and the **Compromise of 1850**) that barred the expansion of slavery into newly created territories of the United States, anti-slavery groups galvanized and created a new party, the Republicans. Formally launched in July 1854 at Jackson, Mississippi, by a group of former Whigs, Democrats, and Free-Soilers, the party's founders were firmly linked in common opposition to expanding slavery. This was a popular view in the North, and the Republicans won control of the House of Representatives in 1858. In 1860, the party's second presidential candidate, Abraham Lincoln, was elected president by the electoral votes of the 18 northern states. Lincoln's election in turn galvanized resentments in southern states, dependent on slave labor, against the Republicans. When southern states seceded, Lincoln declared restoration of the Union to be his objective, but anti-slavery Republicans in Congress pressed for emancipation as well as the stated goal of the Civil War. When the South was defeated, enslaved Africans were emancipated, and the Republican party became known as the party that "freed the slaves."

From its inception, the Republican Party appealed to commercial as well as anti-slavery interests. The party's support of powerful industrial and financial businesses coupled with its identification with northern and midwestern farmers garnered it a coalition strong enough to dominate American politics from the end of the Civil War to the New Deal. From 1860 to 1932, the Republicans won 14 of the 18 presidential elections. From 1896 to 1910, the Republicans also controlled both houses of Congress.

During this period of Republican dominance, those few blacks who were enfranchised (mostly in the northern cities) voted for the Republican Party. The reasons were clear. First, in the immediate aftermath of the Civil War, the short-lived **Reconstruction** period, one wing of the Republican Party—the "Radical Republicans"—sought to extend not only emancipation and political rights to the formerly enslaved, but also to secure racial justice by providing economic oppor-

tunities as well. Their most important measures were the Reconstruction Acts of 1868 and 1876, which mandated universal manhood suffrage and placed the South under a military government. Their most famous unfulfilled promise was to give every former slave family "40 acres and a mule" so that they finally had a genuine chance to prosper. In reality, however, economic opportunity was denied, and Reconstruction was terminated only 10 years after the end of the war when the Compromise of 1877 restored southern white dominance and the **Democratic Party** in the South.

Second, in the immediate post-Reconstruction period, every four years the Republicans in ritual-like fashion called in party platforms for congressional action for ending lynching and disenfranchisement and for providing "equal justice for all men, without regard to race and color." In fact, however, Republican pledges were not redeemed because blacks had nowhere else to turn. For all the magic of the name of Lincoln, no twentieth-century Republican had sought to walk in Lincoln's image as a responsible leader for blacks. With neither party ready to make the fundamental racial commitments that might have changed black voting patterns, those few blacks who could vote remained passively with the Republicans. It would take a crisis of major proportions to move blacks into the Democratic Party.

The Great Depression and the Hoover administration gave blacks such a crisis and ample reason to turn their backs on the GOP. The overtly pro-big-business policies of the party, its harsh attitude toward labor, and its apparent unwillingness to combat the Depression through government programs could hardly be attractive to blacks, a group disproportionately afflicted in the economic crisis. In addition, Republican president Herbert Hoover made mistakes on racial questions and uttered racial slurs through both his administrations in the late 1920s and early 1930s.

Still the memory of the "party of Lincoln" was so strong that a majority of black voters supported Hoover in 1932. It was in 1936, after experiencing the economic benefits of Franklin D. Roosevelt's New Deal when blacks joined the Democratic coalition of Catholics, Jews, farmers, organized labor, intellectuals, northern urbanites, and southern whites.

Beginning with the New Deal, the Republicans became the minority party for more than 40 years. Between 1932 and 1980, the Republican Party won only four presidential elections and controlled Congress for only four years (1947–1949 and 1953–1955). In the 1950s, the party of big business that had vigorously opposed the New Deal began largely to accept an expanded role of government in solving the nation's socioeconomic woes and regulating the economy.

When Republican nominee Dwight Eisenhower was elected president in 1952, his election marked the dominance of the party's liberal-moderate wing as opposed to its conservative wing. Even with the moderates in control, the Republicans remained clearly the more conservative of the two parties on questions of regulation of the economy, foreign policies, and taxes for rich corporations and individuals, but one aspect of its moderation in the 1950s was in the area of civil rights. Thus throughout the 1950s both parties appeared relatively equally identified with the cause of civil rights. Eisenhower, for example, signed the first civil rights acts since Reconstruction (the relatively weak **Civil Rights Act of 1957** and **Civil Rights Act of 1960**) and sent federal troops to Little Rock, Arkansas, to enforce a school desegregation order. In this context, polls showed that American public opinion remained sharply divided on the question of which party was "good for civil rights" throughout the 1950s. As a result of neither party's firm commitment to the cause of civil rights for people of color, a substantial minority of blacks continued to vote for the Republican party as late as 1960. In the contest that year between Republican presidential nominee Richard Nixon and Democratic presidential nominee John Kennedy, 32 percent of black voters cast their ballots for Nixon, who narrowly lost.

Conservatives regained control of the Republican Party in 1964. Seeking a way to widen the party's appeal, the conservatives turned to what came to be known as the "southern strategy"—appealing especially to white southerners (but also conservative white-collar suburbanites, blue-collar workers, and race segregationists in every region) who were hostile to the increasingly pro–civil-rights stance of the Democrats during the 1960s. The 1964 Republican presidential nominee, Arizona senator Barry Goldwater, one of only eight senators outside the South to vote against the Civil Rights Act of 1964, proved to be the first of many Republican nominees who sought to perfect this strategy. Goldwater emphasized his preference for a minimalist role for the federal government in domestic affairs, including the handling of race questions. Segregationists throughout the nation interpreted Goldwater's minimalist approach to mean that those "governments closest to the people" could continue their long-standing racist laws, policies, and practices.

Although the 1964 election was a landslide for the Democrats, a new trend was in the making. Of the six states carried by Goldwater in the election, five were in the Deep South (Mississippi, Alabama, South Carolina, Louisiana, and Georgia), the first time these states had been won by a Republican since Reconstruction (when former Confederates could not vote). But even as Goldwater represented the future of the "southern strategy," he also broke the African-American tie to the Republican party. Forty percent of African Americans had voted for Eisenhower in 1956, and nearly a third had voted for Nixon in 1960, but Goldwater's candidacy began the pattern of Republican presidential nominees winning virtually no support from African Americans—never more than 15 percent since 1964.

Republicans, however, more than made up for the party's loss of black support. Encouraged by the strong showing of Alabama governor George Wallace (then a staunch segregationist) in Democratic primaries in 1968, Republican nominee Richard Nixon moved further rightward and went after white southerners' votes by using race-coded issues such as "law and order," school busing, and welfare. This strategy began to pay off in 1968. Retaining its longtime support among both big and small business and affluent white Americans, the Republicans gained new support from a growing number of groups previously associated with the Democratic Party—especially blue-collar workers, evangelical Christians, and southern Democrats. Nixon narrowly won the election in 1968 but was reelected by a landslide in 1972. As a result of the Watergate scandal, Nixon resigned the presidency in 1974 and was succeeded in office by the first appointed vice president, Gerald Ford. In the immediate post-Watergate atmosphere, Ford was defeated in 1976 by moderate southern Democrat Jimmy Carter, who was defeated four years later by Republican nominee Ronald Reagan.

What Nixon had begun, Reagan perfected in the 1980s. His campaigns vastly expanded the use of race-coded messages to win support from a growing number of grassroots groups. At the heart of Republican politics in the 1980s was an appeal to whites who were disturbed about race., If others could not perceive this, the Invisible Empire, Knights of the **Ku Klux Klan** (KKK)—the nation's long-standing most openly anti-black and anti-Jewish organization—was not hampered by such confusion. In September 1980, the KKK's newspaper, declared Reagan its favorite candidate, asserting that "the Republican platform reads as if it were written by a Klansman."

Elected in 1980 and reelected in a landslide in 1984, Reagan sharply cut back on civil rights enforcement, staunchly supported conservative positions on moral issues such as abortion, retrenched the rights of organized labor, lowered taxes for corporations and the wealthy, significantly reduced spending on social services, and launched a massive peacetime buildup of the U.S. military establishment. His vice president, George Bush, won the presidential election in 1988. Although Congress continued to be controlled by the Democrats in the 1980s, the Republicans began to make gains in congressional, state, and local elections. As Republican pundit and author Kevin Phillips concluded in his book, *The Politics of the Rich and Poor*, one record of the Reagan–Bush years was a decline in the American standard of living, an intensification of the concentration of wealth, and rapidly growing inequality between the top fifth and the remaining 80 percent of the American population.

In 1992, Republicans lost their first presidential election in 12 years to William Jefferson Clinton, a moderate southern Democrat whom some Republicans accused of stealing the party's conservative themes, messages, and ideas. By 1994, Clinton had low scores in public opinion polls, and the Republicans won a majority in both houses of Congress for the first time since 1954. Republican control of Congress ushered in an exceptionally accommodating attitude toward big business and a rigidly conservative social policy agenda. In 1996, although the Republicans again lost the presidential contest, the party retained control of Congress.

As the twentieth century drew to a close, fissures were evident in the Republican's post-1968 coalition. Conservative religious groups who had been attracted to the party by its opposition to abortion, support for school prayer, and other conservative moral stances made a concerted effort to expand their influence within the party. This effort led to heightening conflict between these members of the "religious Right" and more traditional fiscal conservatives in the party, whose major concerns were matters such as taxes and federal regulation of business. Latino and white women's support for the party declined, and African-American support remained abysmally low in the last presidential election of the twentieth century. **See also** Political Leadership; Political Participation; Poverty; Religion and African-American Politics. **See** Emancipation Proclamation and "The Little Rock School Crisis" in Appendix 1. (LFW)

BIBLIOGRAPHY

Carmines, Edward G. and James Stinson. *Issue Evolution: Race and the Transformation of American Politics.* Princeton, NJ: Princeton University Press, 1989.

Edsall, Thomas and Mary Edsall. *Chain Reaction: The Impact of Race, Rights, and Taxes on American Politics.* New York: W.W. Norton, 1991.

Phillips, Kevin. *The Emerging Republican Majority.* New Rochelle, NY: Arlington House, 1969.

———. *The Politics of the Rich and Poor: Wealth and the American Electorate in the Reagan Aftermath.* New York: Random House, 1990.

Pohlman, Marcus. *Black Politics in Conservative America.* New York: Longman, 1990.

Rees, Matthew. *From the Deck to the Sea: Blacks and the Republican Party.* Wakefield, NH: Longwood Academic, 1991.

Stanley, Harold. *Voter Mobilization and the Politics of Race: The South and Universal Suffrage, 1952–1984.* New York: Praeger, 1987.

Tate, Katherine. *From Protest to Politics: The New Black Voters in American Elections.* Cambridge, MA: Harvard University Press, 1994.

Walton, Hanes. *Black Republicans: The Politics of the Blacks and Tans.* Metuchen, NJ: Scarecrow Press, 1975.

Hiram Rhoades Revels (1822–1901)

Hiram R. Revels, a Republican from Mississippi, was the first African American to serve in the United States Senate. Revels was elected in 1870 and served until 1871. From 1869 to 1870, Revels served in the Mississippi State Senate. An ordained African Methodist Episcopal minister, Revels was active in the abolitionist movement. In 1861, he helped organize two Negro regiments of the United States Army. After his service in the U.S. Senate, Revels became president of Alcorn State University.

BIBLIOGRAPHY

Wharton, Vernon L. *The Negro in Mississippi.* Westport, CT: Greenwood, 1984.

Reverse Discrimination

Reverse discrimination is a backlash against the preferential treatment of minorities and women in employment, contract awards, or businesses, for example, mandated by law. Such laws stem from **affirmative action** programs, initiated under the **Civil Rights Act of 1964**, which take race and gender into account when fashioning remedies to overcome the long-term effects and burdens of racism and sexism.

By the 1980s, however, increasing numbers of Americans began to view affirmative action programs as "reverse discrimination" against white males. Discrimination against white males, they argued, will not increase fairness and at the same time overlooks merit. Additionally, the argument for reverse discrimination maintains that if it was once wrong to use labels to discriminate against a group, then it should also be wrong to use those same labels to help a group. Instead, the Reagan administration called for a color-blind society, where laws should be neutral and where employment or treatment should be granted on the basis of individual merit and qualification. (VDD)

BIBLIOGRAPHY

Carney, Dan. "Effort to Ban Racial Preference at Federal Level Restarted." *Congressional Quarterly Weekly Report* 55, no. 25 (June 21, 1997): 1454.

Dovidio, John. "'Aversive' Racism and the Need for Affirmative Action." *The Chronicle of Higher Education* 43, no. 46 (July 25, 1997): A60.

Durstewitz, Jeff. "Why this White Male Is Angry." *Emerge* 6, no. 7 (May 1995): 44.

Fullinwider, Robert K. *The Reverse Discrimination Controversy.* Lanham, MD: Rowman & Littlefield, Inc., 1980.

Garland, Susan B. and Amy Borrus. "The GOP Assault on Affirmative Action Is Getting Serious." *Business Week* 3553 (November 17, 1997): 55.

Goldman, Alan H. *Justice and Reverse Discrimination.* Princeton: Princeton University Press, 1979.

Greenwalt, R. Kent. *Discrimination and Reverse Discrimination.* New York: McGraw-Hill Co., 1983.

Mollins, Carl. "A White Male Backlash: Critics Attack Affirmative Action as Reverse Discrimination." *MacLean's* 108, no. 12 (March 20, 1995): 22.

Reibstein, Larry. "What Color is An A?" *Newsweek* 131, no. 1 (December 29, 1997): 76.

Urofsky, Melvin I. *Affirmative Action on Trial.* Lawrence: University Press of Kansas, 1997.

"Ward Connerly's Trumpet Blast." *The Economist* 342, no. 8010 (March 29, 1997): 34.

Reynolds v. Sims (1964)

Reynolds v. Sims, 377 U.S. 533 (1964), was a reapportionment case that helped clarify the doctrine initiated by the Supreme Court in *Baker v. Carr*. The case came from Alabama, which had not redistricted its state legislature since the 1900 census. As a result, in the state house, one urban district had 16 times the population of a rural district. The state senate was even more malapportioned, with the most populous district having 41 times the population of the least populous rural district. As a result, rural districts and interests had far greater representation and power than urban districts. The

Supreme Court ruled that the Equal Protection Clause of the **Fourteenth Amendment** required that state legislatures should be apportioned on the basis of population. As a reaction to the reapportionment decisions, a constitutional amendment to strip the courts of jurisdiction over reapportionment was introduced and narrowly failed to be ratified. Chief Justice Earl Warren argued that the reapportionment cases were the most important of his tenure because they would break the hold of rural districts over the state legislatures and further minority rights. (RLP)

BIBLIOGRAPHY
Cortner, Richard C. *The Apportionment Cases.* Knoxville: University of Tennessee, 1970.

Condoleezza Rice (1954–)

Born in Alabama, Condoleezza Rice received her Ph.D. in international studies from the University of Denver in 1981. She taught political science at Stanford University from 1981 to 1989. President George Bush selected her to be his advisor on Soviet affairs in 1989 and she joined the National Security Council. (JCW)

BIBLIOGRAPHY
"Chevron Names Stanford Professor to its Board." *Los Angeles Times* (May 8, 1991): D3.

Norman Rice (1943–)

In 1990 Norman Rice became the first black mayor of Seattle. He served until 1997. Emphasizing affordable housing, crime, employment, and education, Rice scored an impressive upset victory winning a majority of voters in the 75 percent white city of Seattle. Rice earned a reputation as a collaborator by promoting school improvements, community policing, and low-income housing. He narrowly lost the Democratic nomination for governor in 1996. Having lost the nomination, Ricke took a post with a private company in the banking industry. (CC)

BIBLIOGRAPHY
Winn, Mylon. "The Election of Norman Rice as Mayor of Seattle." *PS: Political Science and Politics* (June 1990): 36–38.

Rice v. Arnold (1952)

This case involved the use of the Miami Springs Country Club golf course by a black man, Joseph Rice. The course was segregated in that blacks and whites were not able to use it simultaneously. Rice sued for use of the facilities at all times. The circuit court and Florida Supreme Court denied a writ of mandamus (an order that instructs a government official to do something that is part of their duties), arguing that the city could not adopt any policy that did not execute lawful segregation.

In *Rice v. Arnold,* 342, U.S. 946 (1952), the petition for writ of certiorari was denied by the Supreme Court, stating that the judgment of the lower court was based upon a nonfederal ground adequate to support the law. (CJM)

BIBLIOGRAPHY
NAACP. *NAACP 1940–1955 Legal File: Discrimination—Golf Courses, 1947–1952.* Frederick, MD: University Publications of America, 1992.

City of Richmond v. Croson (1989)

The city of Richmond had established a **racial set-aside** program in which a certain number of subcontracting jobs within larger construction contracts awarded were required to be given to minority business enterprises. In *City of Richmond v. Croson,* 448 U.S. 469 (1989), a contractor that had won a construction contract with the city challenged the program as being unconstitutional. The U.S. Supreme Court ruled that while such programs are not unconstitutional per se, each program should be evaluated using strict scrutiny. The Court stated that if strict scrutiny were applied to state-sponsored Title VI programs, in most cases, the programs would not be valid. Justice Sandra Day O'Connor, writing for the four-justice plurality, argued that set-asides are suspect racial classifications that should be given strict judicial scrutiny. While *Croson* did not make unconstitutional all set-aside programs established under **Title VI of the Civil Rights Act of 1964**, it did make it more difficult to craft such a program that would withstand the greater scrutiny called on by the Court.

BIBLIOGRAPHY
Duncan, Nicole. "*Croson* Revisited: A Legacy of Uncertainty in the Application of Strict Scrutiny." *Columbia Human Rights Law Review* 26 (Spring 1995): 679–712.
Sonn, Paul K. "Fighting Minority Underrepresentation in Publicly Funded Construction Project after *Croson.*" *Yale Law Journal* 101 (May 1992): 1577–1606.

Randall Robinson (1946–)

Randall Robinson, executive director of TransAfrica since 1977, came to national prominence through his organizing the pro-sanction protests outside the South African Embassy in 1985. Born in Richmond, Virginia, Robinson studied at Virginia Union University, Harvard Law School, and in Tanzania. After working in Boston as a civil rights attorney, he moved to Washington, D.C., in 1975 to work for Congressman William Clay. Robinson and Howard Wolpe were leaders in the struggle for sanctions against South Africa in 1986. In 1994, he underwent a 27–day hunger strike to focus attention on political repression in Haiti, a factor in subsequent U.S. intervention. (ISM)

BIBLIOGRAPHY
Cheers, Michael D. "TransAfrica: The Black World's Voice on Capitol Hill." *Ebony* 42 (July 1987): 108–14.

Rodney King Verdict and Riots

Rodney King was a black Los Angeles motorist who was brutally beaten in 1991 by four white Los Angeles police officers. The assault was caught on a private videotape and was given worldwide publicity, provoking outrage and condemnation of police brutality and subsequently leading to the arrest and trial of the officers. On April 29, 1992, a suburban all-white Simi Valley jury acquitted all four white officers. The verdict was the impetus for the ensuing riots, looting, and violence across the South Central section of Los Angeles. In June 1992, Mayor **Tom Bradley** spearheaded the passage of Proposition F which reformed the LAPD by removing civil service protection for the police chief, limiting the chief to one 10–year term, and providing more civil authority over the department. In response to public outrage, the officers involved in the beating were retried for violating the civil rights of King. Two of the officers were found guilty and sentenced in August 1993 to two and a half years in prison. (EC)

BIBLIOGRAPHY

Sitkoff, Howard. *The Struggle for Black Equality.* revised edition. New York: Hill & Wong, 1993.

Carl T. Rowan (1925–)

Carl T. Rowan, an award-winning journalist and author of several books, has won five Emmys, a Peabody, and the Columbia University-E.I. Du Pont Silver Baton. He also has 44 honorary degrees, and writes a syndicated column for King Features. Born into poverty in Tennessee during World War II, Rowan began breaking racial barriers when he became one of the first African-American Navy officers in 1944. In 1963 Rowan was appointed ambassador to Finland, and in 1964 he was appointed head of the U.S. Information Agency a post he held until 1965. (VDD)

BIBLIOGRAPHY

Rowan, Carl T. *Breaking Barriers: A Memoir.* Boston: Little Brown & Company, 1991.

Runyon v. McCrary (1976)

Michael McCrary, a black child, was denied admission to all-white private schools run by Russell and Katherine Runyon in Virginia. The schools claimed they were private and had the right to discriminate as "private clubs." In *Runyon v. McCrary,* 427, U.S. 160 (1976), the Supreme Court stated that the schools were not private clubs, but open to the public and operated by private individuals. The civil rights statutes guaranteed African Americans the right to make and enforce contracts. Since the private schools had made contracts only with white families and refused to contract with black families, the owners had violated the civil rights of African-American citizens. (FHJ)

BIBLIOGRAPHY

Kaczorowski, Robert J. "The Enforcement Provisions of the Civil Rights Act of 1866: A Legislative History in Light of *Runyon v. McCrary.*" (Reconstructing Reconstruction) *Yale Law Journal* 98, no. 3 (January 1989): 565–95.
McClellan, James. "The Foibles and Fables of *Runyon.*" (Symposium on the Reconsideration of Runyon v. McCrary) *Washington University Law Quarterly* 67, no. 1 (Spring 1989): 13–45.

Bobby L. Rush (1946–)

Bobby Rush, a politician and organizer, was head of the Illinois **Black Panthers** in 1968. The Democrat became a Chicago alderman (1983–1993) where he was an active in education and housing and community development issues. He was elected to the House of Representatives in 1992. As a member of the powerful House Commerce Committee, he secured an Enterprise Zone designation for Illinois to help create 20,000 jobs and pump $100 million into the economy. (EC)

BIBLIOGRAPHY

Duncan, Phillip D. and Christine C. Lawrence. *Politics in America 1998: The 105th Congress.* Washington, DC: Congressional Quarterly Press, 1997, 445–47.

John Brown Russwurm (1799–1851)

In 1827, John Russwurm created *Freedom's Journal,* one of the United States' first African-American newspapers. In 1829, he moved to Liberia, where he became superintendent of schools. Soon after, Russwurm became editor and publisher of the *Liberia Herald,* working for the paper from 1830 to 1834. Russwurm then became governor of the Maryland colony in Palmas, Africa, serving the territory and the Maryland State Colonization Society from 1836 to 1851. In this role, he helped unite the colony and Liberia, promoted trade and agriculture, managed the 1843 census, and established a court system with presiding judges.

BIBLIOGRAPHY

Brewer, William M. "John Brown Russwurm." *Journal of Negro History* (1928): 413–22.
Shick, Tom W. *Behold the Promised Land: A History of Afro-American Settler Society in 19th Century Liberia.* Baltimore: John Hopkins University, 1980.

Bayard Rustin (1912–1987)

Bayard Rustin was born in 1912 in West Chester, Pennsylvania. Rustin was raised a Quaker with a fundamental belief in equality of everyone. In the 1930s he became a member of the Youth Communist League, but Russia's abandonment of civil rights programs during World War II led Rustin to change his view and oppose communism. Rustin was committed to a universalist civil rights program and objected to what he deemed the narrowing of the civil rights agenda after the death of **Martin Luther King, Jr.** Rustin was a

Bayard Rustin was a central figure in the Montgomery Bus Boycott and the chief organizer of the 1963 March on Washington. *Library of Congress.*

central figure in the **Montgomery Bus Boycott** and the chief organizer of the 1963 **March on Washington**. In 1965 he became executive director of the A. **Philip Randolph** Institute. Rustin's stand against **affirmative action** programs made him unpopular with **James Farmer** and other civil rights lead-ers but had great influence with current African-American intellectuals such as William Julius Wilson. (FAS)

BIBLIOGRAPHY

Anderson, Jervis. *Bayard Rustin: Troubles I've Seen: A Biography.* New York: HarperCollins, 1997.

Peter Salem (d. 1816)

Peter Salem, born a slave, was given his freedom in order to enlist in the Framingham, Massachusetts, Minutemen. Credited with killing Royal Marine Major John Pitcairn at Bunker Hill, he became a Revolutionary War hero. He also served at the Battles of Lexington, Concord, and Saratoga. (GAA)

BIBLIOGRAPHY

Franklin, John Hope and Alfred A. Moss, Jr. *From Slavery to Freedom: A History of Negro Americans*. 7th ed. New York: McGraw-Hill, 1994.

Quarles, Benjamin. *The Negro in the American Revolution*. New York: W.W. Norton, 1973.

Edith S. Sampson (1901–1979)

Edith Sampson was the first woman to receive a Master of Laws degree from Loyola University. She was appointed an official representative to the United Nations in 1950 by President Harry S. Truman and was elected associate judge of the municipal court of Chicago in 1962, the first black woman to ever serve as a circuit court judge. (JCW)

BIBLIOGRAPHY

"Edith Sampson." *Jet* 88, no. 16 (August 28, 1995): 19.

David Satcher (1941–)

David Satcher was appointed Surgeon General of the United States by President Bill Clinton in 1998. Prior to this appointment, Satcher was the director of the Centers for Disease Control (1994–1998). From 1972 to 1975 he was the director of the King-Drew Medical Center. Satcher was also president of the Morehouse College School of Medicine in Atlanta, Georgia.

BIBLIOGRAPHY

"Introducing David Satcher, M.D.: CDC Director." *Ebony* 49, no. 3 (January 1994): 80–82.

Augustus Savage (1925–)

Following a long tenure as a journalist and newspaper publisher, Gus Savage was elected to the U.S. House of Representatives in 1980 from a largely African-American district in Chicago, Illinois. His victory in 1980 came after two unsuccessful attempts against the Chicago machine that controlled most of politics in the Chicago area. In Congress, his fiery personality made it difficult for him to work well, even with his fellow African-American congressmen and Democrats. Savage has consistently made anti-Semitic statements and formed a close relationship with the **Nation of Islam** leader **Louis Farrakhan**. He was defeated for reelection in the 1992 primary by Mel Reynolds, who later won the seat in the general election. (CEM)

BIBLIOGRAPHY

Barone, Michael. *The Almanac of American Politics*. Washington, DC: National Journal, 1990.

Ehrenhalt, Alan. *Politics in America*. Washington, DC: Congressional Quarterly, 1983.

Kurt L. Schmoke (1949–)

In 1987, Kurt L. Schmoke became the first elected African-American mayor of Baltimore, the city of his birth, where he was educated in the city's public schools. In November 1995, Kurt L. Schmoke was elected to his third term. After graduating from Yale University and Harvard Law School in 1971 and becoming a Rhodes Scholar in 1976 , Schmoke began to practice law for a large firm in Baltimore, but soon found himself part of President Jimmy Carter's White House Domestic Policy Staff. He went on to serve as an assistant United States attorney in 1981, and was then elected Baltimore's state attorney, thus becoming Baltimore's chief prosecuting officer. He held this post until be became mayor.

Schmoke's three terms as mayor have been marked with a number of initiatives. One of his recurrent emphases has been on the nexus of issues surrounding education, including literacy, school budgets, and business partnerships. As a former prosecutor, Schmoke has helped to lead the way in such law enforcement programs as community policing, video camera surveillance, and bike patrols. Perhaps his most politically controversial stance has been his position on illegal drugs, a matter he presents as less a question of crime and punishment, and more a question of public health. As part of his efforts to slow the spread of infectious diseases such as AIDS, Schmoke has helped to implement a large needle-exchange program. (AJC)

BIBLIOGRAPHY

Janofsky, Michael. "Baltimore Grapples with Idea of Legalizing Drugs." *New York Times* (April 20, 1995): A16.

Kerr, Peter. "The Unspeakable Is Debated: Should Drugs Be Legalized?" *New York Times* (May 15, 1988): A1.

Valentine, Paul W. "Baltimore Patrolling Some Streets By Camera." *Baltimore Sun* (January 20, 1996): B3.

School Board of City of Richmond, Virginia et al. v. State Board of Education of Virginia (1973)

The Supreme Court, in *School Board of City of Richmond, Virginia et al. v. State Board of Education of Virginia*, 412 U.S. 92 (1973), affirmed a Court of Appeals decision which held that a district judge cannot compel a state to structure its internal government to achieve racial balance in the assignment of pupils to public schools. The district judge had obliged three school districts including Richmond to consolidate in order to create a greater degree of integration. Where the district judge had cited the effective implementation of the **Fourteenth Amendment**, the Supreme Court agreed with the Court of Appeals that the principle of federalism incorporated in the Tenth Amendment took precedence. (CJM)

BIBLIOGRAPHY

McGough, Lucy S. and Frank T. Read. *Let Them Be Judged: The Judicial Integration of the Deep South*. Metuchen, NJ: The Scarecrow Press, Inc., 1978.

Robert C. Scott (1947–)

Robert C. Scott, a Democrat from Virginia, was elected to the United States House of Representatives in 1992. Prior to being elected to Congress, Scott was a member of the Virginia State House of Representatives from 1978 to 1983 and the Virginia State Senate from 1983 to 1992. The most liberal member of the Virginia delegation to Congress, Scott serves on the Education and the Workforce Committee and the Judiciary Committee. He has easily won reelection in each election since 1992. **See also** Congressional Black Caucus.

BIBLIOGRAPHY

Barone, Michael. *The Almanac of American Politics*. Washington, DC: National Journal, 1998.

Stanley Scott (1933–1992)

Stanley Scott received his B.A. from Lincoln University in Missouri. He became an assistant director of communications under President Nixon and served as assistant to the president under Ford. He has been an executive at Phillip Morris since 1977 and has held the office of vice president and director of corporate relations. (JCW)

BIBLIOGRAPHY

"Stanley Scott Succumbs to Cancer in New Orleans." *Jet* (April 20, 1992): 16.

Bobby Seale (1936–)

The founding chairman of the **Black Panther Party** for Self-Defense, Bobby Seale became politically active while attending Merritt College where he met **Huey P. Newton** in 1966. Seale crafted the Black Panthers' political program demanding full employment, decent housing, free health care,

education, the cessation of police brutality, the release of black prisoners, and the 40 acres and a mule promised by the federal government after the **Civil War.** In his eight years as chairman, Seale developed a free breakfast program and led an armed group onto the floor of the California Legislature to protest legislation prohibiting the Panthers from carrying loaded weapons.

Seale was arrested after the 1968 Democratic Convention for conspiracy to incite a riot as a member of the infamous "Chicago Eight" who were protesting the Vietnam War. Seale was defeated in his 1973 bid to become mayor of Oakland, and after resigning from the Panthers, he founded a grassroots community organization in Philadelphia, called REACH, which he currently directs. (CC)

BIBLIOGRAPHY

Seale, Bobby. *A Lonely Rage: The Autobiography of Bobby Seale*. New York: Times Books, 1978.

———. *Seize the Time: The Story of the Black Panther Party and Huey P. Newton*. New York: Random House, 1970.

Segregation/Integration/Separation

Segregation: Segregation is the term used to refer to the separation of people by restricting one group to certain defined residential areas, separate institutions (schools, churches, hospitals, etc.) or facilities (public parks, playgrounds, conveniences, restaurants, etc.) on the basis of characteristics like race, ethnicity, color, religion, culture, or a combination of these. Segregation has been and often still is, a public policy (if not de jure, then de facto), a social system, and an ideology that discriminates against the segregated group, is imposed by force, and is often claimed to be beneficial for the segregated group in maintaining its distinctive cultural values. Segregation inevitably functions to preserve the economic,

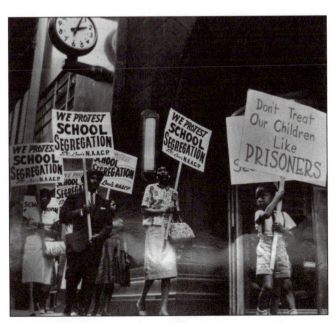

Marchers protest the segregation of St. Louis schools in the 1960s. *National Archives.*

political and social advantages of a politically dominant group. Segregation typically has appeared where multiracial communities exist and large-scale racial mixing has not occurred (as in Brazil, with its ideology of "racial democracy," and in Hawaii, where social but no legal discrimination exists).

However, in the twentieth century, segregation has primarily been understood in terms of white population groups attempting to preserve dominance over others through social and legal color bars. Surprisingly, the use of the term segregation for such a racial color bar is comparatively recent, first coming into widespread use in the United States after 1890 and in South Africa around the time of the 1910 union. (Of course, discrimination as such existed before the term segregation.) The most prominent examples were the system of legally enforced segregation along racial and ethnic lines, termed Apartheid, in force in South Africa from 1948 until 1991, and the racial segregation of public institutions and facilities in the southern states of the U.S. from the late nineteenth century until the 1950s. These two forms of segregation, the "**Jim Crow**" legislation in the American South and Apartheid in South Africa, are modern phenomena, associated with structural processes of modernization, economic specialization, and urbanization—processes which oddly enough, according to modernization theory, were supposed to eradicate such discriminatory practices. Apartheid ended with the releasing of Nelson Mandela from prison and his African National Congress election win in 1994, establishing the first majority-black government. Segregation in the American South officially ended when President Lyndon Johnson signed the **Civil Rights Act of 1964**, under which discrimination on the basis of race in federal programs, voting, education, and the use of public institutions and facilities was forbidden.

The mechanisms of such segregation vary widely. In South Africa, Apartheid legislation for total residential, educational, and facilities segregation was enacted nationally from 1948 onwards, modeled in many instances on similar laws in the American South. In the American South, despite the **Emancipation Proclamation** (January 1, 1863) and the period of **Reconstruction** following the **Civil War** (1861–1865) which included a Civil Rights Bill (1866, subsequently vetoed by President Andrew Johnson) and the Sumner Act (1875, but declared unconstitutional by the Supreme Court 1883), segregation had become the norm by 1876 with the Hayes-Tilden Compromise. This electoral compromise resulted in local autonomy being returned to southern states, the ending of the **Freedmen's Bureau** and the withdrawal of federal troops from southern states. These events in turn led to the practical denial of the **Fourteenth** (granting citizenship to blacks) and **Fifteenth** (the right to vote) **Amendment**s and to the passing of many discriminatory state laws. These were the infamous "**Jim Crow**" enactments which divided southern society in half along racial lines, reducing blacks to second-class citizenship, segregating public institutions, and prohibiting intermarriage. The southern states' continuous enactment of segregation laws was subsequently encouraged by the decision of the U.S. Supreme Court, in *Plessy v. Ferguson*, 162 U.S. 537 (1896), to declare that the provision of separate but equal facilities was not a violation of the right to equal protection under the law, according to the Fourteenth Amendment.

This **de jure segregation** remained in force in the American South until the 1950s, when the **civil rights movement** was triggered by opposition to segregated public transport. Thus from 1955 to approximately 1965 the goals of the civil rights movement were largely defined in terms of overcoming segregation and promoting integration, primarily by integrating public facilities and by black enfranchisement. This applied to blacks as well as other minorities under the rubric of civil rights. However, by the mid-1960s, even **Martin Luther King, Jr**. was aware that de facto segregation remained and that its root cause, racism, was as powerful in the North where powerful political and economic structures preserved segregated housing and educational policies.

The largely nonviolent, reformist approach to removing segregation by legislation advocated by Martin Luther King, Jr. and his followers, was eclipsed following his assassination in 1968, by radical Afro-American movements, some calling for revolution, others for separation. The decade from 1970 to 1980 saw the social consequences of the civil rights movement being hammered out. Unfortunately this led, particularly in the North, to further de facto segregation. This was to continue through the 1980s, with urban segregation increasing, polarization occurring between African Americans and other minority groups, and the troubling growth of an African-American "underclass." All minority groups, but particularly blacks, were, often with Asians and Hispanics, residentially segregated in large metropolitan areas. This has clear class and economic bases, although most researchers would still attribute significant weight to white prejudice and fear.

Integration: Minorities have, in general, had two options open to them, namely separation from, or integration into, the mainstream. The latter being the assertion and exercise of social, political, and economic rights, guaranteed under the U.S. Constitution. The former option has not generally been viewed as realistic, though it has been advocated by black nationalists (see below). The latter option, integration, has been understood and actualized in three basic ways. The earliest and most dominant option was that assimilation (or "Anglo-conformity"), one that was taken up by white national (ethnic) minorities, but one which largely excluded racial minorities such as African Americans. The second option was to be both part of the larger society and at the same time to preserve one's ethnic identity and culture, an approach described as "integration-at-a-distance," or as amalgamation, the integration of the best features of the various peoples into a new nation, an approach often associated with the French-American Hector St. John de Crévecoeur who in his *Letters from an American Farmer* (1782) wrote of "individuals of all nations . . . melted into a new race of men." The third option, that of accommodation, or cultural pluralism, probably always existed, but has only become prominent recently as society and immigrants themselves rejected the "melting pot" thesis and now seek to preserve their own cultures and traditions. This approach recognizes the diversity of peoples and cultures and views society as a mosaic or patchwork quilt of nations within a nation, such as is officially advocated in Canada. In the United States, historically this option only envisioned the European nations as participants, though it is presently undergoing a revival and expansion.

Integration, then, has had diverse meanings. The move for integration as assimilation reached its zenith during the years 1954 to 1963, when a coalition of black and white reformers called for the United States to live up to its constitutional ideals. The climax of this movement for integration came with the 1963 centennial anniversary march on Washington and Martin Luther King, Jr.'s, "**I Have a Dream**" speech and its consequences, the civil rights legislation enacted in 1964, 1967, 1968, and with amendments, in 1982. Integration as amalgamation has not expanded to include involuntary immigrants such as African Americans, or even recent dark-skinned immigrants from the Caribbean. Thus most attempts made up to the 1980s to redress the effects of segregation were aimed at promoting integration in these first two senses. However, this was predicated on the assumption that American society would and could see beyond race. When it became apparent that this was not the case, black radicalism grew in tandem with black pride and culture movements as did similar Hispanic and Asian movements.

Separation: Despite various Civil Rights Acts passed during the 1960s, the slow pace of change, and the failure of political movements to change the socio-economic position of the poor African American led to a conscious abandonment of integration as a goal. As black-white reformist coalitions crumbled, militant African American leadership emerged and the focus now was on "black pride" and **black power,** and many urban ghettos erupted in violence by the decade's end. Meanwhile, college enrollment of African Americans was increasing and African-American studies departments were being founded, from some of which would emerge theories of the Afrocentric origins of Western civilization.

Arguments for racial separation and solidarity tend to emerge when racial equality is perceived to have failed. The ideas of self-acceptance and racial solidarity were old ideas, powerfully advocated a century ago by **Booker T. Washington**. His self-help philosophy was carried by lower-class blacks in northern cities who flocked to **Marcus Garvey**'s "Back-to-Africa" movement during the 1920s, by independent black churches during the 1930s-1940s, and in recent times, by the **Nation of Islam**. As the African-American middle class expanded, the lower classes remained or fell back, leading sociologist William Julius Wilson to speak of the existence of a growing underclass of minorities, particularly of African Americans. This was the scenario during the 1970s and the 1980s. However, while great advances were made during these decades in dealing with racial and ethnic prejudice, African Americans (together with other minorities) were divided on

how to approach the broader structural issues created by segregation and integration. Should equality be attained through group-based, that is, **affirmative action** programs or rather by the impartial application of already existing (presumed color-blind) laws? Such questions arose from the mixed results of federal attempts to enforce desegregation programs, resulting in backlash, particularly in white working-class suburbs, to enforced school integration, the reversal of affirmative action university application processes in the **Allan Bakke** case and finally the 1996 election vote on the California voters' ballot.

Along with an emphasis on separation has come an awareness of multiculturalism, a term coined during the last decade in response to the presence of more vocal African-American, Hispanic, and Asian political pressure groups. These represent the expression of racial, ethnic, national, and cultural awareness that has reacted to the perceived failure of liberal integrationist visions and to the persistent racism which held that others needed to integrate by conforming to, and accepting the norm of, a majority-Anglo and white society. (ISM)

BIBLIOGRAPHY

Cell, John W. *The Highest Stage of White Supremacy: The Origins of Segregation in South Africa and the American South*. New York: Cambridge University Press, 1982.

Fredrickson, George. *Black Liberation*. New York: Oxford University Press, 1995.

Gordon, Milton, ed. "America as a Multicultural Society." *The Annals of the American Academy of Political and Social Science* 454 (March 1981): 1–205.

Myrdal, Gunnar. *The American Dilemma: The Negro Problem and American Democracy*. New York: Harper, 1944.

Takaki, Ronald. *A Different Mirror: A History of Multicultural America*. Boston: Little, Brown, 1993.

Wilson, Julius. *The Declining Significance of Race*. Chicago: University of Chicago Press, 1978.

Yetman, Norman, ed. *Majority and Minority*, 5th ed. Allyn & Bacon, 1991.

Separate But Equal

In 1896, the U.S. Supreme Court ruled that it was constitutional for states to require separate railway cars for whites and blacks, as long as the cars were equal. The concept was applied to public facilities and schools until 1954, when the Supreme Court pronounced that in public schools, separate was inherently unequal. In 1892, Homer Plessy was convicted for riding in a white railway car, violating an 1890 Louisiana law requiring "separate but equal" cars by race. The case came before the Supreme Court as *Plessy v. Ferguson*, 163 U.S. 537 (1896). The Court ruled that the Louisiana law was constitutional, as long as the separate facilities were equal.

The **National Association for the Advancement of Colored People (NAACP)** targeted the *Plessy* case, and achieved several victories by demanding "equal" facilities. After World War II, the NAACP turned to the "separate" aspect. They triumphed in 1954, when the Supreme Court ruled in *Brown v. Board of Education* that "separate but equal" had no place in public education. The struggles of the late 1950s and 1960s

George E.C. Hays, Thurgood Marshall, and James Nabrit (from left to right) congratulate each other on the steps of the Supreme Court after their victory in the landmark 1954 case, *Brown v. Board of Education, Topeka*, which overturned the judicial doctrine of Separate But Equal. *Library of Congress.*

erased official racial segregation in all areas of American public life. (AD)

BIBLIOGRAPHY

Thomas, Brook, ed. *Plessy v. Ferguson: A Brief History with Documents*. Boston: Bedford Books, 1997.

Assata Shakur (1937–)

Assata Shakur was born JoAnne Chesimard in Queens, New York. She was a member of the **Black Panther Party** and was imprisoned for the alleged murder of a state trooper in 1973. She escaped from prison in 1979 and is currently living in exile in Cuba.

BIBLIOGRAPHY

Shakur, Assata. *Assata: An Autobiography*. Westport, CT: L. Hill, 1987.

Shaw v. Reno, North Carolina (1993)

Shaw v. Reno, North Carolina, 92 U.S. 357 (1993), is a Supreme Court case which established that the creation of majority-black districts may violate a person's right to a color-blind electoral process. Because of its population increase, North Carolina gained an extra seat in the House of Representatives. Ruth Shaw and other white citizens claimed that the state had violated the **Fourteenth** Constitutional **Amendment** by racially classifying citizens in order to draw two majority-black districts (the 1st and the 12th) in 1990. Moreover, the plaintiffs claimed that the uncommon boundaries of the districts were too complex for citizens to know who represented them.

North Carolina argued that race-consciousness was unavoidable because of the **Voting Rights Act**'s legal protection of racial minorities; the law prohibits any state district plan that decreases black voting power. The shape of districts, the respondents suggested, was not due to race but to the political concerns of incumbents.

A five-member majority agreed that the right to eliminate color bias is violated by the creation of racial gerrymanders. In the Court's view "when a district is so bizarre on its face that it cannot be explained on grounds other than race," it must be narrowly tailored to pursue a compelling state interest. Though signaling their belief that such gerrymanders bore an "uncomfortable resemblance to political apartheid," the Court initially declined to decide whether North Carolina's plan was unconstitutional. After further litigation, however, the same judges concluded that the 1st and 12th districts were racial gerrymanders. (KC)

BIBLIOGRAPHY

Peacock, Anthony A., ed. *Affirmative Action and Representation: Shaw v. Reno and the Future of Voting Rights*. Durham, NC: Carolina Academic Press, 1997.

Sheet Metal Workers v. EEOC (1986)

Sheet Metal Workers v. EEOC, 478 U.S. 421; 106 Sup. Ct. 3019 (1986), is a Supreme Court case in which plaintiffs claimed that there was discrimination against blacks and Hispanics in areas of recruitment, selection, training, and admission to the union. The remedy included a 29.23 percent nonwhite membership goal. Four members of a six-member plurality held that Section 706(g) of **Title VII** does not prohibit a court from ordering affirmative race-conscious relief as a remedy where an employer or labor union has engaged in persistent discrimination and the membership goal was proper under 706(g) and did not violate the equal protection component of the due process clause of the Constitution. (PLF)

BIBLIOGRAPHY

Reske, Henry J. "Hiring Quotas Are Affirmed." (*Sheet Metal Workers v. EEOC, Local No. 93 v. Cleveland*, U.S. Supreme Court) *Pennsylvania Law Journal-Reporter* 9 (July 7, 1986): 1.

Shelley v. Kraemer (1948)

Shelley v. Kraemer, 334 U.S. 1 (1948), involved an African-American couple who bought a home in St. Louis despite a restrictive covenant that forbade the selling of the home to blacks. While restrictive covenants were discriminatory, white homeowners argued that such contracts were private and therefore beyond the reach of the Equal Protection Clause of the **Fourteenth Amendment**. The Supreme Court ruled that restrictive covenants involved state action because courts had to enforce them. Thus, such contracts were forbidden under the Fourteenth Amendment. This was an important precedent for attacking racial discrimination. (RLP)

BIBLIOGRAPHY

Irons, Peter. *The Courage of Their Convictions: Sixteen Americans Who Fought Their Way to the Supreme Court*. New York: Penguin Books, 1990.

Vose, Clement E. *Caucasians Only: The Supreme Court, the NAACP, and the Restrictive Covenant Cases*. Berkeley: University of California Press, 1959.

Shepherd v. Florida (1950)

In 1949, four black men in central Florida were accused of kidnapping and raping a white woman. The men were beaten during their detention and denied access to an attorney. Despite the efforts of the **National Association for the Advancement of Colored People (NAACP)**, the accused were rushed to trial, found guilty, and sentenced to death. In *Shepherd v. Florida*, 341 U.S. 50 (1950), the U.S. Supreme Court ruled that the men had not received a fair trial and a new trial was ordered. Before it could commence, Sheriff Willis McCall shot and killed Shepherd and injured another defendant in an alleged escape attempt. (CE)

BIBLIOGRAPHY
Lawson, Steven, David Colburn, and Darryl Paulson. "Groveland: Florida's Little Scottsboro." *Florida Historical Quarterly* 65 (July 1986): 1–26.

Shuttlesworth v. Birmingham Board of Education (1958)

Frustrated by the failure of city officials in Birmingham, Alabama to implement the **Brown v. Board of Education** decision requiring the desegregation of public schools, the Reverend Fred L. Shuttlesworth decided to challenge Alabama's Pupil Placement Law. In 1957, Shuttlesworth unsuccessfully attempted to register four black students in the city's largest all-white high school. In the resultant court case, *Shuttlesworth v. Birmingham Board of Education*, 358 U.S. 101 (1958), the U.S. Supreme Court ruled against Shuttlesworth, upholding Alabama's Pupil Placement Law which gave local officials broad powers in determining which schools students would attend. (LPM)

BIBLIOGRAPHY
Bartley, Numan V. *The Rise of Massive Resistance: Race and Politics in the South During the 1950s*. Baton Rouge: Louisiana State University Press, 1969, 291–92.

Benjamin "Pap" Singleton (ca. 1809–1892)

Benjamin Singleton was a Nashville slave who escaped to Canada and later settled in Detroit, Michigan. After the **Civil War,** Singleton dedicated himself to removing blacks from the brutality they endured from the former slave states. He believed that he had a divine mandate to lead blacks to an all-black promised land on earth which he had located in Kansas. By 1879 masses of blacks, known as Exodusters, filled Singleton's Kansas colonies. He also attempted unsuccessfully to move blacks to Cyprus and Africa. (EC)

BIBLIOGRAPHY
Painter, Nell Irvin. *Exodusters: Black Migration to Kansas after Reconstruction*. New York: Knopf, 1977.

Sipuel v. Board of Regents of The University of Oklahoma (1948)

Sipuel v. Board of Regents of the University of Oklahoma, 332 U.S. 631 (1948), is another in a long line of school desegregation cases that culminated in the **Brown v. Board of Education** decision. Sipuel applied for admission to the School of Law of the University of Oklahoma in the spring of 1946 but was turned down solely because of her color. In reversing the State Supreme Court of Oklahoma, the Court held that the "petitioner is entitled to secure legal education afforded by a state institution" under the auspices of the **Fourteenth Amendment**. (CJM)

BIBLIOGRAPHY
D'Amato, Anthony A., Rosemary Metrailer, and Stephen L. Wasby. *Desegregation from Brown to Alexander*. Carbondale, IL: Southern Illinois University Press, 1977.
Greenberg, Jack. *Race Relations and American Law*. New York: Columbia University Press, 1959.

Sit-Ins

Sit-ins are nonviolent demonstrations of direct action used as a form of protest. The technique of sit-ins was developed in the 1930s by labor unions, which would have employees occupy administrative and plant facilities. The protest requires that participants physically occupy an area without directly confronting authorities. If authorities attempt to remove protesters, the protesters neither comply nor resist. The **Congress of Racial Equality (CORE)** and the **National Association for the Advancement of Colored People (NAACP)** effectively used sit-ins to draw national attention to the **civil rights movement**. The results of the protests were that jails would become overrun with arrested demonstrators, clogging the usual flow of justice; more important, the protests often highlighted the mindless violence of the police and others who sought to remove the protesters.

BIBLIOGRAPHY
Meier, August and Elliot Rudwick. *CORE: A Study in the Civil Rights Movement*. Urbana: The University of Illinois Press, 1973.

Slavery

Slavery as an institution in the western hemisphere dates back to 1517 when a Catholic bishop named Bartolomeo de Las Casas wrote to King Charles I of Spain requesting that Spanish immigration to the Americas be encouraged by utilizing Africans as slaves. He hoped to relieve the burden on Native Americans as a labor source. The result of his actions was the North Atlantic slave trade. Several European nations joined the profitable venture of shipping slaves to the "New World" in what became known as the Middle Passage. As a result, African slavery became an entrenched labor source in the colonies. In the United States, slavery grew haphazardly as each colony developed a statutory framework. Between 1663 and 1750 all of the original 13 colonies enacted laws establishing slavery. American notions of race had reduced Africans to a second-class status with the vast majority being locked in a cruel form of chattel or property slavery by the American Revolution. In 1783, during the constitutional convention, American leaders established constitutional protections for the institution in the form of the Fifth Amendment and the controversial **three-fifths clause**. This rule reduced blacks to

This drawing from an 1856 issue of the *Illustrated London News* depicts a scene from a Richmond, Virginia, slave auction. *Library of Congress.*

three-fifths of a person when calculating representation and taxation.

When Eli Whitney introduced the cotton gin in 1793, slavery shifted from the eastern seaboard to the gulf region with the beginnings of the Cotton Kingdom, an area dominated by cotton growers. The Cotton Kingdom resulted in exponential growth in the number of slaves, although the slave trade had been abolished in 1808. With the **Missouri Compromise** of 1820, the nation codified the split between the North and South with the South hitching its economic survival to slavery while the North advocated wage labor. Between 1830 and 1860, a mass organized effort to end slavery was waged by black and white abolitionists. They turned the issue into a moral crusade, which eventually forced governmental action. In 1863, Lincoln signed the **Emancipation Proclamation,** promising freedom to all slaves of states in rebellion to the union. Finally, in December 1865 the U.S. ratified the **Thirteenth Amendment,** officially ending slavery in the United States. (AAB)

BIBLIOGRAPHY

Filler, Louis. *Slavery in the United States.* New Brunswick, NJ: Transaction, 1998.

Foner, Eric. *Slavery and Freedom in the 19th Century.* New York: Oxford University Press, 1994.

Franklin, John Hope. *From Slavery to Freedom.* New York: McGraw-Hill, 1994.

Robert Smalls (1839–1915)

Robert Smalls, born in Beaufort, in the Sea Islands of South Carolina, was elected to the Republican convention in June 1864. He was state constitutional convention delegate in 1868; he was also elected to the state House of Representatives (1868–1870). Smalls was a member of the state Senate (1870–1874), and he was elected to Congress from the 5th District (1874–1878), and (1882–1886). In Congress he resisted the removal of federal troops from the South, opposed racial discrimination in the armed forces, sought legislation

guaranteeing equal accommodations for all railroad passengers regardless of their color, and advocated integration of eating establishments in the District of Columbia. In 1889 President Benjamin Harrison appointed Smalls collector of the port of Beaufort. (EC)

BIBLIOGRAPHY

Uya, Okon Edet. *From Slavery to Public Service: Robert Smalls, 1839–1915.* New York: Oxford University Press, 1971.

Smith v. Allwright (1944)

Smith v. Allwright, 321 U.S. 649 (1944), was an important voting rights case that helped abolish the all-white primary. After the passage of the **Fifteenth Amendment** following the **Civil War,** African Americans were guaranteed the right to vote in general elections. Political parties, however, were considered private entities. As a result, they could establish their own rules for membership. The state Democratic parties in the South forbade African Americans from joining the party and thus from voting in the primaries. Because the South was overwhelmingly dominated by the Democratic Party, the Democratic primary was tantamount to the ultimate election. Thus, the all-white primaries effectively disenfranchised African-American voters.

In the *Smith v. Allwright* decision, the Supreme Court overturned a previous decision, *Grovey v. Townsend* (1935), that allowed white primaries and expanded a more recent precedent, *United States v. Classic* (1941), which authorized Congress to regulate primaries as well as general elections. The Court ruled that the state, Texas in this case, required certain election procedures. Thus, the Court held that these state requirements supported racial discrimination in violation of the **Fourteenth Amendment** and constituted state action within the meaning of the Fifteenth Amendment. This was an important victory for the nascent civil rights movement and it provided a precedent for an expanded view of state action. The Democratic Party in Texas attempted to circumvent the decision by establishing private clubs and country organizations, which could legally restrict membership to whites. The Court eventually ruled that these organizations and clubs were functioning as political parties and could not exclude African Americans in *Terry v. Adams* (1953). (RLP)

BIBLIOGRAPHY

Epstein, Lee and Walker, Thomas G. *Constitutional Law for a Changing America: Rights, Liberties, and Justice.* 2nd ed. Washington, DC: CQ Press, 1995, 775–83.

Greenberg, Jack. *Crusaders in the Court.* New York: Basic Books, 1994.

Hugh H. Smythe (1914–)

Hugh Smythe was born in Pittsburgh, Pennsylvania, and he received a Ph.D. in anthropology from Northwestern University. He taught at Fisk University and did sociological research for the **National Association for the Advancement of Colored People (NAACP).** He joined the faculty of Brooklyn College in 1953 after a two-year teaching assignment in Japan. He served as the U.S. ambassador to Syria from 1965 to 1969. (JCW)

BIBLIOGRAPHY

Walton, Hanes. *African American Power and Politics.* New York: Columbia University Press, 1997.

Sniadach v. Family Finance Corp. of Bay View et al. (1968)

Sniadach v. Family Finance Corp. of Bay View et al., 395 U.S. 337 (1968), is a case that involved the taking of property and procedural due process required by the **Fourteenth Amendment**. Under Wisconsin law, a creditor may move to garnish the wages of a debtor by contacting the latter's employer and thereby setting in motion the process by which wages are frozen. Sniadach sued for violation of the Fourteenth Amendment's procedural due process requirement. The Court reversed the Wisconsin Supreme Court's decision, arguing that the Wisconsin law violated due process because it did not require proof that an actual debt existed. (CJM)

BIBLIOGRAPHY

Richardson, Susanne. "Trustee Process against Earnings in Vermont." *Vermont Law Review* 5, no. 1 (Spring 1980): 133–60.

South Carolina v. Katzenbach (1966)

An early challenge to the **1965 Voting Rights Act**, *South Carolina v. Katzenbach*, 383 U.S. 301 (1966), was a complaint against then Attorney General Nicholas Katzenbach's execution of the law. Although the U.S. Constitution gives states the power to administer voting rules and procedures, Section V of the VRA requires federal approval of proposed changes in election law. South Carolina argued that because the law's remedies were extraordinary and applied only to states in the South, Congress had overstepped its authority. The Court concluded that the **Fifteenth Amendment** grants Congress the power to make laws to prevent states from discriminating against black voters. In Chief Justice Earl Warren's words "exceptional conditions can justify legislative measures not otherwise appropriate." Moreover, since voter turnout determined coverage under Section V of the VRA, the Court found that it was a valid means of prohibiting voter discrimination. (KC)

BIBLIOGRAPHY

Grofman, Bernard, Lisa Handley, and Richard G. Niemi. *Minority Representation and the Quest for Voting Equality.* New York: Cambridge University Press, 1992.

Southern Christian Leadership Conference (SCLC)

The Southern Christian Leadership Conference (SCLC) was established in 1957 as a nonviolent, direct-action civil rights organization. While the first executive director of the SCLC was the Reverend Wyatt Tee Walker, the key leader of the organization was Dr. **Martin Luther King, Jr.** The organization sponsored a number of events beginning in 1957 including

a Prayer Pilgrimage to Washington, D.C., that attracted more than 25,000 participants and a youth march of more than 40,000 marchers. The SCLC used peaceful methods such as boycotts and **sit-ins** to pressure businesses and government to change their discriminatory practices. After the passage of the **Civil Rights Act of 1964** and the **Voter Rights Act of 1965**, the group began to expand its focus and operations to include northern cities. For more than four decades, the Southern Christian Leadership Conference has been a leading civil rights organization. Today, it is headed by Martin Luther King, Jr.'s son, Martin Luther King III. **See also** Civil Rights Movement; Joseph E. Lowery.

BIBLIOGRAPHY

Fairclough, Adam. *To Redeem the Soul of America: The Southern Christian Leadership Conference and Martin Luther King, Jr.* Athens: University of Georgia Press, 1987.
Garrow, David J. *Bearing the Cross.* New York: Viking, 1988.

Southern Regional Council

The Southern Regional Council (SRC) is a private nonprofit organization based in Atlanta, Georgia. The SRC originally began in 1919 as the Commission on Interracial Cooperation (CIC) with leaders from both the black and white communities in southern states who wanted to work for improved race relations. In 1944, the organization changed its name and clarified its mission. The new SRC sought "to attain through research and action the ideals and practices of equal opportunity." In the 1960s the SRC worked to end segregation and discrimination in the South. It published numerous studies and directed the **Voter Education Project** which was headed by **Vernon Jordan**. (VDD)

BIBLIOGRAPHY

Blumberg, Rhoda Lois. *Civil Rights: The 1960s Freedom Struggle.* New York: Macmillan, 1991.

Southern Strategy

The Southern Strategy was a technique used by Richard Nixon before the 1968 and 1972 presidential elections in order to secure a strong bloc of electoral votes from the southern states. He tried to reach out to middle-class southern suburban whites without portraying himself as a proponent of segregation. Using positions such as "anti-crime" and "anti-civil disorder" which played on the race issue, Nixon hoped to secure both conservatives and moderates to vote Republican. This technique was also employed by Ronald Reagan in the 1980 presidential election. (JCW)

BIBLIOGRAPHY

Aistrup, Joseph A. *The Southern Strategy Revisited: Republican Top-Down Advancement in the South.* Lexington, KY: University Press of Kentucky, 1996.

Spallone v. United States (1990)

The United States sued the city of Yonkers, New York, and its housing authority for violating **Title VIII of the Civil Rights Act of 1968** and the Equal Protection Clause of the **Four-**

teenth Amendment, on the grounds that the city deliberately caused the segregation in its housing. The judge in the case found the city and the members of the city council in contempt for failing to desegregate the city's housing. As a result, the judge imposed a fine of a million dollars a day against the city and fined the council members personally for failing to vote for desegregation. However, in *Spallone v. United States,* 493 U.S. 265 (1990), the U.S. Supreme Court ruled that the fines imposed upon the individual members of the city council were unconstitutional because they prevented the members from voting freely without concern for their own financial well-being. The Court reversed the earlier decision, stating that the judge had overstepped his bounds in imposing the fines. **See also** the text of the Fourteenth Amendment in "Civil War Amendments" in the Documents section.

BIBLIOGRAPHY

Friedman, Barry. "When Rights Encounter Reality: Enforcing Federal Remedies" *Southern California Law Review* 65 (January 1992): 735–80.

Robertson, J. Robert. "The Effects of Consent Decrees on Local Legislative Immunity." *University of Chicago Law Review* 56 (Summer 1989): 1121–52.

Mabel Staupers (1898–)

Born in Barbados in 1898, Mabel Staupers moved to the United States where she earned a nursing degree in 1917. In the 1920s she helped organize black nursing programs. During World War II, she served as an advisor to U.S. Attorney General James Magee on black nursing concerns. (AAB)

BIBLIOGRAPHY

Staupers, Mabel. *No Time for Prejudice: A Story of the Integration of Negroes in Nursing in the United States.* New York: Macmillan, 1961.

Bennett Stewart (1912–1988)

Bennett Stewart was born in Alabama, and he graduated from Miles College. He served as an alderman in Chicago city council from 1971 to 1978 and was elected to Congress as a Democratic representative from Illinois in 1978. After serving one term he became interim director of the Chicago Department of Inter-Governmental Affairs.

BIBLIOGRAPHY

Christian, Charles. *Black Saga, the African American Experience.* New York: Houghton Mifflin, 1995.

Carl Stokes (1927–1996)

Carl Stokes, a Democrat, was mayor of Cleveland from 1966 to 1971, becoming the first black to be elected to head a major American city. He was assistant city prosecutor in Cleveland from 1958 to 1962. He served in the Ohio House of Representatives from 1962 to 1966. From 1972 to 1980, he was a television newscaster in New York City. From 1983 until his death he served as a judge on the Cleveland Municipal Court. (EC)

BIBLIOGRAPHY

Nelson, William. "The Rise and Fall of Black Politics in Cleveland." In Michael Preston, Lenneal J. Henderson, Jr., and Paul Puryear, eds. *The New Black Politics: The Search for Political Power,* 2nd ed. New York: Longman, 1987, 172–99.

Louis Stokes (1925–)

Louis Stokes was born in Cleveland, Ohio. He has been a lawyer and United States Congressman. He received his undergraduate training at Western Reserve University, now Case Western Reserve, in Cleveland. He served time in the army and then earned his J.D. at Marshall College of Law of Cleveland State University in 1953. In 1968 he was elected a member of Congress as a Democrat and was re-elected in every subsequent election through 1998. He was a member of the **Black Caucus** and a powerful member of the following committees: Committee on Appropriations; Subcommittee on Labor, Health and Human Services, and Education, District of Columbia. He was chairman of the Appropriations Subcommittee on VA, HUD and Independent Agencies, and chairman of the House Permanent Select Committee on Intelligence and the Committee on Standards of Official Conduct (Ethics Committee, House Select Committee on Assassinations). He retired at the end of 1998. (FAS)

BIBLIOGRAPHY

Barone, Michael et al. *The Almanac of American Politics 1998.* New York: Times Books, 1998.

Chuck Stone (1924–)

As a journalist, political activist, educator, theoretician, and organizer in the **black power** movement of the 1960s, Chuck Stone worked to fundamentally change America's consciousness on race relations. The first African American ever hired to do news commentary on American television and chief administrative assistant to U.S. Representative Adam Clayton Powell, Jr., Stone was a chief architect behind the Black Power Conferences in Washington (1966), Newark (1967), Philadelphia (1968), and Atlanta (1970). In 1991 he became the first black chaired professor at an American journalism school when he was named Walter Spearman Professor of Journalism at the University of North Carolina. (RAM)

BIBLIOGRAPHY

Jackson, Dennis. "'The Outspoken Mr. Stone': A Conversation with Chuck Stone." *The Black Scholar* 27, no. 1 (Spring 1997): 38–57.

James Stone (ca. 1840s–1862)

James Stone was the first black man to fight for the Union in the **Civil War** by passing as white. He enlisted in the First Fight Artillery of Ohio and his racial identity was revealed after his death. (JCW)

BIBLIOGRAPHY

Christian, Charles. *Black Saga, the African American Experience.* New York: Houghton Mifflin, 1995.

Student Nonviolent Coordinating Committee (SNCC)

The Student Nonviolent Coordinating Committee (SNCC) was founded on the campus of Shaw University in 1960. During its formation, Ella Baker, the executive secretary of the **Southern Christian Leadership Conference**, played a key role. The organization selected **Stokely Carmichael** as head on May 19, 1966, succeeding Jake Lewis. The SNCC's ideas differed from the traditional civil rights organizations by placing student activism over legislation. The tactics of SNCC included **sit-ins**, freedom rides, and voter registration projects. Carmichael grew tired of the tactics employed by the SNCC and left in May 1967. H. Rap Brown then became the head of the organization. In 1969 the name was changed to Student National Coordinating Committee and became more confrontational. Shortly thereafter the group became defunct. (DH)

BIBLIOGRAPHY
Sitkoff, Harvard. *The Struggle for Black Equality.* New York: Hill and Wang, 1981.

Students for a Democratic Society (SDS)

Students for a Democratic Society (SDS), one of the more radical, sometimes violent, New Left organizations spawned in the 1960s, began as the Student League for Industrial Democracy. In 1960, the organization was renamed SDS when student leaders Al Haber and Tom Hayden, both of the University of Michigan, took a more activist stance. SDS utilized college campuses in a national movement to attack poverty, the Vietnam War, racism, and other social injustices in American society. (VDD)

BIBLIOGRAPHY
Gitlin, Todd. *The Sixties: Years of Hope, Days of Rage.* New York: Bantam Books, 1989.

Louis Wade Sullivan (1933–)

Louis Sullivan served as secretary of the United States Department of Health and Human Services (HHS) from 1989 to 1993, making him the first African American appointed to a cabinet-level position in the Bush administration. Prior to his government service, Sullivan taught medicine at Harvard Medical School, the New Jersey College of Medicine, Boston University, and Morehouse College. Initially, Sullivan was a controversial figure as secretary of HHS because of his stances against abortion and fetal-tissue research; however, he became an effective advocate for preventative medicine and minority health issues. In 1993, he returned to Morehouse School of Medicine.

BIBLIOGRAPHY
"Dr. Louis Sullivan." *Emerge* (January 1994): 26–27.
Pollner, Fran. "Dr. Sullivan: Hitting His Stride." *Medical World News* 31, no. 1 (January 8, 1990): 30–38.
Smothers, Ronald. "New Faces for 4 Cabinet Posts." *Washington Post* (December 23, 1989): A25.

Swann v. Charlotte-Mecklenberg Board of Education (1971)

In its *Swann v. Charlotte-Mecklenberg Board of Education,* 402 U.S. 1 (1971), decision, the U.S. Supreme Court ruled that students could be bused to achieve racial integration. As busing occurred in cities around the United States during the 1970s, violent protests often resulted. In the 1990s, busing remained a hotly debated topic, and many cities revised or terminated their busing schemes.

Only 490 of 20,000 black students in the Charlotte-Mecklenburg system attended school with white students in 1965. Charlotte attorney Julius Chambers decided to take action. Chambers convinced 10 black families, including that of James Swann, to file suit. The school board's plan featured geographic attendance zones. Students could attend any school in the district, but they had to provide their own transportation. Chambers and the 10 families challenged the plan in North Carolina courts in 1965–1966, and lost. Decisions favoring integration in 1968 convinced Chambers to push on. That September, Swann plaintiffs took their case to the federal district court in Charlotte.

Judge James McMillan ruled in favor of the plaintiffs, and ordered the school board to prepare a new plan for integration. When they responded unsatisfactorily, McMillan crafted an alternative. It integrated all 105 district schools by pairing white suburban schools with black urban schools, busing about 10,000 students for integration purposes.

In May 1970, the U.S. Court of Appeals partially overturned McMillan's decision, ruling against the busing of elementary students. In June, the Supreme Court agreed to hear the case. Chief Justice Warren Burger agreed with the Court of Appeals. However, after months of debate, he endorsed a decision favorable to McMillan's entire plan. The Supreme Court approved of busing to achieve racial integration on April 20, 1971. Plans similar to Charlotte's were implemented across the country, and busing joined **affirmative action** as one of the most controversial racial issues in America. (AD)

BIBLIOGRAPHY
Schwartz, Bernard. *Swann's Way: The School Busing Case and the Supreme Court.* New York: Oxford University Press, 1986.

Sweatt v. Painter (1950)

Four years before the Supreme Court outlawed segregation in public schools in **Brown v. Board of Education**, it struck a blow at the concept of "separate but equal" in the state-supported higher education.

Herman Sweatt had applied to the law school at the University of Texas in 1946 but was denied admission on the basis of his race. Under an earlier Court decision, **Missouri ex. Rel. Gaines v. Canada** (1938), states were required to furnish an accredited law school education for African Americans not admitted to the state university. The alternative devised in Texas would have provided Sweatt with separate law classes held in the state capitol building.

Thurgood Marshall, in behalf of the **NAACP Legal Defense Fund**, represented Sweatt before the Supreme Court. The Court, in *Sweatt v. Painter*, 339 U.S. 629 (1950), ruled unanimously that the African-American law school was not in any way equal to the University of Texas Law School. Even if the school had equal facilities, which it did not, it could not provide the intangible benefits of an established law school, including the advantages of faculty reputation, alumni connections, history, and tradition. The Court ruled that the Equal Protection clause of the **Fourteenth Amendment** required that Sweatt be admitted to the traditionally all-white law school of the University of Texas. (MWA)

BIBLIOGRAPHY

Lively, Donald E. *The Constitution and Race*. New York: Praeger, 1992.

Nieman, Donald G. *Promises to Keep: African-Americans and the Constitutional Order, 1776 to the Present*. New York: Oxford, 1991.

Tennessee v. Garner (1985)

In *Tennessee v. Garner*, 471 U.S. 1 (1985), the U.S. Supreme Court ruled that it is unconstitutional for a police officer to shoot a fleeing suspect who does not pose an immediate danger to the officer or public. The case involved Edward Garner, a black 15–year-old who was killed while trying to escape the scene of a suspected burglary. The case created the Garner Standard, which limits the circumstances under which a police officer can use deadly force against a fleeing person suspected of a felony. **See also** Crime and Punishment. **See** the text of the Fourteenth Amendment in "Civil War Amendments" in Appendix 1. (JCW)

BIBLIOGRAPHY

Edwards, George Clifton, Jr. "The Shot in the Back Case: *Tennessee v. Garner.*" *New York University Review of Law and Social Change* 14, no. 3 (Summer 1986): 733–37.

Tighe, Frank P., III. "Fourth Amendment Limitations on a Peace Officer's Use of Deadly Force to Effect an Arrest." *Loyola University of Chicago Law Journal* 17, no. 1 (Fall 1985): 151–70.

Mary Church Terrell (1863–1954)

Mary Church Terrell was the first president of the **National Association of Colored Women**, serving from 1896 to 1901, and a founding member of the **National Association for the Advancement of Colored People (NAACP)**. Terrell was also the first African-American woman to serve on the Washington, D.C., Board of Education. She was also active in the founding of the Women's International League for Peace and Freedom. An advocate of women's rights and involved in the struggle for woman suffrage, Terrell was active in the National Woman's Party and worked for reforms as a member of the Republican Party.

BIBLIOGRAPHY

Shepperd, Gladys B. *Mary Church Terrell.* Baltimore: Human Relations Press, 1959.

Terrell, Mary Church. *A Colored Woman in a White World.* New York: G. K. Hall, 1996.

Third Parties

Third parties in the United States have been sporadic and intermittent and have generally had a negligible effect on the political system. No minor party has ever come close to winning the presidency, and only eight minor parties have won so much as a single state's votes in the Electoral College.

Third parties do, however, generate controversy, and at times pose promising challenges to the parties that dominate the two-party electoral system, the Republicans and the Democrats. During presidential elections, third parties have also affected the African-American community. In the 1850s, a third political party—the **Republican Party**—gained widespread popularity because of its opposition to **slavery**. The Republicans took six years to win the White House, electing Abraham Lincoln of Illinois as the first first Republican president in 1860. The rise of the Republicans left the two-party system intact because the Republican Party supplanted the Whig Party as the majority opposition to the Democrats.

In the twentieth century, third parties met with limited success in 1968 and 1992, when third party candidates for president received more than 10 percent of the popular vote. For African Americans, both of these third party candidacies were negative ones. In 1968, the American Independent Party (AIP) enjoyed a measure of success because its leader, Alabama Governor George Wallace, held a firm geographic base in the South, and attacked an emotional issue, civil rights. Wallace, nationally known for his racist positions and anti-integration activities as governor, had widespread support from white lower-class voters in his presidential bid. In 1992, Ross Perot, a Texas billionaire with a folksy manner, ran as a candidate for president under the third party ticket called United We Stand America. Perot gained popularity by making the country's budget deficit the central issue of his campaign. He did, however, fall into disfavor with the African-American electorate when, during his second bid for the presidency in 1996, he made derogatory remarks about the black community in an address to the **National Association for the Advancement of Colored People (NAACP)** convention delegates. Today, Perot's third party continues and has been renamed the Reform Party. The Green Party, the Libertarian Party, the Communist Party USA, and Natural Law Party also run as third parties in current American elections. **See also** Democratic Party. (VDD)

BIBLIOGRAPHY

Abramson, Paul R., John H. Aldrich, Phil Paolino, and David W. Rhode. "Third Party and Independent Candidates in American Politics: Wallace, Anderson, and Perot." *Political Science Quarterly* 110, no. 3 (Fall 1995): 1–20.

Bartley, Numan V. and Hugh D. Graham. *Southern Politics and the Second Reconstruction*. Baltimore: The Johns Hopkins University Press, 1975.

Black, Earl and Merle Black. *Politics and Society in the South*. Cambridge, MA: Harvard University Press, 1987.

Mayhew, David R. *Placing Parties in American Politics*. Princeton: Princeton University Press, 1986.

Thirteenth Amendment

Ratified on December 6, 1865, the Thirteenth Amendment was the first of three constitutional changes regarding **slavery** passed following the **Civil War**. The amendment outlaws slavery or the involuntary servitude of any person in the United States without due process of law. As a condition for rejoining the Union, the former states of the Confederacy had to ratify each of the Civil War amendments.

BIBLIOGRAPHY

Hoemann, George H. *What God Hath Wrought*. New York: Garland Publishers, 1987.

Schleichert, Elizabeth. *The 13th Amendment*. Hillside, NJ: Enslow Publishers, 1998.

Clarence Thomas (1948–)

Clarence Thomas is the second African American appointed to the U.S. Supreme Court. Thomas was confirmed in 1991 after a series of contentious confirmation hearings. Thomas was considered one of the brightest stars of a growing number of African-American conservatives. He was appointed assistant secretary of education by President Ronald Reagan in 1981, and served chair of the **Equal Employment Opportunity Commission (EEOC)** from 1982 to 1990 . His tenure as chair of the EEOC was controversial because Thomas frequently took positions that were at odds with traditional civil rights groups, most notably his opposition to **affirmative action**.

Justice Clarence Thomas, a political conservative appointed to the Court by President George Bush in 1991, was a controversial replacement for retiring Justice Thurgood Marshall. *Courtesy of U.S. Supreme Court.*

In 1990, President George Bush appointed Thomas to the Court of Appeals for the District of Columbia. In 1991, Bush appointed Thomas to the Supreme Court seat vacated by **Thurgood Marshall**, the first African-American justice. Thomas's record, ideology, and judicial philosophy were almost the direct opposite of Marshall's. Thomas's confirmation hearings turned into a national spectacle when University of Oklahoma law professor **Anita Hill** charged that Thomas had sexually harassed her when they worked together at the Department of Education and the EEOC. Thomas categorically denied the charges, claiming that it was "a high tech lynching." He narrowly won confirmation by a vote of 52–48, the largest vote ever cast against a successful nominee. Since reaching the Supreme Court, Thomas has fulfilled predictions that he would be conservative. He has supported a limited role for the Court and limitations on the expansion of constitutional rights. (RLP)

BIBLIOGRAPHY

Thomas, Susan. "Clarence Thomas." In Leon Friedman and Fred I. Israel, eds. *The Justices of the United States Supreme Court: Their Lives and Major Opinions*, 5th ed. New York: Chelsea House Publishers, 1997.

Bennie G. Thompson (1949–)

Prior to securing a seat in the U.S. House of Representatives in a special election in 1993, Bennie Thompson was a public school teacher in the Mississippi Delta. He won the seat vacated by newly appointed Secretary of Agriculture **Michael (Mike) Espy**. Thompson has been very active in the agriculture committee, where he has sought to improve conditions in his rural district. **See also** Congressional Black Caucus. (CEM)

BIBLIOGRAPHY

"Regional Reports: South." *National Minority Politics* 4, no. 10 (March 1993): 12–13.

Thornburg v. Gingles (1986)

Thornburg v. Gingles, 478 U.S. 30 (1986), is one of a series of cases dealing with legislative redistricting, in which the U.S. Supreme Court further interpreted the 1982 revisions in section 2 of the **Voting Rights Act of 1965.** In so doing, the Court gave the constitutional basis from which a claimant could challenge the integrity of a legislative district based on race or create a district based on race. Based on these Court decisions, the most important characteristic for justifying a new district was the ability of a racial group to show that the group was large enough (yet compact enough) to form a majority, and that the group could be politically cohesive within the new district. The group also needed to show that minority candidates in the existing district usually lost elections because of racially polarized bloc voting. *Gingles*, however, has come under fire in more recent Court decisions such as *Shaw v. Reno* **(1996). See also** Voting Rights Act Amendments of 1982. (CEM)

BIBLIOGRAPHY

Kilgore, Sue T. "Between the Devil and the Deep Blue Sea." *Catholic University Law Review* 46 (Summer 1997): 1299–1348.

Miller, Andrew P. and Mark A. Packman. "Amend Section 2 of the Voting Rights Act." *Emory Law Journal* 36 (Winter 1987): 1–74.

Thorpe v. Housing Authority of the City of Durham (1969)

Thorpe, a black woman in Durham, North Carolina, had a month-to-month lease with a federally assisted public housing project in her area; this lease provided 15 days notice if either party wished to terminate. The day after being elected president of the tenant's organization, Thorpe was unexpectedly given notice to vacate, which she refused to do, bringing the matter to court instead. The district court held the woman's eviction was legal, agreeing with the Housing Authority that it fell within their right to remove her. Thorpe argued that her eviction was based on her color and organizational activities, and therefore violated her **Fourteenth** and **First Amendment** rights. On appeal, the Supreme Court agreed with Thorpe's reasoning and reversed the lower court decision. In doing so, the Court, in *Thorpe v. Housing Authority of the City of Durham*, 393 U.S. 268 (1969), decided that tenants of federally assisted housing projects could not be evicted without proper notification of the reason and without a hearing. The ruling applied to all tenants, regardless of gender, race, faith, or other similar designations unless sufficient merit warranted action.

BIBLIOGRAPHY

D'Amato, Anthony A., Rosemary Metrailer, and Stephen L. Wasby. *Desegregation from Brown to Alexander*. Carbondale: Southern Illinois University Press, 1977.

Three-Fifths Clause

The three-fifths clause was a compromise struck at the Constitutional Convention of 1787 between slave-holding and free states over issues of taxation and representation. The central issue was how the federal government should count black slaves in the South. Although southern states favored counting blacks to determine the state's political representation in Congress, they vehemently opposed counting blacks as part of a state's population for the calculation of any per capita tax. Thus, southern delegates forged an agreement with their northern colleagues to count black slaves as three-fifths of a person for both taxation and representation. (KC)

BIBLIOGRAPHY

McKissick, Floyd B. *Three-Fifths of a Man*. New York: Macmillan, 1969.

Dwight Tillery (1948–)

Dwight Tillery was born in 1948 in Cincinnati, Ohio. He received his J.D. from the University of Michigan in 1972 and was a professor at the University of Cincinnati from 1975 to 1978. From 1983–1985 he served as senior assistant attorney general for the state of Ohio. He was a city councilman in Cincinnati and was elected mayor in 1991, a post he still holds. Prior to being elected mayor, he taught business law at Miami University in Oxford, Ohio. (JCW)

BIBLIOGRAPHY

"Public Service Salute." *Jet* 15 (June 1992): 34.

Title I of the Civil Rights Act of 1964

Title I of the **Civil Rights Act of 1964**, barred unequal application of voter registration requirements to ensure that black voters were not discriminated against. This title also spelled out the procedure for appealing voter disqualification. While it did not abolish literacy tests sometimes used to disqualify African Americans and poor white voters, it ensured that any tests would be applied to all voters equally.

BIBLIOGRAPHY

Whalen, Charles and Barbara Whalen. *The Longest Debate: A Legislative History of the 1964 Civil Rights Act*. Cabin John, MD: Seven Locks Press, 1985.

Title IV of the Civil Rights Act of 1964

Title IV of the **Civil Rights Act of 1964** required the commissioner of education to undertake a survey and report to the president on "lack of availability of equal educational opportunities for individuals by reason of race, color, religion, or national origin in public educational institutions at all levels in the United States." It authorized but did not require the creation of special training institutes to improve the ability of educators and school personnel to deal effectively with educational problems brought on by desegregation. It also authorized but did not require withdrawal of federal funds from programs that practiced discrimination. Lastly, this title authorized the attorney general to undertake civil actions to enforce desegregation where communities were unwilling or unable to enforce the laws themselves.

BIBLIOGRAPHY

Whalen, Charles and Barbara Whalen. *The Longest Debate: A Legislative History of the 1964 Civil Rights Act*. Cabin John, MD: Seven Locks Press, 1985.

Title VI of the Civil Rights Act of 1964

According to Title VI of the **Civil Rights Act of 1964**, no person in the United States shall, on the ground of race, color, or national origin, be excluded from participation in, be denied the benefits of, or be subjected to discrimination under any program or activity receiving federal financial assistance. Title VI is, generally, remedial rather than punitive in purpose; it prohibits racial discrimination in any program funded by federal financing. One of its objectives is to assure nondiscrimination in acquisition of housing. It imposes upon federal officials not only the duty to refrain from participation in discriminatory practices, but the affirmative duty to police operations and prevent such discriminations by state or local agencies. The purpose of Title VI is to rule out discrimination by cutting off federal funds to those activities that continue to discriminate contrary to Title VI mandates. Although the law was never considered by Congress as covering race discrimination in employment, it has been used to redress it. (PLF)

BIBLIOGRAPHY

Halpern, Stephen C. *On the Limits of the Law: The Ironic Legacy of Title VI of the 1964 Civil Rights Act*. Baltimore: Johns Hopkins University Press, 1995.

Title VII of the Civil Rights Act of 1964

Title VII of the **Civil Rights Act of 1964** seeks to end employment discrimination based on race, color, religion, national origin, and sex. It set up the **Equal Employment Opportunity Commission (EEOC)** and empowered the EEOC to investigate charges of discrimination, to require record keeping and reporting, and to refer cases of substantiated discrimination to the attorney general. Congress chose the Commerce Clause of the United States Constitution as grounds for its interference in state civil rights actions because the Supreme Court had granted Congress extensive freedom in economic matters.

Arguing for passage of the bill, Senator Hubert Humphrey, a Minnesota Democrat, cited statistics on the economic plight of blacks, noting, among other points, that 20 percent of black female high school graduates entered domestic service, and a black man with a college degree earned less than a white male high school dropout. Opponents framed their arguments in terms of a loss of control, declaring that neither individuals nor states would have protection from encroaching national government.

Title VII has been amended a number of times. In 1989, after a series of Supreme Court cases attempted to end many of the protections of Title IV, and after Republican Presidents Ronald Reagan and George Bush staffed the Equal Employment Opportunity Commission (EEOC) with affirmative action opponents, Justice **Thurgood Marshall** believed that Americans had come full circle. The **Civil Rights Act of 1991** restored most of these protections, and the success of Title VII has been documented by scholars who contend that it has resulted in increased economic prosperity and racial equality. (EP)

BIBLIOGRAPHY

Altschiller, Donald, ed. "The Supreme Court and Civil Rights: Has the Tide Turned?" *The Reference Shelf: Affirmative Action*. New York: H.W. Wilson, 1991, 35–38.

Edsall, Thomas Byrne and Mary D. Edsall. *Chain Reaction: The Impact of Race, Rights, and Taxes on American Politics*. New York: W.W. Norton, 1992.

Schwartz, Bernard, ed. *Statutory History of the United States: Civil Rights, Part II*. New York: Chelsea House, 1970.

Title VIII of the Civil Rights Act of 1964

Title VIII of the **Civil Rights Act of 1964** mandated that the secretary of commerce conduct a survey of registration and voting statistics in geographic areas as recommended by the Commission on Civil Rights. Data to be collected included the number of people of voting age (correlated by race, color, and national origin), and a determination of who among these people was registered to vote. This information was to be collected in conjunction with the U.S. Census.

BIBLIOGRAPHY

Loevy, Robert, ed. *The Civil Rights Act of 1964 : The Passage of the Law that Ended Racial Segregation*. Albany: SUNY Press, 1997.

Kwame Toure. *See* Stokely Carmichael

Edolphus "Ed" Towns (1934–)

Edolphus Towns, a Democrat from New York, was first elected to the U.S. House of Representatives in 1982. Before entering Congress, Towns served as the deputy president of the borough of Brooklyn, New York, from 1976 to 1982. In Congress, Towns serves on the Commerce Committee and the Government Reform and Oversight Committee. **See also** Congressional Black Caucus.

BIBLIOGRAPHY

Jennings, C. "Representative Edolphus Towns." *Journal of the American Academy of Nurse Practitioners* 7, no. 6 (1995): 273.

Trafficante et al. v. Metropolitan Life Insurance Co. (1972)

In *Trafficante et al. v. Metropolitan Life Insurance Co.*, 409 U.S. 205 (1972), two tenants, one black and the one white, filed complaints with the secretary of Housing and Urban Development alleging that the tenants' landlord racially discriminated against nonwhites, and that they themselves were injured in that (1) they had lost the social benefits of living in an integrated community, (2) they missed certain advantages that would accrue if they had lived with minority groups, and (3) they had suffered hardships from being stigmatized as residents of a "white ghetto." The U.S. Supreme Court ruled unanimously in favor of the plaintiffs. (CJM)

BIBLIOGRAPHY

Galub, Arthur L. *The Burger Court, 1968–1984*. Millwood, NY: Associate Faculty Press, 1984.

TransAfrica

Founded in 1976 by the **Black Congressional Caucus**, and incorporated on July 1, 1977, with **Randall Robinson** as the first executive director, TransAfrica regards itself as the black American lobby for African and Caribbean affairs. The 1984 protests outside the South African Embassy—the longest continuing demonstration in the U.S.—first gave TransAfrica major prominence and resulted in the Free South Africa Movement. Such public pressure campaigns have been used as models to influence American policy in Africa and the Caribbean. In 1993, a foreign policy institute, TransAfrica Forum, was created. TransAfrica has about 20,000 members in 12 chapters nationwide. (ISM)

BIBLIOGRAPHY

"Challenging U.S. Policy Toward Africa: Conversations with Randall Robinson." *Journal of International Affairs* 46, no. 1 (Summer 1992): 145–56.

Cheers, D. Michael. "TransAfrica: The Black World's Voice on Capital Hill." *Ebony* 42 (July 1987): 108–14.

William Monroe Trotter (1872–1934)

William Monroe Trotter was a journalist and social reformer who opposed **Booker T. Washington**'s program of accommodation. Trotter founded the *Boston Guardian* newspaper, a militant paper, and helped organize the **Niagara movement**, the forerunner of the **National Association for the Advancement of Colored People (NAACP)**. However at the formation of the NAACP he refused to join because he perceived it as too moderate. He was a radical integrationalist who advised blacks to fight for their rights. Many of the tactics he proposed such as getting arrested to draw attention to the issue were adopted by civil rights leaders in the 1960s. (AAB)

BIBLIOGRAPHY

Fox, Stephen R. *The Guardian of Boston: William Monroe Trotter.* New York: Atheneum, 1970.

Sojourner Truth (1797–1883)

Sojourner Truth was born a slave; her given name was Isabella Van Wagenen. She was freed by the New York State Emancipation Act of 1827, and she changed her name in the 1830s while traveling the country advocating for abolition. Working with others like James and Lucretia Mott and Harriet Beecher Stowe, Truth was one of her era's most prominent civil rights activists. Truth was also active in the women's rights and suffrage movements. She was a leading voice for minority women in these movements. She lobbied Congress until her death for free land in the west for former slaves.

Former slave Sojourner Truth (shown here with Abraham Lincoln) was a prominent nineteenth-century civil rights and women's rights activist. *Library of Congress.*

BIBLIOGRAPHY

Gilbert, Olive. *Narrative of Sojourner Truth.* New York: Penguin, 1998.
Mabee, Carleton. *Sojourner Truth.* New York: New York University Press, 1993.

Harriet Tubman (ca. 1820–1913)

Harriet Tubman was born Araminta Ross on a plantation in Dorchester County, Maryland. She escaped from slavery in 1850, against the wishes of her husband, a freed slave. She became a member of the Underground Railroad and made 19 successful "trips" with freed slaves. Her activities in freeing slaves earned her the nickname "Moses." During the **Civil**

Harriet Tubman successfully led many slaves out of bondage on the Underground Railroad. *Library of Congress.*

War, she was a nurse and a scout. After the war, Tubman returned home to Auburn, New York, and in 1869, married Nelson Davis. In 1908, Tubman opened a nursing home for elderly African Americans. She joined Susan B. Anthony and other suffragettes in fighting for women's rights. Tubman died on March 10, 1913. (FAS)

BIBLIOGRAPHY

Sterling, Dorothy. *Freedom Train: The Story of Harriet Tubman.* Garden City, NY: Doubleday, 1954.

Walter R. Tucker (1958–)

Walter Tucker was born in California, graduated from the University of Southern California, and earned a law degree from Georgetown Law Center. He was appointed deputy district attorney for Los Angeles County and was elected to the House of Representatives as a Democrat from California in 1992. (JCW)

BIBLIOGRAPHY

Hall, Carla. "Tucker's Career Blossomed Despite Scandal." *Los Angeles Times.* (August 12, 1994.): p A24.

Tureaud v. Board of Supervisors of Louisiana State University et al. (1954)

In 1953, A.P. Tureaud, Jr. became the first black undergraduate to attend a major southern white university. Tureaud's father, the civil rights lawyer, A.P. Tureaud, had petitioned successfully in federal district court to have his son admitted to Louisiana State University. The appeals court, however, decided in favor of LSU and Tureaud, Jr. was expelled from school. Before the Supreme Court could hear *Tureaud v. Board of Supervisors of Louisiana State University,* 347 U.S. 971 (1954), Tureaud, Jr. decided to enroll at Xavier University in New Orleans. The case was remanded to the State Court of Appeals in light of **Brown v. Board of Education Topeka** (1954). (WPS)

BIBLIOGRAPHY

Fairclough, Adam. *Race & Democracy: The Civil Rights Struggle in Louisiana, 1915–1972.* Athens: University of Georgia Press, 1995.
Greenberg, Jack. *Crusaders on the Courts: How a Dedicated Band of Lawyers Fought for the Civil Rights Revolution.* New York: Basic Books, 1994.

Benjamin Sterling Turner (1825–1894)

Benjamin Turner, a Republican from Alabama, was elected to the United States House of Representatives in 1871 and served until 1873. Prior to entering Congress, Turner served as a tax collector for Dallas County in 1867 and was a member of the Selma, Alabama, city council from 1869 to 1871.

BIBLIOGRAPHY

Rees, Matthew. *From the Deck to the Sea.* Wakefield, NH: Longwood Academic, 1991.

Walton, Hanes. *Black Republicans.* Metuchen, NJ: Scarecrow, 1975.

Henry McNeal Turner (1834–1915)

Henry McNeal Turner was a long-time bishop in the **African Methodist Episcopal (A.M.E.) Church**. He was born to free parents in South Carolina. During the **Civil War** he served as a chaplain and was elected as a republican to the Georgia Constitution Convention in 1867. He served in the state legislature from 1868 to 1870. He steadfastly believed that the oppressions inflicted upon African Americans were God's calling for the best of the race to emigrate to Africa and evangelize the continent. To that end he was active with the **American Colonization Society. (WPS)**

BIBLIOGRAPHY

Angell, Stephen Ward. *Bishop Henry McNeal Turner and African-American Religion in the South.* Knoxville: The University of Tennessee Press, 1992.

Trimiew, Darryl M. *Voices of the Silenced: The Responsible Self in a Marginalized Community.* Cleveland: The Pilgrim Press, 1993.

James Milton Turner (ca. 1840–1915)

James Milton Turner was born a slave in Missouri but his father purchased his freedom in 1844. He managed to receive an education at a secret slave school run by Roman Catholic nuns and believed he should share that education with other freedmen. After teaching in Kansas City and Boonville, he joined the **Freedmen's Bureau** and was responsible for opening 32 black schools by 1870. In spite of white opposition, Turner managed to construct a number of school buildings and provide education for a number of freedmen. He served as resident minister to Liberia from 1871 to 1878. He was president of the Freedman's Oklahoma Association which helped blacks move to the Oklahoma territory. He practiced law including representing Negro members of the Cherokee nation in the 1886 land claim. (FAS)

BIBLIOGRAPHY

Kremer, Gary R. *James Milton Turner and the Promise of America: The Public Life of a Post-Civil War Black Leader.* Columbia University of Missouri Press, 1991.

Nat Turner (1800–1831)

Born on a plantation in Southampton County, Virginia, Nat Turner spent many of his early years acting as a preacher for his fellow slaves. Turner's strong beliefs and powerful presence soon gained him support and followers. In 1831, Turner gathered these supporters together to lead an uprising against the plantation; Turner and his fellow slaves successfully escaped, capturing weapons and killing about 50 whites in their revolt. After a countywide manhunt, most of the escapees were recaptured, including Turner, who was hanged. Turner's uprising had a number of long-standing ramifications; not only did widespread terror and long-term fear of more uprisings sweep the South as a result, but southern states also took on new, more severe slave code laws and put an end to organized southern emancipation groups as a result. **See also** Slavery.

BIBLIOGRAPHY

Bisson, Terry. *Nat Turner.* New York: Chelsea House, 1988.

Duff, John B. *The Nat Turner Rebellion.* New York: Harper & Row, 1971.

Turner v. Fouche (1970)

In *Turner v. Fouche,* 396 U.S. 346 (1970), a group of black residents of Taliaferro County, Georgia, challenged the constitutionality of the school board selection process, which provided that a grand jury would choose five property owners to serve on the school board. No African Americans served on the school board and only a few served on the grand jury, although 60 percent of the county's residents and all of the students in the public schools were black. The U.S. Supreme Court found that the selection procedures used by the grand jury, and the requirement that school board members be property owners, violated the **Fourteenth Amendment. See** the text of the Fourteenth Amendment in "Civil War Amendments" in Appendix 1.

BIBLIOGRAPHY

Alschuler, Albert W. "Racial Quotas and the Jury." *Duke Law Journal* 44 (February 1995): 704–41.

Turner v. Murray (1968)

Willie Lloyd Turner, who was black, was sentenced to death for the murder of a white jewelry-store owner; the murder occurred during the robbery of the store. At the time of his trial, Turner requested that the judge question prospective jurors about prejudice toward a black defendant accused of killing a white man. The judge refused, and Turner then appealed, on the grounds that he had been deprived of a fair and impartial jury. In *Turner v. Murray,* 476 U.S. 28 (1968), the U.S. Supreme Court agreed and vacated Turner's sentence but allowed the verdict of guilty to stand. **See also** Crime and Punishment.

BIBLIOGRAPHY

Bennett, Nancy. "A Defendant's Right to an Impartial Jury." *Oklahoma City University Law Review* 12, no. 1 (Spring 1987): 205–22.

Wyckoff, Maria. "Sixth Amendment—Right to Inquire into Jurors' Racial Prejudices." *Journal of Criminal Law and Criminology* 77, no. 3 (Fall 1986): 713–42.

Tuskegee Institute

The Tuskegee Institute (today Tuskegee University) is located in Tuskegee, Alabama. Its first president was **Booker T. Washington.** Resulting from a deal struck between local blacks and white politicians, Tuskegee Institute was established by the state legislature in 1880 as the Tuskegee State Normal School, and opened the following year with the goal of providing industrial and agricultural training for blacks. In 1893, it was incorporated as the Tuskegee Normal and Industrial Institute and by 1900 it had a library funded by philanthropist Andrew Carnegie, 167 teachers, and almost 1,500 students. Today it is a university with over 3,700 students and 326 faculty, and it awards bachelor's, master's, and doctoral degrees. (ISM)

BIBLIOGRAPHY

Harlan, Louis R. *Booker T. Washington: The Wizard of Tuskegee, 1901–1915*. New York: Oxford University Press, 1983.

Norrell, Robert J. *Reaping the Whirlwind: The Civil Rights Movement in Tuskegee*. New York: Vintage Books, 1985.

Washington, Booker T. *Up from Slavery*. Garden City, NY: Doubleday & Co., 1901.

In March 1939, President Franklin D. Roosevelt greets Dr. George Washington Carver on a visit to the Tuskegee Institute in Tuskegee, Alabama. *National Archives.*

U

Uncle Tom

Selling over 300,000 copies in its first year, Harriet Beecher Stowe's1852 novel *Uncle Tom's Cabin* is credited with helping to start the **Civil War,** and certainly heightened pre-war tensions between the North and the South over **slavery.** In the book, Tom's owner describes him as a "good, steady, sensible, and pious fellow." Even after being sold to Simon Legree, the epitome of a cruel slave owner, Tom continues to exhibit these characteristics. This refusal to rebel or to hate defines the twentieth-century racial stereotype of an "Uncle Tom" as a black who appeases the whites who oppress him, thus seemingly contributing to his own oppression. (EP)

BIBLIOGRAPHY

Stowe, Harriet Beecher. *Uncle Tom's Cabin or Life among the Lowly.* New York: Bantam Books, 1994.

Underground Railroad

The Underground Railroad was a loosely organized and clandestine network of aid and assistance that helped fugitive slaves reach safety and freedom in Canada or the free states of the North. The Underground Railroad had its origins in the colonial period, but it was most active in the three decades before the Civil War, from about 1830 to 1865. It is estimated that as many as 100,000 enslaved African Americans escaped bond-

Harriet Tubman (far left) led this group of slaves to freedom in Canada. *Library of Congress.*

age via the Railroad between the 1780s and the 1860s. Although legend has depicted the Underground Railroad as a highly organized enterprise with "conductors" and "stations," most assistance was given by anti-slavery individuals, both black and white, who provided food, shelter, and information to fugitives as they made their way north. Abolitionists, members of religious groups that opposed slavery, and former slaves, such as **Harriet Tubman**, who led more than 300 people to safety, were all involved in the effort to bring escaped slaves to freedom. (JAW)

BIBLIOGRAPHY

Blockson, Charles L. *The Underground Railroad.* New York: Prentice-Hall, 1987.

Sawyer, Kem Knapp. *The Underground Railroad in American History.* Springfield, NJ: Enslow Publishers, 1997.

United States Commission on Civil Rights

The United States Commission on Civil Rights is an independent, bipartisan agency first established under the Civil Rights Act of 1957. In 1981, President Ronald Reagan appointed **Clarence Pendleton** to be the Commission's first African-American chairman. Both Pendleton and Reagan clashed ideologically with commission members, all presidential appointees serving six-year terms. In 1983, following an attempt by Reagan to dismiss three of the commissioners on the six-member panel, Congress established a new Commission under the Civil Rights Act of 1983. Although the Commission's duties and powers remained the same, its membership changed from six to eight members, four of whom are appointed by the president and four by Congress. The Commission's duties are numerous. Since its inception in 1957, it has published more than 70 reports containing recommendations to Congress and the president and over 160 other public reports and studies on civil rights matters. (VDD)

BIBLIOGRAPHY

Devroy, Ann. "Longtime Bush Ally to Head Rights Unit; President Aims to Make Commission 'Respectable Again,' Aides Say." *Washington Post* (March 22, 1989): A9.

Haveman, Robert H. *A Decade of Federal Antipoverty Programs: Achievements, Failures, and Lessons.* New York: Academic Press, 1977.

Miller, Jeffrey. "Claremont Professor Takes Helm of Civil Rights Panel." *Los Angeles Times* (September 25, 1988): 10.

"Reagan Praises Civil Rights Chief as Apostle of Justice." Associated Press (June 6, 1988).

Roderick, Kevin and Claudia Luther. "Reagan's Appointment of Asian-American Met with Praise." *Los Angeles Times* (August 17, 1988): 3.

United States v. Adams, Bordenave, and Mitchell (1943)

United States v. Adams, Bordenave, and Mitchell, 319 U.S. 312 (1943), was a case involving three black soldiers who were convicted of rape within the confines of Camp Claiborne in Louisiana. They were sentenced to death by a district court. However, **Thurgood Marshall** and the **National Association for the Advancement of Colored People (NAACP)** appealed on the grounds that the local court did not have jurisdiction in the case. The U.S. Supreme Court ruled that the district court was outside its jurisdiction, and the three men were returned to the Army for court-martial. **See also** Crime and Punishment. (CJM)

BIBLIOGRAPHY

Bardolph, Richard. *The Civil Right Record.* New York: Crowell, 1970.

United States v. Classic et al. (1941)

United States v. Classic, 313 U.S. 299 (1941), is significant as a prominent precursor to the Supreme Court's landmark ruling in *Smith v. Allwright* (1944), which banned the white primary, a primary election in which only whites could vote, throughout the South. The case involved a 1940 Democratic primary for a congressional seat in Louisiana. The district court held that "primaries" were not covered under the Constitution and therefore remained under state rather than federal jurisdiction. The U.S. Supreme Court reversed the lower court's decision, holding that Article I, Section 4 of the Constitution covered "primaries" as well as "general elections." (CJM)

BIBLIOGRAPHY

Bixby, David M. "The Roosevelt Court, Democratic Ideology, and Minority Rights! Another Look at *United States v. Classic.*" *Yale Law Journal* 90, no. 4 (March 1981): 741–815.

United States v. Cruikshank (1876)

In the late 1800s two African-American men, Levi Nelson and Alexander Tillman, sued claiming that they had been unjustly and unconstitutionally persecuted as a result of the Enforcement Act of 1870. In *United States v. Cruikshank,* 92 U.S. 542 (1876), the U.S. Supreme Court found that the **Fourteenth Amendment** provided blacks with equal protection under the law, thereby setting a benchmark as one of the earliest civil rights cases. As a result, African Americans' rights as citizens were reaffirmed, as well as their entitlement of protection from injustices against their lives, liberty, or property. However, in its ruling the Supreme Court also stated that the Fourteenth Amendment did not add anything to the rights of one citizen against those of another, which provided an "escape clause" of sorts for many states. **See also** Crime and Punishment. **See** the text of the Fourteenth Amendment in "Civil War Amendments" in Appendix 1.

BIBLIOGRAPHY

Kaczorowski, Robert J. *The Politics of Judicial Interpretation.* New York: Oceana Publications, 1985.

United States v. Paradise (1987)

In 1972, the courts found that Alabama's Public Safety Department "systematically excluded blacks from employment" and placed the department under court order to remedy the situation. Later, the courts found that none of Alabama's black state troopers ranked even as high as corporal and ordered a one-black-for-one-white promotion policy. In *United States v. Paradise,* 480 U.S. 149 (1987), the Supreme Court rejected Alabama's request to end the quotas. Writing for the Court, Justice William Brennan declared the existence of "a compelling governmental interest in eradicating the Department's pervasive, systematic, and obstinate discriminatory exclusion of blacks." (EP)

BIBLIOGRAPHY

O'Brien, David M. *Constitutional Law and Politics: Civil Rights and Civil Liberties.* Vol 2. New York: W.W. Norton, 1991.

United States v. Reese (1875)

To ensure the voting rights of newly freed slaves, Congress enacted the Enforcement Act of 1870, which "provided that citizens of the United States, without distinction of race, color, or previous condition of servitude, shall, if otherwise qualified to vote in state, territorial, or municipal elections, be entitled and allowed to vote at all such elections." The federal government sought to punish two inspectors of a municipal election in Kentucky for refusing to receive and count the vote of William Garner, a U.S. citizen of African descent. But in *United States v. Reese,* 92 U.S. 214 (1875), the U.S. Supreme Court ruled that the act passed by Congress did not provide for the punishment of the offense and therefore was unenforceable against the inspectors.

BIBLIOGRAPHY

Barker, Lucius J. and Mack H. Jones. *African Americans and the American Political System.* Englewood Cliffs, NJ: Prentice Hall, 1994.

Young, James Van. *Landmark Constitutional Law Decisions: Briefs and Analyses.* Lanham, MD: University Press of America, 1993.

United States v. State of Alabama (1960)

In *United States v. State of Alabama,* 362 U.S. 602 (1960), the United States brought suit against voting registrars of the state of Alabama claiming that they had violated the **Civil Rights Act of 1957** by systematically depriving black voters of their right to vote. Alabama argued that the act did not authorize legal action against the state. Before the case was heard in court, the passage by Congress of the **Civil Rights Act of**

1960 specifically authorized such actions against the states, making the case moot. (JCW)

BIBLIOGRAPHY

Bardolph, Richard, ed. *The Civil Rights Record*. New York: Crowell, 1970.

United Steelworkers of America v. Weber (1979)

In response to a collective-bargaining agreement, the United Steelworkers of America and Kaiser Aluminum and Chemical Corporation developed a voluntary **affirmative action** program. Weber, a white male employee, sued, claiming discrimination under **Title VII of the Civil Rights Act of 1964** because of disputes over seniority and job training. In *United Steelworkers of America v. Weber*, 443 U.S. 193 (1979), the Supreme Court disagreed, stating that Title VII of the Civil Rights Act of 1964 "does not condemn all private, voluntary, race-conscious affirmative action programs." The Court's decision gave protection to certain affirmative action policies. (EP)

BIBLIOGRAPHY

Urofsky, Melvin I. *A March of Liberty: A Constitutional History of the United States*. Vol II: *Since 1865*. New York: Alfred A. Knopf, 1988.

Universal Negro Improvement Association (UNIA)

On August 1, 1914, **Marcus Garvey** created the Universal Negro Improvement and Conservation Association and African Communities League (later the Universal Negro Improvement Association—UNIA) in Jamaica. The UNIA's plan of action was based on three broad principles—racial pride, racial self-help, and racial separation. With headquarters located in Harlem, Garvey's UNIA instructed Africans of the diaspora (i.e., living outside of Africa) to be proud of their African heritage. This message was so appealing that within a year of Garvey's arrival in Harlem, the organization grew to 996 branches in 43 different countries. The UNIA became the largest organization of African Americans in the United States. In 1919, the UNIA established the Negro Factories Corporation, which included grocery stores, a black doll factory, a steam laundry, a tailoring establishment, restaurants, a hotel, and a printing press. The Black Star Lines was Garvey's plan for an African-operated steamship line linking Africans of the diaspora in industry and commerce. Despite its grand design and the fact that many members of the UNIA bought stock in the Black Star Lines, the UNIA never achieved its main aims, a situation that led to the eventual downfall of Garvey on charges of fraud. The UNIA still exists as a political organization in Jamaica. (RAM)

BIBLIOGRAPHY

Lewis, Rupert. *Marcus Garvey: Anti-Colonial Champion*. Trenton, NJ: Africa World Press, 1988.

Urban Development Action Grant (UDAG)

In 1970, Congress approved the Urban Development Action Grant (UDAG) to stimulate private investment in distressed communities. Focusing on urban renewal that displaced mostly poor and minority people, the UDAG program provided much more local discretion over how the federal funds would be spent than the other urban renewal programs it replaced. However, instead of revitalizing inner city areas, many mayors used the funds to build festival malls, to expand convention centers, and to build infrastructure that would support business and investment. The program was not renewed. (VDD)

BIBLIOGRAPHY

Caves, Roger W., ed. *Exploring Urban America: An Introductory Reader*. Thousand Oaks, CA: Sage Publications, 1996.

Urban Renewal

In 1945, United States Senators Robert Taft, Robert Wagner, and Allen Ellender introduced the first piece of urban renewal legislation to Congress. The idea of federal involvement in the rejuvenation of the nation's inner cities was an outgrowth both of New Deal ideas about improving the economic and social conditions of the nation's poor and of urban leaders' concerns over the increasing suburbanization of the country's white population. Worried that the nation's increasingly blighted inner cities were undermining property values and increasing social problems like crime and delinquency, federal officials and civic leaders conceived of urban renewal as a way to revitalize the rapidly emptying central business district and to stimulate the national economy. The first piece of urban renewal legislation, the Wagner-Ellender-Taft Housing Act of 1949, assisted urban redevelopment projects by providing local authorities with federal funds to acquire slum properties, clear them of existing buildings, and then sell the land to private developers.

Although a triumph for all people concerned with the nation's ailing inner cities, passage of this legislation marked the beginning of an uneasy alliance between liberal housing advocates, who envisioned public housing as the central focus of federal redevelopment efforts, and profit-minded businesspeople and civic leaders, who saw economic redevelopment as the central goal of the legislation. The 1949 act made housing its primary goal, requiring that most redevelopment take place in residential areas and that "decent, safe, and sanitary" housing be provided for those displaced. Local civic and business leaders, however, maneuvered their way around these provisions, carrying out instead a widespread program of "slum clearance." For their part, federal officials were eager to demonstrate tangible results from the new legislation, and thus made little pretense of enforcing federal legislative requirements concerning replacement housing.

A further impediment to the bill's emphasis on the construction of public housing was the act's requirement that local communities request federal assistance for the construction of public housing. Because most communities associated public housing with minority housing, few initiated such requests.

As a result, out of the 810,000 public housing units authorized by the urban renewal legislation, only 320,000 were constructed in the coming decade.

In 1954, federal officials made substantive changes to the 1949 Housing Act in an effort to make it even more attractive to local communities. The Housing Act of 1954, which changed the name of the program from urban redevelopment to urban renewal, gave local governments greater control over renewal projects and shifted emphasis away from housing by allowing a growing number of the redevelopment plans to be nonresidential in character. These changes signaled a shift in the focus of the program from providing low-income housing to stimulating commercial redevelopment. Increasingly, local business and civic leaders saw urban renewal as a way to free up inner city lands for private development and clear out mostly black neighborhoods that might threaten surrounding property values. While many cities gained attractive hotels, civic arenas, and office buildings as a result of the legislative changes, they also destroyed existing inner-city neighborhoods and, in many cases, created housing crises. In Atlanta, Georgia, for example, between 1957 and 1967, city authorities oversaw the destruction of more than 20,000 housing units, mostly occupied by black residents. It constructed only 5,000 new public housing units in their place, instead using the cleared land to construct a stadium, a new civic center, and acres of parking lots to accommodate commuter traffic. Buoyed by the popularity of urban renewal projects among city leaders, the Kennedy administration, after taking office in 1961, increased funding for the program. More funding meant more projects, so that by the end of the 1960s practically every major city in the United Sates had at least one urban renewal project underway.

At the same time, a growing number of civil rights activists began to protest the discriminatory enactment of federal urban policies, complaining that "urban renewal" often simply meant "Negro removal." Advocates of fair-housing legislation observed that urban renewal projects typically were sited in neighborhoods heavily populated by African Americans and other minorities. In addition, in the increasingly rare instances when urban renewal projects did include provisions for public housing units, displaced residents typically were resegregated into already overcrowded sections of the inner city. Critics of urban renewal charged local authorities with constructing unappealing multi-unit projects of extremely high density in an effort to save money, to limit black residential expansion, and to house as many displaced persons as possible. The Pruitt-Igoe public housing project in St. Louis, Missouri, consisting of 33 eleven-story buildings, represented the prototypical public housing project—highly acclaimed by architects in the 1950s but neglected and virtually unlivable within little more than a decade.

President John F. Kennedy responded to the public outcry against housing discrimination by appointing **Robert Weaver** as the first black director of the U.S. Housing Agency and signing Executive Order 11603 in 1962, requiring all federal agencies to prevent discrimination in federally supported housing projects. Because this order was rarely enforced by federal housing agencies, civil rights groups continued their pressure for a law banning racial discrimination in housing. President Lyndon B. Johnson took two decisive steps toward the improvement of housing conditions in the inner city. In 1965, he established the Department of Housing and Urban Development (HUD) to coordinate and oversee all federal housing programs, and, in the same year, launched the Model Cities program to encourage neighborhood groups to assume a leading role in renewal efforts.

Congressional approval of the 1968 Fair Housing Act marked another step toward federal recognition of the problems inherent in the enforcement of previous urban renewal legislation. The new housing act made it unlawful to discriminate against any potential buyer or tenant on the basis of race and banned the popular practice among real estate agents of "blockbusting," or attempting to promote panic selling by making predictions about the changing racial composition of a neighborhood. Like its legislative predecessors, however, the Fair Housing Act fell short of its goal of open housing because of its weak enforcement provisions. In addition to its inability to assess damages or otherwise penalize a violator, HUD could only investigate complaints brought to its attention by victims of discrimination. Until HUD finally established a system of monitoring compliance with its regulations in 1979, the fight against housing discrimination remained in the hands of community activists.

Meanwhile, the increasingly conservative political climate of the 1970s hastened the federal government's retreat from the problems of urban housing. The Housing Act of 1974, signed into law by President Richard Nixon, redefined the federal role in public housing from that of a builder of low-income housing to that of a facilitator. The federal government essentially handed over its role to private industry, simply offering tax incentives and other benefits to help lower rents for low-income households. Discrimination in housing programs only worsened in the 1980s under the Reagan administration, as HUD's ability to detect housing discrimination became even more circumscribed and as federal funding declined sharply. Finally, amid increasing evidence of discrimination in federal housing policies, Congress passed the Fair Housing Amendments Act in 1988, strengthening HUD's enforcement powers and shifting the responsibility for bringing complaints from victims to the agency itself. In addition, the Financial Institutions Reform, Recovery, and Enforcement Act of 1989 provided for an Affordable Housing Program that increased funding to lenders willing to finance low-income housing projects.

Despite such ongoing reform efforts at the federal level to correct the problems of discrimination in urban renewal and public housing projects, African Americans and other minorities still remain primarily responsible for lodging complaints against discrimination in federal projects. Beginning in the late 1960s and 1970s, community-based action and civil

175

rights groups assumed a leading role in fighting private-sector disinvestment and discrimination by inaugurating a program of community reinvestment. For example, the Association of Community Organizations for Reform Now (ACORN) set up local chapters across the country devoted to stimulating reinvestment in inner-city neighborhoods. In the 1970s and 1980s, organizations like ACORN combined efforts with Community Development Corporations, or CDCs, which initially were funded by the Office of Economic Opportunity. With this federal assistance, CDCs hoped to mobilize black communities in a fight to restore the economic vitality of their neighborhoods. As these community-based organizations matured, they moved from angry confrontations with city officials to the painstaking task of piecing together grants from city and federal agencies and from private foundations, businesses, and churches to reinvest in their own communities. By pooling their resources, these coalitions have succeeded in creating new jobs and stimulating economic development in low-income neighborhoods.

Beginning in the late 1980s, another strategy in the project of urban redevelopment appeared through the formation of Business Improvement Districts, or BIDs. In these specially designated districts, downtown property owners and tenants agree to authorize the city to levy additional taxes on BID members, who in turn use the additional funds collected to provide their district with needed services. As of the late 1990s, the results of this approach are still ambiguous. Critics of BIDs cite the potential for increased social divisions within the city as a result of BID members' efforts to clean up their own neighborhoods, while ignoring the problems of others. At the same time, proponents of BIDs argue that a stronger urban economy will mean greater prosperity for the entire downtown area, which may help in the creation of new jobs by attracting new businesses.

In the final analysis, any revitalization of the inner city owes its success as much to these kinds of community-based efforts as to any federally administered programs. The record on urban renewal itself is fairly dismal. From the 1949 enactment of the Housing Act to 1961, urban renewal projects accounted for the destruction of some 150,000 buildings and the displacement of approximately 500,000 people. Less than 10 years later, these figures had risen to 400,000 and 1.4 million, respectively. Not only did urban renewal schemes typically destroy more housing than they replaced, but by displacing many poor blacks into already crowded ghetto neighborhoods, these projects often shifted the problems of instability and urban blight from one neighborhood to another. (LPM)

BIBLIOGRAPHY

Anderson, Martin. *The Federal Bulldozer: A Critical Analysis of Urban Renewal, 1949–1962.* Cambridge, MA: MIT Press, 1964.

Hays, R. Allen. *The Federal Government and Urban Housing: Ideology and Change in Public Policy.* Albany: State University of New York, 1985.

Hirsch, Arnold R. and Raymond A. Mohl. *Urban Policy in Twentieth Century America.* New Brunswick, NJ: Rutgers University Press, 1993.

Massey, Douglas S. and Nancy A. Denton. *American Apartheid: Segregation and the Making of the Underclass.* Cambridge, MA: Harvard University Press 1993.

Pack, Janet Rothenberg. "BIDs, DIDs, SIDs, SADs: Private Governments in Urban America." *Brookings Review* 10, no. 4 (Fall 1992): 18–21.

Teaford, Jon C. *The Rough Road to Renaissance: Urban Revitalization in America, 1940–1985.* Baltimore: Johns Hopkins University Press, 1990.

Vasquez v. Hillery (1986)

The accused was convicted of first-degree murder and for the next 16 years unsuccessfully pursued appeals claiming that his right to equal protection had been violated because blacks were systematically excluded from the grand jury. In *Vasquez v. Hillery*, 474 U.S. 254 (1986), the Supreme Court held that even if there had been systematic exclusion of blacks from the grand jury, the conviction after a fair trial purged any **Fourteenth Amendment** claim occurring from the grand jury portion of the trial. (PLF)

BIBLIOGRAPHY

"Jury Exclusion for Race Bars Second Conviction." (*Vasquez v. Hillery*) *New York Law Journal* 195 (January 15, 1986): 1.

Stewart, David O. "Defendant's Rights." (Three Supreme Court Decisions) *ABA Journal* 72 (March 1, 1986): 102 (2).

Denmark Vesey (ca. 1767–1822)

Denmark Vesey was born a slave in St. Thomas in what was then the Danish Virgin Islands. In 1783, his owner brought him to Charleston, South Carolina. Shortly afterward, Vesey won a street lottery for $1,500 and purchased his freedom. He became a successful carpenter. However, he brooded over his inability to free his wife and children and over the existence of **slavery** in general. The example of the 1783 Haitian slave revolt inspired him. In 1821, he began plotting his own rebellion. Along with other freed slaves, he hoped to burn Charleston to the ground, kill all whites, and free all slaves. The revolt was set for June 16, 1822, but one of the plotters leaked the plans and Vesey and his conspirators were rounded up and hanged. (FAS)

BIBLIOGRAPHY

Edwards, Lillie J. *Denmark Vesey*. New York: Chelsea House, 1990.

Lofton, John. *Denmark Vesey's Revolt*. Kent, OH: Kent State University Press, 1983.

Vietnam War

The Vietnam War lasted from 1959 to 1975, the longest war in American history. It sparked violent controversy among Americans and changed the course of American politics, poisoning the general atmosphere and often seeming to make rational discourse impossible. The **civil rights movement** was no exception to the general rule of the period.

Most African Americans were opposed to confusing the issues of the Vietnam War and civil rights. However, **Martin Luther King, Jr.** believed that the Vietnam War was intimately connected with the civil rights movement because civil rights for African Americans were intrinsically linked with human rights around the world. By 1967, King had become a major anti-Vietnam War advocate and was deeply involved in the peace movement. African Americans were clearly over-represented in the military and on the front lines, and African-American veterans received less education than non-veterans, made no income advances over those who were not in the military, and suffered a greater percentage of casualties, including fatalities, than other American soldiers.

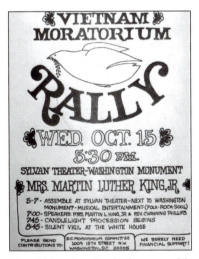

Many African-American leaders opposed the Vietnam War because they believed it was wasting black lives and depriving black communities of the money they needed to develop. *National Archives.*

Noting that the Vietnam War drew money away from President Lyndon Johnson's War on Poverty, King saw racism, militarism, and economic exploitation as related phenomena. Blacks were being exploited in the Vietnam War by being sent to slaughter and by losing money to war that could have been used to build up their communities. Moreover, J. Edgar Hoover, the director of the Federal Bureau of Investigation, used the Vietnam War as a further excuse to increase his campaign against the civil rights movement. Malcolm X had warned African Americans that they had no interest in the Vietnam War and that their energies should go into winning the war in black communities. Boxer Muhammad Ali took this message to heart, stating that "No Cong has ever called me Nigger!" and refusing to be drafted. Although he ultimately won the legal battle, he lost his boxing title without taking a punch in the ring.

Hoover harassed King for the rest of King's life. Some trace King's growing radicalism to his involvement in the peace movement as well as his growing agreement with Malcolm X's message. Certainly, King became more open to Black Power themes and more hostile to white capitalism. The war diverted American efforts from needed reforms, cost almost 60,000 lives, and diverted the normal development of political movements. It took a proportionately greater toll on African Americans than on others but cost all Americans a great deal in the long run. (FAS)

BIBLIOGRAPHY

Loch, Jeff. "MIA: African American Autobiography of the Vietnam War." *African American Review* 37, no. 3 (1997): 105–23.

Malcolm X. *The Autobiography of Malcolm X, with Alex Haley.* New York: Ballantine Books, 1965.

O'Reilly, Kenneth. "The Boss: J. Edgar Hoover and the Great American Inquisition." *Policy Studies Journal* 21, no. 3 (1996): 609–14.

Teachman, Jay D. and R.A. Call Vaughn. "The Effect of Military Service on Educational, Occupational, and Income Attainment." *Social Science Research* 25, no. 1 (1996): 1–31.

Village of Arlington Heights v. Metropolitan Housing Corporation (1977)

The Metropolitan Housing Corporation, a nonprofit developer sought to build high-density, low-income housing in the village of Arlington Heights, Illinois. The application for applicable permits were denied because the project violated zoning practices established by the village. The Housing Corporation challenged the constitutionality of the restrictive zoning practices, claiming that the ordinance was discriminatory and violated the Equal Protection Clause of the **Fourteenth Amendment.** In *Village of Arlington Heights v. Metropolitan Housing Corporation,* 429 US 252 (1977), the U.S. Supreme Court ruled that while the zoning practices of the village did bar the particular plan put forth by the corporation, the zoning practices themselves were not discriminatory and did not violate the equal protection clause. **See** the text of the Fourteenth Amendment in "Civil War Amendments" in Appendix 1.

BIBLIOGRAPHY

Barker, Lucius J. and Twiley W. Barker, Jr. *Civil Liberties and the Constitution.* Englewood Cliffs, NJ: Prentice Hall, 1994.

Cordy Tindell Vivian (1942–)

Cordy Tindell Vivian was born in Howard County, Missouri. He received two doctorates, one in 1984 from the New School for Social Research and another in 1987 from Western Illinois University (where he had received his bachelor's degree). Vivian has been active in civil rights and in church affairs. He is a past national director of the National Baptist Convention and a member of a number of civil rights organizations. He participated in the **March on Washington** in 1963, was an organizer for the **Southern Christian Leadership Conference (SCLC),** and is an author and editor of note. He has been named among the "100 Most Successful Blacks" by *Ebony* magazine.

BIBLIOGRAPHY

Walker, Lydia. *Challenge and Change.* Aldparetta, GA: W.H. Wolfe Assoeul, 1913.

Voter Education Project (VEP)

Begun in 1961, the Voter Education Project (VEP) was a joint effort between the federal government and civil rights organizations to boost black registration in the South. Rather than promoting protest against social and economic **discrimination,** the VEP's main goal was gaining black representation in politics. Between 1962 and 1964, the program added more than 287,000 new black voters to registration lists. Although the federal government supported the VEP, it did little to protect workers who met strong resistance in rural areas.

BIBLIOGRAPHY

Lawson, Steven F. *Black Ballots: Voting Rights in the South.* New York: 1976.

Voting Rights Act of 1965

The Voting Rights Act of 1965 was landmark legislation passed by Congress for the purpose of assuring black registration and voting in the South. Although Congress had passed two civil rights bills in 1957 and 1960 to protect the rights of black voters, some states still took measures to limit black participation. Following the March 1965 assault on voting rights marchers by Alabama state troopers, President Lyndon Johnson pushed for the swift passage of a bill to guarantee black voting rights. The Voting Rights Act was passed by both houses of Congress by August. The law was considered to be sweeping in scope and strong in remedy. Section 2 of the act applied to the entire county, and provided legal relief for minorities who experience political discrimination on the basis of race. The law specifically prohibits state actions adopted with the purpose of abridging the rights of blacks to vote. In certain cases, the attorney general could send federal election officials to states to guarantee fair voting practices.

Perhaps the most controversial part of the act was Section 5, which applied only to states where turnout in the 1964 presidential election had been less than 50 percent. This clause targeted most states in the South, where the problems of black registration were most pronounced. For these states, the law suspended literacy tests and froze all other legislation regarding voting and elections. For any covered state government to change an election law or procedure, the attorney general had to certify that the proposed changes would not cause harm to minority voters. If the attorney general was satisfied, the change would be approved (or pre-cleared) for the state to enact.

The legislation had immediate impact. Millions of African Americans were registered in the first few months after the law's passage. In 1975 and 1982, the act was amended to protect the rights of Mexican Americans and other language minorities in southwestern states.

BIBLIOGRAPHY

Garrow, David J. *Protest at Selma.* New Haven, CT: Yale University Press, 1978.

Parker, Frank R. *Black Votes Count*. Chapel Hill: University of North Carolina Press, 1990.

Voting Rights Act Amendments of 1982

The most recent alterations to the **Voting Rights Act of 1965** were the 1982 amendments that expanded protections for minority voting rights against state legislation. The amendments were largely informed by *Mobile v. Bolden*, a case in which the U.S. Supreme Court concluded an electoral system or law violated the Voting Rights Act only if it was adopted with the intent to discriminate. Congress amended Section 2 of the act to prohibit state actions with either intent or purpose of limiting the opportunity of minorities to choose a candidate of their choice. An important qualification on this amendment was the Dole Proviso, which stated that nothing in the amendment established or supported a requirement for proportional representation for minorities. Minority plaintiffs in many states sued governments under the plan and used evidence of systematic under-representation of minority candidates to demonstrate the effect of limited voting rights. (KC)

BIBLIOGRAPHY

Grofman, Bernard, Lisa Handley, and Richard G. Niemi. *Minority Representation and the Quest for Voting Equality*. New York: Cambridge University Press, 1992.

David Walker (1785–1830)

David Walker was born in Wilmington, North Carolina, of a slave father and a free African-American mother. During his travels in the South, Walker witnessed the brutality and horrors of **slavery** firsthand, which made him determined to fight slavery and its inhumanity. In 1827, at the age of 30, he left the South and settled in Boston, where he became a leader in Boston's Colored Association. In 1829, Walker wrote an anti-slavery pamphlet called *An Appeal to the Colored Citizens of the World,* urging American slaves to fight for their freedom. Its publication and subsequent popularity marked the beginning of the radical anti-slavery movement in the United States. Walker died in 1830 under mysterious circumstances, reportedly of poisoning. (EC)

BIBLIOGRAPHY

Turner, James. *David Walker's Appeal, to the Colored Citizens of the World, Introduction.* Baltimore: Black Classic Press, 1993.

Josiah Thomas Walls (1842–1905)

Josiah T. Walls, an African-American Republican from Florida, was elected to the United States House of Representatives in 1871. He served in Congress until 1873, at which time he lost his seat as a result of a contested election. Walls was re-elected in 1873 and remained in Congress until 1876. Walls was a delegate to the 1868 Florida constitutional convention and a member of the Florida State Senate (1869–1872).

BIBLIOGRAPHY

Klingman, Peter D. *Josiah Walls: Florida's Black Congressman of Reconstruction.* Gainesville: University Press of Florida, 1976.

War on Poverty

The "War on Poverty" is the popular name for a barrage of anti-poverty programs unleashed by the U.S. federal government between 1964 and 1972. The Economic Opportunity Act of 1964 initiated the War on Poverty; it poured resources for community development, job training, and housing into local communities. While the New Deal in the 1930s and the privatized welfare benefits won by organized labor in the 1940s and 1950s failed to address the status of people of color in any fundamental way, the War on Poverty—the centerpiece of President Lyndon Baines Johnson's Great Society programs—targeted them for inclusion.

The core anti-poverty program was community action, which was under the jurisdiction of the new Office of Economic Opportunity (OEO). The OEO, in turn, delegated responsibility to Community-Action Agencies (CAAs). CAAs established neighborhood health centers, emergency food and medical services, job and literacy training, counseling for alcoholics and drug addicts, and other assistance efforts. CAAs also supplied resources to local civil rights organizations, which used these resources to pursue the struggle for political equality.

A second focus of the War on Poverty was job training, which ultimately led to **affirmative action.** Existing job-training programs were expanded, and new programs were added. The Job Corps, the Neighborhood Youth Corps, the Manpower Development and Training Act (MDTA), Jobs in the Business Sector (JOBS), and the other programs all targeted job training to African-American youth.

A third focus was increasing housing for the poor and improving the quality of life in inner cities. Toward this end, Congress in 1968 enacted a Model Cities program. Congress also created the Department of Housing and Urban Development (HUD) to administer housing programs and signal the nation that urban aid would have a special place at the federal level. Other key reform targets in this area were health care and education. In 1965, the Medicaid and Medicare programs were created to improve health care for the poor and elderly, and the Elementary and Secondary Education Act, which greatly increased federal support for poor school districts, was passed.

Although the War on Poverty did not seriously dent the forces that generate want nor create a society of racial equality, it did alleviate many of the consequences of poverty in America. Millions of people, most of them elderly, were able to escape poverty; others whose incomes remained below the poverty line found medical care, food, housing assistance, and income security at a level unprecedented in America's past.

Overall, the War on Poverty coupled with the strong economy of the 1960s managed to cut the poverty rate from the mid-double digits in the 1960s to the high single digits in the early 1970s. Poverty among blacks shrank from 54.9 percent in 1959 to 29.3 percent in 1974 and among whites from 16.5 percent to 7.3 percent during the same period. Among children, poverty rates declined from 27 percent in 1960 to 15 percent in 1974, a decisive (though short-lived) improvement; federal grants helped bring the percentage of black 18– to 24–year olds enrolled in college up from 13 percent in 1965 to 22.6 percent by 1975, a trend that, if it had continued, would have produced racial parity in education by 1983; and affirmative action provided black, Latino, and female college graduates opportunities that had previously eluded them and reduced racial and gender wage differentials.

These trends not only slowed after the mid-1970s but for people of color began to reverse. Some concluded that the War on Poverty had been a dismal failure; others concluded that although some programs had not worked, there had been some inspiring successes. What was certain was that long before the conservative decade of the 1980s, the War on Poverty had been effectively gutted. The OEO and several key antipoverty programs had been abolished and spending had slowed in the 1970s. During President Ronald Reagan's and George Bush's administrations, additional programs were eliminated or sharply cut back; and in 1996 Democratic President Bill Clinton signed a Republican-initiated measure that virtually eliminated the remnants of many War on Poverty programs and ended the federal government commitment, which had been in place since the New Deal, to guaranteeing at least a modicum of income security to all citizens. Although poverty levels remained dramatically high in the late 1990s, the forces in what was known as the War on Poverty had surrendered. (LFW)

BIBLIOGRAPHY

Katz, Michael. *The Undeserving Poor: From the War on Poverty to the War on Welfare.* New York: Pantheon Books, 1989.

Piven, Frances and Richard Cloward. *Regulating the Poor: The Functions of Public Welfare.* New York: Vintage, 1971.

Quadagno, Jill. *The Color of Welfare: How Racism Undermined the War on Poverty.* New York: Oxford University Press, 1994.

Schwarz, John. *America's Hidden Success: A Reassessment of Twenty Years of Public Policy.* New York: Norton, 1983.

Wards Cove Packing Company v. Antonio (1989)

Nonwhite Alaskan cannery workers claimed discrimination due to unfair promotional practices by which they claimed that they were systematically excluded from higher paying jobs in *Wards Cove Packing Company v. Antonio,* 490 U.S. 642 (1989). According to Barker and Barker, the workers gathered a substantive body of evidence to support their case; nevertheless, the Supreme Court rejected their arguments, contending that the absence of minorities in skilled jobs simply "reflects a dearth of qualified nonwhite applicants." Supporters of **affirmative action** were devastated by Justice Byron White's claim that the burden of proof "remains with the plaintiff at all times." (EP)

BIBLIOGRAPHY

Barker, Lucius J. and Twiley W. Barker, Jr. *Civil Liberties and the Constitution: Cases and Commentaries.* Englewood Cliffs, NJ: Prentice Hall, 1994.

Epstein, Lee and Thomas G. Walker. *Constitutional Law for a Changing America: Rights, Liberties, and Justice.* 2nd ed. Washington, DC: CQ Press, 1995.

Booker Taliaferro Washington (1856–1915)

Booker T. Washington was an educator and powerful advocate for southern black educational and economic self-help programs in the post **Civil War** period. The most influential black in the United States of his time, he believed that blacks would gain wider and more rapid acceptance in southern communities if they provided the services and products whites needed. In 1881, Washington established and became the head of the Tuskegee Institute in Tuskegee, Alabama. The Institute offered African Americans practical training in various trades and professions. By Washington's death in 1915, Tuskegee Institute had over 100 buildings, a faculty of 200, a student body of 1,500, and an endowment of $2 million. In 1900, Washington established the National Negro Business League to provide an economic base for further black advancement. In 1906, he turned down an offer of a cabinet post in the Roosevelt administration.

Booker T. Washington, one of the most important post-Civil War black leaders, was conciliatory and gradualist in his approach to civil rights, believing that African Americans had to gradually earn the respect of whites and political rights through their own efforts at economic and social advancement. *Library of Congress.*

Washington was conciliatory in his approach to civil rights, believing that blacks had to gradually earn the respect of whites and political rights through their own efforts at economic and social advancement. This approach, summed up in his speech at the opening of the 1895 Atlanta Cotton States Exposition, turned black intellectuals against him, especially **W.E.B. Du Bois,** who accused Washington of downplaying civil rights, and of "practically accepting the alleged inferiority of the Negro races." Civil Rights leaders of the 1960s viewed Washington's approach as reactionary. However, by the late 1980s, many militants, disillusioned with government-sponsored welfare programs, began to endorse economic strategies for black advancement similar to Washington's.

Born into slavery at Hale's Ford, Virginia, Washington graduated in 1876 from the Hampton Normal and Agricultural Institute in Virginia. He died November 14, 1915, at Tuskegee. (ISM)

BIBLIOGRAPHY

Harlan, Louis R. *Booker T. Washington: The Making of a Black Leader, 1856–1901*. New York: Oxford University Press, 1972.

Washington, Booker T. *Up From Slavery*. Garden City, NY: Doubleday & Co., 1901.

Harold Washington (1922–1987)

Harold Washington, a Democrat, was elected in 1983 as the first black mayor of Chicago, where he made significant structural and programmatical reforms. He outlawed patronage hiring and firing, imposed a $1500 cap on campaign contributions from companies doing business with the city, increased racial and ethnic diversity in the city administration, and aided women and minorities in competing with white male contractors. He appointed Chicago's first black police chief and tried to provide city services more equitably to the black community. Washington had served in the Illinois House of Representatives (1965–1976); in the Illinois Senate (1976–1980); and represented the Illinois 1st Congressional District in the U.S. House of Representatives (1981–1983). In Congress, Washington fought to extend the **Voting Rights Act of 1965** in 1982, he supported a nuclear freeze and a 20 percent cut in defense spending, and he was secretary of the **Congressional Black Caucus**. (EC)

BIBLIOGRAPHY

Starks, Robert T. and Michael B. Preston. "Harold Washington and the Politics of Reform in Chicago: 1983–1987." In Rufus P. Browning, Dale R. Marshall, and David H. Tabb, eds. *Racial Politics in American Cities*. New York: Longman, 1990.

Walter Edward Washington (1915–)

Walter Washington was elected mayor of the District of Columbia in 1974 and served until 1979. Before becoming its mayor, Washington served as the District's Commissioner, having been appointed to this position by President Lyndon Baines Johnson in 1967. From 1966 to 1967, he was the chairman of the New York City Housing Authority. Washington was Executive Director of the **National Association for the Advancement of Colored People (NAACP)** from 1961 until 1965.

BIBLIOGRAPHY

Picott, J. Rupert, ed. *Walter Washington*. Washington DC: ASALH, 1976.

Washington v. Davis (1976)

Washington v Davis, 426 U.S. 229 (1976), involved a challenge that a written test for applicants for the Washington, D.C., police force was discriminatory on racial grounds because more than four times as many African Americans failed the examination as whites. The Supreme Court dismissed the challenge claiming that this represented de facto discrimination, (discrimination that has its basis in something other than merely race) and that to attack de facto discrimination, the applicants needed to show that the city clearly intended to discriminate under the equal protection clause of the **Fourteenth Amendment**. (RLP)

BIBLIOGRAPHY

Epstein, Lee and Thomas G. Walker. *Constitutional Law for a Changing America: Rights, Liberties, and Justice*. 2nd ed. Washington, DC: CQ Press, 1995.

Maxine Waters (1938–)

In 1991, Maxine Waters became the U.S. representative from the 35th District of South Central Los Angeles. Her political career began in 1976 as an Assemblywoman in the California Assembly. Maxine Waters is described as unequivocally "unapologetic," "intractable," and "recalcitrant" when finding ways to focus national interest upon improving the lives of women, African Americans, and the poor. Throughout her political career Waters has tried to authentically represent the interests of those most disenfranchised in American society, and to this end she has successfully pushed through Congress the Gang Prevention and Youth Recreation Act (1995) and the Job and Life Skills Improvement Act (1997). She advocates for the rehabilitation of national and state prison systems, gun control, and the abandonment of capital punishment. Waters' foreign policy initiatives include extensive work with **Randall Robinson** and Trans-Africa concerning political turmoil in South Africa and Haiti. (RAM)

BIBLIOGRAPHY

Gill, Laverne McCain. *African American Women in Congress: Forming and Transforming History*. New Brunswick, NJ: Rutgers University Press, 1997.

Watson v. Fort Worth Bank and Trust (1988)

In *Watson v. Fort Worth Bank and Trust*, 487 U.S. 977 (1988), the plaintiff sued her employer after she was passed over several times for promotion in favor of white employees. She claimed that her employer lacked clear promotion standards and allowed supervisors to make subjective promotion decisions. The Supreme Court noted that facially neutral policies can sometimes have a discriminatory effect, a "disparate impact," as when supervisors have latent prejudices or hold racial stereotypes. However, they concluded that the burden resides exclusively with the plaintiff to identify specific employment practices which lead to statistical outcomes clearly establishing a pattern of discrimination. (FHJ)

BIBLIOGRAPHY

Alessandra, Anita M. "When Doctrines Collide: Disparate Treatment, Disparate Impact, and *Watson v Fort Worth Bank & Trust*." *University of Pennsylvania Law Review* 137, no. 5 (May 1989): 1755–90.

Halverson, Karen. "Title VII: Application of Impact Analysis to Subjective Employment Criteria." [Case note]. *Harvard Civil Rights—Civil Liberties Law Review* 24, no. 1 (Winter 1989): 264–75.

Melvin L. Watt (1945–)

After graduating from Yale Law School, Melvin Watt began his practice as a civil rights attorney during the **civil rights movement** of the 1960s. In 1992, he was elected to the U.S. House of Representatives from North Carolina as a Democrat. Upon entering the House, he was selected to serve on the Steering and Policy Committee and the Banking and Finance Committee. He used his membership on these committees to continue his efforts as a civil rights advocate by sponsoring legislation including a bill to continue funding Legal Services lawyers. A consistently liberal voter, Watt has voted against nearly every measure to increase penalties for crimes. He continues to serve on the Banking and Financial Services and also serves on the Judiciary Committee. **See also** Congressional Black Caucus. (CEM)

BIBLIOGRAPHY
Barone, Michael. *The Almanac of American Politics.* Washington, D.C.: National Journal, 1998.
"North Carolina." *Congressional Quarterly Weekly Report* 50, no. 44 (November 7, 1992): 44–45.

J.C. Watts (1956–)

At the end of the 1990s, J.C. Watts from Oklahoma was the only African-American Republican serving in the U.S. House of Representatives; he was elected in 1994 to a vacant seat. Watts, a Christian conservative, became a national spokesman for the Republican Party, addressing the Republican National Convention and delivering the Republican Response to the President Bill Clinton's 1996 State of the Union address. A native of Oklahoma, Watts was a star athlete at the University of Oklahoma and played professional football in Canada before opening a real estate and petroleum marketing firm in 1986. In 1990, he was elected to the Oklahoma Corporation Commission, where he served as chair from 1992 to 1994. In the House, he serves on the National Security Committee and the Transportation and Infrastructure Committee.

BIBLIOGRAPHY
McCoy, Frank. "Thanks But No Thanks." *Black Enterprise* 25, no. 12 (July 1995): 22.
Watts, J.C. "Republican Response to the State of the Union Address." *Vital Speeches of the Day* 63, no. 10 (1997): 296–98.

Robert C. Weaver (1907–1997)

Robert C. Weaver was born in Washington, D.C., and died in New York City. He was an adviser to three presidents in the course of a distinguished career that saw him as director of the **National Association for the Advancement of Colored People (NAACP),** the first African American in the president's cabinet (secretary of Housing and Urban Development under Lyndon Johnson), and president of Baruch College among many other vital jobs. At the start of his career, Weaver was part of President Franklin Roosevelt's "Black Cabinet," a group of men who served as informal advisors. He served in a number of government posts for Roosevelt. Weaver was also a professor at Hunter College and Carnegie-Mellon University. His B.A., M.A., and Ph.D. were from Harvard. Weaver wrote four books addressing several topics including urban renewal, federalism, and discrimination in housing. Weaver also served on the agency that helped New York City recover from its financial crisis in the 1970s. Weaver spent his life breaking down racial barriers in American life. (FAS)

BIBLIOGRAPHY
Williams, Alma Renee. "Robert C. Weaver: From the Black Cabinet to the President's Cabinet." Ph.D. dissertation, Washington University, 1978.

Wellington E. Webb (1941–)

Wellington Webb was elected mayor of Denver, Colorado, in 1991, having previously run unsuccessfully in 1983, and was re-elected in 1995. Prior to serving as Denver's mayor, Webb was city auditor from 1988 to 1992. From 1973 to 1977, Webb served in the Colorado House of Representatives, and chaired the House Democratic Caucus in 1975. Webb was also chairperson of the United Negro College Fund from 1973 to 1975. After serving as the state chair for President Jimmy Carter's campaign in 1976, Webb served as regional director of the U.S. Department of Health, Education and Welfare from 1977 until 1980 when he accepted a state cabinet post.

BIBLIOGRAPHY
Tucker, Deborah L. *To Make a Mayor.* Lantham, MD: University Press of America, 1995.

Welfare

Although many think of welfare policies as only those government actions aimed at alleviating the plight of the poor, welfare actually is more accurately defined as all actions pursued under government authority designed to affect the free play of the economic market in the interests of addressing economic inequality in capitalist systems. Thus some welfare policies are aimed at the poor, but other policies are also designed for the middle class.

For example, the federal government promotes the social welfare of the middle class in a variety of ways. Pensions and medical care for retired persons help the middle class by relieving them of the burden of caring for their elderly relatives; tax expenditures (such as the exemption from taxation of payments that employers and employees make for pensions and health insurance and tax deductions of payments for home mortgage interest) make it easier and less expensive for working Americans to save for retirement, obtain health care, and buy homes. Tax expenditures mainly benefit the middle class and the more affluent and are less visible than welfare programs that provide direct payments or services. However, tax expenditures represent a heavy investment, costing the federal government in excess of $300 billion a year. Because white Americans are more likely to be affluent than are people of color, middle-class whites benefit most from tax expenditures—a factor partially explaining the strong popularity of tax expenditures and why Congress rarely considers reducing them.

By contrast, currently and historically, the group that has received the least welfare is the working poor. These people—who earn incomes below or just above the poverty line—often work in jobs that do not provide pensions or health care and often are renters because they cannot afford to buy homes. Consequently, the working poor cannot benefit from tax expenditures, and yet they cannot get assistance through programs that are largely restricted to the nonworking poor. Food stamps and the Earned Income Tax Credit (EITC) are two programs, however, that assist the working poor. EITC, implemented in 1976, provides a modest wage supplement for the working poor through the tax code. Food stamps also supplement the income of poor workers.

Participants celebrate the adoption of the welfare plank at the National Women's Conference. *National Archives.*

Although these two programs supply limited assistance to the working poor, their plight has worsened in the closing years of the twentieth century. As a result of the declining wages of less-educated workers and the failure of the minimum wage to keep pace with inflation in the 1970s, 1980s, and 1990s, studies show that the fastest growing group of poor people in the United States are the working poor. Disproportionately composed of people of color, the working poor's very limited support from government is an ironic development in a country that claims to value work so highly.

Neither the relatively substantial welfare that goes to the middle class nor the very limited support for the working poor has garnered the attention of most Americans. Instead, when Americans think of welfare, they usually point to programs that assist the nonworking poor, especially programs for poor children and the parents who take care of them. These programs have a relatively recent vintage in the United States and remain meager compared to similar programs in the advanced industrialized democracies of Western Europe.

Indeed, for much of American history, the federal government was not involved in caring for the poor. Instead, local governments, private charities, and philanthropically inclined rich individuals were the only sources of help for America's poor. It took an economic crisis of major proportions, the Great Depression of the 1930s, to bring the federal government into creating policies to assist the poor and promote economic security.

During the Depression, misfortune became so widespread that **poverty** and dependency were accepted as problems inherent in the capitalist economic system. Many on the left adopted the view was that workers suffered from unforeseen market forces they could not control and that these forces could produce involuntary unemployment: economic need was not necessarily a sign of individual failure. For Americans, this was a dramatic new idea about individual need. By the time President Franklin D. Roosevelt (FDR) took office in 1933, the question was not whether there would be a public welfare system, but how generous or restrictive that system would be and who it would help.

The answer to the first of these questions was provided in the Social Security Act of 1935. The central idea behind the act was that the federal government had the ability and the responsibility to create a healthy economy and play a role in providing for individual economic security. But the Social Security Act (and other parts of FDR's New Deal) did not wholly transform American ideas about government's responsibility toward individuals in need. Suspicion of unearned handouts continued, and many critics wanted eligibility for services and benefits to be conditioned on past employment and individual work histories.

The Social Security Act reflected these criteria. It created two separate categories of welfare: contributory and noncontributory. Contributory programs are financed by taxation, forcing working Americans to set aside a portion of their current earnings to provide income and benefits during their retirement years. Social Security (old-age pensions) and Medicare (health care benefits for the elderly) are premier examples of such programs. Noncontributory programs are programs to which beneficiaries are not required to contribute; they are also known as "public assistance programs" or, derisively, as "welfare." Until 1996, the premier example of a noncontributory program was Aid to Families with Dependent Children (AFDC, originally called Aid to Dependent Children or ADC in the Social Security Act of 1935). Other noncontributory programs are Medicaid (a program providing medical services to low-income persons), food stamps (coupons that can be exchanged for food in most grocery stores), and housing assistance. To receive assistance from a noncontributory program, a person or family must meet a means test (a procedure that requires applicants to demonstrate a financial need for assistance).

The segmentation of welfare into these two main categories in 1935 has had an important effect on American social policy ever since. Given the two types of programs, the tendency has been to consider one type (contributory) as programs for the "deserving poor," and the other (noncontributory) for the "undeserving poor."

Buttressing this tendency is the reality that contributory and noncontributory welfare policies serve radically different clienteles. The two strongest and most generous contributory policies (Social Security and Medicare) serve the elderly. These programs have significantly reduced the poverty rate among the elderly and are politically popular. Their popularity stems from a variety of circumstances: first, the elderly are widely seen as a deserving population (because they are not expected to work due to their age). Second, because a work history is required for receiving Social Security benefits and Medicare, people tend to be supportive of helping past workers. Third, the elderly are a very large politically powerful group. There were more than 32 million Americans over the age of 65 in 1996, and the elderly vote in higher numbers than other age grouping in the population. Just as important, the elderly have developed strong and sophisticated lobbying organizations (most notably, the American Association of Retired Persons—AARP) that can influence policy making and mobilize elderly Americans to defend these programs against proposals to cut them. Fourth, because Social Security and Medicare are universal programs (that is, they are available to *all* former workers and their spouses over the age of 65, whether they are poor or not), they are popular with a wide swath of people in virtually every racial, gender, and class group. Yet it is important to note that contributory welfare programs such as Social Security and Medicare continue to benefit whites disproportionately, because whites compose a larger share of the recipients than their share in the population and have a longer life expectancy than people of color (and thereby whites tend to draw benefits longer). Consequently, contributory programs have escaped being stigmatized as programs committed to helping poor people of color and often are not even thought of as "welfare" in the minds of many Americans.

Just as contributory programs have remained exceptionally popular, noncontributory ones, conversely, have become increasingly unpopular and have been at the center of heated debate. Conservatives, especially, have attacked noncontributory programs for decades. They argue that rather than helping the poor to become self-sufficient, noncontributory programs encourage them to become dependent.

AFDC in particular was singled out, and in the 1970s and 1980s it became the most unpopular social spending program in the country. By not allowing AFDC benefits to keep pace with inflation, the federal government allowed the real value of these benefits to drop by roughly 40 percent in the 1970s and 1980s. As a result, overall spending on welfare for the nonworking poor plunged in the 1980s and 1990s.

In the 1990s, one means conservatives proposed to undercut such programs further was to replace existing welfare programs such as AFDC with aid directly to the states through block grants. In 1996, with Republicans in control of Congress, AFDC was abolished and replaced by the Temporary Assistance to Needy Families (TANF) block grant. Eligibility for TANF is determined by means testing (as it was for AFDC), but unlike AFDC, TANF ended the federal guarantee to all citizens of at least a modicum of economic security not dependent upon the market.

TANF has not only ended the individual entitlement to benefits, but it also requires the head of each family receiving welfare to work within two years or lose assistance, requires teen parents to live with a responsible adult, and establishes a lifetime limit of five years on the receipt of assistance. States are allowed to cap the aid of parents on welfare who have additional children, impose shorter time limits than five years, and exclude teen parents from assistance altogether. Under TANF, spending on welfare for the nonworking poor is expected to fall further. This dramatic reform of noncontributory welfare raises many new questions about whether there will be enough jobs paying a living wage for welfare recipients, whether the block grants to states will provide adequate funds in the future, and whether states will be able to administer welfare effectively. These concerns suggest that the 1996 law may turn out to be little more than a prelude to a round of future welfare reform.

What is already clear, however, is that TANF plunges the nation's nonworking poor into a completely new policy context. A number of reasons explain why it was possible to alter the nation's main noncontributory program so dramatically. First, the recipients of AFDC are widely viewed as undeserving, because they do not work. Second, they have little political muscle. Not only do poor people vote at a lower rate than do more affluent citizens, but also, as a result of their meager resources for organizing, welfare recipients have no lobby like the elderly's AARP. Thus they have little political power to resist cuts in their benefits and have played only the most limited part in recent debates about welfare. Third—and relatedly—the nonworking poor are disproportionately people of color and women, the groups that conservatives have found easy to stigmatize. For instance, conservatives have promoted the view that blacks in particular prefer welfare to work, ignoring the reality that blacks have never composed the majority of welfare recipients and that blacks are disproportionately represented among the welfare clientele simply because they are also much more likely to be poor than white Americans. Much of their poverty is the result of disadvantages that stem from racism as well as the position of people of color in the labor market. African Americans, Latinos, and Native Americans in particular tend to be economically less well off than white Americans. They are more likely than whites are to be stuck in low-wage, dead-end jobs, more likely to become unemployed and to remain unemployed for longer periods of time, and more likely to work in jobs that do not provide access to government-subsidized private pensions and health care services. Women, too, are more likely to be poor than men are, leading policy analysts in recent decades to talk about the "feminization of poverty." This problem is especially acute for single mothers, who are more than twice as likely to fall below the poverty line than the average American.

In the late 1990s, the typical welfare recipient in the United States was a 29–year-old white woman with two children who received less than $300 a month in benefits. Yet, because politicians, media commentators, and academics alike have focused disproportionately on poor blacks as welfare recipients and have distorted the level of the meager and declining benefits going to the poor, support for welfare for the working and nonworking poor has grown ever more precarious. Indeed since its inception, welfare policy in the United States has been confounded by the politics of race. **See also** Political Participation; Racism. (LFW)

BIBLIOGRAPHY

Katz, Michael. *The Undeserving Poor: From the War on Poverty to the War on Welfare.* New York: Pantheon, 1989.

Light, Paul. *Artful Work: The Politics of Social Security Reform.* New York: Random House, 1985.

Marmor, Theodore R., Jerry L. Mashaw, and Phillip L. Harvey. *America's Misunderstood Welfare State.* New York: Basic Books, 1990.

Patterson, James T. *America's Struggle against Poverty, 1900–1994.* Cambridge, MA: Harvard University Press, 1994.

Piven, Frances Fox and Richard A. Cloward. *Regulating the Poor.* New York: Pantheon, 1971.

Schwarz, John E. *America's Hidden Success: A Reassessment of Twenty Years of Public Policy.* New York: W.W. Norton, 1988.

Weir, Margaret, ed. *The Social Divide: Political Parties and the Future of Activist Government.* Washington, DC: The Brookings Institution, 1988.

Ida B. Wells (1862–1931)

Ida B. Wells was a journalist and political reformer who campaigned from the 1890s through the 1920s against the lynching of African Americans. She was part owner of and a reporter for *Free Speech,* a Memphis, Tennessee, newspaper. In 1892, after three of her friends were lynched in Memphis, Wells began to investigate lynching and other violence against African Americans. Her speaking tours against lynching in New York and England led to the establishment of many anti-lynching organizations. She moved to Chicago in 1894 and married Ferdinand L. Barnett, a lawyer and journalist. In 1909, Wells-Barnett helped found the **National Association for the Advancement of Colored People (NAACP).** She was also an ardent campaigner for the suffragist movement. (EC)

BIBLIOGRAPHY

Duster, Alfreda, ed. *Crusade for Justice: The Autobiography of Ida B. Wells.* Chicago: University of Chicago Press, 1970.

Clifton Reginald Wharton, Jr. (1926–)

Clifton Wharton is an educator, business executive, and administrator. Wharton served as the first African-American president of Michigan State University (1970–1978), and he was the first African-American chancellor of the State University of New York (1978–1987). In 1987, he became the CEO of the Teachers Insurance Annuity Association and College Retirement Fund (TIAA–CREF), the nations's largest private pension system. Wharton served briefly as deputy secretary of State under President Bill Clinton (1992–1993), becoming the highest ranking African American in the State Department's history. During his tenure, Wharton worked to reform the Agency for International Development (AID) and to redirect foreign aid procedures. (EC)

BIBLIOGRAPHY

Wharton, Jr., Clifton. "Clifton Wharton, Jr.: America's Most Powerful Black Executive." *Black Enterprise* 23 (February 1993): 134.

Alan Dupree Wheat (1951–)

Alan Wheat (D-MO) was elected to the United States House of Representatives in 1983 and served until 1994. During his first term in Congress, Wheat earned a seat on the highly prestigious House Rules Committee. From 1977 to 1982, he was a member of the Missouri General Assembly. Wheat made an unsuccessful bid for the U.S. Senate in 1994.

BIBLIOGRAPHY

Cooper, Kenneth J. "Wheat Seeks to Add One More in U.S. Senate." *Emerge* 5, no. 6 (March 1994): 17.

Whitcomb v. Chavis (1971)

African-American residents of Marion County, Indiana, challenged the state statute that established the county as a multimember district for the purposes of electing state senators and representatives. A multimember district consists of a single district from which several representatives to the same body are chosen. This differs from a single member district in which multiple districts are drawn and a single representative is elected from each one. Plaintiffs argued that the use of a multimember district voting scheme diluted African-American votes, especially those of the inner city. They argued that single-member districts would ensure the election of at least one African-American representative, while the current system produced none. In *Whitcomb v. Chavis,* 415 U.S. 972 (1971), the United States Supreme Court rejected the claims of African-American plaintiffs and ruled that the multimember district did not infringe upon their voting rights.

BIBLIOGRAPHY

Barker, Lucius J. and Jesse J. McCorry, Jr. *Black Americans and the Political System.* Cambridge, MA: Winthrop Publishers, 1976.

George H. White (1852–1918)

George White was born a slave in North Carolina. He graduated from **Howard University** in 1877 and passed the North Carolina bar in 1879. He was elected to Congress in 1897 and served two terms where he actively supported anti-lynching legislation. He founded Whitesboro, an all-black town in New Jersey, in 1903.

BIBLIOGRAPHY

Ragsdale, Bruce and Joel Treese. *Black Americans in Congress 1870–1989.* Washington DC: U.S. Government Printing Office, 1990.

Michael R. White (1951–)

Michael White was born in Cleveland, Ohio, and served on the Cleveland city council from 1977 to 1984. He was a member of the state senate from 1984 to 1989. In 1989, he was elected mayor of Cleveland. A popular politician and recognized as one of the leaders of Cleveland's renaissance, White was re-elected mayor in 1997 for a third term.

BIBLIOGRAPHY

Walton, Hanes. *African American Power and Politics.* New York: Columbia University Press, 1997.

Walter Francis White (1893–1955)

Two years after graduating from Atlanta University in 1916, Walter F. White was appointed assistant secretary of the **Na-**

tional Association for the Advancement of Colored People **(NAACP)**. For the next four decades, White would work for NAACP, investigating lynchings and race riots and struggling to keep the organized solvent during the Depression. In 1931, he became executive secretary of NAACP (a post he held until his death in 1955) and focused the organization on fighting for constitutional rights. He also authored several books on race in America, including *Rope and Faggot* (1921), *The Fire in the Flint* (1924), *Flight* (1926), *A Rising Wind* (1948), and *How Far the Promised Land?* (1955). As executive secretary of NAACP, White worked with the Roosevelt and Truman administrations to secure legislation against **poll tax**. In 1945 and 1948 he served as an advisor to the U.S. delegation to the United Nations.

BIBLIOGRAPHY

Cannon. Poppy. *A Gentle Knight.* New York: Rinehart, 1956.

White, Walter F. *A Man Called White.* New York: Viking, 1948.

White v. Register (1973)

In *White v. Register,* 412 U.S. 755 (1973), the U.S. Supreme Court established that historical evidence could be considered to show racial discrimination in the political arena. Blacks and Mexican Americans in two Texas counties sued to invalidate multi-member legislative districts because they limited minority representation. While the Court ruled that the U.S. Constitution did not outlaw multi-member districts, it turned to a "blend of history and an intensely local appraisal of the design and impact of the [political] system" and concluded that minorities had less opportunity than other groups to elect candidates of their choice. Accordingly, the Court upheld the plaintiffs' claim "in the light of past and present reality, political and otherwise." (KC)

BIBLIOGRAPHY

Grofman, Bernard, Lisa Handley, and Richard G. Niemi. *Minority Representation and the Quest for Voting Equality.* New York: Cambridge University Press, 1992.

Lawrence Douglas Wilder (1931–)

When L. Douglas Wilder won the election for governor of Virginia in 1989, he became the first African American to be elected governor of a state. Wilder was named after **Frederick Douglass** and Paul Laurence Dunbar. Wilder had a distinguished career leading to his election as governor. He had been lieutenant governor of Virginia and the first black state senator in Virginia since **Reconstruction**. Wilder served as governor from 1990 to 1994. Wilder was also a presidential candidate and a candidate for the U. S. Senate, but both runs were unsuccessful. Currently Wilder writes a monthly newspaper column in Virginia.

BIBLIOGRAPHY

Edds, Margaret. *Claiming the Dream.* Chapel Hill, NC: Algonquin Books, 1990.

J. Ernest Wilkins (1894–1959)

J. Ernest Wilkins was born in Farmington, Missouri. He was a lawyer, a veteran of World War I, and a government official. He graduated from the University of Illinois in 1918, received his J.D. from the University of Chicago Law School after serving in the infantry in France, and in 1941 became president of the Cook County Bar Association. Wilkins's notable service for equal rights led to his appointment by President Dwight Eisenhower in 1953 as vice chairman of the Commission on Government Contracts. Wilkins's duties required him to oversee the fairness of hiring and promotions in companies that had government contracts. In 1954, Wilkins became the first African American appointed to a sub-Cabinet position when Eisenhower named him assistant secretary of Labor, a position he held until his retirement in 1958. (FAS)

BIBLIOGRAPHY

Fenno, Richard Francis. *The President's Cabinet.* New York: Vintage Books, 1959.

Roger Wilkins (1927–)

During the Johnson Administration (1963–1969) Roger Wilkins served as assistant attorney general and lobbied members of Congress for such notable causes as the food stamp program. Wilkins, a journalist, lawyer and writer, is a history professor at George Mason University, in northern Virginia. (VDD)

BIBLIOGRAPHY

Wilkins, Roger. *A Man's Life.* New York: Simon & Schuster Trade, 1982.

Roy Wilkins (1901–1981)

Roy Wilkins was executive director of the **National Association for the Advancement of Colored People (NAACP)** from 1965 to 1977. Before assuming these duties, Wilkins previously served as the organization's executive secretary from 1955 to 1964 and as assistant secretary from 1931 to 1949. He also served as president of the **Leadership Conference on Civil Rights** in 1969.

BIBLIOGRAPHY

Wilkins, Roy and Tom Mathews. *Standing Fast: The Autobiography of Roy Wilkins.* New York: Viking Press, 1982.

Eddie N. Williams (1932–)

Eddie Williams received his B.S. degree from University of Illinois at Urbana in 1954. He was a staff assistant for the U.S. Senate Committee on Foreign Relations and served as a foreign service officer for the State Department from 1961 to 1968. He joined the **Joint Center for Political and Economic Studies** in 1972, and oversaw the growth of the center from a $500,000 operation to an organization with a budget of more than $6.5 million and nearly 50 employees. As president, Williams has focused the Joint Center on producing reports and research that would help black politicians and public policy analysts. (JCW)

BIBLIOGRAPHY

French, Mary Ann. "The Think Tank, after the Deluge." *Washington Post* (March 23, 1995): C1.

Singletary, Michelle. "Eddie Williams, The Guiding Force at the Center." *Washington Post* (March 10, 1997): F9.

Franklin H. Williams (1917–)

Franklin Williams graduated from Fordham Law School in 1945. He served as West Coast regional director of the **National Association for the Advancement of Colored People (NAACP)** and was named ambassador to Ghana in 1965 by President Lyndon Baines Johnson. Upon his return to the United States he became president of the Phelps-Stokes fund, an organization designed to increase opportunities for African Americans and Native Americans. (JCW)

BIBLIOGRAPHY

Robinson, Walter. "New Prospects at the Barnes? (Franklin H. Williams, Barnes Foundation's New Trustee)." *Art in America.* 77, no. 3 (March 1989): 21.

George Washington Williams (1849–1891)

In 1862, George Washington Williams enlisted in the 6th Massachusetts Regiment, eventually earning a promotion to the staff of General N. J. Jackson. Despite his outstanding military service and the recommendation of numerous white officers, Williams was denied entry into the regular army. Running unsuccessfully for the Ohio State Legislature in 1877, he served in the office of the auditor and for the federal Internal Revenue Service. In 1879, he was elected to the Ohio legislature and served a single term. Appointed minister to Haiti in 1885, he served one year. In 1890, he was selected to be part of the U.S. delegation to the World Congress of Foreign Ministers in London. Williams became one of the first scholars of African-American history and wrote two important works, *The History of the Negro Race in America* and *A History of the Negro Troops in the War of Rebellion.*

BIBLIOGRAPHY

Franklin, John Hope. *George Washington Williams: A Biography.* Chicago: University of Chicago Press, 1985.

Hosea Williams (1926–)

Hosea Williams was a project director for the **Southern Christian Leadership Conference (SCLC)** and became executive director in 1971. He led the historic civil rights march on Selma, Alabama, in 1965. He is active in local politics, having served in the Georgia General Assembly as well as the Atlanta City Council.

BIBLIOGRAPHY

Garrow, David J. *Bearing the Cross: Martin Luther King, Jr., and the Southern Christian Leadership Conference.* New York: Vintage Books, 1988.

Margaret Ann "Maggie" Williams (1954–)

Margaret Williams was born in Kansas City, Missouri, and received her B.A. from the University of Pennsylvania. She was the communications director for the Children's Defense

Fund from 1984 to 1989 and a member of the Clinton/Gore campaign in 1992. She was appointed chief of staff to First Lady Hillary Rodham Clinton in 1993. (JCW)

BIBLIOGRAPHY

Sherrill, Martha. "Hillary Clinton's Stealth Communicator." *The Washington Post* (February 11, 1993): D1.

Williams v. Illinois (1970)

Williams was convicted of petty theft in Illinois and given the maximum sentence, one year in prison. Although indigent, he was also assessed a $500 fine and $5 court costs. After serving his sentence, Williams was forced to remain in jail to "work off" his fine and costs, at the rate of $5 per day, forcing him to serve an additional 101 days. In *Williams v. Illinois,* 399 U.S. 235 (1970), the Supreme Court found that Williams' equal protection rights under the **Fourteenth Amendment** had been violated because he was forced to serve a sentence beyond the statutory maximum purely because of his inability to pay the fine. **See also** Crime and Punishment. **See** the text of the Fourteenth Amendment in "Civil War Amendments" in Appendix 1.

BIBLIOGRAPHY

Mackey, David S. "Rationality Versus Proportionalilty: Reconsidering the Constitutional Limits on Criminal Sanctions." *Tennessee Law Review* 51 (Summer 1984): 623–79.

Williams v. Mississippi (1898)

Henry Williams, who was black, was indicted and convicted by an all-white jury in Mississippi and sentenced to death for murder. In *Williams v. Mississippi,* 170 U.S. 213 (1898), Williams appealed, claiming that his **Fourteenth Amendment** rights had been violated because he had been denied due process and equal protection. The jurors in Williams' trial were supposed to have been chosen from a list of voters who met race-neutral qualifications, but in fact no registration book of voters was used when the jurors were selected.

The U.S. Supreme Court upheld the verdict and the death sentence, stating that no Fourteenth Amendment rights were violated unless the discrimination was part of the state constitution or the laws of the state. In this case, the discrimination was in the administration of the Mississippi law and, therefore, not considered unconstitutional. **See also** Crime and Punishment. **See** the text of the Fourteenth Amendment in "Civil War Amendments" in Appendix 1.

BIBLIOGRAPHY

"Developments in the Law: Race and the Criminal Process." *Harvard Law Review* 101 (May 1988): 1479–93.

James Finley Wilson (1881–1952)

James F. Wilson, in 1920, was elected as first vice president of the National Negro Press Association. He served as its president from 1921 until 1924. In 1922, Wilson was elected Grand Exalted Ruler of the Elks' worldwide organization. While leading the Elks, he was instrumental in initiating programs that focused on civil liberties, education, health, and problems of the African-American community. Wilson also served as president of the Colored Voters League of America in 1933, as well as president of the International Association of Colored People of the World in 1945.

BIBLIOGRAPHY

Adams, Russell. *Great Negroes: Past and Present.* Chicago: Afro-American Publishing Company, Inc., 1984.

Wesley, Charles H. *History of the Improved Benevolent and Protective Order of Elks of the World, 1898–1954.* Washington DC: Association for the Study of Negro Life and History, 1955.

Lionel J. Wilson (1915–1998)

Lionel Wilson received his law degree from Hastings College of Law in 1949. After 10 years in private practice, he was appointed a judge of the Oakland Piedmont municipal court in 1960. In 1964, he was appointed to the state superior court. He was elected mayor of Oakland, California, in 1977 and served three terms.

BIBLIOGRAPHY

Woody, Bette. *Managing Crisis Cities.* Westport, CT: Greenwood Press, 1982.

Womanism

African-American feminists have long been considered aliens in the black community. For many political activists, feminism is viewed as an impediment to the more important struggle against racism. Nonetheless, black academics and popular writers defend feminism as a liberating force in the black community that holds the potential to free black women from the staggering effects of racism and sexism.

At the same time, however, black feminists look for ways to differentiate themselves from mainstream white feminism. This need to differentiate is what prompted novelist Alice Walker to coin the phrase "Womanism." Feminism, African Americans like Walker found, was essentially a white woman's concern. Womanism, on the other hand, softens the feminist agenda and in the process becomes a black woman's philosophy. Womanists differentiate themselves from feminists by stressing a holistic, nurturing concern for the community, organic connections to a freedom struggle, and a more moderate critique of the nuclear family. (VDD)

BIBLIOGRAPHY

Heywood, Leslie and Jennifer Drake. *Third Wave Agenda: Being Feminist, Doing Feminism.* Minneapolis: University of Minnesota Press, 1997.

Jonathan Jasper Wright (1840–1885)

Jonathan Jasper Wright became the first African American to be admitted to the Pennsylvania Bar in 1866. Upon returning to his native South Carolina, Wright served as a legal advisor to refugees and freedman until 1868. In 1868, Wright was a delegate to the South Carolina state constitutional convention. Appointed to the South Carolina Supreme Court in 1870, he served until his retirement in 1879.

BIBLIOGRAPHY

Rees, Matthew. *From the Deck to the Sea.* Wakefield, NH: Longwood Academic, 1991.

Walton, Hanes. *Black Republicans.* Metuchen, NJ: Scarecrow, 1975.

Wright v. City of Emporia (1972)

The city of Emporia, Virginia, became a politically independent "city" by state law and wanted to create its own school district. Until that time, city students had attended county schools, and the county school system was under a federally mandated desegregation order. In the decision to *Wright v. City of Emporia,* 407 U.S. 451 (1972), the Supreme Court held that a new city system would impede the county's desegregation efforts. The Court concluded that, in determining whether realignment of school districts is in accordance with the requirements of the **Fourteenth Amendment**, courts must be guided not by the motivation of public officials but by the effect of their action. **See** the text of the Fourteenth Amendment in "Civil War Amendments" in Appendix 1. (FHJ)

BIBLIOGRAPHY

Galub, Arthur L. *The Burger Court, 1968–1984.* Millwood, NY: Associate Faculty Press, 1984.

Wygant v. Jackson Board of Education (1986)

Wygant v. Jackson Board of Education, 476 U.S. 267 (1986), was an **affirmative action** case. A collective bargaining agreement in Jackson, Michigan, established a policy-giving preference to minority teachers by requiring the layoffs of white teachers before African-American teachers with less seniority. The Supreme Court held that the collective bargaining agreement violated the equal protection clause of the **Fourteenth Amendment** because it was not a narrowly tailored remedy to combat past discrimination. Once again, the Court endorsed the notion of "last hired, first fired." (RLP)

BIBLIOGRAPHY

Dometrius, Nelson C. and Lee Sigelman. "Modeling the Impact of Supreme Court Decisions: *Wygant v. Board.*" *Journal of Politics* 50, no. 1 (February 1988): 131–49.

Albert R. Wynn (1951–)

Albert R. Wynn is a member of the U.S. House of Representatives for the 4th District in Maryland, which represents some suburbs of Washington, D.C. Wynn first won this seat in 1992. In 1993, he played a major role in creating hearings to investigate allegations of racial bias at the National Institutes of Health. (WWH)

BIBLIOGRAPHY

Brown, Carolyn M. and Donna Mitchell. "Getting a Fair Deal: House Bill Calls for Greater Disclosure of Lending to Small and Minority Businesses." *Black Enterprise* 25, no. 2 (September 1994): 27.

McCoy, Frank. "Bill Faces Major Challenges." *Black Enterprise* 25, no. 3 (October 1994): 24.

Merida, Kevin. "Caucus Deals with Minority Status." *Emerge* 9, no. 2 (November 1997): 26.

Andrew Young (1932–)

Andrew Young was born in New Orleans, Louisiana, in 1932. Young was influenced by Mohandas Gandhi's teaching and decided he wanted to bring about social change through nonviolent means. To pursue that goal, he became a minister and a significant member of the **Southern Christian Leadership Conference (SCLC).** A confidante of **Martin Luther King, Jr.,** he was beaten and arrested while participating in historic civil rights campaigns in Birmingham, Selma, and Chicago as well as in the Poor People's March on Washington, D.C., in 1968. Young was elected to Congress in 1972 and served three terms in the U.S. House of Representatives, after which President Jimmy Carter named him ambassador to the United Nations in 1979. Young was mayor of Atlanta from 1981 to 1989, and is now vice-chairman of Law Companies Group, an engineering and environmental consulting firm in Atlanta. He was also co-chair of the Atlanta Committee for the 1996 Olympic Games. Throughout his career, Young has been a firm advocate of internationalism, arguing that America's problems can only be solved within a world context. The problems of poverty and oppression in the United States, he maintains, are only one part of a worldwide pattern of poverty and oppression. He has remained a firm supporter of the United Nations, maintaining that lack of money and American support have hindered the UN's effectiveness. (FAS)

BIBLIOGRAPHY

Young, Andrew. *An Uneasy Burden.* New York: Reed Publishing, 1996.

Coleman Alexander Young (1918–1997)

Born in Tuscaloosa, Alabama, Coleman Young became the first African-American mayor of Detroit in 1963. A former Michigan state senator and Democratic Party floor leader, Young began his political career as an organizer for the United Auto Workers while working for the Ford Motor Company. Re-elected mayor for an unprecedented five terms, Young eased relations between Detroit residents and police and employed economic development strategies to revitalize the city's ailing economy. In 1993 he did not seek re-election. (VDD)

BIBLIOGRAPHY

Young, Coleman and Lonnie Wheeler. *The Autobiography of Coleman Young.* New York: Viking Penguin, 1994.

Whitney Moore Young, Jr. (1921–1971)

Whitney Young, a civil rights leader, served as the executive director of the **National Urban League** from 1961 until his death. When executive director, he assisted thousands of African Americans to obtain jobs, by establishing on-the-job training programs and Head Start programs and tutoring centers throughout the country. Young worked for the Urban League in St. Paul and Omaha from 1947 to 1953 and was dean of the Atlanta University School of Social Work from 1954 to 1960. He served on several federal commissions concerned with social welfare or race relations during the Kennedy and Johnson administrations. He was the author of *To Be Equal* (1964), and several other books addressing civil rights issues, crime and racism in America. (EC)

BIBLIOGRAPHY

Weiss, Nancy J. *Whitney M. Young, Jr. and the Struggle for Civil Rights.* Princeton: Princeton University Press, 1989.

Appendixes

1

Speeches and Documents

1. An Act to Prohibit the Importation of Slaves (1807)

Be it enacted, by the Senate and House of Representatives of the United States of America in Congress assembled, that from and after the 1st day of January, 1808, it shall not be lawful to import or bring into the United States or the territories thereof, from any foreign kingdom, place, or country, any Negro, mulatto, or person of color with intent to hold, sell, or dispose of such Negro, mulatto, or person of color as a slave, or to be held to service or labor.

Section 2. And be it further enacted, that no citizen or citizens of the United States, or any other person, shall, from and after the 1st day of January, in the year of Our Lord 1808, for himself, or themselves, or any other person whatsoever, either as master, factor, or owner, build, fit, equip, load, or otherwise prepare any ship or vessel, in any port or place within the jurisdiction of the United States, nor shall cause any ship or vessel to sail from any port or place within the same, for the purpose of procuring any Negro, mulatto, or person of color from any foreign kingdom, place, or country, to be transported to any port or place whatsoever within the jurisdiction of the United States, to be held, sold, or disposed of as slaves, or to be held to service or labor. And if any ship or vessel shall be so fitted out for the purpose aforesaid, or shall be caused to sail so as aforesaid, every such ship or vessel, her tackle, apparel, and furniture shall be forfeited to the United States and shall be liable to be seized, prosecuted, and condemned in any of the circuit courts or district courts for the district where the said ship or vessel may be found or seized. . . .

Section 4. And be it further enacted, if any citizen or citizens of the United States, or any person resident within the jurisdiction of the same, shall, from and after the 1st day of January, 1808, take on board, receive, or transport from any of the coasts or kingdoms of Africa, or from any other foreign kingdom, place, or country, any Negro, mulatto, or person of color, in any ship or vessel, for the purpose of selling them in any port or place within the jurisdiction of the United States as slaves, or to be held to service or labor, or shall be in any ways aiding or abetting therein, such citizen or citizens, or person, shall severally forfeit and pay $5,000, one moiety thereof to the use of any person or persons who shall sue for and prosecute the same to effect. And every such ship or vessel in which such Negro, mulatto, or person of color shall have been taken on board, received, or transported as aforesaid, her tackle, apparel, and furniture, and the goods and effects which shall be found on board the same shall be forfeited to the United States and shall be liable to be seized, prosecuted, and condemned in any of the circuit courts or district courts in the district where the said ship or vessel may be found or seized.

And neither the importer, nor any person or persons claiming from or under him, shall hold any right or title whatsoever to any Negro, mulatto, or person of color, nor to the service or labor thereof, who may be imported or brought within the United States, or territories thereof, in violation of this law, but the same shall remain subject to any regulations not contravening the provisions of this act, which the legislatures of the several states or territories at any time hereafter may make for disposing of any such Negro, mulatto, or person of color.

Section 5. And be it further enacted, that if any citizen or citizens of the United States, or any person resident with the jurisdiction of the same, shall, from and after the 1st day of January, 1808, contrary to the true intent and meaning of this act, take on board any ship or vessel from any of the coasts or kingdoms of Africa, or from any other foreign kingdom, place, or country, any Negro, mulatto, or person of color with intent to sell him, her, or them for a slave, or slaves, or to be held to service or labor, and shall transport the same to any port or place within the jurisdiction of the United States and there sell such Negro, mulatto, or person of color so transported as aforesaid for a slave, or to be held to service or labor, every such offender shall be deemed guilty of a high misdemeanor and, being thereof convicted before any court having competent jurisdiction, shall suffer imprisonment for not more than ten years nor less than five years and be fined not exceeding $10,000, nor less than $1,000.

Section 6. And be it further enacted, that if any person or persons whatsoever shall, from and after the 1st day of January, 1808, purchase or sell any Negro, mulatto, or person of color for a slave, or to be held to service or labor, who shall have been imported or brought from any foreign kingdom, place, or country, or from the dominions of any foreign state immediately adjoining to the United States into any port or place within the jurisdiction of the United States, after the last day of December, 1807, knowing at the time of such purchase or sale such Negro, mulatto, or person of color was so brought within the jurisdiction of the United States, as aforesaid, such purchaser and seller shall severally forfeit and pay for every Negro, mulatto, or person of color so purchased or sold as aforesaid $800, one moiety thereof to the United States and the other moiety the same to effect: Provided, that the aforesaid forfeiture shall not extend to the seller or purchaser of any Negro, mulatto, or person of color who may be sold or disposed of in virtue of any regulation which may hereafter be made by any of the legislatures of the several states in that respect, in pursuance of this act, and the Constitution of the United States.

Section 7. And be it further enacted, that if any ship or vessel shall be found, from and after the 1st day of January, 1808, in any river, port, bay, or harbor, or on the high seas, within the jurisdictional limits of the United States, or hovering on the coast thereof, having on board any Negro, mulatto, or person of color for the purpose of selling them as slaves, or with intent to land the same in any port or place within the jurisdiction of the United States, contrary to the prohibition of this act, every such ship or vessel, together with her tackle, apparel, and furniture, and the goods or effects which shall be found on board the same, shall be forfeited to the use of the United States and may be seized, prosecuted, and condemned in any court of the United States having jurisdiction thereof.

And it shall be lawful for the President of the United States, and he is hereby authorized, should he deem it expedient, to cause any of the armed vessels of the United States to be manned and employed to cruise on any part of the coast of the United States, or territories thereof, where he may judge attempts will be made to violate the provisions of this act, and to instruct and direct the commanders of armed vessels of the United States all such ships or vessels, and moreover to seize, take, and bring into any port of the United States all ships or vessels of the United States, wheresoever found on the high seas, contravening the provisions of this act, to be proceeded against according to law. And the captain, master, or commander of every ship or vessel so found and seized as aforesaid shall be deemed guilty of a high misdemeanor, and shall be liable to be prosecuted before any court of the United States having jurisdiction thereof; and being imprisoned not less than two years and not exceeding four years.

Approved, March 2, 1807

2. *Freedom's Journal*—The First Negro Newspaper (1827)

To Our Patrons,

In presenting our first number of our patrons, we feel all the diffidence of persons entering upon a new and untried line of business. But a moment's reflection upon the noble objects which we have in view by the publication of this journal; the expediency of its appearance at this time, when so many schemes are in action concerning our people, encourage us to come boldly before an enlightened public. For we believe that a paper devoted to the dissemination of useful knowledge among our brethren, and to their moral and religious improvement, must meet with the cordial approbation of every friend to humanity.

The peculiarities of this journal render it important that we should advertise to the world our motives by which we are actuated and the objects which we contemplate.

We wish to plead our own cause. Too long have others spoken for us. Too long has the public been deceived by misrepresentations in things which concern us dearly, though, in the estimation of some, mere trifles; for though there are many in society who exercise toward us benevolent feelings, still (with sorrow we confess it) there are others who make it their business to enlarge upon the least trifle which tends to the discredit of any person of color, and pronounce anathemas and denounce our whole body for the misconduct of this guilty one. We are aware that there are many instances of vice among us, but we avow that it is because no one has taught its subjects to be virtuous; many instances of poverty, because no sufficient efforts accommodated to minds contracted by slavery and deprived of early education have been made, to teach them how to husband their hard earnings and to secure to themselves comforts.

Education being an object of the highest importance to the welfare of society, we shall endeavor to present just and adequate views of it, and to urge our brethren the necessity and expediency of training their children, while young, to habits of industry, and thus forming them for becoming useful members of society. It is surely time that we should awake from this lethargy of years and make a concentrated effort for the education of our youth. We form a spoke in the human wheel, and it is necessary that we should understand our [de]pendence on the different parts, and theirs on us, in order to perform our part with propriety.

Though not desirous of dictating, we shall feel it our incumbent duty to dwell upon the general principles and rules of economy. The world has grown too enlightened to estimate any man's character by his personal appearance. Though all men acknowledge the excellency of Franklin's maxims, yet comparatively few practice upon them. We may deplore, when it is too late, the neglect of these self-evident truths, but it avails little to mourn. Ours will be the task of admonishing our brethren on these points.

The civil rights of a people being of the greatest value, it shall ever be our duty to vindicate our brethren, when oppressed, and to lay the case before the public. We shall also urge upon our brethren (who are qualified by the laws of the different states) the expediency of using their elective franchise, and of making an independent use of the same. We wish them not to become the tools of party.

And as much time is frequently lost, and wrong principles instilled, by the perusal of works of trivial importance, we shall consider it a part of our duty to recommend to our young readers such authors as will not only enlarge their stock of useful knowledge but such as will also serve to stimulate them to higher attainments in science.

We trust, also, that through the columns of the *Freedom's Journal* many practical pieces, having for their bases the improvement of our brethren, will be presented to them from the pens of many of our respected friends, who have kindly promised their assistance.

It is our earnest wish to make our journal a medium of intercourse between our brethren in the different states of this great confederacy; that through its columns an expression of our sentiments on many interesting subjects which concern us may be offered to the public; that plans which apparently are beneficial may be candidly discussed and properly weighed; if worthy, receive our cordial approbation, if not, our marked disapprobation.

Useful knowledge of every kind and everything that relates to Africa shall find a ready admission into our columns; and as that vast continent becomes daily more known, we trust that many things will come to light proving that the natives of it are neither so ignorant nor stupid as they have generally been supposed to be.

And while these important subjects shall occupy the columns of the *Freedom's Journal*, we would not be unmindful of our brethren who are still in the iron fetters of bondage. They are our kindred by all the ties of nature; and though but little can be effected by us, still let our sympathies be poured forth, and our prayers in their behalf ascend to Him who is able to succor them.

From the press and the pulpit we have suffered much by being incorrectly represented. Men whom we equally love and admire have not hesitated to represent us disadvantageously without becoming personally acquainted with the true state of things, nor discerning between virtue and vice among us. The virtuous part of our people feel themselves sorely aggrieved under the existing state of things—they are not appreciated.

Our vices and our degradation are ever arrayed against us, but our virtues are passed by unnoticed. And what is still more lamentable, our friends, to whom we concede all the principles of humanity and religion, from these very causes seem to have fallen into the current of popular feeling and are imperceptibly floating on the stream—actually living in the practice of prejudice, while they abjure it in theory and feel it not in their hearts. Is it not very desirable that such should know more of our actual condition, and of our efforts and feelings, that in forming or advocating plans for our amelioration, they may do it more understandingly? In the spirit of candor and humility we intend by a simply representation of facts to lay our case before the public, with a view to arrest the progress of prejudice and to shield ourselves against the consequent evils. We wish to conciliate all and to irritate none, yet we must be firm and unwavering in our principles and persevering in our efforts.

If ignorance, poverty, and degradation have hitherto been our unhappy lot, has the eternal decree gone forth that our race alone are to remain in this state, while knowledge and civilization are shedding their enlivening rays over the rest of the human family? The recent travels of Denham and Clapperton in the interior of Africa, and the interesting narrative which they have published; the establishment of the republic of Haiti after years of sanguinary warfare; its subsequent progress in all the arts of civilization; and the advancement of liberal ideas in South America, where despotism has given place to free governments and where many of our brethren now fill important civil and military stations, prove the contrary.

The interesting fact that there are 500,000 free persons of color, one-half of whom might peruse, and the whole be benefited by the publication of the Journal; that no publication, as yet, has been devoted exclusively to their improvement; that many selections from approved standard authors, which are within the reach of few, may occasionally be made; and, more important still, that this large body of our citizens have nor public channel—all serve to prove the real necessity, at present, for the appearance of the *Freedom's Journal*.

It shall ever be our desire so to conduct the editorial department of our paper as to give offense to none of our patrons, as nothing is further from us than to make it the advocate of any partial views, either in politics or religion. What few days we can number have been devoted to the improvement of our brethren; and it is our earnest wish that the remainder may be spent in the same delightful service.

In conclusion, whatever concerns us as a people will ever find a ready admission into the *Freedom's Journal*, interwoven with all the principal news of the day.

And while everything in our power shall be performed to support the character of our journal, we would respectfully invite our numerous friends to assist by their communications, and our colored brethren to strengthen our hands by their subscriptions, as our labor is one of common cause and worthy of their consideration and support. And we most earnestly solicit the latter, that if at any time we should seem to be zealous or too pointed in the inculcation of any important lesson, they will remember that they are equally interested in the cause in which we are engaged, and attribute our zeal to the peculiarities of our situation and our earnest engagedness in their well-being.

Freedom's Journal **was edited by Samuel Cornish and John Russwurm**

3. Antebellum Songs of the Underground Railroad

Go Down Moses

When Israel was in Egypt's land,
Let my people go;
Oppressed so hard they could not stand,
Let my people go.
Chorus:
Go down, Moses, way down in Egypt's land;
Tell old Pharaoh, to let my people go.

Thus saith the Lord, bold Moses said,
Let my people go;
If not I'll smite your firstborn dead,
Let my people go.
No more shall they in bondage toil,
Let my people go;
Let them come out with Egypt's spoil,
Let my people go.
O'twas a dark and dismal night,
Let my people go;
When Moses led the Israelites,
Let my people go.
The Lord told Moses what to do,
Let my people go;
To lead the children of Israel through,

Let my people go.
O come along, Moses, you won't get lost,
Let my people go;
Stretch out your rod and come across,
Let my people go.
As Israel stood by the water side,
Let my people go;
At the command of God it did divide,
Let my people go.
And when they reached the other side,
Let my people go;
They sang a song of triumph o'er,
Let my people go.
You won't get lost in the wilderness,
Let my people go;
With alighted candle in your breast,
Let my people go.
O let us all from bondage flee,
Let my people go;
And let us all in Christ be free,
Let my people go.
We need not always weep and moan,
Let my people go;

And wear these slavery chains forlorn,
Let my people go.
What a beautiful morning that will be,

Let my people go;
When time breaks up in eternity,
Let my people go.

Steal Away

Steal away, steal away,
Steal away to Jesus.
Steal away, steal away home
I ain't got long to stay here.
My Lord calls me
He calls me by the thunder;
The trumpet sounds it in my soul;

I ain't got long to stay here.
Follow the drinking gourd
Follow the drinking gourd,
Follow the drinking gourd,
For the old man is a-waiting
For to carry you to freedom,
Follow the drinking gourd.

4. Emancipation Proclamation (1863)

Whereas, on the 22nd day of September, in the year of our Lord 1862, a proclamation was issued by the President of the United States, containing, among other things, the following to wit:

That on the 1st day of January, in the year of our Lord 1863, all persons held as slaves within any state or designated part of a state, the people whereof shall then be in rebellion against the United States, shall be then, thenceforward, and forever free; and the executive government of the United States, including the military and naval authority thereof, will recognize and maintain the freedom of such persons and will do no act or acts to repress such persons, or any of them, in any efforts they may make for their actual freedom.

That the executive will, on the 1st day of January aforesaid, by proclamation, designate the state and parts of the states, if any, in which the people thereof, respectively, shall then be in rebellion against the United States; and the fact that any state or the people thereof shall on that day in good faith represented in the Congress of the United States by members chosen thereto at elections wherein a majority of the qualified voters of such states shall have participated shall, in the absence of strong countervailing testimony, be deemed conclusive evidence that such state and the people thereof are not then in rebellion against the United States.

Now, therefore, I, Abraham Lincoln, President of the United States, by virtue of the power in me vested as commander in chief of the Army and Navy of the United States, in time of actual armed rebellion against the authority and government of the United States, and as a fit and necessary war measure for suppressing said rebellion, on this 1st day of January, in the year of the Lord 1863, and in accordance with my purpose so to do, publicly proclaimed for the full period of 100 days from the day first above mentioned, order and designate as the states and parts of states wherein the people thereof, respectively, are this day in rebellion against the United States the following, to wit:

Arkansas, Texas, Louisiana (except the parishes of St. Bernard, Plaquemines, Jefferson, St. John, St. Charles, St. James, Ascension, Assumption, Terrebonne, Lafourche, St. Mary, St. Martin, and Orleans, including the city of New Orleans), Mississippi, Alabama, Florida, Georgia, South Carolina, North Carolina, and Virginia (except the forty-eight counties designated as West Virginia, and also the counties of Berkeley, Accomac, Northampton, Elizabeth City, York, Princess Anne, and Norfolk, including the cities of Norfolk and Portsmouth), and which excepted parts are for the present left precisely as if this proclamation were not issued.

And, by virtue of the power and for the purpose aforesaid, I do order and declare that all persons held as slaves within said designated states and parts of states are, and henceforward shall be, free; and that the executive government of the United States, including the military and naval authorities thereof, will recognize and maintain the freedom of said persons.

And I hereby enjoin upon the people so declared to be free to abstain from all violence, unless in necessary self-defense; and I recommend to them that, in all cases when allowed, they labor faithfully for reasonable wages.

And I further declare and make known that such persons of suitable condition will be received into the armed service of the United States to garrison forts, positions, stations, and other places, and to man vessels of all sorts in said service.

And upon this act sincerely believed to be an act of justice, warranted by the Constitution upon military necessity, I invoke the considerate judgment of mankind and the gracious favor of Almighty God.

Proclaimed by President Abraham Lincoln on Januray 1, 1863

5. Civil Rights Act (1866)

An Act to Protect all Persons in the United States in their Civil Rights, and Furnish the Means of their Vindication

Be it enacted by the Senate and House of Representatives of the United States of America in Congress assembled, that all persons born in the United States and not subject to any foreign power, excluding Indians not taxed, are hereby declared to be citizens of the United States and such citizens, of every race and color, without regard to any previous condition of slavery or involuntary servitude, except as a punishment for crime whereof the party shall have been duly convicted, shall have the same right, in every state and territory in the United States, to make and enforce contracts; to sue; be parties, and give evidence; to inherit, purchase, lease, sell, hold, and convey real and personal property; and to full and equal benefit of all laws and proceedings for the security of person and property as is enjoyed by white citizens, and shall be subject to like punishment, pains, and penalties, and to none other, any law, statute, ordinance, regulation, or custom to the contrary notwithstanding.

Section 2. And be it further enacted, that any person who, under color of any law, statute, ordinance, regulation, or custom, shall subject, or cause to be subjected, any inhabitant of any state or territory to the deprivation of any right secured or protected by this act, or to different punishment, pains, or penalties on account of such person having at any time been held in a condition of slavery or involuntary servitude, except as a punishment for crime whereof the party shall have been duly convicted, or by reason of his color or race, than is prescribed for the punishment of white persons, shall be deemed guilty of a misdemeanor, and, on conviction, shall be punished by fine not exceeding $1,000 or imprisonment not exceeding one year, or both, in the discretion of the court.

Section 3. And be it further enacted, that the district courts of the United States, within their respective districts, shall have, exclusively of the courts of the several states, cognizance of all crimes and offenses committed against the provisions of this act, and also, concurrently with the circuit courts of the United States, of all causes, civil and criminal, affecting persons who are denied or cannot enforce in the courts or judicial tribunals of the state or locality where they may be any of the rights secured to them by the 1st Section of this act; and if any suit or prosecution, civil, or criminal, has been or shall be commenced in any state court, against any such person, for any cause whatsoever, or against any officer, civil or military, or other person, for any arrest or imprisonment, trespasses, or wrongs done or committed by virtue or under color of authority derived from this act or the act establishing a bureau for the relief of freedom and refugees, and all acts amendatory thereof, or for refusing to do any act upon the ground that it would be inconsistent with this act, such defendant shall have the right to remove such cause for trial to the proper district or circuit court in the manner prescribed by the "Act relating to habeas corpus and regulating judicial proceedings in certain cases," approved March 3, 1863, and all act amendatory thereof. . . .

And with a view to affording reasonable protection to all persons in their constitutional rights of equality before the law, without distinction of race or color, or previous condition of slavery or involuntary servitude, except as a punishment for crime, whereof the party shall have been duly convicted, and to the prompt discharge of the duties of this act, it shall be the duty of the circuit courts of the United States and the superior courts of the territories of the United States, from time to time, to increase the number of commissioners so as to afford a speedy and convenient means for the arrest and examination of persons charges with a violation of this act; and such commissioners are hereby authorized and required to exercise and discharge all the powers and duties conferred on them by this act, and the same duties with regard to offenses created by this act, as they are authorized by law to exercise with regard to other offenses against the laws of the United States.

Section 8. And be it further enacted, that whenever the President of the United States shall have reason to believe that offenses have been or are likely to be committed against the provisions of this act within any judicial district, it shall be lawful for him, in his discretion, to direct the judge, marshal, and district attorney of such district to attend at such place within the district, and for such time as he may designate, for the purpose of the more speedy arrest and trial of persons charged with a violation of this act; and it shall be the duty of every judge or other officer, when any requisition shall be received by him, to attend at the place and for the time therein designated.

Section 9. And be it further enacted, that it shall be lawful for the President of the United States, or such person as he may empower for that purpose, to employ such part of the land or naval forces of the United States, or of the militia, as shall be necessary to prevent the violation and enforce the due execution of this act.

Section 10. And be it further enacted, that, upon all questions of law arising in any cause under the provisions of this act, a final appeal may be taken to the Supreme Court of the United States.

6. Civil War Amendments to the Constitution: Amendments XIII (1865), XIV (1868), and XV (1870)

Amendment XIII

Passed by Congress February 1, 1865. Ratified December 18, 1865.

Section 1. Neither slavery nor involuntary servitude, except as a punishment for crime whereof the party shall have been duly convicted, shall exist within the United States or any place subject to their jurisdiction.

Section 2. Congress shall have power to enforce this article by appropriate legislation.

Amendment XIV

Passes by Congress June 16, 1866. Ratified July 28, 1868.

Section 1. All persons born or naturalized in the United States and subject to the jurisdiction thereof are citizens of the United States and of the state wherein they reside, No state shall make or enforce any law which shall abridge the privileges or immunities of citizens of the United States; nor shall any state deprive any person of life, liberty, or property without due process of law; nor deny to any person within its jurisdiction the equal protection of the laws.

Section 2. Representatives shall be apportioned among the several states according to their respective numbers, counting the whole number of persons in each state, excluding Indians not taxed. But when the right vote at any election for the choice of electors for President and Vice-President of the United States, representatives in Congress, the executive and judicial officers of a state, or the members of the legislature thereof, is denied to any of the male inhabitants of such state, being twenty-one years of age, and citizens of the United States, or in any way abridged, except for participation in rebellion or other crime, the basis of representation therein shall be reduced in the proportion which the number of such male citizens shall bear to the whole number of male citizens twenty-one years of age in such state.

Section 3. No person shall be a senator or representative in Congress, or elector of President and Vice-President, or hold any office, civil or military, under the United States, or under any state, who, having previously taken oath as a member of Congress, or as an officer of the United States, or as a member of any state legislature, or as an executive or judicial officer of any state to support the Constitution of the United States, shall have engaged in insurrection or rebellion against the same or given aid or comfort to the enemies thereof. But Congress may, by a vote of two-thirds of each house, remove such disability.

Section 4. The validity of the public debt of the United States, authorized by law, including debts incurred for payment of pensions and bounties for services in suppressing insurrection or rebellion, shall not be questioned. But neither the United States nor any state shall assume or pay any debt or obligation incurred in aid of insurrection or rebellion against the United States, or any claim for the loss or emancipation of any slave; but all such debts, obligations, and claims shall beheld illegal and void.

Section 5. The Congress shall have power to enforce, by appropriate legislation, the provisions of this article.

Amendment XV

Passed by Congress February 27, 1869. Ratified March 30, 1870.

Section 1. The right of citizens of the United States to vote shall not be denied or abridged by the United States or by any state on account of race, color, or previous condition of servitude.

Section 2. The Congress shall have power to enforce this article by appropriate legislation.

7. Excerpt from "Address to the People of the United States" by Frederick Douglass (1883)

It is our lot to live among a people whose laws, traditions, and prejudices have been against us for centuries, and from these they are not yet free. To assume that they are free from these evils simply because they have changed their laws is to assume what is utterly unreasonable and contrary to facts. Large bodies move slowly. Individuals may be converted on the instant and change their whole course of life. Nations never. Time and events are required for the conversion of nations. Not even the character of a great political organization can be changed by a new platform. It will be the same old snake though in a new skin.

Though we have had war, reconstruction, and abolition as a nation, we still linger in the shadow and blight of an extinct institution. Though the colored man is no longer subject to be bought and sold, he is still surrounded by an adverse sentiment which fetters all his movements. In his downward course he meets with no resistance, but his course upward is resented and resisted at every step of his progress. If he comes in ignorance, rags, and wretchedness, he conforms to the popular belief of his character, and in the character he is welcome. But if he shall come as a gentleman, a scholar, and a statesman, he is hailed as a contradiction to the national faith concerning his race, and his coming is resented as impudence. In the one case he may provoke contempt and derision, but in the other he is an affront to pride and provokes malice. Let him do what he will, there is at present, therefore, no escape for him. The color line meets him everywhere, and in a measure shuts him out from all respectable and profitable trades and callings.

In spite of all your religion and laws, he is a rejected man. He is rejected by trade unions of every trade, and refused work while he lives and burial when he dies; and yet he is asked to forget his color and forget that which everybody else remembers. If he offers himself to a builder as a mechanic, to a client as a lawyer, to a patient as a physician, to a college as a professor, to a firm as a clerk, to a government department as an agent or an officer, he is sternly met on the color line, and his claim to consideration is some way is disputed on the ground of color.

Not even our churches, whose members profess to follow the despised Nazarene, whose home, when on earth, was among the lowly and despised, have yet conquered this feeling of color madness, and what is true of our churches is also true of our courts of law. Neither is free from this all-pervading atmosphere of color hate. The one describes the Deity as impartial, no respecter of persons,

and the other the Goddess of Justice as blindfolded, with sword by her side and scales in her hand, held evenly between high and low, rich and poor, white and black; but both are the images of American imagination rather than American practices.

Taking advantage of the general disposition in this country to impute crime to color, white men color their faces to commit crime and wash off the hated color to escape punishment. In many places where the commission of crime is alleged against one of our color, the ordinary processes of the law are set aside as too slow for the impetuous justice of the infuriated populace. They take the law into their own bloody hands and proceed to whip, stab, shoot, hang, or burn the alleged culprit, without the intervention of courts, counsel, judges, juries, or witnesses. In such cases it is not the business of the accusers to prove guilt, but it is for the accused to prove his innocence, a thing hard for any man to do, even in a court of law, and utterly impossible for him to do in these infernal lynch courts.

A man accused, surprised, frightened, and captured by a motley crowd, dragged with a rope around his neck in midnight-darkness to the nearest tree, and told in the coarsest terms of profanity to prepare for death, would be more than human if he did not, in his terror-stricken appearance, more confirm suspicion of guilt than the contrary. Worse still, in the presence of such hell-black outrages, the pulpit is usually dumb, and the press in the neighborhood is silent or openly takes the sides with the mob. There are occasional cases in which white men are lynched, but one sparrow does not make a summer. Everyone knows that what is called lynch law is peculiarly the law for colored people and for nobody else.

If there were no other grievance that this horrible and barbarous lynch-law custom, we should be justified in assembling, as we have now done, to expose and denounce it. But this is not all. Even now, after twenty years of so-called emancipation, we are subject to lawless raids of midnight riders, who, with blackened faces, invade our homes and perpetrate the foulest of crimes upon us and our families. This condition of things is too flagrant and notorious to require specifications or proof. Thus in all the relations of life and death we are met by the color line. It hunts us at midnight, it denies us accommodation in hotels and justice in the courts; excludes our children from schools, refuses our sons the chance to learn trades, and compels us to pursue only such labor as will bring the least reward.

While we recognize the color line as a hurtful force, a mountain barrier to our progress, wounding our bleeding feet with its flinty rocks at every step, we do not despair. We are a hopeful people. This convention is a proof of our faith in you, in reason, in truth, and justice; our belief that prejudice, with all its malign accompaniments, may yet be removed by peaceful means; that, assisted by time and events and the growing enlightenment of both races, the color line will ultimately become harmless. When this shall come it will then only be used, as it should be, to distinguish one variety of the human family from another. It will cease to have any civil, political, or moral significance, and colored conventions will then be dispensed with as anachronisms, wholly out of place—but not till then.

Do not marvel that we are not discouraged. The faith within us has a rational basis and is confirmed by facts. When we consider how deep-seated this feeling against us is; the long centuries it has been forming; the forces of avarice which have been marshaled to sustain it; how the language and literature of the country have been pervaded with it; how the church, the press, the playhouse, and other influences of the country have been arrayed in its support, the progress toward its extinction must be considered vast and wonderful.

If liberty, with us, is yet but a name, our citizenship is but a sham, and our suffrage thus far only a cruel mockery, we may yet congratulate ourselves upon the fact that the laws and institutions of the country are sound, just, and liberal. There is hope for a people when their laws are righteous, whether for the moment they conform to their requirements or not. Constitution and its righteous laws, it will not do to reproach the colored people of this country with keeping up the color line; for that people would prove themselves scarcely worthy of even theoretical freedom, to say nothing of practical freedom, if they settled down in silent, servile, and cowardly submission to their wrongs from fear of making their color visible.

They are bound by every element of manhood to hold conventions in their own name and on their own behalf, to keep their grievances before the people and make every organized protest against the wrongs inflicted upon them within their power. They should scorn the counsels of cowards and hang their banner on the outer wall. Who would be free, themselves must strike the blow. We do not believe, as we are often told, that the Negro is the ugly child of the national family, and the more he is kept out of sight the better it will be for him. You know that liberty given is never so precious as liberty sought for and fought for. The man outraged is the man to make the outcry. Depend upon it, men will not care much for a people who do not care for themselves. . . .

In conclusion upon this color objection, we have to say that we meet here in open daylight. There is nothing sinister about us. The eyes of the nation are upon us. Ten thousand newspapers may tell if they choose of whatever is said and done here. They may commend our wisdom or condemn our folly, precisely as we shall be wise or foolish. We put ourselves before them as honest men and ask their judgment upon our work.

Delivered in Louisville, Kentucky, September 1883

8. "The Road to Negro Progress" by Booker T. Washington (1893)

Mr. President and Gentlemen of the Board of Directors and Citizens:

One-third of the population of the South is of the Negro race. No enterprise seeking the material, civil, or moral welfare of this section can disregard this element of our population and reach the highest success. I but convey to you, Mr President and Directors, the sentiment of the masses of my race when I say that in no way have the value and manhood of the American Negro been more fittingly and generously recognized than by the managers of this magnificent exposition at every stage of its progress. It is a recognition that will do more to cement the friendship of the two races than any occurrence since the dawn of our freedom.

Not only this, but the opportunity here afforded will awaken among us a new era of industrial progress. Ignorant and inexperienced, it is not strange that in the first years of our new life we began at the top instead of at the bottom; that a seat in Congress or the state legislature was more sought than real estate or industrial skill; that the political convention or stump speaking had more attractions than starting a dairy farm or truck garden.

A ship lost at sea for many days suddenly sighted a friendly vessel. From the mast of the unfortunate vessel was seen a signal; "Water, water; we die of thirst." The answer from the friendly vessel at once came back: "Cast down your bucket where you are." A second time the signal, "Water, water, send us water!" ran up from the distressed vessel, and was answered: "Cast down your bucket where you are." And a third and fourth signal for water was answered: "Cast down your bucket where you are." The captain of the distressed vessel, at last heeding the injunction, cast down his bucket, and it came up full of fresh, sparkling water from the mouth of the Amazon River.

To those of my race who depend on bettering their condition in a foreign land or who underestimate the importance of cultivating friendly relations with the Southern white man, who is their next-door neighbor, I would say: Cast down your bucket where you are; cast it down in making friends, in every manly way, of the people of all races by whom we are surrounded. Cast it down in agriculture, mechanics, in commerce, in domestic service, and in the professions. And in this connection it is well to bear in mind that whatever other sins the South may be called to bear, when it comes to business, pure and simple, it is in the South that the Negro is given a man's chance in the commercial world, and in nothing is this exposition more eloquent than in emphasizing this chance.

Our greatest danger is that, in the great leap from slavery to freedom, we may overlook the fact that the masses of us are to live by the productions of our hands and fail to keep in mind that we shall prosper in proportion as we learn to dignify and glorify common labor, and put brains and skill into the common occupations of life; shall prosper in proportion as we learn to draw the line between the superficial and the substantial, the ornamental gewgaws of life and the useful. No race can prosper till it learns that there is as much dignity in tilling a field as in writing a poem. It is at the bottom of life we must begin, and not at the top. Nor should we permit our grievances to overshadow our opportunities.

To those of the white race who look to the incoming of those of foreign birth and strange tongue and habits for the prosperity of the South, were I permitted I would repeat what I say to my own race, "Cast down your bucket where you are." Cast it down among the 8 million Negroes whose habits you know, whose fidelity and love you have tested in days when to have proved treacherous meant the ruin of your firesides. Cast down your bucket among these people who have, without strikes and labor wars, tilled your fields, cleared your forests, built your railroads and cities, and brought forth treasures from the bowels of the earth and helped make possible this magnificent representation of the progress of the South. Casting down your bucket among my people, helping and encouraging them as you are doing on these grounds, and, with education of head, hand, and heart, you will find that they will buy your surplus land, make blossom the waste places in your fields, and run your factories.

While doing this, you can be sure in the future, as in the past, that you and your families will be surrounded by the most patient, faithful, law-abiding, and unresentful people that the world has seen. As we have proved our loyalty to you in the past, in nursing your children, watching by the sickbed of your mothers and fathers, and often following them with tear-rimmed eyes to their graves, so in the future, in our humble way, we shall stand by you with a devotion that no foreigner can approach, ready to lay down our lives, if need be, in defense of yours; interlacing our industrial, commercial, civil, and religious life with yours in a way that shall make the interests of both races one. In all things that are purely social we can be as separate as the fingers, yet one as the hand in all things essential to mutual progress.

There is not defense or security for any of us except in the highest intelligence and development of all. If anywhere there are efforts tending to curtail the fullest growth of the Negro, let these efforts be turned into stimulating, encouraging, and making him the most useful and intelligent citizen. Effort or means so invested will pay a thousand percent interest. These efforts will be twice blessed — "blessing him that gives and him that takes."

There is no escape, through law of man or God, from the inevitable:

> The laws of changeless justice bind
> Oppressor with oppressed;
> And close as sin and suffering joined
> We march to fate abreast

Nearly 16 million hands will aid you in pulling the load upward, or they will pull against you the load downward. We shall constitute one-third and more of the ignorance and crime of the South, or one-third its intelligence and progress; we shall contribute one-third to the business and industrial prosperity of the South, or we shall prove a veritable body of death, stagnating, depressing, retarding every effort to advance the body politic.

Gentlemen of the exposition, as we present to you our humble effort at an exhibition of our progress, you must not expect over-much. Starting thirty years ago with ownership here and there in a few quilts and pumpkins and chickens (gathered from miscellaneous sources), remember: the path that has led from these to the invention and production of agricultural implements, buggies, steam engines, newspapers, books, statuary, carving, paintings, the management of drugstores and banks, has not been trodden without contact with thorns and thistles. While we take pride in what we exhibit as a result of our independent efforts, we do not for a moment forget that our part in this exhibition would fall far short of your expectations but for the constant help that has come to our educational life, not only from the Southern states but especially from Northern philanthropists who have made their gifts a constant stream of blessing and encouragement.

The wisest among my race understand that the agitation of questions of social equality is the extremest folly, and that progress in the enjoyment of all the privileges that will come to us must be the result of severe and constant struggle rather than of artificial forcing. No race that has anything to contribute to the markets of the world is long in any degree ostracized. It is important that all privileges of the law be ours, but it is vastly more important that we be prepared for the exercise of those privileges. The opportunity to earn a dollar in a factory just now is worth infinitely more than the opportunity to spend a dollar in an opera house.

In conclusion, may I repeat that nothing in thirty years has given us more hope and encouragement and drawn us so near to you of the white race as this opportunity offered by the exposition; and here bending, as it were, over the altar that represents the results of the struggles of your race and mine, I pledge that, in your effort to work out the great and intricate problem which God has laid at the doors of the South, you shall have at all times the patient, sympathetic help of my race; only let this be constantly in mind that, while from representations in these buildings of the product of field, of forest, of mine, of factory, letters, and art, much good will come—yet far above and beyond material benefits will be that higher good, that let us pray God will come, in a blotting out of sectional differences and racial animosities and suspicions, in a determination to administer absolute justice, in a willing obedience among all classes to the mandates of law. This, coupled with our material prosperity, will bring into our beloved South a new heaven and a new earth.

Delivered in Atlanta, September 18, 1893

9. Excerpt from *The Souls of Black Folk* by W. E. B. Du Bois (1903)

Between me and the other world there is ever an unasked question: unasked by some through feelings of delicacy; by others through the difficulty of rightly framing it. All, nevertheless, flutter round it. They approach me in a half-hesitant sort of way, eye me curiously or compassionately, and then, instead of saying directly, How does it feel to be a problem? they say, I know an excellent colored man in my town; or, I fought at Mechanicsville; or, Do not these Southern outrages make your blood boil? At these I smile, or am interested, or reduce the boiling to a simmer, as the occasion may require. To the real question, How does it feel to be a problem? I answer seldom a word.

And, yet, being a problem is a strange experience—peculiar even for one who has never been anything else, save perhaps in babyhood and in Europe. It is in the early days of rollicking boyhood that the revelation first bursts upon one, all in a day, as it were. I remember well when the shadow swept across me. I was a little thing, away up in the hills of New England, where the dark Housatonic winds between Hoosac and Taghkanic to the sea. In a wee wooden schoolhouse, something put it into the boys' and fills' heads to buy gorgeous visiting cards—ten cents a package—and exchange. The exchange was merry, till a girl, a tall newcomer, refused my card,—refused it peremptorily, with a glance. Then it dawned upon me with a certain suddenness that I was different from the others; or like, mayhap, in heart and life and longing, but shut out from their world by a vast veil.

I had thereafter no desire to tear down that veil, to creep through; I held all beyond it in common contempt and lived above it in a region of blue sky and great wandering shadows. That sky was bluest when I could beat my mates at examination time, or beat them at a foot race, or even beat their stringy heads. Alas, with the years all this fine contempt began to fade; for the worlds I longed for, and all their dazzling opportunities, were theirs, not mine. But they should not keep these prizes, I said; some, all, I would wrest from them. Just how I would do it I could never decide—by reading law, by healing the sick, by telling the wonderful tales that swam in my head—some way.

With other black boys the strife was not so fiercely sunny; their youth shrink into tasteless sycophancy or into silent hatred of the pale world about them and mocking distrust of everything white; or wasted itself in a bitter cry—Why did God make me an outcast and a stranger in mine own house? The shades of the prison house closed round about us all: walls strait and stubborn to the whitest, but relentlessly narrow, tall, and unscalable to sons of night who must plod darkly on in resignation, or beat unavailing palms against the stone, or steadily, half-hopelessly, watch the streak of blue above.

After the Egyptian and Indian, the Greek and Roman, the Teuton and Mongolian, the Negro is a sort of seventh son, born with a veil, and gifted with second-sight in this American world—a world which yields him no true self-consciousness, but only lets him see himself through the revelation of the other world. It is a peculiar sensation, this double-consciousness, this sense of always looking at oneself through the eyes of others, of measuring one's soul by the tape of a world that looks on in amused contempt and pity. One ever feels his twoness—an American, a Negro; two souls, two thoughts, two unreconciled strivings; two warring ideals in one dark body, whose dogged strength alone keeps it from being torn asunder.

The history of the American Negro is the history of this strife, this longing to attain self-conscious manhood, to merge his double self into a better and truer self. In this merging he wished neither of the older selves to be lost. He would not Africanize America, for America has too much to teach the world and Africa. He would not bleach his Negro soul in a flood of white Americanism, for he knows that Negro blood has a message for the world. He simply wishes to make it possible for a man to be both a Negro and an American, without being cursed and spit upon by his fellows, without having the doors of opportunity closed roughly in his face.

This, then, is the end of his striving: to be a co-worker in the kingdom of culture, to escape both death and isolation, to husband and use his best powers and his latent genius. These powers of body and mind have in the past been strangely wasted, dispersed, or forgotten. The shadow of a mighty Negro past flits through the tale of Ethiopia the Shadowy and of Egypt the Sphinx. Throughout history, the powers of single black men flash here and there like falling stars, and die sometimes before the world has rightly gauged their brightness.

Here in America, in the few days since Emancipation, the black man's turning hither and thither in hesitant and doubtful striving has often made his very strength to lose effectiveness, to seem like absence of power, like weakness. And yet it is not weakness—it is the contradiction of double aims. The double-aimed struggle of the black artisan—on the one hand to escape white contempt for a nation of mere hewers of wood and drawers of water, and on the other hand to plow and nail and dig for a poverty-stricken horde—could only result in making him a poor craftsman, for he had but half a heart in either cause.

By the poverty and ignorance of his people, the Negro minister or doctor was tempted toward quackery and demagogy; and, by the criticism of the other world, towards ideals that made him ashamed of his lowly tasks. The would-be black savant was confronted by the paradox that the knowledge his people needed was a twice-told tale to his white neighbors, while the knowledge which would teach the white world was Greek to his own flesh and blood. The innate love of harmony and beauty that set the ruder souls of his people a-dancing and a-singing raised but confusion and doubt in the soul of the black artist; for the beauty revealed to him was the soul-beauty of a race which his larger audience despised, and he could not articulate the message of another people. This waste of double aims, this seeking to satisfy two unreconciled ideals has wrought sad havoc with the courage and faith and deeds of ten thousand thousand people—has sent them often wooing false gods and involving false means of salvation, and at times has even seemed about to make them ashamed of themselves.

Away back in the days of bondage, they thought to see in one divine event the end of all doubt and disappointment; few men ever worshipped Freedom with half such unquestioning faith as did the American Negro for two centuries. To him, so far as he thought and dreamed, slavery was indeed the sum of all villainies, the cause of all sorrow, the root of all prejudice; Emancipation was the key to a promised land of sweeter beauty than ever stretched before the eyes of wearied Israelites. In song and exhortation swelled one refrain—Liberty; in his tears and curses the God he implored had Freedom in His right hand. At last it came,—suddenly, fearfully, like a dream. With one wild carnival of blood and passion came the message in his own plaintive cadences:

> Shout, O children!
> Shout, you're free!
> For God has bought you liberty!

Years have passed away since then — ten, twenty, forty; forty years of national life, forty years of renewal and development, and yet the swarthy specter sits in its accustomed seat at the nation's feast. In vain do we cry to this our vastest social problem:

> Take any shape but that, and my firm nerves
> Shall never tremble!

The nation has not yet found peace from its sins; the freedman has not yet found his promised land. Whatever of good may have come in these years of change, the shadow of a deep disappointment rests upon the Negro people, a disappointment all the more bitter because the unattained ideal was unbounded save by the simple ignorance of a lowly people.

The first decade was merely a prolongation of the vain search for freedom, the boom that seemed ever barely to elude their grasp, like a tantalizing will-o'-the-wisp, maddening and misleading the headless lost. The holocaust of wars, the terrors of the Ku Klux Klan, the lies of carpetbaggers, the disorganization of industry, and the contradictory advice of friends and foes left the bewildered serf with no new watchword beyond the old cry for freedom. As the time flew, however, he began to grasp a new idea. The ideal of liberty demanded for its attainment for is attainment powerful means, and these the Fifteenth Amendment gave him. The ballot, which before he had looked upon as a visible sign of freedom, he now regarded as the chief means of gaining and perfecting the liberty with which war had partially endowed him. And why not? Had not votes made war and emancipated millions? Had not votes enfranchised the freedmen? Was anything impossible to a power that had done all this? A million black men started with renewed zeal to vote themselves into the kingdom.

So the decade flew away, the revolution of 1876 came, and left the half-free serf weary, wondering, but still inspired. Slowly but steadily, in the following years, a new vision began gradually to replace the dream of political power—a powerful movement, the rise of another ideal to guide the unguided, another pillar of fire by night after a clouded day. It was the ideal of "book learning"; the curiosity, born of compulsory ignorance, to know and test the power of the cabalistic letters of the white man, the longing to know. Here at last seemed to have been discovered the mountain path to Canaan; longer than the highway of Emancipation and law, steep and rugged, but straight, leading to heights high enough to overlook life.

Up the new path the advance guard toiled, slowly, heavily, doggedly; only those who have watched and guided the faltering feet, the misty minds, the dull understandings of the dark pupils of these schools know how faithfully, how piteously this people strove to learn. It was weary work. The cold statistician wrote down the inches of progress here and there, noted also where here and there a foot had slipped or someone had fallen. To the tired climbers, the horizon was ever dark, the mists were often cold, the Canaan was always dim and far away. If, however, the vistas disclosed as yet no goal, no resting place, little but flattery and criticism, the journey at least gave leisure for reflection and self-examination; it changed the child of Emancipation to the youth with dawning self-consciousness, self-realization, self-respect.

In those somber forests of his striving, his own soul rose before him and he saw himself—darkly as through a veil; and yet he saw in himself some faint revelation of his power, of his mission. He began to have a dim feeling that, to attain his place in the world, he must be himself, and not another. For the first time he sought to analyze the burden he bore upon his back, that deadweight of social degradation partially masked behind a half-named Negro problem.

He felt his poverty; without a cent, without a home, without land, tools, or savings, he had entered into competition with rich, landed, skilled neighbors. To be a poor man is hard, but to be a poor race in a land of dollars is the very bottom of hardships. He felt the weight of his ignorance, not simply of letters but of life, of business, of the humanities; the accumulated sloth and shirking and awkwardness of decades and centuries shackled his hands and feet. Nor was his burden all poverty and ignorance. The red stain of bastardy, which two centuries of systematic legal defilement of Negro women had stamped upon his race, meant not only the loss of ancient African chastity but also the hereditary weight of a mass of corruption from white adulterers, threatening almost the obliteration of the Negro home.

A people thus handicapped ought not to be asked to race with the world, but rather allowed to give all its time and thought to its own social problems. But alas! while sociologists gleefully count his bastards and his prostitutes, the very soul of the toiling, sweating black man is darkened by the shadow of a vast despair. Men call the shadow prejudice and learnedly explain it as the natural defense of culture against barbarism, learning against ignorance, purity against crime, the "higher" against the "lower" races. To which the Negro cries Amen! and swears that to so much of this strange prejudice as is founded on just homage to civilization, culture, righteousness, and progress he humbly bows and meekly does obeisance.

But before that nameless prejudice that leaps beyond all this, he stands helpless, dismayed, and well-nigh speechless; before that personal disrespect and mockery, the ridicule and systematic humiliation, the distortion of fact and wanton license of fancy, the cynical ignoring of the better and the boisterous welcoming of the worse, the all-pervading desire to inculcate disdain for everything black, from Toussaint to the devil—before this there rises a sickening despair that would disarm and discourage any nation save that black host to whom "discouragement" is an unwritten word.

But facing of so vast a prejudice could not but bring the inevitable self-questioning, self-disparagement, and lowering of ideals which ever accompany repression and breed in an atmosphere of contempt and hate. Whisperings and portents came borne upon the four winds: Lo! we are diseased and dying, cried the dark hosts; we cannot write, our voting is vain; what need of education since we must always cook and serve? And the nation echoed and enforced this self-criticism, saying: Be content to be servants, and nothing more; what need of higher culture for half-men? Away with the black man's ballot, by force or fraud—and behold the suicide of a race! Nevertheless, out of the evil came something of good—the more careful adjustment of education to real life, the clearer perception of the Negroes' social responsibilities, and the sobering realization of the meaning of progress.

So dawned the time of Sturm und Drang: storm and stress today rocks our little boat on the mad waters of the world sea; there is within and without the sound of conflict, the burning of body and rending of soul; inspiration strives with doubt, and faith with vain questionings. The bright ideals of the past—physical freedom, political power, the training of brains and the training of hands—all these in turn have waxed and waned, until even the last grows dim and overcast. Are they all wrong—all false? No, not that, but each alone was oversimple and incomplete—the dreams of a credulous race-childhood, or the fond imaginings of the other world which does not know and does not want to know our power. To be really true, all these ideals must be melted and welded into one.

The training of the schools we need today more than ever—the training of deft hands, quick eyes and ears, and, above all, the broader, deeper, higher culture of gifted minds and pure hearts. The power of the ballot we need in sheer self-defense, else what shall save us from a second slavery? Freedom, too, the long-sought, we still seek—the freedom of life and limb, the freedom of work and think, the freedom to love and aspire. Work, culture, liberty, all these we need, not singly but together, not successively but together, watch growing and aiding each, and all striving toward that vaster ideal that swims before the Negro people, the ideal of human brotherhood, gained through the unifying ideal of race; the ideal of fostering and developing the traits and talents of the Negro, not in opposition to or contempt for other races but rather in large conformity to the greater ideals of the American republic, in order that some day on American soil two world races may give each to each those characteristics both so sadly lack.

We, the darker ones, come even now not altogether empty-handed: there are today no truer exponents of the pure human spirit of the Declaration of Independence than the American Negroes; there is not true American music but the wild sweet melodies of the Negro slave; the American fairy tales and folklore are Indian and African; and, all in all, we black men seem the sole oasis of simple faith and reverence in a dusty desert of dollars and smartness. Will America be poorer if she replace her brutal, dyspeptic blundering with lighthearted but determined Negro humility? or her coarse and cruel wit with loving jovial good-humor? or her vulgar music with the soul of the Sorrow Songs?

Merely a concrete test of the underlying principles of the great republic is the Negro Problem, and the spiritual striving of the freedmen's sons is the travail of souls whose burden is almost beyond the measure of their strength, but who bear it in the name of an historic race, in the name of this the land of their fathers' fathers, and in the name of human opportunity.

10. Principles of the Niagara Movement (1905)

The members of the conference, known as the Niagara Movement, assembled in annual meeting at Buffalo, July 11, 12, and 13, 1905, congratulate the Negro Americans on certain undoubted evidences of progress in the last decade, particularly the increase of intelligence, the buying of property, the checking of crime, the uplift in homelife, the advance in literature and art, and the demonstration of constructive and executive ability in the conduct of great religious, economic, and educational institutions.

At the same time, we believe that this class of American citizens should protest emphatically and continually against the curtailment of their political rights. We believe in manhood suffrage; we believe that no man is so good, intelligent, or wealthy as to be entrusted wholly with the welfare of his neighbor.

We believe also in protest against the curtailment of our civil rights. All American citizens have the right to equal treatment in places of public entertainment according to their behavior and deserts.

We especially complain against the denial of equal opportunities to us in economic life; in the rural districts of the South this amounts to peonage and virtual slavery; all over the South it tends to crush labor and small business enterprises; and everywhere American prejudice, helped often by iniquitous laws, is making it more difficult for Negro Americans to earn a decent living.

Common-school education should be free to all American children, and compulsory. High-school training should be adequately provided for all, and college training should be the monopoly of no class or race in any section of our common country. We believe that, in defense of its own institutions, the United States should aid common-school education, particularly in the South, and we especially recommend concerted agitation to this end. We urge an increase in public high-school facilities in the South, where the Negro Americans are almost wholly without such provisions. We favor well-equipped trade and technical schools for the training of artisans, and the need of adequate and liberal endowment for a few institutions of higher education must be patent to sincere well-wishers of the race.

We demand upright judges in courts, juries selected without discrimination on account of color, and the same measure of punishment and the same efforts at reformation for black as for white offenders. We need orphanages and farm schools for dependent children, juvenile reformatories for delinquents, and the abolition of the dehumanizing convict-lease system.

We note with alarm the evident retrogression in this land of sound public opinion on the subject of manhood rights, republican government, and human brotherhood; and we pray God that this nation will not degenerate into a mob of boasters and oppressors, but rather will return to the faith of the fathers, that all men were created free and equal, with certain unalienable rights.

We plead for health—for an opportunity to live in decent houses and localities, for a chance to rear our children in physical and moral cleanliness.

We hold up for public execration the conduct of two opposite classes of men: the practice among employers of importing ignorant Negro American laborers in emergencies, and then affording them neither protection nor permanent employment; and the practice of labor unions of proscribing and boycotting and oppressing thousands of their fellow toilers simply because they are black. These methods have accentuated and will accentuate the war of labor and capital, and they are disgraceful to both sides.

We refuse to allow the impression to remain that the Negro American assents to inferiority, is submissive under oppression, and apologetic before insults. Through helplessness we may submit, but the voice of protest of 10 million Americans must never cease to assail the ears of their fellows so long as America is unjust.

Any discrimination based simply on race or color is barbarous, we care not how hallowed it be by custom, expediency, or prejudice. Differences made on account of ignorance, immorality, poverty, or disease may be legitimate methods of reform, and against them we have no word of protest; but discriminations based simply and solely on physical peculiarities, place of birth, color [of] skin, are relics of that unreasoning human savagery of which the world is and ought to be thoroughly ashamed.

We protest against the "Jim Crow" car, since its effect is and must be to make us pay first-class fare for third-class accommodations, render us open to insults and discomfort, and to crucify wantonly our manhood, womanhood, and self-respect.

We regret that this nation has never seen fit adequately to reward the black soldier who, in its five wars, have defended their country with their blood and yet have been systematically denied the promotions which their abilities deserve. And we regard as unjust the exclusion of black boys from the military and Navy training schools.

We urge upon Congress the enactment of appropriate legislation for securing the proper enforcement of those articles of freedom, the Thirteenth, Fourteenth, and Fifteenth Amendments of the Constitution of the United States.

We repudiate the monstrous doctrine that the oppressor should be the sole authority as to the rights of the oppressed. The Negro race in America, stolen, ravished, and degraded, struggling up through difficulties and oppression, needs sympathy and receives criticism; needs help and is given hindrance; needs protection and is given mob violence; needs justice and is given charity; needs leadership and is given cowardice and apology; needs bread and is given a stone. This nation will never stand justified before God until these things are changed.

Especially are we surprised and astonished at the recent attitude of the Church of Christ—of an increase of a desire to bow to racial prejudice, to narrow the bounds of human brotherhood, and to segregate black men in some outer sanctuary. This is wrong, unchristian, and disgraceful to the 20th century civilization.

Of the above grievances we do not hesitate to complain, and to complain loudly and insistently. To ignore, overlook, or apologize for these wrongs is to prove ourselves unworthy of freedom. Persistent, manly agitation is the way to liberty, and toward this goal the Niagara Movement has started and asks the cooperation of all men of all races.

At the same time we want to acknowledge with deep thankfulness the help of our fellowmen from the Abolitionist down to those who today still stand for equal opportunity and who have given and still give of their wealth and of their poverty for our advancement.

And while we are demanding, and ought to demand, and will continue to demand the rights enumerated above, God forbid that we should ever forget to urge corresponding duties upon our people:

The duty to vote.
The duty to respect the rights of others.
The duty to work.
The duty to obey the laws.
The duty to be clean and orderly.

The duty to send our children to school.

The duty to respect ourselves, even as we respect others.

This statement, complaint, and prayer we submit to the American people and to Almighty God.

11. Executive Order 9981 Desegregating the Armed Forces (1948)

Whereas it is essential that there be maintained in the armed services of the United States the highest standards of democracy, with equality of treatment and opportunity for all those who serve in our country's defense:

Now, Therefore, by virtue of the authority vested in me as President of the United States by the Constitution and the statutes of the United States, and as Commander in Chief of the armed services, it is hereby ordered as follows:

1. It is hereby declared to be the policy of the President that there shall be equality of treatment and opportunity for all persons in the armed services without regard to race, color, religion, or national origin. This policy shall be put into effect as rapidly as possible, having due regard to the time required to effectuate any necessary changes without impairing efficiency or morale.

2. There shall be created in the national military establishment an advisory committee to be known as the President's Committee on Equality of Treatment and Opportunity in the Armed Services, which shall be composed of seven members to be designated by the President.

3. The committee is authorized on behalf of the President to examine into the rules, procedures, and practices of the armed services in order to determine in what respect such rules, procedures and practices may be altered or improved with a view to carrying out the policy of this order. The committee shall confer and advise with the secretary of defense, the secretary of the Army, the secretary of the Navy, and the secretary of the Air Force, and shall make such recommendations to the President and to said secretaries as in the judgment of the committee will effectuate the policy hereof.

4. All executive departments and agencies of the federal government are authorized and directed to cooperate with the committee in its work, and to furnish the committee such information or the services of such persons as the committee may require in the performance of its duties.

5. When requested by the committee to do so, persons in the armed services or in any of the executive departments and agencies of the federal government shall testify before the committee and shall make available for the use of the committee such documents and other information as the committee may require.

6. The committee shall continue to exist until such time as the President shall terminate its existence by executive order.

Issued by President Harry S. Truman on July 26, 1948

12. "The Little Rock School Crisis" by Dwight D. Eisenhower (1957)

For a few minutes this evening I want to speak to you about the serious situation that has arisen in Little Rock. To make this talk I have come to the President's office in the White House. I could have spoken from Rhode Island, where I have been staying recently; but I felt that, in speaking from the house of Lincoln, of Jackson, and of Wilson, my words would better convey both the sadness I feel in the action I was compelled today to take and the firmness with which I intend to pursue this course until the orders of the federal court at Little Rock can be executed without unlawful interference.

In that city, under the leadership of demagogic extremists, disorderly mobs have deliberately prevented the carrying out of proper orders from a federal court. Local authorities have not eliminated that violent opposition, and, under the law, I yesterday issued a proclamation calling upon the mob to disperse. This morning the mob again gathered in front of the Central High School of Little Rock obviously for the purpose of again preventing the carrying out of the court's order relating to the admission of Negro children to that school.

Whenever normal agencies prove inadequate to the task and it becomes necessary for the executive branch of the federal government to use its powers and authority to uphold federal courts, the President's responsibility is inescapable. In accordance with that responsibility, I have today issued an executive order directing the use of troops under federal authority to aid in the execution of federal law at Little Rock, Arkansas. This became necessary when my proclamation of yesterday was not observed, and the obstruction of justice still continues.

It is important the reasons for my action be understood by all our citizens.

As you know, the Supreme Court of the United States has decided that separate public educational facilities for the races are inherently unequal, and, therefore, compulsory school segregation laws are unconstitutional. Our personal opinions about the decision have no bearing on the matter of enforcement, the responsibility and authority of the Supreme Court to interpret the Constitution are very clear. Local federal courts were instructed by the Supreme Court to issue such orders and decrees as might be necessary to achieve admission to public schools without regard to race—and with all deliberate speed.

During the past several years, many communities in our Southern states have instituted public-school plans for gradual progress in the enrollment and attendance of school children of all races in order to bring themselves into compliance with the law of the land. They thus demonstrated to the world that we are a nation in which laws, not men, are supreme. I regret to say that this truth—the cornerstone of our liberties—was not observed in this instance.

It was my hope that this localized situation would be brought under control by city and state authorities. If the use of local police powers had been sufficient, our traditional method of leaving the problems in those hands would have been pursued. But when large gatherings of obstructionists made it impossible for the decrees of the court to be carried out, both the law and the national interest demanded that the President take action.

Here is the sequence of events in the development of the Little Rock school case.

In May of 1955, the Little Rock School Board approved a moderate plan for gradual desegregation of the public schools in that city. It provided that a start toward integration would be made at the present term in high school, and that the plan would be in full operation by 1963. Here I might say that, in a number of communities in Arkansas, integration in the schools has already started and without violence of any kind. Now, this Little Rock plan was challenged in the courts by some who believed that the period of time as proposed in the plan was too long.

The United States court at Little Rock, which has supervisory responsibility under the law for the plan of desegregation in the public schools, dismissed the challenge, thus approving a gradual rather than an abrupt change from the existing system. The court found that the School Board had acted in good faith in planning for a public-school system free from racial discrimination. Since that time, the court has, on three separate occasions, issued orders directing that the plan be carried out. All persons were instructed to refrain from interfering with the efforts of the School Board to comply with the law.

Proper and sensible observance of the law then demanded the respectful obedience which the nation has a right to expect from all its people. This, unfortunately, has not been the case at Little Rock. Certain misguided persons, many of them imported into Little Rock by agitators, have insisted upon defying the law and have sought to bring it into disrepute. The orders of the court have thus been frustrated.

The very basis of our individual rights and freedoms rests upon the certainty that the President and the executive branch of government will support and insure the carrying out of the decisions of the federal courts, even, when necessary, with all the means at the President's command. Unless the President did so, anarchy would result. There would be no security for any except that which each one of us could provide for himself. The interest of the nation in the proper fulfillment of the law's requirements cannot yield to opposition and demonstrations by some few persons. Mob rule cannot be allowed to override the decisions of our courts.

Now let me make it very clear that federal troops are not being used to relieve local and state authorities of their primary duty to preserve the peace and order of the community. Nor are the troops there for the purpose of taking over the responsibility of the School Board and the other responsible local officials in running Central High School. The running of our school system and the maintenance of peace and order in each of our states are strictly local affairs, and the federal government does not interfere except in a very few special cases and when requested by one of the several states. In the present case, the troops are there pursuant to law, solely for the purpose of preventing interference with the orders of the court.

The proper use of the powers of the executive branch to enforce the orders of a federal court is limited to extraordinary and compelling circumstances. Manifestly, such an extreme situation has been created in Little Rock. This challenge must be met and with such measures as will preserve to the people as a whole their lawfully protected rights in a climate permitting their free and fair exercise.

The overwhelming majority of our people in every section of the country are united in their respect for observance of the law—even in those cases where they may disagree with that law. They deplore the call of extremists to violence.

The decision of the Supreme Court concerning school integration, of course, affects the South more seriously than it does other sections of the country. In that region I have many warm friends, some of them in the city of Little Rock. I have deemed it a great personal privilege to spend in our Southland tours of duty while in the military service and enjoyable recreational periods since that time. So, from intimate personal knowledge, I know that the overwhelming majority of the people in the South—including those of Arkansas and of Little Rock—are of goodwill, united in their efforts to preserve and respect the law even when they disagree with it. They do not sympathize with mob rule. They, like the rest of our nation, have proved in two great wars their readiness to sacrifice for America.

A foundation of our American way of life is our national respect for law. In the South, as elsewhere, citizens are keenly aware of the tremendous disservice that has been done to the people of Arkansas in the eyes of the nation, and that has been done to the nation in the eyes of the world.

At a time when we face grave situations abroad because of the hatred that Communism bears toward a system of government based on human rights, it would be difficult to exaggerate the harm that is being done to the prestige and influence, and indeed to the safety, of our nation and the world. Our enemies are gloating over this incident and using it everywhere to misrepresent our whole nation. We are portrayed as a violator of those standards of conduct which the peoples of the world united to proclaim in the Charter of the United Nations. There they affirmed "faith in fundamental human rights" and "in the dignity and worth of the human person" and they did so "without distinction as to race, sex, language or religion."

And so, with deep confidence, I call upon the citizens of the state of Arkansas to assist in bringing to an immediate end all interference with the law and its processes. If resistance to the federal court orders ceases at once, the further presence of federal troops will be unnecessary, and the city of Little Rock will return to its normal habits of peace and order, and a blot upon the fair name and high honor of our nation in the world will be removed.

Thus will be restored the image of America and of all its parts as one nation, indivisible, with liberty and justice for all.
Delivered in Washington, DC, September 24, 1957

13. Excerpts from the Writings of Elijah Muhammad

"The Black Man Must Know the Truth," Chapter 1 of *Our Saviour Has Arrived*

No. 1—TO KNOW THE TRUTH of the Presence of the God of Truth and that His Presence is the Salvation of the Lost and Found people of America is to know your life and its happiness.

No. 2—TRUTH is in favor of you and me, for the truth of our enemies that we have been serving in the U.S.A. for over 400 years who we did not know to be our enemies by nature, is the truth that the Black Man must have knowledge of to be able to keep from falling into the deceiving traps that are being laid by our enemies, to catch us to go their way which is opposed to the right way of the righteous, of whom we are members.

No. 3—THE ARCH DECEIVER. We are warned throughout the Bible and Holy Quran to shun this deceiver if we are members of the Black Nation (the righteous). There is nothing that is left of the truth of these people that God has not made manifest. And I am teaching you daily of this people. There are some Black Americans who will, after knowledge, sympathize with the arch deceiver (the devil) for the sake of advantage. Even some of our highly educated people will accept speaking in defense of this arch enemy of ours, for the sake of trying to gain their respect and sympathy so they can gain higher places with this arch deceiver. And some of them will tell me and the Believers of Islam that they do not believe in any religion and in no God of religion. The Bible foretold that this kind of talk against the truth would come in the last days; that the fool will say in his heart "there is no God." This prophecy is now being fulfilled among even our most educated class of people.

You cannot see the Hereafter unless you believe in righteousness and unless you are a submissive one to the God and Author of righteousness, because righteousness is the type of world that we will have to live under, after the destruction of this evil and deceitful world.

No. 4—THE CHRISTIAN CHURCH. There are "die hards" in the Christian church. Slowly but surely the Spirit of Allah is making manifest to the Black Man that the church and its religion called Christianity is the chain that binds the Black Man in mental slavery (seeking salvation where there is none), and thinking that they must die first to get to heaven. This is really a misunderstanding, because heaven is a condition of life and not a special place. Heaven is enjoying peace of mind and contentment with the God of the righteous and the Nation of the righteous. It can be here in America, in the isles of the Pacific, or on the continents of Asia and Africa, but it is only a condition of life.

Black Christian believers are warned in the Bible in the 18th Chapter of Revelation (last book) to come out of her ("her" means the way and belief of the white race and the so-called Christian religion), that you be not partakers with them in their Divine plagues of God upon her (U.S.A.). This is the religion that the prophets prophesies to you that the enemy will deceive you with. Christianity was not the teachings of Jesus. Their theologians and religious scientists will agree with us, in a show-down, that it was the religion of Jesus, for the religion of Jesus was Islam as it was the religion of Moses and all the prophets of God. The Holy Quran teaches us that the prophets' religion was none other than Islam, the religion of Truth, Freedom, Justice, and Equality. This, the Christians preach with their mouths, but they do not practice Truth, Freedom, Justice, and Equality with us, the Black people. Since knowledge of them, we do not want to follow them in any religion, because they are not by nature made to lead people into righteousness.

No. 5—REVOLUTION between white and Black is due to the work of Allah and His Truth among the Black people of America. Never before in all your life have you seen the white man so anxious to keep the Black Man near him in his society and especially in Christianity, the great false, deceiving religion. He even offers to bribe any Black people of note and for accepting his invitation and high places, they are reduced by a sudden fall to the level of his grace and shame.

No. 6—LEADERS. We, the Black Nation, today with the knowledge of the truth cannot accept leaders made and offered to us for our guidance. I warn each of you to no more accept the white man's made or chosen leaders for you. This is what has kept us bound in the mental chains of slavery since the days of slavery. Our leaders are by their choice. These kind of leaders are Uncle Toms, who are licking the boots of the white man for his pleasure and wealth, regardless to what happens to you and me for they care not.

No. 7—ABRAHAM'S PROPHECY. But I ask you to remember this: In the parable in the Bible of the rich man and Lazarus—which means none other than the white and Black people of America, the rich man died (deprived of authority and wealth). In the anguish of the torment of his loss of wealth and power, the parable refers to the rich man as being in hell. And, in this condition, the beggar (Lazarus) saw no hope to beg any longer, that once rich man for some of his sumptuous table food. Then, he turned to go for self (Abraham's bosom).

The prophecy which Abraham was the recipient of only means that after 400 years of our enslavement, all these things are coming to pass. I ask you to be in time and accept the truth and do not mix up the truth with falsehood while you know it, for the sake of untrue friendship.

What the Muslims Want

This is the question asked most frequently by both the whites and the blacks. The answers to this question I shall state as simply as possible.

1. We want freedom. We want a full and complete freedom.

2. We want justice. Equal justice under the law. We want justice applied equally to all, regardless of creed or class or color.

3. We want equality of opportunity. We want equal membership in society with the best in civilized society.

4. We want our people in America whose parents or grandparents were descendants from slaves, to be allowed to establish a separate state or territory of their own—either on this continent or elsewhere. We believe that our former slave masters are obligated to provide such land and that the area must be fertile and minerally rich. We believe that our former slave masters are obligated to maintain and supply our needs in this separate territory for the next 20 to 25 years—until we are able to produce and supply our own needs.

Since we cannot get along with them in peace and equality, after giving them 400 years of our sweat and blood and receiving in return some of the worst treatment human beings have ever experienced, we believe our contributions to this land and the suffering forced upon us by white America, justifies our demand for complete separation in a state or territory of our own.

5. We want freedom for all Believers of Islam now held in federal prisons. We want freedom for all black men and women now under death sentence in innumerable prisons in the North as well as the South.

We want every black man and women to have the freedom to accept or reject being separated from the slave master's children and establish a land of their own.

We know that the above plan for the solution of the black and white conflict is the best and only answer to the problem between two people.

6. We want an immediate end to the police brutality and mob attacks against the so-called Negro throughout the United States.

We believe that the Federal government should intercede to see that black men and women tried in white courts receive justice in accordance with the laws of the land — or allow us to build a new nation for ourselves, dedicated to justice, freedom and liberty.

7. As long as we are not allowed to establish a state or territory of our own, we demand not only equal justice under the laws of the United States, but equal employment opportunities—NOW!

We do not believe that after 400 years of free or nearly free labor, sweat and blood, which has helped America become rich and powerful, that so many thousands of black people should have to subsist on relief, charity or live in poor houses.

8. We want the government of the United States to exempt our people from ALL taxation as long as we are deprived of equal justice under the laws of the land.

9. We want equal education—but separate schools up to 16 for boys and 18 for girls on the condition that the girls be sent to women's colleges and universities. We want all black children educated, taught and trained by their own teachers.

Under such schooling system we believe we will make a better nation of people. The United States government should provide free, all necessary text books and equipment, schools and college buildings. The Muslim teachers shall be left free to teach and train their people in the way of righteousness, decency and self-respect.

10. We believe that intermarriage or race mixing should be prohibited. We want the religion of Islam taught without hindrance or suppression.

These are some of the things that we, the Muslims, want for our people in North America.

What the Muslims Believe

1. WE BELIEVE in the One God Whose proper Name is Allah.

2. WE BELIEVE in the Holy Quran and in the Scriptures of all the Prophets of God.

3. WE BELIEVE in the truth of the Bible, but we believe that it has been tampered with and must be reinterpreted so that mankind will not be snared by the falsehoods that have been added to it.

4. WE BELIEVE in Allah's Prophets and the Scriptures they brought to the people.

5. WE BELIEVE in the resurrection of the dead—not in physical resurrection—but in mental resurrection. We believe that the so-called Negroes are most in need of mental resurrection; therefore, they will be resurrected first.

Furthermore, we believe we are the people of God's choice, as it has been written, that God would choose the rejected and the de-spised. We can find no other persons fitting this description in these last days more than the so-called Negroes in America. We believe in the resurrection of the righteous.

6. WE BELIEVE in the judgment; we believe this first judgment will take place as God revealed, in America . . .

7. WE BELIEVE this is the time in history for the separation of the so-called Negroes and the so-called white Americans. We believe the black man should be freed in name as well as in fact. By this we mean that he should be freed from the names imposed upon him by his former slave masters. Names which identified him as being the slave master's slave. We believe that if we are free indeed, we should go in our own people's names—the black peoples of the earth.

8. WE BELIEVE in justice for all, whether in God or not; we believe as others, that we are due equal justice as human beings. We believe in equality—as a nation—of equals. We do not believe that we are equal with our slave masters in the status of "freed slaves."

We recognize and respect American citizens as independent people and we respect their laws which govern this nation.

9. WE BELIEVE that the offer of integration is hypocritical and is made by those who are trying to deceive the black peoples into believing that their 400-year-old open enemies of freedom, justice and equality are, all of a sudden, their "friends." Furthermore, we believe who declared ourselves to be righteous Muslims, should not participate in wars which take the lives of humans. We do not believe this nation should force us to take part in such wars, for we have nothing to gain from it unless America agrees to give us the necessary territory wherein we may have something to fight for. . . .

11. WE BELIEVE our women should be respected and protected as the women of other nationalities are respected and protected.

12. WE BELIEVE that Allah (God) appeared in the Person of Master W. Fard Muhammad, July, 1930; the long-awaited "Messiah" of the Christians and the "Mahdi" of the Muslims.

We believe further and lastly that Allah is God and besides HIM there is no God and He will bring about a universal government of peace wherein we all can live in peace together.

African-American Organizations

A. Philip Randolph Educational Fund
260 Park Avenue South, 6th Floor
New York, NY 10010
(212) 533-8000
President: Norman Hill

The A. Philip Randolph Educational Fund was founded in 1964 to end prejudice and discrimination towards African Americans, as well as assist in defending their human rights and civil liberties.

A. Philip Randolph Institute
260 Park Avenue South, 6th Floor
New York, NY 10010
(212) 533-8000
President: Norman Hill

Founded in 1964. Works toward political action, social change, and cooperation between labor groups and the African-American community. Also focuses on voter registration, labor education, and trade union leadership. Offers research, a speakers' bureau, and education programs.

AFNA National Education and Research Fund
117 South 17th Street, Suite 1200
Philadelphia, PA 19103
(215) 854-1470
(215) 854-1487 Fax
Web site: http://www.quikpage.com/A/afra/

The AFNA National Education and Research Fund was founded in 1968 as the American Foundation of Negro Affairs. Seeks to improve communication skills, reasoning, and self-image of young African Americans. Provides detailed educational planning to achieve its goals.

African American Institute
Chanin Building
380 Lexington Avenue
New York, NY 10168-4298
(212) 949-5666
(800) 745-3899
(212) 682-6174 Fax
Web site: http://www.interaction.org/mb/aai.html
Senior Vice President: Frank Ferrari

Founded in 1952 to improve understanding about African Americans and Africa. Supports conferences, media, congressional workshops, and various seminars, as well as providing training, developmental assistance, and informational activities. Publishes annual reports and related materials.

African American Labor Center
1925 K Street NW, Suite 300
Washington, D.C. 20006
(202) 778-4600
(202) 778-4601 Fax
Executive Director: Byron W. Charlton

Founded in 1964, the African American Labor Center assists in the development of sound labor organizations and other groups beneficial to the community. Offers education in leadership, vocations, credit unions, social programs, union medical, and communication. Helps initiate visitor programs so that African and American unionists can familiarize themselves with one another's politics, economics, and business philosophies.

African American Library and Information Science Association
c/o UCLA Center for African American Studies Library
P.O. Box 951545
Los Angeles, CA 90095-1545
(310) 825-6060
(310) 206-3421 Fax
E-Mail: imz@ucla.edu
President: Itibari Zulu
Web site: http://www.sscnet.ucla.edu/caas/library

Founded in 1993, the African American Library and Information Science Association works toward assisting and empowering African Americans, as well as sharing their heritage with them. Supplies collections containing black works and references, promotes various community literacy programs, and publishes *Lexicon of African American Subject Headings*.

African American Museum
1765 Crawford Road
Cleveland, OH 44106
(216) 791-1700
(216) 791-1774 Fax
Web site: http://www.ben.net/aamuseum/

Founded in 1957, the group focuses on promoting the study of African Americans, their achievements, and their history. Also strives for equality issues and to better race relations. Provides speakers, classes, and library holdings while also sponsoring African-American History Week and publishing the bimonthly *African American Museum Newsletter*.

African Cultural Foundation
731 Rock Creek Church Road NW
Washington, D.C. 20010-1616
(202) 882-2232
Deputy Director: Dr. Mohamed Saidu

Founded in 1982 as a multinational organization. Goals include the promotion of African cultural, social, political, and economic conditions worldwide and an increase in informational communication among races and people. Sponsors a discussion forum on cultural, philosophical, and political issues relevant to people of African descent. Also provides employment assistance, counseling and tutoring services, and tours of Africa.

The African Fund
198 Broadway
New York, NY 10038
(212) 962-1210
Executive Secretary: Jennifer Davis

Founded in 1966 as the African Legal Defense and Aid Fund, The African Fund focuses on defending human and civil rights, especially through legal assistance, medical relief, and research. Supports U.S. legislation that furthers the group's goals. Offers various publications.

Afro American Cultural Foundation
10 Fiske Plaza, Suite 204-206
Mount Vernon, NY 10550
Executive Director: Charles Smith

The Afro American Cultural Foundation was founded in 1969. The group seeks to improve African-American self-esteem, as well as the opinion and attitude of other races toward them. Also tries to increase awareness about national issues. Provides workshops, lectures, seminars, speakers, historical and economic research programs, and biographical archives. Special programs include an annual workshop called the Institute of Racism, plus the Students Essay Oratorical Content, and the Committee on Higher Education for Minorities. Publishes *Black Survival Seminar, Guide Book to Black Organizations in Westchester County,* and *New Black Image,* as well as other resources.

Afro American Historical and Genealogical Society
P.O. Box 73086
Washington, D.C. 20056
(202) 234-5350
(202) 829-8970
President: Barbara Dodson Walker

Founded in 1977 to support African-American history, genealogy, and culture. Conducts seminars and workshops, as well as providing archive material. Collects and maintains preserved documents of significance to the African-American community.

Afro American Historical Society Museum
1841 Kennedy Blvd.
Jersey City, NJ 07305
(201) 547-5262
(201) 547-5392 Fax
Contact: Theodore Brunson

Founded in 1977 to help preserve and share African-American history and culture. Conducts research on prevalent African-American topics, provides library holdings, organizes exhibits, and holds fund-raising activities.

Afro American Police League
P.O. Box 49122
Chicago, IL 60649
(312) 753-9454
Executive Officer: Edgar Gosa

The Afro American Police League was formed in 1968 as the Afro American Patrolmen's League. The group works to improve communication among officers, as well as educate the public about the role of law enforcement. Also focuses on police brutality, legal services, and law and order legislation.

Alliance of Minority Women for Business and Political Development
815 Thayer Avenue, Suite 202A
Silver Spring, MD 20910
(301) 565-0527
President: Brenda Alford

Formed in 1982 as the Task Force on Black Women Business Owners. Seeks to unite black women business owners and entrepreneurs to help meet their needs. The group represents members before regulatory agencies, the federal government, and private industry. Provides information and training on management, credit card and capital spending, marketing, government contracting, and business legislation.

American Association for Affirmative Action
11 East Hubbard Street, Suite 200
Chicago, IL 60611
(312) 329-2512
Executive Director: Judith Burnison

Founded in 1974 to promote affirmative action and equal opportunity, especially in the areas of education and employment. Also acts as a liaison with federal, state, and local organizations.

American Association of Blacks in Energy
927 15th Street NW, Suite 200
Washington, D.C. 20005
(202) 371-9530
(202) 371-9218 Fax

Founded in 1977 to represent the black community in issues involving energy use, research, and technology. Assists African Americans in gaining employment within the energy field. Works with the Development of Energy, Department of the Interior, Department of Commerce, the Small Business Administration, and other agencies in order to support policy-making activities, provide energy research, and inform the public on legislation. Publishes a quarterly newsletter, *Energy News.*

American Baptist Black Caucus
c/o Dr. Gillette O. James
Beth Eden Baptist Church
10th & Adeline Streets
Oakland, CA 94607
(510) 444-1625
(510) 832-2730
(510) 444-7405 Fax
Web site: http://www.betheden.com/Black_Caucus

Founded in 1968, the group represents approximately 750,000 individuals from African-American congregations of American Baptist Churches. Strives for unity among blacks and whites, scholarship aid for disadvantaged students, and resources for inner-city business and religious projects. Also seeks support for black colleges and universities, equal black representation, and open hiring policies. Publishes the quarterly *Black Caucus Newsletter* and the monthly *In Mission.*

American Civic Association
131 Front Street
Binghamton, NY 13905
(607) 723-9419
Executive Director: Irene Krome

Founded in 1939, the American Civic Association works to assist naturalized, foreign-born American citizens with problems associated with their origins. Supports citizenship and language programs, as well as helping immigrants integrate into American society.

American Civil Liberties Union
132 West 43rd Street
New York, NY 10036
(212) 944-9800
Web site: http://www.aclu.org/

Founded in 1920 to support rights guaranteed by the Constitution and the Declaration of Independence. Focuses on issues concerning freedom of speech, due process, and racial equality. Also works on court cases, legislation, and public protests that meet their goals. Offers various publications.

American Civil Liberties Union Foundation
132 West 43rd Street
New York, NY 10036
(212) 944-9800
Executive Director: Ira Glasser

Founded in 1966 as the Roger Baldwin Foundation of the American Civil Liberties Union (ACLU). The foundation works as a division of ACLU; it provides legal defense, research, and educational programs in support of ACLU, and also assists in local legal defence agencies to become self-supporting and self-sufficient.

American Institute for Economic Development
422 First Street SE, Suite 210
Washington, D.C. 20003
(202) 667-9833
President: Freddie John Martin

Founded in 1983. Membership includes federal government funding sources, corporations and businesses, and interested private sector parties. Seeks to provide economic prosperity for minority communities.

Association for Multicultural Counseling and Development
c/o American Association for Counseling and Development
5999 Stevenson Avenue
Alexandria, VA 22304
(703) 823-9800
(800) 545-AACD
Web site: http://edap.bgsu.edu/AMCD/
Executive Director: Patrick J. McDonough

The Association for Multicultural Counseling and Development was formed in 1972 as the Association for Non White Concerns in Personnel and Guidance. The organization works toward bettering human and civil rights, as well as for more understanding among races. Seeks to improve minority education opportunities and to help social services, community agencies, and other relevant parties in affecting change.

Association for the Study of Afro American Life and History
1407 14th Street NW
Washington, D.C. 20005
(202) 667-2822
(202) 387-9802 Fax
Web site: http://www.artnoir.com/asalh/
Executive Director: Karen McRae

Founded in 1915. Goals include racial harmony, promotion of black historical research, and advancement of African-American heritage programs. Encourages educational pursuits involving African Americans. Works with a variety of government organizations and other groups in order to further its goals. Publications include *Journal of Negro History, Negro History Bulletin,* brochures, and textbooks.

Association of African American People's Legal Council
13902 Robson Street
Detroit, MI 48227
(313) 837-0627
President: William Bert Johnson

The Association of African American People's Legal Council was founded in 1959 as a group of African-American attorneys. Works toward providing equal justice for African Americans. Also provides free legal counsel to blacks and creates reports on international inequality.

Association of Black Catholics Against Abortion
1011 1st Avenue
New York, NY 10022
(212) 371-1000
(212) 319-8265 Fax
President: Dr. Dolores Bernadette Grier

Founded in 1988 by black Catholics in opposition to abortion. The group conducts educational programs about abortion, child rearing, family issues, and related issues. Supports voter registration and strives for legislative change.

Association of Urban Universities
501 I Street SW
Washington, D.C. 20036
(202) 863-2027
President: James B. Harrison

Formed in 1976, the Association of Urban Universities, was known previously as the Committee of Urban Program Universities. Functions as a collection of urban area universities seeking to assist students in their educational needs. Has supported federal legislation concerning the Urban Grant University Program, as well as Title XI of the Higher Education Act and other legislative interests that supports the group's goals.

Black Affairs Center for Training and Organizational Development
c/o Margaret V. Wright
10918 Jarboe Court
Silver Spring, MD 20901
(301) 681-9827
(301) 681-3186 Fax
President: Margaret V. Wright

Formed in 1970. Supports social change, education, multicultural skills development, and other issues through training programs and consultation services. Focuses programs on topics such as women's issues, drugs and alcohol, stress management, single parenting, teen sex, day care, sexual harassment, and concerns of the aging. Publications include *BAC Update* and *National Minority Business Association.*

Black American Response to the African Community
127 North Madison Avenue, Suite 400
Pasadena, CA 91101
(818) 584-0303
Executive Director: Frank E. Wilson

Formed in 1984 to provide assistance to drought and famine victims in Africa. Provides emergency relief in the areas of water irrigation, medical needs, housing, food, and regeneration projects. Maintains Family Network Program in order to help orphans and the National Education Task Force to help educate Americans about problems in Africa. Raises money through television documentaries, benefit movie premieres, art exhibits, collection boxes, and other donations.

Black Americans for Life
419 7th Street NW, Suite 500
Washington, D.C. 20004
(202) 626-8800
Web site: http://www.nrlc.org/outreach/bal.html

Works for pro-life and pro-family issues. Supports the rights of the unborn and abortion alternatives within the black community. Provides information on resources and speakers.

Black Citizens for a Fair Media
156-20 Riverside Drive, No. 13L
New York, NY 10032
(212) 568-3168
President: Emma L. Bowen

Black Citizens for a Fair Media was founded in 1971. Seeks to improve the image of African Americans in the media. Also works toward programming, training, and hiring of blacks, as well as monitoring FCC standards for equal opportunity.

Black Community Crusade for Children
25 E Street NW
Washington, D.C. 20001
(202) 628-8787
(202) 662-3530 Fax
E-mail: africa@webcom.com
Web site: http://www.childrensdefense.org/bccc.html

Membership in the Black Community Crusade for Children consists of black clergy, educators, officials, and community leaders seeking to assist children. Focuses on building community, providing spiritual, character, and leadership development, working on interracial and interethnic communication, and offering related programs. Maintains Freedom Schools, which offers meals and economic and cultural achievement opportunities.

Black Employees of the Library of Congress
1412 Arcadia Avenue
Capitol Heights, MD 20743
(202) 287-7571
Executive Director: Howard R.L. Cook

Founded in 1970 with membership consisting of African American employees of the Library of Congress. Works toward providing racial equality throughout the U.S. Conducts research, provides in-formation on minority employment and black worker court litigation, and works with the Senate and House Appropriations Subcommittees. Publishes *Ethnic Brotherhood.*

Black, Indian, Hispanic, and Asian Women in Action
122 West Franklin Avenue, Suite 306
Minneapolis, MN 55404
(612) 870-1193
(612) 870-0855 Fax
Executive Director: Alice O. Lynch

Founded in 1983. Advocates educational programs for Black, Indian, Hispanic, and Asian women. Also focuses on issues concerning family violence, chemical dependency, social change, and physical, mental, and emotional health. Manages library holdings and publishes a quarterly newsletter called *Unison.*

Black Resources Information Coordinating Services
614 Howard Avenue
Tallahassee, FL 32040
(904) 576-7522
President: Emily A. Copeland

Provides various information services, seminars, and workshops to support African-American genealogy, ethnic heritage, and history. Maintains a library housing more than 8,000 resources. Assists in research work. Publications include *Big Brass, Guide to Afro American Resources, Media Showcase,* and *Minority Information Trade Annual.*

Black Revolutionary War Patriots Foundation
1612 K Street NW, Suite 1104
Washington, D.C. 20006
(202) 452-1776
(202) 728-0770
Web site: http://www.blackpatriots.org/
President: Maurice A. Barboza

Founded in 1985, the Black Revolutionary War Patriots Foundation is also known as the Patriots Foundation. The organization works to raise funds for the construction and maintenance of a memorial in Washington, D.C., that is dedicated to black patriots of the American Revolutionary War.

Black Silent Majority Committee of the USA
P.O. Box 5519
San Antonio, TX 78201
(210) 340-2424
(210) 340-3816 Fax
Director: Clay Clarbourne

Founded in 1970 as the National Black Silent Majority Committee. Works in support of improved race relations worldwide and school prayer; opposes forced busing and similar issues. Strives to illustrate African Americans as upstanding Americans that support patriotic causes, religious morals, and so on. Publishes booklets, brochures, and other materials.

Black Veterans for Social Justice
686 Fulton Street
Brooklyn, NY 11217
(718) 935-1116
(718) 935-1629
President: Job Mashariki

Formed in 1979 to help black veterans in issues concerning civil rights, unjust dishonorable discharges, and Veterans Administration benefits. Seeks to overcome discrimination, provide educational programs, and provide counseling services. Offers community workshops and assistance to black veterans harmed by Agent Orange.

Black Women in Church and Society

c/o Interdenominational Theological Center
671 Bekwith Street SW
Atlanta, GA 30314
(404) 527-7740
(404) 527-0901 Fax
Web site: http://www.atlantahighered.org/institutions/itc.htm

Formed in 1982. Supports African-American women serving in leadership roles in the church and society. Conducts research, sponsors charitable events, and maintains library holdings on black theology, feminism, and womanist movements.

Black Women Organized for Educational Development

518 17th Street, Suite 202
Oakland, CA 94612
(510) 763-9501
(510) 763-4327 Fax
Executive Director: Frankie Arrington

Black Women Organized for Educational Development was founded in 1984 to promote the empowerment of low income and socially disadvantaged women. Provides various programs seeking to improve the social and economic well-being of disadvantaged women, as well as a mentor program for junior high teen women in low-income urban areas. Offers support groups, maintains the Black Women's Resource Center, and publishes the quarterly *BWOED Newsletter.*

Black Women's Roundtable on Voter Participation

1629 K Street NW, Suite 801
Washington, D.C. 20006
(202) 659-4929
(202) 659-5025 Fax
Web site: http://www.telecity.org/concernedwomen/
Executive Director: James Ferguson

Founded in 1983 as a division of the National Coalition on Black Voter Participation. Focuses on gaining social justice and economic equality through political participation. Activities include voter registration, education, and empowerment programs, women's leadership skills development, discussion groups on the influence of women voting. Supports groups with similar goals.

Black World Foundation

P.O. Box 2869
Oakland, CA 94609
(510) 547-6679
(510) 547-6679 Fax
President: Robert Chrisman

Founded in 1969. Develops and distributes African-American educational materials to help promote black cultural and political awareness. Publications include the quarterly *The Black Scholar* and *Listing of Black Books in Print.*

Blacks Against Nukes

3728 New Hampshire Avenue NW, Suite 202
Washington, D.C. 20010
Contacts: Brenda and Gregory Johnson

Blacks Against Nukes was formed in 1981. Seeks to inform individuals against the dangers of nuclear war, nuclear energy, and radiation. Supports alternate energy resources and works towards gaining government funding for blacks seeking to purchase solar energy projects. Provides seminars, workshops, and speakers.

Blacks in Government

1820 11th Street NW
Washington, D.C. 20001-5015
(202) 667-3280
(202) 667-3705 Fax
Web site: http://www.bignet.org/
President: Oscar Ason

Founded in 1975 by employees or retired employees of local, state, and federal government agencies. Seeks to improve the status of African Americans within the U.S. government. Provides training programs geared toward instilling liberty and a feeling of well being, as well as seminars and workshops. Publishes a quarterly newsletter, *Blacks in Government News.*

Caribbean Action Lobby

c/o Oswald B. Silvera
1534 Bedford Avenue
Brooklyn, NY 11216
(718) 467-1777
Contact: Oswald B. Silvera

Founded in 1980. Works to educate Caribbean immigrants in America on topics such as voting, U.S. immigration laws, and American government. Also seeks to sensitize and inform government officials on issues affecting Caribbean immigrants. Provides educational workshops, seminars, and activities, as well as lobbying on pertinent issues.

Center for Educating African American Males

Morgan State University
Jenkins Building, Room 308 B
Cold Spring Lane and Hillen Road
Baltimore, MD 21239
(410) 319-3275
(410) 319-3871 Fax
Director: Dr. Spencer H. Holland

Founded in 1990 by African-American males seeking to help male youths. Promotes African-American academic achievement while also providing positive role modeling in the community. Publishes *Project 2000 Focus*, an annual newsletter.

Center on Budget and Policy Priorities

236 Massachusetts Avenue NE, Suite 305
Washington, D.C. 20002
(202) 544-0591
Web site: http://www.cbpp.org/
Director: Robert Greenstein

The Center on Budget and Policy Priorities was founded in 1981. The organization provides information on federal and state spending, specifically on its effects on moderate-and low-income families. Focuses on poverty, social programs, defense spending, tax policy, hunger and nutrition issues, minimum wage, unemployment, and military retirement.

Citizens' Commission on Civil Rights

1201 16th Street NW, Suite 424
Washington, D.C. 20036
(202) 822-7708

E-mail: citizens@cccr.org
Web site: http://www.cccr.org/
Chairperson: Arthur Flemming

Founded in 1982 with a membership consisting of bipartisan former federal cabinet officials. Goals include monitoring federal government legislation concerning discrimination, furthering civil rights, and formulating policy recommendations.

Coalition of Black Trade Unionists

P.O. Box 66268
Washington, D.C. 20035
(202) 429-1203
(202) 429-1102 Fax
President: William Lucy

Formed in 1972, the Coalition of Black Trade Unionists consists of 76 separate unions combined for a united front in favor of black organized labor. Works for voter registration and education, better employment opportunities, and economic development.

Commission for Racial Justice

105 Madison Avenue
New York, NY 10016
(212) 683-5656
Executive Director: Dr. Benjamin F. Chavis, Jr.

The Commission for Racial Justice was founded in 1963 with the purpose of representing members of the United Church of Christ on racial justice issues, especially those in black communities. Publications include the weekly *Civil Rights Journal, Commission News,* and *The Black Family: An Afro Centric Perspective.*

Conference of Prince Hall Grand Masters

4th & State Street
Pine Bluff, AR 71601
(501) 534-5467
(501) 868-5572
(501) 535-3581 Fax
Contact: Howard L. Woods

Founded in 1919, the group provides leadership and other resources for the betterment of the black community. Offers seminars, workshops, and training programs to train progressive leaders. Works with charity functions. Publishes *Conference of Grand Masters and Prince Hall Masonic Directory.*

Congress of National Black Churches

1225 I Street NW, Suite 750
Washington. D.C. 20005
(202) 371-1091
(202) 371-0908 Fax
Web site: http://www.cnbc.org/
Executive Director: H. Michael Lemmons

Formed in 1978 to promote unity, charity, and fellowship. Seeks to provide a united front on issues such as economic development, antidrug campaigns, and leadership training. Publishes *Visions,* a quarterly newsletter.

Congress of Racial Equality (CORE)

817 Broadway, 3rd Floor
New York, NY 10003
(212) 598-4000
(212) 598-4141 Fax
National Chairman: Roy Innis
Web site: http://www.core-online.org/

Founded in 1942 as a black nationalist organization. Seeks black political power in areas where they do not demographically dominate while also conducting research on the issue. Provides a speakers' bureau and sponsors charitable programs. Publications include *CORE Magazine, Correspondent, Equal Opportunity Journal, Population Studies,* and *Profiles in Black.*

Congressional Black Associates

2236 Sam Rayburn Building
Washington, D.C. 20515
(202) 225-5601
President: Samuel E. Thomton III

Founded in 1979 by black congressional staff members. Provides information to the African-American community on federal government operations. Strives to raise the social, political, and economic status of African Americans, as well as sharing and highlighting the black American experience. Offers seminars, a placement service, and publications such as the quarterly *News from Congressional Black Associates.*

Congressional Black Caucus

319 Cannon HOB
Washington, D.C. 20515
(202) 225-3315
Web site: http://drum.ncsc.org/~carter/CBC.html
Chairman: Donald M. Pane

Founded in 1971 as a collection of black members of the U.S. House of Representatives. Seeks to work with black officials throughout the government to meet the legislative concerns of African Americans. Focuses on issues such as employment, welfare reform, health development, and international affairs. Publications include *Black Staff Directory* and a quarterly newsletter, *For the People.*

Cooperative Assistance Fund

2100 M Street NW, Suite 306
Washington, D.C. 20037
President: Herman Wilson

The Cooperative Assistance Fund was founded in 1968 with the purpose of utilizing private investment capital for the benefit of low-income community economic development. Conducts research and works for other development money sources.

Council for a Black Economic Agenda

1367 Connecticut Avenue NW
Washington, D.C. 20036
(202) 331-1103
Executive Officer: Paul Pride

Founded in 1984. Works to assist African Americans in becoming economically self-sufficient. To accomplish its goals, the organization seeks to lessen black dependence on certain government programs, assist in urban development projects, strive for tax write-off legislation for small businesses in economically repressed areas, and assist in public housing management. Also strives to gain government assistance in areas such as day care, foster care, adoption, unemployment compensation, education, and job training.

Council for African American Progress

P.O. Box 946
Little Rock, AR 72203-0946
(501) 376-7415
Contact: Wayne E.X. Burt

Promotes African-American culture and heritage through the support of educational, social, political, economic, and substance abuse prevention programs. Backs multicultural curriculums in education while also promoting the celebration of African-American holidays.

Department of Civil Rights, AFL-CIO

815 16th Street NW
Washington, DC 20006
(202) 637-5270
Web site: http://www.aflcio.org/
Director: Richard Womack

Founded in 1955. Functions as a liaison between women's and civil rights groups and government offices connected to equal opportunity issues. Assists in implementing state and federal equal opportunity laws, as well as in developing affirmative action programs. Also provides information on civil rights, speakers for unions and other organizations, and helps resolve difficulties involving Title VII of the 1964 Civil Rights Act and Executive Order 11246.

Ethiopian Community Mutual Assistance Association

554 West 114th Street, Suite 2R
New York, NY 10025
(212) 749-5957
President: Fetene Hailu

Founded in 1981 to advance the economic and social needs of Ethiopians living in America. Focuses on immigration, civil rights, historical identity, cultural communication and understanding, and refugee rights.

Free African Liberation Organization African Liberation Movement

P.O. Box 64
Adelphi Station
Brooklyn, NY 11238
(718) 237-2651
Founder: Ameer Mustafa Ali Hassan

Formed in 1989 with a membership consisting of Americans descended from African slaves. Goals include attaining political independence, gaining national sovereignty, and providing economic reparations. Maintains a speakers' bureau, offers reference holdings, and publishes *Nationalist View.*

Institute for Black Leadership Development and Research

1028 Dole Human Development Center
University of Kansas
Lawrence, KS 66045
(913) 864-3990
(913) 864-5323 Fax
Program Assistant: Diana Horton

Formed in 1988 to develop leadership skills in the African-American community and for the betterment of society. Provides research, training, and reference holdings on a variety of topics, including leadership, aging, multiculturalism, developmental disabilities, and substance abuse. Publications include the *Narratives of African Americans in Kansas: Beyond the Exodus Movement* and *The Role of Higher Education in Alcohol and Other Drug Abuse Prevention.*

Institute for the Advanced Study of Black Family Life and Culture

175 Filbert Street, Suite 202
Oakland, CA 94607
(510) 836-3245

(510) 836-3248 Fax
Executive Director: Wade Nobles

Goals of the Institute for the Advanced Study of Black Family Life and Culture include reclaiming traditional African-American culture, strengthening black families, and revitalizing the African-American community. Conducts research in the areas of teenage pregnancy, substance abuse, child rearing practices, and mental health issues. Maintains a speakers' bureau, publishes *African American Families Issues, Insights, and Direction,* and sponsors the HAWK Federation, a training program dedicated to providing character development to black children within the schools.

International Black Women's Congress

1081 Bergen Street
Newark, NJ 07112
(201) 926-0570
(201) 926-0818 Fax
President: Dr. La Francis Rodgers Rose

Founded in 1983 to help African-American women gain assistance in employment needs, education, and other issues. Offers support groups, charity programs, and a speakers' bureau. Publications include *Black Women's Health and Social Policy, International Black Women's Directory, Oni Newsletter, Political Socialization of Black Women: Empowerment,* and *River of Tears: Politics of Black Women's Health.*

International Campaign to Free Geronimo Ji Jaga Pratt

P.O. Box 3585
Oakland, CA 94609
Chairperson: Muhjah Shakir

Founded in 1988 to help obtain freedom for Geronimo Pratt, a former Black Panther deputy of defense, who the group believes was wrongly framed for robbery and murder by the Los Angeles Police Department and the FBI. Provides educational programs, a speakers' bureau, and other forms of public awareness resources to achieve its goals.

Interreligious Foundation for Community Organization

c/o Rev. Lucius Walker
402 West 145th Street, 3rd Floor
New York, NY 10031
(212) 926-5757
Web site: http://www.ifconews.org/
Executive Director: Rev. Lucius Walker

Founded in 1967. Focuses on political organization, housing, education, job training, and legal aid. Provides technical and financial assistance to community organizations, as well as helping poor and other troubled communities to assist themselves.

Jack and Jill of America Foundation

c/o Violet D. Greer
PO Drawer 3689
Chattanooga, TN 37404
(615) 624-6097
Board Secretary: Violet D. Greer

Founded in 1968. Works to improve educational, social, cultural, and civic opportunities for minority youths, as well as providing educational grant monies to community projects and monitoring relevant legislative issues. Provides college prep, preschool, and other programs.

Joint Center for Political and Economic Studies

1090 Vermont Avenue NW, Suite 1100
Washington, D.C. 20005-4961
(202) 789-3500
(202) 789-6390 Fax
President: Eddie N. Williams
Web site: http://www.jointctr.org

The Joint Center for Political and Economic Studies was founded in 1970 as a nonpartisan organization seeking to provide information on African-American elected and appointed public officials. Also focuses on black voting, public policy issues, and topics that affect socially and economically disadvantaged communities.

Lawyers Committee for Civil Rights Under Law

1400 I Street NW, Suite 400
Washington, D.C. 20005
(202) 371-1212
Director: Barbara R. Arnwine

Founded in 1963, the Lawyers Committee for Civil Rights Under Law provides legal assistance to African Americans and other minority groups living in urban regions. Focuses on issues such as employment, voting rights, civic liberties, housing, and discrimination.

Leadership Conference on Civil Rights

1629 K Street NW
Suite 1010
Washington, D.C. 20006
Chair: Dorothy L. Height
Executive Director: Wade Henderson
Web site: http://www.lccr.org11ccr.html

Founded in 1950 as the Civil Rights Mobilization. Works on issues such as civil rights, social and economic legislation, and enforcement of preexisting laws. Reviews civil rights activities of government offices such as the U.S. Department of Justice and the U.S. Department of Education. Previous studies included examining President Reagan's tax and budget programs in light of social welfare, housing, education, and similar areas.

Lincoln Institute for Research and Education

1001 Connecticut Avenue NW, Suite 1135
Washington, D.C. 20036
(202) 223-5112
President: J.A. Parker

The Lincoln Institute for Research and Education was formed in 1978. Evaluates public policy issues affecting middle-class black Americans, as well as other theories and programs the group feels may be harmful to the long-range interests of African Americans. Provides research findings to government officials and the public to help overcome problems facing blacks. Supports private enterprise, a growing economy, and strong national defense, while also providing research and education programs, conferences, and seminars. Publishes *Lincoln Review,* a quarterly journal.

Minority Caucus of Family Service America

34 1/2 Beacon Street
Boston, MA 02108
(617) 523-6400
(617) 525-3034 Fax
Executive Director: Mark Allen

Formed in 1969, the Minority Caucus of Family Service America was known previously as the Black Caucus of Family Service Association of America and the Minorities Caucus of Family Service Association of America. Works toward overcoming racism. Also works with policy-making groups. Divisions include the Minority Resource Council and Task Force to Eradicate Institutional Racism.

NAACP Legal Defense and Educational Fund

99 Hudson Street, 16th Floor
New York, NY 10013
(212) 219-1900
Web site: http://www.ldfla.org/
Contact: Julius LeVonne

Founded in 1939. Strives to provide legal support in the areas of constitutional rights, employment, education, housing, voting, health care, and other areas. Has also worked to abolish capital punishment and to gain prison reform. Provides court action funding, education scholarships, and informative reports.

National Alliance of Black Organizations

3724 Airport Blvd.
Austin, TX 78722
(512) 478-9802
(512) 478-9804 Fax
President: M.J. Anderson, Sr.

Founded in 1976 as a committee representing various black organizations and associations. Supports voting and charity functions. Also acts as a forum for exchanging ideas on prevalent issues.

National Alliance of Black School Educators

2816 Georgia Avenue NW
Washington, D.C. 20001
(202) 483-1549
(202) 483-8323 Fax
Web site: http://www.nabse.org/
Executive Director: Dr. Ernest Holmes

The National Alliance of Black School Educators was founded in 1970 as the National Alliance of Black School Superintendents. Works to eliminate racism within education and to raise the educational standards of African-American students. Works with a number of local, state, and federal agencies to further the goals of black education; also involves itself with pertinent legislation matters. Sponsors workshops, encourages research, and supports meaningful black American curriculum.

National Association for Black Veterans

P.O. Box 11432
Milwaukee, WI 53211
(414) 265-8940
(414) 342-5000
(800) 842-4597
(414) 332-4627 Fax
Executive Officer: Thomas H. Wynn, Sr.

The National Association for Black Veterans was founded in 1970 as Interested Veterans of the Central City. Represents black veterans before the Veterans Administration. Also works to gain honorable discharge for veterans unjustly dismissed from service and, through the Readjustment Counseling Program, to defend incarcerated veterans. Holds workshops dealing with Post Traumatic Stress Disorder, as well as other training services. Helps elderly and homeless African-American veterans. Publishes the monthly newspaper *Eclipse.*

Appendix 2: African-American Organizations

National Association for Equal Opportunity in Higher Education
Lovejoy Building
400 12th Street NE, 2nd floor
Washington, D.C. 20002
(202) 543-9111
President: Dr. Samuel L. Myers

Founded in 1969. Seeks to gain more government and private organization support for African-American universities and colleges. Also strives to increase black leadership in educational organizations, commissions and federal boards. Provides placement services and various publications.

National Association for the Advancement of Black Americans in Vocational Education
c/o Dr. Ethel O. Washington
P.O. Box 04437
Detroit, MI 48204
(313) 494-1660
(313) 494-1132
President: Dr. Ethel O. Washington

Founded in 1977, the group seeks to instill national leadership and increase the impact of black American education funding, as well as better recruitment and hiring possibilities and improve other areas affecting blacks. Provides workshops, placement services, and training models to further their goals. Publications include *Conference Proceedings* and a quarterly newsletter.

National Association for the Advancement of Colored People (NAACP)
Washington Bureau
1025 Vermont Ave NW, Suite 1120
Washington, DC 20005
(202) 638-2269
President: Kweisi Mfume

The National Association for the Advancement of Colored People seeks to gain equality through the democratic progress. NAACP focuses on eliminating racial discrimination in housing, voting, schools, transportation, the court system, employment, prisons, and other areas. Provides day care services, job assistance and referrals, informative seminars, and a law library. Supports the NAACP National Housing Corporation, which helps with low- and moderate-income housing development.

National Association of Black County Officials
440 1st Street NW, Suite 500
Washington, D.C. 20001
(202) 347-6953
(202) 393-6596 Fax
Web site: http://www.nobco.org/
Executive Director: Maria Desenna Lopes

Founded in 1975, the National Association of Black County Officials focuses on providing planning and management assistance. Also works on resolving local, state, and national problems. Holds seminars and training sessions. Supports open communication. Publishes *County Compass* and *County to County.*

National Association of Blacks in Criminal Justice
North Carolina Central University
Criminal Justice Building, Room 106
P.O. Box 19788
Durham, NC 27707
(919) 683-1801

(919) 683-1903 Fax
Web site: http://www.nabcj.org/

Founded in 1972 as a collection of criminal justice professionals concerned with the impact of justice issues on the African-American community. Works with local, state, and federal justice organizations to improve minority recruitment and related issues. Provides conferences, career development training, and community group assistance. Publications include *Local Criminal Justice Issues Newsletter, NABCJ Annual Report, NABCJ Minority Criminal Justice Personnel Directory,* and other newsletter and reports.

National Association of Blacks within Government
1820 11th Street NW
Washington, D.C. 20001-5015
(202) 667-3280
(202) 667-3705 Fax

Formed in 1982, the National Association of Blacks within Government seeks to make African Americans more employable within the government. Also strives to prepare black youths for government and private sector employment. Offers an annual seminar focused on producing interpersonal, management, learning, and other skills within young African Americans.

National Association of Black Women Attorneys
724 9th Street NW, Suite 206
Washington, D.C. 20001
(202) 637-3570
(202) 637-4892 Fax
President: Mabel D. Haden

The National Association of Black Women Attorneys was founded in 1972. Seeks to promote the opportunities of women through law, aid in civil and human rights cases, and provides expanded opportunities for African-American women lawyers.

National Association of Negro Business and Professional Women's Clubs
1806 New Hampshire Avenue NW
Washington, D.C. 20009
(202) 483-4206
President: Jacquelyn Gates

Formed in 1935, the group seeks to gather professional black women in a united front in favor of improved social and civic conditions. Also focuses its efforts on employment, education, health, housing, legislation, and aged disabled issues. Provides consumer education services, prison reform programs, and a speakers' bureau.

National Association of State Universities and Land Grant Colleges
1307 New York Avenue NW, Suite 400
Washington, D.C. 20005-4701
(202) 778-0818
(202) 296-6458 Fax
Web site: http://www.nasulgc.org
President: Robert L. Clodius

Founded in 1962. Focuses on the effect that federal and state legislation has on higher education, curriculum, enrollment, and other topics prevalent to education. Operates committees on black colleges, federal relations, and Senate lobbying.

National Black Caucus of Local Elected Officials
1301 Pennsylvania Avenue NW, Suite 550
Washington, D.C. 20004
(202) 626-3000

(202) 626-3191
(202) 626-3101 Fax
E-mail: gordon@NLC.org
Contact: Mary France Gordon

Founded in 1970 as a collection of elected African-American municipal and county officials. Goals include improving government organizational structure, supporting legislative and economic policies that are beneficial to the black community, and dealing with problems of its members. Publishes *Constituency,* a monthly journal, and *Newslines,* a monthly newsletter.

National Black Caucus of State Legislators

Hall of States
444 North Capitol Street NW, Suite 622
Washington, D.C. 20001
(202) 624-5457
(202) 508-3826 Fax
President: Lois Deberry

Founded in 1977 to help communication and networking among black state legislators and federal and state officials. Conducts seminars, operates a speakers' bureau, arranges meetings between government groups, and maintains numerous committees dedicated to assisting others and improving the welfare of U.S. citizens. Publishes the *Directory of Black States Legislators* and a quarterly newsletter, the *Legislator.*

National Black Child Development Institute

1023 15th Street NW, Suite 600
Washington, D.C. 20005
(202) 387-1281
(202) 234-1738 Fax
Web site: http://www.nbcdi.org/
Executive Director: Evely K. Moore

The National Black Child Development Institute was founded in 1970. Seeks to improve the quality of life for young African Americans. Focuses on issues concerning child care, health, child welfare, and education. Works toward and campaigns for policies that will assist black children. Publications include the quarterly *Child Health Talk.*

National Black Law Student Association

1225 11th Street NW
Washington, D.C. 20001
Web site: http://www.tc.umn.edu/nlhome/g015/blsa/blsa.html
Chairperson: Brian Roberts

Founded in 1967. Supports the needs of black law students while also strengthening their relationship with attorneys, the legal system, and society. Seeks to work for the benefit of the black community, as well as illustrate the professional competence of African Americans. Formerly known as the Black American Law Student Association.

National Black Leadership Roundtable

1424 Longworth House Building
Washington, D.C. 20515
President: Eleanor Holmes

Founded in 1983 as a compilation of representatives from various black organizations. Supports economic, political, and other issues important to the black community. Backs elected officials sensitive to the needs of African Americans. Provides a forum for members.

National Black on Black Love Campaign

1000 East 87th Street
Chicago, IL 60619
(312) 978-0868
(312) 978-7082 Fax
Executive Director: Geri Duncan Jones

Founded in 1983, the National Black on Black Love Campaign seeks to spread the concepts of love and respect to oppose crime, especially black-against-black crimes. Supports youth organizations, seminars, a speakers' bureau, and charity programs. Other activities include No Crime Day and Adopt a Building.

National Black Republican Council

375 South End Avenue, Plaza 400-84
New York, NY 10280
(212) 662-1335
Chairman: Fred Brown

The National Black Republican Council was founded in 1972. The group works to gain the election of more African-American Republicans at the national, state, and local levels. Operates a speakers' bureau.

National Black Sisters' Conference

3027 4th Street NE
Washington, D.C. 20017
(202) 529-9250
(202) 529-9370 Fax
E-mail: nbsc@igc.apc.org
President: Sr. Patricia Chappell

Founded in 1968. Offers retreats, consulting, and programs in leadership and cultural understanding. Goals include developing the resources of African-American Catholic women, combating racism, and serving the black community. Provides educational and spiritual programs. Publishes *Joint Black Clergy and Black Sisters, Naming and Claiming Our Resources, Tell It Like It Is,* a quarterly newsletter titled *Signs of Soul,* and other books and articles.

National Black Survival Fund

P.O. Box 3885
Lafayette, LA 70502-3885
(318) 232-7672
Chairman: A.J. McKnight CS

The National Black Survival Fund was formed in 1982. Seeks to improve the economic and educational status of poor African Americans so they can become self-sustaining. Tries to overcome discrimination, along with subjects they feel severely threaten the stability of the black community, such as economic recession and cutbacks in federal funding. Maintains the Food for Survival Program, the Health Care for Survival Program, and the Jobs for Survival Program.

National Black United Front

P.O. Box 4700665
Brooklyn, NY 11247
(718) 467-0258
Web site: http://www.nbufront.org/
Contact: Elizabeth Butler

The National Black United Front was founded in 1980. It seeks to unite African Americans for the purpose of eliminating racism, sexism, and violence. Focuses on issues such as police brutality, unemployment, economics, and racist groups. Provides charity programs and publishes *The Front Page,* a quarterly newsletter. Participates in boycotts, demonstrations, and electoral politics.

217

Appendix 2: African-American Organizations

National Black United Fund
40 Clinton Street
Newark, NJ 07102
(201) 643-5122
(800) 223-0866
(201) 648-8350 Fax
E-mail: nbuf@tnt.org
Web site: http://www.nbuf.org/
President: William T. Merritt

Formed in 1972, the National Black United Fund provides financing to programs assisting African-American communities. Supports projects in the areas of education, health, human services, economic development, social justice, arts, culture, and emergency needs. Supports volunteerism, self-help, and mutual aid. Backs the National Black United Federation of Charities, which the group also founded.

National Black Women's Consciousness Raising Association
1906 North Charles Street
Baltimore, MD 21218
(410) 727-8900
(410) 789-3553

The National Black Women's Consciousness Raising Association was founded in 1975. The group focuses on women's rights and issues, specifically in relation to black women. Offers educational and informational workshops, seminars, and the BWCR semiannual newsletter. Acts as a support group for women.

National Black Women's Political Leadership Caucus
3005 Bladensburg Road NE, No. 217
Washington, D.C. 20018
(202) 529-2806
Executive Director: Junita Kennedy Morgan

The National Black Women's Political Leadership Caucus was founded in 1971. Goals of the group include participation in the political and economic process by black women, as well as education for female African Americans in the role of national, state, and local government. Activities include speaker training, research, placement services, charity work, workshops, and children's services.

National Black Youth Leadership
250 West 54th Street, Suite 800
New York, NY 10019
(212) 541-7600
Executive Director: Dennis Rahim Watson

Founded in 1983, the National Black Youth Leadership works for developing black youth leadership, development, and education. Seeks to inform people about multiculturalism, cultural diversity, and racism. Sponsors drug abuse awareness programs. Advises parents and teachers in the importance of assisting young adults.

National Business League
1511 K Street NW, Suite 432
Washington, D.C. 20005
(202) 737-4430
(202) 466-5487 Fax
President: Sherman Copilin

Formed in 1900, the National Business League was formerly known as the National Negro Business League. The organization supports economic development, small business management and ownership, and corporate free enterprise as it pertains to minorities.

Also provides committees on women in business, policy review, black issues, and similar topics. Publications include *Corporate Guide for Minority Venders, National Memo,* and *President's Briefs.*

National Caucus and Center on Black Aged
1424 K Street NW, Suite 500
Washington, D.C. 20005
(202) 637-8400
(202) 347-0895 Fax
President: Samuel J. Simmons

Founded in 1970 out of a merger of the National Center on Black Aged and the National Caucus on the Black Aged. Focuses on improving the status of low-income senior citizens by working with state and federal agencies in improving economic, health, and social standards. Provides community awareness material, an employment program for older citizens, and rental housing for the elderly. Also offers training in nursing home administration, housing management, long-term care, and commercial property maintenance.

National Center for Urban Environmental Studies
James Office Building, Room 405
Annapolis, MD 214011
(301) 841-3612
President: Larry Young

Formed in 1975. The National Center for Urban Environmental Studies was previously known as the Joint Center for Urban Environmental Studies and later as Center for Urban Environmental Studies. Strives to assist urban legislators in health, energy, and urban environmental policy issues. Monitors relevant legislation and conducts environmental programs for elected officials.

National Coalition for Quality Integrated Education
1201 16th Street NW, Room 424
Washington, D.C. 20036
(202) 822 7708
Director: Dr. Arthur Flemming

Founded in 1975 as the National Center for Quality Integrated Education. Focuses on improving and desegregating elementary and secondary schools in America. Also coordinates, supports, and encourages legislative involvement by citizens.

National Coalition of 100 Black Women
38 West 32nd Street, 16th Floor
New York, NY 10001-3816
Chairman: Jewell Jackson McCabe

Founded in 1981. Focuses on issues such as economic development, health, housing, criminal justice, employment, voting, education, the arts, and family issues. Provides career networking and leadership development. Supports role modeling and mentorship programs to provide assistance to young students, college aged women, recent graduates, and teen mothers. Provides communication links for black women to corporations and political groups. Publishes *National Coalition of 100 Black Women Statement,* a semiannual newsletter.

National Coalition of Blacks for Reparations in America
P.O. Box 62622
Washington, D.C. 20029-2622
(202) 635-6272
(504) 357-7909
Web site: http://www.ncobra.com/
Contact: Hannibal T. Afrik

Founded in 1989, the National Coalition of Blacks for Reparations in America seeks to gain reparations from the U.S. government, other governments, and businesses that profited from labor provided by African slaves. Provides statistics, a speakers' bureau, educational and research programs, and publications such as *ENCOBRA* and *Reparation/NCOBRA NEWS.*

National Coalition on Black Voter Participation

1629 K Street NW, Suite 801
Washington, D.C. 20006
(202) 659-4929
(202) 659-5025 Fax
Executive Director: Sonia R. Jarvis
Web site: http://www.bigvote.org

National Coalition on Black Voter Participation was formed in 1976. Supports and tries to increase black voter registration, participation in the electoral process, nonpartisan participation, and citizen empowerment programs. Conducts training programs, distributes resource materials, and collects voting data. Sponsors Operation Big Vote and the Black Women's Roundtable on Voter Participation. Publications include *How to Organize and Implement a Successful Nonpartisan Voter Participation Campaign* and *Operation Big Vote Newsletter.*

National Coalition to End Racism in America's Child Care System

22075 Koths Street
Taylor, MI 48180
(313) 295-0257
President: Carol Coccia

Founded in 1984 as a coalition of adoption support groups, child care agencies, politicians, and concerned individuals seeking to house foster and adoption children in supportive homes, regardless of race. Provides educational resources to political groups, private and public organizations, and the media. Offers a quarterly newsletter, *The Children's Voice.*

National Conference of Black Lawyers

2 West 125th Street
New York, NY 10027
(212) 864-4000
(212) 829-5182 Fax
Director: Adjoa Aiyetero
Web site: http://www.geocities.com/capitolhill/lobby/9470

Formed in 1968 as a collection of American and Canadian attorneys seeking to use their legal expertise to assist the black community. Focuses on voting rights, international affairs, poverty, and community organization needs. Also researches racism, provides continuing legal training to members, maintains a legal library, and publishes the quarterly *Notes.* Offers a speakers' bureau which addresses civil rights, criminal justice, and international human rights issues.

National Conference of Black Mayors

1422 West Peachtree Street NW, Suite 800
Atlanta, GA 30309
(404) 892-0127
(404) 876-4597 Fax
Web site: http://www.votenet.com/members/b/l/a/blackmayors/
Executive Director: Michelle D. Kourouma

Founded in 1974, the National Conference of Black Mayors works to improve executive management, assist communities, and promote industry, employment, and investment. Also supports the

activities of African-American elected officials. Provides workshops and publications.

National Conference of Black Political Scientists

c/o Shiela Ards
Hubert Humphrey Institute
University of Minnesota
Minneapolis, MN 55455
(612) 625-9505
(612) 625-6351 Fax
E-mail: sards@hhh.umn.edu
Web site: http://power.ncat.edu/ncobps/default.htm

National Conference of Black Political Scientists was founded in 1969. Supports research in the area of black politics, while also seeking to improve the political life of African Americans. Publications include the *National Political Science Review.*

National Council of African American Men

1028 Dole Human Development Center
University of Kansas
Lawrence, KS 66045
(913) 864-3990
(913) 864-5323 Fax
Program Assistant: Diana Horton

Founded in 1989 to foster leadership skills within the African-American community. Supports positive family and community development by seeking to empower black men to assume responsibility within their lives. Other goals include the acquisition of more accurate, positive African-American scholarship and literature. Publishes semiannual *Journal of African American Male Studies.*

National Council on Black Aging

P.O. Box 51275
Durham, NC 27717
(919) 493-4858
(919) 493-4858 Fax
Director: Dr. Jaquelyne J. Jackson

Founded in 1975, the National Council on Black Aging conducts research and reviews policies affecting older blacks and other minorities. Manages a speakers' bureau, holds lectures, and publishes *Journal of Minority Aging.*

National Council of Negro Women

1001 G Street NW, Suite 800
Washington, D.C. 20006
(202) 628-0015
(202) 785-8733 Fax
Web site: http://www.ncnw.com/
President: Dorothy I. Height

Founded in 1935. Helps develop and support black female leaders, as well as working on a number of women's issues. Maintains the Women's Center for Education and Career Advancement, as well as the Bethune Museum and Archives for Black Women's History. Works to improve the economic and social condition of women in developing countries. Publishes *Black Woman's Voice* and *Sisters Magazine.*

National Forum for Black Public Administrators

777 North Capital Street NE, Suite 807
Washington, D.C. 20002
(202) 408-9300
(202) 408-8558 Fax

Web site: http://www.nfbpa.org
Executive Director: James Wright

Founded in 1983 with the goal of increasing the role of African Americans in public administration. Provides training programs. Works with the Leadership Institute of Small Municipalities, the National Minority Business Development Forum, the Executive Leadership Institute, and the Mentor Program. Also focuses on homicide and environmental issues. Publications include the *Forum,* a quarterly newsletter.

National Hook Up of Black Women

c/o Wynetta Frazier
5117 South University Avenue
Chicago, IL 60615
(312) 643-5866
President: Wynetta Frazier

Founded in 1975. Provides a communications link for African-American women serving in leadership roles. Represents women, families, and the black community to overcome economic, educational, and social difficulties. Works with elected and appointed African-American women officials. Publications include *Hook Up News and Views*, a quarterly newsletter.

National Housewives' League of America for Economic Security

3240 Gilbert Avenue
Cincinnati, OH 45207
513 281-8822
President: Magnolia R. Silmond

Formed in 1933 as the National Housewives League of America. Supports black-owned and -operated businesses to help strengthen the community's economic base. Holds committees on consumer education, research, trade, youth issues, and world affairs.

National Organization of Black County Officials

440 First Street NW, Suite 500
Washington, D.C. 20001
(202) 347-6953
Web site: http://www.nobco.org/
Contact: Crandall O. Jones

The National Organization of Black County Officials was founded in 1975 to assist African-American county officials exchange ideas and use their influence to overcome state and national problems. Conducts seminars and offers a quarterly newsletter, *County Compass.*

National Political Congress of Black Women

1625 I Street NW, Suite 1018
Washington, D.C. 20006
(202) 775-8650
Web site: http://www.natpolcongblackwomen.com/
Chairperson: Shirley Chisholm

Founded in 1984 as a nonpartisan organization dedicated to encouraging political involvement by African-American women. Provides training programs in activities in the fields of fund raising, campaigning, public speaking, and other areas of use to black women running for offices.

National Rainbow Coalition

30 West Washington Street, Suite 300
Chicago, IL 60602
(312) 855-3773

Web site: http://www.archive.org/pres96/dolesville/rainbow.html
President: Jesse L. Jackson, Jr.

Founded in 1984. Seeks to end economic, racial, and sexual discrimination and violence. Works for tax reform, greater political and economic opportunity, an unpolluted environment, and peace driven foreign policy. Also strives for greater voter participation and rights.

National Trust for the Development of African American Men

7411 Riggs Road, Suite 424-426
Adelphi, MD 20783-4246
(301) 445-3077
E-mail: tnt@tnt.org
Web site: http://tnt.org/
President: Garry A. Mendez, Jr.

The National Trust for the Development of African American Men was founded in 1989 by people seeking to improve self-esteem among African-American men. Supports traditional African values. Provides research and educational programs, children's services such as teaching and monitoring projects, and various publications in the form of brochures and pamphlets.

National Urban League

500 East 62nd Street
New York, NY 10021
(212) 310-9000
(215) 593-8250 Fax
Web site: http://www.nul.org/
President: Hugh Price

The National Urban League was formed in 1910 as the National League on Urban Conditions Among Negroes. Main goal of the group is the elimination of racism, segregation, and discrimination within the United States. Focuses on issues concerning health, family planning, law and consumer affairs, housing, employment, education, social welfare, mental illness, labor difficulties, veterans' affairs, youth problems, community development, and minority business support. Publications include *BEEP Newsletter, Community Surveys and Reports, Urban League News,* and *Urban League Review.*

New Afrikan People's Organization

13206 Dexter Avenue
Detroit, MI 48238
(313) 883-3312
Chairperson: Chokwe Lumumba

Formed in 1984 with the purpose of founding an independent black nation in America's Deep South. Monitors legislation and collects information to meet its goals. Maintains the People's Low Cost Survival Programs, as well as Malcolm X Community Centers. Also provides speakers, food and clothing to needy people, youth programs; publishes a monthly newspaper, *By Any Means Necessary.*

Operation Big Vote

c/o National Coalition on Black Voter Participation
1629 K Street NW, Suite 801
Washington, D.C. 20006
(202) 659-4929
(202) 659-4929 Fax
Web site: http://www.bigvote.org/

Founded in 1976 as a program of the National Coalition on Black Voter Participation. Seeks to increase African-American voter participation by promoting interest among registered voters and providing educational information to all voting age blacks. Promotes citizen empowerment programs, local fund raising, and self-sufficiency among African Americans.

Operation PUSH—People United to Save Humanity
930 East 50th Street
Chicago, IL 60615
(312) 373-3366
Contact: Willie Barrow

Founded in 1971 as a national and international human rights group dedicated to providing economic and educational equality for African Americans, Hispanics, and the poor. Promotes social and community responsibility. Publications include *The Push Servant* and the *Voice of Excellence.*

Organization of African American Veterans
P.O. Box 873
Fort Huachuca, AZ 85613
(520) 458-7245

Founded in 1978, the Organization of African American Veterans has a membership composed of African-American veterans and active black personnel from all branches of the U.S. military. Promotes the physical, mental, social, and economic rehabilitation of veterans, while also obtaining comprehension, medical care, employment, and business assistance for these individuals. Supports and represents veterans and the families of veterans in benefit claims cases, as well as striving for beneficial legislation.

Parker Coltrane Political Action Committee
P.O. Box 76204
Washington, D.C. 20013
(313) 961-5610
Contact: John Matlock

The Parker Coltrane Political Action Committee was founded in 1981. The group encourages and assists African Americans and progressive candidates in gaining public office in the southern United States. Provides campaign contributions, technical assistance, and training in order to achieve its goals.

Planning and the Black Community
Department of the Army
P.O. Box C 3755
Seattle, WA 98124-2255
(206) 764-3614
Contact: Horace H. Foxall

Founded in 1980 by members of the American Planning Association to focus on issues relevant to the African-American community. Examines, formulates, and shares policy issues related to black citizens. Works to strengthen communication among black social workers, economists, public officials, and various organizations. Also focuses on employment an education issues.

Potomac Institute
1785 Massachusetts Avenue NW, Suite 401
Washington, D.C. 20036
(202) 332-5566
Web site: http://www.potomacinstitute.com/
Contact: Harold C. Flemming

Founded in 1961 with the purpose of providing equal opportunities for minorities. Offers research services to government and private organizations. Focuses on issues such as affirmative action, civil rights, school desegregation, education, housing, urban growth, and black business support.

Programs for Research on Black Americans
5006 Institute for Social Research
University of Michigan
P.O. Box 1248
Ann Arbor, MI 48106-1248
(313) 763-0045
(313) 763-0044 Fax
Web site: http://www.isr.umich.edu/rcgd/prba/
Director: James S. Jackson

Formed in 1976. Collects and analyzes data on African Americans based on national and international studies to support various projects. Focuses research on mental health and mental disorders among black Americans. Provides research and training opportunities for black social scientists and students.

Project on Equal Education Rights
c/o NOW LDEF
1333 H Street NW, 11th Floor
Washington, D.C. 20005
(202) 682-0940
Web site: http://www.nowldef.org/html/issues/njep/index.htm
Director: Eleanor Hinton Hoytt

Founded in 1974 as an educational division of the NOW Legal Defense and Education Fund. Supports a stronger stand on Title IX and other laws against sex discrimination in schools. Provides information on Congress, federal agencies, and the courts as it relates to equality within education.

Sisterhood Agenda
1721 Chapel Hill Road
Durham, NC 27707
(191) 493-8358
(919) 493 2524
sisagenda@mindspring.com
Web site: www.sisagenda.hom.mindspring.com
Executive Director: Angela D. Coleman

Founded in 1994, the Sisterhood Agenda is a non-profit organization that seeks to increase the opportunities for women of African descent. It sponsors various educational programs, including a speakers' bureau and forums.

Southern Christian Leadership Conference (SCLC)
334 Auburn Avenue, NE
Atlanta GA 30303
(404) 522-1420
(404) 659-7390
President: Martin Luther King III

Founded by Dr. Martin Luther King, Jr. in 1957, the SCLC is a national civil rights organization with affiliated groups that operate mainly out of churches. The organization sponsors programs that teach the nonviolent methodology that Dr. King employed in the 1960s as well as programs on voter registration, educational opportunities, and economic empowerment.

Southern Poverty Law Center (SPLC)
1001 South Hull Street
Montgomery, AL 36104
(205) 264-0286
(205) 264-0629
Web site: www.splcenter.org
President: Joseph J. Levin, Jr.

Founded in 1971, the Southern Poverty Law Center is active in the struggle to protect the legal and civil rights of poor people. The SPLC publishes the *monthly Klanwatch Intelligence Report*, and several other less frequent items, including *SPLC Report* and *Teaching Tolerance*.

TransAfrica
1744 R Street, NW
Washington, DC 20009
(202) 797-2301
(202) 797-2382
President: Randall Robinson

Founded in 1977, TransAfrica is a nonprofit organization concerned with the human and political rights of people in Africa and the Caribbean. The organization is also concerned with the rights of people of African descent in the United States. The organization publishes a semiannual journal entitled *TransAfrica News*.

Twenty-first Century Foundation
100 E. 85th Street
New York, NY 10028
(212) 249-3612
(212) 472- 0508
President: Robert S. Browne

Founded in 1971, this nonmembership organization works to develop an endowment to support other black charitable organizations.

United American Progress Association (UAPA)
701 East 79th Street
Chicago IL 60619
(773) 268-1873
(773) 651-1436
President: Webb Evans

Founded in 1961, the UAPA is a coalition of businesses, churches, and others in the African American community that encourages the support of local black owners and the local black community. The UAPA works in conjunction with Operation PUSH.

United Black Church Appeal (UBCA)
c/o Christ Church
860 Forest Avenue
Bronx, NY 10456
(718) 665-6688
President: Wendell Foster

Founded in 1980, the organization is dedicated to using the power of black church leadership to increase the political and economic awareness of the black community. The UBCA also works to improve local neighborhoods by working with youth to prevent drugs and gangs and also to build pride in black heritage.

United Negro College Fund (UNCF)
8260 Willow Oak Corporation Drive
Fairfax, VA 22031
(703) 205-3432
(703) 205-3575
Web site: www.uncf.org
President: William H. Gray III

Founded in 1944, the UNCF is an educational assistance organization that raises money to support the 41 historically black colleges and universities in the United States.

Youth Organizations U.S.A
P.O. Box 526
12 Tenalfy Road
Englewood, NJ 07631
(201) 836-1838
(201) 894-5117
President: Anne M. Garfield

Founded in 1981, the organization promotes coalitions that support programs for black youths. The group organizes programs that develop self-esteem as well as intervene in destructive behavior, including conflict resolution and drug abuse prevention.

Zeta Phi Beta Sorority
1734 New Hampshire Avenue, NW
Washington, DC 20009
(202) 387-3103

A national Negro sorority, Zeta Phi Beta sponsors programs that teach leadership and work for civil rights.

3
Tables

African-American Members of the U.S. House of Representatives

Name	State	Party	Dates
Joseph H. Rainey	South Carolina	Republican	1870–1879
Jefferson F. Long	Georgia	Republican	1870–1871
Robert B. Elliot	South Carolina	Republican	1871–1874
Robert C. DeLarge	South Carolina	Republican	1871–1873
Benjamin S. Turner	Alabama	Republican	1871–1873
Josiah T. Walls	Florida	Republican	1871–1873
Richard H. Crane	South Carolina	Republican	1873–1875; 1877–1879
John R. Lynch	Mississippi	Republican	1873–1877; 1882–1883
James T. Rapier	Alabama	Republican	1873–1875
Alonzo J. Ransier	South Carolina	Republican	1873–1875
Jeremiah Haralson	Alabama	Republican	1875–1877
John A. Hyman	North Carolina	Republican	1875–1877
Charles E. Nash	Louisiana	Republican	1875–1877
Robert Smalls	South Carolina	Republican	1875–1879
James E. O'Hara	North Carolina	Republican	1883–1887
Henry P. Cheatham	North Carolina	Republican	1889–1893
John M. Langston	Virginia	Republican	1890–1891
Thomas E. Miller	South Carolina	Republican	1890–1891
George W. Murray	South Carolina	Republican	1893–1895; 1896–1897
George W. White	North Carolina	Republican	1897–1901
Oscar DePriest	Illinois	Republican	1929–1935
Arthur W. Mitchell	Illinois	Democrat	1935–1943
William L. Dawson	Illinois	Democrat	1943–1970
Adam C. Powell, Jr.	New York	Democrat	1945–1967; 1969–1971
Charles C. Diggs, Jr.	Michigan	Democrat	1955–1980
Robert C. Nix	Pennsylvania	Democrat	1958–1978
Augustus F. Hawkins	California	Democrat	1963–1990
John Conyers, Jr.	Michigan	Democrat	1965–
William L. Clay	Missouri	Democrat	1969–
Louis Stokes	Ohio	Democrat	1969–1998
Shirley A. Chisholm	New York	Democrat	1969–1982
George W. Collins	Illinois	Democrat	1970–1972
Ronald V. Dellums	California	Democrat	1971–1997
Ralph H. Metcalfe	Illinois	Democrat	1971–1978
Parren H. Mitchell	Maryland	Democrat	1971–1986
Charles B. Rangel	New York	Democrat	1971–
Walter E. Fauntroy	District of Columbia	Democrat	1971–1990
Yvonne B. Burke	California	Democrat	1973–1979
Cardiss Collins	Illinois	Democrat	1973–1997
Barbara C. Jordan	Texas	Democrat	1973–1978
Andew J. Young	Georgia	Democrat	1973–1977
Harold E. Ford	Tennessee	Democrat	1975–

African-American Members of the U.S. House of Representatives (continued)

Name	State	Party	Dates
Bennett M. Steward	Illinois	Democrat	1979–1980
Julian C. Dixon	California	Democrat	1979–
William H. Gray	Pennsylvania	Democrat	1979–1991
Mickey Leland	Texas	Democrat	1979–1989
Melvin Evans	Virgin Islands	Republican	1979–1980
George W. Crocker, Jr.	Michigan	Democrat	1980–1990
Mervyn M. Dymally	California	Democrat	1981–1992
Augustus Savage	Illinois	Democrat	1981–1992
Harold Washington	Illinois	Democrat	1981–1983
Katie B. Hall	Indiana	Democrat	1982–1984
Major R. Owens	New York	Democrat	1983–
Edolphus Towns	New York	Democrat	1983–
Alan Wheat	Missouri	Democrat	1983–1983
Charles A. Hayes	Illinois	Democrat	1983–1992
Alton R. Waldon, Jr.	New York	Democrat	1986–1987
Mike Espy	Mississippi	Democrat	1987–1993
Floyd H. Flake	New York	Democrat	1987–1997
John Lewis	Georgia	Democrat	1987–
Kweisi Mfume	Maryland	Democrat	1987–1993
Donald M. Payne	New Jersey	Democrat	1989–
Craig A. Washington	Texas	Democrat	1989–
Barbara R. Collins	Michigan	Democrat	1991–1997
Gary A. Franks	Connecticut	Republican	1991–1997
William J. Jefferson	Louisiana	Democrat	1991–
Eleanor H. Norton	District of Columbia	Democrat	1991–
Maxine Waters	California	Democrat	1991–
Lucian E. Blackwell	Pennsylvania	Democrat	1991–
Sanford Bishop	Georgia	Democrat	1993–
Corrine Brown	Florida	Democrat	1993–
Eva M. Clayton	North Carolina	Democrat	1993–
James E. Clyburn	South Carolina	Democrat	1993–
Cleo Fields	Louisiana	Democrat	1993–
Alcee L. Hastings	Florida	Democrat	1993–
Earl F. Hilliard	Alabama	Democrat	1993–
Eddie B. Johnson	Texas	Democrat	1993–
Cynthia McKinney	Georgia	Democrat	1993–
Carrie Meek	Florida	Democrat	1993–
Mel Reynolds	Illinois	Democrat	1993–1995
Bobby L. Rush	Illinois	Democrat	1993–
Robert C. Scott	Virginia	Democrat	1993–
Walter R. Tucker III	California	Democrat	1993–
Melvin Watt	North Carolina	Democrat	1993–
Albert R. Wynn	Maryland	Democrat	1993–
Bennie G. Thompson	Mississippi	Democrat	1993–
Juanita Millender–McDonald	California	Democrat	1995–
Jesse L. Jackson, Jr.	Illinois	Democrat	1995–
Elijah E. Cummings	Maryland	Democrat	1995–
J.C. Watts	Oklahoma	Republican	1995–
Chaka Fattah	Pennsylvania	Democrat	1995–
Sheila Jackson Lee	Texas	Democrat	1995–
Danny K. Davis	Illinois	Democrat	1997–
Julia M. Carson	Indiana	Democrat	1997–
Carolyn C. Kilpatrick	Michigan	Democrat	1997–
Harold E. Ford, Jr.	Tennessee	Democrat	1997–
Donna Christian–Green	Virgin Islands	Democrat	1997–
Barbara Lee	California	Democrat	1998–

African-American Members of the U.S. Senate

Name	State	Party	Dates
Edward W. Brooke	Massachusetts	Republican	1967–79
Blanche K. Bruce	Mississippi	Republican	1875–81
Carol Moseley–Braun	Illinois	Democrat	1993–99
Hiram R. Revels	Mississippi	Republican	1870–71

Part 2
Asian Americans

Introduction
The Politics of Asian Americans

by Don Toshiaki Nakanishi

Large-scale immigration from Asia since the enactment of the **Immigration and Nationality Act of 1965** has had a dramatic impact on many states and regions across the United States, as well as on the Asian-American population. From a largely native-born group of 1.5 million in 1970, Asian Americans experienced extraordinary growth and diversification to reach 7.2 million in 1990, of which 66 percent were foreign born. Recent projections estimate that Asian Americans will continue to increase to nearly 12 million by 2000, and to 20 million by 2020.

Because of their recent demographic growth and concentration in certain key electoral states such as California, New York, and Texas, a number of political writers and scholars have speculated about whether Asian Americans will become a major new force in American electoral politics, perhaps akin to American Jews, Many believe that if Asian Americans come to represent a proportion of the electorate that is comparable to, if not greater than, their share of the total population, then they could become a highly influential "swing vote" in critical local, state, and presidential elections. In California, for example, if Asian Americans, who represent 1 in 10 residents of the state, also became 1 in 10 of the state's voters (who will continue to control the nation's largest number of seats in Congress and the most presidential electoral college votes), then they could play a strategically important role in national and local elections.

During the 1980s and 1990s, there has been an unmistakable increase in the political participation of Asian Americans in electoral politics. The 1998–1999 edition of the *Asian Pacific American Political Almanac and Resource Guide* listed more than 2,000 Asian-American elected and major appointed officials for 33 different states, as well as the federal government. In comparison, the first edition of this political directory, published in 1978, listed several hundred politicians, primarily holding offices in the states of Hawaii and California. The vast majority of those earlier officials were second- and third-generation Asian Americans, primarily Japanese Americans. In contrast, a growing number of recently elected officeholders have been immigrants such as **Jay Kim** of Walnut, California, the first Korean American elected to Congress; **David Valderrama**, the first Filipino American elected as a delegate to the Assembly of Maryland; and city councilman Tony Lam of Westminster, California, the first Vietnamese

American elected to public office. In the past few years, Asian-American candidates also have run well-financed, professional mayoral campaigns in some of the nation's largest cities, including Los Angeles, San Francisco, and Oakland. In November 1996, **Gary Locke** was elected governor of the state of Washington and became the first Asian-American elected governor of one of the continental states. **Benjamin Cayetano**, **John Waihee**, and **George Ariyoshi** have served as governor of Hawaii.

This seemingly optimistic assessment of Asian-American electoral achievements, however, is predominately among the most actively involved leaders. Beyond this is the reality of an immigrant-dominated population that has yet to reach its full political potential, especially in transforming its substantial population growth into comparable proportions of individuals who register to vote and actually vote during elections. In California, for example, the more than 3 million Asian Americans may represent 1 in 10 residents, but it is estimated that they are no more than 1 in 20 of the state's registered voters and 3 in 100 of those who actually vote. Indeed, as many studies have shown, Asian-American citizens have one of the lowest rates of voter registration, lower than that of whites and African Americans, and comparable to that of Latin Americans.

This overview explores both the enormous potential and the current status of political activity among Asian Americans. It begins by offering a framework for understanding minority and ethnic group politics, based on the Asian-American political experience, which goes beyond the customary preoccupation with electoral politics in the field of political science. It argues that Asian Americans, as well as other immigrant and minority groups, have traditionally pursued a range of political activities other than electoral politics to advance their group interests and to confront societal issues that are potentially damaging or harmful to their group standing and livelihood. The discussion then examines several key characteristics of the dynamic growth and diversification of the Asian-American population during the 1980s and 1990s, especially those characteristics that have had an impact on their political participation. The overview concludes by assessing the various countervailing factors that will likely influence the ability of Asian Americans in reaching their full political potential.

The Multiple Forms of Asian-American Politics

Asian-American politics has received limited scholarly attention. Early works such as Morton Grodzins' *Americans Betrayed* (1949) and Roger Daniels' *Politics of Prejudice* (1968) focused on how American political institutions, especially the major political parties and West Coast state legislatures, had a decisive impact on creating and maintaining a system of exclusion and discrimination against Asian Americans. Until recently, there were few studies on the flip side of that structural condition, namely how Asian Americans responded to such treatment and, more generally, how they pursued a variety of political activities in both the domestic and nondomestic arenas during the course of their historical experiences.

Although there has been an extreme paucity of serious academic work devoted to the political behavior and involvement of Asian Americans until recently, it has become apparent to most political commentators and practitioners that Asian Americans are becoming increasingly visible and influential actors in American politics. At no other period in the more than 150-year historical experience of Asians in U.S. society have so many individuals and organizations participated in such a wide array of political and civil rights activities, especially in relation to the American political system but also in relation to the recent tumultuous events in the People's Republic of China, Philippines, Korea, Pakistan, and other ancestral homelands in Asia. In traditional electoral politics, what had become a routine occurrence in Hawaii by the 1970s, namely the election of Asian Americans to public office, has become a less-than-surprising novelty in the so-called mainland states with the election and appointment of Asian Americans to federal, state, and local positions from Washington state to Delaware. And perhaps most significantly, Asian Americans have demonstrated that they, too, have the organizational and leadership skills, the financial resources, the interethnic networks, and a growing sense of political efficacy to assert their policy positions and to effectively confront broader societal issues that are damaging to their group interests. Three widely reported grassroots campaigns of recent years illustrate this new collective determination: the successful drive by Japanese Americans to gain redress and reparations for their **World War II** incarceration; the successful mobilization of Asian Americans in coalition with other groups in defeating the nomination of Daniel Lundgren for California state treasurer; and the national movement to appeal and overturn the initial light sentences that were given to two unemployed Detroit auto workers who, in 1982, used a baseball bat to kill a Chinese American named Vincent Chin. (In the **Chin murder case**, the two men mistook Chin for being Japanese, and therefore, someone who was viewed as having taken away their jobs.)

The emergence of Asian Americans in American politics probably could not have been foreseen. Early Chinese and Japanese immigrants, for example, were disenfranchised and excluded from fully participating in American life because of a plethora of discriminatory laws and policies, perhaps the most crucial being *Ozawa v. United States* (1922), which forbade Asian immigrants from becoming naturalized citizens. This legal barrier prevented early Asian immigrants from being involved in electoral politics in any way, and it substantially delayed the development of their electoral participation and representation until the second and subsequent generations during the post–World War II period—more than 100 years after their initial period of immigration. And although the news media in the United States have often touted them as America's "**model minority**"—a label that Asian-American leaders and scholars have criticized because of its simplistic implication that other minority groups can overcome racial and other discriminatory barriers simply by following the example of Asian Americans—this reputed success has disguised their historical lack of access to and influence in the nation's most significant decision-making arenas and institutions. Asian-American leaders and civil rights groups have remained vigilant in seeking the elimination of structural barriers, such as unfair redistricting plans and inaccessibility to bilingual ballots, that have prevented Asian Americans from exercising their full voting rights.

Although electoral politics has become an increasingly significant focus of attention, it represents only one of several major forms of political participation that have been and continue to be pursued by Asian Americans. First, as the highly visible and determined responses in 1989 and thereafter by Chinese foreign students and Chinese Americans alike to the repression of the prodemocracy movement in the People's Republic of China demonstrate, Asian Americans have long been concerned about and affected by events, issues, and relationships that are international in nature, particularly as they relate to their ancestral homelands. They have been active transnational participants in major revolutionary, nationalistic, and independence movements that have emerged in their respective homelands during the past century, and they have sought to contribute to subsequent national development efforts in those countries. They probably have also been affected to a greater extent than other American minority groups by the dramatic shifts in bilateral relations between the United States and their homelands, such as the confinement of Japanese Americans in **internment camps** during World War II or the thwarting of Asian-American leftist activities during the McCarthy era and other "cold war" periods in American diplomatic history. At present, interest among different sectors of the Asian-American population in Asian-oriented issues ranges from restoring democratic rule to both right-wing and Communist political systems in Asian countries to playing a greater role in United States–Pacific Rim relationships in trade, cultural exchanges, and economic development activities. In the past, Asian Americans have not been as successful as other American immigrant groups in lobbying American foreign policy decision-making. However, this should not minimize the significance Asian-oriented political involvement has had and will continue to have for Asian Americans and, more specifically, in competing with domestic-oriented political issues in mobilizing Asian-American communities.

At the same time, Asian Americans, like other American racial minorities that have been historically disenfranchised from the American electoral system, have engaged in an array of nonelectoral political activities to advance or protect their group interests. As recent scholarship has documented, Asian Americans have been active participants in labor-organizing efforts on the West Coast, Hawaii, New York, and the Rocky Mountain states, and indeed they were at the forefront in creating labor unions for agricultural workers in California and Hawaii. Like other racial minorities, Asian Americans also have a long history of seeking social justice and equal treatment by continuously engaging in legal challenges against discriminatory laws and practices in education, employment, housing, land ownership, immigration, and other significant public policy issues. Many of their most significant legal cases, including *Korematsu v. United States* (1943), *Lau v. Nichols* (1974), or *Equal Employment Opportunity Commission v. University of Pennsylvania* (1989), have become landmark civil rights decisions. Although electoral participation is increasing among Asian Americans, it is clear that nonelectoral political participation is still vigorously pursued by the Asian-American community. In recent years, Asian Americans have formed a number of their own organizations that parallel broader social movements in American society dealing with civil rights, women's issues, immigration legislation, and nuclear proliferation, and they have established an assortment of leftist organizations that continue a long-standing Marxist sector in Asian-American communities. They have also launched major nationwide campaigns seeking justice for individuals such as Chol Soo Lee and **Iva Ikuko Toguri D'Aquino** (commonly known as Tokyo Rose), who were viewed as victims of discriminatory legal treatment; they have also protested the Soviet downing of Korean Air Lines flight 007, the imprisonment of Chinese-American human rights activist Henry Wu by the government of the People's Republic of China, and the assassinations of Philippines exile Benigno Aquino and Chinese-American journalist Henry Liu.

Viewing Asian-American politics in this multifaceted manner involving domestic and nondomestic orientations, as well as electoral and nonelectoral types, goes beyond what is customary considered under the general rubric of minority politics. However, such an expanded framework is necessary to highlight the fact that electoral politics is only one of several major competing forms of political activity that the diverse ethnic groups and special interests of the Asian-American population have pursued and will likely continue to pursue in the future. A broader view that recognizes their extensive historical record, as well as their abundant contemporary examples, of both nondomestic and nonelectoral political activities should guard us against making unwarranted generalizations about their overall political behavior based

solely on their relatively low rates of electoral participation in the past as well as the present. Instead, taking these nonelectoral and nondomestic activities into account should serve to focus our attention on the structural and legal barriers that led to their historical condition of being disenfranchised from the American electoral system—and that continue to have lasting consequences.

The New Asian-American Population: Growth and Diversity

The Asian-American population has undergone a series of dramatic demographic transformations during the 1980s and 1990s that have greatly augmented their numbers and led to their increased internal heterogeneity. These demographic trends have had and will continue to have a significant impact on their electoral participation and more generally on issues dealing with their access, representation, and influence in both public and private institutions and sectors. To begin with, Asian Americans are the country's fastest growing group, having doubled from 1.5 million nationally in 1970 to 3.5 million in 1980, and then doubling again to 7.2 million in 1990. Recent projections estimate that Asian Americans will continue to increase to 12 million by 2000, and to nearly 20 million by 2020. This substantial increase can be attributed in large measure to the Immigration Act of 1965 (which eliminated the discriminatory quota provisions of the **Immigration Act of 1924**), the Indochinese Refugee Resettlement Program Act of 1975, and the **Refugee Act of 1980**. These latter two legislative measures permitted the migration and entry of close to 1 million refugees from Southeast Asia.

In reversing a four-decade longitudinal trend, Asians now represent the largest group of legal immigrants to the United States. For example, between 1931 and 1960, when the provisions of the 1924 National Origins Act were in effect, 58 percent of the legal immigrants were from Europe, 21 percent from North America, 15 percent from Latin America, and the smallest portion, 5 percent, were from Asia. However, this situation was nearly the opposite by the reporting period 1980–1984. Legal immigration from Europe had decreased to 12 percent of the overall total, North America to 2 percent, while Latin America had increased to 35 percent and Asian immigration had substantially increased to 48 percent of the country's total legal immigrants.

During the decade from 1970 to 1980, and continuing into the 1990s, the Asian-American population also dramatically shifted from being largely American born to predominantly foreign born, as a result of this upsurge in international migration. For example, according to the 1990 census, 65.6 percent of all Asian Americans across the nation were foreign born; with 79.9 percent of the Vietnamese, 72.7 percent of the Koreans, 64.4 percent of the Filipinos, 75.4 percent of the Asian Indians, and 69.3 percent of the Chinese having been born outside the United States. Only the Japanese Americans, with 32.4 percent foreign born, had more native-born individuals in its population. In marked contrast, 8.7 percent of the whites, 7.2 percent of the African Americans, and 38.5 percent of the Hispanic/Latino population were foreign born. In California in 1994, 64.5 percent of the state's Asian Americans were foreign born in comparison to 44.3 percent of the Hispanics, 20.8 percent of the whites, and 3.7 percent of the African Americans. Recent population projections estimate that the percentage of foreign-born Asian Americans will remain in the majority for several decades to come.

From the 1970s through the 1990s, the relative representation of different ethnic and national groups within the rapidly evolving Asian-American population also changed significantly. For example, in 1970, Japanese Americans were the largest Asian American ethnic group. By 1980, however, both Chinese Americans (812,178) and Filipino Americans (781,894) surpassed Japanese Americans (716,331); other Asian-American groups, such as Asian Indian Americans (387,223), Korean Americans (357,393), and Vietnamese Americans (245,025), grew rapidly as well through immigration. By 1990, both Chinese Americans (1,645,472) and Filipino Americans (1,406,770) had grown to be nearly twice as large as Japanese Americans (847,562), who experienced relatively little immigration from Japan and a gradually declining birth rate. The other three major Asian-American groups—Asian Indian Americans (815,447), Korean Americans (798,849), and Vietnamese Americans (614,547)—also recorded substantial population gains by 1990. It is projected that by 2000 Japanese Americans will fall further down the population scale, with practically all other major Asian-American groups outnumbering them, and Filipino Americans replacing Chinese Americans as the largest Asian-American ethnic group.

California, with a population of nearly 3 million Asian Americans in 1990, is the state with the largest population of Asian Americans. Of all the Asian Americans in the United States, 40 percent live in California. They now outnumber the state's African-American population and are second to the rapidly growing Latino populace, which continues to be California's single largest population of color. By 2000, it is estimated that more than 5 million of the nation's projected population of 12.1 million Asian Americans will be Californians. New York (which has the second largest Asian-American population), Hawaii, Texas, Washington, and Illinois are also expected to experience continued growth and diversification of their Asian-American communities.

The Asian-American population, as many studies have shown, should not be conceptualized as a single, monolithic entity. It has become an extremely heterogeneous population, with respect to ethnic and national origins, cultural values, generation, social class, religion, and other socially differentiating characteristics. At the same time, for any specific Asian-American group such as Chinese Americans, the within-group differences can be quite pronounced, reflecting different historical waves of immigration and different segments of a class hierarchical structure.

Differences in educational attainment levels provide a glimpse of this internal diversity. For example, Table 1 provides 1990 census data on educational attainment levels for adult males and females, 25 years of age and older, for six ethnic categories of Asian Americans, African Americans, American Indians, Hispanics, non-Hispanic whites, and others. Asian Americans and individuals of Hispanic origin appear to be at polar extremes of the educational continuum, with the former having a seemingly unrivaled percentage of college graduates, and the latter exhibiting a disturbingly unmatched percentage of individuals with fewer than eight years of formal schooling.

Table 1. Educational Attainment Levels for Males and Females, 25 Years and Older, California, 1990

	% Eight Years or Less of Schooling	% Non-High School Graduate	% College Graduate
ASIAN PACIFICS			
Males	11%	19%	39%
Females	17%	26%	31%
AFRICAN AMERICANS			
Males	7%	25%	15%
Females	7%	24%	14%
AMERICAN INDIANS			
Males	9%	27%	12%
Females	9%	30%	10%
HISPANICS/LATINOS			
Males	35%	55%	8%
Females	35%	55%	6%
NON-HISPANIC WHITES			
Males	4%	13%	33%
Females	4%	15%	23%
OTHERS			
Males	39%	60.4%	6%
Females	41%	61%	4%
TOTAL POPULATION			
Males	11%	23%	27%
Females	11%	25%	20%

Source: 1990 Census of Population, Social and Economic Characteristics, California, 1993.

However, Table 2, which differentiates the monolithic Asian category among 11 different ethnic groups, illustrates the necessity for recognizing and analyzing the internal heterogeneity of this population. Several Asian groups, for example, such as the Cambodians, Hmongs, and Laotians, clearly do not reflect high educational attainment levels and generally have far fewer college graduates and proportionately more people who are not high school graduates (and more people with fewer than eight years of schooling) than Asians as a whole, as well as other ethnic and racial populations. At the same time, other groups that appear to have stronger group-level academic profiles, such as the Chinese, Koreans, Thais, and Asian Indians, still had large numbers of individuals who did not attain high educational levels. Approximately one in four women of these four groups, 25 years of age and older, had not completed high school, and more than one in 10 of them had fewer than eight years of schooling. Such between- and within-group differences in educational attainment levels, as well as other quality of life indicators, are expected to continue among Asian Americans in the future.

Table 2. Educational Attainment Levels for Asian Pacific American Males and Females, 25 Years and Older, California, 1990

	% Eight Years or Less of Schooling	% Non-High School Graduate	% College Graduate
ASIAN INDIANS			
Males	2%	15%	72%
Females	16%	27%	42%
CAMBODIANS			
Males	45%	56%	8%
Females	66%	77%	3%
CHINESE			
Males	14%	23%	44%
Females	21%	31%	32%
HMONGS			
Males	49%	60%	7%
Females	65%	85%	2%
JAPANESE			
Males	3%	8%	44%
Females	5%	11%	30%
KOREANS			
Males	5%	11%	45%
Females	13%	24%	27%
LAOTIANS			
Males	45%	57%	7%
Females	65%	76%	6%
PACIFIC ISLANDERS			
Males	8%	24%	12%
Females	10%	28%	9%
FILIPINOS			
Males	8%	14%	35%
Females	11%	18%	41%
THAIS			
Males	6%	15%	43%
Females	18%	28%	27%

Source: 1990 Census of Population, Social and Economic Characteristics, California, 1993.

The combination of unprecedented demographic growth, along with extraordinary internal diversification, has a number of implications for Asian-American electoral participation. On the one hand, there is no question that as Asians have come to represent an increasingly sizable proportion of the population in certain states (most notably California) and in specific urban areas such as Los Angeles and San Francisco, topics such as redistricting, bilingual ballots, and fair political representation that were previously rarely considered have now become critical policy issues for Asian Americans. In earlier periods, their population size and density might not have been substantial enough for Asians to place special emphasis on these issues or to seek participation in the rough-and-tumble political decision-making process associated with creating political districts. But the demographic patterns that existed in the 1990s and are forecast for the twenty-first century justified and necessitated enhanced involvement and monitoring of these processes. Indeed, during reapportionment hearings at the beginning of the 1990s, a number of Asian communities from across the nation, from the Silicon Valley in Northern California to Queens and Chinatown in New York, expressed deep concern about potential gerrymandering practices and the possible dilution of Asian electoral strength. Unlike in previous years, Asian-American leaders actively participated in these hearings.

On the other hand, their unusual internal heterogeneity will challenge leaders and organizers of different Asian sectors and communities—who are often separated by both real and symbolic boundaries of national origins, language, culture, social class, religion, and other characteristics—to find common ground on key policy issues, to cope with the uneven political development and maturation of different ethnic groups, and to seek effective mechanisms for pursuing their shared interests in a unified manner on both a continuous and ad hoc manner. Although this may appear to be visionary, there are enough examples from the 1980s and 1990s, be it in terms of their concerted lobbying activities against university admissions quotas, anti-Asian violence, or unfair immigration policy legislation, to illustrate the potential and necessity of such collective endeavors. And, finally, it is highly likely that the term "Asian American," which has been imbued with constantly changing strategic, ideological, and tactical connotations since it was first articulated in the 1960s, will undergo further reconsideration in response to the conditions of the 1990s.

Conclusion: The Future of Asian-American Politics

In the 1990s, many outside political observers and media commentators optimistically predicted that Asians will soon become a major new force in American politics, especially because of their extraordinary demographic growth and concentration in certain key electoral states such as California, Texas, and New York. Many analysts believe that if, like American Jewish voters, Asian Americans come to represent a proportion of the electorate that is comparable to their numbers in the total population, they could become a highly influential "swing vote" in critical local, state, and presidential elections.

Although the future course of Asian-American political involvement cannot be easily forecast, it does appear that the ability of this population to realize its full electoral potential will be influenced by an array of currently visible trends. To begin with, for many Asian immigrant and refugee groups, homeland issues continue to dominate their ethnic political leadership agendas and the front pages of their vernacular media, and such issues will compete with, if not at times overwhelm, efforts to steer the ever-growing numbers of naturalized citizens toward greater involvement in the American electoral system. In this respect, these groups are involved in a very familiar (yet normally conflict-filled process) that other earlier American immigrant populations have endured, of coming to grips with and seeking a balance between their domestic and nondomestic political orientations. At the beginning of the 1990s, groups such as the **Korean American Coalition** and the Taiwanese American Citizens League, both of Los Angeles, were founded to enhance the participation of members of their communities—composed largely of immigrants—in American electoral politics and to address major domestic civil rights issues facing their ethnic groups. Both have gained footholds in their respective ethnic community power structures, which are dominated by elderly leaders whose attention is geared far more toward resolving highly volatile situations in their countries of origin. Major social conflicts such as the **Los Angeles riots** in 1992 in which more than 2,000 Korean and other Asian business establishments were seemingly targeted and destroyed, can sometimes serve to accelerate the development of a domestic-oriented leadership agenda and organizations. New political directions such as inter-ethnic coalition-building may come to be viewed as even more compelling. Developments in the upcoming decades will probably provide us with important answers about how the leaders of these and other Asian immigrant and refugee communities reach a meaningful accommodation between their domestic issues and their homeland concerns.

Conventional wisdom assumes that interest towards nondomestic or homeland politics is limited to the initial immigrant generation, and that involvement declines with succeeding, acculturated generations, However, there is much to suggest that such a linear conceptualization fails to consider changing conditions (in California and elsewhere) for Asian Americans and other groups in society. For example, large numbers of second- and third-generation Asian Americans, particularly those in business, law, and academics, are visibly involved in emerging Rim affairs, and they are more generally involved in the structural transformations that are occurring as a result of the internationalization of regional political economies. In the 1990s, some Asian-American leaders have used their real and symbolic linkages with Pacific Rim issues to define a unique and highly significant niche in American domestic politics and business affairs. At the same time, the continued interest and involvement of groups as diverse as American Jews, Poles and other Eastern Europeans, Ukrainians, Cubans, Greeks, Armenians, Chicanos, and African Americans with their "homeland" issues demonstrates that acculturation does not automatically signal the end of involvement.

In addition, the ability of Asian Americans to reach their full electoral potential also will be determined by the extent to which they mature politically beyond their most visible, and recently most controversial, manner in which they have participated in recent American electoral politics, namely by giving money. During the 1980s and 1990s, Asian Americans became increasingly recognized as a major new source of campaign funds, a veritable mountain of gold for Democratic and Republican prospectors across the nation. Indeed, during election periods, there is a staggering number of fund-raising activities in Asian-American communities. In the 1988 and 1992 presidential elections, it is estimated that Asians contributed more than $10 million, divided almost equally between Republican and Democratic candidates; this was second only to the American Jewish population in the amount of campaign money raised by an ethnic or racial group. For longtime political allies and friends such as former Los Angeles mayor Thomas Bradley, contributions from Asians usually amounted to more than 10 percent of their total campaign war chests.

This emerging view of Asian Americans as the new political moneybags of American politics had a mixed reaction even before the November 1996 presidential election focused media and partisan attention on the activities of Asian and Asian-American donors and fund-raisers such as **John Huang**. For some Asian-American leaders, the wooing of Asian Americans by the two major political parties was viewed positively, especially in light of the decades-long history of disenfranchisement and the general lack of outreach and recruitment activities by party officials in the past, particularly in California. Other Asian-American community leaders, however, argued that Asians may be the victims of something akin to political consumer fraud. They claim that Asians have not received the types of political benefits and goods—be it greater access or more high-level decision-making appointments— that they sought or were promised when they contributed to party coffers.

Although political contributions will undoubtedly continue to play an inordinate role in American politics, it would be unfortunate and misguided if Asian Americans, by their own volition or at the encouragement of politicians and party officials, largely restricted their participation in American electoral politics to giving money. In recent years, many Asian-American organizations in California and elsewhere, such as the **Asian Pacific Legal Center of Southern California**, **Korean American Coalition**, **Leadership Education for Asian Pacifics**, and the Chinese Voter Education Committee of San Francisco, have undertaken innovative projects and activities like leadership training symposia and voter education drives that go beyond the limited and narrow development of Asian Americans being political donors. Many of these efforts fall under the general rubric of political education and are variously directed at uplifting the political awareness, efficacy, and participation of the diverse sectors of the Asian population in different political activities, be they as seemingly simple and fundamental (such as registering to vote) or more complex and involved (such as running for public office). These activities are far removed from the glamorous side of politics. Instead, they are geared toward the long-range development of a political infrastructure for the Asian population. Indeed, as Asian Americans attempt to enhance their representation and influence in electoral politics in California and nationally in the coming decades, it will be necessary to engage in these and other innovative political education endeavors to reverse their low rates of voter registration, which work against the realization of their full electoral potential.

Although there has been a visible increase in political involvement and representation by Asian Americans in all forms of political activity during the 1980s and 1990s, it would be highly remiss to conclude that they have now become a powerful and unified political entity, or that they are now capable of competing equally with other political actors—be they other immigrant and minority groups or special interests—in realizing their specific political goals. In comparison with other more established political actors such as American Jews and African Americans, Asian Americans still have not fully developed and used the wide array of real and symbolic resources that are needed to compete on an equal basis with other groups, and their various levels of internal diversity have often prevented them from being a unified political actor that is suggested by the overarching umbrella label of "Asian Americans." In some of the smaller California suburban cities such as Gardena and Monterey Park and to a lesser extent the big cities such as San Francisco, Seattle, and Los Angeles, Asian Americans have become increasingly viable and recognized political participants. However, in most areas of the country (aside from Hawaii) and at higher levels of state and federal decision-making, they remain largely ignored and underrepresented. No Asian American has yet to be a cabinet member of any presidential administration. Indeed, for a variety of reasons, they have not been able to cultivate sufficiently a statewide or national political presence, or an explicit set of national priorities, that is recognized when major policy issues dealing with the poor, the elderly, or even United States relations with Asia are debated and implemented. At best, their present impact on American politics has been regional and sporadic rather than national and continuous.

The start of the new century, which is widely viewed in optimistic terms for Asian Americans because of seemingly positive demographic trends, will be a provocative and significant time to witness and analyze because of the extraordinary challenges and opportunities it will undoubtedly present for Asian Americans in realizing their full electoral potential. Whether or not they will become a significant swing vote in states such as California is nearly impossible to predict. However, our ability to raise and seriously entertain such a question in the context of the historical conditions of disenfranchisement and exclusion that Asian Americans faced in the past is quite revealing in itself.

Bibliography

Arax, Mark. "Group Seeks to Reverse Voter Apathy by Asians." *Los Angeles Times* (March 3, 1986): 1, 3.

Bai, Su Sun. "Affirmative Pursuit of Political Equality for Asian Pacific Americans: Reclaiming the Voting Rights Act." *University of Pennsylvania Law Review* 139, no. 3 (1991): 731–767.

Cain, Bruce E. "Asian-American Electoral Power: Imminent or Illusory?" *Election Politics* 5 (1988): 27–30.

Carmody, Deirdre. "Secrecy and Tenure: An Issue for High Court." *New York Times* (December 6, 1989): B8.

Chen, Marion, Woei-Ming New, and John Tsutakawa. "Empowerment in New York Chinatown: Our Work as Student Interns." *Amerasia Journal* 15 (1989): 299–306.

Chin, Rocky. "The Long Road-Japanese Americans Move on Redress." *Bridge* 7 (1981): 11–29.

Chuman, Frank. *The Bamboo People: Japanese Americans and the Law*. Del Mar, CA.: Publisher's, Inc., 1976.

Chun, Ki-Taek. "The Myth of Asian Pacific American Success and Its Educational Ramifications." *IRCD Bulletin* 15 (1980): 1–12.

Clifford, Frank. "Contributors to Mayoral Race Seek a Friendly Ear." *Los Angeles Times* (March 11, 1985): 1, 3, 14.

——. "Barriers to Power for Minorities." *Los Angeles Times* (May 7, 1990): 1, 24, 25.

Coffman, Tom. *Catch a Wave: A Case Study of Hawaii's New Politics*. Honolulu: University of Hawaii Press, 1973.

Cooper, Richard T. "How DNC Got Caught in Donor Dilemma." *Los Angeles Times* (December 23, 1996): A-1.

Daniels, Roger. *The Politics of Prejudice*. New York: Atheneum, 1968.

De Vera, Arleen. "Without Parallel: The Local 7 Deportation Cases, 1949–1955." *Amerasia Journal* 20 (1994): 1–26.

DeWitt, Howard. *Violence in the Fields: California Filipino Farm Labor Organizing During the Great Depression*. Saratoga, CA: Century Twenty-One Publishing, 1980.

Din, Grant. "An Analysis of Asian/Pacific American Registration and Voting Patterns in San Francisco." Unpublished M.A. thesis, Claremont Graduate School, 1984.

Erie, Steven P. and Harold Brackman. *Paths to Political Incorporation for Latinos and Asian Pacifics in California*. Berkeley: The California Policy Seminar, 1993.

Espiritu, Yen. *Asian Pacific American Panethnicity: Bridging Institutions and Identities*. Philadelphia: Temple University Press, 1992.

Fawcett, James T. and Benjamin Carino, eds. *Pacific Bridges*. Staten Island, NY: Center for Migration Studies, 1987.

Griffiths, Stephen. "Emigrant and Returned Migrant Investment in a Philippine Village." *Amerasia Journal* 5 (1976): 45–67.

Grodzins, Morton. *Americans Betrayed*. Chicago: University of Chicago Press, 1949.

Gurwitt, Rob. "Have Asian Pacific Americans Arrived Politically? Not Quite." *Governing* (November 1990): 32–38.

Hatamiya, Leslie T. *Righting a Wrong: Japanese Americans and the Passage of the Civil Liberties Act of 1988*. Stanford: Stanford University Press, 1993.

Horton, John. *The Politics of Diversity*. Philadelphia: Temple University Press, 1995.

Ichioka, Yuji. "The Early Japanese Quest for Citizenship: The Background of the 1922 Ozawa Case." *Amerasia Journal* 4 (1977): 1–22.

———. *The Issei*. New York: Free Press, 1988.

Irons, Peter. *Justice at War*. New York: Oxford University Press, 1983.

Jo, Yung-Hwan, ed. *Political Participation of Asian Pacific Americans: Problems and Strategies*. Chicago: Pacific/Asian Pacific American Mental Health Research Center, 1980.

Jurergensmeyer, Mark. "The Ghadar Syndrome: Nationalism in an Immigrant Community." *Center for South and Southeast Asian Studies Review* 1 (1978): 9–13.

Karnow, Stanley. "Apathetic Asian Pacific Americans? Why Their Success Hasn't Spilled Over into Politics." *Washington Post* (November 29, 1992): C1–2.

Kim, Hyung-Chan and Nicholas Lai. "Chinese Community Resistance to Urban Renewal." *Journal of Ethnic Studies* 10 (1982): 67–81.

Kwoh, Stewart and Mindy Hui. "Empowering Our Communities: Political Policy." In *The State of Asian Pacific America: Policy Issues to the Year 2020*. Los Angeles: LEAP Asian Pacific American Public Policy Institute and the UCLA Asian Pacific American Studies Center, 1993, 189–197.

Kwong, Peter. *Chinatown, New York: Labor and Politics, 1930–1950*. New York: Monthly Review Press, 1981.

Lai, Him Mark. "China Politics and United States Chinese Communities." In Emma Gee, et al., eds. *Counterpoint: Perspectives on Asian America*. Los Angeles: UCLA Asian American Studies Center 1976, 152–159.

Lien, Pei-te. "Ethnicity and Political Participation: A Comparison between Asian and Mexican Americans." *Political Behavior* 16, no. 2 (1994): 237–264.

Lim, Derrick. "Learning from the Past: A Retrospective Look at the Chol Soo Lee Movement." Unpublished M.A. thesis, University of California, Los Angeles, 1985.

Lin, Sam Chu. "Candidates Keeping Tabs on Asian Pacific American Trends." *Asianweek* (November 2, 1995): 10.

Low, Victor. *The Unimpressible Race: A Century of Educational Struggle by Chinese in San Francisco*. San Francisco: East–West Publishers, 1982.

Lyu, Kingsley. "Korean Nationalist Activities in Hawaii and the Continental United States, 1900–1945, Part I and II." *Amerasia Journal* 4 (1977): 23–90.

McKee, Delber. "The Chinese Boycott of 1905–1906 Reconsidered, The Role of Chinese Americans." *Pacific Historical Review* 55 (1986): 165–191.

Miller, John. "Asian Pacific Americans Head For Politics." *The American Enterprise* 6 (1995): 56–58.

Nakanishi, Don T. "Asian Pacific American Politics: An Agenda for Research." *Amerasia Journal* 12 (1986): 1–27.

———. "A Quota on Excellence? The Debate on Asian American Admissions." *Change* (November/December 1989): 38–47.

———. "Surviving Democracy's 'Mistake': Japanese Americans and Executive Order 9066." *Amerasia Journal* 19 (1993): 7–35.

———. "When Numbers Do Not Add Up: Asian Pacific Americans and California Politics." In Michael B. Preston, Bruce E. Cain, and Sandra Bass, eds. *Racial and Ethnic Politics in California*. vol. 2. Berkeley: Institute of Governmental Studies Press, University of California, Berkeley, 1998, 3–44.

———. and James Lai. *1998–1999 National Asian Pacific American Political Almanac and Resource Guide*. Los Angeles: UCLA Asian American Studies Center, 1998.

——— and Tina Yamano Nishida, eds. *The Asian Pacific American Educational Experience*. New York: Routledge, 1995.

Saxton, Alexander. "The Army of Canton in the High Sierra." *Pacific Historical Review* 35 (1966): 141–152.

———. *The Indispensable Enemy*. Berkeley: University of California Press, 1971.

Scharlin, Craig and Lilia V. Villanueva. *Philip Vera Cruz: A Personal History of Filipino Immigrants and the Farmworkers Movement*. Los Angeles: UCLA Asian Pacific American Studies Center and UCLA Labor Center, 1992.

Stokes, Bruce. "Learning the Game." *National Journal* 43 (October 22, 1988): 2649–2654.

Takagi, Dana. *Retreat from Race*. New Brunswick, NJ: Rutgers University Press, 1992.

Tam, Wendy. "Asians—A Monolithic Voting Bloc?" *Political Behavior* 17, no. 2 (1995): 223–249.

Tsai, Shih-Shan Henry. "The Emergence of Early Chinese Nationalist Organizations in America." *Amerasia Journal* 8 (1981): 121–144.

Uyeda, Clifford. "The Pardoning of 'Tokyo Rose': A Report on the Restoration of American Citizenship to Iva Ikuko Toguri." *Amerasia Journal* 5 (1978): 69–94.

Wang, L. Ling-Chi. "*Lau v. Nichols*: History of a Struggle for Equal and Quality Education." In Emma Gee, et al., eds. *Counterpoint: Perspectives on Asian America*. Los Angeles: UCLA Asian Pacific American Studies Center, 1976, 240–263.

——. "The Structure of Dual Domination: Toward a Paradigm for Study of the Chinese Diaspora in the United States." *Amerasia Journal* 21, nos. 1/2 (1995): 149–169.

Weglyn, Michi. *Years of Infamy*. New York: William Morrow, 1976.

Yoneda, Karl. *Ganbatte*. Los Angeles: UCLA Asian Pacific American Studies Center, 1983.

Yu, Renqiu. "Chinese American Contributions to the Educational Development of Toisan, 1910–1940." *Amerasia Journal* 10 (1983): 47–72.

Abe v. Fish and Game Commission (1935)

The main question the court considered in *Abe v. Fish and Game Commission,* 9 Cal. App. 2nd (1935), was whether Section 990 of the Fish and Game Code violated the equal protection clause of the Fourteenth Amendment. Section 990 limited the license to fish to persons who had lived in the United States for a period of a year; however, the Superior Court of San Diego ruled that Section 990 was void because it discriminated between residents and nonresidents of the United States.

The plaintiff, T. Abe, owner of a fishing boat, required a crew of six to bring in fish from waters off the coast of California. The defendants charged that none of the crew members had resided in California; therefore none were eligible to obtain a commercial fishing license. In the opinion of the court, Section 990 held a double standard, bringing about unequal exaction from one class while not imposing it on the majority. (FHM)

BIBLIOGRAPHY

Chuman, Frank F. *The Bamboo People.* Del Mar, CA: Publisher's Inc., 1976.

———. *T. Abe v. Fish and Game Commission of the State of California.* 9 Cal. App. 2nd (1935).

Acheson v. Murakami (1949)

Acheson v. Murakami, 176 F. 2d 953 (1949), was a federal court case handed down by the U.S. 9th Circuit Court of Appeals. It reinstated Miye Mae Murakami as a U.S. citizen. She had renounced her U.S. citizenship with 5,700 other Japanese Americans during **World War II.** The courts found that there were cruel treatments conducted at the **internment camps** and the atmosphere created an influence of duress. The court ruled that her renunciation was not voluntary, and so her citizenship was restored.

BIBLIOGRAPHY

tenBroek, Jacobus, Edward N. Barnhart, and Floyd W. Matson. *Prejudice, War, and the Constitution.* Berkeley: University of California Press, 1970.

Affirmative Action

The term "affirmative action" has many meanings. The first use of the term was in the National Labor Relations Act of 1935, known as the Wagner Act. Under the law, employers were required to engage in "affirmative action," which meant that they should rehire those employees who had been fired because they were union members and hire in the future without regard to union membership. At this time, the term "affirmative action" meant that employers should voluntarily comply with the law.

The next use of "affirmative action" came on March 6, 1961, when President John F. Kennedy issued Executive Order 10925. Under this order, businesses receiving contracts with the federal government were not only prohibited from discriminating in employment but also required to "take affirmative action to ensure that employees are treated during employment without regard to their race, creed, color, or national origin." This requirement was understood at the time to mean that employers should desegregate their businesses by putting an end to all-black and all-white work units, departments, or companies. On June 22, 1963, Kennedy issued Executive Order 11114, which empowered federal agencies to terminate contracts with businesses that disobeyed Executive Order 10925.

The term "affirmative action" next appeared in Title VII of the Civil Rights Act of 1964. Passed on July 2, the statute empowered courts to require employers found guilty of discrimination to engage in "such affirmative action as may be appropriate, which may include reinstatement or hiring of employees with or without back pay."

On September 24, 1965, President Lyndon B. Johnson issued Executive Order 11246, which modified Executive Order 10925 by applying affirmative action to the recruitment, screening, and selection of new employees. By 1966, the Equal Employment Opportunity Commission (EEOC), which was given the power to enforce Title VII, asked employers who were found to have engaged in discrimination to draw up "affirmative action plans," that is, changes in policies, practices, and procedures that were judged responsible for the discrimination in a manner similar to Executive Order 11246. On October 13, 1967, Johnson signed Executive Order 11375, which extended affirmative action to cover sex discrimination. On August 8, 1969, President Richard M. Nixon extended affirmative action to all federal employees under the jurisdiction of the U.S. Civil Service Commission, in Executive Order 11478.

During Johnson's term of office, affirmative action took on a more precise meaning. On May 28, 1968, the U.S. Department of Labor issued guidelines that for the first time required contractors to write affirmative action programs. When the order was revised on February 5, 1970, an administrative definition of an "affirmative action program" was at last provided: "An affirmative action program is a set of specific and result-oriented procedures to which a contractor commits himself to apply every good faith effort. The objective of those procedures plus such efforts is equal employment opportunity."

These guidelines mean that federal contractors must analyze their workforce to determine whether there are patterns of exclusion or underemployment of minorities or women; if so, changes should be made in personnel policies, practices, or procedures that are deemed responsible for the anomalous patterns, including goals and timetables, and they should be implemented in good faith. Failure to make an analysis or to correct deficiencies is then assumed to be operating in bad faith, thus placing a contract in jeopardy. To determine anomalies, statistics are used. If an employer hired skilled workers in the Detroit metropolitan area, for example, that employer's percentage of black and female skilled workers should be the same as the percentage of black and female skilled workers in the labor market of the Detroit metropolitan area, as derived from the latest U.S. census. For example, if auto company A hired 1 percent blacks, auto company B hired 30 percent blacks, but the Detroit labor pool had 15 percent blacks, then company A had a 14 percent deficiency to correct, whereas company B would presumably need to hire more white workers. Company A would then have a goal of hiring at least 15 percent blacks; the timetable for achieving the goal would be based on turnover statistics, with hiring tilted toward hiring more blacks qualified for skilled labor jobs but without excluding qualified whites. Once again, the aim of affirmative action was desegregation, that is, ending the practice of having some companies ethnically identifiable on the basis of their hiring patterns.

There are three forms of what has been called "corrective action." "Remedial action" is retrospective, that is, when a violation of equal opportunity laws occurs, courts are empowered to require a remedy, such as back pay for a victim of unequal pay. "Affirmative action" is prospective, that is, it involves agencies and employers in changing discriminatory policies, practices, and procedures to achieve equal opportunity at some time in the future. "Nondiscrimination" is what agencies and employers are supposed to do in the present tense—hire, promote, and otherwise treat qualified persons without regard to ethnicity, race, and sex.

Congress extended the concept of affirmative action in Section 503(a) of the Rehabilitation Act of 1973. Passed on September 26, the law requires federal construction contractors "to take affirmative action to employ and advance qualified handicapped individuals." The legislation was considerably broadened in the Americans with Disabilities Act of 1990.

The new methodology of affirmative action caught the attention of many civil rights leaders, government agencies, and those opposed to progress in achieving ethnic, racial, and gender equality. Although the term was applied only to matters of employment, it came to be applied to corrective actions in other spheres. Among them were broadcast licensing, college admissions, housing project regulations, minority contractor set-asides—a policy whereby a specific number or percentage of a contract is renewed for special categories of contractors—school desegregation and busing plans, and voting reapportionment. In these areas, there was no federal administrative or statutory requirement to engage in affirmative action, although federal nondiscrimination requirements apply.

There are four ways in which affirmative action comes about. One is when an agency or company voluntarily adopts an affirmative action plan. A second source is court action, when a violation of equal opportunity has occurred. A third source of affirmative action is the requirement of federal agencies and federal contractors under Executive Order 11246, as amended. Finally, the U.S. Civil Service Commission, before it was abolished, integrated affirmative action methodology into the merit system, such that the application of merit system principles accomplishes the goal of affirmative action.

However, affirmative action has not always been implemented in a manner consistent with federal guidelines. Some voluntary affirmative action plans have been implemented by overzealous personnel officers, who have promoted less-qualified minorities or women to satisfy public relations objectives, thereby incurring the wrath of white males who feel they are the victims of "reverse discrimination." Courts have imposed quotas on recalcitrant employers; an example would be, in those states where blacks are less than half the workforce, requiring the state to hire one black firefighter to every white firefighter until the overall percentage of black firefighters equals the state's percentage of blacks in the population. Companies seeking to be federal contractors have been denied eligibility by the U.S. Department of Labor when their percentage of black skilled employees has fallen below the percentage of blacks in the population regardless of the percentage of black skilled workers in the workforce. Government employees, expecting to be subject to civil service regulations, often complain that "affirmative action" prevails over merit principles in conditions of work, although the culprit is often politics, not affirmative action. In addition, there are numerous examples of agencies or companies that make very little progress toward affirmative action goals yet remain federal contractors. In short, many observers are dissatisfied with the way in which affirmative action has been handled in practice.

People dissatisfied with affirmative action, primarily white males, have launched challenges in court, although the U.S. Supreme Court has never invalidated an affirmative action plan monitored by the U.S. Department of Labor under Executive Order 11246, as amended. Instead, judges have supported affirmative action narrowly tailored to remedy specific deficiencies in reasonable periods of time, but they have struck down inept efforts at "affirmative action" in the areas not covered by the executive order. The first major case to be tried by the Supreme Court was *University of California v. Bakke,* 438 U.S. 265(1978). In this case, the University of California at Davis opened a new School of Medicine and evaluated prospective students in separate categories based on their ethnic/racial backgrounds. In 1978, a divided court ruled that the practice of considering admissions in segregated pools of applicants violated the equal protection clause of the Fourteenth Amendment, but that the school would otherwise be justified in considering racial diversity as one among several criteria to use in determining who should be admitted. As a result of *Bakke,* civil rights advocates began to stress "diversity" rather than "affirmative action" as a goal—without necessarily defining "diversity" or considering that implementation of a policy of diverse admissions to college might result in discrimination, such as in a state where the population is notably lacking in racial diversity. The Supreme Court has continued to narrow the range of circumstances in which affirmative action can be used, and their rejection of a U.S. Department of Transportation affirmative action plan [*Adarand Constructors v. Pena,* 515 U.S. 200 (1995)] left many wondering if the Court was ready to end affirmative action altogether. In addition, court challenges to excessively broadly conceived efforts to promote diversity have been successful in recent years, most notably in the closely watched case of *Hopwood v. Texas,* 78 F3d 932 (1996).

In response to various criticisms of the way in which affirmative action has been implemented, President Bill Clinton ordered a review of the matter upon taking office in 1993. A report by the President's Committee on Affirmative Action, entitled *Affirmative Action Review* (1995), prompted Clinton to establish four standards for "mending" affirmative action: Affirmative action (1) should not establish quotas; (2) should not establish preferences for the unqualified; (3) should not involve reverse discrimination; and (4) should be abolished when the goal of affirmative action has been accomplished. Although these standards had long governed the implementation of affirmative action by federal agencies, this was the first time that a president of the United States declared that these principles should be followed. (MH)

BIBLIOGRAPHY

Andritzky, Frank W. and Joseph G. Andritzky. "Affirmative Action: The Original Meaning." *Lincoln Law Review* 17, no. 2 (1987): 249–273.

Carter, Stephen L. *Reflections of an Affirmative Action Baby.* New York: Basic Books, 1991.

Ezorsky, Gertrude. *Racism and Justice: The Case for Affirmative Action.* Ithaca, NY: Cornell University Press, 1991.

Glazer, Nathan. *Affirmative Discrimination: Ethnic Inequality and Public Policy.* New York: Basic Books, 1975.

Kahlenberg, Richard D. *The Remedy: Class, Race, and Affirmative Action.* New York: Basic Books, 1996.

President's Committee on Affirmative Action. *Affirmative Action Review: Report to the President.* Washington, D.C.: President's Committee on Affirmative Action.

Sturm, Susan and Lani Guinier. "The Future of Affirmative Action: Reclaiming the Innovative Ideal." *California Law Review* 84, no. 4 (July 1996): 953–1036.

Agricultural Workers Organizing Committee (AWOC)

The Agricultural Workers Organizing Committee (AWOC) was a predominantly Filipino farm workers union in California. It was created in 1959 by the AFL-CIO and led by Larry Itliong. After 1924 Filipino workers began immigrating to the United States to take advantage of the labor shortage caused by a ban on Asian immigration. Many of them worked on farms in California and were called "'pinoys.'" Unions tried to organize them but, because of the power of the Associated Farmers of California, the Filipino workers were afraid to join a union. However, in 1940s Filipino workers began demanding better wages and improved working conditions. They still did not formally organize until 1959, when Itliong formed the organizing committee. In 1965 AWOC started the famous Delano Grape strike, which lasted for seven months. Cesar Chavez and the National Farm Workers Association joined the strike; in 1966, after the strike, the two unions joined to form the **United Farm Workers Organizing Committee.**

BIBLIOGRAPHY

Hess, Gary R. "The Forgotten Asian Americans: The East Indian Community in the United States." In Norris Hundley, Jr., ed. *The Asian American.* Santa Barbara, CA: Clio Books, 1976.

John Aiso (1909–1987)

After graduating cum laude from Brown University, John Aiso studied law at Harvard Law School. He was drafted into the army in 1941, and taught Japanese in the Army Intelligence School. After the war, he served as commissioner in the Superior Court of California, before becoming a Superior Court judge. In 1968 he became a judge in the California Court of Appeals.

BIBLIOGRAPHY

Morrison, Patt and Sontiago O'Donnell. "John Aiso, Prominent Nisei and Jurist, Dies after Mugger's Attack." *Los Angeles Times* (December 31, 1987). II:2.

———. *John Aiso and the M.I.S.: Japanese-American Soldiers in the Military Intelligence Service, World War II.* trans. into English by Haruo Kugizck; ed. by John Aiso. Los Angeles: Military Intelligence Service Club of Southern California, 1988

Daniel K. Akaka (1924–)

Born September 11, 1924, of Chinese-Hawaiian ancestry, Daniel Kahikina Akaka was elected to the U.S. House of Representatives from Hawaii in 1976, appointed to replace deceased Senator **"Spark" Matsunaga** in 1990, and elected senator in 1990 and 1996. His legislative accomplishments include amending the Native American Programs Act in 1987 to enable Samoans and other Pacific Islanders to benefit from provisions of the law, adoption of the **Native Hawaiian Health Care Act of 1988**, passage of the joint resolution of Congress in 1993 apologizing to native Hawaiians for American complicity in the overthrow of the independent Hawaiian monarchy in 1893, and the establishment of the Kaho'olawe Island Conveyance Commission in 1990, which resulted in the formation of the Kaho'olawe Island Reserve Commission. The commission is supervising the transformation of the island, used by the U.S. Navy for target practice from 1942 to 1990, into a Native Hawaiian cultural preserve. **See also** Annexation of Hawaii. (MH)

BIBLIOGRAPHY

Altonn, Helen. "Akaka Summed Up Nicely: His Friends Call His Gentlemanly Manner His Greatest Political Asset." *Honolulu Star-Bulletin* (October 30, 1990): A1, A4.

Alien Land Act of 1920

After the California Alien Land Act of 1913 was passed, numerous court cases challenged the constitutionality of the law. As a result, the act was amended several times, and in 1920, new legislation was passed to replace the 1913 law. The Alien Land Act of 1920 permitted aliens who were ineligible for citizenship (and thus ineligible to own land) to lease land for farming. Japanese farmers began leasing land in California for farming, and they began making sharecropping deals in which Japanese would become tenant farmers on farms owned by Americans. However, sharecropping contracts were outlawed in 1923, in an amendment to the Alien Land Act of 1920, and Japanese farmers continued to be prohibited from owning land until after **World War II**, when the U.S. Supreme Court ruled in *Oyama v. California* (1948) that the California Alien Land Law was unconstitutional. **See also** Proposition 13; Proposition 15 (1945).

See specific land ownership cases: *Frick v. Webb* (1923); *Fujii Sei v. State of California* (1952); *Jordan v. Tashiro* (1928); *Morrison v. People of the State of California* (1933); *Porterfield v. Webb* (1923); *State of California v. Hayao Yano and Tetsubumi Yano* (1922); *Terrace et al. v. Thompson, Attorney General of Washington* (1923).

BIBLIOGRAPHY

Chuman, Frank F. *The Bamboo People: The Law and Japanese Americans*. Del Mar, CA: Publisher's Inc., 1976.

Alien Land Laws

Beginning in 1889, western states began enacting laws to prohibit aliens from owning land. In 1909, the Alien Land Bill was defeated in the California assembly, but in 1913 the California Alien Land Act was passed, and it was amended several times during the next 10 years. Oregon, Idaho, Arizona, and Washington state all passed similar laws preventing aliens from owning property. Asian Americans challenged the constitutionality of these laws in several Supreme Court cases, and in 1946 the California Alien Land Law was ruled unconstitutional in a landmark decision by the Supreme Court. The case, *Oyama v. California* (**1948**), finally made it possible for Asian Americans to own property in the United States. **See also** Alien Land Act of 1920; Proposition 13; Proposition 15 (1945). **See** California Alien Land Act of 1920 in Appendix 1.

See specific land ownership cases: *Frick v. Webb* (1923); *Fujii Sei v. State of California* (1952); *Jordan v. Tashiro* (1928); *Morrison v. People of the State of California* (1933); *Porterfield v. Webb* (1923); *State of California v. Hayao Yano and Tetsubumi Yano* (1922); *Terrace et al. v. Thompson, Attorney General of Washington* (1923).

BIBLIOGRAPHY

Chuman, Frank F. *The Bamboo People: The Law and Japanese Americans*. Delmar, CA: Publisher's Inc., 1976.

Alliance of Asian Pacific Labor (AAPL)

The Alliance of Asian Pacific Labor (AAPL) was established in 1987 as an umbrella organization for Japanese, Chinese, Filipino, Korean, Vietnamese, and Indian laborers living on the West Coast. The organization has assisted with union activities among Asian Americans. The group is also interested in Asian-American civil rights and in eradicating racism against Asian-American laborers. The AAPL has also been involved in helping Asian Americans gain a political presence as well. The organization registers voters, works on redistricting, and targets selected issues that will impact the Asian-American community. AAPL is also interested in becoming to a national organization to assist Asian-American laborers. **See also** Asian-American Relations with Other Minorities; Political Participation.

BIBLIOGRAPHY

Wong, Kent. *In the State of Asian America: Activism and Resistance in the 1990s*. Boston: South End Press, 1994.

Amendment of 1884

This legislation amended the **Immigration Act of 1882** (Chinese Exclusion Act). It represented the first attempt by the United States to single out a group because of race. It suspended the immigration of Chinese laborers for 10 years. The amendment, in turn, broadened the act by restricting immigration of "hucksters, peddlers, or those engaged in taking, drying, or otherwise preserving shell or other fish for home consumption or exportation." **See also** Immigration Restriction Movement.

BIBLIOGRAPHY

McClain, Charles J. *In Search of Justice*. Berkeley: University of California Press, 1994.

Amerasian Homecoming Act of 1987

The Amerasian Homecoming Act of 1987 was created to assist children fathered overseas by U.S. soldiers during the **Vietnam War.** The act allowed such children to emigrate to the United States from Vietnam and to bring with them one set of immediate family members, such as a spouse and children or a mother and siblings. This broadness in the act's scope sought to avoid breaking up families. Though criticized by detractors as liable to misuse, Vietnam veterans and their supporters hailed this first postwar venture between the two countries as a victory. Underestimating the response such an invitation would elicit, the act originally specified a departure deadline of March 1990. A large number of would-be immigrants, however, necessitated that the act be amended to extend this deadline indefinitely.

BIBLIOGRAPHY

Bass, Thomas A. *Vietnamerica: The War Comes Home.* New York: Soho Press, 1996.

American Citizens for Justice

A community group organized in Detroit, Michigan, in 1982 became known as American Citizens for Justice. The group was formed after Ronald Ebens and his stepson, Michael Nitz, beat Vincent Chin, a Chinese-American man, to death outside a nightclub. The primary goal of the organization was to ensure that the two men were properly tried and sentenced for murder. When Ebens and Nitz were given only fines and no jail time, the American Citizens for Justice demanded that the case be retried. The case was retried in district court in 1984, and Ebens and Nitz were found guilty, but their convictions were overturned on a technicality in 1986. **See also** Vincent Chin.

BIBLIOGRAPHY

Wei, William. *The Asian American Movement.* Philadelphia: Temple University Press, 1991.

American Loyalty League (ALL)

The American Loyalty League (ALL) was founded in Fresno, California, in 1923. The League—whose founders included **Thomas T. Yatabe**—was established as a civil rights organization for Japanese Americans. The goals of the group included the fuller participation of Japanese Americans in politics, economics, and society in general. The ALL was the forerunner of the **Japanese American Citizens League (JACL).** In 1930, the original Fresno chapter changed its name and affiliation to JACL.

BIBLIOGRAPHY

Daniels, Roger. *The Politics of Prejudice.* Berkeley: University of California Press, 1977.
O'Brien, Daniel J. and Stephen S. Fugita. *The Japanese American Experience.* Bloomington: Indiana University Press, 1991.

Angel Island

The Angel Island Processing and Detention Center, a notorious San Francisco arrival point for Chinese immigrants, was originally built to replace a converted warehouse at the Pacific Mail Steamship Wharf that had been established following the mandates of the Chinese Exclusion Act (**Immigration Act of 1882**). Complaints of crowding and poor conditions at the warehouse facility resulted in a boycott of U.S. goods by the Chinese government in protest. An inspection of the warehouse by U.S. Immigration Commissioner General Frank Pearce Sargent led to the facility's closure and recommendations for a new center. Following congressional appropriation of $200,000 in 1903, construction began in 1905

and was completed in 1908. Upon commencing operations in January 1910, Angel Island served as the major West Coast center for incoming Asian immigrants.

Criticism of Angel Island's processing was widespread, however. Investigation of immigrants' entrance claims by U.S. authorities could take months or even years to complete, subjecting Chinese immigrants to harsh conditions, isolation, humiliation, and sometimes leading to suicide. Such harsh treatment gained Angel Island the nickname the "Isle of the Immortals" among the Chinese and the "Ellis Island of the West" among Americans. On November 4, 1940, the final Chinese detainees were transferred to other facilities and Angel Island's facilities were permanently closed down. In 1976, the California

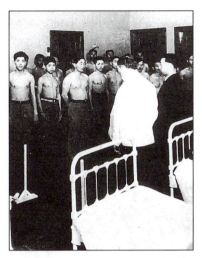

New immigrants from Asia are examined by the medical staff at Angel Island before being admitted to the United States. *National Archives.*

State Legislature allocated $250,000 to preserve Angel Island's buildings so that future generations could learn from the words of frustration, pain, and anguish etched by Chinese immigrants on the former center's walls.

BIBLIOGRAPHY

Chen, Jack. *The Chinese in America.* New York: Harper & Row, 1980.
Lai, H.M. "Island of Immortals." *California Historical Society* 1 (Spring 1978): 88–103.

Angell Treaty of 1880

The so-called Angell Treaty is named after James B. Angell, a distinguished jurist and president of the University of Michigan, who headed a delegation appointed by President Rutherford B. Hayes to negotiate a treaty with the Chinese government concerning migration of Chinese laborers. The treaty allowed the United States to limit and regulate the immigration of Chinese laborers but not actually to suspend it. Furthermore, the treaty guaranteed Chinese laborers and visitors to the United States the treatment due to citizens of a most favored nation. It also included provisions that the U.S. government would protect those Chinese currently in the country and that the government of China would be informed of all changes in U.S. immigration policy. Additionally, the delegation was able to negotiate a commercial treaty in the 48 days it was in China.

BIBLIOGRAPHY

Shih-Shan Henry Tsai. *The Chinese Experience in America.* Bloomington: Indiana University Press, 1986.

Annexation of Hawaii

Proposals to have the United States annex the Hawaiian Islands emerged from some members of the expatriate community in the independent kingdom of Hawaii during the last half of the nineteenth century, but the matter gained urgency in 1891 with the passage of the McKinley Act, which granted subsidies to domestic sugar growers in the United States, thus threatening to undersell Hawaii's principal export. In 1893, **Queen Liliuokalani** accepted a petition from citizens of the monarchy to change the constitution, which favored the interests of the expatriates by restricting the right to vote to persons with financial means. Thirteen conspirators, led by Lorrin A. Thurston, then plotted the overthrow of the monarchy in consultation with U.S. minister of Hawaii, John Stevens; they included six Caucasian citizens of Hawaii, five American citizens, one English citizen, and one German citizen. On January 16, 1893, Stevens ordered 162 troops from the SS *Boston* to disembark, seize the government building, raise the United States flag, and place the queen under house arrest until she relinquished sovereignty. The conspirators, forming the **Committee of Safety**, then declared a Provisional Government on January 17, pending annexation by the United States.

Although Stevens recognized the new Provisional Government, neither outgoing President Benjamin Harrison nor incoming President Grover Cleveland did. Cleveland dispatched James H. Blount to engage in secret negotiations to restore the monarchy. Since Washington turned down the request for annexation, the Provisional Government declared itself to be the Republic of Hawaii on July 4, 1894, continuing martial law, and emissaries were sent to Washington to lobby for annexation, even though the McKinley Act was abolished in 1894, removing one of the principal pretexts for annexation.

The lobbying effort paid off after William McKinley was elected president in 1896 and the United States launched the Spanish-American War in 1898. On July 7, 1898, McKinley signed a joint resolution of both houses of Congress, known as the Newlands Resolution, declaring Hawaii to be a part of the territory of the United States, effective August 12, 1898, though there was no corresponding vote in Hawaii to accept or reject the action. American troops remained on the islands to enforce the annexation, which to this day has been rejected by some observers as an act illegal under international law. **See also** Annexation Club; Home Rule Party; Native Hawaiians Study Commission. (MH)

BIBLIOGRAPHY

Budnick, Rich. *Stolen Kingdom: An American Conspiracy*. Honolulu: Aloha Press, 1992.

Osborne, Thomas J. *"Empire Can Wait": American Opposition to Hawaiian Annexation*. Kent, OH: Kent State University Press, 1981.

Pratt, William J. *Expansionists of 1899: The Acquisition of Hawaii and the Spanish Islands*. New York: Quadrangle Books, 1936.

Anti-Coolie Clubs

Predominant in the late nineteenth and early twentieth centuries, anti-coolie clubs sought to drive Chinese immigrants out of the United States. The first of these appeared in California in the 1850s; club members were determined to force Chinese miners out of their jobs by employing both legal and illegal means, such as boycotting, and violence.

The Central Pacific Anti-Coolie Association of 1862 quickly spread from San Francisco through the Bay Area, combining in 1876 with similar groups to form the Anti-Chinese Union, a group whose roster included prominent businessmen and legislators. The Anti-Chinese Union's explicit goals included opposing the hiring of Chinese and Chinese-American workers and boycotting items sold and produced by those who employed Chinese workers. By the early 1900s, membership in these organizations waned as legislation began to reflect popular dissatisfaction with such discrimination. **See also** Cubic Air Ordinance; Foreign Miners Tax; League of Deliverance.

BIBLIOGRAPHY

Kung, S.W. *Chinese in American Life*. Seattle: University of Washington Press, 1962.

Sandmeyer, Elmer C. *The Anti-Chinese Movement in California*. Chicago: University of Illinois Press, 1939.

Antimiscegenation Laws

"Miscegenation" refers to sexual behavior involving persons of different racial backgrounds. The practice of miscegenation began almost as soon as English colonists met Native Americans on a social basis and continued when Africans were imported as slaves into the colonies. In many cases, the product of miscegenation was a child of mixed race born out of wedlock, although in some instances the couples sought recognition of their union by church and state.

By the 1660s, the colonial legislatures of tobacco-growing Maryland and Virginia banned interracial sex and marriage, seeking primarily to separate blacks and whites. In the early 1700s, antimiscegenation laws were adopted in Delaware, Massachusetts, and the southern colonies. Initially, the ban was on both interracial sex and interracial marriage. By the middle of the nineteenth century antimiscegenation laws had been adopted by 38 states, although Iowa and Kansas repealed these laws before the Civil War and eight northern states followed suit in the two decades immediately after the Civil War. By 1951, 29 states still prohibited miscegenation. Although the focus of the law was on marriage more than sexual behavior, interracial adultery and fornication were still prosecuted in most of these states.

The California Supreme Court ruled in *Perez v. Sharp*, 32 Cal. 2d 711 (1948), that the state's antimiscegenation law was unconstitutional, violating the equal protection clause of the Fourteenth Amendment. Although no other state court made a similar ruling, 10 western states abolished their antimiscegenation laws from 1953 to 1963. The U.S. Supreme Court invalidated the ban on interracial cohabitation in

McLaughlin v. Florida, 379 U.S. 184 (1964); three years later, the Court struck down the prohibition on interracial marriage in *Loving v. Virginia,* 388 U.S. 1 (1964). In the latter case, a white man and a black woman went from Virginia to the District of Columbia to obtain a marriage license, but they were found guilty of the Virginia antimiscegenation law when they returned to Virginia to establish their marital abode. The Court ruled that the couple was entitled to equal protection of the law, which was denied solely because of the race of the marriage partners. Thereafter, challenges invalidated the remaining antimiscegenation laws as well as prohibitions on interracial adoptions. (MH)

BIBLIOGRAPHY

Applebaum, Harvey M. "Miscegenation Statutes: A Constitutional and Social Problem." *Georgetown Law Review* 53, no. 1 (Fall 1964): 49–91.

Bell, Derrick A., Jr. "Right to Interracial Sex and Marriage." In *Race, Racism and American Law.* Boston: Little, Brown, 1973.

Hernton, Calvin C. *Sex and Racism in America.* New York: Grove Press, 1966.

Smith, John David, ed. *Racial Determinism and the Fear of Miscegenation Post-1900: Race and "The Negro Problem."* New York: Garland, 1993.

Daniel T. Aoki (1918–1986)

Daniel Toshimichi Aoki was president of the 442nd Veterans Club and campaign manager for John Burns (Democrat), who became Hawaii's delegate to Congress and then governor of Hawaii. Aoki was administrative aide to Governor Burns, Senator **Daniel Inouye**, and Governor **George Ariyoshi. See also** 442nd Regimental Combat Team. (MH)

BIBLIOGRAPHY

Burris, Jerry. "Dem Leader Dan Aoki Dies at 68." *Honolulu Advertiser* (June 12, 1986): A3.

Hooper, Paul and Dan Boylan. "Interviews with Dan Aoki." Honolulu: Hamilton Library, University of Hawaii at Manoa, 1977, 10 audio cassettes.

George Ariyoshi (1926–)

George Ariyoshi practiced law in Hawaii from 1953 to 1970, where he also served in the Hawaii House of Representatives from 1954 to 1958, and in the Territory of Hawaii Senate in 1958. Following Hawaii's transition to U.S. statehood, Ariyoshi, a Democrat, became a member of the Hawaiian State Senate, where he remained from 1958 to 1970. While there, he acted as both chairman of the Ways and Means Committee and as Senate majority leader. Ariyoshi served as Hawaii's lieutenant governor from 1970 to 1973, and in 1973 became acting governor. In 1974 he was elected governor and served until 1986. While governor, he oversaw Hawaii's rapid growth in population and development. An adept politician, he was regarded as a coalition builder during his tenure in office.

BIBLIOGRAPHY

Coffman, Tom. *Catch a Wave: A Case Study of Hawaii's New Politics.* Honolulu, 1973.

Asakura v. City of Seattle et al. (1924)

R. Asakura was a Japanese alien working as a pawnbroker in Seattle, Washington. In 1921 the city of Seattle passed a law that prohibited aliens from acquiring a license to work as a pawnbroker. Asakura objected that the law was unconstitutional, and he appealed to the superior court. Asakura maintained that the law violated his Fourteenth Amendment rights and the treaty between the United States and Japan, which governed commerce between Japanese and American persons. The court ruled in favor of Asakura, but its decision was reversed when the case was appealed to the Supreme Court of Washington State. The case then went before the U.S. Supreme Court, on a writ of error. In *Asakura v. City of Seattle et al.,* 265 U.S. 332 1924, the Court decided on the sole question of whether the ordinance violated the treaty between the United States and Japan; the Court held that a treaty was a supreme law that could not be overruled by the laws of individual states.

BIBLIOGRAPHY

Consulate-General of Japan. *Documentary History of Law Cases Affecting Japanese in the United States, 1916–1924.* San Francisco: Consulate-General of Japan, 1925.

Asian-American Movement

Ignited by the African-American civil rights movement of the 1960s, the Asian-American movement was a made up of largely middle-class reform-minded Asian Americans who sought racial equality, social justice, and political empowerment. The movement tried to become Pan-Asian by tying together the diverse cultural groups including Chinese, Filipino, Korean, and Japanese Americans. The problem, as seen by the reformers, was that they were neither Asian nor American because both cultures did not accept them.

Active in the civil rights movement and the protests against the **Vietnam War,** the members of the Asian-American movement were estranged from other ethnic minorities who treated them as only token minorities. The movement was successful in accomplishing some of its goals early on including the Supreme Court cases *Lau v. Nichols* **(1974),** which demanded bilingual education, and *Wards Cove v. Antonio,* which ruled that employment discrimination against Filipinos violated constitutional protection. However, even the success in these cases did not bring Asian Americans into greater working alliances with other minorities.

The movement suffered from a number of failings including the lack of a national leader with the recognition of Martin Luther King, Jr., Malcolm X, Rudolfo "Corky" Gonzalez, or Russell Means. Additionally, Asian Americans constituted only 1 percent of the population and so their struggles were often ignored by the press and others in U.S. society. Finally, the movement lacked a specific agenda that could unite its constituents. The result was a fragmented approach to problems that continues to this day.

BIBLIOGRAPHY
Wei, William. *The Asian American Movement*. Philadelphia: Temple University Press, 1993.

Asian-American Political Coalition

Operating from New Jersey, the Asian-American Political Coalition is a private, nonprofit organization dedicated to raising political awareness and participation in the Asian-American community. It publishes the bimonthly newsletter *Asian Voice*.

BIBLIOGRAPHY
Sy, Levin. *National Asian Pacific American Political Almanac*. Los Angeles: University of California, 1996.

Asian-American Relations with Other Minorities

Asian Americans have been heralded for their educational achievements and applauded for their economic success. Moreover, they have been identified under the banner of the **model minority** stereotype. This stereotype attempts to paint a positive image of all Asian Americans as industrious, intelligent, and hardworking. Advocates of this model claim that educational, occupational, and economic status are strong indicators of Asian success in a society that historically has limited their assimilation in mainstream society. Asian Americans fit the model minority stereotype because the majority of their population has overcome the obstacles that plague other minority groups in American society. Part of their success is based on their small but growing population that does not pose a threat to mainstream society. In contrast, other minority populations, such as the African Americans and Latinos, have much larger populations and consequently are perceived as more of a threat to mainstream society, and this perception increases and intensifies discriminatory practices on a larger scale.

The model minority stereotype has negative images that have an adverse impact on other ethnic groups. Society interprets the Asian-American success as validation that mainstream America is an open society with opportunities for other minority groups to succeed. However, the model minority image represents a constant danger that other minority groups could be perceived as less successful and be blamed for their lack of achievement and failure, thus becoming scapegoats. Therefore, it could be an unfair assessment to compare the much larger populations of the African-American and Latino communities with the model minority image of Asian Americans because of the frequent discriminatory activities targeting the former groups. This environment can create anti-Asian sentiment within the African-American and Latino communities, whose lack of success is measured by the loss of illusionary opportunities in society in comparison to Asian Americans.

The model minority stereotype also adversely affects Asian Americans. Primarily, the stereotype perpetuates the illusion that social ills (such as poverty, crime, and homelessness) that adversely affect African Americans and Latinos are nonexistent among Asian Americans. As their population continues to increase, the "model minority" myth continues to belie many serious issues confronting the Asian-American community. Various subtle forms of discrimination are increasingly apparent such as economic, political, legal, educational, and housing discrimination that has at times led to violence against Asian Americans. Asian Americans often are challenged by employment concerns regarding the "glass ceiling," adverse hiring and promotion practices, and limitations on career choices. From a political perspective, Asia Americans are rarely elected to public office and are often underrepresented in government institutions. They have also been challenged educationally by colleges and universities that have established quota systems resulting in the denial of opportunities for qualified Asian-American students. In all of these areas, Asian Americans have passively endured these subtle discriminatory practices. Traditionally, Asian Americans have not had much experience with public protests of their grievances, but in more recent years they have taken a proactive position by legally and politically challenging discriminatory practices.

While a general consensus persists in mainstream society regarding the success of Asian Americans, their history in the United States portrays a different scenario. Similar to the experiences of African Americans and Latinos, Asian-Americans' historical experiences have been marred by negative stereotypes and discriminatory practices that still persist. All three minority subpopulations are heterogeneous groups. Within each and among the subpopulations, there are differences regarding ethnicity, income, and immigration histories.

Like African Americans and Latinos, Asian Americans have a unique physical appearance. Their facial characteristics make them visible in American society. As a result, they tend to be categorized as a single ethnic group, with no regard for their distinct language and culture. This is exacerbated by the misconception that they are new immigrants leading to anti-Asian-American sentiments in society.

Historically, the first significant wave of Asians to arrive in the United States were the Chinese. They came to work in the California gold mines in the 1850s and later in building the American railroad system. By the early twentieth century, the small Asian population increased with the immigration of Japanese, Filipinos, Koreans, and Asian Indians. To restrict the influx of Asian immigration to the United States and eliminate Asian competition with American workers, local and federal government authorities established immigration legislation that discriminated against the growing Asian subpopulation. For example, in 1855 California passed a head tax law, placing a fee of $55 on every Chinese immigrant. By 1858 the state enacted another law that prohibited Chinese immigration into California. However, in 1876 the U.S. Supreme Court ruled both laws unconstitutional. In 1882, the United States passed the Chinese Exclusion Act (**Immigration Act of 1882**), which prohibited immigration for 10 years and eliminated Chinese descendants from acquiring U.S. citizenship after the act became effective. The act was extended in 1892, 1902, and 1904. In 1943 this act was discontinued by congressional repeal (through the **Immigration Act of 1943**, the so-called Magnuson Act) and a quota system for Chinese immigrants was implemented instead.

The Japanese, Filipinos, and Koreans also experienced negative treatment by the U.S. legal system. In the case of the Japanese, they immigrated to the United States at the turn of the twentieth century and settled on the West Coast. When they arrived they were accused of taking jobs and wages away from mainstream American workers. This led to the creation of the **Immigration Act of 1917**, which prohibited Japanese and other Asians from immigrating to the United States. As a result of highly restrictive immigration laws established by Congress in the 1920s, Asian immigration dramatically decreased. For example, the National Origins Act (**Immigration Act of 1924**) prohibited all types of Japanese immigration: barring Japanese wives of American husbands, Japanese aliens, and individuals of Japanese ancestry from immigrating to the United States.

After the bombing of **Pearl Harbor** on December 7, 1941, the federal government's regulation of Asians increased with the establishment of Japanese **internment camps.** In the name of national security, the U.S. government relocated people of Japanese background to camps. Their property was disposed of but not their history, culture, or language. In contrast, African Americans were "interned" without compensation and with hard labor for hundreds of years under the organized structure of slavery. They also lost their history, language, culture, and family. However, unlike African Americans who were promised "40 acres and a mule" but never received retribution, the Japanese were successful in winning reparations for the hardship they endured.

In the case of the Filipino and Korean immigrants, their experience with United States immigration laws met with mixed results. Prior to the 1920s, Chinese and Japanese immigration represented the largest number of Asian immigration to the United States, with Filipinos and Koreans immigrating in smaller numbers. During this period the United States held the Philippine Islands as a territory; therefore, Filipinos were exempt from the Immigration Act of 1917 and the National Origins Act of 1924, and they were allowed to immigrate to the United States. They currently represent the second largest Asian subpopulation in the United States. Upon their entry into the United States, Filipinos worked on the Hawaiian sugar plantations and as field laborers in the California agricultural industry. However, their increasing numbers led to anti-Filipino sentiment. In a partial response to these tensions, Congress passed the **Tydings–McDuffie Act** in 1934, which granted deferred independence to the Philippine Islands and restricted their immigration numbers to an annual quota of only 50 being allowed entry into the United States.

As for the Korean subpopulation, they came to the United States as political exiles in 1885 in search of a better lifestyle and standard of living. Their numbers increased between 1903 and 1905 as they settled in Hawaii and California. However, instead of an improved standard of living, they were relegated to low wages and poor living conditions because of the fear of deportation. It was not until the passage of the **Immigration and Nationality Act of 1965** which liberalized immigration that there was an increase in Korean immigration to the United States.

Immigration legislation that restricts Asian immigration and threatens existing immigrants with deportation (in addition to anti-Asian sentiments from other ethnic groups) continues to exist. While this is not as blatant as the threat of harassment and protest endured by Latinos and African Americans, it is just as real.

The various Asian immigrant groups have also experienced economic, political, and educational discrimination that has at times been magnified by violence. Institutionalized discrimination has shaped economic discrimination, leading to limited economic opportunities and relatively limited success for Asian Americans in mainstream society. The impetus for anti-Asian-American sentiment and stereotypical images has been the fear of mainstream America workers' that they would be displaced in employment opportunities. In addition, African Americans and Latinos fear that Asian Americans would take over their neighborhood businesses. These fears result from anti-Asian stereotypical images and their proposed socioeconomic threat to mainstream society. For example, according to the U.S. Commission on Civil Rights in 1992, while Asian Americans are represented in greater numbers than other ethnic minorities in white-collar occupations, they suffer from discrimination that limits their mobility within these occupations.

For Asian Americans, their occupational success when compared to African Americans and Latinos should be qualified. Asian Americans themselves have bought into the myth of the model minority, thus creating a false sense of achievement that conceals the degree of underemployment experienced by their subpopulation. As Asian Americans accept the stereotypical image of themselves, they believe that they are more successful than they actually are. While Asian Americans are represented in high-status occupations, in reality they are placed in lower-level professional positions.

As a result, Asian Americans peak early in their professional positions, thus reaching the "glass ceiling" early on their careers. This places them at a career disadvantage when they attempt to progress to higher managerial positions. Despite their qualifications, Asian Americans are aware that the negative stereotypical images have limited their rise into advanced professional occupations.

Asian-American men are less likely to be in management positions than white men with the same qualifications. For example, Asian Americans were less successful in moving from professional to managerial positions than were either white Americans or other ethnic minority groups. When Asian Americans lack opportunities for promotion and advancement they tend to cluster in technical jobs, which gives the appearance to the rest of society that Asians Americans excel in this field. Moreover, in the nation's largest companies, only 0.6 percent of the senior management positions were held by African Americans, 0.4 percent by Latino Americans, 0.3 percent by Asian Americans, and 3 to 5 percent by women. While making up less than 50 percent of the workforce, white males occupy up to 95 percent of managerial positions.

A consequence of the glass-ceiling impact is that Asian Americans, like African Americans and Latinos, are in fewer white-collar management and professional positions than their white counterparts. As a result of limited occupational mobility, economic discrimination thus reinforces societal negative beliefs regarding Asian Americans. For instance, in 1996, more than 90,000 complaints of discrimination were filed with the Equal Employment Opportunity Commission. However, only 3 percent of those were alleged for "reverse discrimination," and most of those were found to be without merit. The Glass Ceiling Commission found that there was still great disparity between the numbers of management positions held by women and minorities and those held by white men.

With the exception of Cuban Americans, the Asian subpopulations are the second most economically successful ethnic groups in mainstream society. A much higher percentage of Asian Americans are middle class and white collar than in other ethnic populations; as a consequence, their "success" has made Asian Americans the model minority.

There are at least three factors accounting for higher incomes among the Asian-American subpopulations. First, in a majority of Asian-American households both spouses work. Second, when Asian-American children become of age they tend to live at home while being employed, thus adding significantly to the household income. Third, on average, the Asian family is much larger, resulting in more wage earners per household. Consequently, the income data for Asian Americans do not reflect the fact that there are more wage earners per Asian-American household.

Asian Americans' income compared to that of other minorities illustrates that the median income of Asian Americans is higher than that for African Americans and Latino Americans. The Asian net gain in income between 1980 and 1994 was equal to whites. However, comparing the increase in the Asian-American poverty rate relative to their income reveals that the Asian-American population can be characterized between those growing richer and those who remain poor. In general, the Asian subpopulation's economic success reinforces the model minority myth, an image that belies their challenge for integrating fully in higher-level professional positions in mainstream America.

In terms of the American political arena, Asian subpopulations have not fared well. Unlike African Americans, who have made great strides to be visible and represented in political office and in the Democratic Party, Latinos and Asian Americans have not had the same success. Despite their increasing populations, Asian Americans are relatively absent from the political arena. For example, with the exception of Hawaii, very few Asian Americans have been elected to public office. According to the U.S. Commission on Civil Rights in 1992, 10 percent of the California population is Asian American; yet, only two Asian Americans from California serve in Congress, only one has been elected to a state position, and no Asian American served in the California legislature at the time of the report. In New York City, with an Asian-American population of more than a half million, no Asian American has ever been elected to city council.

The underrepresentation of Asian subpopulations in the political arena can be attributed to discriminatory political practices embedded in the model minority stereotype. Accordingly, Asian Americans are labeled as being politically silent on issues, thereby limiting their participation in the political process. Like African Americans and Latinos, Asian Americans have been subject to gerrymandering practices that weaken their voting power. However, unlike African Americans who mainly identify with and have received support from the Democratic Party, Asian Americans have been overlooked by both political parties, which have neglected to establish any political agendas inclusive of Asian-American issues.

Political progress against discriminatory practices targeting Asian-American subpopulations have also been limited by the lack of effective political organization in many of their communities. However, in 1986 the Asian-American Voters Coalition was created to consolidate the diverse Asian subpopulations into an effective pan-Asian voting bloc. This coalition could have an important impact on elections held in such states as California, Texas, New York State, and Illinois, where large numbers of Asian Americans reside.

From an education perspective, Asian Americans are regarded to be the most educated ethnic subpopulation in mainstream society. Their success rate in matriculating from high school and college is higher than whites, African Americans, and Latinos. Between 1980 and 1990, however, a 10.2 percent increase in the number of white high school graduates brought the two groups closer to parity. However, the increase in the number of Asian-American high school graduates between 1980 and 1990 was only 47 percent of the increase in the white population, indicating possible problems in the areas of education for Asian Americans.

In 1994, 41.2 percent of Asian Americans had completed four or more years of college. While this figure appears to reflect no limitations to Asian Americans obtaining educational success, it fails to reveal the discrimination of restrictive admission policies targeting Asian-American college applicants. Although there was more than a 70 percent increase in Asian-American college applicants between 1980 and 1990, the number of Asian-American students admitted to college decreased by almost 80 percent.

A discovery of lower admission rates for Asian Americans at Ivy League institutions reveals that while Asian Americans possessed the academic qualifications equal to their white counterparts, they were denied admission more frequently. The justification for creating a quota system that limits rather than increases the admission of qualified Asian students is that it would minimize reverse discrimination claims by qualified white college applicants.

However, in light of the model minority stereotype, the high levels of scholastic achievement by Asian Americans present a scenario that discrimination is nonexistent. Yet Asian Americans are confronted with discriminatory practices in higher education—as they are increasingly admitted to institutions of higher learning, the anti-Asian sentiment also grows.

In the late 1990s, Asian Americans responded to the attack on affirmative action and California's Proposition 209. Many Asian Americans believe that they must defend and promote the civil and political rights of their ethnic subpopulations within the context of promoting a multiracial democracy in the United States. Issues of particular concern to the Asian-American communities include college admissions and employment policies. College-educated Asian Americans earn 11 percent less than college-educated whites. Although Asian Americans admit that affirmative action is an imperfect mechanism for them, it is a necessary tool to level the playing field. The Asian-American community was divided in its response to California's Proposition 209, also known as the California Civil Rights Initiative, which sought to eliminate preferential treatment based on race, gender, or ethnicity in public education, public employment, and public contracting. Critics of affirmative action attempted to persuade Asian Americans to support the abolishment of affirmative action, claiming that eliminating the program would be more advantageous to Asian Americans in the areas of education and employment. Critics further invoked the model minority myth of Asian-American achievement and assimilation into mainstream society as evidence that affirmative action programs are no longer needed—and in fact that they impede opportunities for "qualified" Asian Americans. On the other hand, advocates of affirmative action pointed out that America has not achieved a strictly merit-based and color-blind society, especially in light of discrimination in college admissions and hiring processes. Like other ethnic groups in America, the Asian subpopulations have benefited from affirmative programs; therefore they believed that they have an obligation to support the legacy of those activists who worked and died for the civil rights movement. Asian Americans acknowledged that affirmative action programs are not flawless and may require some reform; they also acknowledged, however, that California's Proposition 209 is not about change or reform, it is about abolition. Contrary to the model minority myth, Asian Americans do not have a level playing field in society, and therefore they viewed California's proposition 209 as too radical.

As a result, Asian Americans are reconsidering whether they want to support abolishing affirmative action programs that they have benefited from, without room for reform or fine-tuning. Is the 8 percent increase in school admissions of Asian Americans worth the price of declining admissions for African American and Latino students, while virtually eliminating Native American students? What is "merit," and will abolishing affirmative action obtain it? An injury to one is an injury to all—that is the recurrent theme in Asian-American testimony on affirmative action. The proposition process created much resentment against California Governor Pete Wilson's attempts to turn hard-won gains of Asian Americans into a wedge against Latinos and African Americans.

Asian-American support for affirmative action is hardly uniform or universal. Asian-American support for affirmative action is gaining momentum. It manifests a higher patriotism, a vision of a society that is truly democratic and representative of such diverse ethnic groups as Latinos, African Americans, Native Americans, Asian Americans, and white ethnic groups.

Even as excessive negative beliefs have moved some to violence against Asian Americans, a series of more subtle and invidious beliefs have emerged. For example, the model minority becomes the "yellow peril" when Asian Americans are accused of taking jobs from white Americans, African Americans, and Latinos. Also, tensions between Japan and the United States have created various waves of "Japan bashing." Asians' occupational niche as a middleman minority group that sells to non-Asians has created the same kinds of negative beliefs that emerge against all middleman minority groups—that they are clannish, secretive, dishonest, and devious. The Chinese were labeled with these negative epithets early on, but in the 1980s and 1990s these beliefs have been revived with a new intensity as Asian Americans have established small businesses in the neighborhoods of other disadvantaged minority groups, particularly those of African Americans and Latinos. These beliefs have created a sometimes volatile mix of resentment that erupts into violence, as the Korean merchants learned in the **Los Angeles riots of 1992**.

Typically, the model minority does not protest as loudly as others to discriminatory treatment, but this treatment is a fact of life for Asian Americans today, more than 100 years since they began emigrating to the United States. Anti-Asian graffiti, flyers, racial bigotry, and violence consistently plague the diverse Asian-American communities; all these factors work to discourage them from obtaining economic, political, and educational success.

Historically, Asians have not mounted highly visible or violent protests against those who discriminate against them. Indeed, part of the reason why Asian Americans are considered the model minority is, no doubt, their relatively low-key protests against discrimination. For example, the internment of Japanese Americans did not generate confrontation, except in the court system. Earlier laws that restricted the rights of Chinese and Japanese Americans were often accepted and only later challenged in court. Asian-American middlemen minorities in inner-city neighborhoods have countered violence with civil protest (marches and court actions) but not confrontation. The harassment and, at times, violence against Asian Americans who enter non-Asian neighborhoods are usually uncontested.

In measuring whether Asian Americans are the model minority it could be argued that their educational, occupational, and economic status is an indicator of success, especially in light of efforts to limit Asian-American presence in, and assimilation into, mainstream American society. Asian Americans fit the model minority stereotype because many have overcome the odds and succeeded. Beneath the surface, however, the model minority image has negative repercussions for not only Asian Americans but other ethnic groups as well.

The subtlety of much discrimination—for example, college admissions practices, corporate glass ceilings, and gerrymandering of voting districts, coupled with the sporadic acts of violence against Asian Americans by angry whites and disadvantaged minorities—makes it difficult to mount a concerted corrective effort, especially by a largely politically passive model minority that is not perceived to have problems. By the end of the 1990s, considerable effort was made by governmental and legal agencies to be more conscious of, and to correct for, past and present discrimination against African Americans, Latinos, and Native Americans, but comparatively little effort was made on behalf of, or by, Asian Americans.

Historically, Asians have not been prone to visible protests, but in the 1970s, 1980s, and 1990s, legal and political challenges to discriminatory practices have been mounted, indicating that Asians will no longer passively accept discrimination. **See also** Immigration Act of 1907; Immigration and Nationality Act of 1952; Immigration and Nationality Act of 1990; Immigration Policy; Immigration Restriction Movement; Los Angeles Riots (1992); Model Minority; Philippine Naturalization. (MKT)

BIBLIOGRAPHY

Aguirre, Adalberto, Jr. and Jonathan H. Turner. *American Ethnicity: The Dynamics and Consequences of Discrimination*. 2nd ed. New York: McGraw Hill, 1995.

Hurk, Won and Kim Kwang. "The Success Image of Asian Americans: Its Practical and Theoretical Implications." *Ethnic and Racial Studies* 12 (1989): 512–538.

Kitano, Harry and Roger Daniels. *Asian Americans: Emerging Minorities*. Englewood Cliffs, NJ: Prentice-Hall, 1988.

Knoll, Tricia. *Becoming Americans: Asian Sojourners, Immigrants, and Refugees in the Western United States*. Portland, OR: Coast to Coast Books, 1982.

Osaka, Masako. "Japanese-Americans: Melting into the All-American Pot?" In Melvin Holli and Peter Jones, eds. *Ethnic Chicago*. Grand Rapids, MI: Eerdmans Publishing, 1984.

Suzuki, Bob. "Asians." In Arthur Levine and Associates, eds. *Shaping Higher Education's Future: Demographic Realities and Opportunities, 1990–2000*. San Francisco: Jossey-Bass, 1989.

Takagi, Dana. "From Discrimination to Affirmative Action: Facts in the Asian American Admissions Controversy." *Social Problems* 37 (1990): 578–592.

Thomas, Gail. "Notes on Asian American Employment." In Gail Thomas, ed. *Race and Ethnicity in America: Meeting the Challenge in the 21st Century*. Washington, D.C.: Taylor & Francis, 1995.

U.S. Census Bureau. *Recent Activities Against Citizens and Residents of Asian Descent*. Washington, D.C.: U.S. Government Printing Office, 1986.

U.S. Department of Labor. *Preliminary Report on Discrimination in the Workplace and the Existence of the "Glass Ceiling."* Washington, D.C.: U.S. Government Printing Office, 1991.

Asian Americans for Community Involvement

Asian Americans for Community Involvement is a nonprofit organization founded in 1973. Based in Santa Clara County, California, the group provides social and human services to Asian Pacific immigrants. It is the largest organization of its kind in the United States. In addition to its work with immigrants, the organization was the catalyst in changes adopted by the state of California in regard to textbook adoption. In 1976, it successfully lobbied the state board of education to ensure that multicultural groups are surveyed before a textbook is adopted. Asian Americans for Community Involvement encourages self-help, ethnic pride, and economic and social justice.

BIBLIOGRAPHY

Sy, Levin. *National Asian Pacific American Political Almanac*. Los Angeles: University of California, 1996.

Asian Americans for Equality (AAFE)

A leftist civil rights organization that formed in 1979 out of the Asian American for Equal Employment (1974–1979), the Asian Americans for Equality (AAFE) is a class-conscious revolutionary group with broad civil and political agendas. Twenty-six members of the original founding group left to for the **Chinese American Democratic Rights Association (CADRA)** because of a split in the direction of the organizations. Violence ensued between the two groups with the AAFE attempting to silence CADRA. The AAFE gained greater political clout in 1986 with the decline of the Communist Worker's Party and its 1984 endorsement of Jesse Jackson for president of the United States. The group remains based in New York City and actively encourages its members to join and participate in the Democratic Party and labor unions to increase its own influence.

BIBLIOGRAPHY

Wei, William *The Asian American Movement*. Philadelphia: Temple University Press, 1993.

Asian Law Alliance

The Asian Law Alliance is a nonprofit legal organization that was founded in 1977 in San Jose, California. The group's efforts are directed at the provision of equal access for Asians to the legal system. The alliance promotes self-reliance and an improved level of life. The group also makes available multilingual and culturally sensitive legal services. The organization provides programs in legal counseling, community education, and organization within the community.

BIBLIOGRAPHY

"Supervisors Pass Program to Deport Jailed Immigrants; Santa Clara County Plan Draws Fire From Bot." *The San Francisco Chronicle* (April 1, 1998): A13.

Asian Law Caucus

Formed in 1972 as an Oakland-based nonprofit organization dedicated to providing legal services to Asian Americans in financial straits, the Asian Law Caucus later relocated to San Francisco, where it continued to work for civil, constitutional, and immigration rights as well as improved labor, employment, and housing conditions. It was party to two important Supreme Court decisions in *Korematsu v. United States* **(1944)** and *Hirabayashi v. United States* **(1934),** both involving Japanese internment during **World War II**. Other major cases included *Chan v. Scott* (1972), *Ping Yuen Tenants Association v. San Francisco Housing Authority* (1978), *International Molders' and Allied Workers' Union v. Nelson* (1982), *Ha et al. v. T&W Fashion* (1983), *EEOC v. Tortilleria La Mejor* (1987), and *Vietnamese Fishermen's Association of America v. Admiral Paul Vost* (1989). In addition to courtroom advocacy, the Asian Law Caucus has supported bilingual balloting, unionization, minimum wage and back-pay entitlements, and adequate tenant housing. **See also** Dennis Hayashi; Paul M. Igasaki.

BIBLIOGRAPHY
Wei, William. *The Asian American Movement.* Philadelphia, PA: Temple University Press, 1993.

Asian Pacific American Labor Alliance (APALA)

The Asian Pacific American Labor Alliance (APALA) was formed in 1922 by Asian Pacific American labor activists and the American Federation of Labor–Congress of Industrial Organizations (AFL-CIO). APALA organizes workers and trains union leaders. The initial chapters of the organization were located in Washington state, California, New York, Washington D.C., Massachusetts, and Hawaii.

BIBLIOGRAPHY
Dine, Philip. "Asian-American Group Puts Spotlight on Immigrant Workers." *St. Louis Post-Dispatch* (May 31, 1996): C1.

Asian Pacific American Legal Center of Southern California

The Asian Pacific American Legal Center of Southern California was founded in 1983 to give the Asian Pacific American community legal services and educational opportunities. The organization was founded by private donors, foundation grants, and state allocations. Headquartered in Los Angeles, the center offers free help to low-income groups. The center also advises on family law and domestic violence, immigration, housing, employment, government services, and other issues. The organization also pays attention to racial incidents in the U.S. society to publicize the wrongs.

BIBLIOGRAPHY
Kang, K. Connie. "Hate Crimes against Asians in Southland Rose in 1995." *Los Angeles Times* (August 2, 1996): A3.
Richardson, Lisa. "Little Change Seen in Hate Crimes against Asians." *Los Angeles Times* (September 9, 1997): B1.

Asian Pacific Democratic Club

Formed in 1992 in the Bay Area of San Francisco, the Asian Pacific Democratic Club is a progressive organization involved in electoral politics. Serving the Asian-American community on issues like immigration and voting rights, the organization seeks to empower Asian Americans and encourages activity at the local, state, and national levels.

BIBLIOGRAPHY
Ward, Mike. "Protests Fail to Change Council's Immigration Stand." *Los Angeles Times* (June 12, 1996): 9–1.

Asian/Pacific Women's Network

The Asian/Pacific Women's Network was founded in 1979 to promote the interests of Asian Pacific women nationwide. The network works towards social justice and economic mobility for the women. Besides the national network, there are state and local chapters found in several states. Public awareness of Asian Pacific women's issues is central to the organization. The group sponsors educational programs as well.

BIBLIOGRAPHY
Davidson, Joanne. "The Achieving Women Honored." *Denver Post* (June 19, 1995): F4.

Asian Women United

Founded in 1976 to promote equal educational opportunity and oppose racial discrimination and stereotyping, Asian Women United works closely with schools, universities, and like-minded organizations to develop educational resources and sponsor community projects. The group has funded and produced such publications as *Making Waves: Writing by and about Asian American Women*, *With Silk Wings: Asian American Women at Work*, *Dear Diane: Letters From Our Daughters*, and *Dear Diane: Questions and Answers for Asian-American Women*.

BIBLIOGRAPHY
Wei, William. *The Asian American Movement.* Philadelphia, PA: Temple University Press, 1993.

Asiatic Exclusion League

The Asiatic Exclusion League was based in San Francisco, with A.E. Yoell as its secretary. Yoell spread rumors that East Indians were untrustworthy and a menace to communities. He helped foster anti-Asian sentiment, which led to the **Bellingham** (Washington) **Riot of 1907** in which whites forced Indian lumber workers out of the city and across the Canadian border. In 1909 Yoell also appealed to officials in Washington, D.C., about the increasing Indian immigration into California, claiming that the immigrants were stealing jobs from white citizens and spreading disease. The league continued to back bills that would limit Asian immigration. They were especially concerned that Indians might not be included in anti-Asian legislation. Daniel O'Keefe, commissioner general of immigration for California, ignored their protests, and the league turned its attention to Hart H. North, the San Francisco commissioner of immigration. In 1910 they petitioned President William Howard Taft to remove North from his post, claiming he was profiting from East Indian labor. Eventually their protests drew the attention of H.A. Millis, superintendant of immigration of the U.S., who headed a commission to investigate the East Indian community. By 1911 North was ousted. By 1917 East Indian immigration to the U.S. was effectively ended. However, the exclusion league continued to harass Indians and to prevent them from owning or leasing land in California. Finally, in 1923 the U.S. Supreme Court ruled in *United States v. Bhagat Singh Thind* that Indians could not become naturalized citizens of the United States and thus could not own land under the **California Alien Land Act of 1913**. **See also** Immigration Restriction Movement; San Francisco School Board Crisis of 1906.

BIBLIOGRAPHY
Hess, Gary R. "The Forgotten Asian Americans: The East Indian Community in the United States." In Norris Hundley, Jr., ed. *The Asian American*. Santa Barbara, CA: Clio Books, 1976.

Assembly Centers

After President Franklin Roosevelt had signed **Executive Order 9066** into law, assembly centers were created up and down the West Coast. The order called for the removal of all persons of Japanese ancestry from California, Oregon, Washington state, and part of Arizona to relocation camps. After the attack on Pearl Harbor by the Japanese, the president was advised to have the military remove all Japanese Americans from the West Coast. On March 24, 1942, the U.S. military began evacuating people of Japanese ancestry and taking them to assembly centers. Assembly centers were set up in all four states and served as temporary centers before the Japanese Americans were taken to **internment camps** (relocation centers). From March to September of 1942, more than 110,000 persons were evacuated and brought to assembly centers. **See** Executive Order 9066 in Appendix 1.

BIBLIOGRAPHY
Christgau, John. *Enemies*. Ames: Iowa State University Press, 1985.

Association of Indians in America

Founded in 1967 in New York City, the Association of Indians in America sought to promote the professional, social, and cultural goals of its diverse Asian Indian membership. Already active for years, in 1971 the group created a formal charter, established chapters in cities nationwide, and formed several subsidiaries including the Council on Medical Affairs, Engineers Council, Council on Trade, and Council on Trade and Tourism. The group waged a successful 1980 campaign to have Asian Indians classified separately from Caucasians for purposes of U.S. government polling, worked to influence economic relations between the United States and Indian countries, and provided delegates to various congressional hearings. In addition, the group conducted study programs, sponsored cultural and charity programs, and staged national conferences. The organization eventually changed its name to the Association of Asian Indians in America, which currently claims over a thousand members.

BIBLIOGRAPHY
Saran, Parmatma and Edwin Eames. *The New Ethnics*. New York: Praeger, 1980.

Association of Korean Political Studies in North America

The organization was founded in 1973 as the Association of Korean Political Scientists in North America. The association changed its name to broaden the membership to non-Korean political and social scientists. The group researches professional interests, including Korean political studies, and holds conferences.

BIBLIOGRAPHY
Montrey, Charles B. *Asian American Informative Directory*. Detroit, MI: Gale, 1994.

B

Bellingham Riot of 1907

The Bellingham riot was one of the largest uprisings in the Pacific Northwest by white working men opposing Asian Indian immigrant workers. Several hundred Indians, mostly Sikhs, arriving at the turn of the century, worked in the lumber mills of Bellingham, Washington. The **Asiatic Exclusion League** was crucial in fostering anti-Asian sentiment, thus forcing officials to exclude Indians from the work force. On the evening of September 5, 1907, Indian workers were driven from their tenements and most fled to Canada. (FHM)

BIBLIOGRAPHY

Jensen, Joan. *Passage From India: Asian Indian Immigrants in North America.* New Haven, CT: Yale University Press 1988.

Berger v. Bishop (1903)

E. Faxon Bishop, secretary of the C. Brewer and Company, was accused of violating the act of 1903, which stated that illegal aliens could not enter the United States if they had been paid in advance for contract labor in the United States. A reward was offered for bringing suit against persons in violation of the act. Thus, in *Berger v. Bishop* (1903), Frederick V. Berger filed suit against Bishop, when he discovered that Bishop had illegally gone to Korea to recruit contract laborers. Bishop had given money to David Deshler in Inchon to find Korean laborers and to pay their passage to the United States. The operation was discovered when a boat carrying 113 Koreans docked in Honolulu on April 30, 1903, and the Board of Special Inquiry began investigating how the passengers had paid for their travel. Bishop admitted in court that he had paid for their passage, but he was found not guilty of violating the 1903 act because he had recruited the laborers in 1902, before the act went into effect.

BIBLIOGRAPHY

Choy, Bong-youn. *Koreans in America.* Chicago: Nelson-Hall, 1979.

Bilingual Education Act of 1974

In 1974, Congress established the Bilingual Education Act to provide equal educational opportunity for all children in the United States. The act sought to meet this need in two ways: first, by creating educational programs that used bilingual educational techniques and, second, by providing financial assistance to local and state educational programs. The federal appropriation in 1974 was $135,000,000.

Children who may participate in bilingual education programs are those who were not born in the United States, whose native language is not English, or who came from an environment where the English language is not dominant. Although the bilingual education programs are primarily for children with limited spoken English, children whose language is English may voluntarily enroll on a limited basis so that they may better understand their classmates' cultural heritage.

Part A of the Bilingual Education Act provides details on the funds available for grants. Upon application from a state education agency, the commissioner for bilingual education at the Department of Education will determine the necessity of the proposed program. If bilingual education programs are sought by schools serving predominately American Indian children, then the commissioner will make payments to the secretary of the interior to carry out the necessary programs. Part B concerns administrative details such as the requirements for the office of the commissioner as well as requiring a national assessment every five years on the children, activities, and teachers of bilingual education programs.

The act also provides that a National Advisory Council on Bilingual Education composed of 15 members appointed by the secretary of education will convene at least four times a year; the membership will represent segments of the population of persons with limited speaking ability and different geographic regions in the United States. Research projects will also be carried out under this act to develop the effectiveness of bilingual education programs. **See also** Multiculturalism. (FHM)

BIBLIOGRAPHY

Kim, Hyung-Chan, ed. *Asian Americans and the Supreme Court: A Documentary History.* New York: Greenwood Press, 1992.

Julia Chang Bloch (1942–)

Julia Chang Bloch was the first U.S. ambassador of Asian ancestry. She immigrated from China to the United States at age nine and eventually earned a master's degree in government and East Asia studies from Harvard. She began her political career as a congressional staffer for the Senate Select Committee on Nutrition and Human Needs in 1971. Prior to her ambassadorship to Nepal (1989–1993), Chang Bloch was responsible for numerous public diplomacy tasks, including administering the world's largest food aid program. In the late 1990s, she was the president of the U.S.–Japan Foundation. (PL)

BIBLIOGRAPHY

Henry, Jim. "Julia Chang Bloch." In Helen Zia and Susan B. Gall, eds. *Notable Asian Americans*. New York: Gale Research, 1995.

Carlos Bulosan (1911–1956)

Carlos Bulosan, a writer, poet, and activist, was born in Binalonan in the Philippines on November 2, 1911. He came from a poor peasant family but at the age of 16 was writing poetry, fiction, and essays. He left his native land and arrived in Seattle, Washington, in 1930 seeking to fulfill his dream of equality among men and freedom for all. By 1947 he was recognized as one of the most prolific writers in the United States, with his face appearing on covers of many magazines. He contributed articles to numerous magazines including *Harper's Bazaar* and *The New Yorker*. His most famous contribution was the "Freedom from Want" essay that accompanied Norman Rockwell's classic depiction of the four freedoms in the *Saturday Evening Post*. His other famous literary works are *Laughter of My Father* and *America Is in the Heart*. In the 1950s, *Look* magazine would hail *America Is in the Heart* as one of the 50 most important American books ever published. It was translated into different languages and sold around the world. This quasi-autobiographical piece bore witness to the racism that Bulosan encountered, leading him to the conclusion that it was a crime to be Filipino in California—because, among other reasons, they were subject to unreasonable searches, and they could not marry white women. The Filipino was a victim of exploitation and discrimination by labor contractors, farmers, gamblers, racist vigilantes and state laws.

Bulosan longed to become part of the United States but was part of an oppressed and exploited minority. He wrote for the labor movement, which became his weapon against injustice and his key to American life. He was active in the United Cannery, Agricultural, Packing and Allied Workers of America, which represented fish cannery workers in Seattle and packing house workers in Salinas, California. He served as editor of *The New Tide*, a labor movement publication. The final decade of his life saw his decline into poverty, alcoholism, loneliness, and obscurity. He died of exposure on a Seattle street on September 11, 1956. (CGM)

BIBLIOGRAPHY

Evangelista, Susan. *Carlos Bulosan and His Poetry: A Biography and Anthology*. Seattle: University of Washington Press, 1985.

Kim, Elaine H. *Asian American Literature: An Introduction to the Writings and Their Social Context*. Philadelphia: Temple University Press, 1982.

Wong, Sau-ling Cynthia. *Reading Asian American Literature: From Necessity to Extravagance*. Princeton, NJ: Princeton University Press, 1993.

Burlingame Treaty (1868)

Negotiated in 1868 between the United States and China under the Ch'ing Dynasty to amend the 1852 Reed Treaty and named after Anson Burlingame, the U.S. negotiator, the Burlingame Treaty declared that the United States and its citizens abroad would respect China's territorial rights under the Chinese Emperor, particularly with respect to matters of trade, commerce, and navigation. The treaty further included goodwill provisions aimed at improving relations between the two countries. In what many considered the most significant section of the Burlingame Treaty, Article V provided for unhampered migration between China and the United States for citizens of either country for purposes of residence, travel, or business. While the treaty's trade and territory rights and other articles held fast in later years, the provisions of Article V often did not, as open migration became subject to anti-immigration biases and erosive legislation. **See** selections from the Burlingame Treaty (1868) in Appendix 1.

BIBLIOGRAPHY

Williams, Frederick Wells. *Anson Burlingame and the First Chinese Mission to Foreign Powers*. New York: Scribner's, 1912.

Cable Act of 1922

The Cable Act, passed by Congress in 1922, stipulated that a female citizen who married an alien would lose her own citizenship, and that a female could not gain citizenship by marriage. This proved to be particularly discriminatory toward Asian women because persons of Asian ancestry were already ineligible for citizenship, and the act was a further means of preventing naturalization and citizenship for Asian people. The law was changed in 1931, after much lobbying on the part of the **Japanese American Citizens League**.

BIBLIOGRAPHY

Hosakawa, Bill. *Nisei: The Quiet Americans.* New York: William Morrow, 1969.

Lee, Rose Hum. *The Chinese in the United States.* Hong Kong: Hong Kong University Press, 1960.

California Oriental Exclusion League

Formed in September 1919 in Sacramento, California, the California Oriental Exclusion League was founded by State Controller John S. Chambers and State Senator J. M. Inman, with the latter serving as president of the organization. The group sought the repeal of the **Gentlemen's Agreement** of 1907. In addition, the anti-Japanese organization supported the exclusion of picture brides and Japanese immigrants. It supported a constitutional amendment that limited U.S. citizenship to children whose parents were both eligible for U.S. citizenship. Furthermore, the group sought to deny all Asians citizenship in the United States. **See also** Immigration Restriction Movement.

BIBLIOGRAPHY

Miller, Stuart C. *The Unwelcome Immigrant.* Berkeley: University of California Press, 1969.

California Police Tax

During the 1870s the California state legislature passed a multitude of anti-Chinese laws. The California Police Tax, also know as the Chinese Police Tax, required that any Chinese person over the age of 18 who was not engaged in fishing or mining pay a monthly tax of four dollars. In their court challenges to this tax, the Chinese relied upon the Fourteenth Amendment; eventually the tax was declared unconstitutional because it denied due process and equal protection of the law. **See also** Foreign Miners Tax. (FHM)

BIBLIOGRAPHY

Storti, Craig. *Incident at Bitter Creek: The Story of the Rock Springs Chinese Massacre.* Ames: Iowa State University Press, 1991.

Benjamin Jerome Cayetano (1939–)

Benjamin Jerome Cayetano was elected governor of Hawaii during the 1996 elections, and he is the highest ranking Filipino-American elected official. Born in Honolulu on November 14, 1939, he grew up in pool halls, loved fast cars, spent a night in jail, and barely graduated from high school. His career path included stints as a junkyard parking attendant, an electrician's apprentice, a truck driver, and a member of a state highway crew. After he passed the draftsman's exams, discrimination prevented him from getting a job, and he swore he would not go back to Hawaii until he was a lawyer. He went to the University of California, Los Angeles, and Loyola University School of Law and earned his degree in 1971.

Cayetano returned to Hawaii and launched his political career. Starting in 1974 he served two terms in the state House of Representatives and two terms in the state Senate, ran for lieutenant governor in 1986, and was reelected in 1990. Cayetano has led the fight for education reform and has helped put into effect state-funded after-school programs for working families. (CGM)

BIBLIOGRAPHY

Silva, John. "Straight Outta Kalihi." *Filipinas* (May 1996): 32–34, 257.

Zia, Helen and Susan B. Gall, ed. *Notable Asian Americans.* Detroit: Gale Research, 1995.

Chae Chan Pin v. United States (1889)

In 1887 Chae Chan Pin, a California resident for over 10 years, left for China. While he was away, the **Scott Act of 1888** was passed which voided all certificates of identity issued under the Chinese Exclusion Act (**Immigration Act of 1882**). When he tried to re-enter the United States, his certificate to return was deemed invalid, and he was denied entry. Chae Chan Pin took the case to court, but in *Chae Chan Pin v. United States,*

(1889), also known as the "Chinese Exclusion Case," the U.S. Supreme Court found in favor of the U.S. government, stating that in the interest of security, the government could bar anyone from entry into the United States.

BIBLIOGRAPHY

Konvitz, Milton R. *The Alien and the Asiatic in American Law.* Ithaca, NY: Cornell University Press, 1946.

June Chan (1956–)

Chan is a cofounder of the Asian Lesbians of the East Coast (ALOEC). Founded in 1983, ALOEC is a political and cultural support group for Asian lesbians located in New York City. Born in Manhattan, Chan also works as a laboratory technician at Cornell Medical College in Manhattan where she conducts research in neurobiology. She has also worked for the Committee for Abortion Rights and Against Sterilization Abuse.

BIBLIOGRAPHY

Aguilar-San Juan, Karin. *The State of Asian American Activism.* Boston: South End Press, 1994.

Sherman, Phillip. *Uncommon Heroes: A Celebration of Heroes and Role Models for Gay and Lesbian Americans.* New York: Fletcher Press, 1994.

Chang Chan v. John D. Nagle (1925)

In 1924, Chang Chan and three other Asian-American men petitioned John Nagle, commissioner for the Port of San Francisco, and other officials for the release from detention of four Chinese women whom the men claimed to be their wives. Preliminary courts ruled that such detention was justified because the women did not arrive with proper immigration visas, and because the **Immigration Act of 1924** required the secretary of labor to detain such wives regardless of the status of their husbands if the wives themselves were ineligible for citizenship. In *Chang Chan v. John D. Nagle,* 268 U.S. 346 (1925), the U.S. Supreme Court upheld the lower court's decision by asserting that foreign-born women ineligible for U.S. citizenship did not become U.S. citizens simply by marrying U.S. residents. The Court based this denial of admission on the Chinese Exclusion Act (**Immigration Act of 1882**), the 1924 act, and the **Cable Act of 1922. See also** Immigration Restriction Movement.

BIBLIOGRAPHY

Konvitz, Milton R. *The Alien and the Asiatic in American Law.* Ithaca, NY: Cornell University Press, 1946.

Elaine Chao (1953–)

Arriving from Taiwan in 1961 at the age of eight, Elaine Chao grew up to became a banker and then the highest ranking Asian Pacific American presidential appointee in the executive branch, as director of the Peace Corps and deputy secretary of transportation, in the Bush administration. From 1992 to 1996 she was president of United Way of America. A distinguished fellow at the Heritage Foundation, Ms. Chao presents a conservatism that sees each ethnic group contributing to a merit standard that is uniquely American. (KM)

BIBLIOGRAPHY

Beargie, Tony. "Elaine Chao Tapped for FMC Leadership." *American Shipper* (May 1988): 8.

Zia, Helen and Susan B. Gall, eds. *Notable Asian Americans.* Detroit, MI: Gale, 1995.

Elaine Chao was the director of the Peace Corps from 1990 to 1993. *Courtesy of U.S. House of Representatives.*

Lily Lee Chen (1938–)

Lily Lee Chen made history on the evening of November 28, 1983, when she became the first Chinese-American woman to serve as a mayor of a U.S. city. Born in Tianjin, China, Chen made her political debut as an international goodwill ambassador from Taiwan at age 17. Chen rose from her job as an entry-level social worker to a variety of administrative positions in Los Angeles County prior to her election to the city council of Monterey Park, California. Her long and distinguished tenure in public service has been highlighted by the pioneering work in Asian-American social services, the rights of women and children, and aggressive voter registration campaigns targeting new immigrants. (PL)

BIBLIOGRAPHY

Chen, Lily Lee. *Politics Is in My Blood: An Autobiography.* Taipei, Taiwan: Business Weekly, forthcoming.

Cheung Sum Shee et al. v. Nagle, Commissioner of Immigration for the Port of San Francisco (1924)

Cheung Sum Shee, wife of a Chinese merchant residing in the United States, was denied entry into the United States when she arrived with her children on July 11, 1924. The United States secretary of labor stopped their entrance on the grounds of the recently passed **Immigration Act of 1924.** Together with other wives and their children, Cheung Sum Shee was heard by the Supreme Court in 1925. In the opinion to *Cheung Sum Shee et al. v. Nagle, Commissioner of Immigration for the Port of San Francisco,* 45, 268, U.S. 336 (1924), delivered by Justice James C. McReynolds, it was decided that the Immigration Act of 1924 did not prevent the wives and children of merchants already residing in the United States from seeking permanent residence in the United States. Thus, Cheung Sum Shee and her children were permitted entry.

BIBLIOGRAPHY

Konvitz, Milton. *The Alien and the Asiatic in American Law.* Ithaca, NY: Cornell University Press, 1946.

Chew Heong v. United States (1884)

Chew Heong, a Chinese laborer living in the United States, left for Hawaii in June 1881 and was denied reentry in 1884. While he was away, the Chinese Exclusion Act (**Immigration Act of 1882**) was passed, which mandated that Chinese laborers had to have a certificate of residence in order to be readmitted to the United States. As Chew did not have a certificate, he was denied entry. In *Chew Heong v. United States,* 112 U.S. 536 (1884), the U.S. Supreme Court found that when Chew left, he was acting under the assumption that the treaty of 1880 between the United States and China was still in force; therefore, he would be allowed to return.

BIBLIOGRAPHY

Konvitz, Milton. *The Alien and the Asiatic in American Law*. Ithaca, NY: Cornell University Press, 1946.

Vincent Chin (d. 1982)

Vincent Chin, a Chinese American, was beaten to death by two unemployed auto workers in 1982. The workers, Ronald Ebens and Michael Nitz, were tried and convicted of manslaughter in 1983, but they were sentenced to only three years probation and fined $3,780 each.

The incident arose on July 19, 1982, in a bar in Michigan where both parties were customers. Ebens began to make racial remarks toward Chin. Apparently believing Chin to be Japanese, Ebens subsequently blamed Chin for his unemployment, upon which a fight erupted among Ebens, Nitz, and Chin. The men took their fight outside, and Ebens struck Chin several times with a baseball bat in a nearby parking lot. That night, Chin died from severe injuries sustained from the beating.

In 1984, Ebens and Nitz were charged by the U.S. Justice Department with violating Chin's civil rights. In their defense, Ebens and Nitz claimed that the incident was not motivated by the race, color, or national origin of Vincent Chin. Nitz was acquitted, but Ebens was convicted. However, in 1986, Ebens' conviction was overturned by the Court of Appeals for the 6th Circuit. A year later, in his retrial in Cincinnati, Ebens was acquitted. **See also** American Citizens for Justice. (JK)

BIBLIOGRAPHY

Cummings, Judith. "Detroit Asian-Americans Protest Lenient Penalties for Murder." *The New York Times* (April 26, 1983): A16.

Holusha, John. "Two Fined in Detroit Slaying Are Indicted by Federal Jury." *The New York Times* (November 3, 1983): A26.

Chin Bak Lan v. United States (1902)

Chin Bak Lan entered the United States from Canada in 1901; he was arrested and brought before a commissioner of a federal court who ordered that he be deported. The case came before the U.S. Supreme Court because Chin Bak Lan claimed he was a United States citizen (although he could not verify this), and because he charged that commissioners did not have the authority to deport people. In *Chin Bak Lan v. United States* 186 U.S. 193 (1902), the Supreme Court ruled that the burden of proving citizenship lay with the citizen and that the com-

missioner, acting on behalf of the Chinese Exclusion Act (the **Immigration Act of 1882**), had the authority to deport illegal aliens.

BIBLIOGRAPHY

Konvtiz, Milton R. *The Alien and the Asiatic in American Law*. Ithaca, NY: Cornell University Press, 1946.

Chin Yow v. United States (1907)

When Chin Yow attempted reentry to the United States after a trip to China, his claims of U.S. citizenship and San Francisco residency were denied. Yow claimed in court that authorities had denied him any chance to obtain witnesses to testify to his citizenship, or to petition for habeus corpus, thereby preventing his detention. Yow was held for deportation on the Pacific Mail Steamship Company under the Chinese Exclusion Act (**Immigration Act of 1882**), which prevented Chinese laborers from immigration to the United States and becoming naturalized citizens. If Yow's citizenship could be proven, however, such forcible deportation would violate the 1868 **Burlingame Treaty** and other legislation. In *Chin Yow v. United States,* 208 U.S. 8 (1907), the U.S. Supreme Court found for Yow, ruling that he had been held improperly and denied due legal process. While the government possessed the right to expel illegal aliens, the Court said, it must first allow an individual the chance to prove citizenship. **See also** Immigration Restriction Movement.

BIBLIOGRAPHY

Konvitz, Milton R. *The Alien and the Asiatic in American Law*. Ithaca, NY: Cornell University Press, 1946.

Chinese American Citizens Alliance (CACA)

Originally started in 1895 as the fraternal order of the Native Sons of the Golden State, the Chinese American Citizens Alliance (CACA) is one of the longest-running civil rights organizations in the United States. It was founded in San Francisco by a small group of young second-generation Chinese Americans, against a backdrop of rampant discrimination and racial exclusion by the all-white **Native Sons of the Golden West**. With a growing number of lodges established elsewhere in California and across the nation, the new organization name was invented for lodges outside of California in 1915 and was officially adopted for the entire organization in 1929.

The founding members' objectives, to foster assimilation into American society and to seek justice and equality, are evidenced in the organization's preamble: ". . . to promote the general welfare and happiness of its members and the Chinese communities, to quicken the spirit of American patriotism, to insure the legal rights of its members and to secure equal economical and political opportunities for its members."

Throughout its history, CACA has vigorously fought against every attempt to disenfranchise citizens of Chinese ancestry. It spearheaded the abolition of forced separation of American citizens from their wives by the **Immigration Act of 1882** (Chinese Exclusion Act) and the **Immigration Act of 1924**. In the 1920s and early 1930s, the alliance helped desegregate Chinese students in San Francisco by working with parents to fight compulsory busing. It also opposed the "Cinch Bill" of 1925, which was to block the manufacture, sale, and use of herbal medicine. In more recent times, CACA has joined with other civil rights groups to continue its efforts toward shaping immigration legislation as well as protesting against biased business codes and discriminatory school admission policies, among other agendas.

In its role of fostering assimilation, CACA has organized and sponsored many bilingual citizenship classes, voter registration campaigns, and programs for the elderly and youth. In addition to the traditional means of encouraging voting participation and endorsing candidates, the alliance also encourages members to run for political office and seek political appointments. Another sign of social change in the century-old organization is the inclusion of women. Membership in the organization was originally confined to native-born Chinese males, as a gesture of recognition for their accomplishments in the community. Women could not be admitted as full members until 1977. By the end of the 1990s, about half of lodge presidents were women. (PL)

BIBLIOGRAPHY

Centennial Celebration and 43rd Biennial National Convention Yearbook. San Francisco, CA: Chinese American Citizens Alliance. August 13–19, 1995.

Chung, Sue Fawn. "The Chinese American Citizens Alliance: An Effort in Assimilation, 1895–1965." In *Chinese America: History and Perspectives.* San Francisco: Chinese Historical Society of America, 1987.

Interview with Winston Wu, President, Los Angeles Lodge, March 29, 1996.

Chinese American Democratic Rights Association (CADRA)

The Chinese American Democratic Rights Association (CADRA) a left-wing group, was formed by 26 disgruntled members of **Asian Americans for Equality** (AAFE) in January 1979. The group disagreed with the new direction that the AAFE wanted to take. Violence ensued between the two groups. CADRA is still active today in the New York City area.

BIBLIOGRAPHY

Wei, William *The Asian American Movement.* Philadelphia: Temple University Press, 1993.

Chinese Boycott of 1905

In 1904 the United States refused to renegotiate a treaty with China after the Gresham-Yang Treaty was not renewed. The Ch'ing government tried to send over drafts of a new treaty, but President Theodore Roosevelt's administration refused to cooperate. This, together with the ever-increasing restrictions on Chinese individuals in the United States, caused Chinese merchants in China to decide to boycott U.S. goods. The boycott was very organized and soon spread to all the major ports in China, and initially had an adverse effect on U.S. trade. The Roosevelt administration protested and the Ch'ing gov-

ernment, possibly fearing political repercussions, decided to oppose the boycott. In the end, the United States relaxed some of its immigration laws and the boycott was ended. **See also** Immigration Restriction Movement.

BIBLIOGRAPHY

McKee, Delber L. *Chinese Exclusion versus the Open Door Policy, 1900–1906: Clashes over China Policy in the Roosevelt Era.* Detroit, MI: Wayne State University Press, 1977.

Chinese Consolidated Benevolent Associations (CCBA)

Also known as the Chinese Six Companies, this organization was formed in California in 1862 as an umbrella association of all of the existing Asian organizations in California. After the enactment of the Chinese Exclusion Act (the **Immigration Act of 1882**), the Chinese Consolidated Benevolent Association (CCBA) was formally created. The goal of the organization was to battle anti-Chinese laws and to provide legal support for its members. The association also created a Chinese-language school and collected fees for exit permits from Chinese wishing to return to China. Soon, Chinese Consolidated Benevolent

In November 1936, an elderly Chinese man sits outside the offices of a mutual aid society in Sacramento, California. *Library of Congress.*

Associations were formed in New York, Honolulu, Vancouver, Portland, and Seattle. Like their Japanese counterpart, the Japanese Association in America, the groups hired Euro-American lawyers to defend their clients against discriminatory laws. For example, in ***Yick Wo v. Hopkins*** (1886), CCBA provided a lawyer to Yick Wo, a Chinese laundryman in San Francisco; the lawyer helped him to defeat a discriminatory law in front the U.S. Supreme Court. In the 1930s CCBA in New York came under attack by its own community. An ordinance passed during the Great Depression required all one-person laundries in New York City to pay an annual fee. The CCBA required the laundry owners to pay the fee before they would investigate the law. The laundry owners formed the Chinese Hand Laundry Alliance (CHLA) and convinced the city's aldermen to reduce the fee. CCBA labeled CHLA a communist organization. However, the two joined forces during **World War II** to form the All Chinatown Anti-Japanese Patriotic Organization.

BIBLIOGRAPHY

Shih-Shan, Henry Tsai. *The Chinese Experience in America.* Bloomington: Indiana University Press, 1986.

Chinese Exclusion Act. *See* Immigration Act of 1882

"Chinese Exclusion Case." *See Chae Chan Pin v. United States*

Chinese for Affirmative Action

Formed in 1969, this San Francisco-based, grassroots community activist organization was originally composed mostly of recent college graduates working for better jobs and benefits for immigrant Chinese. The group maintains a skills bank to help upgrade the employment skills of Chinese immigrants. The organization continues to expand its charter to serve as an advocacy group for larger issues facing the Chinese in the United States. In 1974, Henry Der, the executive director, expanded the mission formally to fight for Chinese-American rights. Chinese for Affirmative Action acts as a clearinghouse for social and political issues and empowerment. The organization was a prime advocate for the Voting Rights Act of 1975 and its extension in 1981. The group also sponsored the program "Break the Silence," an anti-Chinese violence conference in May 1986.

BIBLIOGRAPHY
Wei, William *The Asian American Movement.* Philadelphia: Temple University Press, 1993.

Chinese Student Protection Act of 1992

The Chinese Student Protection Act was legislation that permitted Chinese students and scholars to remain in the United States and apply for permanent residency. The act was spurred by the 1989 Tiananmen Square incident. President George Bush signed the bill after being presented with it twice. It allowed students who resided in the United States continuously since April 11, 1990, to apply for permanent residency. In its final form, the act was expanded to include other categories of legal Chinese immigrants.

BIBLIOGRAPHY
United States, House, Committee on the Judiciary. *Chinese Student Protection Act of 1992: Report.* Washington, D.C., 1992.

Chong Chum v. Kohala Sugar Company (1892)

Chong Chum, a Chinese laborer, was a contract worker for the Kohala Sugar Company, which had sponsored his passage to Hawaii. However, he was forced to sign a contract with the sugar company before coming to Hawaii, which allowed the company to withhold a part of his wages until enough money was collected for his return fare to China. In 1892 he brought suit against the company alleging that by withholding his wages, the company was violating his constitutional rights. In Chong Chum v. Kohala Sugar Company (1892), the U.S. Supreme Court decided in favor of Chong.

BIBLIOGRAPHY
Kuykendall, Ralph S. *The Hawaiian Kingdom.* Honolulu: University of Hawaii Press, 1967.

Herbert Y.C. Choy (1916–)

Born on a sugar plantation in Hawaii, Herbert Choy received his degree from the University of Hawaii and his J.D. from Harvard in 1945. After a brief stint in the military, he went into private practice. In 1976 President Richard Nixon appointed him to the 9th Circuit Court of Appeals, making him the first Asian American to serve on a U.S. federal court.

BIBLIOGRAPHY
Jackson, Robert. "Herbert Choy Makes a First for the U.S. Court of Appeals." *Rocky Mountain News* (May 21, 1996): USA.

Judy Chu (1953–)

Judy Chu has served on the city council of Monterey Park, California, and has also been the city's mayor. First elected to the council in 1988, Chu was a key figure as the city wrestled with substantial population change, which resulted, according to *Asian Week* (May 24–30, 1996) and the 1990 census, in Monterey Park becoming the first U.S. city with an Asian majority. Chu has been a leader in forging intergroup alliances (e.g., between Latinos and Asians) in the racially and ethnically mixed area. Chu is also a professor of psychology at East Los Angeles College; she received her Ph.D. from the California School of Professional Psychology (Los Angeles). (ALA)

BIBLIOGRAPHY
John Horton. *The Politics of Diversity: Immigration, Resistance, and Change in Monterey Park, California.* Philadelphia: Temple University Press, 1995.

Chy Lung v. Freeman (1876)

After arriving in San Francisco, Chy Lung, a Chinese woman, was detained by the California Commissioner of Immigration. The ship's captain was ordered to pay $500 in gold for all the women on board. California laws passed in 1873 gave the commissioner the right to use precautionary measures when dealing with female Chinese immigrants, who were often (falsely) suspected of being prostitutes. The boat captain challenged the validity of the commissioner's actions, and the matter was brought to court.

The lower court found that the Commissioner's actions were justifiable under the California laws. These laws permitted immigration officers to board ships, demand immigration examinations, and charge fees for the treasury. However, in *Chy Lung v. Freeman,* 92 U.S. 275 (1876), the U.S. Supreme Court stated that the commissioner's actions had violated the equal protection clause of the Fourteenth Amendment, as well as the guidelines set by the **Burlingame Treaty** (1868). **See also** *In Re Ah Fong* (1874).

BIBLIOGRAPHY
McClain, Charles. *In Search of Equality.* Berkeley: University of California Press, 1994.

Citizens Committee to Repeal Chinese Exclusion

The Citizens Committee to Repeal Chinese Exclusion was founded on May 25, 1943. More than 250 Americans joined in a campaign to revoke the Chinese Exclusion Act (**Immigration Act of 1882**). Since the committee was formed when China was an ally in **World War II**, pro-Chinese sentiment was prevalent and support came from many corners—the Congress of Industrial Organizations, the Federal Council of Churches, and even some traditionally pro-exclusion groups such as the American Federation of Labor. On November 26, 1943, the **Immigration Act of 1943** repealed the Chinese Exclusion Act. **See also** Immigration Restriction Movement. (FHM)

BIBLIOGRAPHY

Riggs, Fred W. *Pressures on Congress: A Study of the Repeal of Chinese Exclusion.* Westport, CT: Greenwood Press, 1972.

Civil Liberties Act of 1988

During **World War II,** Americans of Japanese ancestry residing on the West Coast and Aleuts in Alaska were interned by the American military. Although the **Japanese American Evacuation Claims Act of 1948** provided some compensation, the amounts were not enough for those displaced to recover the resulting wartime losses.

Many Japanese Americans continued to seek redress for another reason: They maintained that there was no wartime necessity for their internment, unlike the situation in Alaska, and military authorities suppressed evidence that the relocation was unnecessary. Japanese-American agitation led Congress to establish the **Commission on Wartime Relocation and Internment of Civilians**, which filed reports in 1983 and in 1984 recommending that each person relocated or interned during the war should be paid $20,000. Meanwhile, the **National Council for Japanese-American Redress** filed a class-action lawsuit in 1983, asking for $24 million in damages.

Congress passed the Civil Liberties Act of 1988, which authorized the U.S. attorney general to pay $20,000 in damages to all interned Japanese or their immediate family heirs, with a total ceiling of $1.25 billion. The act, adopted on August 10, also provided payments of $12,000 to each Aleut who was similarly relocated (up to a ceiling of $5 million); $1.4 million for wartime damage to Aleut church property; $15 million for the loss of Aleut lands that resulted from designating part of Attu Island as a part of the National Wilderness Preservation System; and $5 million to aid elderly, disabled, and seriously ill Aleuts and to provide scholarships for Aleuts, for the improvement of Aleut community centers, and for Aleut cultural preservation.

No funds were appropriated until November 21, 1989. The first letters of apology were sent out in October 9, 1990. Recipients gave up their rights to make any claims for future recovery of damages. **See also** Civilian Exclusion Orders; Executive Order 9066; Internment Camps/Relocation Centers; *Korematsu v. United States* (1943); National Council for Japanese-American Redress; Redress Movement. **See** Executive Order 9066; Civil Liberties Act (1988) in Appendix 1. (MH)

BIBLIOGRAPHY

Commission on Wartime Relocation and Internment of Civilians. *Personal Justice Denied.* Washington, D.C.: Commission on Wartime Relocation and Internment of Civilians, 1983.

Esther, Scott and Calvin Naito. *Against All Odds: The Japanese American's Campaign for Redress.* Cambridge, MA: Case Program, Kennedy School of Government, Harvard University, 1990.

Hohri, William Minoru. *Repairing America.* Pullman: Washington State University Press, 1988.

Irons, Peter. *Justice at War.* New York: Oxford University Press, 1983.

Franklin, John Hope. *Reconstruction: After the Civil War.* Chicago: University of Chicago Press, 1961.

Civilian Exclusion Orders

After **Executive Order 9066** was signed by President Franklin Roosevelt, civilian exclusion orders were issued in 1942 by General John L. DeWitt, commanding that persons of Japanese ancestry be removed from areas of California, Oregon, Washington state, and Arizona. The five orders were organized as Numbers 1 to 5, with each number targeting specific areas where Japanese Americans lived, including Bainbridge Island (in Washington state) and the wharf areas of San Francisco. Persons of Japanese ancestry were taken to **assembly centers** while awaiting relocation. **See also** Internment Camps and specific internment and exclusion order cases: *Ex Parte Endo* (1944); *Hirabayashi v. United States* (1943); *Inouye Yuichi et al. v. Clark* (1947); *Korematsu v. United States* (1943); *Minoru Yasui v. United States* (1943). **See** Executive Order 9066 in Appendix 1.

BIBLIOGRAPHY

DeWitt, John L. *Final Report: Japanese Evacuation from the West Coast, 1942.* Washington, D.C.: U.S. Government Printing Office, 1943.

Weglyn, Michi. *Years of Infamy.* New York: William Morrow, 1976.

Combined Asian-American Resources Project

A group established by San Francisco writers, including Jeffrey Chan, Frank Chu, and Lawson Inada, founded the Combined Asian-American Resources Project in 1969. The group's goals in establishing the group were to record oral histories of Chinese Americans, to organize teachers of Asian-American studies, and to help publish books the group deemed important. The group was extremely influential in getting a number of Asian-American author's books published including Louis Chu's *Eat a Bowl of Tea* (1961) and Monica Sone's *Nisei Daughter* (1953).

BIBLIOGRAPHY

Chu, Louis. *Eat a Bowl of Tea.* Boston: Little Brown, 1961.

Sone, Monica. *Nisei Daughter.* Boston: Little Brown, 1953.

Commission on Asian American Affairs

The Commission on Asian American Affairs was created in 1972 as a liaison group between Asian Pacific American communities and the state governments. The organization attempted to make the needs of the communities clear to the state. It also monitored the state's actions to make sure the needs were met effectively. The commission has worked with other groups on the passage of redress and reparation for Japanese Americans sent to **internment camps** during **World War II,** on the 1991 Civil Rights Act, and on citizenship for Filipino war veterans. **See also** Redress Movement.

BIBLIOGRAPHY

Abe, Debby. "Minorities Seek Better 'Climate.'" *The News Tribune* (Tacoma, WA) (February 19, 1995): B1.

Commission on Wartime Relocation and Internment of Civilians (CWRIC)

The Commission on Wartime Relocation and Internment of Civilians (CWRIC), established in 1980, investigated the **World War II** relocation of Japanese Americans. The CWRIC concluded that there was no military justification for the internment, and that racism and hysteria—not military conditions—were the key reasons for the evacuation. The CWRIC recommended a variety of reparations, including cash payments to relocation camp survivors; the redress money was finally approved in 1988.

Mainstream historical scholarship supported the CWRIC assessment, and only a few prominent figures—such as John McCloy, who had been assistant secretary of war at the time of the internment—opposed the CWRIC report. Research by scholar Peter Irons has convincingly refuted the claims of these few remaining opponents; Irons uncovered documents showing that military officials had fabricated the case for internment and had hidden contrary evidence. (Irons' findings were so compelling that they were the basis for a rare writ that successfully called for the overturn of the wartime convictions of three Japanese Americans who had conducted a legal test of the military orders.) **See also** Civilian Exclusion Orders; Civil Liberties Act of 1988; Executive Order 9066; *Hirabayashi v. United States* (1943); Japanese American Evacuation Claims Act of 1948; *Korematsu v. United States* (1943); *Minoru Yasui v. United States* (1943); War Relocation Authority. **See** Executive Order 9066 in Appendix 1. (ALA)

BIBLIOGRAPHY

Daniels, Roger. *Asian America: Chinese and Japanese in the United States Since 1850.* Seattle and London: University of Washington Press, 1988.
McClain, Charles, ed. *The Mass Internment of Japanese Americans and the Quest for Legal Redress.* New York: Garland, 1994.

Committee of Safety

The Committee of Safety was formed in Honolulu, Hawaii, on June 13, 1893. Its main objective was to overthrow the Hawaiian government of Queen Liliuokalani. A number of members from the former Annexation club joined the group, including Lorrin A. Thurston, William Smith, and Henry Cooper. As soon as the queen stated her intentions of creating a new authoritarian constitution, the Committee of Safety took swift action and organized the overthrow of the monarchy.

The committee initially oversaw the day-to-day operations of the Hawaiian provisional government and helped to reorganize and maintain the islands after the queen's forced departure. On July 4, 1894, this government was replaced by the new official government called the Republic of Hawaii, and Sanford Dole was named as its first president. Soon after, President Grover Cleveland publicly recognized the new Hawaiian government and arranged for an exchange of delegates. In August 1898, the Committee of Safety helped formalize the annexation of the Hawaiian Islands and assisted it in becoming a territory of the United States. **See also** Annexation of Hawaii.

BIBLIOGRAPHY

Kuykendall, Ralph S. and A. Grove Day. *Hawaii: A History.* New York: Prentice Hall, 1948.

Confession Program

The Confession Program was initiated by the U.S. Department of Justice in 1955 to discover Chinese residents in the United States who had entered the country illegally. The program granted immunity to anyone who confessed their illegal status. However, it also allowed the government to revoke citizenship from anyone who had obtained it illegally, although the immigrant would be allowed to reapply for it later. The program caused great consternation among Chinese residents, who feared that they might be forced to confess.

BIBLIOGRAPHY

Chen, Jack. *The Chinese of America.* New York: Harper and Row, 1980.
Sung, B. L. *The Story of the Chinese in America.* New York: Macmillan, 1967.

Conservatism

Of the ethnic groups in the United States the Asian/Pacific Islander Americans represent the only group that is statistically as conservative or more conservative than the white American majority. Asians are culturally among the most conservative of major racial and ethnic groups. Statistically, Asians have a very low rate of arrest for most crimes, despite the stereotype of Asian gangs (which actually compose a very small percentage of the Asian-American population). Asian Americans have a low rate of teen and unwed pregnancy, and a high rate of births to married couples who are over the age of 25. The practice of arranged marriages is still followed to some degree in most Asian nations, and Western-style dating is still relatively new to Asian cultures.

The short-lived television sitcom *All-American Girl* (starring Margaret Cho), which reflected a stereotype of Asians parents as domineering, expecting their children to have only the highest academic standards, and to date only suitable men, reflects some of the conservative values still common among

Asian families. Asians have high median household incomes, high median education levels, and Asian-American students receive relatively high grades and test scores. However, unlike Jews, who as a religious group are also highly educated and conservative, Asians are not overwhelmingly liberal politically, except among the mostly English-speaking Japanese and Asian Indians.

In recent presidential and congressional elections, most national polls showed Asians often favoring Republicans (see Table 1). In a 1994 *New York Times* poll of the vote for Congress, only white Protestants and "born again" Christians polled more conservatively than Asians. A Voters News Service poll showed Asians to be the only racial group that favored the Republican Bob Dole over Bill Clinton in 1996, while a CNN–*Time* poll showed Asians favoring Dole by a couple of more points than the small white margin did. At the local level, a 1993 exit poll of the New York City mayoral election showed most Asian ethnic groups (with the exception of Asian Indians) favored the conservative Republican Rudolph Guliani over liberal Democrat David Dinkins as mayor in a race that was close citywide (Table 2).

Table 1. 1992 Congressional Election

Group	% of Vote	% Voting Republican
Whites	79	50
White Protestants	41	57
White Born Again Christians	20	66
Blacks	13	11
Hispanics	5	28
Jews	4	21
Gays and Lesbians	3	23
Asians	1	51

Source: "Portrait of the Electorate: Who Voted for Whom in the House," *New York Times* (November 13, 1994): 15.

Table 2. 1993 New York Mayoral Race

Asian-American Group	% Members of Democratic Party	% Voting for Guiliani
Chinese	38	70
Filipinos	24	80
Koreans	30	71
Southern Asians	62	36

Source: AALDEF Outlook (Spring 1994).

Even in cities and races where Asians favor Democrats overall, Asians are generally a few points more likely to favor the conservative candidate than white Americans, in contrast to other minorities who are, in general, strongly in favor of the liberal candidate.

Asian-American political organizations did their own polls of Asian Americans during the 1996 presidential election in many major metro areas of the country. They found

Asians to favor Democrats, and questioned the validity of national polls that may have undersampled Asians. However, the same ABC news poll which showed Asians favoring the Republicans nationally by 49 to 41 also showed that Asians in California and Hawaii (states with the largest Asian populations) strongly favored the Democratic candidate by 53 to 42. Thus another pattern may be of Asians favoring Democrats in urban strongholds, but not in the suburbs, where the other half of Asians live. The Chinese American Voters Education Committee found that Asians were nearly twice as likely to be Democrats than Republicans in Alameda and San Francisco counties in 1996. However, this was much less than the 3 to 1 margin for the general population, so they were still less liberal, and not more conservative than the general population.

Among Asians, the Chinese, Koreans, and Vietnamese are the most conservative and Republican. Many have fled communism, or come from a nation like South Korea which is threatened by communism. Consequently, many have a dim view of the leftist philosophies. Such Asians are, or were probably supportive of defense spending, the U.S. presence in Asia, and of operations such as Desert Storm and the **Vietnam War**. A Republican Committee poll found that majorities of all Asian ethnic groups favored a tax cut, even among the most liberal ethnic Asians.

Asian parents often steer their children into fields such as medicine, music, or engineering. In contrast to other minorities in education, Asians spend more time worrying about how hard their children study, and that they seek to get the highest grades and test scores, rather than pressing for forced busing, affirmative action, multicultural curriculum, or giving preference to the hiring of Asian/Pacific American teachers or administrators. The traditional Asian style of education emphasizes rote memorization, individual achievement, and striving to score at the top of the class or to get into one of the most elite colleges; this style emphasizes much different values than some education reform movements that promote tests without a single correct answer, study that deemphasizes memorization, classroom dynamics that emphasize group achievement, and a curriculum that stresses self-esteem over academic performance. One Boston education official on Public Radio International noted the conflict between the values she was teaching in the American classroom and the expectations of a Chinese immigrant mother who wanted her daughter to pay absolute respect to the teacher and score at the top of her class. Some communities such as Bellevue, Washington, and Cupertino, California, are magnets for Asian parents seeking middle-class communities with good schools.

Indeed, Asians are behind African Americans on most measures of these race and politically based educational initiatives, though they are ahead of white Americans in terms of grades. Asian parents may question the value or legality of preferential affirmative action that they perceive as giving admissions to less qualified minorities. It is this conservatism that may have much to do with statistics that show a long life expectancy, high household incomes, relatively low rates of divorce and single-parent families, and high academic achievement.

One of the most visible conservative Asian Americans was **S.I. Hayakawa,** who gained fame as the university president who pulled the plug on the sound system of campus protesters at San Francisco State College during the late 1960s. More recently, he was one of the primary sponsors of the English First movement. **Dinesh D'Souza,** an Asian Indian immigrant, wrote *Illiberal Education,* a prominent book attacking affirmative action and multiculturalism. Ramesh Ponneru, a South Asian, is on the staff of the conservative National Review. Chinese-American Arthur Hu, a columnist for *Asian Week,* has played a prominent role in criticizing racial preferences in admissions at the University of California. Asians such as **Elaine Chao** and Ken Masugi held important policy positions in the Bush administration. **Jay Kim,** the first Korean American elected to Congress, is a Republican. **Matthew Fong,** California's former state treasurer, spoke out against bilingual education and **affirmative action.**

However, there are few truly prominent conservative Asian Americans on the scale of African-American conservatives such as Thomas Sewell, Walter Williams, or Shelby Steele in academia or in Republican politics. Asian-American conservatism is more a phenomenon of everyday choices of average Asian-American families with traditional values rather than a movement of the academic or political elite. **See also** Liberalism among Asian Americans; Model Minority. (AH)

BIBLIOGRAPHY

Aguilar-San Juan, Karin. *The State of Asian America.* Boston, MA: South End Press, 1994.

Espiritu, Yen Le. *Asian American Panethnicity.* Philadelphia: Temple University Press, 1992.

Lien, Pei-te. *The Political Participation of Asian Americans.* New York: Garland, 1997.

Liu, Eric. *The Accidental Asian.* New York: Random House, 1998.

Ng, Franklin. *Asian American Interethnic Relations and Politics.* New York: Garland, 1998.

Takahashi, Jere. *Nisei/Sansei: Shifting Japanese American Identities and Politics.* Philadelphia: Temple University Press, 1997.

Coolie Bill (1862)

"Coolie" was a term given to menial laborers, many of whom were transported from China. The Coolie Bill was put forth to the California House of Representatives by Democrat George B. Tingely in 1852. It proposed giving Chinese laborers fixed wage contracts for 10 years or less to come to the United States, as a way to solve the labor shortage problem in California. The bill met with a great deal of opposition, especially from California governor John Bigler, who disapproved of financing Chinese immigration. In addition, the bill had few supporters at the 1852 Democratic State Convention, and thus it did not pass.

BIBLIOGRAPHY

Melendy, H. Brett. *The Oriental American.* Boston: Twayne Publishers, 1972.

Cubic Air Ordinance

In 1870 an investigation of San Francisco's Chinatown living quarters was requested by the Anti-Coolie League. The result of the investigation led the San Francisco Board of Supervisors to pass a municipal ordinance called the Lodging House Ordinance, more popularly known as the Cubic Air Ordinance. The requirements were that for each adult there would be at least 500 cubic feet of air space in sleeping quarters. Either a landlord or lodger in violation could be fined anywhere from $10 to $500 or face imprisonment. On the first day that the ordinance was enforced, 51 Chinese were fined $10 a day; however, on the second day 50 others refused to pay the fine and instead went to jail. Soon the jails were stuffed beyond capacity; subsequently, the Cubic Air Ordinance was loosely enforced. **See also** Anti-Coolie Clubs. (FHM)

BIBLIOGRAPHY

Sandmeyer, Elmer C. *The Anti-Chinese Movement in California.* Urbana: University of Illinois, 1973.

D

Daihyo Sha Kai (Representative Body)

Daihyo Sha Kai was formed by people of Japanese ancestry who were sequestered at the Tule Lake Segregation Center. Under **Executive Order 9066,** people of Japanese descent were evacuated from their homes in the states of Washington, Oregon, California, and Arizona, and taken to **assembly centers**. Some of these Japanese refused to declare their allegiance to America and disavow their loyalty to the Emperor of Japan; they were considered disloyal to the United States and were taken to the Tule Lake center. The Daihyo Sha Kai organization was formed to address concerns about the poor living conditions in the Tule Lake camp. After appointing representatives, meetings were held with the camp administration to discuss possible living condition improvements. **See also** Hokuku Seinen-Dan (Young Men's Organization to Serve Our Mother Country); No-No Boys. **See** Executive Order 9066 in Appendix 1.

BIBLIOGRAPHY

Girdner, Audrie and Anne Loftis. *The Great Betrayal: Evacuation of the Japanese-Americans During World War II*. New York: Macmillan, 1969.

Thomas, Dorothy and Richard Nishimoto. *The Spoilage*. Berkeley: University of California Press, 1969.

Iva Ikuko Toguri D'Aquino (1916–)

On July 5, 1941, Toguri sailed to Japan to care for an ailing relative and to visit her parents' homeland. She was not happy in Japan and almost immediately wrote to her family about her plans to return to the United States. But the Japanese attack on **Pearl Harbor** stranded her, like approximately 10,000 other Japanese Americans in Japan at the time. The local police and *kempeitai,* or military police, demanded that she renounce her U.S. citizenship. Toguri began to work for the Domei News Agency, monitoring the airwaves for U.S. movements in the Pacific. In June 1943, she also began working as a typist for Radio Tokyo, which was responsible for English-language radio broadcasts in the Pacific, including anti-American propaganda. Even though she had no broadcast experience, Toguri was chosen to read script for Radio Tokyo's program "Zero Hour," which played popular music mixed with news and propaganda. During her broadcasts, she used the stage names "Tokyo Rose" and "Orphan Ann."

When **World War II** ended, Toguri believed that she would be able to return quickly to the United states with her new husband, Felipe d'Aquino, whom Toguri had married in 1945. However, after giving several interviews as to why she had been part of Radio Tokyo broadcasts, she was arrested and charged with treason. She was convicted on one count of treason and served six years in a federal prison in West Virginia. **See also** Edison Uno.

BIBLIOGRAPHY

Duus, Masayo. *Tokyo Rose: Orphan of the Pacific.* New York: Harper & Row, 1983

Gunn, Rex B. *They Called Her Tokyo Rose.* Santa Monica, CA: Gunn, 1977.

Howe, Russell Warren. *The Hunt for "Tokyo Rose."* Lanham, MD: Madison Books, 1990.

Taraknath Das

A revolutionary in India, Taraknath Das came to the United States seeking asylum from the Indian police. He attended the University of Washington, and in 1908 he began publishing *Free Hindustan*. He banded with other revolutionaries on the West Coast and continued to write and give speeches to enlist U.S. support for Indian home rule. During **World War II**, Das was among the East Indian voices in the United States who supported the Indian National Congress.

BIBLIOGRAPHY

Melendy, H. Brett. *Asians in America.* Boston: Twayne, 1977.

Day of Remembrance

The first Day of Remembrance occurred in Seattle, Washington, on Thanksgiving Day, 1978. The purpose of the event was to remember the signing of **Executive Order 9066,** which ordered the relocation and detention of Japanese-American citizens living in West Coast states during **World War II.** The day allowed citizens of Japanese-American heritage to grieve and to show symbolic disapproval of the internment. After the first year, the Day of Remembrance became an annual event and is now observed on February 12 in most American cities. Some Japanese Americans perform burial rites and other ceremonies, others visit the Puyallup Assembly Center, a well-known detention center, and participate in a reenactment of the forced relocation. The Day of Remembrance has not, however, attracted widespread participation in all Japanese-American communities. **See also** Assembly Centers; Interment Camps/Relocation Centers. **See** Executive Order 9066 in Appendix 1.

BIBLIOGRAPHY
Takami, David. *Executive Order 9066*. Seattle: Wing Luke Asian Museum, 1992.

Denationalization Act of 1944

The Denationalization Act amended the Nationality Act of 1940. The Nationality Act allowed U.S. citizens to renounce their citizenship during wartime. It was signed by President Franklin D. Roosevelt. The legislation was drafted with Japanese Americans in mind. The act was inspired by the actions of the militantly pro-Japanese faction of internees, the **Hokuku Seinen-Dan,** and the U.S. government's fear of "subversive elements" among Japanese Americans. **See also** Public Law 405.

BIBLIOGRAPHY
Daniels, Roger. *Asian America: Chinese and Japanese in the United States since 1850*. Seattle: University of Washington Press, 1980.

Displaced Persons Act of 1948

The Displaced Persons Act of 1948, signed by President Harry Truman in June 1948, allowed 205,000 people who had been displaced by **World War II** to emigrate to the United States. Initially the bill affected only Europeans, but an amendment made to the bill in 1950 allowed Chinese persons already living in the United States to remain. This was important to many Chinese residing in the United States who were apprehensive about returning to communist China after the war. **See also** Immigration Policy.

BIBLIOGRAPHY
Kung, S.W. *Chinese in American Life*. Seattle: University of Washington Press, 1962.

Nelson K. Doi (1922–)

Nelson Kiyoshi Doi, a veteran of **the 442nd Regimental Combat Team** in **World War II**, began his political career by being elected student body president at the University of Hawaii in 1945. He then won election to the Hawaii Territorial Senate from 1954 to 1959 and the state senate from 1959 to 1969. He next served as senior justice of the Third Circuit Court, Hilo. In 1974, he was elected lieutenant governor, which meant he was also the state's chief elections officer; in this capacity he made many speeches opposing the requirement to provide voter assistance and to print ballots in languages other than English. In 1976, he unsuccessfully ran for mayor of Honolulu. In 1978, he retired from politics, serving as a part-time family court judge. In 1985–1987, he directed the highest trial court of the Marshall Islands, and he served as honorary chair of the gubernatorial campaign of Cecil Heftel in 1986. (MH)

BIBLIOGRAPHY
"Back in Kamuela, Nelso Doi's Restless." *Honolulu Star-Bulletin* (March 3, 1983): D1-D2.
Brown, Stuart Gerry. "Interview with Nelson K. Doi." Honolulu: Hamilton Library, University of Hawaii at Manoa, 1977, one audio cassette reel.

Dinesh D'Souza (1961–)

Born in 1961 to a Catholic family in India, D'Souza came to the United States for his high school education and remained for college, at Dartmouth, where he earned notoriety as an iconoclastic conservative journalist. After graduation he developed his journalistic skills and became a noted lecturer and author, also serving in the Reagan White House. A fellow at the American Enterprise Institute, he is author of numerous books of political and religious commentary, including *Illiberal Education: The Politics of Race and Sex on Campus* and *The End of Racism*. (KM)

BIBLIOGRAPHY
D'Souza, Dinesh. *The End of Racism*. New York: Free Press, 1996.
———. *Illiberal Education: The Politics of Race and Sex on Campus*. New York: Vintage, 1992.
———. *Ronald Reagan: How an Ordinary Man Became an Extraordinary Leader*. New York: Free Press, 1997.

El Monte Berry Strike of 1933

During the harvest season of 1933, the communist-organized Cannery and Agricultural Workers (composed mainly of Mexican workers) went on strike, leaving the Japanese farmers in El Monte, California, to rely on family and friends to help with the harvest. Despite **alien land laws** prohibiting Japanese farmers from owning land, Japanese *issei* controlled 80 percent of the 600–700 acres of land in El Monte. However, because most of the leases to the Japanese were in violation of the law, the landowners feared repercussions if news should spread about these illegal land arrangements; as a result, the Japanese farmers were helped and supported during the strike by the white landowners, the police, and the sheriff's department.

BIBLIOGRAPHY

Hoffman, Abraham. "The El Monte Berry Picker's Strike, 1933.*" Journal of the West* 12, no. 1 (January 1973): 71–84.
Spaulding, Charles B. "The Mexican Strike at El Monte, California." *Journal 18* (August 1934): 571–580.

Eldridge v. See Yup Company (1859)

Eldridge v. See Yup Company (1859) was one of the earliest court cases in the United States involving Chinese Americans. It involved a dispute over land where Chinese Americans had erected a Buddhist temple. Eldridge charged that Buddhist practices were contrary to American lifestyles, and that the land could not be used for this purpose. The lower court ruled that the Chinese occupants of the land had to cease religious practices in the temple because these acts were "heathenish and superstitious." However, the California Supreme Court disagreed with the lower court's ruling and stated that Chinese Americans, like other U.S. citizens, were free to practice their own religion.

BIBLIOGRAPHY

Barth, Gunther. *Bitter Strength.* Cambridge, MA: Harvard University Press, 1964.

Emergency Detention Act of 1950

The Emergency Detention Act of 1950 gave the president of the United States the right to detain and arrest anyone who was identified as a threat to the internal security of the United States. Such persons included communists and foreign spies.

The act, which was passed through and overrode President Harry Truman's veto, remained in effect from 1950 to 1971. The act was seen as a threat by the Asian-American community; in 1968, with the help of Senator **Daniel Inouye** (D-HI), the **Japanese American Citizens League** began working to have the bill repealed. In 1971 Congress and President Richard Nixon approved its repeal.

BIBLIOGRAPHY

Hutchinson, E.P. *Legislative History of American Immigration Policy, 1798–1965.* Philadelphia: University of Pennsylvania Press, 1981.

Emergency Service Committee

The Emergency Service Committee was founded by Japanese Americans in Hawaii to promote patriotism and to improve morale within the community after the Japanese attack on **Pearl Harbor.** They helped support agencies such as the Red Cross. The committee's members also joined Japanese-American regiments. They also served as a liaison with Hawaii's white community.

BIBLIOGRAPHY

Okihiro, Gary Y. *Cane Fires.* Philadelphia: Temple University Press, 1991.

Enemy Alien Control Unit

The Enemy Alien Control Unit was established as a branch of the U.S. Justice Department in the early 1940s as a result of the Japanese attack on **Pearl Harbor.** The unit was given the authority to detain and prosecute any alien suspected of conducting espionage or of being disloyal to the United States. The group concentrated its efforts on persons of Asian descent living on the West Coast and in Hawaii and Alaska. The creation of this special unit marked one of the earliest responses to the Japanese and to Japanese Americans following the bombing of Pearl Harbor, and it was soon followed by the establishment of Japanese **assembly centers** and **internment camps** in 1942.

BIBLIOGRAPHY

Girdner, Audrie and Ann Loftis. *The Great Betrayal.* New York: Macmillan, 1969.

tenBroek, Jacobus, Edward N. Barnhart, and Floyd W. Matson. *Prejudice, War, and the Constitution*. Berkeley: University of California Press, 1970.

March Kong Fong Eu (1922–)

March Kong Fong Eu received her Ph.D. from Stanford University in 1956 and was elected to the California state legislature in 1966. She went on to serve three terms in the legislature, and in 1975, she was elected secretary of state for California. She was the first Asian-American woman to ever hold this position.

BIBLIOGRAPHY

"Eu Resigns to Take Ambassadorship." *San Francisco Chronicle* (Feb 11, 1994) A21.

Lyons, Steve. "March Fong Eu, Ed. D.: Breaking Barriers to Serve." *Access* (July 1997).

"March Fong Eu" *Marquis Who's Who*. Chicago: Reed Elsevier, 1999.

Ex Parte Endo (1944)

Ex Parte Endo, 323 U.S. 283 (1944), was a Japanese-American internment case. Mitsuye Endo had been caught attempting to escape from an **internment camp.** Endo had been placed in the camp even though she had gone through the established government procedures and had been classified as loyal to the United States. Endo, a California state government employee who had lived her whole life in the United States, was a Methodist and had a brother in the armed forces; she was recruited for this test case to challenge the law.

In an attempt to avoid a judicial challenge to its power to detain Japanese Americans, the government offered to release Endo if she agreed not to return to the restricted area of the West Coast. Endo refused and spent two more years in an internment camp. The U.S. government had a weak case and thus concentrated its efforts on the other internment cases, leading the U.S. Supreme Court to side with Endo and grant her a writ of habeas corpus. The Court unanimously held that the government did not have the authority to detain persons who had been classified as loyal.

The decision was announced the same day as the ***Korematsu v. United States* (1943)**, which upheld the evacuation and detention of Japanese Americans. The *Endo* decision was a small victory for Japanese Americans, but a footnote to the more important *Korematsu* decision. Indeed, in the *Endo* decision, Justice William O. Douglas did not directly confront the constitutional issue of whether the detention of Japanese Americans was legal, thus limiting the extent of the victory. (RLP)

BIBLIOGRAPHY

Irons, Peter. *Justice at War*. New York: Oxford University Press, 1983.

Executive Order 9066

On February 19, 1942, two months after the bombing of **Pearl Harbor**, Executive Order 9066 was issued by President Franklin D. Roosevelt. The order required that all persons of

Signed by President Franklin Roosevelt in 1942, Executive Order 9066 sent this family, like all persons of Japanese ancestry living on the West coast, to internment camps. *National Archives.*

Japanese ancestry living in California, Oregon, Washington state, and southern Arizona be confined in detention camps. This gave the secretary of war the authority to send thousands of Americans to concentration camps. Temporary **assembly centers** were quickly built and administered by the **War Relocation Administration**. Permanent **internment camps/relocation centers** were completed in the central United States by August 1942. After the end of **World War II,** it was revealed that a report prepared by the Federal Bureau of Investigation several months prior to the Pearl Harbor bombing (the **Munson report**) found that there was no danger of collaboration between the Japanese and Japanese Americans. **See also** Civilian Exclusion Orders; Public Proclamation No. 1; Public Proclamation No. 2; Public Proclamation No. 3; Public Proclamation No. 4. **See** specific internment and exclusion order cases: *Ex Parte Endo* (1944); *Hirabayashi v. United States* (1943); *Inouye Yuichi et al. v. Clark* (1947); *Korematsu v. United States* (1943); *Minoru Yasui v. United States* (1943). **See** Executive Order 9066 in Appendix 1.

BIBLIOGRAPHY

DeWitt, John L. *Final Report: Japanese Evacuation from the West Coast, 1942*. Washington, D.C.: U.S. Government Printing Office, 1943.

Executive Order 9102

Executive Order 9102 was signed on March 18, 1942, by President Franklin D. Roosevelt to create the **War Relocation Authority (WRA),** a federal department focused on moving people of Japanese descent living in the United States into **relocation centers.** The order came as a result of anti-Japanese sentiment brought on by the bombing of **Pearl Harbor,** as well as unfounded American fears of espionage and sabotage conducted by Japanese immigrants in the United States. Milton Stover Eisenhower was named the WRA's first director; he served until being replaced on June 17, 1942, by Dillon S. Myer.

More than 110,000 Japanese Americans and Japanese immigrants were forced to move because of the order, most finding themselves in **assembly centers** and then in **internment camps,** under military jurisdiction. Under Executive Order 9102, Japanese Americans were allowed a five-day period after receiving relocation notification to sell, loan, store, or otherwise maintain any real estate, possessions, or other properties the families could not carry; this did little to quiet the resentment, anguish, and discomfort caused by the relocation. Property losses were high among encamped Japanese. On December 18, 1944, the United States Supreme Court declared the forced detainment of law-abiding U.S. citizens to be unconstitutional. On the same day, all internment camps in the United States were finally closed, and on June 30, 1946, the War Relocation Authority was officially terminated.

BIBLIOGRAPHY

Chan, Sucheng. *Asian Americans.* Boston: Twayne, 1991.

Daniels, Roger. *Asian America.* Seattle: University of Washington Press, 1988.

Executive Order 9814

Executive Order 9814 as signed by President Harry Truman in 1946 set up a panel to review the cases of all U.S. citizens who had violated the 1940 Selective Training and Service Act. Upon review, the board made recommendations to the attorney general as to whether or not clemency should be granted to those persons found in violation of the law. In 1947 President Truman granted pardons to 265 Japanese Americans in Presidential Proclamation 2762, as well as to numerous others who had been found in violation of the law. **See also** *Tamesa Minoru v. United States* (1945).

BIBLIOGRAPHY

O'Brien, David J. and Stephen S. Fugita. *The Japanese American Experience.* Bloomington: Indiana University Press, 1991.

Exeter Riot of 1929

In 1929 an anti-Filipino riot occurred in Exeter, California, a small rural community located in the San Joaquin Valley. A mob of approximately 300 people stormed a fig farm that employed Filipinos and burned down the ranch, driving the farmworkers out of town. There are conflicting accounts of how the riot actually began. Some stated that the mob only gathered after an Italian man was stabbed, other reports mentioned that the quarrel began because white women were seen with Filipino men. In any event, the taunts started to fly, and the Filipinos bore the brunt of the riot.

The riot showed that Californians had a new concern with a third wave of Asian immigrants. Although the working men who were questioned after the riot all stated that they refused to work the jobs the Filipinos worked, most still saw the Filipino workers as an economic threat. Powerful agribusiness groups pressured politicians to stop Filipino immigration because they saw the rising Filipino labor unions as a threat to stability in the fields. **See also** Filipino-Americans; Tacoma Race Riot of 1885; Watsonville Anti-Filipino Riot (1930). (FHM)

BIBLIOGRAPHY

Lasker, Bruno. *Filipino Immigration.* New York: Arno Press, 1969.

Fair Play Committee (FPC)

In the Heart Mountain (Wyoming) Center (one of the **internment camps** for people of Japanese descent), a group of internees created the Fair Play Committee (FPC), to organize an antidraft movement among the Japanese-American community at the camp. Starting in 1944, FPC held meetings and published bulletins, arguing that the draft violated their constitutional rights. Several members of the group were sent to another segregation camp; eventually more than 60 men in the group refused induction. These men were brought to trial in Cheyenne and were sentenced to three years in federal prison. The movement continued in Heart Mountain and other camps; in all, 287 men were sentenced for draft evasion. In 1944 the seven leaders of the FPC, most of whom opposed the draft, were arrested, tried, and sentenced to four years in Fort Leavenworth Federal Prison. They served 18 months, because an appeal court reversed the decision, and President Harry Truman pardoned the resisters. **See also** No-No Boys; *Okamoto Kiyoshi v. United States* (1945).

BIBLIOGRAPHY

Chuman, Frank F. *The Bamboo People.* Del Mar, CA: Publisher's Inc., 1976.

Nelson, Douglas W. *Heart Mountain: The History of an American Concentration Camp.* Madison: Department of History, University of Wisconsin, 1976.

Farrington v. Tokushige (1927)

Beginning in 1920, Hawaii's territorial government imposed a series of requirements to restrict private language schools, mostly attended by Japanese Americans. In 1922, *Hawai'i Hochi* editor "Fred" Kinsaburo Makino championed a lawsuit against the requirements, which affected some 160 schools enrolling approximately 20,000 Asian Americans. The case eventually went to the U.S. Supreme Court. In the decision to the case, *Farrington v. Tokushige*, 273 U.S. 284 (1927), the U.S. Supreme Court invalidated the requirements, a ruling that affected 22 states with similar restrictions that had originally been imposed during World War I to ban the teaching of German. (MH)

BIBLIOGRAPHY

Kimura, Yukiko. "Sociological Significance of the Japanese Language Campaign in Hawaii." *Social Process in Hawaii* 20: (1979) 47–51.

Okihiro, Gary Y. *Cane Fires: The Anti-Japanese Movement in Hawaii, 1865–1945.* Philadelphia: Temple University Press.

Fiancees Act of 1946

The Fiancees Act, which allowed U.S. servicemen to bring foreign-born fiancees into the United States, was adopted on June 26, 1946. Its provisions expanded the **War Brides Act of 1945** by exempting up to 5,000 alien women engaged to marry U.S. servicemen from the national quota system for immigration. Large numbers of Chinese women used this act in order to immigrate to the United States by marrying Chinese-American servicemen, thus correcting a gender imbalance caused by the immigration policies of the United States. **See** War Brides Act (1945) in Appendix 1.

BIBLIOGRAPHY

Bennett, Marion T. *American Immigration Policy.* Washington, D.C.: Public Affairs Press, 1963.

Hutchinson, E.P. *Legislative History of American Immigration Policy, 1789–1965.* Philadelphia: University of Pennsylvania Press, 1981.

Fifteen Passenger Bill of 1879

The Fifteen Passenger bill which passed both the House and the Senate in 1879, stated that no ships entering the United States could carry more that 15 Chinese passengers. The bill was intended to slow Chinese immigration to the West Coast, and it was initially put forth in a memorial by the Oregon Legislature. Despite congressional support, the bill was ultimately vetoed by President Rutherford B. Hayes.

BIBLIOGRAPHY

Hutchinson, E.P. *Legislative History of American Immigration Policy, 1798–1965.* Philadelphia: University of Pennsylvania Press, 1981.

Filipino Americans

Filipino Americans are the second largest group of Asian immigrants in the United States. They come from the Republic of the Philippines, a former colony of Spain and then the United States. Filipinos are of Malay stock, with Chinese, Spanish, American, and East Indian influences. They have lived in the United States for more than 200 years, but only after 1965 has much attention been paid to them. At the time of the 1990 census, they numbered 1.4 million. Although Asians geographically, Filipinos are different from most Asians socially and culturally. They are a highly westernized immigrant group, speaking English well, and familiar with the U.S. lifestyle. The majority are well-educated professionals.

The first permanent Filipino settlement began in the late eighteenth century, long before American involvement with the Philippines. The so-called "manilamen" who were forced to build and crew Spanish galleons jumped ship in Mexico and Louisiana and made their way to the bayous. They established villages outside of New Orleans as early as 1763 and made their livelihood in the fishing and shrimping industries.

The mass immigration of Filipinos to the United States did not occur until the beginning of the twentieth century. The first wave began in 1903 when the **Pensionado Act of 1903** provided support to send young Filipinos to the United States for education on American life. The "pensionados," as these young Filipinos were called, studied in institutions such as Harvard, Stanford, Cornell, and the University of California at Berkeley. They founded Filipino student organizations, some of which are still in existence, and they sent glowing reports back home about educational opportunities in the United States.

Harry Kitano divides Filipino immigration into four historical periods. The first generation immigrating in the 1920s and 1930s was mostly male and employed in agricultural labor. With restrictions on Japanese immigration, Filipino labor was sought for Hawaiian pineapple plantations. Filipinos also worked in Seattle and Alaska canneries, but those jobs were for short periods.

The second period was when women were allowed to come into the United States with their husbands, because married men were considered to be better workers than bachelors. The third wave consisted of the post–**World War II** arrivals which included many war veterans. This third generation, although more assimilated, faced job discrimination and social exclusion. As more Filipinos were born in the United States, contact with the native land and culture diminished substantially. The fourth wave came after 1965 when the educated, upwardly mobile professionals and entrepreneurs came into this country. Today 64 percent of Filipinos live in California and Hawaii. **See also** Agricultural Workers Organizing Committee; Carlos Bulosan; Exeter Riot of 1929; Pablo Manlapit; Irene Natividad; Philippine Naturalization; Phillip Villamin Vera Cruz; Watsonville Anti-Filipino Riot (1930); *Roque Espiritu de la Ysla v. United States* (1935). (CGM)

BIBLIOGRAPHY

Kitano, Harry and Roger Daniels. *Asian Americans: Emerging Minorities.* Englewood Cliffs, NJ: Prentice Hall, 1995.

Knoll, Tricia. *Becoming Americans: Asian Sojourners, Immigrants and Refugees in the Western United States.* Portland, OR: Coast to Coast Books, 1982.

Min, Pyong Gap. *Asian Americans: Contemporary Trends and Issues.* Thousand Oaks, CA: Sage Publications, 1995.

Schaefer, Richard T. *Racial and Ethnic Groups.* New York: Harper Collins, 1993.

Wong, Sau-ling Cynthia. *Reading Asian American Literature: From Necessity to Extravagance.* Princeton, NJ: Princeton University Press, 1993.

Filipino Repatriation Act of 1935

The Filipino Repatriation Act of 1935 was a consequence of increased Filipino immigration to the United States and the effect of the **Tydings–McDuffie Act (1934),** which gave the Philippines commonwealth status for 10 years. Filipino nationalists would hail this legislation as a step on the road to independence, but the act had been inspired in a large part by anti-Filipino sentiments in the United States. At the onset of the Great Depression, many Americans came to believe that the unemployment situation could be eased by eliminating immigrant labor, and the racial prejudice to which Filipinos had long been subjected boiled over into several acts of violence. The Tydings-McDuffie Act allowed only 50 Filipinos per year to enter the United States. Legislators attempted not only to end Filipino immigration, but also to secure the removal of Filipinos already in the country. Thus, in 1935 the Repatriation Act was signed, which provided free transportation back to the Philippines for those immigrants who were ready to leave. (CGM)

BIBLIOGRAPHY

Stern, Jennifer. *The Filipino Americans.* New York: Chelsea Publishers, 1989.

Hiram Leong Fong (1907–)

After graduating from Harvard Law School, Leong Fong returned to his native Hawaii to work in private practice. In 1938 he won election to the territorial legislature as a Republican and in 1958, he became a U.S. Senator. He was reelected in 1964. During his first two terms, Fong was relatively liberal on domestic issues, which helped him to maintain good relations with the International Longshoremen's and Warehousemen's Union, who had supported his candidacy in 1958. While in the Senate, Fong worked on the 1965 Voting Rights Act and served as member of the Judiciary Committee's Immigration and Naturalization Subcommittee. He was reelected again in 1970 but his support was waning, and he retired from the Senate in 1977.

BIBLIOGRAPHY

Chan, Sucheng. *Asian Americans.* Boston: Twayne, 1991.

Melendy, H. Brett. *The Oriental Americans.* NY: Twayne, 1971.

Matthew K. Fong (1953–)

Matthew K. Fong, the son of former Democratic assemblywoman and five-time California Secretary of State March Fong Eu, served as California's state treasurer from 1995 to 1999. In 1998, he ran a competitive (though unsuccessful) election bid to unseat Democratic Senator Barbara Boxer. Prior to his service as state treasurer, Fong was vice-chairman of California's State Board of Equalization, a statewide administrative entity. Serving on the board from 1991 to 1994, Fong managed a variety of tax programs involving more than $36 billion annually. A lawyer, Fong worked in private practice with the international firm of Sheppard, Mullin, Richter, and Hampton from 1985 to 1990. He served in the United States Air Force from 1975 to 1980 and has been in the Air Force Reserve since then. Fong was awarded the United States Air Force Meritorious Service Medal for his years of service.

BIBLIOGRAPHY

Weng, Cheong Heng "California Urges Listing on Both Sides of Pacific." *Business Times* (April 5, 1996): 15.

Fong Yue Ting v. United States (1893)

Fong Yue Ting v. United States, 149 U.S. 698 (1893), involved three Chinese men who had failed to apply for or obtain a certificate of residence in the United States. This requirement followed the passage of the **Geary Act of 1892**, which required all Chinese laborers living in the United States to apply for a residency certificate within one year or be subject to deportation. The three men had been arrested for not possessing a residency certificate and were awaiting deportation. When their case was brought before the U.S. Supreme Court in 1893, it was found that two of the men had simply never applied for a certificate, and the third had failed to find a white witness who could verify his residency. The men were deported. **See also** Immigration Act of 1882; Immigration Restriction Movement.

BIBLIOGRAPHY

Konvitz, Milton R. *The Alien and the Asiatic in American Law*. Ithaca, NY: Cornell University Press, 1946.

Tung, William L. *The Chinese in America, 1820–1973*. Dobbs Ferry, NY: Oceana Publications, 1974.

Foran Act of 1885

The Foran Act of 1885, introduced by Democrat Michael Foran of Ohio, attempted to stop labor contractors from paying the passage of foreigners to come to the United States. Before this, it was common practice for companies to send labor recruiters abroad to round up foreign labor and pay their passage to the United States. Even after the bill passed, however, this practice continued.

BIBLIOGRAPHY

Chan, Sucheng. *Asian Americans*. Boston: Twayne, 1991.

Foreign Miners Tax

The Foreign Miners Tax was established in 1850. It was one of a number of California taxes which unfairly discriminated against Chinese and Mexican workers. In its first draft, the tax imposed a $20 monthly tax on aliens who were mining in California. This tax directly affected Mexican miners, many of whom refused to pay the tax, causing mobs of angry white Americans to drive many of the foreign-born miners out of the state.

In 1852, in response to the substantial increase in Chinese miners working in California, the legislature redrafted the Foreign Miners Tax. This new tax demanded a monthly mining fee of $3 from all foreign born miners. The new tax law was distributed in English, Spanish, and Chinese in order to reach targeted ethnic groups. This tax, along with other anti-Chinese activity in California, contributed to the foundation of the anti-Chinese movement which led legal and hostile action against Chinese Americans. In 1870, the Foreign Miners Tax was declared unconstitutional. Until that point, it had continued to promote anti-Chinese sentiment in California as well as provide a sizable source of revenue to the state. **See also** Anti-Coolie Clubs; California Police Tax; *Lin Sing v. Washburn* (1863); Workingmen's Party of California. **See** "Disgraceful Persecution of a Boy" by Mark Twain (1870) in Appendix 1.

BIBLIOGRAPHY

McClain, Charles. *In Search of Equality*. Berkeley: University of California Press, 1994.

442nd Regimental Combat Team

After **Pearl Harbor** was bombed on December 7, 1941, University of Hawaii students of Japanese ancestry rallied to the support of the United States by forming the Varsity Victory Volunteers in February 1942 and offering to assist the war effort in any way possible. The unit so impressed Assistant Secretary of War John J. McCloy that in January 1943 he authorized the activation of the 100th Infantry Battalion, composed primarily of Japanese Americans in Hawaii who were in the army before the Pearl Harbor bombing. A presidential order of January 1943 also enabled Japanese Americans in Hawaii and within **relocation camps** in the western United States to volunteer to serve in a new army unit, the 442nd Regiment. Both units, numbering almost 3,000 soldiers, were dispatched in February 1943 for basic training.

The 100th Infantry Battalion was first deployed to North Africa in August 1943. In March 1944, the 442nd Regiment was attached to the 34th (Texas) Division and was assigned to Anzio, alongside the 100th Battalion. The regiment fought valiantly throughout Italy and achieved considerable notoriety in September 1994, when it rescued 211 Texans of the 141st Infantry (the "Lost Battalion") in the Vosges Mountains of France.

The 442nd Regimental Combat Team adopted the slogan "Go for Broke" because of its willingness to endure great risks in order to prove that Japanese Americans were completely loyal to the United States. With a casualty rate of more than 300 percent (approximately 600 dead and 9,000 wounded), soldiers of the 442nd received one Congressional Medal of Honor, one Distinguished Service Medal, 47 Distinguished Service Crosses, 350 Silver Stars, 810 Bronze Stars, and 3,600 Purple Hearts. The 100th Battalion received similar honors. (MH)

BIBLIOGRAPHY

Chang, Thelma. *"I Can Never Forget": Men of the 100th/442nd*. Honolulu: Sigi Productions, 1991.

Matsuo, Dorothy. *Boyhood to War: History and Anecdotes of the 442nd Regimental Combat Team.* Honolulu: Mutual Publishing Company, 1992.

Frick v. Webb (1923)

In the early 1920s Raymond L. Frick was told it was against the law for him to sell his shares of stock in the Merced Farm Company, which owned 2,000 acres of land in California, to N. Satow, who was a Japanese citizen. This transaction would be in violation of California's **Alien Land Act of 1920**, which made it illegal to sell stock in any company that owned agricultural land to someone who was ineligible for citizenship. U.S. Webb, the attorney general of California, told Frick that if he went ahead with the deal the government would have the right to confiscate his shares in the Merced Farm Company. Frick, and Satow took the matter to court, claiming that the California Alien Land Act was in violation of the 1921 Treaty of Commerce and Navigation between the United States and Japan. They lost the case. They then appealed to the Supreme Court; in *Frick v. Webb,* 263 U.S. 326 (1923), the Court ruled that the 1921 treaty between the United States and Japan was only concerned with trade between the two countries and not land ownership, and that the Alien Land Law did not infringe on the due process and equal protection clauses of the Fourteenth Amendment. **See** California Alien Land Act of 1913 in Appendix 1.

BIBLIOGRAPHY

Chuman, Frank. *The Bamboo People.* Del Mar, CA: Publisher's Inc., 1976.

Ichihashi, Yamato. *Japanese in the United States.* Stanford, CA: Stanford University Press, 1932.

Fujii Sei v. State of California (1952)

After hearing several cases and continually upholding the constitutionality of the **California Alien Land Act of 1913**, the Supreme Court of California ruled in *Fujii Sei v. State of California* (1952) that the land act was in violation of the U.S. Constitution. Fujii Sei was a Japanese citizen who had grown up in the United States; he decided to buy land in California. However, because he was ineligible for citizenship in the United States, such a purchase was illegal under the California Alien Land Act. When the state tried to take the land from Fujii, he took the matter to court. He was encouraged by the recent case of *Oyama v. California*, in which the Supreme Court had struck down the constitutionality of the Alien Land Act, stating that it violated Oyama of equal protection under the laws of California. Thus, after losing in the state superior court, Fujii took his case before the state supreme court, which ruled in his favor. **See also** Alien Land Laws; *Masoaka v. State of California* (1952). **See** California Alien Land Act of 1920 in Appendix 1.

BIBLIOGRAPHY

Chuman, Frank F. *The Bamboo People: The Law and Japanese-Americans.* Del Mar, CA: Publisher's Inc., 1976.

Francis Fukuyama (1952–)

A student of political development and Soviet foreign policy, Fukuyama used his education in political philosophy to propose his controversial "end of history" thesis, which speculated that democracy and free markets are the universally accepted political goals in the modern world. All wars and other international competition at least implicitly assume these ends. After serving in the Bush administration State Department, he presented this argument in *The End of History and the Last Man* (1992). (KM)

BIBLIOGRAPHY

Fukiyama, Francis. *The End of History and the Last Man.* New York: Avon, 1993.

——. *Trust: The Social Virtues and the Creation of Prosperity.* New York: Free Press, 1996.

Geary Act of 1892

The Geary Act of 1892 was a supplement to the original Chinese Exclusion Act (**Immigration Act of 1882**). The 1882 act, which was enacted to curb Chinese immigration, expired in 1892. The Geary Act stipulated that all persons of Chinese ancestry residing in the United States were required to apply for a certificate of residence within one year after the bill was passed, and that each Chinese resident must have a white witness attest to their residency. The bill also prohibited Chinese laborers from entering the United States and gave the U.S. government the right to deport anyone who was residing in the United States illegally. In addition, the Geary Act stated that Chinese persons who were found without a certificate could be jailed, fined, or deported. The Chinese government complained to the U.S. government about the passage of the Geary Act; the constitutionality of the act was challenged and upheld by the U.S. Supreme Court in *Fong Yue Ting v. United States* **(1893). See also** Immigration Restriction Movement; McCreary Amendment to the Geary Act of 1892. **See** The Chinese Equal Rights League (1892) in Appendix 1.

BIBLIOGRAPHY

Konvitz, Milton R. *The Alien and the Asiatic in American Law*. Ithaca, NY: Cornell University Press, 1946.

Tung, William L. *The Chinese in America, 1820–1973*. Dobbs Ferry, NY: Oceana Publications, 1974.

General Deficiency Appropriation Account Act of 1904

The General Deficiency Appropriation Account Act of 1904 was created to strengthen existing Chinese exclusion acts of the time. The act was issued by the U.S. government in part as a response to the termination of the 1894 Chinese-American Treaty. The treaty was terminated by Chinese nationalists who felt that elements of the treaty were unfair. During deliberations for the 1904 act, Congressman Edward James Livernash of California attempted to include provisions that would prevent Chinese workers from serving on U.S. merchant ships, but this effort was unsuccessful. After further discussions, the General Deficiency Appropriation Account Act was drafted on April 17, 1904. As a result, Chinese immigrants in American Pacific Island territory holdings were prohibited from moving to the U.S. mainland. **See also** Immigration Restriction Movement.

BIBLIOGRAPHY

Coolidge, Mary R. *Chinese Immigration*. New York: Henry Holt, 1909.

McKee, Delbar L. *Chinese Exclusion and the Open Door Policy*. Detroit, MI: Wayne State University Press, 1977.

Gentlemen's Agreement

The "Gentlemen's Agreement" is the name given to an immigration-restriction accord reached between the United States and Japan in 1908. Japan agreed to stop issuing passports to Japanese laborers seeking to emigrate to the United States; in exchange, the United States would not prevent the immigration of parents, wives, and children of immigrants already in America.

The agreement was sparked by efforts of the San Francisco School Board to segregate Japanese-American (and Chinese-American) students from white pupils. In October 1906 Japanese-American children had been ordered to attend the Chinese-American school. News of the segregation spread to Japan, and President Theodore Roosevelt found himself facing an international incident. Although Roosevelt was not favorably disposed toward Japanese immigrants, he seemed to have been more tolerant than most of his contemporaries, and he was well aware that Japan had become a military power. Unlike China, whose emigrants could be treated with impunity, Japan could not be safely dismissed, and Roosevelt sought to strike a deal that satisfied the wishes of California racist as well as Japanese insistence on respect.

After convincing the San Francisco School Board to rescind their segregation order, the agreement was reached through the exchange of a series of notes between the United States and Japan, running from late 1907 through early 1908. Ironically, although Californians seemed to believe that this would end Japanese immigration, it instead helped to rectify the high male-female ratio, permitting Japanese immigrants to establish a self-sustaining community that doubled in size during the following two decades.

The push for immigration restrictions was fueled by hysterical warnings about the "yellow peril": Japanese immigrants who would bring crime and corruption into a "white man's" country. About a century later, however, Japanese Americans surpass whites in income and educational levels, have low rates of crime, and show high rates of intermarriage. Today, as new voices again warn that immigrants (now primarily from Asia and Latin America) will be unable to integrate into American society, it is useful to remember the similar warnings of an earlier era, and how spectacularly wrong those claims turned out to be. **See also** Immigration Act of 1907; Immigration Act of 1917; Immigration Act of 1924; Immigration Restriction Movement; Japanese Americans; San Francisco School Board Crisis of 1906; San Francisco School Segregation Order of 1906. (ALA)

BIBLIOGRAPHY

Daniels, Roger. *Asian America: Chinese and Japanese in the United States since 1850.* Seattle and London: University of Washington Press, 1988.

Hing, Bill Ong. *Making and Remaking Asian America through Immigration Policy, 1850–1990.* Stanford, CA: Stanford University Press, 1993.

Ghadar Revolutionary Party

The Ghadar Revolutionary Party grew out of the Hindu Association of the Pacific Coast, which was begun in 1913 by Har Dayal, a young revolutionary. Dayal was offered a teaching position at Stanford University in 1911, but the offer was rescinded once the university learned of his radical views. Soon after, Dayal began giving revolutionary speeches to Indian laborers on the West Coast, many of whom had encountered racism in the United States. Through Dayal's leadership, the Ghadar Revolutionary Party was formed, and although Dayal was forced to leave the United States in 1914, the party continued. Through the assistance of the German government, the Ghadar Revolutionaries conspired to return to India to start a revolution there. The party received money and arms through the German consulate in San Francisco. However, in 1917, one of the conspirators was arrested in New York and the leaders of the German plot were arrested in Chicago and San Francisco. They were tried in 1917 and all except one American were found guilty.

BIBLIOGRAPHY

Brown, Emily C. *Har Dayal: Hindu Revolutionary and Rationalists.* Tucson: University of Arizona Press, 1975.

Puri, Harish K. *Ghandar Movement: Ideology, Organization, and Strategy.* 2nd ed. Amrisar, Punjab: Buru Nanak Dev University Press, 1993.

Gong Lum et al. v. Rice et al. (1927)

In *Gong Lum et al. v. Rice et al.,* 275 U.S. 78 (1927), the U.S. Supreme Court affirmed the decision of the Mississippi Supreme Court, which had previously decided that Martha Lum, a child born in the United States but of Chinese descent, was not denied equal protection of the law by being classed by the state as a colored person; therefore, it remained the right of the state to assign her to a public school separate from white students. (FHM)

BIBLIOGRAPHY

Kim, Hyung-Chan, ed. *Asian Americans and the Supreme Court: A Documentary History.* New York: Greenwood Press, 1992.

Wendy Lee Gramm (1945–)

Wendy Lee Gramm, Asian American wife of U.S. Senator Phil Gramm (R-TX), acted as assistant professor of economics at Texas A&M University from 1971 to 1978. From 1978 to 1982, Gramm served at the Institute of Defense Analysis, then in 1984 went to work for the Federal Office of Management and Budget. In February 1988, President George Bush appointed Gramm to the Commodity Futures Trading Commission, where she served for the duration of Bush's Presidency. Gramm currently sits on the board of the Chicago Mercantile Exchange.

BIBLIOGRAPHY

Chen, Lilliana, et al. "The 25 Most Influential Asian Americans." *A Magazine: Inside Asia America* (January 31, 1997): 53–67.

Soong, Tina. "Wendy Lee Gramm Captivates APA Women in New Orleans." *AsianWeek* (April 28, 1995): 4.

Great Strike of 1909

Japanese workers for the Hawaiian sugar planters went on strike at the Aiea Plantation in May 1909. They were striking for higher wages and better living conditions, and soon Japanese workers from a number of other plantations followed suit. The Hawaiian Sugar Planters' Association refused to negotiate and brought in scabs (nonunion replacement workers). The Japanese workers were arrested and some were evicted from their homes. In August 1909, after one of the strikers was wounded while attacking an editor for the local newspaper, the Japanese workers decided to call off the strike and in November of that same year, the Hawaiian Sugar Planters' Association raised Japanese laborers wages.

BIBLIOGRAPHY

Takaki, Ronald. *Pau Hana: Plantation Life and Labor in Hawaii.* Honolulu: University of Hawaii Press, 1983.

Guey Heung Lee v. Johnson (1971)

In 1971 the San Francisco Unified School District reassigned Chinese pupils to different public schools in an attempt to desegregate the school system. Until that time, most Chinese students had attended an exclusively Asian school. The Chinese parents protested, stating that their children learned about their cultural heritage in that school, and that by reassigning their children, they would lose this valuable part of their curriculum. The case went before the U.S. Supreme Court in 1971, and in *Guey Heung Lee v. Johnson,* 404 U.S. 1215 (1971), the Court found in favor of the San Francisco Unified School District. **See also** Multiculturalism.

BIBLIOGRAPHY

Appleton, Nicholas. *Cultural Pluralism in Education.* New York: Longman, 1983.

Hampton v. Wong Mow Sun (1976)

Wong Now Sun and others applied for positions in the Civil Service Commission and were denied. Despite their qualifications, the agency claimed that it would not hire Sun and the others because federal jobs were only provided to "American citizens." In response, Sun and the others filed suit against the commission on the basis that such hiring practices were arbitrary, discriminatory, and contrary to due process legislation.

In court, the government argued that exclusionary clauses were necessary to preserve policy making and national security issues. Government attorneys also added that the exclusionary clauses encouraged immigrants to obtain legal U.S. citizenship through naturalization.

After hearing arguments, the district court found in favor of the government, but the case was appealed to the court of appeals and the United States Supreme Court. In *Hampton v. Wong Mow Sun,* 426 U.S. 88 (1976), the Court stated that while the government had the right to protect its security and regulate matters pertaining to aliens, it did not have the right to deprive constitutional rights. As a result, the lower court's ruling was overturned.

BIBLIOGRAPHY

Mutharika, A. Peter. *The Alien under American Law.* New York: Oceana Publications, 1981.

Ross Masao Harano (1942–)

Ross Harano is president of the World Trade Center Chicago Association (WTCCA). He is also the chairperson of the Chicago Chapter of the Japanese American Citizens League. Harano was born in California in Fresno Fairgrounds. The fairgrounds was an **assembly center** for Japanese Americans interned during **World War II.** Harano started off in insurance but switched to banking where he became the vice president at the Bank of Chicago in 1978, and at the Community Bank of Edgewater in 1980. In 1988, he joined the office of the attorney general of Illinois where he served as the equal opportunity officer. Then he became the president of the WTCCA in 1993.

BIBLIOGRAPHY

Yates, Ronald E., "Trade Center Has Global Ambitions—in the Midwest." *Chicago Tribune* (April 4, 1993): 1, 12.

Hare–Hawes–Cutting Act (1933)

Congress passed the Hare-Hawes-Cutting Act in 1933, promising political independence to the Philippine Islands in 1943. The purpose of the bill may have been to prevent Filipino immigration to the United States, but businesses that had invested heavily in the Philippines were alarmed at the prospect of losing large sums of money once the islands were granted independence. In Europe, it was unheard of for a government to grant independence to a colony, but the United States was in the midst of the Great Depression, and granting independence to the Philippines may have seemed economically beneficial at the time. When the bill was first introduced, the Democrats in Congress tended to be for Philippine independence, while the Republicans were against it. The bill passed the House easily, and it passed the Senate after a few amendments were added. One amendment was an extension of the waiting time to 10 years, slightly longer than the eight years of the original bill. **See also** Filipino Americans; Filipino Repatriation Act of 1935; Immigration Restriction Movement; Jones Act of 1916; Philippine Naturalization; Tydings–McDuffie Act (1934).

BIBLIOGRAPHY

Friend, Theodore. *Between Two Empires: The Ordeal of the Philippines, 1929–1946.* New Haven, CT: Yale University Press, 1965.
Kirk, Grayson V. *Philippine Independence.* New York: Farrar and Rinehart, 1936.

Lon S. Hatamiya (1959–)

After unsuccessful runs in 1990 and 1992 as a Democrat for the California State Legislature, Lon Hatamiya continued to work for the California Democratic Party and for agricultural groups in California. A year after beginning work in 1991 for the California Agricultural Education Foundation's Leadership Program, Hatamiya was appointed by the California State Assembly to the Rural Economic Development Infrastructure Panel. At the same time, Hatamiya sat on the Executive Committee of the California Democratic Party, where he co-chaired the Party's Finance Committee. In 1993, President Bill Clinton appointed him administrator of the U.S. Department of Agriculture's Agricultural Marketing Service.

BIBLIOGRAPHY

Trammell, Jeffrey B. and Gary T. Osifishin. *The Clinton 500.* Washington, D.C.: Almanac Publishing, 1994.

Hawaii. *See* Annexation of Hawaii

Hawaii Seven

Seven people were arrested in Hawaii in 1953 and charged with conspiring to overthrow the government. In arresting the seven, the Federal Bureau of Investigation evoked the Smith Act, which made it illegal to conspire to teach or advocate the overthrow of the government. Five of the seven had already been arrested once before, after being questioned by the House Committee on Un-American Activities in 1950. They were part of a group who had refused questioning, named the **Reluctant Thirty-Nine.** (They were later acquitted of any wrongdoing.) Among the Hawaii Seven were several self-proclaimed communists, a fact that came out during the trial in 1953. All seven were found guilty of the charges, but the decision was reversed by the U.S. circuit court of appeals in 1958, which stated that teaching communism in its abstract form was not the same as conspiring against the government.

BIBLIOGRAPHY

Daws, Gavan. *Shoal of Time*. Honolulu: University Press of Hawaii, 1968.

Wright, Theon. *The Disenchanted Isles*. New York: Dial Press, 1972.

Hawaiian Homes Commission Act of 1920

On July 9, 1921, the **Organic Act** of Hawaii was amended to allow native Hawaiians to obtain homesteads in the Territory of Hawaii, with 99-year leases at a cost of $1 per year. The amendment is known as the Hawaiian Homes Commission Act of 1920.

Plots of land, from 20 to 1,000 acres, were to be awarded by the Hawaiian Homes Commission, consisting of the governor of Hawaii and four persons appointed by the governor, three of whom were required to be native Hawaiians. The law also established a revolving loan fund of up to $1 million for homesteaders seeking capital to build houses, purchase livestock, or acquire equipment for agricultural cultivation. To obtain money for the fund, however, the commission leased land to non-Hawaiians, and the land available has been considerably less than the demand by native Hawaiians, who often must be on waiting lists for decades. **See also** Hawaiian Native Claims Settlement Act (1975). (MH)

BIBLIOGRAPHY

U.S. Commission on Civil Rights, Hawaii Advisory Committee. *A Broken Trust: The Hawaiian Homelands Program: Seventy Years of Failure of the Federal and State Governments to Protect the Civil Rights of Native Hawaiians*. Washington, D.C.: U.S. Commission on Civil Rights.

Hawaiian Native Claims Settlement Act (1975)

The Hawaiian Native Claims Settlement Act offered a settlement to Hawaiian natives for their loss of property and identity at the hands of U.S. intervention. In 1893 the United States overthrew the Hawaiian monarchy and laid claims to the islands, displacing native persons and destroying their homes. In 1920, the first bill to compensate Hawaiians, known as the Hawaiian Homes Commission Act, offered land to anyone who was at least half Hawaiian. Then in 1974, Matsunaga and Mink, the Representatives from Hawaii, put forth the Hawaiian Native Claims Settlement Act, which offered to compensate anyone who could prove they had any native Hawaiian lineage. In 1975 a bill by the same name was proposed by Representative Lloyd Meeds (D-WA) and hearings were held in Hawaii. It was determined that a fund called the Hawaiian Native Fund should be created and run by all persons who could established their native Hawaiian identity.

BIBLIOGRAPHY

U.S. Congress. *House Committee on Interior and Insular Affairs, Hawaiian Native Claims Settlement Act, Part I, Hearings Before the Subcommittee on Indians Affairs on H.R. 1944, 94th. Congress, 1st Session, Washington, D.C.* Washington, D.C.: U.S. Government Printing Office, 1974.

Samuel Ichiye Hayakawa (1906–1992)

Samuel Ichiye (S.I.) Hayakawa was a semanticist who gained national prominence as president of San Francisco State College (later renamed San Francisco State University) during the era of student protest in the 1960s. With the cameras of national news organizations rolling, Hayakawa personally pulled out the connections of the audio system at a student protest, thus propelling himself into the public eye.

His conservative views had attracted the attention of then-Governor Ronald Reagan, who had appointed Hayakawa as president of San Francisco State. Hayakawa's notoriety gained at the college helped him eventually win one of California's seats in the United States Senate in 1976. His Senate years were undistinguished, and he left Congress in 1983. In the 1980s, he became honorary chair of U.S. English, an organization dedicated to making English the official language.

Born in Vancouver, British Columbia, to Japanese immigrants, Hayakawa earned his Ph.D. from the University of Wisconsin in 1935, and he later wrote a successful textbook on language. Before entering politics, he taught at the University of Wisconsin, Illinois Institute for Technology, and San Francisco State.

Hayakawa's conservatism put him at odds with many Japanese Americans, particularly when he supported their detainment in **internment camps** during **World War II.** (He himself was not interned.) *Sansei* (third-generation Japanese Americans) were probably most likely to distance themselves from him, while many *nisei* (second generation) seemed to view him more ambivalently. (ALA)

BIBLIOGRAPHY

King, Wayne. "Hayakawa Resists Idea of Dropping Out of Race." *The New York Times* (January 24, 1982): 24.

Dennis Hayashi (1952–)

In 1993, President Clinton announced that Dennis Hayashi had been appointed the new director of the Office for Civil Rights. Hayashi had spent the majority of his career at the **Asian Law Caucus,** a nonprofit law firm that focuses on defending the civil rights of the Asian Pacific Islander Community in the United States He personally focused on employment and racial discrimination cases. Hayashi represented **Fred Korematsu** in the attempt to turn over the ruling in *Korematsu v. United States* **(1944).** He was elected the national director of the **Japanese American Citizens League** in 1991. He has also been director for the National Asian Pacific American Association, the San Francisco Legal Assistance Foundation, and the Coalition of Asian Pacific Americans.

BIBLIOGRAPHY

Hilts, Philip J. "Hospital Is Object of Rights Inquiry," *The New York Times* (February 6, 1994): 29.

Chung, L.A. "S.F. Lawyer Named to Health Post, Appointment of Dennis Hayashi Is Highest for Asian American." *The San Francisco Chronicle* (May 6, 1993): A2.

Joseph Heco (1837–1897)

Joseph Heco, also known as Hikozaemon (or Hizoko Hamada), was rescued at sea from his sinking ship by an American sailing vessel in 1850. Heco was taken to San Francisco, but he later moved to Baltimore, where he received an education. In 1858 he became the first Japanese to be naturalized as a U.S. citizen, but in 1862 he returned to Japan and opened an import-export business. He also ran the first privately published newspaper in Japan, *Kaigai Shimbum.*

BIBLIOGRAPHY

Kuroda, Andrew Y. "Joseph Heco and the Joseph Heco Society." *Pacific Citizen* 2, no. 9 (January 1987): 18, 20–21.

Hidemitsu Toyota v. United States (1925)

In *Hidemitsu Toyota v. United States,* 268 U.S. 402 (1925), the U.S. Supreme Court upheld the circuit court decision to cancel Toyota Hidemitsu's certificate of citizenship granted to him by the district court. Toyota came to the United States from Japan in 1913 and served in the U.S. Coast Guard for 10 years. He was granted naturalization in Massachusetts, because all serving aliens with honorable discharges were granted naturalization. The Federal Circuit Court of Appeals for the 1st Circuit revoked the citizenship by claiming it was illegally obtained. The U.S. Supreme Court said the distinction of race and color in naturalization was to be upheld. A person born of the Japanese race could not be naturalized.

BIBLIOGRAPHY

Konvitz, Milton R. *The Aliens and the Asiatic in American Law.* Ithaca, NY: Cornell University Press, 1946.

Wilson, Robert A. and Bill Hosokawa. *East to America.* New York: William Morrow and Co., 1980.

Hirabayashi v. United States (1943)

On March 24, 1942, General John Lesene DeWitt handed down a curfew for all Japanese Americans or individuals of Japanese ancestry that were living in Military Area No. 1, which encompassed southern Arizona, all the coastal region of the three pacific coast states (California, Oregon, and Washington), and Seattle, Washington which was under his jurisdiction. On May 9, 1942, Gordon Kiyoshi Hirabayashi failed to meet the 8:00 P.M. to 6:00 A.M. curfew. As a result, Hirabayashi was brought up on misdemeanor charges, of which he was later convicted; because of this, the issue was brought before the United States Supreme Court on appeal.

In *Hirabayashi v. United States,* 320 U.S. 81 (1943), Hirabayashi's attorney's argued that it was beyond Congress's legislative power to issue military commanders the right to impose curfews and that such actions violated the Fifth Amendment, which guaranteed equal rights for United States citizens of different races. The Court denied the argument, saying that the curfew was a result of **Executive Order 9066** and enacted because of the need to protect the country from possible espionage and sabotage. As a result, the misdemeanor charges were reinstituted. In 1984, the case was repetitioned by a group of individuals stating that the 1942 curfews were unnecessary and illegal, especially in light of the eventual abolition of the military zones in which they were established; the plea was denied later that year. In 1986, the case was again reopened, after revelations that that the government had knowingly and willingly concealed information regarding the perceived danger posed by Japanese Americans during the war. Evidence presented by the legal historian Peter Irons showed that government officials had concealed evidence and had lied to the Supreme Court. This newly discovered evidence led to all convictions being vacated by 1988, on order from the 9th Circuit Court of Appeals. The government did not appeal, and the Supreme Court has never reheard the cases of Hirabayashi, **Fred Korematsu**, or **Minoru Yasui**. **See also** Commission on Wartime Relocation and Internment of Civilians; *Korematsu v. United States* (1943); *Minoru Yasui v. United States* (1943).

BIBLIOGRAPHY

Chuman, Frank. *The Bamboo People: The Law and Japanese-Americans.* Del Mar: Publisher's Inc., 1976.

Irons, Peter. *Justice at War: The Story of the Japanese American Internment Cases.* New York: Oxford University Press, 1983.

Irene Y. Hirano (1948–)

In 1975, Irene Y. Hirano became director of T.H.E. Clinic for Women, a nonprofit clinic, where she would serve for the next 13 years. In 1976, she was selected by the governor to chair the California Commission on the Status of Women. In 1980 she cochaired the National Asian Women's Network. Hirano was a driving force in the National Conference of the Asian/Pacific American Education Equity Project which held a conference in Washington, D.C., from August 15 to 17, 1980. The conference examined the status of Asian-American women and was analogous to the Houston conference on the status of women held in 1979. She was a cofounder of Leadership Education for Asian Pacifics, a group dedicated to expanding leadership among Asian Americans. In 1985, she became director of the Japanese-American National Museum located in Los Angeles, California; a post she still holds.

BIBLIOGRAPHY

Zia, Helen and Susan B. Gall, eds. *Notable Asian Americans.* Detroit, MI: Gale, 1995.

Ho Ah-Kow v. Mathew Nunan (1879)

Ho Ah-Kow v. Mathew Nunan, 12 Fed Cas. 252 (1879), involved a Chinese prisoner, Ho Ah-kow, who was ordered under the **Queue Ordinance** of 1876 to have his hair cut to one inch from his scalp. The ordinance, which stated that all male prisoners in San Francisco must have their hair cut to a specified length, was ruled unconstitutional in 1879 by the U.S. Circuit Court of California. Sheriff Mathew Noonan, who had cut Ho Ah-kow's hair, was ordered to pay $10,000 in retribution.

BIBLIOGRAPHY

Sawyer, L.S.B. *Reports of Cases Decided in the Circuit and District Courts of the United States for the Ninth Circuit.* San Francisco: A.L. Bancroft and Company, 1880.

Hokuku Seinen-Dan (Young Men's Organization to Serve Our Mother Country)

The Hokuku Seinen-Dan was originally formed as a study group of Japanese culture and history at the Tule Lake Relocation Center in 1944. The Japanese-American men and women at the Tule Lake Camp had been singled out by the **War Relocation Authority** because of their refusal to swear allegiance to the United States or to renounce their allegiance to the Emperor of Japan. Thus, in forming the Hokuku Seinen-Dan, they were preparing for their eventual return to Japan. Despite leader Reverend Aramaki's efforts to cultivate membership, the group numbered only about 500 people. **See also** Daihyo Sha Kai (Representative Body); Denationalization Act of 1944; No-No Boys; Public Law 405.

BIBLIOGRAPHY

Nishimoto, Richard and Dorothy S. Thomas. *The Spoilage: Japanese-American Evacuation and Resettlement During World War II.* Berkeley: University of California Press, 1969.

Home Rule Movement

The Home Rule Movement grew out of the land use movement that successfully had adopted the Hawaiian Land Use Law (1961). The act treats all land (public and private) as a public resource as opposed to a commodity that may be freely traded. Based upon land law in England, the provisions of the law require the legal protection of land against unregulated commercial exploitation. The law was passed in response to the rapid growth of cities like Honolulu, which caused the increase in formerly agricultural lands being sold and developed for commercial purposes.

The goal of the movement was to create a balance among the four basic types of land use (conservation, agricultural, rural, and urban). The Land Use Commission, which was authorized by the 1961 act, was charged with the responsibility of maintaining the balance. However, economic pressures often led to the conversion of lands for urban (commercial) use at the expense of the other residents. In 1973, however, developers were prevented from turning 2,300 acres of farmland into a housing project. This decision helped to reinvigorate the continuing issue of urbanization in the islands and has generally made it more difficult (though not impossible) for developers to have land rezoned.

BIBLIOGRAPHY

Callies, David L. *Regulating Paradise: Land Use Controls in Hawaii.* Honolulu: University of Hawaii Press, 1984.
Horwitz, Robert H. and Norman Meller. *Land and Politics in Hawaii.* Honolulu: University of Hawaii Press, 1966.

Home Rule Party

In 1895, the Home Rule Party was established in Hawaii for the purpose of overthrowing the current government, the Republic of Hawaii, so as to restore Queen Liliuokalani to power. The party believed that the Republic of Hawaii was dominated by Anglos wishing to overturn and exploit the traditions of the native Hawaiian culture. As a result, the party began an aggressive political campaign, drawing on the slogan "nana I ka ili," Hawaiian for "look to the skin," to gather support.

In 1900, the group gained a party majority in both houses of the Hawaiian territorial legislature; in this first campaign, the party successfully won 14 of 27 seats in the Hawaiian Territorial House of Representatives and nine of 13 seat in the Territorial Senate. The group also sought to fight provisions of Hawaii's **Organic Act of 1900,** which decreed that citizens of the Republic of Hawaii would automatically become citizens of the Territory of Hawaii, although some measures were also made in the act to exclude Asian-Hawaiians from citizenship. After debate, the party was successful in influencing Congress to counter some of the act's legislation by allowing native Hawaiians voting rights. In 1904, however, the Home Rule Party's influence declined and began to dissipate as former Hawaiian Prince Jonah Kuhio, a major party contributor, divided the native vote by supporting the Republic party and the Big Five sugar companies.

BIBLIOGRAPHY

Kuykendall, Ralph S. and A. Grove Day. *Hawaii: A History.* New York: Prentice-Hall, 1948.

Florence Makita Hongo (1928–)

A founder in 1969 of the Japanese American Curriculum Project (later renamed the Asian American Curriculum Project), an organization dedicated to the education and betterment of Asian Americans, Florence Makita Hongo remained active into the 1990s as a member, consultant, and activist. Hongo and other educators produced the 1970 book *Japanese Americans: The Untold Story,* among the first histories of its kind printed in English, shedding particular light on the treatment of Asians in U.S. **internment camps** during **World War II.** Hongo contributed to two history texts: *The Education of Asian and Pacific Americans* (1982) and *Strength in Diversity: A Study Guide for Elementary Schools on Japanese American Women* (1990), and served as editor for the 1985 work *Japanese American Journey: The Story of a People.*

BIBLIOGRAPHY

O'Brien, David J. and Stephen S. Fugita. *The Japanese American Experience.* Bloomington: Indiana University Press, 1991.

Thomas Hsieh

Thomas Hsieh was the founder of the Asian Pacific Caucus of the Democratic Party and has served on the Democratic National Committee for a number of years. In 1985, he was elected to the board of supervisors for the city and county of San Francisco. On the board, he chairs the budget committee and the transportation authority committee.

BIBLIOGRAPHY

Unterburger, Amy L. *Who's Who Among Asian Americans*. Detroit: Gale, 1994

John Huang (1949–)

John Huang, a naturalized U.S. citizen, was born in mainland China and raised in Taiwan. He became the central figure in an investigation of illegal campaign contributions to the Democratic National Committee (DNC) and the election coffers of President Bill Clinton. In 1969 Huang immigrated to the United States, where he earned a business degree from the University of Connecticut in 1971. During the 1980s, Huang worked in Hong Kong in the banking industry where he met James Riady—an acquaintance of then Governor Clinton of Arkansas—who was connected to the Lippo Group. In 1990, Huang became head of the Lippo Group's U.S. operations. A large contributor to Democratic Party candidates, Huang secured a senior position in the Commerce Department in 1994, serving until December 1995. In December, Huang joined the DNC as a vice chairman with the specific purpose of raising funds from Asian Americans.

BIBLIOGRAPHY

Abse, Nathan. "Q&A: John Huang." *The Washington Post* (May 13, 1997): A8.

Morgan, Dan. "Clashing Sketches of Fund-Raiser Begin to Emerge." *The Washington Post* (October 18, 1996): A35.

Hung Wai Ching

Hung Wai Ching served as the executive secretary of the University of Hawaii's branch of the YMCA from 1938 to 1941. During **World War II,** he assisted in heading the morale section of the Office of Military Governor. When Japanese Americans were discharged from the Hawaii Territorial Guard in January 1942, Ching helped form the **Varsity Victory Volunteers,** an organization that consisted of former Japanese-American soldiers and other Japanese Americans who provided noncombat labor for the U.S. military. Ching was also able to convince Assistant Secretary of War John McCloy and President Franklin D. Roosevelt to return Japanese Americans to active combat duty. Following their decision to allow this, Ching helped with the formation of the **442nd Regimental Combat Battalion.**

BIBLIOGRAPHY

Duus, Masayo. *Unlikely Liberators: The Men of the 100th and 442nd.* Honolulu: University of Hawaii Press, 1987.

Ng, Franklin, ed. *The Asian American Encyclopedia.* New York: Marshall Cavendish, 1995.

I

Paul M. Igasaki (1955–)

Igasaki is currently the acting commissioner of the United States Equal Employment Opportunity Commission. Igasaki, born in Chicago, was the executive director of the **Asian Law Caucus** before that. The Asian Law Caucus is a San Francisco-based civil rights and legal advocacy organization that has represented Asian Americans for 21 years. He has also served as the Washington, D.C., representative for the **Japanese American Citizen's League,** a group that lobbies for the interests of Japanese Americans. Igasaki has worked for the Legal Services of northern California where he was a Reginald Herbert Smith Fellow. He was director of the Private Bar Involvement Project, which worked to increase resources in legal services offices. Starting in 1985, he served as the liaison to Chicago's Asian-American community.

BIBLIOGRAPHY

Lash, Steve. "EEOC Won't Seek Funds for 'Testers,' Practice of Hiring Actors to Uncover Job Bias Criticized by Republicans." *The Houston Chronicle* (April 2, 1998): 6.

Immigration Act of 1882

Popularly known as the Chinese Exclusion Act, the immigration law of 1882 prohibited Chinese laborers from entering the United States for a period of 10 years. The first immigration restriction law aimed at a particular nationality, the act's prohibition of Chinese immigration was extended for a further 10 years by the 1892 **Geary Act**, and then made permanent by a third Chinese exclusion statute in 1902. The Immigration Act of 1882 was the result of growing anti-Chinese sentiment in the West, particularly California. In need of labor, particularly to build railroads, the new state of California welcomed Chinese immigrants in the 1850s. However, by the 1880s, over 100,000 Chinese immigrants were living on the Pacific coast, and this explosive growth fueled the racism that led to anti-Chinese riots in San Francisco in 1877-78. In 1879, the California State Constitution was altered to prohibit the hiring of Chinese workers. Although there was little direct competition between Chinese and white laborers, native-born Americans and European immigrants found the Chinese to be ideal scapegoats for their own economic frustrations. By 1882, the cause of Chinese exclusion was widely popular, and Congress was simply responding to prevailing sentiment on the West coast when it passed the Immigration Act. Although anti-Chinese racism died down after the turn of the century, the exclusion statutes remained in effect until their repeal in 1943, when Chinese immigration was allowed under the quota system established for other nationalities in the 1920s. (JAW)

BIBLIOGRAPHY

Chan, Sucheng, ed. *Entry Denied: Exclusion and the Chinese Community in America, 1882-1943.* Philadelphia: Temple University Press, 1991.

Gyory, Andrew. *Closing the Gate: Race, Politics, and the Chinese Exclusion Act.* Chapel Hill: University of North Carolina Press, 1998.

Immigration Act of 1907

The Immigration Act of 1907 was passed by Congress on February 20, 1907. It had 44 sections. Section One explicitly authorized the president to exclude Japanese and Koreans from admission into the continental United States. Section Two listed 20 different classes of people to be denied entry into the country. Section 30 also authorized the president to enter into international agreements that would prevent the immigration of aliens who were excluded from admission into the United States.

It was based on this provision that the agreement with Japan, to be known as the **Gentlemen's Agreement** of 1908, would be signed. It terminated all labor immigration from Japan but allowed the entry of wives and children of Japanese residents of the United States. Thus, between 1900 and 1920, many Japanese men took advantage of the window of opportunity and summoned their wives from Japan. The Gentlemen's Agreement explicitly only allowed immigrants to receive passports if they fit the designation of "relatives," "former residents," or settled agriculturalists. (CGM)

BIBLIOGRAPHY

Hing, Bill Ong. *Making and Remaking Asian American through Immigration Policy, 1850–1990.* Stanford, CA: Stanford University Press, 1993.

Kim, Hyung-chan. *A Legal History of Asian Americans, 1790–1990.* Westport, CT: Greenwood Press, 1994.

Immigration Act of 1917/Barred Zone Act of 1917

The Immigration Act of 1917, also known as the Barred Zone Act of 1917, passed on February 5, 1917. It was Congress's response to the clamor against immigrants from Asia and southern and Eastern Europe. This law included the controversial requirement that would exclude aliens who could not read and understand at least 30 words in some language or dialect, thus creating a literacy test for entry into the United States.

The law also created and delineated an "Asiatic barred zone," thus extending the Chinese exclusion laws to other Asians. This barred zone drew an imaginary line from the Red Sea to the Mediterranean, Aegean, and Black Seas, through the Caucasus Mountains and the Caspian Sea along the Ural River, and then through the Ural Mountains. All peoples living in areas west of the line which came to be called the barred zone were denied entry in the United States. The zone covered "Asia" from Arabia to Indochina, as well as the adjacent islands. It included India, Burma, Thailand, the Malay states, the East Indian Islands, Asiatic Russia, the Polynesian Islands, and parts of Arabia and Afghanistan. China and Japan did not have to be included since they were already covered by the Chinese Exclusion Act (**Immigration Act of 1882**) and the **Gentlemen's Agreement.** Taken all together, these three laws declared inadmissible all Asians except teachers, merchants, and students. Only Filipinos and Guam residents who were under U.S. jurisdiction at that time were not included in this barred zone law. **See also** Immigration Policy. (CGM)

BIBLIOGRAPHY

Hing, Bill Ong. *Making and Remaking Asian Americans through Immigration Policy, 1850–1990.* Stanford, CA: Stanford University Press, 1993.

Kim, Hyung-chan. *A Legal History of Asian Americans, 1790–1990.* Westport, CT: Greenwood Press, 1994.

Immigration Act of 1924

The Immigration Act of 1924 barred the entry of those ineligible for citizenship into the United States. In effect it denied entry to virtually all Asians, including the Japanese who were not originally barred. This was a reaction to the influx of Japanese "picture brides" who were able to enter the country as a result of the **Gentlemen's Agreement** that admitted relatives; this influx had led to an increase in the number of Japanese-American children born in America, thereby raising xenophobic feelings of Anglo U.S. citizens. The act stopped Japanese immigration entirely by barring the entry of "aliens ineligible to citizenship." In effect it nullified the Gentlemen's Agreement and denied admission even to wives of U.S. citizens. The ensuing great protest forced the government to allow for those who had married U.S. citizens before 1924 to enter. However, various provisions of the act were stringent and made it difficult even for naturalized citizens to travel abroad. Thus if Chinese women went to China for a visit, even though they were born in the United States and therefore by *jus soli* were U.S. citizens, they still had a hard time reentering the country. They would have to show conclusive evidence that they were U.S. citizens. The daughters of Chinese men who were citizens had to prove their relationship to their fathers, and fathers had to prove equally that they were bona fide U.S.-born citizens.

The law only affected Asians at first, but it was soon applied to people from southern and Eastern Europe, people with different and supposedly inferior cultures and genes. A fear of foreigners grew, fueled by economic fears of being outworked and undercut by people with a lower standard of living and also by a fear of incoming radicals, especially Russians from the Revolution of 1917. This prejudice was leveled not only against nonwhites, but also whites who were not Anglo-Saxon or Nordic.

This law also introduced a national origins quota system, which used the country of birth to determine whether an individual could enter as a legal alien into the United States. The quota set was based on the number of previous immigrants and their descendants to determine how many from a certain country could enter annually. This system heavily favored immigrants from Great Britain, Ireland, and Germany. But these quotas were usually unfilled, with low numbers of would-be immigrants and high quota levels. On the other hand, other countries had low quotas and high numbers wishing to emigrate. The restrictions of the act were not repealed until the passage of the **Immigration and Nationality Act of 1952/ McCarran-Walter Act of 1952. See also** Immigration Restriction Policy. (CGM)

BIBLIOGRAPHY

Hing, Bill Ong. *Making and Remaking Asian American through Immigration Policy, 1850–1990.* Stanford, CA: Stanford University Press, 1993.

Kim, Hyung-chan. *A Legal History of Asian Americans, 1790–1990.* Westport, CT: Greenwood Press, 1994.

Immigration Act of 1943 (Magnuson Act)

Warren Magnuson from Washington state introduced a bill to repeal some 15 different Chinese laws. The bill became law on December 17, 1943, with the official title, "To repeal the Chinese Exclusion Acts, to establish quotas, and for other purposes." It marks the beginning of a long legislative process that would bring about the removal of race and ethnicity as immigration and naturalization criteria.

The law had three main sections: the first one enumerated all the Chinese exclusion laws that had been repealed. Some critics insisted that the law still had racist qualities since the second section assigned an annual Chinese quota based upon the number of Chinese in America in 1920; in addition, 75 percent of the quota was allocated to Chinese who were born and resided in China and the remainder was applied to Chinese in other countries, like Canada. The third section made Chinese and persons of Chinese descent eligible for naturalization. (CGM)

BIBLIOGRAPHY

Hing, Bill Ong. *Making and Remaking Asian American through Immigration Policy, 1850–1990.* Stanford, CA: Stanford University Press, 1993.

Kim, Hyung-chan. *A Legal History of Asian Americans, 1790–1990.* Westport, CT: Greenwood Press, 1994.

Immigration and Nationality Act of 1952

The Immigration and Nationality Act of 1952 (known as the McCarran-Walter Act) is considered the first general immigration act since 1924. As one of the most comprehensive immigration acts passed by Congress, it codified all existing immigration laws and organized them under different classifications. It continued to use the national origins model with several major innovations. First, it removed all racial and ethnic barriers to immigration and naturalization and provided for family reunification. It also allowed female citizens to bring in their alien husbands to the United States on a nonquota basis.

The McCarren-Walter Act, passed over President Harry Truman's veto, reimposed the quota system of immigration into the United States in order to bar the entry of "undesirables," specifically those labeled communists. In retaining the quota system, it still used the 1920 census to determine the size of the quota. However, there were concessions to common sense: for the first time, the Japanese were allowed to become citizens, and were awarded an annual quota of 115, considered a small liberalization of immigration policy; special provisions were enacted to allow 120,000 soldiers to return home with their foreign-born wives; displaced persons or refugees from Western Europe and Russia were permitted to enter without waiting to qualify under the quota. The McCarren-Walter Act also authorized the deportation of aliens and naturalized citizens for communist and communist-front affiliations. This would be reversed in 1953 by the **Refugee Relief Act.**

A precursor to the McCarren-Walter Act was the Mundt-Nixon Act, which required communists to register with the government. Likewise, in September 1950, Senator Patrick McCarren (D-NV) of the Internal Security Subcommittee, in his effort to blacklist communists, successfully pushed Congress to override measures such as Truman's veto of the McCarren Internal Security Act. It was a grab bag of anticommunist measures such as requiring communist organizations to publish their records; authorizing punishment of communists who advocated totalitarian dictatorship in the United States; barring communists from employment in defense plants and from obtaining passports; and establishing a bipartisan Subversive Activities Control Board to aid in the work of exposing communists. In the same legislation, Congress barred any person who had been a member of a totalitarian organization from entering the United States. (CGM)

BIBLIOGRAPHY

Harmann, Susan. *Truman and the 80th Congress.* Columbia: University of Missouri Press, 1971.

Hing, Bill Ong. *Making and Remaking Asian American through Immigration Policy, 1850–1990.* Stanford, CA: Stanford University Press, 1993.

Kim, Hyung-chan. *A Legal History of Asian Americans, 1790–1990.* Westport, CT: Greenwood Press, 1994.

The Lamp and the Law: The McCarren-Walter Act of 1952. Hollywood, CA: American Civil Liberties Union, 1955.

McDonald, Forrest. *The Torch is Passed: The United States in the 20th Century.* Reading, MA: Addison Wesley, 1968.

Immigration and Nationality Act of 1990

The Immigration Act of 1990, which was signed into law on November 29, 1990, is considered the second longest in the history of Congressional legislation on immigration in America. It is also considered an improvement over the 1965 Immigration Act. It is organized into eight different titles, emphasizing attracting persons who possess desirable occupational skills or economic resources. It still provides for the unification of families and close relatives of U.S. citizens, and, to a lesser extent, permanent residents. This law for the first time establishes a category for the issuance of permanent visas to investors who establish or invest in new, job-creating enterprises.

The 1990 act increased the number of immigrants allowed to come into the U.S. from 290,000 to 700,000. Of this number, 465,000 were set aside for family-sponsored immigrants, while 140,000 were designated for employment-based immigration. A total of 55,000 were also set aside for the spouses and children of new legalized aliens, and the number of family preference visas cannot drop below 226,000 per year. One special provision known as diversity visas was included in the law to allow 40,000 Western Europeans to come into the country between 1992 and 1994 because they were not able to take advantage of the family preference system. Of these 40,000, 16,000 were allocated to the natives of Ireland as an accommodation to Senator Edward Kennedy, who together with other members of Congress was responsible for pushing through the provisions of the 1990 legislation.

Supporters of the law had the following goals in mind: (1) to eliminate family reunification as the principle basis of immigration policy in the U.S. since there were too many Asian and Latin American immigrants coming into the United States through the family preference and the immediate relative system; (2) attract skilled workers in short supply in the United States; and (3) change laws that had worked to exclude Western Europeans.

The new law also had a provision that beginning in 1995, allocated 55,000 annual visas to natives of so-called low-admission countries. However, countries such as India, Korea, the People's Republic of China, the Philippines and Taiwan were excluded from this category. Although the family preference system was retained and allowed Asian Americans to bring in family members, the diversity visa provisions favored non-Asian immigrants. Unaddressed were heavy backlogs of petitions filed by Asian Americans for their immediate family members. For example, petitions for brothers and sisters of

Filipino Americans have a 20-year waiting period, and those filed by Asian Indians have an 11-year waiting period. (CGM)

BIBLIOGRAPHY

Carrion, Ramon. *USA Immigration Guide.* Clearwater, FL: Sphinx Publishing, 1994.

Hing, Bill Ong. *Making and Remaking Asian American through Immigration Policy, 1850–1990.* Stanford, CA: Stanford University Press, 1993.

Kim, Hyung-chan. *A Legal History of Asian Americans, 1790–1990.* Westport, CT: Greenwood Press, 1994.

Immigration Policy

Immigration is the term used to describe the mass movement of people from one country to another. The decision to leave one's country of origin to take up residence in another has political, social, and economic implications for both the receiving and sending country. Costs and benefits accrue to both home (the country of emigration) and host (the country of immigration). The home country loses some of its best talent through the phenomenon called the "brain drain." Emigrants may take all of their assets along with them, thus causing a shortfall in capital. The decision to leave family behind causes prolonged separation and even the deterioration of family life. However, the home country benefits from emigration if population pressures are alleviated. In addition, emigrants who have left family behind may send back earnings, thus boosting the economy of their native country.

It is not easy to leave one's country and enter another. Conditions such as wars, natural disasters, or persecution push people to flee those situations. There are people with a title and wealth in their home country who leave in order to ex-

Although Chinese immigration to the U.S. was later restricted, Chinese laborers played a key role in the construction of the transcontinental railroad. *Library of Congress.*

pand their fortune. Some flee from poverty in search for a better life for themselves and their children. The choice of destination often depends on the perception as to where the greater freedom and the better life can be found; because of

this, developing countries usually lose their people to developed countries.

The host country benefits when the best talents of other countries become assets to their society. Some of these immigrants are willing to do the work that the native population may not want to do. Some immigrants bring their financial resources along with them and invest in the country they come into, thus increasing the investments available to the domestic economy. Because they come from a different background, they bring along their diverse cultures, customs, and practices that enhance the domestic culture.

However, host countries can also look at immigration as a burden on society. There are social costs involved in making available diverse services that the society is not used to providing. During difficult economic times, immigrants serve as convenient scapegoats for domestic problems, especially when they are perceived to be taking away limited resources from the native population. This can bring about feelings of prejudice and acts of discrimination.

Sovereign nations pride themselves on being able to control their borders, limiting the number of people who come through those borders, and determining the kinds of people they accept and under what conditions they are accepted. The development of immigration policies to control the flow of people is considered; a national prerogative. Some countries have looser policies; others are more restrictive. Those who fulfill criteria set for entry are considered legal immigrants. There are those immigrants who enter a country to work and then return to their home country at the end of the season or after earning a decent wage. These are temporary immigrants who have no intentions of establishing permanent residence in the country where they work. Those who enter a country outside of set criteria are considered illegal immigrants.

Americans recognize that their nation was built by immigrants who had fled to this country from Europe because of religious and political persecution, and there is sometimes sympathy toward newcomers who have chosen to come to U.S. shores to avoid similar persecution. However, concern over the flow of immigrants has followed the economic cycle. When the economy is in good shape, there is no perceived threat from immigrants, and they are not a target of restrictive public policy, but when the economy is sluggish immigrants become convenient scapegoats to blame for economic problems.

American immigration history can be divided into the following periods: the open door era (1776–1881), the era of regulation (1882–1916), the era of restriction (1917–1964), and the era of liberalization (since 1965).

There have been different waves of immigration into the United States. The first wave came from Europe, while the more recent wave comes from the developing countries. In the past laws often favored European immigrants over non-European ones. New immigrants encountered ambivalence, intolerance, or social discrimination.

Discrimination against those who were nonwhite began to grow in the late 1800s, but as far back as the late eighteenth century, the **Naturalization Act of 1790** employed explicitly racist criteria, limiting citizenship to free white persons. When policy makers were called upon to define further what was meant by "white," it was applied to those considered Caucasian. But members of some races such as Indians of the subcontinent and Middle Easterners considered themselves, and were considered by others, to be Caucasians. So the term further came to be applied to "other whites" who are easily assimilated into the larger community, although courts usually rejected the efforts of South Asians to enjoy equal rights with those of European ancestry.

The history of American legislation toward immigrants began in 1814 when the War of 1812 was ended by the Treaty of Ghent. The war had brought immigration to a complete halt and the end of the war marked the beginning of the first great wave of immigration, which included English, Polish, Germans, Dutch, and Irish.

The Chinese Exclusion Act (**Immigration Act of 1882**) made Chinese immigration to the United States illegal, making Chinese the first people declared undesirable by the U.S. Congress. This law was extended until 1943, even though it was originally intended to last only for 10 years. In 1921, the **Quota Immigration Act** introduced the quota system, which heavily favored northern and Western European immigrants and slammed the door on Eastern and southern Europeans and immigrants from all other countries, especially Asia.

The next major piece of legislation was the McCarran-Walter **Immigration and Nationality Act of 1952**. The act permitted Asian immigration; stopped sexual discrimination by allowing alien husbands of citizens to enter as nonquota immigrants; clarified legislation pertaining to the admission of former members of totalitarian political parties; and recognized the need to codify all existing immigration statutes. However, it also retained the national origins quota system and used the 1920 census for setting quotas, instead of using the latest census. Thus the quotas were still low for non-European groups, while still heavily biased toward northwestern Europe. It still heavily restricted Asian immigration.

The Immigration and Nationality Act of 1965 eliminated the national origins quotas. Substituted was an overall immigration quota of 170,000 per year. The quota for the western hemisphere was fixed at 120,000 per year. A system of preferences was introduced, with preference given to relatives and those with special skills. The law also stipulated that no one country could have more than 20,000 immigrants per year.

In 1986, the Immigration Reform and Control Act (IRCA) was signed. The act provided for implementation of employer sanctions, which made it a federal offense for an employer to knowingly hire an illegal alien; an amnesty or "legalization status" for illegals who could prove that they had been in the United States prior to January 1, 1982; and a loophole to allow temporary work visas for seasonal agricultural workers.

Despite the implementation of such legislation, immigration continues to be a controversial issue.

Today's immigrants can be classified into various categories. There are those who possess legal resident status because they have close family ties (children, spouses, siblings) to American citizens, or legal alien residents, and (to a lesser extent) to immigrants with particularly valuable skills and talents not available in the United States. There are also those who are undocumented, either evading inspection when crossing into the country at the borders (such as Mexicans), or entering the country with a visa and then remaining beyond the limits of their stay (overstaying aliens). After 1965 the new wave of immigrants who came from third world countries were nonwhite and were more susceptible to racial or ethnic discrimination because of their different skin colors, languages, and cultures.

Aversion and suspicion toward the new immigrants are on the rise. Immigrants have been accused of taking away jobs that rightfully belong to native-born Americans. Immigrants are also held responsible for lowering the standard of living, because they are willing to work for less, willing to take on jobs that others do not want because of difficult conditions and low pay. Immigrants also are sometimes ridiculed for differences in dress or practices. Partly in response to hostility, immigrants have often lived in ethnic enclaves, such as Chinatowns, Japantowns, and Koreatowns.

As a result of the growing hostility toward immigrants, some policy makers have proposed greater control over borders, harsher penalties for illegal aliens, and new efforts to deprive illegal immigrants of all types of medical, health, and social welfare benefits. Although such solutions seem to have popular appeal during tough economic times, there is fear that such treatment will be applied to legal nonwhite immigrants as well, thus aggravating racial prejudice and discrimination. Others suggest attacking the root cause of immigration by supporting economic development efforts in home countries, thereby making emigration from developing countries a less attractive option. This requires strengthening the economies of the sending countries through trade, aid, and investment.

See also Asian-American Relations with Other Minorities; Displaced Persons Act of 1948; Immigration Act of 1907; Immigration Act of 1917/Barred Zone Act of 1917; Immigration and Nationality Act of 1952; Immigration and Nationality Act of 1990; Immigration Restriction Movement; Refugee Act of 1980; Tydings–McDuffie Act of 1934; War Brides Act of 1945.

See "Disgraceful Persecution of a Boy" by Mark Twain (1870); A Letter on Chinese Immigration by John Stuart Mill (1869); and Irwin Convention (1885) in Appendix 1.

See individual immigration cases: *Berger v. Bishop* (1903); *Chae Chan Pin v. United States* (1889); *Chang Chan v. John D. Nagle* (1925); *Cheung Sum Shee et al. v. Nagle, Commissioner of Immigration for the Port of San Francisco* (1924); *Chew Heong v. United States* (1884); *Chin Bak Lan v. United States* (1902); *Chin Yow v. United States* (1907); *Chy*

Lung v. Freeman (1876); *Fong Yue Ting v. United States* (1893); *In Re Ah Fong* (1874); *In Re Look Tin Sing* (1884); *Kawakita Tomoya v. United States* (1952); *Kimm v. Rosenberg* (1959); *Kwock Jan Fat v. White, Commissioner of Immigration* (1920); *Lee Kum Hoy, Lee Kum Cherk, and Lee Moon Wah v. John L. Murff* (1957); *Lem Moon Sing v. United States* (1895); *Li Sung v. United States* (1900); *Nishimura v. United States* (1892); *Nishikawa v. Dulles* (1958); *Ng Fung Ho et al. v. White, Commissioner of Immigration* (1917); *Okimura Kiyokura v. Acheson, Secretary of State* (1952); *Quon Quon Poy v. Johnson* (1926); *Roque Espiritu de la Ysla v. United States* (1935); *Takao Ozawa v. United States* (1922); *Tang Tun v. Harry Edsell* (1906); *United States v. Ju Toy* (1905); *United States v. Jung Ah Lung* (1888); *United States v. Sakharam Ganesh Pandit* (1926); *United States v. Sing Tuck* (1904); *United States v. Wong Kim Ark* (1898); *Webb v. O'Brien* (1923); *White v. Chin Fong* (1920); *Wong Wing v. United States* (1895); *Yamataya Kaoru v. Thomas M. Fisher* (1903). (CGM)

BIBLIOGRAPHY

Hing, Bill Ong. *Making and Remaking Asian Americans through Immigration Policy 1850–1990.* Stanford, CA: Stanford University Press, 1993.

Kaye, Barbara. *America Fever: The Story of American Immigration.* Greenleaf, NY: Four Winds Press, 1970.

Kim, Hyung-chan. *A Legal History of Asian Americans, 1790–1990.* Westport, CT: Greenwood Press, 1994.

Long, Robert Emmet. *Immigration to the United States.* New York: H.W. Wilson, 1992.

McClellan, Grant S. *Immigrants, Refugees, and U.S. Policy.* New York: H.W. Wilson, 1981.

Immigration Restriction Movement

Efforts at restricting immigration of Asian Americans can be divided into two periods: the largely successful efforts of the late nineteenth and early twentieth centuries, and the so-far unsuccessful efforts of the last two decades of the twentieth century. Open racial prejudice drove much of the earlier efforts, and the decline of support for such attitudes has helped to undercut the more recent attempts. This essay will review major developments in the first wave of immigration restrictions (from the mid-nineteenth century to 1924), and then discuss some of the most important elements of the current immigration restriction movement.

Although there were always periodic complaints about immigrants—Benjamin Franklin complained about German immigrants, and the Irish were targets of particularly virulent prejudice in the nineteenth century—immigration remained unrestricted for the first 100 years after independence.

Chinese immigration in the mid-nineteenth century helped spur more vigorous opposition to immigration. Organized labor, recognizing the Chinese as unwelcome competition that depressed wages, led the effort for limitations, but employers successfully opposed their efforts. By 1870, however, with the completion of the Union-Central Pacific Railroad resulting in 10,000 unemployed—that is, unnecessary—Chinese workers, pressures for Chinese exclusion swelled.

This cartoon shows Dennis Kearney in jail for inciting violence at anti-Chinese rallies in the 1880s. *Library of Congress.*

Opposition to the Chinese was at first confined largely to the western United States, but it gradually expanded to the entire country, until Congress passed the Chinese Exclusion Act (**Immigration Act of 1882**), which reduced Chinese immigration to a trickle. In 1904, Congress passed legislation extending Chinese exclusion indefinitely, even as European immigration grew to record levels.

By that time, concern over Asian immigration was increasingly focusing on Japan. Given Japan's growing military power, however, American presidents were hesitant to support openly humiliating immigration policies, and restriction of Japanese immigration was less overt than it had been for the Chinese. In 1907 and 1908, the United States and Japan carried out discussions that culminated in the **Gentlemen's Agreement**, in which Japan agreed to stop issuing passports to laborers seeking to travel to the United States. Apparently not foreseen by many negotiators, however, was the provisions that allowed thousands of current Japanese immigrants to return to Japan and bring back wives, helping the Japanese-American population to increase by more than 100 percent in the next 20 years. Efforts to limit Japanese immigration continued, culminating in the **Immigration Act of 1924**, which barred the immigration of "aliens ineligible for citizenship" and effectively made Japanese and most other Asians ineligible for immigration.

Only Filipinos escaped the restrictions of the 1924 legislation, which ended most Asian immigration for several decades. Filipino immigration continued to grow for another decade, but that too was eventually dramatically reduced by the **Tydings–McDuffie Act of 1934**.

The combination of the Great Depression, **World War II**, and immigration laws effectively ended the need for an immigration restriction movement during the middle of the twentieth century. Changing times, however, led to landmark immigration reform with the passage of the Immigration and Nationality Act of 1965, opening up the way for substantial legal immigration form Latin America, Asia, and Africa. Many reformers appeared to believe that reform of immigration laws would not lead to dramatic changes in the composition of immigration, but the result was very different. The new law gave preference to family members of American residents, and new immigrants found that, in a relatively short time, they could then gain authorization for the immigration of their own family members. Those family members in turn gained authorization for the immigration of other family members, and this "chain migration" helped fuel an enormous surge in immigration from areas that had previously sent relatively few immigrants to the United States.

By the 1980s, the actual number of immigrants had reached levels not seen since the turn of the century, although the relative number of immigrants (i.e., measured as a percentage of the population) was much smaller than during the earlier era of high immigration. This enormous surge of immigration sparked vigorous debate over the wisdom of immigration policy, and a new immigration restriction movement began to gain strength. Public opinion data showed that majorities or pluralities of Americans favored reductions in immigration, but the surveys also suggested that immigration was not an issue that most Americans found to be very important.

In the late 1990s, calls for reducing immigration included economic and cultural arguments. Although both perspectives seek more restrictive immigration laws, they have significant differences and need to be examined separately.

Those motivated by economic concerns (who, for convenience, will be called "economic restrictionists") are often much more moderate in their calls for immigration reductions. In some cases, these restrictionists suggest that significant reduction in immigration may not be necessary, as long as the composition of immigration is changed substantially. Economic restrictionists argue that the current immigration imposes net costs (i.e., the total dollar costs of immigrants exceed the total dollar benefits) on the United States, because large numbers of current immigrants come with few skills and low levels of education. As a result, economic restrictionists argue, the current wave of immigrants will consume more in public services and government benefits than they will pay in taxes.

Not all economic restrictionists take this position, however. Perhaps the most notable economic restrictionist, George Borjas, has found that immigrants may actually make a net contribution to the public treasury, when all factors are considered.

Borjas argues, however, that immigration policy should nevertheless be changed. He contends that the total economic contribution of immigrants represents such a tiny portion of the total national economy that it would not be missed if immigration is significantly reduced, while immigration is harmful to Americans on the bottom of the economic ladder. Although affluent Americans—such as those who employ immigrants as low-paid maids or nannies—receive substantial benefits from immigration, poor Americans lose jobs

because employers opt for immigrants who are willing to work for extremely low wages. Borjas charges that current immigration policy benefits the wealthy at the expense of the poor—often African Americans.

Neither economic restrictionist position necessarily implies a substantial drop in total immigration, however. Borjas and others have suggested that immigration laws be changed to give more preference to those with skills needed in the United States.

Were this approach to be adopted, immigration from Asia would not necessarily decline dramatically. While significant numbers of Asian immigrants do come with few skills and little or no education, many others come with advanced degrees and training. The composition of Asian immigration would be altered somewhat, but, unlike immigration from Latin America, overall levels might not be substantially reduced.

While many economic restrictionists stress that they seek a color-blind immigration policy, those motivated by cultural concerns (who, for convenience, will be called "cultural restrictionists") take a very different approach. Although cultural restrictionists often cite the arguments of economic restrictionists, cultural restrictionists are most concerned about the social and cultural impact of immigration. Cultural restrictionists believe that non-European immigrants will be unable to adapt to American society and will instead push drastic and undesirable change onto American society. Some cultural restrictionists doubt that such change will occur, but they believe that the result will be bitter fighting between different ethnic and racial groups. These restrictionists believe that, one way or another, high levels of non-European immigration will destabilize America.

The cultural restrictionist argument is directly contradicted by the experiences of long-established Asian Americans (primarily Japanese Americans and some Chinese Americans). Although prejudice and discrimination continues, long-resident Asian-American families have integrated successfully and are often now held up as role models for other immigrants. While most Asian Americans are recent immigrants or the children of immigrants—and so are still in the process of acculturation—available evidence suggests that they too are adjusting well to their new country.

Partly because of the success of acculturation, the immigration restriction movement has had limited success as of 1997. Although there is widespread support for greater limits on welfare benefits for immigrants (most immigrants were already unable to qualify for the range of benefits available to citizens), reductions in immigration meets with more resistance. Many Americans appear to support immigration reductions, but there is relatively little elite support for the cultural restrictionist view that those not of European ancestry are unlikely to become good Americans.

Cultural restrictionist claims have repeatedly been contradicted by the evidence. Despite dire warnings about the impact of Irish, Italian, Greek, and other immigrants—each of whom, when they represented the newest group of immigrants, were seen as racially different from the majority of Americans—all of these national groups were able to adapt well to this country. Cultural restrictionists warn that the situation is different this time, because the numbers are greater, but in fact immigrants make up a much smaller percentage of the population than they did in the early twentieth century, and in the 1980s and 1990s immigrants seemed to be acculturating faster than earlier generations did.

Economic restrictionists have more support, but their claims are not undisputed. Perhaps most important, the relevant data are not very good. No definitive analysis can be made of the economic impact of immigration, because the necessary information is not available or is unreliable. Given this, it is not surprising that other analysts have concluded that immigration is not causing undue harm to poor Americans, and that immigrants provide a substantial economic benefit to the country.

The immigration restriction movement will undoubtedly continue to attract supporters as long as immigration levels remain high, and Asian Americans will continue to play a central role in the controversy. Changes in immigration policy will not come easily, but they are not out of the question. However, by the end of the twentieth century, few political leaders had been swayed by the most dire warnings of advocates of immigration restriction. **See also** Asian-American Relations with Other Minorities; Asiatic Exclusion League; Burlingame Treaty (1868); Chinese Boycott of 1905; Citizens Committee to Repeal Chinese Exclusion; Displaced Persons Act of 1948; Fiancees Act of 1946; General Deficiency Appropriation Account Act of 1904; Immigration Act of 1882; Immigration Act of 1907; Immigration Act of 1924; Immigration Act of 1943 (Magnuson Act); Immigration and Nationality Act of 1952; Immigration and Nationality Act of 1965; Immigration and Nationality Act of 1990; Immigration Restriction Movement; Quota Immigration Act of 1921; Refugee Act of 1980; War Brides Act of 1945.

See "Disgraceful Persecution of a Boy" by Mark Twain (1870); "A Letter on Chinese Immigration" by John Stuart Mill (1869); and Irwin Convention (1885) in Appendix 1.

See individual immigration cases: *Berger v. Bishop* (1903); *Chae Chan Pin v. United States* (1889); *Chang Chan v. John D. Nagle* (1925); *Cheung Sum Shee et al. v. Nagle, Commissioner of Immigration for the Port of San Francisco* (1924); *Chew Heong v. United States* (1884); *Chin Bak Lan v. United States* (1902); *Chin Yow v. United States* (1907); *Chy Lung v. Freeman* (1876); *Fong Yue Ting v. United States* (1893); *In Re Ah Fong* (1874); *In Re Look Tin Sing* (1884); *Kawakita Tomoya v. United States* (1952); *Kimm v. Rosenberg* (1959); *Kwock Jan Fat v. White, Commissioner of Immigration* (1920); *Lee Kum Hoy, Lee Kum Cherk, and Lee Moon Wah v. John L. Murff* (1957); *Lem Moon Sing v. United States* (1895); *Li Sung v. United States* (1900); *Ng Fung Ho et al. v. White, Commissioner of Immigration* (1917); *Nishimura v. United States* (1892); *Nishikawa v. Dulles* (1958); *Okimura Kiyokura v.*
Acheson, Secretary of State (1952); *Quon Quon Poy v. Johnson* (1926); *Roque Espiritu de la Ysla v. United States* (1935); *Takao Ozawa v. United States* (1922); *Tang Tun v. Harry Edsell* (1906); *United States v. Ju Toy* (1905); *United States v. Jung Ah Lung* (1888); *United States v. Sakharam Ganesh Pandit* (1926); *United States v. Sing Tuck* (1904); *United States v. Wong Kim Ark* (1898); *Webb v. O'Brien* (1923); *White v. Chin Fong* (1920); *Wong Wing v. United States* (1895); *Yamataya Kaoru v. Thomas M. Fisher* (1903). (ALA)

BIBLIOGRAPHY

Beck, Roy. *The Case against Immigration: The Moral, Economic, Social, and Environmental Reasons for Reducing Immigration Back to Traditional Levels*. New York: W.W. Norton, 1996.

Borjas, George. *Friends or Strangers: The Impact of Immigrants on the U.S. Economy*. New York: Basic Books, 1990.

———. "Know the Flow." *National Review* (April 17, 1995): 44–51.

Briggs, Vernon M., Jr. *Mass Immigration and the National Interest*. Armonk, NY: M.E. Sharpe, 1992.

Brimelow, Peter. 1995. *Alien Nation: Common Sense about America's Immigration Disaster*. New York: Random House, 1995.

Chan, Sucheng. *Asian Americans: An Interpretive History*. New York: Twayne, 1991.

Hing, Bill Ong. *Making and Remaking Asian Americans through Immigration Policy, 1850–1990*. Stanford, CA: Stanford University Press, 1993.

Simon, Julian. *The Economic Consequences of Immigration*. Cambridge: Basil Blackwell, 1989.

Simon, Rita J. "Old Minorities, New Immigrants: Aspirations, Hopes, and Fears." *Annals of the American Academy of Political and Social Science* 530 (November 1993): 61–73.

Williamson, Chilton, Jr. *The Immigration Mystique: America's False Consciousness*. New York: Basic Books, 1996.

In Re Ah Chong (1880)

In Re Ah Chong, 2 F 733 (1880), involved a Chinese man, Ah Chong, who was arrested for fishing off the coast of California and selling his catch. He was found guilty of violating an 1880 California law that prohibited foreigners from fishing in California waters and from selling fish caught in California waters. Ah Chong appealed on the grounds that his imprisonment was in violation of the **Burlingame Treaty** of 1868 and of his Fourteenth Amendment rights. The United States Circuit Court ruled that the California law prohibiting aliens from fishing was a violation of the Fourteenth Amendment to the U.S. Constitution. **See also** Burlingame Treaty in Appendix 1.

BIBLIOGRAPHY

Sandmeyer, Elmer C. "California Anti-Chinese Legislation and the Federal Courts: A Study in Federal Relations." *Pacific Historical Review* 5, no. 3 (1936): 189–211.

Sawyer, L.S.B. *Reports of Cases Decided in the Circuit and District Courts of the United States for the Ninth Circuit*. San Francisco: A.L. Bancroft, 1882.

In Re Ah Fong (1874)

On August 24, 1873, a group of 21 Chinese women arrived in San Francisco and were detained by the commissioner of immigration, who sought to expel them from the United States.

The case was brought to court, on a writ of habeas corpus, in order to gain the release of the women who were being held against their will. The petition was filed jointly by the Pacific Mail Steamship Company, which owned the boat on which they had sailed, and a Chinese woman who was representing the other females. The commissioner of immigration argued that he had acted within the law, and stated that a 1870 California state law allowed for the removal of immigrants who were lewd, idiotic, deaf, dumb, crippled, or otherwise unable to support themselves. The women's case was not successful the first time, so another writ of habeas corpus was filed. *In Re Ah Fong,* IF Cas 213 (1874), was heard by the U.S. Court of Appeals, which ruled that the state statute on which the commissioner had based his claims violated the **Burlingame Treaty** of 1868, as well as the Fourteenth Amendment to the U.S. Constitution and the Civil Rights Act of 1870. As a result, all 21 women were released, except one whose case was later heard by the Supreme Court in *Chy Lung v. Freeman* **(1876).**

BIBLIOGRAPHY

McClain, Charles. *In Search of Equality.* Berkeley: University of California Press, 1994.

In Re Look Tin Sing (1884)

The case *In Re Look Tin Sing,* 21 Fed 905 (1884), was a habeas corpus claim made on behalf of Look Tin Sing. Look had been born in Mendocino, California; at the age of nine he was sent to China by his father to receive an education. When Look returned to the United States five years later in 1882, he was denied entry. His denial of entry was based upon the first Exclusion Act (**Immigration Act of 1882**), which prevented Chinese from becoming citizens through naturalization. However, his parents argued that Look Tin Singwas a citizen of the United States as defined by the Fourteenth Amendment, which states in part that "all persons born or naturalized in the United States, and subject to its jurisdiction thereof, are citizens of the United States." The trial judge and the court of appeals agreed with Look's' position that he was a citizen.

BIBLIOGRAPHY

McClain, Charles J. *In Search of Equality.* Berkeley: University of California Press, 1994.

In Re Tiburcio Parrott (1880)

In 1879 the California legislature passed a law stating that it was illegal for any company to employ Chinese workers. Tiburcio Parrott was the president and director of the Sulphur Quicksilver Mining Company; he was arrested soon after section 2 of Article XIX was passed. He sued, stating that the law was unconstitutional and violated the **Burlingame Treaty.** *In Re Tiburcio Parrott,* IF 481 (1880), made it to the circuit court in Washington, D.C., which declared the law unconstitutional.

BIBLIOGRAPHY

Sawyer, L.S.B. *Reports of Cases Decided in the Circuit and District Courts of the United States for the Ninth Circuit.* San Francisco: A.L. Bancroft and Company, 1882, pp. 349–389.

Indochina Migration and Refugee Assistance Act of 1975

The Indochina Migration and Refugee Assistance Act of 1975 was intended to update the Migration and Refugee Assistance Act of 1962. The government broadened the term "refugee," which had previously only applied to those persons fleeing from persecution because of race, color, religion, or political beliefs. The 1975 act also included people emigrating from Vietnam, Laos, and Cambodia, and appropriated $455 million in order to help with the resettlement costs for Indochinese refugees in the United States. However, these funds were discontinued in 1977.

The 1975 act continued the 1962 act's stipulation that the president hold a membership in the Intergovernmental Committee for European Migration, and that the United States assist in the movement of refugees and provide developing nations with money and manpower. The 1975 act also approved funding for this committee, for the High Commissioner of the United Nations for Refugee Assistance, and for particular refugee groups when the need arose and when such assistance was congruent with U.S. security interests.

BIBLIOGRAPHY

Kitano, Harry H.L. and Roger Daniels. *Asian Americans: Emerging Minorities.* Englewood Cliffs, NJ: Prentice Hall, 1988.

Daniel Inouye (1924–)

After serving in **World War II**, Daniel Inouye returned to Hawaii where he finished college at the University of Hawaii. He then went on to receive his law degree at George Washington University in 1952. He returned to Hawaii and worked in private practice for several years before being elected to the territorial house of representatives. He served three terms and was elected to the territorial senate. In 1959 Hawaii became the 50th state and Inouye was soon elected to the U.S. House of Representatives. In 1962 he became a U.S. senator. He followed the policies of John F. Kennedy and Lyndon Johnson and was a civil rights supporter. He went on to serve on the Watergate Committee and was the first congressman to call for President Richard Nixon's resignation. He has worked to advance Asian-American causes and was the cosponsor of the **Commission on Wartime Relocation and Internment of Civilians**. He was instrumental in the **redress movement**, which gave compensation to all Japanese Americans who had been interned during World War II. **See also** Civil Liberties Act of 1988.

BIBLIOGRAPHY

Hosokawa, Bill. *JACL, In Quest of Justice.* New York: William Morrow, 1982.
Inouye, Daniel and Lawrence Elliot. *Journey to Washington.* Englewood Cliffs, NJ: Prentice-Hall, 1967.

Inouye Yuichi et al. v. Clark (1947)

Many Japanese Americans who were evacuated from their homes and taken to **internment camps/relocation centers** during **World War II** were asked to renounce their American citizenship, or to renounce their allegiance to the Emperor of Japan. Inouye and three others had renounced their citizenship. In *Inouye Yuichi et al. v. Clark,* 73 F. Supp. 1000 (1947), this action was deemed illegal by the Circuit Court, and Yuichi had his citizenship restored.

BIBLIOGRAPHY
Chuman, Frank F. *The Bamboo People: The Law and Japanese-Americans.* Del Mar, CA: Publisher's Inc., 1976.

Internment Camps/Relocation Centers

In 1942 **Executive Order 9066** gave the secretary of war the power to begin designating areas as relocation centers or internment camps, and organizing the evacuation of all persons of Japanese American descent from the West Coast. A civilian agency, the **War Relocation Authority** (WRA), administered the evacuation program, and ran the 10 concentration camps, called "projects," located in Arkansas, Arizona, California, Colorado, Idaho, Wyoming, and Utah. Each camp held between 8,000 and 20,000 Japanese Americans; the people lived in makeshift barracks and ate in large mess halls or cooked over potbellied stoves in their cabins. Many people lost all their possessions during the evacuation, which they either sold quickly for little money or gave to white neighbors to keep. **See also** Civilian Exclusion Orders; Commission on Wartime Relocation and Internment of Civilians; Executive Order 9102; Japanese American Evacuation and Settlement Study; Japanese American Evacuation Claims Act of 1948; Loyalty Oath/Test; Poston Strike; Public Law 503; Redress Movement; War Agency Liquidation Division. **See** specific internment and exclusion order cases: *Ex Parte Endo* (1944); *Hirabayashi v. United States* (1943); *Inouye Yuichi et al. v. Clark* (1947); *Korematsu v. United States* (1943); *Minoru Yasui v. United States* (1943). **See** Civil Liberties Act (1988) and Executive Order 9066 in Appendix 1.

BIBLIOGRAPHY
Baker, Lillian. *The Concentration Camp Conspiracy: A Second Pearl Harbor.* Lawndale, CA: AFHA Publication, 1981.
Spicer, Edward T. et al. *Impounded People.* Tucson: University of Arizona Press, 1968.

J

Japanese American Citizens League (JACL)

The Japanese American Citizens League (JACL) has been a leading organization fighting for equal rights for Japanese Americans. Attracting controversy and criticism—often from Japanese Americans—throughout his history, JACL probably faced its most critical challenges during **World War II.**

Growing out of efforts beginning in 1918, JACL had its first national meeting in Seattle in 1930. In its early years, JACL worked to overturn laws that hampered or prevented Japanese-American citizenship.

The attack on **Pearl Harbor** forever changed Japanese Americans and JACL. The Federal Bureau of Investigation interrogated and detained scores of *issei* (first-generation Japanese Americans) community leaders, and JACL—headed by *nisei* (second generation)—was often the only functioning organization left in many Japanese-American communities.

After the order for the evacuation of Japanese Americans from the West Coast, JACL held an emergency meeting at which they made the fateful decision to comply with the order. The league's decision was controversial then and still is today, although it is difficult to see how opposition would not have been counterproductive, given the tremendous racism facing Japanese Americans at the time.

For individual members of JACL, another monumental decision came a few months later, in November 1942, when **Mike Masaru Masaoka** convinced JACL delegates to push for the right for Japanese-American citizens to serve in the military, as they had been able to do before the attack on Pearl Harbor. When the delegates returned to their internment camps and relocation centers, some were physically attacked, and JACL's policy of cooperation with the authorities contributed to a plunge in membership.

After the war, JACL membership rebounded vigorously, and the organization continued its work against discriminatory laws. During the 1960s and 1970s, there were further challenges to JACL's dominance, as the *sansei* (third-generation Japanese Americans) began to reach adulthood and challenged their *nisei* elders for leadership, sometimes echoing the World War II criticisms that JACL was too conservative. JACL has also managed to weather this storm, and it and its newspaper (*Pacific Citizen*) seem to have become institutions in most Japanese-American communities. **See also** 442nd Regimental Combat Team; Dennis Hayashi; Paul M. Igasaki; Internment Camps/Relocation Centers; Japanese-American Creed; Japanese Americans; Lillian Chiyeko Kimura; National Committee for Redress; Proposition 13; Redress Movement; Masao Satow. (ALA)

BIBLIOGRAPHY

Chuman, Frank F. *The Bamboo People: The Law and Japanese-Americans.* Del Mar, CA: Publisher's Inc., 1976.

Daniels, Roger. *Asian American: Chinese and Japanese in the United States Since 1850.* Seattle and London: University of Washington Press, 1988.

Hosokawa, Bill. *JACL In Quest of Justice: The History of the Japanese American Citizens League.* New York: William Morrow, 1982.

Japanese-American Creed

The Japanese American Creed was written in 1940 by **Mike Masaru Masaoko** of the **Japanese American Citizens League** as a statement of loyalty to the United States. The creed pledged that Asian Americans would uphold the ideals of American democracy and freedom as well as the ideals of fair and equal treatment for all people. Masaoko and others hoped the document would help quiet fears and anti-Asian sentiment caused by Japanese involvement in **World War II**.

On May 9, 1941, the Japanese-American creed was officially documented in the *Congressional Record.* The creed pointed out several cases in which U.S. citizenship created a sense of national pride among Asian immigrants, who had gained liberties and opportunity through citizenship. The document also mentioned the need for tolerance and acceptance from the American people, and the need to overcome all forms of discrimination.

BIBLIOGRAPHY

Girdner, Audrie and Ann Loftis. *The Great Betrayal: Evacuation of the Japanese-Americans During World War II.* New York: Macmillan, 1969.

tenBroek, Jacobus, Edward N. Barnhart, and Floyd W. Matson. *Prejudice, War, and the Constitution.* Berkeley: University of California Press, 1970.

Japanese-American Evacuation and Settlement Study

The Japanese American Evacuation and Resettlement Study was conducted by the University of California at Berkeley to study the sociological implications of the evacuation and internment during **World War II** on Japanese Americans. The project began in the spring of 1942 under the guidance of sociologist Dorothy Swaine Thomas, who recruited students and professors to help her conduct interviews and compile data on former evacuation camp internees. The group worked closely with the **War Relocation Authority,** the agency that had been responsible for rounding up Asian Americans living on the West Coast, and for relocating them to **internment camps**.

In 1943, the group established an office in Chicago to track former Japanese-American internees living in Midwestern and Eastern cities. While conducting interviews, some of the researchers came under threat by former internees who questioned the researcher's intentions and targeted them as government informants. In spite of this danger, researchers continued to gather data until the mid 1940s.

The study helped provide an overall view of the harsh conditions inside the relocation camps, as well as the physical, psychological, social, and economic impact on the internees. The first publication from the research appeared in 1946 as *The Spoilage*. It concentrated on the camp experiences at Tule Lake, California. Another book, *The Salvage* was published in 1952, which described those former internees who had settled in the Midwest. Other books based on this research include *Americans Betrayed: Politics and the Japanese Evacuation,* which analyzed the legal, political, and business implications of the relocation, and *Prejudice, War, and the Constitution*. A number of the journals, diaries, reports, and other documents from the study were deposited in the archive of the Bancroft Library at the University of California, Berkeley.

BIBLIOGRAPHY

Girdner, Audrie and Ann Loftis. *The Great Betrayal: Evacuation of the Japanese-Americans During World War II*. New York: Macmillan, 1969.

tenBroek, Jacobus, Edward N. Barnhart and Floyd W. Matson. *Prejudice, War, and the Constitution*. Berkeley: University of California Press, 1970.

Japanese American Evacuation Claims Act

(1948)

The Japanese American Evacuation Claims Act, signed by President Harry Truman in 1948, allowed Japanese Americans who had lost property while in **internment camps** during **World War II** to be compensated for their losses. The **Japanese American Citizens League** had urged its members to demand compensation for the property they had been forced to abandon after **Executive Order 9066** was signed. Harold Ickes, the United States secretary of the interior, worked on behalf of an evacuation claims bill to present to Congress and then to the president. Once the act was signed, however, the process moved slowly and proving claims was initially very costly to the United States government. In 1951 the bill was amended slightly to allow the U.S. attorney general to settle

claims up to $2,500 immediately. However, Japanese Americans were paid the 1941 value of their houses; in addition, most of the elderly Japanese claimants accepted a low monetary settlement because they did not want to engage in a lengthy suit with the government. In 1956 President Dwight Eisenhower amended the bill again, in order to expedite the settlement of claims of Japanese-owned businesses, some of which had been confiscated from Japanese Americans under the Trading with the Enemy Act. **See also** Commission on Wartime Relocation and Internment of Civilians; Redress Movement; War Relocation Authority. **See** Executive Order 9066 in Appendix 1.

BIBLIOGRAPHY

Girdner, Audrie and Anne Loftis. *The Great Betrayal: Evacuation of the Japanese-Americans During World War II*. New York: Macmillan, 1969.

Hosokawa, Bill. *JACL In Quest of Justice: The History of the Japanese American Citizens League*. New York: William Morrow, 1982.

Japanese American Research Project

In 1960 Wakamatsu Shigeo, president of the **Japanese American Citizen League** (JACL), put forth the idea of surveying and collecting oral histories, documents, and memorabilia from first-generation (*issei*) and second-generation (*nisei*) Japanese Americans, in order to compile a history of this ethnic group. The goals were outlined at the 1962 JACL convention, and members donated money to the project, which later became known as the Japanese American Research Project. Some of the money was donated to UCLA, which cosponsored the project, and grant money was raised from the Carnegie Corporation and the National Institute of Mental Health. Several important books on Japanese-American culture have been published as a result of the project. **See also** Japanese Americans.

BIBLIOGRAPHY

Radin, Charles A. "Study Disputes Popular View on Bomb, Cancer." *The Boston Globe* (October 14, 1995): D2.

Japanese Americans

The Japanese-American story is one of devoted workers becoming full citizens in a formerly hostile land.

Following Commodore Matthew Perry's opening of Japan to the West in 1853, Japanese began to come to North America, although in far lower numbers than the Chinese. These first adventurers included students, merchants, and agricultural workers; the number of such immigrants increased in the 1890s. The U.S. **annexation of Hawaii** in 1898 made the 60,000 Japanese there (mostly agricultural workers) eligible to enter the United States. The immigrants settled chiefly in California and other western states.

Under U.S. law and Japanese practice the immigrants could not be naturalized, and they were subject to discriminatory practices and laws, somewhat mitigated by the Fourteenth Amendment. In 1906, to avoid an international crisis,

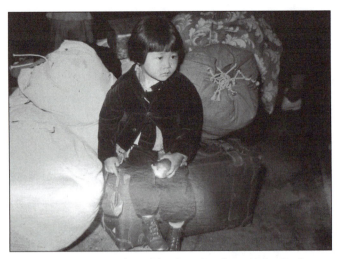

In 1942, a Japanese-American girl waits to be taken with her family to a relocation camp. *National Archives.*

President Theodore Roosevelt intervened when Asian schoolchildren were denied the right to attend San Francisco public schools. Roosevelt's **Gentlemen's Agreement** of 1907 with Japan restricted Japanese immigration and facilitated the return of settlers. But the arrival of "picture brides" transformed the mostly male population; the adventurers became family men and settlers, in self-contained communities. The **Immigration Act of 1924** set quotas on immigration to the United States and absolutely prohibited immigration from Asia.

Subsequently, tensions grew between the generations, with the older *issei* (first generation) pitted against the Americanizing *nisei* (second generation). Some parents sent their children to Japan for education in the Japanese heritage (*kibei*). The *nisei* **Japanese American Citizens League** emphasized the devotion of its membership to America. Japanese success, especially in California agriculture, provoked resentment, and Japan's brutal imperialism of the 1930s inspired fear. The growing Americanization of Japanese Americans was put to the ultimate test by Japan's attack on **Pearl Harbor**, resulting in the relocation of 110,000 Japanese—two-thirds of whom were American citizens—into **internment camps** during **World War II.**

The postwar Japanese Americans made the best of their situation, building on the Japanese virtues of *gaman* (perseverance) and *enryo* (self-denial). Most Japanese returned to the West Coast, often encountering discriminatory laws, which were gradually repealed. The **Japanese American Evacuation Claims Act of 1948** provided some compensation for losses incurred by the relocation. The McCarran–Walter **Immigration and Nationality Act of 1952** permitted naturalization of Japanese immigrants.

From their agricultural and small business roots, Japanese Americans have flourished to make their mark in all the professions, from architect to astronaut, from actor to economist. Defying stereotyping as the "**model minority**" or the "quiet Americans" (in the subtitle of Bill Hosokawa's 1969 history, *Nisei*), Japanese Americans are an ethnic minority whose diversity makes it even smaller as a group. Of the 10 million Asian Americans in the 1990 census, Japanese numbered 850,000, while in 1960 they had represented 52 percent of the total Asian population. The high intermarriage rate exceeds 50 percent in some metropolitan areas.

The Japanese have become more politically active, tending to vote Democratic (unlike most other Asian Americans), especially in Hawaii, which has been represented by Japanese Americans such as Senator **Daniel Inouye** and Congresswoman **Patricia Saiki**. Even the formerly anti-Asian state of California elected semanticist and university president **S.I. Hayakawa** to the U.S. Senate (1972–1982) as a Republican.

The civil rights activism of the 1960s encouraged many in this younger generation (the *yonsei*) to become more politically involved. This activism led to the redress law (**Civil Liberties Act of 1988**) signed by President Ronald Reagan, which apologized for the World War II relocation and made payments of $20,000 to Japanese who had been relocated and interned.

Will Japanese Americans look to their ancestral culture or to their identity as citizens? The same question arises in their attitude toward race and ethnic preferences, which aids minority-owned small businesses but definitely harms Asians in university admissions. The Japanese-American ambivalence on racial preferences reflects the ambivalence of America on these questions. **See also** Asian-American Relations with Other Minorities; Commission on Wartime Relocation and Internment of Civilians; Political Participation. (KM)

BIBLIOGRAPHY

Hiraoka, Leona and Ken Masugi. *Japanese-American Internment: The Bill of Rights in Crisis.* Amawalk, NY: Golden Owl, 1994.

Stephan, John J. *Hawaii Under the Rising Sun: Japan's Plans for Conquest After Pearl Harbor.* Honolulu: University of Hawaii, 1984.

Wilson, Robert A. and Bill Hosokawa. *East to America: A History of the Japanese in the United States.* New York: William Morrow, 1980.

Japanese Exclusion League of California

The Japanese Exclusion League of California was a group formed in San Francisco to prevent Japanese immigration and to support the **California Alien Land Act of 1913**, which prohibited aliens from owning land. State Senator J.M. Inman was president of the organization, which was organized in 1920 and formally disbanded in 1924, after the Japanese Exclusion Act was passed.

BIBLIOGRAPHY

Daniels, Roger. *The Politics of Prejudice.* Berkeley, CA: University of California Press, 1962.

Jones Act of 1916/Philippine Autonomy Act of 1916

The Jones Act (also known as the Jones Law of 1916 in Philippine history books) was the United States government's announcement of its intention to create an autonomous and independent Philippines. The preamble declared that independence would be granted to the Filipino people as soon as a stable government was established in the country. Executive power was given to an American governor-general. Legislative power was exercised by a bicameral Philippine legislature, and judicial power was vested upon the U.S. Supreme Court and lower courts.

The Jones Act provided for a bill of rights that safeguarded the rights and liberties of the people such as freedom of religion, speech, and the press, and the right to life, liberty, and the pursuit of happiness. Also it was recognized that voting rights would be extended to the Filipinos, and that this bill of rights would be incorporated in whatever constitution they eventually drew up for themselves.

Prior to this law, the Philippines was ruled by the United States through the **Philippine Commission**, a legislative body dominated by Americans. The Jones Act would replace the commission with a Senate elected by the people. The act would remain in force as the country's de facto constitution until 1934 when it was superseded by the **Tydings-McDuffie Act.** (CGM)

BIBLIOGRAPHY

Zaide, Gregorio F. and Sonia F. Zaide. *History of the Republic of the Philippines.* Manila: National Book Store, 1987.

Jordan v. Tashiro (1928)

In *Jordan v. Tashiro,* 278 U.S. 123 (1928), the state of California tried to prevent a group of Japanese from forming a corporation under which it sought to run the Japanese Hospital of Los Angeles. The state argued that California law prevented them from forming a corporation for these purposes because they were not commercial in nature. The U.S. Supreme Court, however, decided that the treaty provisions with Japan when interpreted liberally did apply to any commercial ventures, including the formation of a corporation. Therefore, the California alien land laws did not apply to the corporation. The Court's opinion upheld the opinion of the California Supreme Court.

BIBLIOGRAPHY

Kim, Hyung-Chan, ed. *Asian Americans and the Supreme Court: A Documentary History.* New York: Greenwood Press, 1992.

Konvitz, Milton R. *The Aliens and the Asiatic in American Law.* Ithaca, NY: Cornell University Press, 1946.

Mubarak Ali Khan

In 1937, Mubarak Ali Khan founded the India Welfare League, which assisted unemployed Asian Indians in the United States and fought for naturalization rights. During the 1940s, Khan engaged in public speaking endeavors in Arizona, Washington, D.C., and New York in order to support Asian-American civil rights. In 1946, after the passage of the Luce-Celler Bill, Khan helped create the Pakistan Welfare League of America to support Muslims in their desires to support Pakistan as a separate nation apart from British colonial territory rule. In 1949, Khan worked with Pakistan's ambassador M.A.H. Ispahani in bettering relations between Asian Indians and Americans.

BIBLIOGRAPHY

Melendy, H. Brett. *Asians in America.* Boston: Twayne, 1977.

Saburo Kido (1902–1977)

Born in Hawaii, Saburo Kido received his law degree in 1926. He practiced law in San Francisco, and in 1930 he became a founding member of the **Japanese American Citizens League (JACL)**. Ten years later, he was elected president of the league. When **World War II** broke out, Kido used his position to try to persuade Japanese Americans to comply with the U.S. government. After the war, he worked successfully to reestablish JACL.

BIBLIOGRAPHY

Hosokawa, Bill. *JACL, In Quest of Justice.* New York: William Morrow and Co., 1982.

Haan Kilsoo

Haan Kilsoo was the leader of the **Sino-Korean People''s League**, which was formed to help the Korean people against the Japanese and to encourage anti-Japanese action in America. The league was organized in Hawaii during **World War II,** and Kilso agitated against Japanese Americans in California and Hawaii.

BIBLIOGRAPHY

Takaki, Ronald. *Strangers from a Different Shore.* Boston: Little Brown and Company.

Elaine H. Kim (1942–)

Eliane Kim, born in New York, is a professor of Asian American Studies at the University of California at Berkeley. She has been a leading national activist and writer in national newspapers and magazines. She was the project director of the Asian Women United of California Project on Asian Women's Education and Employment for the U.S. Department of Education. She has also worked in various ways for the Korean Community Center of the East Bay.

BIBLIOGRAPHY

Kim, Elaine H. "Creating a Third Space." *San Francisco Bay Guardian* (March 10, 1993).

Jay C. Kim (1939–)

Jay C. Kim was elected the nation's first Korean-born congressman in 1992. Prior to this, he was the mayor of Diamond Bar, California, following his election too the city council in 1990. In July 1997, the third-term representative and former owner of a highly successful engineering design firm shocked many constituents when he pleaded guilty to campaign finance violations after a four-year investigation. (PL)

BIBLIOGRAPHY

Eljera, Bert. "Kim Pleads Guilty to Illegal Donations." *Asianweek* (August 8, 1997): 8–9.

Kimm v. Rosenberg (1959)

In 1928 Diamond Kimm left Korea to study in the United States. During his stay in the United States, the Sino-Korean war broke out, so Kimm decided to remain in the United States and find a job. The immigration authorities ordered that he be deported, because his visa was only for the duration of his studies, which he had completed by then. Kimm challenged the immigration authorities and took the matter to court, thinking he could win the case by proving his good character and ethics.

In court, Kimm was asked about his possible communist affiliation; he responded by taking the Fifth Amendment and stating that his past political ties should have little to do with his current desires. Due to this, the court found little evidence to support Kimm's good character and declared he was to be deported. Kimm's lawyers appealed stating that the burden of proof had been placed too heavily on their client and furthermore that his Fifth Amendment rights had been violated. In *Kimm v. Rosenberg,* 363 U.S. 405 (1959), the appeals court overturned the lower court's ruling by a majority.

BIBLIOGRAPHY

Choy, Bong-youn. *Koreans in America.* Chicago: Nelson-Hall, 1979.
Lee, Chong-sik. *The Politics of Korean Nationalism.* Berkeley: University of California Press, 1965.

Lillian Chiyeko Kimura (1929–)

Lillian Kimura, born in California, became the first national woman president of the **Japanese American Citizens League** in 1992. She has received the prestigious order of the Precious Crown, Wisteria, for her work in promoting relations between the United States and Japan. She has served as the associate national executive director of the Young Women's Christian Association (YWCA) for five years. Preceding this, she was the executive of the field services unit of the YWCA. In 1973, she was the first woman to serve as president of the Japanese American Service Committee.

BIBLIOGRAPHY

Clifford, Timothy. "D'Amato on Japan's Greed." *Newsday* (September 11, 1990): 4.
McKenna, Sheila. "Manhattan Profile/Lillian Kimura." *Newsday* (July 1, 1992): 22.

Jean Sadako King (1925–)

Jean Sadako King is the daughter of a Caucasian father and a Japanese mother. She was elected to the Hawaii house of representatives in 1972 and to the state senate from 1974 to 1978; she was elected lieutenant governor in 1978. Defeated as a candidate for governor in the Democratic Party primary in 1982 (when she ran as "Jean King," rather than "Jean Sadako King" as in previous contests), she thereafter retired from politics. While in office, she championed affordable housing, environmental pollution, and sunshine laws. (MH)

BIBLIOGRAPHY

Ronck, Ronn. "Jean King." *Honolulu Advertiser* (August 16, 1979): B1, B4.

Kiyokura Okimura v. Acheson, Secretary of State (1952)

Kiyokura Okimura v. Acheson, Secretary of State, 342 U.S. 899 (1952), involved an American-born Japanese man, Okimura Kiyokura, who had his U.S. citizenship revoked because he served in the Japanese Army during **World War II** and had voted in a Japanese election. Okimura was born in Hawaii in 1921 and was sent to study in Japan (this was a common practice among Japanese-American families). In 1942, after he had started teaching in a Japanese school, he was drafted into the Japanese Army, despite his protest that he was a U.S. citizen. After the war, Okimura stayed in Japan and trained to be a Buddhist monk; he also voted in a local election there. In 1949 he was refused permission to return to the United States; he was told that he had relinquished his

citizenship by serving in the Japanese Army and voting in a Japanese election. However, the district court ruled that it was unconstitutional for the U.S. government to revoke Okimura's citizenship. The case was appealed to the Supreme Court, which upheld the district court ruling.

BIBLIOGRAPHY

Chuman, Frank F. *The Bamboo People: The Law and Japanese-Americans.* Del Mar, CA: Publisher's Inc., 1976.

Kiyoshi Okamoto v. United States (1945)

Okamoto Kiyoshi was the organizer of an antidraft movement at the Heart Mountain (Wyoming) **internment camp**. The group, called the **Fair Play Committee**, held meetings and published bulletins, arguing that the draft violated their constitutional rights. Several members of the group were sent to a segregation camp and in 1944, the seven leaders of the committee, including Okamoto, were arrested, tried, and sentenced to four years in Fort Leavenworth Federal Prison. In *Okamoto Kiyoshi v. United States,* 152 F2d 905 (1945), the Federal Circuit Court of Appeals reversed the decision on a technicality, and President Harry Truman later pardoned the resisters.

BIBLIOGRAPHY

Chuman, Frank F. *The Bamboo People: The Law and Japanese-Americans.* Del Mar, CA: Publisher's Inc., 1976.

Kongnip Hyop-Hoe

Kongnip Hyop-Hoe, a **mutual assistance society**, was formed in California by Korean immigrants in 1905. The group published a newspaper in Korean. In 1909 the society decided to join with the Hanin Hapsong Hyophoe (United Korean Society) of Hawaii to form the **Korean National Association (KNA)**. All Korean immigrants were urged to join and pay membership dues. KNA worked to establish Korean independence and provided social services for its members. The association established Korean language schools, offered welfare assistance, and aided Koreans in the United States to better themselves economically and intellectually.

BIBLIOGRAPHY

Mangiafico, Luciano. *Contemporary American Immigrants.* New York: Praeger, 1988.

Koreagate

"Koreagate" came to the attention of the American people in October 1976. The scandal was about whether the South Korean government had financially rewarded policy voting in Congress. The level of suspicion had risen after the lucrative trade of rice between the United States and South Korea. A central figure of the scandal was Park Tong Sun, a Korean resident of Washington, D.C. He was surrounded with accusations that he bribed Congressmen on behalf of South Korea. Another person who was covered with allegations was a Korean-American staffer in the office of house speaker Carl Albert. The staffer was accused of supplying confidential information to the Korean Central Intelligence Agency. Neither person was successfully prosecuted, but Richard Hanna, an

American Congressman of California, was convicted and sentenced for bribery. The situation was coined "Koreagate" after President Nixon's scandal "Watergate." The scandal damaged South Korea's image in the United States and hurt diplomatic relations between the two countries.

BIBLIOGRAPHY
Deming, Angus. "Inside South Korea's CIA." *Newsweek* (November 5, 1979): 62.
Holt, Don, Elaine Shannon, and Henry W. Hubbard. "The Cloud is Lifting." *Newsweek* (April 17, 1978): 49.

Korean American Coalition

The Korean American Coalition was founded in 1983 to serve as an advocacy group for Korean Americans. The coalition is a nonprofit, nonpartisan organization that promotes the advance of Korean Americans in the civic and political worlds. The organization also serves as a means of communication among the ethnic communities of Los Angeles. The organization runs voter education programs as well.

BIBLIOGRAPHY
Doherty, Jake. "Koreatown; Grant Helps Coalition Serve Community." *Los Angeles Times* (October 24, 1993): 9.
Kang, K. Connie. "Voter Registration Crosses Cultural Lines." *Los Angeles Times* (May 9, 1993): B3.

Korean National Association

The Hanin Hapsong Hyophoe (United Korean Society) in Hawaii and the Tac-Hanin Kungmin (Mutual Assistance Society) in California combined forces in 1909, calling themselves the Tac-Hanin Kungmin-hoe (Korean National Association). The group established its headquarters in San Francisco and soon asked all Korean Americans to join and pay dues. The association's main objective was to liberate Korea from Japan; branch offices were opened in Hawaii, Siberia, and Manchuria to aid their cause. After Korea gained its independence from Japan in 1945, the organization ceased to have any real function. **See also** Kongnip Hyop-Hoe; Korean Women's Patriotic Society.

BIBLIOGRAPHY
Choy, Bong-youn. *Koreans in America.* Chicago: Nelson-Hall, 1979.

Korean War (1950–1953)

The Korean War was the conflict between the Democratic People's Republic of Korea (North Korea) and the Republic of Korea (South Korea). The United States and 15 other nations allied under the United Nations sided with South Korea. The People's Republic of China (PRC) sided with North Korea. An estimated 5 million people lost their lives in this war. It stared on June 25, 1950, when North Korea, with the approval of the Soviet Union, launched a surprise attack all along the 38th parallel with the intent of bringing South Korea under its rule. They seized Seoul within only three days, and at that point, South Korea had little hope. The country did not have the military or supplies to hold off the north.

President Harry Truman believed that North Korea's advances had to be stopped. He authorized the use of troops for the conflict without the permission of Congress. U.S. General Douglas MacArthur became the commander-in-chief of the United Nations Command (UNC). North Korea remained strong early, but showed weakness as the UNC landed at Inchon in September of 1950. The bulk of the northern forces were cut in half. The People's Republic became very concerned when MacArthur pushed past the 38th parallel. China had warned the UNC to keep out of North Korea, because they felt it was an immediate threat to Manchuria. Thus, 200,000 Chinese troops were sent into the war and forced MacArthur and the UNC back south of the 38th. The communist forces attempted one last time to overrun the south, but continuous UNC air raids ceased the attempts. MacArthur did not finish the war, because General Matthew B. Ridgeway was appointed into the position of command of the UNC. This was because of MacArthur's attempts to win support of the U.S. people for bombing Manchurian bases. Cease-fire negotiations started in July 1951, but an agreement by both parties did not happen until July 1953. The disagreement was mainly about the exchange of prisoners of war. Dwight Eisenhower, who had been elected president in November 1952, influenced the PRC and North Korea by secretly threatening the use of nuclear bombs. The war established the lengths to which the United States was willing to go to prevent the expansion of communism.

The end of the conflict also meant an ongoing presence in South Korea of U.S. troops and the continued commitment of the United States to stop the spread of communism in future conflicts like Vietnam. American society was also affected, with an increase in the number of Koreans emigrating to the United States after the war.

BIBLIOGRAPHY
Appleman, Roy E. *South to the Naktong, North to the Yalu.* Washington, D.C.: Department of the Army, 1961.
Merrill, John. *Korea: The Peninsular Origins of the War.* Newark: University of Delaware Press, 1989.

Korean Women's Patriotic Society

The Korean Women's Patriotic Society was formed in 1919 in Dinuba, California, with the purpose of uniting the state's various Korean-American groups under one cause. In its first gathering, three different groups, the San Francisco Korean Women's Society, the Sacramento Korean Women's Association, and the Los Angeles Women's Friendship Association, merged to form a joint focus group on issues affecting the Asian-American community. This group, also known as the Korean Women's Patriotic League, soon formed a partnership with the **Korean National Association** to support the Korean independence movement against Japan. The Korean Women's Patriotic Society also raised funds, boycotted Japanese goods, and provided assistance to needy native and American-raised Koreans. **See also** Kongnip Hyop-Hoe; Mutual Assistance Society.

BIBLIOGRAPHY

Okihiro, Gary V. *Margins and Mainstreams*. Seattle: University of Washington Press, 1994.

Fred Toyosaburo Korematsu (1919–)

Fred Korematsu was arrested for remaining in the city of San Leandro, California, and not reporting to an **assembly center**, following the issuance of **Executive Order 9066**, which required all persons of Japanese ancestry to be evacuated from the Western states. Korematsu took his appeal to court several times. His case reached the U.S. Supreme Court in *Korematsu v. the United States* (**1943**), where he argued that the order to evacuate was unconstitutional. The Court ruled against him, stating that the constitutionality of the evacuation law was not relevant to the case; instead, the Court agreed that Korematsu had broken the law by not reporting when it had been deemed militarily necessary by the U.S. government. **See also** *Hirabayashi v. United States* (1943); *Minoru Yasui v. United States* (1943). **See** Executive Order 9066 in Appendix 1.

BIBLIOGRAPHY

Konvitz, Milton, R. *The Alien and the Asiatic in American Law*. Ithaca, NY: Cornell University Press, 1946.

Wilson, Robert A. *East to America*. New York: William Morrow, 1980.

Korematsu v. United States (1943)

Korematsu v. United States, 319 U.S. 432 (1943), arose from an incident in which Japanese-American **Fred Toyosaburo Korematsu** was arrested (and convicted) for remaining in the city of San Leandro, California, and not reporting to an **assembly center**, following the issuance of **Executive Order 9066** and the **Civilian Exclusion Orders**, which required all persons of Japanese ancestry to be evacuated from the Western states. Civilian Exclusion Order No. 34, issued by commanding General J.L. DeWitt on May 3, 1942, had ordered the exclusion of all persons of Japanese ancestry from the San Leandro region. This exclusion was part of a larger order to transport people of Japanese ancestry to **internment camps**.

Korematsu subsequently appealed on two occasions in 1943 to the 9th Circuit Court of Appeals and the U.S. Supreme Court. Both courts, however, affirmed the conviction. When his case reached the U.S. Supreme Court in *Korematsu v. the United States*, Korematsu argued that the order to evacuate was unconstitutional. He asserted that the government's targeting of his ethnic group was so "arbitrary and capricious" a racial discrimination that it violated the due process clause of the First Amendment.

In its decision, the Supreme Court held that the mitigating circumstances of **World War II** justified any infringement of some of the "inherent rights and liberties of individual citizens." The Court accordingly held that the proclamation of evacuation was valid. Justice Robert H. Jackson disagreed with the majority's logic and noted that the internment of 70,000

Japanese Americans was "not unlike that of Hitler in so confining the Jews in his stockades."

The Court stated that the constitutionality of the evacuation law was not relevant to the case; instead, the Court agreed that Korematsu had broken the law by not reporting when it had been deemed militarily necessary by the U.S. government. The Supreme Court also upheld the conviction in a later appeal, finding that the "pressing public necessity" of World War II justified the evacuation and internment of persons of Japanese ancestry. Justice Hugo Black's majority opinion held that, while legal restrictions that infringe upon the civil rights of a single racial group are immediately suspect, the internment of persons of Japanese ancestry regardless of citizenry was constitutional because such persons could pose a potential "menace to the national defense and safety." The majority also maintained that race was not the determining factor of the exclusion, rather that the exclusion was enacted because the United States was at war with Japan.

In 1987, Korematsu's conviction was overturned following his petition for writ of error *coram nobis* (a writ correcting errors of fact so fundamental that they justify vacation of the earlier judgment). Korematsu was one of 12 Japanese Americans to challenge the World War II exclusion orders in court. **See also** Dennis Hayashi; *Hirabayashi v. United States* (1943); *Minoru Yasui v. United States* (1943). **See** Executive Order 9066 in Appendix 1. (JK)

BIBLIOGRAPHY

Harris, Glenn P. "*Hohri v. United States*: Sovereign Immunity." *George Washington Law Review* 55, nos. 4–5. (May–August 1987): 1068–1091.

Konvitz, Milton, R. *The Alien and the Asiatic in American Law*. Ithaca, NY: Cornell University Press, 1946.

Simpson, A.W.B. "Detention without Trial in the Second World War: Comparing the British and American Experiences." *Florida State University Law Review* 16, no. 2 (Summer 1988): 225–267.

Wilson, Robert A. *East to America*. New York: William Morrow, 1980.

K.V. Kumar (1945–)

A strategic planner on minority issues for the 1988 Bush/Quayle presidential campaign, K.V. Kumar was appointed deputy chief to the Director of Systems Management in the Bush administration's Presidential Transition Office's Telecommunications Center. Also during George Bush's presidency, Kumar founded the National Indian American Chamber of Commerce in 1991. Kumar ceased his political activities after the Bush/Quayle ticket failed to secure reelection in 1992. In June 1994, Kumar began extensive volunteer work for the National Head Injury Foundation.

BIBLIOGRAPHY

Zia, Helen and Susan B. Gall. *Notable Asian Americans*. Detroit, MI: Gale, 1995.

Joseph Yoshisuke Kurihara (1895–)

Born in Hawaii, Joseph Kurihara graduated from college in San Francisco. He served in the U.S. Army during World War I and was honorably discharged. After the bombing of **Pearl Harbor**, he was evacuated along with other Japanese Americans and relocated to an **internment camp.** Kurihara was so outraged that at the end of the war he gave up his U.S. citizenship and moved to Japan.

BIBLIOGRAPHY

Thomas, Dorothy S. and Richard Nishimoto. *The Spoilage.* Berkeley: University of California Press, 1946.

Yoneda, Karl G. *Ganhatte: Sixty-Year Struggle of a Kibei Worker.* Los Angeles: Asian American Studies Center, University of California, Los Angeles, 1983.

Kwock Jan Fat v. White, Commissioner of Immigration (1920)

An American-Chinese man, Kwock Jan Fat, left for China in 1915; upon returning to the United States in 1917, he was forbidden to reenter. Before his departure for China, he had filed an application for leave and had obtained three white witnesses to testify as to his identity. The Department of Immigration investigated him and then issued him a permit that allowed his return. However, Kwock was denied reentry to the United States based on erroneous information that had surfaced in his absence. The resulting case, *Kwock Jan Fat v. White, Commissioner of Immigration,* 253 U.S. 454 (1920), was heard by the U.S. Supreme Court, which found that the San Francisco Immigration Office had hidden information from Kwock and denied him his right to a proper hearing.

BIBLIOGRAPHY

Konvitz, Milton R. *The Alien and the Asiatic in American Law.* Ithaca, NY: Cornell University Press, 1946.

Laddaran, Estanislao P. v. Laddaran, Emma P. (1931)

In 1931 Estanislao Laddaran wished to have his marriage to Emma annulled. Since Laddaran was Filipino and Emma was white, the case went to court to determine if the marriage had been legal in the state of California. In *Laddaran, Estanislao P. v. Laddaran, Emma P.* (1931), the California Supreme Court stated that because Filipinos were not Mongolian, the marriage was legal and, therefore could not be annulled.

BIBLIOGRAPHY

Sickels, Robert J. *Race, Marriage, and the Law.* Albuquerque: University of New Mexico Press, 1972.

Cheryl A. Lau (1944–)

Cheryl Lau was a political novice when she became Nevada's first Asian-American secretary of the state in 1991. Born in Hawaii as a third-generation Chinese American, Lau dreamed of teaching music, and she earned a doctoral degree for this. However, her interest in crime and social order prompted her to earn a law degree, which led to her appointment to the office of deputy attorney general in Nevada. Lau took the Republican Party by surprise when she easily won both the primary and general elections in her first contest for office. However, she lost her bids for governor in 1994 and for U.S. Congress in 1996. (PL)

BIBLIOGRAPHY

"Cheryl Lau Marches to Congress." *China Daily News* (June 15, 1996): B14.

Lau v. Nichols (1974)

Lau v. Nichols, 414 U.S. 563 (1974), was a case involving the rights of students of Chinese ancestry. The case originated in San Francisco and involved students who did not speak English. Of the more than 2,800 students in the San Francisco school system who did not speak English, approximately 1,000 were provided with remedial English. The Supreme Court ruled that the failure of the school district to provide remedial English instruction for the rest of the students of Chinese ancestry who did not speak English amounted to a violation of Title VI of the Civil Rights Act and the regulations promulgated from Title VI.

The Court ruled that Title VI regulations required remedial instruction where the inability to understand English excluded children of foreign ancestry from full participation in educational programs. California law required that students demonstrate a proficiency in English to graduate from high school. The Court determined that without remedial instruction, the students in the *Lau* case were denied a "meaningful opportunity to participate in the educational program." The Supreme Court did not order a specific remedy but remanded the case for the fashioning of appropriate relief. The San Francisco school district was ordered to provide bilingual instruction to more than 1,800 non-English-speaking students of Chinese ancestry.

The case was an important extension of the rights of non-English-speaking students. In addition, it was one of a number of cases that allowed the remedial use of race to correct discrimination under Title VI. Congress passed Title VI to authorize the executive branch to halt any federal funds to either public or private schools or activities in which discrimination on the grounds of race, color, or national origin is allowed to continue.

The Department of Health, Education, and Welfare (HEW) broadly interpreted this provision to require special assistance to non-English-speaking students of Chinese ancestry. HEW argued that the Chinese-speaking minority received fewer benefits than the English-speaking majority and thus lacked a meaningful opportunity to participate in the educational program, earmarks of the discrimination Title VI was designed to remedy. The Court unanimously upheld this very broad interpretation, avoiding constitutional grounds and confining the decision to the statute. (RLP)

BIBLIOGRAPHY

Chestnut, Kathi Lee. "Supplemental Language Institution for Students with Limited English-Speaking Ability: The Relationship Between the Right and the Remedy." *Washington University Law Quarterly* 61, no. 2 (1998): 415–34.

Haft, Jonathan. "Assuring Equal Educational Opportunity for Language Minority Students: Bilingual Education and the Equal Education Opportunity Act of 1974." *Columbia Journal of Law and Social Problems* 18, no. 2 (1985): 209–93.

Laundry Ordinances

Because there were so few women on the West Coast during the Gold Rush, Chinese men who did not want to work in sweatshops and factories began making a living washing and ironing clothes. The trend caught on and, as far away as Chicago, Chinese laundries sprang up in great numbers. It soon became one of the few professions that whites permitted Chinese immigrants to hold. However, starting in 1870, discriminatory laws were passed against Chinese laundrymen. In 1870 San Francisco passed a law that laundries using horses for delivery would pay a fee of two to four dollars, and those without a horse

In the 1870s and 1880s, the San Francisco Board of Supervisors passed a number of ordinances discriminating against Chinese laundries. *Library of Congress.*

would pay a $15 fee. The law discriminated against Chinese, who usually did not own horses. Between 1873 and 1884, the San Francisco Board of Supervisors passed 14 ordinances discriminating against Chinese laundrymen.

In 1880 the city passed a law stating that all laundries whose buildings were made of wood must adhere to specific requirements and that the laundry owners needed to obtain permission from the city to operate. This law was contested by Yick Wo, a Chinese man operating a laundry in San Francisco. He was arrested for violating the city ordinance, even though he had obtained permits from the city stating that his business complied with all fire and sanitation codes. He was initially found guilty, but in *Yick Wo v. Hopkins* (**1886**), the U.S. Supreme Court reversed the lower court's ruling stating that the ordinance was unconstitutional.

BIBLIOGRAPHY

McClain, Charles. *In Search of Equality*. Berkeley: University of California Press, 1994.

Leadership Education for Asian Pacifics (LEAP)

The Leadership Education for Asian Pacifics (LEAP), a nonprofit community group founded in 1982, was created to develop and expand leadership roles among the Asian-American community. The organization soon created two subsidiary education groups, the Leadership Management Institute and the Community Development Institute, to facilitate workshops and provide leadership training to Asian Pacific Americans residing in the United States. In 1992, LEAP and the Asian

American Studies Center of the University of California in Los Angeles founded the Asian Pacific American Policy Institute to help further legislative and government participation in Asian-American issues.

BIBLIOGRAPHY

Sy, Levin. *National Asian Pacific American Political Almanac*. Los Angeles: University of California, 1996.

League of Deliverance

Formed in San Francisco in 1882, the League of Deliverance's main objective was to force Chinese people to leave California. The League, which emerged out of unions and trade leagues, organized boycotts to destroy Chinese businesses. The League's leader was Frank Roney, who in 1880 had organized the Seaman's Protective Union, and in 1881 he became president of the San Francisco Representative Assembly of Trades and Labor Unions. He used his position to advance his anti-Chinese agenda, which included replacing Chinese workers with white workers and targeting Chinese goods and stores. The league ceased its operations after the Chinese Exclusion Act (**Immigration Act of 1882**) was passed.

BIBLIOGRAPHY

Saxton, Alexander. *The Indispensable Enemy*. Berkeley: University of California Press, 1971.

Leave Clearance

During **World War II,** the **War Relocation Authority** could allow Japanese Americans to leave the confines of their **internment camp/relocation centers**. The Japanese-American detainees had to apply for this leave clearance in order to work outside the camps for short periods of time. Whether they were granted leave or not was often determined by how they had answered questions about loyalty to the United States and willingness to reject allegiance to the Emperor of Japan. In total, about 6,800 Japanese Americans were granted leave while in relocation centers.

BIBLIOGRAPHY

Myer, Dillon S. *Uprooted Americans*. Tuscon: University of Arizona Press, 1971.

Weglyn, Michi. *Years of Infamy*. New York: William Morrow, 1976.

Bill Lann Lee (1949–)

Bill Lann Lee is the first Asian American to serve in the position of assistant attorney general for civil rights, a position often referred to as "the nation's chief civil rights enforcer." Lee, a Chinese American, was appointed to the post by President Bill Clinton on December 15, 1997. The son of immigrants who ran a small laundry after they came to the United States, Lee decided to pursue civil rights law after witnessing the bigotry faced by his father.

After graduating from Columbia Law School in 1974, Lee served as the associate counsel for the NAACP Legal Defense and Education Fund (1974–1983) and then as western regional counsel for the fund (1988–1997); he was supervising attorney for civil rights litigation at the Center for Law in the Public Interest (1983–1988). In addition, he was counsel for the Asian-American Legal Defense and Education Fund, and an adjunct professor at Fordham University.

Lee's appointment to the civil rights post met with strong opposition from Senate Republicans, and President Clinton named Lee acting assistant attorney general (an appointment that does not require Senate confirmation) after his nomination seemed unlikely to be approved by the Senate. Opponents of Lee's nomination criticized his support for racial preferences in policies such as affirmative action. Although Lee holds the same authority as an appointee who was confirmed by the Senate, some observers believed that his effectiveness would be diminished. (ALA)

BIBLIOGRAPHY

Katyal, Neal K. "Recess Appointment Need not Be Antagonistic." [Report of President Clinton's appointment Of Bill Lann Lee, as acting assistant attorney general for civil rights.] *The National Law Journal* 20, nos. 18–19 (December 29, 1997): A16.

Shaw, Daniel. "Clinton Names Lee Acting AG for Civil Rights; Discrimination Victims Not Aided by Retribution against Him, Says Hatch." *The Los Angeles Daily Journal* 110, no. 243 (December 16, 1997): 1.

Lee Kum Hoy, Lee Kum Cherk, and Lee Moon Wah v. John L. Murff (1957)

Lee Kum Hoy, Lee Kum Cherk, and Lee Moon Wah v. John L. Murff, 355 U.S. 169 (1957), was a case involving a number of Chinese living in Hong Kong who wished to be considered American citizens because they claimed to have an American parent. The U.S. Immigration Service administered blood tests to determine if they were indeed the children of American citizens. The U.S. District Court ruled that Lee Kum Hoy and the others should be allowed to immigrate, but the Immigration Service appealed. The case reached the U.S. Supreme Court in 1957, and it was the Court's opinion that the blood tests given to Lee Kum Hoy and the others were not valid and had perhaps been falsified.

BIBLIOGRAPHY

Kung, S.W. *Chinese in American Life: Some Aspects of Their History, Status, Problems, and Contributions.* Seattle: University of Washington Press, 1962.

Lem Moon Sing v. United States (1895)

On January 20, 1894, Lem Moon Sing (who had been a United States citizen residing in San Francisco, California, since 1892), left the United States to visit his ancestral home of China. While he was out of the country, U.S. lawmakers passed the Exclusion of Chinese Merchant Act, which gave U.S. immigration officers and customs officials binding say on all matters concerning aliens entering the country. When Sing returned to San Francisco on November 3, 1894, he found himself denied entrance into the country because of this new exclusion bill.

Sing took the matter to court, stating that the new act did not apply to him because he was a legal citizen of the United States. Sing's pleas were denied by district courts, leading to an appeal of the case to the U.S. Supreme Court. In *Lem Moon Sing v. United States,* 158 U.S. 538 (1895), the Court stated that aliens within the United States had to be provided the same rights as U.S.-born citizens. However, the Court also decided that aliens outside the country seeking entrance, even those who left the country on their own accord and later sought reentry, should be held under the same entrance stipulations as defined under the exclusion laws. As a result, the lower court finding was reaffirmed, and Lem Moon Sing was not allowed reentrance into the country. The Supreme Court based this finding on precedents established in **Nishimura v. United States (1892). See also** Immigration Restriction Movement.

BIBLIOGRAPHY

McClain, Charles. *In Search of Equality.* Berkeley: University of California Press, 1994.

Tye Leung

In 1912 Tye Leung was the first known Chinese-American woman to vote in a presidential election. She was also the first Chinese American hired to work as an interpreter and assistant to the matrons of the **Angel Island** Immigration Center in San Francisco Bay. The island served as a detention center from 1910 to 1940 for Asian immigrants awaiting entry to the United States, or deportation back to their country of origin.

BIBLIOGRAPHY

Ng, Franklin, ed. *The Asian American Encyclopedia.* New York: Marshall Cavendish, 1995.

Li Sung v. United States (1900)

Li Sung v. United States (1900), which involved the deportation of a Chinese alien, was heard in the U.S. Supreme Court. The Court stated that Congress could require aliens to prove their right to be in the United States. If an Asian laborer lacked a certificate of residence then it would be up to him to prove to the United States that he belonged in the country. The Court also ruled that an alien had no constitutional protection of trial by jury and also was not protected against unreasonable search and seizure and cruel and unusual punishment.

BIBLIOGRAPHY

Konvitz, Milton R. *The Alien and the Asiatic in American Law.* Ithaca, NY: Cornell University Press, 1947.

Liberal Patriotic Association

The Liberal Patriotic Association was formed in Hawaii in 1889. Headed by Robert Wilcox, a Hawaiian native, the group's objective was to overthrow the Hawaiian government, which was led by King Kalakaua. Wilcox held clandestine meetings in order to plot a strategy. Several Chinese residents of Hawaii gave Wilcox money to carry out his plan, and Ho Fon, a journalist, was later convicted of conspiracy and fined. The group disbanded after Wilcox"s attempt to coerce Kalakua into changing the state constitution failed and Wilcox was arrested. He was tried and found not guilty of treason.

BIBLIOGRAPHY
Kuykendall, Ralph S. *The Hawaiian Kingdom.* vol. III: 1874–1893. Honolulu: University of Hawaii Press, 1967.

Liberalism

Asians have generally been stereotyped as being more conservative than most minority groups. However, depending on which subgroup among Asians is being discussed and where they live, many Asians are quite liberal in their politics. While Asians are relatively conservative when it comes to respect for traditional culture, they have a history consistent with that of a disadvantaged minority. Chinese laborers worked under discriminatory wages and conditions and were strongly persecuted by organized labor when the railroad jobs ended. The Japanese were put into **internment camps**—concentration camps—during **World War II.** All Asian groups were faced with discriminatory laws with respect to intermarriage, immigration, and citizenship. Even today, Asians are subject to stereotyping, and have not been represented in fields such as management in proportion to their numbers.

Asian-American liberals are quick to attack the model minority myth of Asian success. In part, the myth undermines efforts to create social programs which directly benefit Asians. Also, the myth undermines the victim based civil rights arguments often used to justify programs other minorities have succeeded in attaining.

Many sectors of Asian Americans are disadvantaged because of language, culture, and poverty. For example, although Asians Americans in many suburbs are affluent, the old core Chinatowns often meet the statistical definition of a ghetto with over 40 percent of families falling under the poverty line. Many of the elderly have no knowledge of English, little formal education, and find it impossible to find employment in the mainstream economy. Asian-American liberals have promoted unionization of restaurant and garment workers who have traditionally been low paid with few benefits and long hours. They have helped Asian-American workers take advantage of their rights by promoting full participation in programs for laid off workers in cities like Boston. Liberals also seek to protect the integrity of communities which may be affected by redevelopment.

Among Asian Americans, the Japanese and South Asian Indians are the most liberal. Many Asian-American Congressmen from California and Hawaii have been Democrats. The fact that most Japanese Americans are native born and Asian Indians have a firm command of the English language may help explain why these two groups more closely resemble Jewish Americans in their political liberalism than other Asian groups.

There also seems to a difference between party identification. According to a Republican National Committee (RNC) poll, only Asian Indian Americans polled more liberal than conservative. However, that was not a good indication of party identification. For example, Japanese Americans polled the second most conservative, but were among the most likely Asian Americans to be Democrats. Also, on specific issues the various ethnic sub-groups seemed strangely split. Vietnamese Americans, for example were the most conservative in the RNC poll, but also the most supportive of the government doing everything it could to advance disadvantaged minorities, while Japanese Americans were the least supportive of **affirmative action** programs, despite their party affiliation.

Many of the most politically active Asian Americans and the vast majority of Asian-American scholars in the areas of politics and history are more liberal than the general Asian-American population. Asian-American activists have an interest in liberal immigration policies and liberal welfare programs because most Asian Americans are immigrants, and many, especially refugees and the elderly, are dependent on government programs for income and health care. Liberal activists are also active in combating stereotypes and fighting race-based violence such as that in the **Vincent Chin murder case**.

Many Asian Americans are active in causes such as feminism and the gay/lesbian movement even though, as a whole, Asian Americans are more likely to embrace traditional roles for women and are generally less tolerant of homosexuality. Although the civil rights movement was seen largely as an African-American event, Asian-American students lead the struggle for ethnic studies programs at schools like San Francisco State College. On campuses, the Asian-American movement was fashioned by Asian-American activists after the civil rights movement.

Ironically, many Asian-American student activists took to the streets to protest the ending of affirmative action in California schools even though the program clearly benefits other minority groups at the expense of Asian Americans. University of California chancellor Chang Lin became one of the most visible supporters of affirmative action, coining the phrase "Diversity is Excellence." His opposition pitted him against African-American regent Ward Connerly who led the movement to end affirmative action. Chinese for Affirmative Action, a liberal, San Francisco-based civil rights organization, defended a consent decree that capped the number of Chinese Americans allowed to attend the prestigious Lowell High School despite the fact that most Asian parents opposed the cap.

In the end, while most Asian Americans tend to be more conservative than their white counterparts, those who are politically active tend to be more liberal. This includes political candidates such as **Michael Woo,** who lost a bid for mayor of Los Angeles in the wake of Rodney King; **Gary Locke** of Washington state, who opposed a conservative woman for governor; and most members of Congress including **Patsy Mink, Robert Matsui, Daniel Inouye** and **Daniel Akaka. See also** Conservatism among Asian Americans; Model Minority. (AH)

BIBLIOGRAPHY
Aguilar-San Juan, Karin. *The State of Asian America.* Boston, MA: South End Press, 1994.

Espiritu, Yen Le. *Asian American Panethnicity*. Philadelphia: Temple University Press, 1992.

Lien, Pei-te. *The Political Participation of Asian Americans*. New York: Garland, 1997.

Liu, Eric. *The Accidental Asian*. New York: Random House, 1998.

Ng, Franklin. *Asian American Interethnic Relations and Politics*. New York: Garland, 1998.

Takahashi, Jere. *Nisei/Sansei: Shifting Japanese American Identities and Politics*. Philadelphia: Temple University Press, 1997.

Channing Liem (1909–1996)

Channing Liem was a longtime Korean expatriate who lived in the United States. He served briefly as the Republic of Korea's ambassador to the United Nations. Liem had been a longtime supporter of the establishment of a nonaligned South Korea. He founded and was president of Han Min Yun, which is a global organization striving for peace and unity in South Korea. Born in Ul Yul, Korea, Liem worked for the U.S. government during **World War II** in the Office of Censorship. He taught political thought and government at such schools as Chatham College and the State University of New York at New Paltz.

BIBLIOGRAPHY

Schwartz, Stephen. "Channing Liem." *The San Francisco Chronicle* (January 31, 1996): A15.

Liliuokalani (1838–1917)

Liliuokalani ascended to the Hawaiian throne when her father King Kalakaua died while traveling in the United States. Her reign, which lasted only from 1891 to 1893, was a controversial one due in large measure to the economic troubles of the kingdom. The economy was in a depression because of the McKinley Tariff of 1890, which raised the tariff on sugar imported from Hawaii. Trying to consolidate her power as opposition grew, she tried to change the Hawaiian constitution to give her more autonomy. However, the **Annexation Club** had convinced the United States government and many Hawaiian landowners to oppose her reign. In January 1893, the **Committee of Safety** overthrew her government. She was held prisoner in the royal palace until she abdicated the throne and signed a pledge to support the Hawaiian Republic. After this, she sought to live the rest of her life in privacy. Her considerable landholdings were placed in trust for the republic's orphans and today is the home of the Queen Liliuokalani Children's Center. **See also** Annexation of Hawaii.

BIBLIOGRAPHY

Dougherty, Michael. *To Steal a Kingdom*. Waimaualo, HI: Island Style Press, 1996.

Lin Sing v. Washburn (1863)

In 1862, a tax was imposed on Chinese Americans living in California. The law stated that all "Mongolians" who were not employed by the rice, sugar, tea or coffee manufacturers or were not paying the California **Foreign Miners Tax**, must pay $2.50 a month. In 1863 Lin Sing objected to the tax and took his case to court, arguing that the tax violated his constitutional rights. In *Lin Sing v. Washburn,* 20 XL. 534 (1863), the California Supreme Court decided that the law was indeed unconstitutional.

BIBLIOGRAPHY

Shih-Shan, Henry Tsai. *The Chinese Experience in America.* Bloomington: Indiana University Press, 1986.

Gary Locke (1950–)

Gary Locke of Washington is the first Chinese-American governor in U.S. history and the first Asian American to be governor of a state other than Hawaii. Born to immigrant parents, Locke grew up in a public housing project. Through part-time jobs, financial aid, and scholarships, he was able to receive a bachelor's degree in political science from Yale University and a law degree from Boston University. Locke won a seat in the Washington House of Representatives in 1982. During his 11 years in the legislature, he rose to chair the Appropriations Committee and was rated the most effective lawmaker from the Puget Sound area. Based on his reputation as a brilliant budget writer and consensus builder, he was elected chief executive of King County by the highest margin ever recorded for that office. When Locke left this office for governorship in 1997, he left a leaner but not meaner government and a nationally acclaimed growth management plan. (PL)

BIBLIOGRAPHY

State of Washington. Official biography of Gary Locke. (1997)

Los Angeles County Anti-Asiatic Society

The Los Angeles County Anti-Asiatic society was formed in 1919 to exclude Japanese and other Asian immigrants from participating in American society. The group also dedicated itself to supporting the **California Alien Land Act of 1913** (which prevented Japanese immigrants from owning or leasing land in the United States) and pushed for other similar and stricter legislation.

The group gained much of its support from the campaign run of U.S. Senate hopeful James D. Phelan, who ran on an anti-Asian ballot; Phelan gained the support of a number of organizations that shared his views. These groups, which included the Native Sons of the Golden West, the American Legion, and a number of labor unions, formed the Anti-Asian Committee, the forerunner of the Los Angeles Anti-Asian Society, in order to back Phelan. This group soon adopted a strict exclusionary philosophy, because they felt that the only way to preserve Western culture was to eliminate all Eastern influences.

The Los Angeles Anti-Asian Society eventually came under the leadership of Sheriff William I. Traeger. Under his guidance the group continued to back Phelan's political efforts and the preservation of racial purity in Western culture. It also fought for the adoption of the 1920 Alien Land Initiative, a bill intended to amend and intensify restriction in the California Alien Land Act of 1913. **See** California Alien Land Act of 1920 in Appendix 1.

BIBLIOGRAPHY

Kim, Hyung-Chan. *Dictionary of Asian American History.* New York: Greenwood Press, 1986.

Modell, John. *The Economics and Politics of Racial Accommodation: The Japanese of Los Angeles, 1900–1942.* Urbana: University of Illinois Press, 1977.

Ng, Franklin, ed. *The Asian American Encyclopedia.* New York: Marshall Cavendish, 1995.

Los Angeles Riot (1871)

In 1871 a riot broke out when an argument started between members of two Los Angeles Chinese tongs (fraternal organizations). The two men began shooting at one another and attracted a crowd at the Calle de los Negros. The crowd quickly got out of control; another group of people arrived on the scene and began attacking the Chinese. They went systematically through the nearby buildings, ransacking apartments and shooting Chinese residents who fled. Nineteen Chinese were killed in the riots, and many others were wounded. The police were called in, and one officer was wounded before the rioting ended four hours later. The riot made international news, and the Chinese government denounced the event. A trial ensued and nine men were found guilty of starting the riot; however, they each served less than a year in jail. In addition, a bill was introduced into Congress to have the government help pay reparations to the victims of the riots, but it was voted down. **See also** Rock Springs Riot.

BIBLIOGRAPHY

Bowman, Lynn. *Los Angeles: Epic of a City.* Berkeley, CA: Howell North Books, 1974.

Kung, S.W. *Chinese in American Life.* Seattle: University of Washington Press, 1962.

Los Angeles Riots (1992)

After the mid-1960s South Central Los Angeles became less African American and more diverse. The increased number of Korean Americans and Latinos moving into the area caused growing tensions. These tensions were exacerbated by the recession of the 1980s and increasing poverty in the area. South Central, which already was a poor area, became even more economically depressed. Various research studies indicated that one of every four African-American men from the area was in jail and that most babies were born to single African-American parents. By the time of the riots, the poverty rate had reached 30 percent and household income was approximately only $7,000. Hostility in the area was mounting as African Americans grew angrier at paying higher insurance and mortgage rates, while they were subject to badly equipped schools and to police brutality.

The catalyst for the 1992 riots occurred when Rodney King, an African-American man, was beaten by police one night after being pulled from his car. America might never have heard of this incident if not for a passerby's videotape of the brutal beatings. While white America was shocked and appalled by the videotape, African Americans were not, because police harassment and brutality had become well known

in the community. The case went to trial, but despite the videotape and a badly injured King as a witness, the court did not punish the policemen, but instead gave them a only a light, symbolic punishment.

Within hours, the depressed and disenfranchised African Americans of South Central and elsewhere in Los Angeles rioted against a system of justice that they felt had not served them for years. Many of the rioters targeted and destroyed the Korean-owned businesses in their neighborhoods. These business had tended to do well, even in depressed areas such as South Central Los Angeles. African Americans resented what they considered to be the high prices these merchants charged and the fact that they did not hire African-American workers. Many African-American and white-owned businesses were also looted and burned, but half of the more than $900 million dollars in damages to the city was suffered by Korean businesses. In the aftermath of the riots, a new trial was ordered for the policemen accused of beating Rodney King; in this second trial, the policemen were found guilty of using excessive force and were sentenced to prison time. **See also** Asian-American Relations with Other Minorities.

BIBLIOGRAPHY

Chang, Edward T. "America's First Multiethnic Riots." *The State of Asian America: Activism and Resistance in the 1990s.* Boston: South End Press, 1994.

Loyalty Oath/Test

In the U.S. **internment camps** during World War II, the U.S. Army and the **War Relocation Authority (WRA)** began to administer the Japanese-American internees a series of questions that were, in theory, meant to aid in the determination of loyalty. Two questions in particular, numbers 27 and 28, were of special concern. Question 27 asked, "Are you willing to serve in the armed forces of the United States on combat duty, wherever ordered?" Question 28 asked, "Will you swear unqualified allegiance to the United States of America and faithfully defend the United States from any or all attacks by foreign or domestic forces; and forswear any allegiance or obedience to the Japanese emperor and to any other foreign government, power or organization?"

Issei, older Japanese men, were apprehensive about answering question 28 because they were too old to fight and were not eligible for citizenship. If they renounced their allegiance to Japan, then they would be citizens of no country. To accommodate this, question 28 was altered for *issei.* It stated that they agreed to abide by U.S. laws and not to interfere with war efforts.

The army and the WRA were unclear on the purpose of the test. More specifically, they did not know what the consequences were of "yes" or "no" answers. Furthermore, they did not know what to do if members of the same family answered the questions differently. In the end, the questions were used to segregate potential enemies from the general Japanese-American population. **No-No Boys,** those people who answered "no" on both questions, were sent to Tule Lake re-

The issue of loyalty has long plagued many Asian immigrants, who were both forbidden to become citizens and scorned for not rejecting their homelands. Here some Asian-American children are part of a group of students pledging allegiance to the flag at a San Francisco school in April 1942. *National Archives.*

location center, which had been designated as a segregation camp with the purpose of repatriation of disloyal Japanese Americans. More than 7,000 Japanese were deported by the government to Tule Lake.

BIBLIOGRAPHY

Girdner, Audrie and Anne Loftis. *The Great Betrayal.* New York: Macmillan, 1969.

O'Brien, David J. and Stephen S. Fugita. *The Japanese American Experience.* Bloomington: Indiana University Press, 1991.

Luce-Cellar Bill (1946)

The Luce-Cellar Bill, also known as the Indian Immigration Act of 1946, was proposed by Claire Booth Luce and Emanuel Cellar. In 1943, the United States government repealed the Chinese Exclusion Act (Immigration Act of 1882), which had prevented Chinese immigration and land ownership in the United States for a half century. The Luce-Cellar Bill attempted eliminate the same type of restrictions for Asian Indians. The original bill died in committee, but with the public support of President Harry Truman, the two cosponsors reintroduced the bill and it became law in 1946. The act specifically permitted Asian Indians to become naturalized citizens and to own land in the U.S.

BIBLIOGRAPHY

Chandrasekhar, R. *From India to America.* La Jolla, CA: Population Review Book, 1982.

Hutchinson, E.P. *Legislative History of American Immigration Policy, 1789–1965.* Philadelphia: University of Pennsylvania Press, 1981.

Kalfred Dip Lum (1899–1979)

After becoming a political science professor at the University of Hawaii in 1928, Kalfred Dip Lum was made executive secretary and chairman of Guomindang's (the Chinese Nationalist Party's) General Branch in Hawaii. In 1931, Lum served as Hawaii's delegate to the National People's Conference in Nanjing, China, which drafted a provisional Chinese constitution; he also received appointment as Guomindang's Commissioner of Overseas Affairs. Lum continued to work for the Guomindang government through the 1930s as inspector for the Chinese Party and Overseas Affairs in the United States and Hawaii, inspector of Chinese Affairs in Southeast Asia in 1935, and Special Mediator in the United States in 1937.

BIBLIOGRAPHY

Jeans, Roger B. *Democracy and Socialism in Republican China.* Lanham, MD: Rowman & Littlefield, 1997.

M

McCarran-Walter Act. *See* Immigration and Nationality Act of 1952

Magnuson Act. *See* Immigration Act of 1943

Pablo Manlapit (1891–1969)

Born on January 17, 1891, Pablo Manlapit arrived as a sugar plantation worker on the island of Hawaii in 1910, but he was fired for strike involvement in 1912. After moving to Honolulu, he organized a series of strikes for plantation workers, including the **sugar strike of 1920**, which for the first time involved both Filipinos and Japanese. For his role in the bloody **sugar strike of 1924**, he was convicted of subornation of perjury regarding testimony about the death of a striker's child. Jailed for two years, he was released on the condition that he would leave Hawaii. After five years of labor organizing in California, he nevertheless returned to Honolulu, where he was arrested in 1934 for overcharging a legal client, and he was then convicted and deported to the Philippines in 1935, where he worked for the government, advised various labor organizations, and died in poverty on April 15, 1969. (MH)

BIBLIOGRAPHY

Kerkvliet, Melinda Tria. "Manlapit's Fight for Justice." *Social Process in Hawaii* 33 (1991): 153–168.

Manlapit, Pablo. *Filipinos Fight for Justice: Case of the Filipino Laborers in the Big Strike of 1924.* Honolulu: Kumalae Publishing Company, 1933.

Beckie Masaki (1957–)

Beckie Masaki is the cofounder and executive director of San Francisco's Asian Women's Shelter. It was founded in 1988 to provide safe shelter and a wide variety of social, economic, and legal services for Asian women. Born in California, Masaki had been working in a shelter since 1983 but opened her own in 1988. She was a winner of the sixth annual Peace Prize from the California Wellness Foundation in 1998.

BIBLIOGRAPHY

Minton, Torri. "Violence Prevention Efforts Rewarded." *The San Francisco Chronicle* (December 4, 1998): A24.

Mike Masaru Masaoka (1915–1991)

Mike Masaoka was the national executive secretary of the **Japanese American Citizens League (JACL)** at a critical moment in Japanese-American history. Masaoka played a key role when JACL decided to cooperate with the internment of Japanese Americans during **World War II,** and he subsequently pushed JACL to support the right of Japanese Americans to serve in the military during the war. When that right was granted, Masaoka was the first to volunteer, becoming part of the famed **442nd Regimental Combat Team**. After the war, Masaoka became a lobbyist for JACL, and he later formed his own Washington, D.C., lobbying firm.

Masaoka, along with JACL, was a controversial figure among Japanese Americans, many of whom opposed what they saw as his excessive patriotism and willingness to work within the established political system. Many are still critical of his wartime efforts to undermine support for Japanese Americans who sought court cases testing the World War II evacuation orders.

For others, however, Masaoka will be remembered as a powerful positive force in Japanese Americans' greatest time of crisis. Faced with deep and widespread racism during the war, and few allies in positions of political power, it seems unlikely that JACL would have been more successful had it called for resistance rather than cooperation. The tremendous postwar success of Japanese Americans is due to least in small part to the choices made by Masaoka and his colleagues. **See also** Civilian Exclusion Orders; Internment Camps/Relocation Centers; Japanese-American Creed; Proposition 15 (1945); Redress Movement. (ALA)

BIBLIOGRAPHY

Daniels, Roger. *Asian American: Chinese and Japanese in the United States since 1850.* Seattle and London: University of Washington Press. 1988.

Drinnon, Richard. *Keeper of Concentration Camps: Dillon S. Myer and American Racism.* Berkeley: University of California Press, 1987.

Hosokawa, Bill. *JACL in Quest of Justice.* NY: William Morrow, 1982.

Masaokka, Mike M. with Bill Hosokawa. *They Call Me Moses Masaoka: An American Saga.* NY: Morrow, 1987.

Masoaka v. State of California (1952)

In *Masoaka v. State of California* (1952), the court reexamined the **Alien Land Law of 1920,** an amendment to the **California Alien Land Act of 1913**, which prevented Japanese Americans from owning or leasing land. The case originated when the sons of Hauye Masoaka tried to transfer the ownership rights of a house they had built to their mother Masoaka, an *issei* woman. However, because Japanese Americans were ineligible for citizenship, they could not buy, sell, or lease land under the Alien Land Laws.

The district court found that the law violated the Fourteenth Amendment of the Constitution, and the court declared that Masoaka was entitled to the land. The decision was appealed by the State of California. The higher court reaffirmed the district court finding, pointing to *Fujii Sei v. the State of California* (1952), which had also provided land title rights to an *issei* in California. All alien laws were later repealed.

BIBLIOGRAPHY

O'Brien, David J. and Stephen S. Fugita. *The Japanese American Experience.* Bloomington: Indiana University Press, 1991.

Masters and Servants Act of 1850

The Masters and Servants Act of 1850 required imported workers to pay transportation costs to Hawaii through lengthy work contracts under penalty of jail sentences. The law was amended three times: in 1867, reducing the jail sentence to a fine; in 1872, allowing workers to prepay transportation costs; and in 1882, prohibiting work contract extension as a penalty for desertion. The law was invalidated in 1900, when Hawaii became a territory of the United States, since it was contrary to provisions in the Peonage Abolition Act of 1867. (MH)

BIBLIOGRAPHY

Beechert, Edward D. (1985). *Working in Hawai'i: A Labor History.* Honolulu: University of Hawaii Press.

Donald Masuda (1961–)

Masuda is a health care professional who cofounded the Gay Asian Pacific Alliance (GAPA) in 1987. GAPA is a nonprofit support group and social service provider located in San Francisco. Masuda also cofounded the GAPA Community HIV project. He was elected to the board of the Alice B. Toklas Democratic Club, a gay political organization in San Francisco. He has also worked for the Asian Task Force and cochaired the Asian Pacific AIDS Coalition.

BIBLIOGRAPHY

Aguilar-San Juan, Karin. *The State of Asian American Activism.* Boston: South End Press, 1994.
Sherman, Phillip. *Uncommon Heroes: A Celebration of Heroes and Role Models for Gay and Lesbian Americans.* New York: Fletcher Press, 1994.

Prema Mathai-Davis (1950–)

Prema Mathai-Davis was the first foreign-born woman to lead the Young Women's Christian Association (YWCA), which was established in 1858. She was selected the YWCA's executive director in 1994. Born in Kerala, India, Mathai-Davis has been the director of New York's Mount Sinai School of Medicine–Hunter College Long Term Care Gerontology Center from 1979 to 1981. After that, she was director of social service programs with the Community Service Society of New York until 1985. She also was the president and chief executive director of the Community Agency for Senior Citizens, Inc. of Staten Island until 1990. Then she became New York City's commissioner in the Department of Aging until assuming her position at the YWCA.

BIBLIOGRAPHY

McNatt, Robert. "Y Chief Preaches Revival Message." [New Executive Profiles]." *Crain's New York Business* (March 7, 1994): 31.
Melwani, Lavina. "YWCA's National Director: An Advocate for Women of All Ages." *India West* (February 11, 1994): 41, 44.

Robert Matsui (1941–)

Robert Matsui has been a Congressman since 1978, representing California's fifth district. He is a senior member of the highly respected House Ways and Means Committee. He was chosen by President Bill Clinton to lead the gathering of support for NAFTA (North Atlantic Free Trade Agreement). Born in California, Matsui served on the Sacramento City Council from 1971 to 1978. Besides his work in support of NAFTA, Matsui has also worked on the Enterprise Capital Formation Act. He has served as the treasurer of the Democratic National Committee since 1991.

BIBLIOGRAPHY

Barone, Michael. *Politics in America.* Washington, D.C.: National Journal, 1998.
Yang, Jeff. "The Power of Two, An Interview with Bob and Doris Matsui." *A. Magazine* 2, no. 3 (December 15, 1993).

"Spark" Masayuke Matsunaga (1916–1990)

Born in Hawaii in 1916, "Spark" Matsunaga held a long career of public service to both Hawaii and the nation. During **World War II,** he served in the highly decorated **100th Infantry Battalion** formed of Americans of Japanese decent. After the war, Matsunaga returned to Hawaii and served as a statehood delegate in 1950 and again in 1954. From 1954 to 1959 he served as a representative to the territorial legislature. In 1962 he was elected to the House of Representatives as a Democrat, to replace **Daniel K. Inouye** who had been elected to the United States Senate. He served in the House from 1963 until 1977. He was elected to the U.S. Senate in 1976 and reelected to the post in 1982 and 1988. He worked tirelessly on behalf of Japanese Americans who sought redress for their internment during World War II and was one of the legislative leaders that brought redress to reality. **See also** Redress Movement,

BIBLIOGRAPHY

Chuman, Frank. *The Bamboo People.* Del Mar, CA: Publisher's Inc., 1976

Matsunaga, Spark M. "An Academy of Peace." *The Futurist* (February 1985): 4+.
Matsunaga, Spark M. and Ping Chen. *Rulemakers of the House.* Urbana: University of Illinois Press, 1976.

McCreary Amendment of 1892

The **Geary Act of 1892** continued earlier laws forbidding Chinese immigration to the United States, but it also stipulated that all people of Chinese ancestry living in the United States must carry a residential permit. Under the Geary Act, Chinese were ordered to obtain a residential permit within a year of the act's enforcement; however, many of these residents had failed to do so by 1893. Because the penalty for not carrying a permit was deportation, the United States did not want to enforce this on a massive scale. So the McCreary Amendment, which extended the deadline for obtaining residential permits by six months, was quickly passed. **See also** Immigration Restriction Movement.

BIBLIOGRAPHY
Coolidge, Mary R. *Chinese Immigration.* New York: Henry Holt, 1909.

Benjamin Menor (1922–)

A long-time practicing lawyer in Hawaii, Benjamin Menor served as Hawaii county attorney from 1953 to 1959. In 1962, Menor became the first Filipino American to be elected to a legislature in the United States, when he was elected to the Hawaii state senate. He did not stand for reelection in 1966 and returned to his law practice. In 1974, Menor became the first Filipino to be appointed judge in the Hawaii Supreme Court.

BIBLIOGRAPHY
Zia, Helen and Susan B. Gall. *Notable Asian Americans.* Detroit, MI: Gale, 1995.

Merchant Marine Act of 1936

Signed into law in June 1936 by President Franklin D. Roosevelt, the Merchant Marine Act was intended to secure more U.S. employment during the Great Depression. The act mandated that 90 percent of the total crews on all U.S. merchant ships be U.S. citizens. This greatly affected the Filipino community, as many were employed at the time as ship workers in the Louisiana Gulf region. Between the years of 1930 and 1935, approximately 5,800 to 7,800 Filipinos were employed on U.S. vessels. On June 29, 1936, the act was put into practice, and many Filipino sailors were suddenly unemployed. In April 1937, Louisiana State Senator Allen Ellender proposed to amend the act to help Filipinos in the New Orleans area who had lost their jobs. Despite his numerous petitions, little was done at the time to make changes. Similar acts and exclusion clauses continued to limit jobs for non-Americans up until the time of **World War II**, when more manpower was needed for the U.S. war effort.

BIBLIOGRAPHY
Melendy, H. Brett. *Asians in America.* Boston: Twayne, 1977.

Dale Minami (1946–)

Dale Minami is a civil rights attorney who has handled some of the most important cases in Asian-American civil rights. In 1972, he became managing attorney for the **Asian Law Caucus.** He headed the fundraising efforts of the organization in order to get the group going. In that same year, he was the lead attorney in *Chan v. Scott*, a class action suit to prevent police from conducting sweeps of Chinese youths suspected of being in gangs. In 1987 he handled the tenure denial case of Don Nakanishi at the University of California, Los Angeles. He chaired the Attorney General's Asian/Pacific Advisory Committee (1988–1990) and was president of the Coalition of Asian Pacific Americans (1988–1992). He serves on the Board of Governors of the Japanese American National Museum and in 1994 was appointed by President Bill Clinton to chair the Civil Liberties Public Education Fund Commission.

BIBLIOGRAPHY
Wei, William. *The Asian American Movement.* Philadelphia: Temple University Press, 1994.
Zia, Helen and Susan B. Gall, eds. *Notable Asian Americans.* Detroit, MI: Gale, 1995.

Norman Y. Mineta (1931–)

Mayor of San Jose, California, from 1971 until 1974, Norman Mineta was elected to the U.S. House of Representatives as a Democrat from California in 1974. With his term beginning in 1975, he became the first non-Hawaiian Asian American to serve in Congress. While in Congress, Mineta has proved to be a moderate voter. His district, which includes much of Silicon Valley in California, had traditionally been Republican territory. However, Mineta has been reelected every cycle without much trouble. Mineta, who was in an **internment camp** in Wyoming during **World War II**, was lead sponsor of the Japanese American Redress bill. In 1995, Mineta left Congress to become a lobbyist for Lockheed Martin. **See also** Redress Movement.

BIBLIOGRAPHY
Barone, Michael. *Politics in America.* Washington, D.C.: National Journal, 1992.

Patsy Takemoto Mink (1927–)

Democratic Congresswoman Patsy Takemoto Mink, a Japanese American, served in the House of Representatives from 1965 to 1977 and then again in 1990. The second woman of Asian ancestry admitted to the bar in Hawaii, she has spent nearly 40 years in politics, including a brief presidential bid in 1972. Mink opposed American involvement in the **Vietnam War**, seeing it as contributing to the "continued slaughter of Asians by Asians." A member of the Budget and Education committees during the Clinton administration, she helped protect an education program for native Hawaiians from budget cuts.

Mink's grandparents came from Japan to work in the sugar cane fields, and five of her relatives served with distinction during **World War II**. As a member of the territorial legislature, she was a leader in the drive for statehood. After leaving the House to run unsuccessfully for the Senate, Mink joined the Carter administration's State Department as an assistant secretary and served on the Honolulu City Council. (JHT)

BIBLIOGRAPHY

Chamberlin, Hope. *A Minority of Members: Women in the U.S. Congress.* New York: Praeger, 1973.

Foerstel, Karen and Herbert N. Foerstel. *Climbing the Hill: Gender Conflict in Congress.* Westport, CT: Praeger, 1996.

Minoru Yasui v. United States (1943)

Minoru Yasui, an American-born individual of Japanese ancestry, was convicted in 1942 of violating a curfew order applying to certain western states. In *Minoru Yasui v. United States,* 320 U.S. 115 (1943), the conviction was upheld by the U.S. Supreme Court.

Public Proclamation No. 3 of the Western Defense Command, 7 Fed. Reg. 2543 (1942) (issued by General John L. DeWitt) ordered all persons of Japanese ancestry living in certain western states to remain in their homes from 8:00 P.M. to 6:00 A.M. On March 28, 1942, Yasui deliberately violated the curfew when he walked into a police station in Portland, Oregon. Yasui was found guilty of violating restrictions imposed on people of Japanese ancestry in the United States. Yasui challenged his conviction, citing that the curfew did not apply to citizens of the United States; he had been born and educated in Oregon and had been a second lieutenant in the U.S. Army. The district court ruled that the order was unconstitutional as applied to American citizens, but it held that Yasui's conduct was a renouncement of his American citizenship. Yasui was given the maximum sentence of one year in prison and a $5,000 fine. The Supreme Court diverged from the lower court's findings, holding that the curfew order was valid as applied to citizens, and thus the issue of citizenship was not relevant to the conviction.

In 1983, Yasui, along with **Fred Korematsu** and **Gordon Hirabayashi**, petitioned federal courts to declare the curfew orders unconstitutional and to set aside their **World War II** convictions for violating curfew and evacuation orders. Both the indictment and judgment were dismissed by the United States District Court for the District of Oregon in 1984. See also *Hirabayashi v. United States* (1943); *Korematsu v. United States* (1943). (JK)

BIBLIOGRAPHY

Kim, Hyung-Chan, ed. *Asian Americans and the Supreme Court: A Documentary History.* New York: Greenwood Press, 1992.

Model Minority

Asian Americans are sometimes considered to be a "model minority," a now-controversial assertion that reveals some of the complexity of the politics of race. Writers point to the high levels of education, income, and occupational status—and low crime rates—of many Asian Americans in arguing that they are a "model minority" that has succeeded primarily because of personal qualities rather than public policy. Their accomplishments, often in the face of substantial prejudice, are said to be the consequence of hard work, thrift, high morals, commitment to education, and other desirable traits.

The notion of Asian Americans as a model minority is generally considered to have begun in the mid-1960s. William Peterson's 1966 *New York Times Magazine* story on the success of Japanese Americans is usually cited as the first to popularize the model minority idea. A *U.S. News and World Report* article later that year highlighted the achievements of Chinese Americans, and, in the 1980s, the accomplishments of Korean, Vietnamese, and other Asian Americans were hailed in a number of stories that appeared in major publications.

Some writers have cited these accomplishments as evidence of the irrelevance of race-conscious policies, such as multicultural education or **affirmative action**, while other analysts have charged that Asian-American success has been deliberately exaggerated to undermine the claims of racial minorities when they call for race-based compensatory policies. The reality is more complex than either view.

The achievements are indeed impressive. Critics note that the higher household incomes for Asian Americans are the result of above-average numbers of family members working, but this obscures the fact that median individual income levels are lower for Asian Americans than for white Americans. Nevertheless, household incomes are an important indicator of accomplishment and are a better measure (than individual income) of the resources that parents can pass on to their children. High Asian-American household incomes bode well for the next generation of Asian Americans.

On the other hand, critics are correct when they note that comparisons of Asian Americans with African Americans or Native Americans are dubious. While Japanese and Chinese Americans did indeed prosper in the face of prejudice and without the aid of public policies, their circumstances were substantially different than those of the other groups. For instance, while Asian immigrants were able to establish language schools and other institutions designed to maintain their culture, American Indian children were removed form their homes and sent to schools that sought to eradicate their heritage. And, while Japanese and Chinese immigrants faced severe prejudice in the workforce, their relatively small numbers enabled substantial percentages of them to find work in the few niches available (such as laundries or gardening)—unlike African Americans, whose much larger numbers overwhelmed the few openings they found.

Furthermore, critics of the model minority concept are correct when they point out that recent Asian immigrants have had more mixed success. Immigrants with little or no education—such as the Hmong from Southeast Asia—have struggled, highlighting the diverse nature of Asian America, and calling into question the usefulness of the term "Asian American."

An even-handed assessment would acknowledge that many—but not all—Asian Americans have had impressive success in this country, but that the Asian-American experience does not provide an adequate basis for evaluating other racial minorities in the United States. **See also** Asian-American Relations with Other Minorities. (ALA)

BIBLIOGRAPHY

Osajima, Keith. "Asian Americans as the Model Minority: An Analysis of the Popular Press Image in the 1960s and the 1980s." In Gary Y. Okihiro et al., eds. *Reflections on Shattered Windows: Promises and Prospects for Asian American Studies*. Pullman: Washington State University Press, 1988.

Peterson, William. "Success Story, Japanese-American Style." *New York Times Magazine* (January 9, 1966): 20–21, 33, 36, 38, 40–41, 43.

Suzuki, Bob. "Education and the Socialization of Asian Americans: A Revisionist Analysis of the 'Model Minority' Thesis." *Amerasia Journal* 4, no. 2 (1977): 23–51.

Morrison v. People of the State of California (1934)

Morrison v. People of the State of California, 291 U.S. 82 (1934), involved two men, George Morrison and H. Doi, who were arrested and charged with failing to comply with the **California Alien Land Act of 1913**. This law stated that no persons who were ineligible for U.S. citizenship could purchase land in California. Doi, who was a Japanese alien, had attempted to acquire land from Morrison. The two men were arrested on conspiracy charges and found guilty of violating the Alien Land Act. They appealed on the grounds that the act violated their Fourteenth Amendment rights. However, the case was heard by the U.S. Supreme Court in 1933, and the Court upheld the constitutionality of the California Land Act. **See** California Alien Land Act of 1920 in Appendix 1.

BIBLIOGRAPHY

Churman, Frank. *The Bamboo People*. Del Mar, CA: Publisher's' Inc., 1976.

Konvitz, Milton R. *The Alien and the Asiatic in American Law*. Ithaca, NY: Cornell University Press, 1946.

Multiculturalism

Multiculturalism, which relates to cultural differences within a society, has been a major political concern throughout American history. Although the word itself has only been a source of controversy since the early 1980s, questions of cultural difference have been central issues from the time Europeans first confronted Native Americans.

In the United States, much of the politics surrounding multiculturalism is fueled by competing views of cultural difference and how American society should deal with it. Looking from the perspective of the motto "*E pluribus unum*" ("From many, one") that appears on the Great Seal of the United States, much of the debate over multiculturalism can be thought of as an argument over the proper balance between the *pluribus* (the diversity in American society) and the *unum* (the common ties that bind society together).

Some of the most prominent views of multiculturalism are examined here. Three broad positions dominate discussions of multiculturalism; in this essay, these positions are labeled liberal multiculturalism, pluralistic multiculturalism, and monoculturalism.

This discussion will be based primarily on the politics of multicultural education, although multiculturalism can be a concern in employment, the arts, social clubs, or virtually any other area of life. In the concluding section, the role of Asian Americans specifically will be considered.

Asian Americans have often struggled to retain aspects of their culture, such as the Japanese tradition of Kabuki theater pictured here. *Library of Congress.*

A key disagreement dividing the three most prevalent views of multiculturalism regards the definition of a distinct cultural group. While many agree that different nationality groups are also different cultural groups, so that Germans, Chinese, and Nigerians would each compose distinct cultural groups, there is much less agreement over whether different ethnic or racial groups are also distinct cultural groups. Do Americans of African, Asian, and European descent belong to one or to three distinct cultural groups?

Liberal multiculturalism argues that most Americans—whatever their ancestry—share a common culture, even though they may be divided into different subcultural groups. For example, Japanese Americans and German Americans can communicate easily with each other (most are native English speakers), have many of the same aspirations, enjoy similar forms of entertainment, and, perhaps most important, share a commitment to certain core political ideas—such as representative government, civil liberties and civil rights, and political equality. Liberal multiculturalists see these shared understandings as elements of a common culture.

Liberal multiculturalists agree that the two groups are likely to differ in many ways—for example, in dietary practices, church memberships, or holiday observances—but these differences are transcended by the shared culture. In some places, such as Bosnia or the Sudan, these differences are far more important, and they can even lead to civil war. What these areas lack—and what the United States has, argue advocates of liberal multiculturalism—is a common culture that surmounts differences and unites a diverse array of people.

Liberal multiculturalism appears to be the dominant perspective in American schools today, where it is common to find an emphasis on treating each student as a unique individual who is shaped but not fully determined by heritage and ancestry. The increasingly widespread efforts to teach about non-European experiences is often accompanied by an emphasis on the principles that all Americans can share and that tie us together. The easy acceptance of Martin Luther King, Jr. as an American hero (rather than just a role model for African Americans) demonstrates the power of liberal multiculturalism.

Another view, here called "pluralistic multiculturalism," denies that there is any meaningful national culture and focuses on the many differences between groups. Pluralistic multiculturalists believe that the shared culture—if, in fact, one even exists—is less consequential than the cultural differences.

Pluralistic multiculturalists often wish to preserve cultural differences. At a minimum, they argue, American society will not allow these differences to become insignificant. If one looks at the dismal treatment of American Indians, African Americans, Latinos, and Asian Americans, they contend, one can see a widespread unwillingness to treat nonwhites fairly. Color-conscious remedies such as multiculturalism are necessary to counter this deeply embedded racial discrimination (often referred to as "institutional racism").

Perhaps the best known—and most controversial—version of pluralistic multiculturalism is known as "Afrocentrism." While there are different versions of Afrocentrism, one of the most prominent is the view that argues that those of African ancestry are fundamentally different from those not of African ancestry. From the perspective of Afrocentrists, liberal multiculturalists fail to comprehend the deep divisions that separate those of different ancestries.

In the popular press, many of the attacks on "multiculturalism" are targeted at Afrocentrism or other versions of pluralistic multiculturalism, which critics charge weaken the ties that bind America together. Some of the harshest views of pluralistic multiculturalists come from liberal multiculturalists, such as Arthur Schlesinger, Jr., whose book *The Disuniting of America* has become one of the most widely quoted works in the debate over multiculturalism.

Pluralistic multiculturalists are often—but not always—politically allied with those who are critical of the economic system of the United States. The latter, who might be called "economic multiculturalists," are often more concerned about economics than culture, and they usually call for a substantial redistribution of resources. This view is widely shared in certain academic disciplines but has yet to win substantial support in the general public; as a result, "economic multiculturalism" has yet to become a substantial political presence.

The monocultural perspective also sees cultural differences as persistent, but it fears rather than celebrates those differences. Monoculturalists usually wish to reduce cultural pluralism (that is, the existence of many different cultural groups) in the United States, and so they advocate substantial reductions in immigration, particularly immigration from Asia, Latin America, and Africa. Unlike the other views described in this essay, monoculturalists oppose multiculturalism, fearing that it threatens a common American culture.

Monoculturalism appeared to make political gains in the 1990s, but it remains a minority player in American conservatism. Patrick Buchanan's fiery speech at the 1992 Republican National Convention was a call to his fellow monoculturalists, but most other Republicans saw it as a disaster that alienated much of the remainder of the electorate, leading monoculturalism to be viewed as a political liability. Whether that will change in the future is uncertain.

Both monoculturalists and pluralistic multiculturalists can be criticized for their understanding of American history. With important exceptions, newcomers to the United States have adapted to the larger society, often overcoming substantial discrimination and, eventually, losing much of their cultural distinctiveness. Each new wave of immigrants has been greeted with fears of cultural pollution (similar to the fears of monoculturalists), but those fears have always been unfounded.

Liberal multiculturalists, in contrast, stress the adaptive power of American society. Some, such as Nathan Glazer and Daniel Patrick Moynihan, argue that considerable subcultural variation remains within a common culture, as immigrants gradually develop an ethnic identity that maintains some sense of distinctiveness, even as they assimilate to the common culture.

Liberal multiculturalists point out the dynamic nature of American society and note that past sources of great difference between groups have often become insignificant today. Even some of the deep-seated societal taboos—such as marriage between Catholics and Protestants—have become widely accepted. While liberal multiculturalists agree that significant differences still separate Americans—perhaps most importantly, the racial divide between black and white—they argue that these divisions can and should be reduced. Underlying liberal multiculturalism is an emphasis on individual rights, which respects differences but also undermines them. Honoring individual rights requires that individuals be treated equally regardless of differences of ancestry or heritage, but it also means that groups will not be allowed to maintain their hold on individuals who wish to break away.

Some liberal multiculturalists cite the Asian-American experiences as evidence for their views. When one examines the experiences of Asian Americans whose families have been in the United States for many decades—say, 50 years or more—one finds the patterns described by liberal multiculturalists. Japanese Americans, for instance, have prospered and become highly integrated into the larger society, despite early twentieth-century laws preventing Japanese immigrants from becoming citizens or owning land, the **World War II** incarceration in **internment camps** of more than 100,000 Japanese Americans (whose "crime" was to be of Japanese descent), and countless other instances of legal and extralegal discrimination. Perhaps most important, rates of intermarriage—marriage between Japanese Americans and non-Japanese Americans—are so high that the continuing distinctiveness of the Japanese-American community is in question. Similar trends can be found in other long-settled Asian-American communities, although the developments are often obscured because all Asian-American groups (except Japanese Americans) contain large numbers of recent immigrants.

This is not to suggest that Asian Americans have been in the vanguard of those advocating multiculturalism. Although Asian Americans have long been aware of the European bias of American education, the first waves of Asian immigrants responded by establishing their own language and cultural schools, rather than attempting to alter the monocultural curriculum that was widespread in public schools in the late nineteenth and early twentieth centuries. While overt Asian-American support for multiculturalism is more evident today, many Asian immigrants appear to be continuing the practice of transmitting their heritage through private institutions.

A few groups, such as the Hmong, have been active in calling for curriculum that gives more attention to their culture, and the hiring of more teachers of Asian ancestry. As with African Americans, many Hmong parents are concerned over difficulties their children have faced in public schools, and they hope that a greater commitment to a culturally sensitive learning environment might reduce some of those problems. In addition, many Asian-American scholars are strong supporters of pluralistic multiculturalism.

It is unclear, however, whether the often-tacit Asian-American support for liberal multiculturalism will change as Asian Americans grow in numbers. Currently, only in certain parts of academia can one find substantial Asian-American support for a more pluralistic multiculturalism, but many first-generation Asian Americans seem to share a widespread immigrant desire to preserve much of their heritage and to resist being engulfed by the culture of their new country. What is clear, however, is that the large influx of Asian (as well as Latino) immigrants will continue to force Americans to confront the challenges of multiculturalism, and America will continue to wrestle with questions of cultural difference as the country enters a new millennium. **See also** Bilingual Education Act; *Guey Heung Lee v. Johnson* (1971); *Lau v. Nichols* (1974). (ALA)

BIBLIOGRAPHY

Asante, Molefi Kete. *The Afrocentric Idea*. Philadelphia: Temple University Press, 1987.

Auster, Lawrence. *The Path to National Suicide: An Essay on Immigration and Multiculturalism*. Monterey, VA: American Immigration Control Foundation, 1990.

Gans, Herbert J. "Symbolic Ethnicity: The Future of Ethnic Groups and Cultures in America."' In Herbert J. Gans, Nathan Glazer, Joseph R. Gusfield, and Christopher Jencks, eds. *On the Making of Americans: Essays in Honor of David Riesman*. Philadelphia: University of Pennsylvania Press, 1979.

Glazer, Nathan and Daniel Patrick Moynihan. *Beyond the Melting Pot: The Negroes, Puerto Ricans, Jews, Italians, and Irish of New York City*. 2nd ed. Cambridge, MA: MIT Press, 1970.

Goldberg, David Theo, ed. *Multiculturalism: A Critical Reader*. Cambridge, MA: Blackwell, 1994.

Gordon, Avery F. and Christopher Newfield, eds. *Mapping Multiculturalism*. Minneapolis: University of Minnesota Press, 1996.

Hollinger, David A. *Postethnic America: Beyond Multiculturalism*. New York: Basic Books, 1995.

Kallen, Horace M. *Cultural Pluralism and the American Idea: An Essay in Social Philosophy*. Philadelphia: University of Pennsylvania Press, 1956.

Ravitch, Diane. "Multiculturalism: *e pluribus plures*." *The American Scholar* 59 (1990): 337–354.

Schlesinger, Arthur, Jr. *The Disuniting of America: Reflections on a Multicultural Society*. Knoxville, TN: Whittle Direct Books, 1991.

Munson Report

In October and November 1941, Curtis B. Munson, a special agent to the state department, analyzed the pro-American sentiment among Japanese Americans living in Hawaii and the West Coast. He completed his investigation just prior to the bombing of **Pearl Harbor.** In a very detailed report, in which he analyzed different generations, he found most Japanese Americans had a great deal of loyalty toward the United States. However, this information was largely ignored when the U.S. government decided to evacuate and relocate all people of Japanese ancestry living on the West Coast shortly after the Japanese attack on Pearl Harbor. **See also** Civilian Exclusion Orders; Executive Order 9066. **See** Executive Order 9066 in Appendix 1.

BIBLIOGRAPHY

Hosokawa, Bill. *Nisei*. New York: William Morrow, 1969.
Weglyn, Michi. *Years of Infamy*. New York: William Morrow, 1976.

Mutual Assistance Society

The Mutual Assistance Society (Tac-Hanin Kungmin) was formed in California in 1905. It was the first Korean political association in the United States; the group's aim was to help liberate Korea from Japan. By 1909 the society had more than 100 members. In that year, the society joined with the Hanin Hapsong Hyophoe (United Korean Society) of Hawaii to form the **Korean National Association. See also** Kongnip Hyop-Hoe.

BIBLIOGRAPHY

Choy, Bong-youn. *Koreans in America*. Chicago: Nelson-Hall, 1979.
Kim, Hyung-chan, ed. *The Korean Diaspora*. Santa Barbara, CA: ABC-Clio Press, 1977.

Naim v. Naim (1953)

On June 26, 1952, Naim Ham Say, a Chinese seaman, and Ruby Elaine Naim, a Caucasian American, were married in North Carolina. Soon after the wedding, the couple moved to Virginia, where they set about to take permanent residence. However, plans were cut short when, on September 30, 1953, Ruby Naim sought an annulment from the marriage; she based her request on claims that the marriage was illegal according to Virginia state law, which presented restrictions on such interracial unions. The Virginia court accepted the annulment, which prompted Naim Ham Say to seek an appeal with the Virginia State Supreme Court. When this court likewise held the annulment, Naim Ham Say sought to pursue the case again, this time in the United States Supreme Court. However, in *Naim v. Naim*, 350 U.S. 891 (1953), the Court refused to rehear the case, stating that such matters were state, not federal, questions. While this decision had minimal impact on marriage practice legislation, it did reflect the ethnic biases still in existence in American society at the time.

In 1967, the U.S. Supreme Court took a different view, holding in *Loving v. Virginia,* 388 U.S. 1, (1967), that a Virginia law banning interracial marriage violated the Fourteenth Amendment's equal protection and due process guarantees; and so, almost 200 years after the nation's founding, all bans on interracial marriage were rendered void.

BIBLIOGRAPHY

Kim, Hyung-Chan. *Dictionary of Asian American History.* New York: Greenwood Press, 1986.

Ng, Franklin, ed. *The Asian American Encyclopedia.* New York: Marshall Cavendish, 1995.

Sickels, Robert J. *Race, Marriage, and Law.* Albuquerque, NM: University of New Mexico Press, 1972.

Philip Tajitsu Nash (1956–)

Philip Nash is a civil rights activist, lawyer, teacher, and writer. He is currently the executive director of the National Asian Pacific American Legal Consortium in Washington, D.C. He has been involved with the Asian American Legal Defense and Educational Fund. He served on the board of the **Japanese American Citizens League** and helped found the Coalition of Asian Pacific American Associations. Nash also cofounded the Inter-Change Consultants, the AmerAsian League, the National Asian Pacific American Law Students Association, and the **National Asian Pacific American Bar Association**.

BIBLIOGRAPHY

Nash, Philip Tajitsu. "Creating Critical Consciousness; Paulo Freire and the Mechanics of Teaching Asian American Studies." In Gary Okihiro, et al., eds. *Reflections on Shattered Windows: Promises and Prospects for Asian American Studies.* Pullman: Washington State University Press, 1988.

National Asian Pacific American Bar Association

This nonprofit, nonpartisan national legal organization represents the interests of Asian Pacific American attorneys and the national Asian community. The bar association is made up of local, regional, and state bar associations and individuals, and it is a national communications network. The group also provides a support group and legally represents those in need.

BIBLIOGRAPHY

Gall, Susan. *The Asian American Almanac.* Detroit, MI: Gale, 1994.

National Asian Pacific American Legal Consortium (NAPALC)

The first pan-Asian legal organization of a national stature, the National Asian Pacific American Legal Consortium (NAPALC) was founded in Washington, D.C., in 1993 by three regionally based civil rights organizations. Its mission is to advance the legal and civil rights of the Asian-American community through litigation, advocacy, public education, and public policy development. The consortium is best known for publishing an annual audit on anti-Asian violence. Other priorities include voting rights, immigrant rights, language rights, **affirmative action**, and fairness and accuracy of the 2000 U.S. Census. (PL)

BIBLIOGRAPHY

Interview with Karen Narasaki, NAPALC Executive Director, June 2, 1996.

National Asian Pacific American Legal Consortium. *Annual Report.* Washington, D.C. 1996.

National Chinese Welfare Council

The National Chinese Welfare Council was founded in 1957 by Chinatown leaders to work toward more favorable immigration laws for the Chinese. The group was formed from the National Conference of Chinese Communities in America. The council also fought for minority rights and an improved political position. The organization is composed of **Chinese Consolidated Benevolent Association (CCBA)** members. New York and San Francisco's CCBAs disagreed with various policies and split from the council in 1992, so the San Francisco CCBA founded the National Chinese Welfare Council of Western United States.

BIBLIOGRAPHY

Mark, Diane Mei Lin and Ginger Chih. *A Place Called Chinese America*. Dubuque, IA: Kendall/Hunt Publishing Co., 1993.
Tsai, Shih-Shan Henry. *The Chinese Experience in America*. Bloomington: Indiana University Press, 1986.

National Committee for Redress

In 1976 **Edison Uno** convinced the **Japanese American Citizens League (JACL)** to ask the U.S. government for compensation for those interred during **World War II.** Uno formed the National Committee for Redress and immediately began enlisting support from the Japanese community. In 1977 Uno died and **Clifford Uyeda** became chairman of the committee. The final plan, which came to include heirs of those who had been interred during World War II, was agreed upon at the 1978 JACL national convention. The committee then turned its attention to the formation of a bill to investigate the treatment of Japanese Americans during World War II; this led to the formation in 1980 of the **Commission on Wartime Relocation and Internment of Civilians. See also** Civilian Exclusion Orders; Civil Liberties Act of 1988; Executive Order 9066; Redress Movement.

BIBLIOGRAPHY

Hosakawa, Bill. *JACL in Quest of Justice.* New York: William Morrow, 1982.

National Council for Japanese-American Redress

Formed in May 1979 under the leadership of William Hohri, the National Council for Japanese-American Redress was a coalition of groups including the Little Tokyo People's Rights Association and the Asian Pacific Student Union. The joint effort sought redress for survivors of the U.S. **internment camps** during **World War II.** In November 1980, the organization held a redress conference in Los Angeles. The group's efforts led to the 1988 **Civil Liberties Act,** signed by President Ronald Reagan, which secured $1.25 billion for the 70,000 survivors of the internment camps. **See also** Redress Movement.

BIBLIOGRAPHY

Wei, William *The Asian American Movement*. Philadelphia: Temple University Press, 1993.

National Democratic Council of Asian and Pacific Americans

The National Democratic Council of Asian and Pacific Americans (NDCAPA) was formed in the aftermath of the 1984 presidential elections. At that time, the Democratic Party decided to dismantle many of its special interests caucuses, including the Asian Pacific Caucus. The party believed that it lost the 1984 elections because it was seen as catering to a myriad of special interests. The NDCAPA was organized by leading Asian and Pacific Americans as an independent national organization of Democrats. The goal was to empower and unite Asian and Pacific Democrats so that they would not be taken for granted by the Democratic Party. In 1988, the group held its first major conference, called Target 88/Margin of Victory, which attracted major candidates and confirmed the influence of the group.

BIBLIOGRAPHY

Wei, William *The Asian American Movement*. Philadelphia: Temple University Press, 1993.

National Reform Party

In 1890 two Hawaiian political organizations banded together into the National Reform Party because they both did not want the Asian Reform Party to win power in the elections. However, the two groups were very different. One, the Hui Kaliaiaina or Hawaiian Political Association, wanted Hawaiian natives to come to power, and the other group, the Mechanics' and Workingmens' Political Protective Association, wanted whites to rule Hawaii. The election was a draw between the National Reform Party and the Asian Reform Party.

BIBLIOGRAPHY

Kuykendall, Ralph S. and A. Grove Day. *Hawaii: A History.* New York: Prentice Hall, 1948.

Native American Programs Act of 1974

The Native American Programs Act was created to help recognize native Hawaiians as official U.S. States citizens, so that they would be eligible for special federal programs. The 1974 act sought to improve upon the Economic Opportunity Act of 1964, which provided federal assistance to groups, by making it more inclusive. The 1974 legislation provided financial assistance through the U.S. Department of Health and Human Services for projects which involved research, education, or which otherwise promoted self-sufficiency among native Pacific Americans. The act also funded up to 80 percent of the costs for public and nonprofit organizations dedicated to helping Samoan and Hawaiian natives.

Several changes were made to the Native American Programs Act after its implementation in 1974. First, in 1975, Alu Like, a nonprofit organization dedicated to helping Pacific Americans, was created to help evaluate need and properly distribute federal funds. In 1987, the definition of Native American Pacific Islanders was broadened to encompass all native Hawaiians, Samoans, and Pacific Island occupants, thereby further extending the jurisdiction of the act. Amendments in 1987 also made it clear that a revolving loan fund of $3 million would be distributed from 1988 to 1990. In 1992, the government again approved $3 million for an additional three-year cycle, which was to be matched equally by the Office of Hawaiian Affairs.

BIBLIOGRAPHY

"Reagan Opposes Amendments." *San Diego Union-Tribune* (September 27, 1986): A18.

Native Hawaiian Health Care Act of 1988

On October 31, 1988, Congress adopted the Native Hawaiian Health Care Act as an amendment to the Indian Health Care Improvement Act of 1976. The law authorized the establishment of health centers incorporating traditional Hawaiian healers and Western-trained health personnel for programs of disease prevention, health promotion, and primary health services other than in-patient services. In 1992, the legislation was reauthorized, setting numerical goals for the reduction of various health conditions by the year 2000 and providing scholarships in health fields to native Hawaiians. (MH)

BIBLIOGRAPHY

Miike, Lawrence. *Current Health Status and Population Projections of Native Hawaiians Living in Hawaii.* Washington, D.C.: Office of Technology Assessment, 1987.

Native Hawaiians Study Commission

The Native Hawaiians Study Commission was a nine-member commission created to study the arising questions of the overthrow of the Hawaiian monarchy in 1893 and its relations to the native Hawaiian property claims. The first commission was appointed by President Jimmy Carter in 1980. It was then replaced with new appointees by President Ronald Reagan in 1981. The commission cleared the United States of direct responsibility of overthrowing **Queen Liliuokalani.** It also said federal action was not necessary in dealing with the property claims. **See also** Annexation of Hawaii.

BIBLIOGRAPHY

United States. Congress. House. Committee on Interior and Insular Affairs. *Native Hawaiian Study Commission Report: Oversight Hearing Before the Committee on Interior and Insular Affairs, House of Representatives, Ninety-Eighth Congress, second session . . . hearing held in Washington, D.C., May 3, 1984,* Washington, U.S. Government Printing Office, 1985.

Native Sons of the Golden West

The Native Sons of the Golden West was founded by General Albert Maver Winn on July 11, 1875. Membership was restricted to white males born in California on or after 1846. Young men were recruited via local newspapers to participate in Independence Day parades to dress in the miner's garb of their forefathers.

Between 1907 and 1920, the organization sought to protect U.S. economic standards from Japanese imperialism by pressuring the federal government to pass immigration laws.

To pursue that goal, the Native Sons opposed granting immigration quotas to Japan, statehood to Hawaii, and citizenship to Asians. **See also** Chinese American Citizens Alliance. (FHM)

BIBLIOGRAPHY

Conmy, Peter T. *The Origin and Purposes of the Native Sons and Native Daughters of the Golden West.* San Francisco: Dolores Press, 1956.

Irene Natividad (1948–)

Irene Natividad, a Filipina activist, feminist, and educator, was born on September 14, 1948. Her father was a chemical engineer who traveled extensively and brought his family to live in many parts of the world. Thus, in addition to English, Natividad became fluent in Spanish, French, Italian, Tagalog, Farsi, and Greek.

Her political activism began in New York City where she worked with waiters and waitresses and organized them to fight against their poor working conditions. Her activism led her in the 1980s to serve as founder and head of the Asian American Professional Women, National Network of Asian Pacific Women and the Child Care Action Campaign. She also chaired the New York State Asian Pacific Caucus from 1982 to 1984, served as deputy chair of the Asia Pacific Caucus of the Democratic National Committee, and served as the Asian-American liaison for the Geraldine Ferraro vice presidential campaign in 1984.

From 1985 to 1988 Natividad chaired the National Women's Political Caucus (NWPC); she was the first Asian-American woman to head a national women's organization. The NWPC is a bipartisan organization whose goal is to place women in political office and to increase women's influence in politics as voters, campaign staff members, and candidates. During the Clinton administration, Natividad was appointed director of Sallie Mae, the quasi-governmental corporation that administers student loans, chaired the National Commission on Working Women, was a director of Global Forum for Women, and was executive director of the Philippine America Foundation, while serving as the principal of her consulting firm, Natividad and Associates. (CGM)

BIBLIOGRAPHY

Brozan, Nadine. ". . . As Another Gets Ready to Broaden the Movement's Base." [Article reprinted from *The New York Times.*] *The Los Angeles Daily Journal* 98 (July 15, 1985): 4.

Zia, Helen and Susan B. Gall, eds. *Notable Asian Americans.* Detroit, MI: Gale Research, 1995.

Naturalization Act of 1790

Signed into law by President George Washington, the Naturalization Act of 1790 was the first U.S. legislation to establish who could and could not become naturalized citizens. The original law was also known as An Act to Establish a Uniform Rule of Naturalization. It stipulated that any free white person who had proof of residence in the United States for two years was eligible for citizenship. In 1795 the residency requirement was changed from two to five years. Persons of

African birth or descent were permitted to become citizens after the Civil War, but Asian Americans, who were neither black nor white, did not become eligible for citizenship until 1952.

BIBLIOGRAPHY

Chuman, Frank F. *The Bamboo People: The Law and Japanese Americans.* Del Mar, CA: Publisher's Inc., 1976.

Ng Fung Ho et al. v. White, Commissioner of Immigration (1922)

Ng Fung Ho, a Chinese laborer, his son, and two other Chinese men were arrested for being in the United States illegally, just before the passage of the **Immigration Act of 1917**. In *Ng Fung Ho et al. v. White, Commissioner of Immigration,* 259 U.S. 276 (1922), the U.S. Supreme Court ruled that aliens thought to be dangerous to the country could be deported at any time, even if they had been detained before the passage of the General Immigration Act of 1917. Because the four Chinese men all maintained that they were U.S. citizens, they had a right to a judicial hearing to determine if they were indeed citizens, but the burden of proof lay on them. The Court also stated that the Chinese did not have the right to be released from custody, and that they could be held until the trial to ascertain their citizenship.

BIBLIOGRAPHY

Konvitz, Milton. *The Alien and the Asiatic in American Law.* Ithaca, NY: Cornell University Press, 1946.

Nishikawa v. Dulles (1958)

In 1939, Mitsugi Nishikawa, a native-born American from California, went to Japan to further his studies; while there, he was forced to serve in the Japanese Army during **World War II.** For a number of years, he worked in this capacity as a mechanic and maintenance man for a Japanese Air Force regiment stationed in China. Nishikawa later stated that he was continuously physically and emotionally abused while serving in this post by soldiers who were angry with his pro-American connections. When the war ended, Nishikawa attempted to return to the United States, but he was denied access under the statement that his American citizenship had been revoked. He tried unsuccessfully to appeal the situation to U.S. Secretary of State John Foster Dulles, after which he sought assistance in court. After both the district court and the court of appeals denied his pleas, the case was moved to the United States Supreme Court. In *Nishikawa v. Dulles,* 356 U.S. 129 (1958), the Court found that there was no evidence that Nishikawa had voluntarily joined the Japanese Army and, as a result, should not have had his U.S. citizenship suspended. The Court also stressed that any American-born citizen could not be constitutionally denied continued citizenship rights.

BIBLIOGRAPHY

Chuman, Frank. *The Bamboo People: The Law and Japanese Americans.* Del Mar: Publisher's Inc., 1976.

Kim, Hyung-Chan. *Dictionary of Asian American History.* New York: Greenwood Press, 1986.

Kim, Hyung-Chan, ed. *Asian Americans and the Supreme Court: A Documentary History.* New York: Greenwood Press, 1992.

Ng, Franklin, ed. *The Asian American Encyclopedia.* New York: Marshall Cavendish, 1995.

Nishimura Ekiu v. United States (1892)

In 1891, Nishimura Ekiu, a Japanese woman, was refused the right to disembark in San Francisco by Commissioner William H. Thornley. Nishimura proved that she had money, a passport, and was married to a man who had lived in the United States for two years. In her writ of habeus corpus, she asserted that she had been unjustly detained and not allowed due process of law. In 1891 the circuit court stated that a tribunal had heard her case and that only the secretary of the treasury, not a court of law, could change the decision of the inspector of immigration. In 1892 the case was appealed to the Supreme Court. As *Nishimura v. United States,* 142 U.S. 651 (1892). In the case, the court affirmed the circuit court's ruling. **See also** Immigration Restriction Movement; *Lem Moon Sing v. United States* (1895).

BIBLIOGRAPHY

Chuman, Frank F. *The Bamboo People: The Law and Japanese-Americans.* Del Mar, CA: Publisher's Inc., 1976.

Konvitz, Milton. *The Alien and the Asiatic in American Law.* Ithaca, NY: Cornell University Press, 1946.

No-No Boys

In 1943, a year after President Franklin D. Roosevelt signed the Japanese-American evacuation order, the government required that all internees answer questionnaires about their loyalty and their willingness to serve in the U.S. armed forces. The purpose of these questionnaires was to draft the Japanese-American boys in the **internment camps**. Question 27 asked men of draft age if they would be willing to serve in the U.S. military, and question 28 asked if they would swear allegiance to the U.S. and forswear allegiance to any other foreign power. The No-No boys were those who answered "no" to both of these questions. In the Heart Mountain (Wyoming) Relocation Center, one group, the **Fair Play Committee**, organized an anti-draft movement. Some of the draft resisters from Heart Mountain and other camps were sent to the Tule Lake segregation center. Others were prosecuted and sentenced for draft evasion, but they were later pardoned by President Truman. **See also** Daihyo Sha Kai (Representative Body); Hokuku Seinen-Dan (Young Men's Organization to Serve Our Mother Country); Loyalty Oath/Test; *Okamoto Kiyoshi v. United States* (1945).

BIBLIOGRAPHY

Takaki, Ronald. *Strangers from A Different Shore.* Boston: Little Brown and Company.

Office of Hawaiian Affairs

The Office of Hawaiian Affairs was created by the 1978 constitutional convention of the State of Hawaii. It was formed to serve all Hawaiians by receiving and administering its share of public land trust funds to improve native Hawaiian conditions under the Admissions Act which originally set forth the provision under which Hawaii was admitted as a state in 1959. The office is a combination of a public trust and a government agency. The office also acts as a principal state agency for programs concerning Hawaiians.

BIBLIOGRAPHY

"Hawaiians to Vote on Ethnicity." *St. Louis Post-Dispatch* (December 31, 1989): 44G.

MacKenzie, Melody Kapilialoha, ed. *Native Hawaiian Rights Handbook.* Honolulu: University of Hawaii Press, 1991.

Office of Redress Administration

The Office of Redress Administration was created as a part of the U.S. Department of Justice in response to the efforts of the **National Committee for Redress** and other groups seeking to amend injustices caused against Japanese Americans during **World War II.** President Ronald Reagan called upon the office to issue and review monetary disbursements entitled to formerly interned citizens of Japanese ancestry, as well as deal with other provisions established in the **Civil Liberties Act of 1988.** The Office of Redress Administration soon started an active working relationship with the **Japanese American Citizens League** and the **National Coalition for Redress and Reparations;** together these three groups successfully located approximately 75,000 Japanese-American citizens who were eligible for benefits because of their forced relocation to **internment camps** during World War II. The office also provided a telephone hotline and workshops to help internment camp survivors in regards to their funding entitlements, as well as to help manage the processing of related paperwork.

BIBLIOGRAPHY

O'Brien, David J. and Stephen S. Fugita. *The Japanese American Experience.* Bloomington: Indiana University Press, 1991.

Wei, William. *The Asian American Movement.* Philadelphia: Temple University Press, 1993.

Angela Eunjin Oh (1955–)

Angela Oh is probably best known as the spokesperson for Korean Americans in Los Angeles in the aftermath of the 1992 riots. More than 2,000 Korean businesses were damaged or destroyed. Afterwards she was appointed by California State Assembly Speaker Willie Brown to co-chair the assembly's Special Committee on the Los Angeles Crisis. Oh also serves as chair of Senator Barbara Boxer's judiciary advisory committee. She has written several articles published in the *New York Times* and the *Los Angeles Times.* She was a board member of the American Civil Liberties Union and president of the Korean Bar Association in 1992.

BIBLIOGRAPHY

Riptson, Ramona. "Ramona Riptson in Conversation with Angela Oh." *Open Forum* 68, no. 4 (Winter 1993): 1–6.

On Lee v. United States (1952)

On Lee was a laundry owner in Hoboken, California. While in the presence of a former employee, Chin Poy, On Lee made incriminating remarks about opium sales. Poy, who was employed at that time as an undercover agent for the Bureau of Narcotics, secretly taped this conversation with Lee and turned it over for evidence. After a second taped conversation between Lee and Poy revealed more connections to opium sales, On Lee was arrested.

Lee was eventually convicted of opium selling. He appealed the verdict, calling into question the search and seizure procedures used against him. On appeal, Lee argued that the use of secret transmission devices, such as the ones used to tape his conversations with Chin Poy, was illegal because it violated his Fourteenth Amendment rights. Lee argued that the opium case should be dropped because evidence used in it constituted entrapment and was considered self-incriminating. The California courts disagreed with On Lee and, in *On Lee v. United States,* 343 U.S. 747 (1952), the U.S. Supreme Court concurred, stating that methods for obtaining evidence in such situations should be viewed on their credibility.

BIBLIOGRAPHY

Lyman, Stanford. *Chinese Americans.* New York: Random House, 1974.

100th Infantry Battalion

The 100th Infantry Battalion, also known as the Purple Heart Battalion because of the extraordinary number of Purple Hearts its members were awarded, was an all-volunteer unit made up of Japanese-American reservists. A segregated Hawaiian outfit, the group saw action in the European theater in Italy, France, and Germany where it earned a reputation as one of the bravest units. **See also** 442nd Regimental Combat Team; "Spark" Masayuke Matsunaga.

BIBLIOGRAPHY

Spickard, Paul R. *Japanese Americans: The Formation and Transformation of an Ethnic Group*. New York: Twayne Publishers, 1996.

Wing Foon Ong (1904–1977)

Wing F. Ong emigrated to the United States in 1918. At the age of 36 he ran for his first elected office in the state of Arizona, but he lost. He left politics temporarily to pursue a law degree. He was then elected to the Arizona House of Representatives, making him the first Chinese American to serve in a state legislature. In 1966, Ong was elected to the state senate after several unsuccessful bids, but he was not reelected in 1968.

BIBLIOGRAPHY

Nagasawa, Richard. *Summer Wind*. Tucson, AZ: Westernlore Press, 1986.

Organic Act of 1900

On July 7, 1898, President William McKinley signed a joint resolution of Congress declaring that the Hawaiian Islands were under the sovereignty of the United States. On April 30, 1900, Congress passed the Organic Act, which established a constitution for the Territory of Hawaii; the law came into effect on July 15, 1900. Thereafter, Hawaii was governed much like a state, with an elective bicameral legislature, but the governor was appointed by the president of the United States. The governor, in turn, reported to the secretary of the interior. In this manner, a primarily nonwhite population was governed by a small white minority.

Several unusual provisions were contained in the Organic Act. Although American citizenship and voting rights were extended to native Hawaiians, Chinese citizens of the formerly independent island nation had to litigate the right to American citizenship; they won their court battles. Although voting required a minimum of one year of residence, members of the armed services were ineligible to vote for the territorial senate. The literacy test for voting applied to those who were literate in English or Hawaiian. Officeholders, including the governor, were required to have a minimum of three years of residence in Hawaii. Jury selection by race was repealed; to serve on a jury, a citizen had to be literate in English, male, and over 21 years of age.

Contract labor was outlawed, thus striking down the condition of legal peonage established by the **Masters and Servants Act of 1850**. Exclusive fishing rights for native Hawaiians were abolished. The federal government took over former government lands, including some lands that were formerly held in common by the Hawaiian monarchs on behalf of the people.

Subsequently, when Congress passed laws, the applicability to the territory of Hawaii was not automatic. The governor or the territorial legislature could request a waiver, which could be granted by the secretary of the interior if local conditions were so different as to preclude implementation of the law. For example, most government functions were centralized in the territorial government. Although counties were established for routine functions regarding sewage, trash collection, and water, no cities were incorporated. The Organic Law was superseded by Hawaii's state constitution on August 15, 1959. (MH)

BIBLIOGRAPHY

George, William H. and Paul S. Bachman. *The Government of Hawaii, Federal, Territorial, and Country*. rev.ed. Honolulu: University of Hawaii, 1940.

Littler, Robert McD.C. *The Governance of Hawaii: A Study of Territorial Administration*. Stanford, CA: Stanford University Press, 1929.

Organization of Asian-American Women

Originally formed as the Organization of Asian Women in 1976, the Organization of Asian American Women focuses its efforts upon the political study of Asian-American women. A network of smaller local chapters, the group works closely with other Asian civil rights organizations to advance its goals. The organization was active in forming the Coalition against Anti-Asian Violence as a result to the **Vincent Chin murder case** in 1986. The group is also producing an audiovisual history of Asian-American women entitled "Tapestry."

BIBLIOGRAPHY

Wei, William *The Asian American Movement*. Philadelphia: Temple University Press, 1993.

Organization of Chinese American Women (OCAW)

The Organization of Chinese American Women (OCAW) was formed in 1977 by a group of established Chinese-American women to advance the cause of Chinese women in the United States and to foster public awareness of their special needs and concerns. With headquarters in Washington, D.C., OCAW distinguishes itself by functioning primarily as a service organization but also monitors legislative and public policies affecting Chinese and Asian-American women.

Over the years, the organization has advanced the interests of the Chinese- and/or Asian-American women in four ways. To encourage the participation of Chinese-American women in positions of leadership, OCAW sponsors a summer intern program for college students, provides annual scholarships for high school students, and offers scholarship for professional Asian-American women to attend leadership conferences. To promote equal rights and opportunities for

Chinese-American women at work, in the community, and at home, the OCAW conducts management, career fulfillment, skills training, and job development seminars and conferences, and cosponsors English classes with the Chinatown Service Center. To facilitate the exchange of knowledge and experience among members as well as build bonds of common interests with others, OCAW publishes a membership directory and reports members' activities in a quarterly national newsletter, *OCAW Speaks*; it also hosts regular luncheons and biennial national conferences. To foster a positive image of Chinese and other Asian Americans, OCAW hosts an annual awards banquet and cosponsors art exhibits, dance performances, book signing receptions, and other cultural events featuring Asian artists and authors.

Membership to OCAW is open to anyone who supports the purpose of the organization. By the late 1990s, OCAW had about 2,000 members; members may be affiliated with one of the seven regional chapters. (PL)

BIBLIOGRAPHY

Correspondence with Pauline Tsui, OCAW cofounder and acting executive director, August 19, 1997.

Organization of Chinese American Women [informational pamphlet]. 1997.

Wei, William. *The Asian American Movement*. Temple University Press, 1993.

Organization of Chinese Americans (OCA)

The Organization of Chinese Americans (OCA) is one of the earliest Asian-American civil rights groups to set up a national office in Washington, D.C. Founded in 1973, OCA has 10,000 members in 40 chapters across the nation and an overseas chapter in Hong Kong. With an annual budget of $300,000, it has grown to be the preeminent Asian-American civil rights organization and an active member of the national civil rights coalition.

OCA's primary objectives are to promote the active involvement of citizens and residents of Chinese and Asian ancestry in local and national affairs; to secure social justice, equal opportunity, and equal treatment; to eliminate prejudice, stereotypes, and ignorance; and to promote the cultural heritage of Chinese and Asian Americans.

Over the years, the organization has helped pass a number of federal legislation vital to the ethnic community. Some examples of the organization's successes include the Hate Crimes Statistics Act of 1990, the **Immigration and Nationality Act of 1990**, and the Voting Rights Improvement Act of 1992. It has also helped defeat proposals to deny federal funds to legal permanent residents and to conduct government business only in English.

In the 1996 election, OCA conducted its first-ever national voter registration drive, sponsored by 18 other major Asian-American groups. Before and during the 1997 congressional hearings on Asian campaign contributions, OCA worked closely with other community organizations to ensure fairness in the investigation and to denounce media stereotyping of the community.

To help achieve its goals, OCA develops local leadership and community involvement through its chapters. Each chapter develops its own outreach programs, which range from holding educational seminars and running Chinese community centers and language schools to assisting in the resettlement of Southeast Asian refugees. OCA chapters also organize social activities for members and celebrate a variety of Chinese and Asian cultural festivals. (PL)

BIBLIOGRAPHY

Interview with Christine Chen, project coordinator, OCA national headquarters, April 24, 1996.

Organization of Chinese Americans. *National Newsletter*. 1996–1999.

Yip, Althea. "Countering Complacency." *Asianweek* (June 21, 1996): 12–13.

Organization of Pan Asian American Women

The Organization of Pan Asian American Women (usually just called Pan Asian) was formed in 1976 at the National Conference on the Educational and Occupational Needs of Asian and Pacific American Women, which was sponsored by the National Institute of Education and held in San Francisco. Pan Asian is a national public policy nonprofit organization that works on issues of special concern to women, including child care, women's equity, and parental leave. In 1980 the group was the leading sponsor of the National Conference of the Asian/Pacific American Education Equity Project.

BIBLIOGRAPHY

Wei, William. *Asian American Movement*. Philadelphia: Temple University Press, 1994.

Oyama v. California (1948)

Fred Oyama was the legal owner of land purchased for him in 1934 by his *issei* father, Oyama Kajiro. With the conclusion of **World War II**, Oyama was denied the use of these lands by the United States government, which stated they had been purchased illegally because the **California Alien Land Law of 1913** prevented *issei* and other aliens ineligible for U.S. citizenship from owning or leasing property in the United States.

Oyama argued this situation to the California District Court, which disagreed with his claims that the 1913 Land Act was unconstitutional. In *Oyama v. California*, 332 U.S. 633 (1948), Oyama argued to the U.S. Supreme Court that his property rights had been violated by wrongful legislation. The Court agreed with him, stating that provisions in the land act were contrary to the Fourteenth Amendment. As a result, Oyama's land was returned to him and the California Alien Land Law was declared unconstitutional.

BIBLIOGRAPHY

Wilson, Robert A. and Bill Hosokawa. *East to America*. New York: William and Morrow, 1980.

Page Law (1875)

The Page Law, passed in 1875, forbid the entry of Chinese, Japanese, and Mongolian contract laborers into the United States. It also excluded women prostitutes and felons. The law did have an effect on the numbers of women admitted to the United States, but not until the Chinese Exclusion Act (**Immigration Act of 1882**) did the immigration authorities have the right to hinder Chinese immigration to the United States.

BIBLIOGRAPHY

Coolridge, Mary Roberts. *Chinese Immigration.* New York: Henry Holt, 1909.

McKee, Delbar L. *Chinese Exclusion and the Open Door Policy.* Detroit, MI: Wayne State University Press, 1977.

Paper Sons

Many Chinese immigrated to the United States illegally by falsifying documents, including U.S. birth certificates. These illegal immigrants were called "paper sons" in the Chinese communities. Many of these "paper sons" arrived shortly after the 1906 San Francisco earthquake and fire, which destroyed all of the immigration records. Immigration officials were aware of the tactics for gaining entry to the United States and would question immigrants for hours about minute details of their villages, houses, and relatives. The Chinese became aware of these interrogations and prepared elaborate histories for immigrants to study prior to their arrival in the United States. Finally, in 1950 the United States granted immunity to those who would come forward and admit their illegal status. However, this "confession program" brought widespread panic in the Chinese community as confessors were forced to implicate relatives and friends. Most of the illegal immigrants were permitted to remain in the United States, but the confessions allowed the U.S. government to deport anyone suspected of being engaged in illegal or subversive activities who was not a legal citizen. The FBI and the Immigration and Naturalization Service (INS) began investigating a number of Chinese Americans, and anyone who supported the Chinese communist government was subject to scrutiny and possible deportation.

BIBLIOGRAPHY

Jackson, Hayes. "Paper Sons." *Humanities* (November/December 1994): 43–47.

Shih-Shan, Henry Tsai. *The Chinese Experience in America.* Bloomington: Indiana University Press, 1986.

Payne-Aldrich Tariff Act

The Payne-Aldrich Tariff Act was signed into law on August 5, 1909. This act allowed for free trade between the United States and the Philippine Islands, thereby overcoming previous restrictions in other existing tariff laws that had applied to Philippine imports to mainland U.S. ports. Also at this time, Congress passed the Philippine Tariff Act, which worked in conjunction with the Payne-Aldrich Tariff Act in providing adequate trading between two areas. On October 3, 1913, the Underwood-Simmons Act replaced the Payne-Aldrich Tariff Act, thereby overcoming quota limitations on sugar and tobacco products. As a result, complete free trade between the United States and the Philippines was finally accomplished.

BIBLIOGRAPHY

Barth, Gunther. *Bitter Strength.* Cambridge, MA: Harvard University Press, 1964.

Pearl Harbor

Pearl Harbor, a large harbor on Oahu in the Hawaiian Islands, has long served as the headquarters for the United States Pacific Fleet. Although the harbor remains an important naval base, it is best known as the target of a Japanese surprise attack on December 7, 1941, which helped propel the United States into **World War II.**

By late 1941, Japanese military leaders had decided to launch the surprise assault on Pearl Harbor, hoping to wipe out the American Pacific Fleet and thereby prevent the United States from becoming a serious obstacle to Japan's efforts to dominate Asia and the South Pacific. Launched on a Sunday morning, when the American readiness was at its lowest level, the assault inflicted substantial losses on the fleet, including the sinking of the battleship *Arizona,* which went down with more than 1,100 men and is today an underwater memorial to Americans who died at Pearl Harbor. However, the Japanese failed to destroy crucial oil storage facilities, as well as the fleet's aircraft carriers, which were far from the harbor at the time of the assault. Carriers subsequently played a critical role in the naval war in the Pacific.

The attack on Pearl Harbor generated overwhelming support for U.S. entry into the war, and Congress passed the declaration of war almost unanimously. While the United States probably would have entered the war even without the attack on Pearl Harbor, it seems likely that U.S. participation in the war would have started much later.

In addition, the attack on Pearl Harbor was helpful to those prejudiced against Japanese Americans. Although even after the attack on Pearl Harbor, some influential government officials—such as J. Edgar Hoover, head of the Federal Bureau of Investigation—doubted that Japanese Americans represented a security threat, public shock over Pearl Harbor and resentment toward Japanese (whom most Americans did not distinguish from Japanese Americans) made it politically easy for President Franklin D. Roosevelt to issue **Executive Order 9066**, the first legal step in the process that resulted in the internment of more than 100,000 Japanese Americans during the war. **See also** Enemy Alien Control Unit; Internment Camps. **See** Executive Order 9066 in Appendix 1. (ALA)

BIBLIOGRAPHY
Prange, Gordon William with Donald M. Goldstein and Katherine V. Dillon. *December 7, 1941: The Day the Japanese Attacked Pearl Harbor*. New York: McGraw-Hill, 1988.
Toland, John. *Infamy: Pearl Harbor and Its Aftermath*. Garden City, NY: Doubleday, 1982.

Pensionado Act of 1903

The Pensionado Act of 1903 provided for government-sponsored education and training for young Filipinos in the United States. The act was legislated at the recommendation of the **Taft Commission,** a four-year study of the Filipino life and economics lead by Judge William Howard Taft. The Philippines had recently been acquired by the United States at the end of the **Spanish-American War**, so in 1900, President William McKinley chose Taft to lead an investigative commission of the Philippines. After the act was passed, Filipino students applied to come to the United States; if chosen, they were housed with U.S. families and enrolled in schools and universities. **See also** Filipino Americans.

BIBLIOGRAPHY
Melendy, H. Brett. *Asians in America*. Boston: Twayne, 1977.

People v. Downer (1857)

People v. Downer (1857) involved the owner of a ship, Stephen Baldwin, who brought 250 Chinese people to California and did not pay the $12,750 in tax that was due. (In 1855 California passed the Passenger Tax Act, which stated that all people ineligible for U.S. citizenship who arrived by sea in California must pay a tax of $50.) The case was first heard in District Court and then appealed to the U.S. Supreme Court in 1857. The Supreme Court decided that the Passenger Tax Act was illegal because Congress was the only legislative group that could regulate commerce with other nations.

BIBLIOGRAPHY
Coolidge, Mary R. *Chinese Immigrants*. New York: Henry Holt, 1909.

People v. Hall (1854)

George W. Hall was convicted of murder based primarily on the testimony presented by a Chinese witness. Because of this, Hall appealed the decision, stating that the testimony should be excluded because of guidelines established in the Civil Practice Act of 1850. According to sections of this act, it was mandated that "no Indian or Negro" was allowed to testify in court proceedings against a white person: Hall argued that Asian were likewise barred under this act, even though they were not explicitly named. In *People v. Hall*, 4 Cal. 399 (1854), under the guidance of Chief Justice Hugh Campbell Murray, the California Supreme Court found that the act's guidelines were indeed generic and were intended to prevent all people of color from giving testimony. As a result, Hall's case was remanded for retrial, and people of Chinese ancestry residing in the United States were prevented from testifying against whites in future criminal and civil cases.

BIBLIOGRAPHY
Chen, Jack. *The Chinese of America*. New York: Harper & Row, 1980.
McClain, Charles. *In Search of Equality*. Berkeley: University of California Press, 1994.

People v. McGuire (1873)

In 1873 a white man named McGuire was convicted of assaulting a Chinese man, Sam Wah. The case was an important one because Wah was permitted to testify against McGuire. Prior to this, Mongolians or Chinese could not be called as witnessed to testify for or against a defendant in California. In 1854 the Supreme Court had upheld that this law violated the Fourteenth Amendment. However, in 1873 the California State Legislature repealed all laws preventing Chinese from testifying against white men. The McGuire case was settled just prior to this law being enacted, but the Supreme Court ordered a new trial on the grounds that the State of California could not supercede the Supreme Court's decisions.

BIBLIOGRAPHY
Shih-Shan, Henry Tsai. *The Chinese Experience in America*. Bloomington: Indiana University Press, 1986.

Perez v. Sharp (1948)

In *Perez v. Sharp* (1948) the law preventing persons of differing races from marrying was ruled unconstitutional by the California Supreme Court. This was especially important to Asian Americans who had been barred from marrying whites and who had tried to have the law overturned numerous times since its inception in 1880. Section 69 of the California Civil Code prohibited whites from marrying "Mongolians." In 1931 Salvador Roldan, a Filipino, won the right to marry Marjorie Rodgers. The judge in the case ruled that Filipinos were Malays and not Mongolians and thus were not prohibited from marrying whites. However, in 1933 the California legislature amended the law to include Malays among the races that whites were forbidden to marry. This change in law was overturned by *Perez v. Sharp*.

BIBLIOGRAPHY

Sickels, Robert J. *Race, Marriage, and the Law.* Albuquerque: University of New Mexico Press, 1972.

Philippine-American War (1898)

The Philippines, a former Spanish colony, was ceded to the United States as part of the concessions of the Spanish defeat during the **Spanish-American War** of 1898. The Filipinos thought that the United States government would give them independence, but the government was not prepared to do that, since the Philippines could be convenient as a source of raw materials, a market for U.S. products, a military base, and a refueling port for U.S. ships on their way to and from Asia. Having the Philippines for a colony could bolster the United States as a world power.

But the Filipinos were not willing to surrender their hard-fought independence from the Spanish, and so, beginning in 1899, they continued their war of independence, now fighting against the United States. The First Philippine Republic under Emilio Aguinaldo was proclaimed in Malolos, Bulacan (just outside of Manila). This republic had its own newspapers, music, literature, educational system, taxation system, and armed forces. The rise of this republic worsened the already deteriorating relationship with the Americans, whom the Filipinos resented for preventing Filipinos from entering Manila after its capture from the Spanish.

But the incident that sparked the war was the killing of a Filipino soldier by a U.S. soldier on February 4, 1899, as the soldier was crossing the San Juan Bridge. By firing the first unprovoked shot, the Americans started what was to be known as the War of Philippine Independence. This incident was telegraphed to President Aguinaldo and he immediately declared war on the United States. However, the Americans would not dignify this struggle and would instead call it a Filipino "insurrection."

The Filipinos attacked Manila but were repulsed. U.S. troops moved northward to capture Malolos, the republic's capital. The Filipinos bravely resisted but were overwhelmed by the superior American forces. Malolos was captured by General Arthur MacArthur on March 31, 1899. Aguinaldo fled and transferred the capital further north to San Fernando, Pampanga. The Filipinos were determined to resist the American incursions to the bitter end.

After two years of battle and further movements of the Filipinos northward, General Aguinaldo was captured. He was brought back to Manila to face MacArthur. Aguinaldo took the oath of allegiance to the United States on April 19, 1901. Although the capture of Aguinaldo marked the end of the Philippine Republic, it did not end the war. Other Filipino leaders took up the cause, although resistance to the much stronger opponent was futile. Some would continue the struggle until 1903. Officially, the Philippine-American War, which would be known in the United States as the Philippine Insurrection, took place from 1899 to 1902, and cost the lives of between 200,000 and 1 million Filipinos. (CGM)

BIBLIOGRAPHY

Pong, Gap Min. *Asian Americans: Contemporary Trends and Issues.* Thousand Oaks, CA: Sage Publications, 1995.

Welch, Richard E., Jr. *Response to Imperialism: The United States and the Philippine American War, 1899–1902.* Chapel Hill: University of North Carolina Press, 1979.

Zaide, Gregorio F. and Sonia F. Zaide. *History of the Republic of the Philippines.* Manila: National Book Store, 1987.

Philippine Commission

The Philippine Commission was a set of U.S. delegations during the time of colonization which prepared the Philippine government for eventual independence. After the **Spanish-American War** of 1898, President William McKinley put together such commissions as fact-finding missions to investigate the conditions in the country so that Philippine political administration could be established.

The resulting administration was a civilian rather than a military one, consisting of a U.S.-selected governor general with veto power. A cabinet was appointed by him, and a general advisory council was elected through a limited vote. The judicial branch was separate.

The first commission established in 1898, known as the Shurman Commission, was headed by Dr. Jacob G. Shurman, then president of Cornell University. Because of the ongoing Philippine-American war, it did not accomplish its mission, but it did submit a report to President McKinley with the following recommendations: that the U.S. government should (1) establish a territorial form of government with a legislature of two houses; (2) withdraw military rule in pacified areas of the country; (3) conserve Philippine natural resources for the Philippines; (4) organize autonomous local government; (5) open free elementary schools; and (6) appoint men of high ability and good character to important government offices.

The Second Philippine Commission was the **Taft Commission** (1900 to 1904), headed by William Howard Taft. Its guiding principles were that the government to be established in the Philippines would be designed not for U.S. satisfaction but for the "happiness, peace, and prosperity of the people of the Philippines." It would instill the U.S. principles of separation of powers, responsible municipal government, due process of law, defense of private property, and free public education. It was more successful than the Shurman Commission. **See also** Jones Act of 1916/Philippine Autonomy Act of 1918. (CGM)

BIBLIOGRAPHY

Welch, Richard E. Jr. *Response to Imperialism: The United States and the Philippine American War, 1899–1902.* Chapel Hill: The University of North Carolina Press, 1979.

Zaide, Gregorio F. and Sonia F. Zaide. *History of the Republic of the Philippines.* Manila: National Book Store, 1987.

Philippine Naturalization

The naturalization of immigrants has been a sensitive issue for many societies. In the United States the **Naturalization Act of 1790** restricted citizenship to "free white persons," thus disallowing blacks and Asians who lived in the country at that time to obtain citizenship. In an 1870 amendment to the act, citizenship was extended to blacks. However, all others were still excluded.

The **Immigration Act of 1924**, which effectively barred the immigration of all Asians (particularly the Japanese) exempted the Filipinos, because the Philippines was an American colony at that time and Filipinos were considered nationals of the United States. Thus the Philippines was allotted a yearly immigration quota of 50 people, which was raised to 100 upon Philippine independence in 1946. The Filipinos who had immigrated before national independence, who held the special status as "nationals" of the United States, were midway between being an alien and a citizen and constantly had to struggle with the dilemma of exclusion and inclusion. As American nationals, they were entitled to U.S. passports and could even enter and leave the country freely without fear of deportation. However, they did not have the full rights of citizenship, and they were often subjected to racial prejudice and sometimes violence. They were also relegated to the most menial and lowest-paying occupations. They were placed under heavy scrutiny because of their alleged immorality, criminality, and inability to assimilate. And except for those few who had served three years in either the Navy or the Marines during World War I, Filipinos were ineligible for citizenship and possessed an ambiguous legal status. They were not entitled to bear arms or to trial by jury. Although they were allowed to take federal civil service exams, the licensing boards of most states prohibited them from practicing many professions. Because they were not citizens, during the hard times of the Depression they did not qualify for benefits under the social programs of the New Deal. **See also** Asian-American Relations with Other Minorities; Filipino Americans; Filipino Repatriation Act of 1935; Jones Act of 1916; Tydings-McDuffie Act (1934). (CGM)

BIBLIOGRAPHY

Jones, Maldwyn Allen. *American Immigration*. Chicago: University of Chicago Press, 1960.
Hofstetter, Richard H. *U.S. Immigration Policy*. Durham, NC: Duke University Press, 1984.
Stern, Jennifer. *The Filipino Americans*. New York: Chelsea Publishers, 1989.

Political Participation

Although Asians have been in the United States for at least 150 years, their history of active participation in mainstream electoral politics is a brief and recent one. Only in the latter part of the twentieth century has there been a gradual removal of protracted legal barriers to immigration, naturalization, property ownership, integration, mixed-race marriage, and voting; prior to that, the nation's prevailing legal, political, and economic systems systematically denied Asian Americans equal opportunity to political participation. Political participation in the lengthy era (up to the late twentieth century) of racial exclusion and alienation usually took the forms of litigation, protest, labor strikes, homeland independence movements, and wartime volunteerism and relief efforts. Asian Americans were not considered a viable political force until the 1980s and 1990s when changes in U.S. immigration policies as well as economic, social, and political forces within and outside the United States converged to forge a new and accelerated era of Asian immigration.

Between 1980 and 1990, the Asian population rose from 3.5 million to 7.3 million. This rate of growth was the fastest among all major population groups during the same period. Moreover, the population explosion has been accompanied by a remarkably high level of socioeconomic achievement in the aggregate. For instance, according to the U.S. Bureau of the Census among persons aged 25 years old and over, the percentage of Asians with four or more years of college (41 percent) was almost twice the percentage of non-Hispanic whites (24 percent); in 1993 their median family income of $49,510 among married couples was $4,270 higher than that of non-Hispanic white married couples.

These figures appear to support the **model minority** thesis and herald the ascendance of political power, yet the current status of Asian Americans is a controversial one. There is no doubt that the legal status of Asians has drastically improved since the nineteenth and early twentieth centuries, when formal and blatant discrimination and exploitation were the norm of practice. Relative to other minority (or even majority) groups, Asians in the aggregate have clearly experienced a remarkable degree of economic success. There is also little doubt that the election and appointment of Asians to federal, state, and local positions in the 1980s and 1990s have become less novel. If naturalization is an indicator of one's desire to become integrated into the American system, scholars concur that Asians in the aggregate have the strongest commitment to do so. In the 1970s, 1980s, and 1990s, Asian immigrants petitioned to become U.S. citizens much sooner and at a higher rate than their counterparts from other areas of the world.

In spite of these indicators of progress, those who anticipate a corresponding growth of Asian participation in the American political power structure have so far been disappointed. In terms of national officeholding, there have only been a handful of Asians—mainly Democrats, of Japanese descent, and from Hawaii or California—who have been elected to positions of power. Among the five voting members of Asian descent in the 105th Congress (1997–1999), for instance, four are Democrats, three are of Japanese ancestry, and two are from California. Results of the 1990 Bureau of Census Civilian Labor Force data (Equal Employment Opportunity File) reveal that only 1.4 percent of all legislators surveyed in the nation were Asians. At the local level, a 1987 Census of Governments reports that .07 percent of all elected officials nationwide were Asians. This figure rose to .13 percent when the same survey was administered in 1992; but it still compared poorly to the .42 percent for American Indians, 1.4 percent for Hispanics, 2.7 percent for blacks, and 95.4 percent for non-Hispanic whites. The situation at the national level seems similar. In the early 1990s, only 45 of the 8,200 staff positions in Congress were held by Asians.

The lack of elected or appointed Asian officials is mirrored by the low levels of voter registration and turnout by the American public of Asian origin. A 1984 analysis of voter registration lists for three areas of high Asian concentration in San Francisco reveals that people with Chinese- and Japanese-American surnames registered to vote at far lower levels (31 percent and 37 percent, respectively) than the 60 percent registration rate found among the general electorate. Similar findings are reported in a 1986 study in Los Angeles, where 43 percent of all Japanese were registered, followed by 35 percent of Chinese, 27 percent of Filipinos, 17 percent of Asian Indians, 13 percent of Koreans, and 4 percent of Vietnamese. A 1984 California statewide ethnicity survey finds that Asians registered at 55 percent and voted at 48 percent in 1984; these rates are about 30 percent lower than those for non-Hispanic whites and blacks. In the 1992 presidential election, a *Los Angeles Times* exit poll indicated that the Asian percentage of the statewide vote share was a dismal 3 percent, despite the group's 7 percent share of adult citizens. An improved Asian vote share was reported by the *Los Angeles Times* exit poll for the 1996 presidential election, where 5 percent of voters identified themselves as Asians. Still, this represents only half of the statewide percentage of adult Asians.

Perhaps by far the most accurate estimate of Asian electoral participation rates is the Current Population Survey (CPS) series taken during the November elections since 1992. In 1992, of the sampled Asian population aged 18 or over in the United States, only 31 percent were registered to vote and 27 percent actually turned out at the polls. In 1994, the figures slid down to 29 percent for registration and 22 percent for voting. A major reason for the low level of participation may be that only about half of the Asian adult population are citizens. When citizenship status along with education and age are taken into account, Asian registration and voting rates increase substantially. However, there is still a 10 percent to 24 percent participation gap between Asians and whites.

Even in one aspect of American politics where Asian have been active—donating disproportionately large amounts of money to political campaigns—reactions to this emerging view of Asians as the "new moneybags" of American politics have not been entirely positive. Beginning in the mid-1980s, journalists note that whereas Asians constituted no more than one-tenth of the population in California, they often contributed 20 percent to 30 percent of the total campaign fund. In the 1988 and 1992 national elections, Democratic and Republican presidential candidates were reported to have received a combined total of more than $10 million from Asians. This makes the Asian-American community second only to the American Jewish community in terms of the amount of campaign money raised by an ethnic minority group. However,

community activists maintain that a deep chasm remains between what is promised and what is delivered to Asians—be it greater access to power or more high-level appointments that involve serious decision making in government operations. Moreover, the higher amount of money donated by Asians as a whole does not necessarily indicate that more Asians are involved in the political process. This is supported by survey studies that find, for example, that Asian respondents in California did not contribute money at a higher rate than their non-Hispanic white counterparts in the 1984 and 1992 presidential campaign. Insiders observe that donation levels vary greatly between ethnic groups and generations. Worst of all, because of the Democratic fund-raising controversy in the 1996 election, many now believe that much of the money donated to or by Asians is on a shaky legal ground, either because it may come from some individuals or entities that are not legally permitted to donate and/or because the money may originate from somewhere in China.

In sum, although progress has been made over the years, observers note that "Asian American politics has remained to an unusual degree 'politics by other means,' i.e., not direct electoral representation but indirect access through campaign contributions, lobbying, litigation, and protest"(Lien, 1997). Furthermore, this "asymmetrical participation" through campaign contributions has not produced very efficacious results in terms of public officeholding and political power. Instead, by the middle of 1997, it had brought harassment, shame, and anger to many long-term participants and community leaders.

Why is the political participation of Asian Americans low in relation to their socioeconomic achievement and population share? Numerous explanations, mostly at the aggregate level, have been proposed to explain the deficit. Externally, some note the legally sanctioned exclusion and discrimination that have, until recently, kept the Asian-American community small and disenfranchised. Others attribute low participation to the legal restraints in the electoral system via the numerous practices of minority-vote dilution. These include the requirements of geographic compactness and the block-voting component in redistricting, and in the problems of accessing a foreign-language ballot. Still others mention the labor market segmentation that is responsible for the underemployment, underpayment, and lack of upward occupational mobility of Asian Americans.

In addition, a few Asian Americans mention the general antipathy they have toward government, which is often an extension of the immigrants' unpleasant or frightening experiences dealing with corrupt regimes in their home countries, or of the continued interference of homeland governments and politics in the host country. Some Asians emphasize cultural impediments—for example, the Buddhist–Confucianist values of hierarchy, reverence for authority, resignation, and passivity are antidemocratic civic traditions that discourage some Chinese, Japanese, and Korean Americans from participating in democratic partisan politics.

The participation potential of Asians may be severely discounted by certain demographic characteristics unique to the group such as minuscule population size, dominance of the foreign-born members of the community, dispersed and skewed population distribution, and internal fragmentation by immigration generation (i.e., the number of generations an individual's family has been in the United States), ethnicity, nationality, religion, language, and social class. These characteristics may mitigate the formation of a common sense of community or minority group identity among Asians in America and hence impede the translation of socioeconomic successes into political actions and gains. (PL)

BIBLIOGRAPHY

Lien, Pei-te. *The Political Participation of Asian Americans: Voting Behavior in Southern California.* New York: Garland Publishing, 1997.

Porterfield v. Webb (1923)

W.L. Porterfield owned land in Los Angeles that he tried to lease to Y. Mizuno for farming. However, under the **California Alien Land Act of 1913**, Mizuno, who was a Japanese citizen ineligible for U.S. citizenship, was not permitted to lease land. Porterfield appealed to the U.S. Supreme Court of California to prevent the California attorney general Ulysses S. Webb from possessing his land. In *Porterfield v. Webb,* 236 U.S. 225 (1923), the court upheld the Alien Land Act, stating that it did not violate the treaty between the U.S. and Japan, nor did it violate the Fourteenth Amendment. **See** California Alien Land Act of 1920 in Appendix 1.

BIBLIOGRAPHY

Chuman, Frank F. *The Bamboo People: the Law and Japanese Americans.* Del Mar, CA: Publisher's Inc., 1976.

Poston Strike

The Poston Strike grew out of turmoil in one of the **World War II** internment camps for Japanese Americans. Although the strike itself was of limited historical significance, it helps to illustrate some of the complexities of the camps.

The genesis of the strike came during the evening of November 14, 1942, when a *kibei* was beaten unconscious in the Poston internment camp in Arizona. (*Kibei* were *nisei*—second-generation Japanese Americans—who had received at least some of their education in Japan.) Camp security officials arrested two popular *nisei*, also *kibei*, and charged them with the beating. In response, many Poston internees demanded the release of the two men; when camp authorities refused, a general strike was called, and all but essential services were suspended. Although some officials called for using the military to quell the protests, the acting administrator opted instead for negotiation, eventually agreeing to release one of the accused and try the other within the relocation center. In addition, stronger relations were forged with leaders of the internees.

The Poston incident is one of those events that graphically demonstrates the tensions within the camps. (Tule Lake and Manzanar were sites of other notable disturbances.) Not only was there the understandable anger over the internment, but there was considerable friction generated by the forced gathering of people who, despite their common ethnic heritage, had many differences. The response to the Poston Strike also illustrates the conflicting pressures on camp administrators and the willingness of some officials to take more thoughtful and effective approaches, rather than bowing to the demands of racially motivated critics. **See also** Internment Camps/Relocation Centers. (ALA)

BIBLIOGRAPHY

Girdner, Audrie and Anne Loftis. *The Great Betrayal: The Evacuation of the Japanese-Americans During World War II.* New York: Macmillan, 1969.
Wilson, Robert A. and Bill Hosokawa. *East to America: A History of the Japanese in the United States.* New York: William Morrow, 1980.

Arati Prabhakar (1959–)

Arati Prabhaker was appointed by President Bill Clinton in 1993 as the first Asian director of the National Institute of Standards and Technology. The institute develops and applies technology, measurements, and standards along with industry to stimulate economic growth. Born in New Delhi, India, Prabhakar's former job was as a congressional fellow at the U.S. Office of Technology Assessment. He then became the director of the Microelectronics Technology Office in the Defense Department's Advanced Research Policy Agency.

BIBLIOGRAPHY

Adam, J.A. "Arati Prabhakar." *IEEE Spectrum* (December 1993): 48–51.

Dith Pran (1942–)

Employed as a photojournalist and assistant to *New York Times* correspondent Sydney Schanberg in Cambodia from 1974 to 1975, Pran became separated from Schanberg during the 1975 invasion of Phnom Penh, when local U.S. Embassy officials rejected Pran's claims of being a journalist for the United States and turned him away. As a consequence, Pran lived as a fugitive from the Khmer Rouge within Cambodia from 1975 to 1979, hungry, poor, and in constant flight from troop movements. Schanberg searched unsuccessfully for his friend and coworker throughout this time. In 1979, Pran managed to escape Cambodia for the United States, where he regained his job as a *Times* photographer. He eventually began speaking publicly about his experiences in Cambodia. These experiences were portrayed in the 1984 film *The Killing Fields*, from which Haing S. Ngor received an Academy Award for his portrayal of Pran.

BIBLIOGRAPHY

Watanabe, Scott. "Dith Pran Speaks at UPS." *International Examiner* (April 16, 1996): 1.

Proposition 13 (1956)

Proposition 13 was created in 1956 by the **Japanese American Citizens League (JACL)**. The document asked the California state legislature to repeal the **California Alien Land**

Act of 1913, which prevented aliens ineligible for U.S. citizenship from owning or leasing land. After final measures were taken, Proposition 13 was placed on the ballot of the November 4, 1956, election. Joe Masaoka and other members of JACL soon began an intense campaign to have the repeal of the act passed into legislation. The group went on to gain 2.5 million votes in California, winning by a 2 to 1 majority. Besides showing the major advances that had been made in Japanese-American rights in the state, the two-thirds voting majority also reflected a growing regard by the general population for Asian-American issues.

BIBLIOGRAPHY
O'Brien, David J. and Stephen S. Fugita. *The Japanese American Experience.* Bloomington: Indiana University Press, 1991.

Proposition 15 (1945)

Proposition 15 was also known as the Validation of Legislative Amendments to Alien Land Law. It was introduced in 1945 to change section 17 of Article 1 of the California Constitution. The amended law was to close all loopholes left in the **Alien Land Act of 1920.** The **Japanese American Citizens League,** under **Mike Masaru Masaoka,** helped persuade voters to turn down Proposition 15.

BIBLIOGRAPHY
Takaki, Ronald. *Strangers from a Different Shore: A History of Asian Americans.* Boston: Little, Brown, 1989.

Public Law 95-145

Public Law 95-145 was approved by Congress and the president in 1977. It was passed to deal with the large influx of Asian refugees from Southeast Asian nations who were fleeing political and economic hardship. The law allowed refugees to become permanent residents upon request. Further, it reduced the number of years a permanent resident who entered under this statute had to wait before applying for U.S. citizenship to only five years of residency.

BIBLIOGRAPHY
Ng, Franklin, ed. *The Asian American Encyclopedia.* New York: Marshall Cavendish, 1995.

Public Law 405

Public Law 405 was adopted on July 1, 1944, in response to growing trouble at the Tule Lake Relocation Center, an **internment camp** for Japanese Americans during **World War II.** The measure, which was drafted by Attorney General Francis Biddle, allowed for the voluntary renunciation of citizenship by Japanese Americans while on U.S. soil when such renunciations were not contrary to national defense. Public Law 405 resulted in thousands of Japanese Americans renouncing their citizenship and seeking repatriation. However, controversies arose after the war when many who had renounced their citizenship claimed that it was not voluntary. The act was repealed on July 25, 1947. **See also** *Acheson v. Murakami* (1949); Denationalization Act of 1944; Hokuku Seinen-Dan.

BIBLIOGRAPHY
tenBroek, Jacobus, Edward N. Barnhart, and Floyd W. Matson. *Prejudice, War, and the Constitution.* Berkeley: University of California Press, 1970.

Public Proclamation No. 1

Public Proclamation No. 1 was issued by General John L. DeWitt in compliance with **World War II** Japanese-American internment orders (directed by **Executive Order 9066**). Established on March 2, 1942, this proclamation created military zones in which the government could exclude and monitor citizens, particularly those of Japanese descent. This legislation came primarily from fears originating from the bombing of **Pearl Harbor,** causing many Americans to fear that Asian Americans along the West Coast were conspiring with the Japanese. The orders designated the western parts of Wash-

In 1942, Japanese Americans line up for transportation to Manzanar Relocation Camp. *Library of Congress.*

ington state, California, and Oregon, as well as the southern half of Arizona, as Military Area No. 1, establishing exclusion zones in these areas to monitor the movement of people of Japanese ancestry. As a result, many Japanese Americans were pushed into the Midwestern and Central regions of the United States. **See also** Internment Camps/Relocation Centers.

BIBLIOGRAPHY
Daniels, Roger. *The Decision to Relocate the Japanese Americans.* Philadelphia: J.B. Lippincott Company, 1975.
Herman, Masako. *The Japanese in America, 1843–1973.* Dobbs Ferry, NY: Oceana Publications, 1974.
Myers, Dillion S. *Uprooted Americans.* Tuscon: University of Arizona Press, 1971.

Public Proclamation No. 2

Public Proclamation No. 2 was a Japanese-American internment order issued by General John DeWitt to follow guidelines established in **Executive Order 9066.** This proclamation, which was created on March 16, 1942, came soon after **Public Proclamation No. 1** and sought to continue efforts in monitoring people of Japanese ancestry in the United States, who were considered by some as possible spies and espionage agents for the Japanese war effort. This order required all people of Japanese descent living on the U.S. West Coast to comply with change of residence notices established under Public Proclamation No. 1. This resulted in the forceful movement of even more Japanese Americans and Japanese immigrants, creating more tension, hostility, and fears towards these people. To facilitate these movements, administrators of the proclamation worked with the **Wartime Civil Control Administration** and Western Defense Command in accomplishing its goals. **See also** Internment Camps/Relocation Centers.

BIBLIOGRAPHY

Daniels, Roger. *The Decision to Relocate the Japanese Americans.* Philadelphia: J.B. Lippincott Company, 1975.

Herman, Masako. *The Japanese in America, 1843–1973.* Dobbs Ferry, NY: Oceana Publications, 1974.

Myers, Dillion S. *Uprooted Americans.* Tuscon: University of Arizona Press, 1971.

Public Proclamation No. 3

Public Proclamation No. 3, a **World War II** internment order, was issued by General John DeWitt under guidelines established in **Executive Order 9066.** This proclamation, which was implemented on March 24, 1942, was the third in a series of four proclamations intended to monitor and hold Japanese Americans, who were inaccurately feared to be loyalists to the Japanese war cause. This proclamation established curfew and travel regulations for all people of Japanese ancestry living in the United States, regardless of whether they were citizens or not. In Military Zone No. 1, a location that included the western parts of California, Oregon, and Washington state, and the southern region of Arizona, a curfew of 8:00 P.M. to 6:00 A.M. was created beginning March 27, 1942. **See also** Internment Camps/Relocation Centers.

BIBLIOGRAPHY

Daniels, Roger. *The Decision to Relocate the Japanese Americans.* Philadelphia: J.B. Lippincott Company, 1975.

Herman, Masako. *The Japanese in America, 1843–1973.* Dobbs Ferry, NY: Oceana Publications, 1974.

Myers, Dillion S. *Uprooted Americans.* Tuscon: University of Arizona Press, 1971.

Public Proclamation No. 4

Public Proclamation No. 4 was the fourth and last in a series of orders created by General John L. DeWitt during **World War II** to follow Japanese-American internment procedures called upon by **Executive Order 9066.** This proclamation came into play on March 27, 1942, to help enforce stricter guidelines against people of Japanese ancestry living in Military Area No. 1, a region that stretched across the United States West Coast. This action prevented all Japanese Americans and aliens of Japanese descent from leaving this area without approval by the U.S. military, cutting away the previous "voluntary" nature of such movements. Of the greatest impact, Public Proclamation No. 4 and its three predecessors directly led to the later forced relocation and internment of Japanese Americans. **See also** Internment Camps/Relocation Centers.

BIBLIOGRAPHY

Daniels, Roger. *The Decision to Relocate the Japanese Americans.* Philadelphia: J.B. Lippincott Company, 1975.

Herman, Masako. *The Japanese in America, 1843–1973.* Dobbs Ferry, NY: Oceana Publications, 1974.

Myers, Dillion S. *Uprooted Americas.* Tuscon: University of Arizona Press, 1971.

Question 28

Question 28 was a controversial loyalty/allegiance statement held on registration questionnaires distributed by the War Department and the **War Relocation Authority** to Japanese-American occupants of World War II **internment camps.** The War Department sought to use the questions to determine whether *nisei* males were fit for the draft, while the War Relocation Authority wished to utilize it as a part of its general resettlement program. These allegiance questions were resented by some Japanese Americans, because the government was asking about their loyalty to the United States while at the same time holding them against their will. Other Japanese Americans found the questions confusing or humiliating. In some cases, swearing U.S. allegiance meant admitting falsely to previous Japanese ties. This confusion caused many of Japanese ancestry to be wrongly identified as "disloyals" or otherwise incriminated. **See also** World War II.

BIBLIOGRAPHY

Girdner, Audrie and Ann Loftis. *The Great Betrayal: The Evacuation of the Japanese-Americans During World War II.* New York: Macmillan, 1969.

tenBroek, Jacobus, Edward N. Barnhart, and Floyd W. Matson. *Prejudice, War, and the Constitution.* Berkeley: University of California Press, 1970.

Queue Ordinance

In 1876 an ordinance was passed in San Francisco that gave prison wardens the right to cut off the queues, or pigtails, of Chinese prisoners. Chinese men were upset by this rule, as this hairstyle was required of men by the Manchu rulers. The ordinance was vetoed by the mayor of San Francisco before it was ever executed. **See also** *Ho Ah-Kow v. Mathew Nunan* (1879).

BIBLIOGRAPHY

McClain, Charles. *In Search of Equality.* Berkeley: University of California Press, 1994.

Quon Quon Poy v. Johnson (1926)

Quon Quon Poy came to the United States in 1924 and claimed he should be allowed to immigrate because his father Quon Mee Sing was a native-born U.S. citizen. A Boston immigration inspector questioned him and Quon Mee Sing. The Board of Special Inquiry held a hearing and decided that Quon Quon Poy should not be permitted to immigrate. In *Quon Quon Poy v. Johnson,* 47, 273 U.S. 352 (1926), the case went before the U.S. Supreme Court on appeal from the district court in Massachusetts; the Supreme Court unanimously decided that there was no evidence that the immigration officer had acted unjustly or had abused his authority.

BIBLIOGRAPHY

Konvitz, Milton. *The Alien and the Asiatic in American Law.* Ithaca, NY: Cornell University Press, 1946.

Quota Immigration Act of 1921

President Warren Harding signed the quota immigration act into law in 1921. Using the 1910 U.S. census, which counted the total number of persons of each foreign nationality residing in the United States, the act allowed a 3 percent increase in the number of residents from each country. The government picked this method because large numbers of English, Irish, Scottish, and Scandinavians had migrated to the United States in 1909 and 1910, and thus the racial makeup of new immigration would continue to be predominantly "white." **See also** Immigration Act of 1924; Immigration Restriction Movement.

BIBLIOGRAPHY

Bennett, Marion T. *American Immigration Policies: A History.* Washington, D.C.: Public Affairs Press, 1963.

Stephenson, George. *A History of American Immigration, 1820–1924.* New York: Russell and Russell, 1964.

R

Reciprocity Treaty of 1875

Negotiated in 1875 between the United States and the kingdom of Hawaii and ratified by the United States Senate in 1876, the Reciprocity Treaty of 1875 gave the United States the authority to use **Pearl Harbor**, in Hawaii, as a military base for 22 years. In return, the United States encouraged investment in the sugar industry and lowered tariffs on Hawaiian sugar imports. To prevent Hawaiian opposition to the treaty, the pact specifically stated that the land used for a military base could not be ceded to the United States and that no other reciprocity treaties would be negotiated with countries other than the United States. Over the 22-year span of the treaty, the sugar industry of Hawaii had phenomenal growth of over 2,000 percent. While the growth helped fuel the Hawaiian economy, it also made it vulnerable to United States tariff policy, as the McKinley Tariff Act of 1890 would show, wherein the tariffs on imported sugar were raised in an attempt to protect domestic sugar products.

BIBLIOGRAPHY

Okihiro, Gary Y. *Cane Fire*. Philadelphia: Temple University Press, 1991.

Red Guard Party

The Red Guard Party was founded in San Francisco's Chinatown in 1969. This radical political group took their name from the Red Guards, shock troops in the Cultural Revolution used by Mao Zedong. The Red Guard Party organized community aid programs. They challenged the **Chinese Consolidated Benevolent Associations** and other traditional power structures. They merged with another communist organization in 1971.

BIBLIOGRAPHY

Wei, William. *The Asian American Movement*. Philadelphia: Temple University Press, 1993.

Redress Movement

The redress movement began on the West Coast in the 1960s, calling for reparations from the U.S. government for all Japanese persons who had been forced to move to **internment camps** during **World War II.** In the 1970s the **Japanese American Citizens League (JACL)** passed its first resolution calling for reparations. Many Japanese Americans were initially fearful of supporting the redress movement, because

Beginning in the 1960s, the redress movement called for the federal government to make reparation to World War II Japanese-American internees, such as the ones shown here at the camp at Poston, Arizona. *Library of Congress.*

they worried that their acceptance into American society would be jeopardized. However, by 1974, redress was a priority of JACL and the concept was being supported by the Japanese community. In 1976, JACL formed the **National Committee for Redress**, and at the 1978 JACL convention in Salt Lake City, the committee passed a resolution stating that the federal government should allocate $25,000 to each person who had been interned at the relocation camps. Thus, the Japanese-American congressional delegation brought the circumstances surrounding the internment camps to the attention of the media, and in 1980 the **Commission on Wartime Relocation and Internment of Civilians** was created. The commission held hearings in several major cities and concluded that the incarceration was the result of "race prejudice and war hysteria." After considerable lobbying efforts on the part of the Japanese-American legislators and activists, the **Civil Liberties Act of 1988** was signed into law. It required that the U.S. government apologize for its actions toward the Japanese-American people, and that $20,000 be paid to all living persons who were interned. **See** Civil Liberties Act (1988) in Appendix 1.

BIBLIOGRAPHY

Daniels, R., S.C. Taylor, and H.H.L. Kitano, eds. *Japanese Americans: From Relocation to Redress*. Seattle: University of Washington Press, 1991.

Reform Society

Tateishi, John. *And Justice for All: An Oral History of the Japanese American Detention Camps*. New York: Random House, 1984.
Weglyn, Michi. *Years of Infamy: The Untold Story of America's Concentration Camps*. New York: William Morrow, 1976.

Reform Society

The Reform Society was founded in 1913 in Hawaii under the original title of the Central Japanese League, a group dedicated to Japanese labor issues and the overcoming of unfair practices by immigration companies. This original group also sought to prevent difficulties that arose from 1894 legislation that mandated Japanese immigrants pay $50 for a certificate of deposit. This certificate was intended to be redeemed later for cash at Hawaiian banks after the immigrants had been transported from Japan, yet few Japanese received refunds. The Central Japanese League fought to have Japan's government return this money, continuing this cause until it was replaced in 1905 by the Reform Society. The Reform Society continued to lobby for the return of deposit funding and, in 1916, was successful in convincing the Japanese government to do so. As a result, the group disbanded, having accomplished its main goal.

BIBLIOGRAPHY
Okihiro, Gary Y. *Cane Fires*. Philadelphia: Temple University Press, 1991.

Refugee Act (1953)

After the Communist Party came to power in China in 1949, many Chinese already living or studying in the United States sought political asylum. Some 2,000 refugees were permitted to immigrate under the Refugee Act, which was passed into law in 1953. Subsequent acts legislated in 1957 and 1959 allowed for another 1,000 refugees to immigrate or change their visa status.

BIBLIOGRAPHY
Chen, Jack. *The Chinese of America*. New York: Harper and Row, 1980.

Refugee Act of 1980

The Refugee Act, signed by President Jimmy Carter in 1980, increased the number of refugees permitted to enter the United States by more than 30,000; the act also created two new bureaus to handle refugee immigration and status in the United States: the Office of the United States Coordination for Refugee Affairs and the Office of Refugee Resettlement. The act also provided for new federal refugee programs and requested that the government budget $200 million in annual funding for these programs. The act was put forth because of the growing number of Vietnamese and Cuban refugees seeking asylum in the United States during the 1970s, and it was an improvement over the Migration and Refugee Assistance Act of 1962. **See also** Immigration Policy; Immigration Restriction Movement.

BIBLIOGRAPHY
Knoll, Tricia. *Becoming Americans*. Portland, OR: Coast-to-Coast Books, 1982.

Wain, Barry. *The Refused: The Agony of the Indochina Refugees*. New York: Simon and Schuster, 1981.

Regan v. King (1942)

Regan v. King (1942) involved the **Native Sons of the Golden West,** a white organization that filed suit in 1942 to take away citizenship from all Japanese Americans. The case arose from the anti-Japanese sentiment on the West Coast that surfaced after the bombing of **Pearl Harbor** and was presented in court while Japanese Americans living on the West Coast were being relocated inland. The case was later dismissed by the U.S. Court of Appeals.

BIBLIOGRAPHY
Girdner, Audrie and Ann Loftis. *The Great Betrayal: The Evacuation of the Japanese-Americans During World War II*. New York: Macmillan, 1969.
tenBroek, Jacobus, Edward N. Barnhart and Floyd W. Matson. *Prejudice, War and the Constitution*. Berkeley: University of California Press, 1970.

Relocation Centers. *See* Internment Camps/ Relocation Centers

Reluctant Thirty-Nine

The Reluctant Thirty-Nine was the nickname for the 39 people who refused to testify in April of 1950 before the House Select Committee to Investigate Un-American Activities. These people, members of the International Longshoremen's and Warehousemen's Union, came under investigation when the Hawaiian-based union was charged as having communist ties, allegations that arose due to a 1949 dockers' strike. Out of the 66 union members called to testify, the Reluctant Thirty-Nine declined to answer questions, stating that doing so was a violation of their Fifth Amendment rights. As a result, all 39 of them were held in contempt of Congress.

The following year, under review of federal judge Delbert Metzer, all contempt charges were dropped, and the 39 union members were acquitted. Many reasoned that the original charges had been wrongly placed because many of the 39 were Japanese Americans, and that the communist allegations were made as retribution to their union activities. Later on, five of the individuals who made up the Reluctant Thirty-Nine became part of the group known as the **Hawaiian Seven,** a number of alleged communist leaders tried for violating the Alien Registration Act of 1940 (also known as the Smith Act).

BIBLIOGRAPHY
Daws, Gavan. *Shoal of Time*. Honolulu: University Press of Hawaii, 1968.

Restrictive Covenants

A restrictive covenant was a discriminatory housing practice that was widely accepted before 1948. Property owners would generally agree at the time of building to exclude nonwhites from the property. The agreement was signed and binding, and those in violation could be taken to court. On the West

Coast, restrictive covenants were often created to keep Asian Americans out of certain neighborhoods. The practice was ruled unconstitutional by the U.S. Supreme Court in the case *Shelley v. Kraemer* (1948).

BIBLIOGRAPHY

Vose, Clement E. *Caucasians Only.* Berkeley: University of California Press, 1959.

Syngman Rhee (1875–1965)

After graduating from school in Korea, Syngman Rhee became involved with the Independence Club, a group that sought an independent Korea, and was arrested in 1897 for agitating for government reform. He spent seven years in jail. Upon his release in 1904, Rhee came to the United States to discuss Korean independence with President Theodore Roosevelt, but he met with indifference from the president. Rhee stayed in the United States, and in 1908, he received his Ph.D. in International Relations from Princeton University. In 1913 he accepted the position of principal of the Korean Compound School in Hawaii. After the 1919 Independence Movement in Korea, Rhee was selected as president of the provisional government, which was based in Shanghai. Rhee established the Comrade Society in Hawaii, whose members worked to aid the provisional government in establishing Korean independence. Rhee was named the first president of the Republic of Korea in 1945, but in 1960, Rhee was smuggled out of the country when his government was overthrown by student revolutionaries. He returned to Hawaii, where he died in 1965.

BIBLIOGRAPHY

Allen, Richard C. *Korea's Syngman Rhee, an Unauthorized Portrait.* Rutland, VT: Charles E. Tuttle, 1960.

Roberts Commission Report

After the Japanese attack on **Pearl Harbor** in 1941, a special committee was appointed to analyze the Japanese Americans living in Hawaii. The commission, chaired by associate justice Owen J. Roberts, put out a report in late January 1942. The commission stated that Japanese Americans reportedly had engaged in covert activities and were possible threats to American safety. This report had a major impact on the way the government perceived Japanese Americans during **World War II** and helped reinforce the decision to place them in **internment camps**. **See also** Executive Order 9066 (text of Executive Order 9066 is in Appendix 1).

BIBLIOGRAPHY

Hosaka, Bill and Wilson, Robert A. *East to America.* NY: William Morrow and Co., 1980.

Robinson v. L.E. Lampton, County Clerk of Los Angeles (1930)

Robinson v. L.E. Lampton, County Clerk of Los Angeles (1930) was a case involving Stella Robinson, a white woman who went to court to prevent her daughter, Ruby, from marrying a Filipino man, Tony V. Moreno. The judge in the case ruled that, because the California Civil Code defined Filipinos to be "Mongolians" (that is, Chinese), they could not marry whites. **See also** *Salvador Roldan v. Los Angeles County* (1931).

BIBLIOGRAPHY

Quinsaat, Jesse, ed. *Letters in Exile.* Los Angeles: Regents of the University of California, 1976.

Rock Springs Riot

In 1855 the small mining town of Rock Springs (in Wyoming Territory) experienced one of the most violent outbreaks of anti-Chinese sentiment. On September 2, more than 600 Chinese miners employed by the Wyoming Coal and Mining Company were fired upon by a white mob incensed by the fact that the Chinese refused to participate in a mine strike. The company had also used the Chinese as strikebreakers; thus, the violence against the Chinese increased as the day passed, and by dusk, 29 Chinese lay dead, and 15 were wounded.

Since Chinese residences in Rock Springs were burned to the ground, most of the Chinese fled to the nearby town of Green River. Federal troops were called to protect the Chinese, and within days they were back on the payroll at the mine. Chinese foreign ministers sought indemnification for the miners' losses. Under pressure from the Chinese government, President Grover Cleveland sent a message to Congress which eventually designated more than $150,000 to the Rock Springs Chinese. (FHM)

BIBLIOGRAPHY

Chan, Sucheng. *Asian Americans: An Interpretive History.* Boston: Twayne Publishers, 1991.
Storti, Craig. *Incident at Bitter Creek: The Story of the Rock Springs Chinese Massacre.* Ames: Iowa State University Press, 1991.

Roque Espiritu de la Ysla v. United States (1935)

Roque Espiritu de la Ysla v. United States, 296 U.S. 575 (1935), arose when the plaintiff, a native-born citizen of the Philippines, applied for United States citizenship. Ysla was denied naturalization by the California state court, which stated that his actions were only an attempt to exploit benefits bestowed upon naturalized U.S. citizens. Ysla continued to argue his cause, stating that he should be provided citizenship and other constitutional rights because he was born in a country owing allegiance to the United States. He was again denied citizenship, at which time Ysla sought appeal. Both the lower courts and the U.S. Supreme Court declined to hear his appeal, stating that the matter was under the jurisdiction of the state court of California and, therefore, the case was already settled.

BIBLIOGRAPHY

Kim, Hyung-chan and Cynthia Mejia. *The Filipinos in America, 1898–1974.* Dobbs Ferry, NY: Oceana Publishing, 1976.

Patricia Fukuda Saiki (1930–)

Patricia Saiki was born in Hilo, Hawaii, on May 28, 1930. She served in the Hawaii legislature from 1968 to 1978. In 1986 Saiki became the first Republican to represent Hawaii and the first Asian-American woman to serve in the U.S. House of Representatives. From 1991 to 1993 Saiki served as the administrator of the Small Business Administration, following an unsuccessful bid for the U.S. Senate. At the Small Business Administration, she oversaw reforms to streamline procedures. In 1994, Saiki was the unsuccessful Republican candidate for governor of Hawaii.

BIBLIOGRAPHY

"Hawaii's Patricia Saiki Sworn in as Chief of SBA." *Wall Street Journal* (April 11, 1991): B2.

"Republicans Select Woman in Hawaii." *New York Times* (September 20, 1994): A19.

Richards, Rhonda. "Small Business Administration Chief Noted for Agency Reform." *USA Today* (December 3, 1992): B4.

Wood, Daniel B. "GOP Has Rare Shot in Hawaii Governor Race." *Christian Science Monitor* (September 23, 1994): 7:1.

Sake Bill (1897)

The Sake Bill was a law passed by the Hawaiian legislature in 1897. The official name was "An Act to Increase the Duty on Liquors, Still Wines, and Other Beverages Made from Materials Other Than Grape Juice." The law, which was designed mostly to tax Japanese sake (which is made from fermented rice), was enacted to discourage Japanese immigration and expansion in Hawaii. President Sanford Ballard Dole of Hawaii vetoed the bill, but it still passed by the legislature and went into effect on July 1, 1897.

BIBLIOGRAPHY

Conroy, Francis Hilary. *The Japanese Expansion into Hawaii, 1868–1898.* San Francisco: R & E Associates, 1973.

Salinas Lettuce Strike (1934)

In August 1934, the Filipino labor union began a strike against the Central California Vegetable Growers and Shippers' Association. The Filipinos demanded higher wages, but the association refused, so 7,000 workers walked off the job when the union's demands for its members were ignored. The strikers were continually harassed by local officials working on behalf of the Growers and Shippers' Association, but the strike crippled the lettuce industry. By September 1934, union leaders decided to end the strike; in negotiations, they successfully obtained a 10-cent-per-hour pay increase for all the Filipino laborers.

BIBLIOGRAPHY

DeWitt, Howard A. "The Filipino Labor Union: The Salinas Lettuce Strike of 1934." *American Journal* 5, no. 2 (1978): 1–21.

Salvador Roldan v. Los Angeles County (1931)

Salvador Roldan v. Los Angeles County (1931) was a case involving a Filipino man, Salvador Roldan, who wished to marry a white woman, Marjorie Rodgers. In 1880, section 69 of the California Civil Code was established to prohibit intermarrying between whites and Chinese (termed "Mongolians" in the code). However, in 1921 a Los Angeles court decided that since Filipinos were not Mongolians, they could indeed marry whites. Anti-Filipino groups and the California attorney general sued Los Angeles County to put an end to this practice. In 1931 Salvador Rolan's case reached the state supreme court, where a judge decided that marriage between a white and a Filipino did not violate sections 60 and 69 of the civil code. This decision was appealed, and in 1933 the majority opinion of the appellate court was that Filipinos were not Mongolians, but Malays, and thus could marry whites. (In 1933 the California legislature amended the law to include Malays among the races that whites were forbidden to marry.) **See also** *Robinson v. L.E. Lampton, County Clerk of Los Angeles* (1930).

BIBLIOGRAPHY

Melendy, H. Brett. "Filipinos in the United States." In Norris Hundley Jr., ed. *The Asian Experience.* Santa Barbara, CA: Clio Press, 1976.

San Francisco School Board Crisis of 1906

Although the climax of the San Francisco School Board crisis was when the **San Francisco School Board School Segregation Order** was passed in 1906, in many ways the crisis had been percolating under the surface of municipal affairs as early as 1892. In the late nineteenth century, as Japanese immigrants began arriving in California in greater numbers, white residents began to agitate increasingly for the school board to establish separate schools for what were called "Mongolian" children. In 1901 the Labor Party continued to argue for separate schooling. For opponents of the Japanese, the legislative cogs turned slowly and four years had passed when finally the California state legislature passed a resolution outlining 10 reasons why Japanese immigrants were undesirable. In 1905 the San Francisco Board of Supervisors provided for the enlargement of the Chinese Oriental School; however, this early plan did not materialize due to lack of funds.

The San Francisco School Board decision began to receive national attention only after the 1906 earthquake. On October 15, 1906, Chinese and Korean students obeyed the order to send their children to the Chinese Oriental School; however, the Japanese asked for the assistance of the Japanese Consul in San Francisco to write a letter of protest. Victor Howard Metcalf, secretary of the Navy, was sent by President Theodore Roosevelt to investigate the matter. When Metcalf returned with a report arguing for full federal protection for the Japanese, Roosevelt ended up having to address privately the California Federation of Labor, the **Asiatic Exclusion League,** and the Building Trade Council and summon the Board of Education to Washington, D.C. In the end, a compromise was reached and the school board rescinded the segregation order while the president promised to end Japanese immigration. (FHM)

BIBLIOGRAPHY

Bell, Reginald. *Public School Education of Second Generation Japanese in California.* New York: Arno Press, 1978.

San Francisco School Board Segregation Order of 1906

On October 11, 1906, the San Francisco School Board passed the School Segregation Order. This municipal order came shortly after the great earthquake of 1906 which leveled San Francisco. During the rebuilding process, it was decided that the Chinese Oriental School could accommodate all Asian children in the city; however, the Segregation Order affected the Japanese the most since they were located furthest from Chinatown. Section 1662 directed all Chinese, Japanese, and Korean children to the Chinese Oriental School. The Japanese parents refused to comply, thus signaling the start of the **San Francisco School Board Crisis of 1906**. (FHM)

BIBLIOGRAPHY

Bell, Reginald. *Public School Education of Second Generation Japanese in California.* New York: Arno Press, 1978.

San Francisco State College Strike (1968–1969)

The San Francisco State college strike was a student strike forcing the campus administrators to initiate the first School of Ethnic Studies established by any college or university in the United States. The principal organizer of the movement was the Third World Liberation Front, which was a coalition of student associations from many ethnic groups within the

college. It was the longest civil rights display (and protest against the **Vietnam War**) in U.S. history. Hundreds of demonstrators were arrested after the California state authorities got involved. Compromises included the School of Ethnic Studies and the first Asian American Studies department in the United States in a college.

BIBLIOGRAPHY

San Francisco State College. Study Team Concerning the San Francisco College Strike. *College in Crisis: A Report to the National Commission on the Causes and Prevention of Violence.* William H. Orrick, Director. Nashville: Aurora Publishers, 1970.

Masao Satow (1908–1977)

Masao Satow graduated from the University of California in 1929 and went on to receive a Bachelor of Theology from Princeton University in 1932. In 1936 he became both the assistant executive secretary of the **Japanese American Citizens League (JACL)** and the chair of the Second Generation Development Program. Satow resumed his work with JACL after being interned during **World War II**, and in 1947 he became the national secretary, a position he held until he retired in 1972.

BIBLIOGRAPHY

O'Brien, David J. and Stephen S. Fugita. *The Japanese American Experience.* Bloomington: Indiana University Press, 1991.

Dalip Singh Saund (1899–1973)

Dalip Singh Saund was born in India in 1899 and educated at the University of Punjab. He came to the United States in 1920 and earned his Ph.D. in mathematics at the University of California, Berkeley. He began speaking about India's problems publicly and helped to organize the India Association. In the early 1940s he became president of the association and began lobbying for U.S. citizenship for Asian Americans. In 1949 Saund was permitted to become a naturalized citizen, and in 1956 he became the first Asian American to be elected to Congress. He went on to serve on the House Foreign Affairs Committee and to oversee a foreign aid program in Asia. In 1957 Saund gave a speech to the Parliament of India, and he denied that Asians, and other nonwhite races in the United States, were mistreated. He retired from Congress in 1962, after losing an election.

BIBLIOGRAPHY

Chan, Suchens. *Asian Americans: An Interpretive History.* Boston: Twayne Publishers, 1991.

Scott Act of 1888

The Scott Act of 1888 was created as an amendment to the Chinese Exclusion Act (**Immigration Act of 1882**), which prevented Chinese laborers from immigrating to the United States for a period of 10 years. The 1882 act also stated that Chinese immigrants already in the United States had to acquire a federal certificate of readmission if they desired to leave the country to visit China and later return to the United States.

On March 12, 1888, the Scott Act was approved, thereby eliminating the issuing of readmission certificates as of November 1 of that year. Not only did this discourage Chinese laborers from leaving the United States, it also banned around 20,000 immigrants who were visiting China from returning to the United States. As a result, many Chinese families found themselves separated or alienated from their homes. The act was soon condemned by the Chinese government, as well as Chinese immigrants who unsuccessfully campaigned in 1889 to have the United States Supreme Court declare the act unconstitutional. The Scott Act was adopted as a result of growing anti-Chinese sentiment in the American West and political pressures during President Grover Cleveland's reelection bid, causing for the act's repeal to be impossible until such social biases changed.

BIBLIOGRAPHY

Chen, Jack. *The Chinese of America.* New York: Harper and Row, 1980.

Lyman, Stanford. *Chinese Americans.* New York: Random House, 1974.

Sidewalk Ordinance of 1983

The 1983 Sidewalk Ordinance was signed by San Francisco mayor Dianne Feinstein. It required merchants in Chinatown and the North Beach area to apply to the city for permits to display merchandise in front of the stores. The purpose was to keep the sidewalks clear for pedestrians. However, many Chinese merchants objected because it interfered with their traditional way of doing business. The ordinance also reminded the community of the Sidewalk Ordinance of 1870 that forbid people who were carrying poles (a customary way for Chinese to carry goods) from using the sidewalks, thus forcing them into the dangerous and dirty streets.

BIBLIOGRAPHY

Ng, Franklin, ed. *The Asian American Encyclopedia.* New York: Marshall Cavendish, 1995.

Sino-Korean People's League

The Sino-Korean People's League was formed to help the Korean people and to encourage anti-Japanese action. The league was organized in Hawaii during **World War II** and it was headed by Haan Kilsoo. Kilsoo cautioned against a Japanese attack on the United States and hypothesized that the Japanese living in the United States would back Japan in the event of hostilities.

BIBLIOGRAPHY

Girdner, Audrie and Ann Loftis. *The Great Betrayal: The Evacuation of the Japanese-Americans during World War II.* New York: Macmillan, 1969.

tenBroek, Jacobus, Edward N. Barnhart, and Floyd W. Matson. *Prejudice, War and the Constitution.* Berkeley: University of California Press, 1970.

Snake River Massacre (1887)

The Snake River Massacre was an anti-Chinese act of violence that occurred in May 1887 north of Hell's Canyon in Idaho. The result was the murder of 10 Chinese miners. They were shot or beaten to death by men who were under the understanding that the miners had great quantities of gold. (Supposedly miners did not trust Western banks, so they would hold on to their gold.) Some of the miners were tortured for information, and all of their bodies were thrown into the river.

BIBLIOGRAPHY

Tsai, Shih-Shan Henry. *The Chinese Experience in America.* Bloomington: Indiana University Press, 1986.

Spanish-American War (1898)

The Spanish-American War was a brief conflict, lasting from April 25 to August 12, 1898. The war's origins lay in the Cuban struggle for independence from Spain, and Americans' sympathy with this struggle. Early in 1898, civil disorder broke out in Cuba, and the USS *Maine* was sent to Cuba to protect U.S. citizens. Then in February 1898 the warship inexplicably exploded and sank off the port of Havana, and many Americans thought Spain was somehow responsible. President William McKinley confronted Spain about ending the unrest in Cuba and about their rule of the island. Spain granted limited powers of government to Cuba, but the U.S. Congress declared that Cuba had a right to its independence. Spain then declared war on the United States on April 24, which was followed by a declaration of war by the United States the next day. The war was completely one-sided, because Spain did not have any kind of military power to contest the U.S. fleets. The U.S. forces easily defeated the Spanish fleet in Manila Bay, in the Philippines, and the Spanish governor-general offered to surrender the colony to Commodore George Dewey. The U.S. domination continued as U.S. troops landed on Santiago's coast and forced the main Spanish fleet out of its harbor. The war officially ended when Admiral Pascual Cervera of Spain surrendered to American General William Shafter on August 13, 1898. In December, Spain signed the **Treaty of Paris,** which gave the Philippines, Puerto Rico, and Guam to the United States. The Filipinos refused to be under the care of the United States, so they formed a resistance. Led by Emilio Aguinaldo of the Katipunan military organization, the Filipinos fought the U.S. troops with guerrilla-style tactics. Aguinaldo was not captured until 1902. **See also** Philippine-American War.

BIBLIOGRAPHY

Graff, Henry F. *America Imperialism and the Philippine Insurrection.* Boston: Little, Brown, 1969.

State of California v. Hayao Yano and Tetsubumi Yano (1922)

Under the **Alien Land Act of 1920**, Hayao Yano was prohibited from owning land himself, so he bought land in the name of his American-born daughter Tetsubumi. In 1922, Yano requested and was denied the right to become the legal guardian of his daughter and his daughter's property. This decision was appealed in *State of California v. Hayao Yano and Tetsubumi Yano* (1922), where it was ruled that the Alien Land Act infringed on the rights of minors. It was also ruled that the elder Yano could be named as his daughter's legal guardian regardless of his citizenship. The result of this decision was that Japanese residents in the United States were suddenly allowed to buy land and transfer it to their American-born children.

BIBLIOGRAPHY

Chuman, Frank F. *The Bamboo People: The Law and Japanese-Americans.* Del Mar, CA: Publisher's Inc., 1976.

Consulate-General of Japan. *Documentary History of Law Cases Affecting Japanese in the United States, 1916–1924.* San Francisco: Consulate-General of Japan, 1925.

State of California v. S.S. Constitution (1872)

On May 3, 1852, the California state legislature passed legislation which required shipmasters to pay $500, or $5 to $10 per passenger, for all aliens transported on their vessels. This money was to be used for immigrant medical care and relief work after being distributed among California's hospitals. Chinese immigrants initially paid about 45 percent of these entrance taxes, but by 1870, this amount had risen to 85 percent, thereby helping to accumulate over $433,600 for the State of California.

When William Hudson, master of the S.S. *Constitution*, failed to pay the tax for four of his passengers from New Granda, the matter was brought to the courts, which examined the legality of the taxation legislation. In *State of California v. S.S. Constitution,* 42 Cal 878 (1872), the court stated that Congress alone, not the states, had the power to regulate commerce issues. The court also stated that while California could place exclusions on immigrants who were likely to become state charges, such as the poor, the sick, and criminals, it could not regulate individuals who did not fall into these categories, such as the passengers of the S.S. *Constitution*.

BIBLIOGRAPHY

Coolidge, Mary Roberts. *Chinese Immigration.* New York: Henry Holt, 1989.

State of California v. Timothy S. Yatko (1925)

In 1925 Timothy S. Yatko, a Filipino man, was found guilty of murdering a white man, Harry L. Kidder. Yatko was married to a white woman, Lola Butler, whom he had allegedly found in bed with Kidder. In *State of California v. Timothy S. Yatko* (1925), the state maintained that Yatko's marriage was illegal, because he was Filipino and Lola Butler was white. At the trial, Butler testified that her husband had stabbed Kidder to death. Yatko was found guilty and was given a life sentence to be served at San Quentin prison.

BIBLIOGRAPHY

Chuman, Frank F. *The Bamboo People: The Law and Japanese-Americans.* Del Mar, CA: Publisher's Inc, 1976.

Sugar Strike of 1909

On May 9, 1909, A'iea sugar plantation workers went on strike, and soon strikes occurred at other plantations throughout Hawaii in what became known as the "Great Japanese Strike." Called by the Japanese Higher Wage Association, the strikers primarily sought to raise the wages of Japanese, by $4 per month, to the level of Portuguese workers. After one month, four strike leaders were arrested, and the strike was over. Although the strike ended without any concessions, management granted all the union demands as an act of "benevolence" in September. (MH)

BIBLIOGRAPHY

Murayama, Milton. *All I Am Asking for Is My Body.* San Francisco: Supa Press, 1975.

Okahata, James H. "Struggle for Equality." In *A History of Japanese in Hawaii.* Honolulu: The United Japanese Society of Hawaii, 1971.

Sugar Strike of 1920

On January 19, 1920, the Filipino Labor Union, led by **Pablo Manlapit**, called a strike, principally demanding higher wages for plantation workers. By February 1, the Japanese Federation of Labor joined the strike, in the first collaboration between the two ethnic groups. Some 165 days later, after 15 Japanese were arrested and misunderstandings arose between Filipinos and Japanese, the strike was called off. Although the strike was a failure, management later granted some of the demands as an act of "benevolence." **See also** Filipino Americans. (MH)

BIBLIOGRAPHY

Beechert, Edward D. *Working in Hawaii: A Labor History.* Honolulu: University of Hawaii Press, 1985.

Fuchs, Lawrence H. *Hawaii Pono: A Social History.* New York: Harcourt, Brace & World, 1961.

Sugar Strike of 1924

During April 1924, Filipino workers on 23 of the 43 Hawaiian plantations went on strike, seeking the same wage demands as the **sugar strike of 1920**. Although Filipinos expected Japanese to strike, too, the latter demurred. Known as the "Filipino Piecemeal Strike," the strikers held out for eight months until September 9, when 16 strikers and four police were killed, and more than 100 strikers were arrested in what is known as the "Hanapepe Massacre." **Pablo Manlapit,** a principal organizer, was also arrested. Management made no concessions. **See also** Filipino Americans. (MH)

BIBLIOGRAPHY

Manlapit, Pablo. *Filipinos Fight for Justice: Case of the Filipino Laborer in the Big Strike of 1924.* Honolulu: Kumalae Publishing Company, 1933.

Reinecke, John E. *The Tragic Filipino Piecemeal Strike of 1920.* Honolulu: Social Science Research Institute, University of Hawaii at Manoa, 1997.

Sugar Strike of 1946

The Sugar Strike of 1946 was a four-month labor strike that occurred against all sugar plantations in the territory of Hawaii, making it one of the largest movements of its nature. The strike was led by the International Longshoremen's and Warehousemen's Union, which united workers from all ethnic groups to participate in the industry-wide strike. The action called for a 16.5-cent-an-hour wage increase, a 40-hour work week, and an end to discriminatory practices; after these demands were denied, over 21,000 employees from 33 sugar plantations walked out of work on September 1, 1946, and refused to return until concessions were made. Union members soon established committees for food collection, picketing, finance, morale, and volunteer organization, as well as forming strategy committees in all local units. In November 1946, settlements were finally made, providing the strikers with many of the conditions they had asked for. The strike also put an end to single class/ethnic group unions in Hawaii, as workers realized that a unified front was the best means to achieve their goals.

BIBLIOGRAPHY

Kuykendall, Ralph S. and A. Grove Day. *Hawaii: A History.* New York: Prentice-Hall, 1948.

Tacoma Race Riot of 1885

The Tacoma race riot involved the Chinese residents of Tacoma, Washington, all of whom were harassed into leaving their homes. In 1884 a "workingmen's union" was formed in Tacoma, led by the mayor of the city, Robert Weisbach. He and other community officials decided to drive the Chinese residents from the city. In February 1885, they formed an anti-Chinese committee and began to boycott Chinese merchants. On October 9, 1885, the committee decided to force all Chinese people from the city by November 1; they went door to door informing the Chinese that they must leave. However, by November 1, only 500 of the 700 Chinese residents had left, so committee members forcibly moved the Chinese people and their belongings to the train station and burned their houses behind them. Ten of the men involved with the anti-Chinese committee were arrested and tried, but none were ever convicted. **See also** Los Angeles Riot (1871); Rock Springs Riot.

BIBLIOGRAPHY

Daniels, Roger, ed. *Anti-Chinese Violence in North America.* New York: Arno Press, 1978.

Taft Commission

In 1898 at the end of the **Spanish-American War**, the United States obtained the Philippines from Spain through the **Treaty of Paris**. The Taft Commission, or the Second **Philippine Commission**, was formed by President William McKinley to examine the newly acquired Philippine Islands. Headed by Judge William Howard Taft, the commission lasted from 1900 to 1904, studying all aspects of the Filipino civic, political, and economic life. The commission reported that they felt the Philippine government should be permitted to govern more independently. It also encouraged the U.S. government to give $1 million to assist with highway and road repairs, and $1 million to complete the reconstruction of Manila harbor. The commission also recommended a reorganization of the Filipino court system and the Filipino Bureaus of Forestry and Mining. They also supported the passage of the **Pensionado Act of 1903**, through which Filipino children were schooled and trained in the United States. **See also** Jones Act of 1916; Philippine America War.

BIBLIOGRAPHY

Taylor, George E.. *The Philippines and the United States: Problems of Partnership.* New York: Frederick A. Praeger, 1964.

Taft-Katsura Agreement of 1905

The Taft-Katsura Agreement was a secret memorandum exchanged by the United States secretary of war, William Taft, and Japan's prime minister, Katsura Taro. The memorandum endorsed the Japanese domination of Korea and the hegemony in the Philippines by the United States. Following the agreement, Japan forced the Korean government into accepting its position as a protectorate under the Protectorate Treaty of 1905. Korea later became a colony of Japan.

BIBLIOGRAPHY

Lee, Yur-Boh and Wayne Patterson, eds. *One Hundred Years of Korean–American Relations, 1882–1982.* University, AL: The University of Alabama Press, 1986.

Shirin R. Tahir-Kheli (1944–)

Shirin Tahir-Kheli was the ambassador at the United States Mission to the United Nations (UN) from 1990 to 1993. He was the first Asian ambassador to represent the United States at the UN. He was also the first Muslim senior government official appointed by the president and confirmed by the Senate. Born in Hyderabad, India, Tahir-Kheli taught at Temple University from 1973 to 1985. He joined the Office of the Secretary of State as a member of the policy planning staff in 1982. Later he became director of political-military affairs from 1984 to 1986. He was the director of the Near East and South Asian Affairs from 1986 to 1989. He is currently a fellow at the Center of International Studies at Princeton University.

BIBLIOGRAPHY

Anderson, Jack. "CIA Fought Clearance for NSC Staffer." *Newsday* (February 10, 1988): 76.

Sakae Takahashi (1919–)

After serving as a first lieutenant and captain with the **100th Infantry Battalion** during **World War II**, Sakae Takahashi won a 1950 seat on the Hawaiian Board of Supervisors. He was appointed the next year to serve as treasurer of the Territory of Hawaii, and was elected to the U.S. Senate in 1954. In the late 1960s, Takahashi was active in opposing private development projects on public lands.

BIBLIOGRAPHY

O'Brien, David J. and Stephen S. Fugita. *The Japanese American Experience.* Bloomington: Indiana University Press, 1991.

Takahashi v. Fish and Game Commission et al. (1948)

Between 1915 and 1943, Torao Takahashi, a resident of California since 1907, had fished off the coast of California, but in 1943 he was denied a commercial fishing license. Prior to **World War II**, California had issued fishing licenses regardless of citizenship status. In 1947, Takahashi brought the matter to the Los Angeles County Court, which granted that law-abiding aliens were entitled to commercial fishing rights. Then the California State Supreme Court, in *Takahashi v. Fish and Game Commission et al.*, 334 U.S. 410 (1948), reversed the county court's decision in favor of a state's rights to conserve the supply of fish along its coast for its citizens. (FHM)

BIBLIOGRAPHY

Kim, Hyung-Chan, ed. *Asian Americans and the Supreme Court: A Documentary History.* New York: Greenwood Press, 1992.

Torao Takahasi v. Fish and Game Commission, 68 S. Ct. 1138, 30 C.2d 719 (1948).

Takao Ozawa v. United States (1922)

Takao Ozawa v. United States, 260 U.S. 178 (1922), concerned Japanese-born Takao Ozawa's petition for United States citizenship, which had been opposed by the United States district attorney for Hawaii in 1914. The U.S. Supreme Court held that individuals of the Japanese race and born in Japan were not eligible for citizenship under the naturalization laws. In its affirmation of the district court, the Supreme Court held that Ozawa did not fit under the category of "white person."

Born in Japan, Ozawa had attended high school and college in California; including his residence in Hawaii, he had been a resident of the United States for 20 years. While the district court of Hawaii noted that Ozawa had met character and education requirements for citizenship, it nevertheless found that he was not eligible for naturalization on the grounds that Ozawa had been born in Japan and was of Japanese ancestry. The district court relied on a federal statute, which stated that naturalization was limited to aliens being "free white persons" and to "aliens of African nativity and to persons of African descent."

In his appeal, Ozawa raised two defenses: that an act of June 29, 1906, conferred the privilege of naturalization without limitation as to race and that persons of Japanese ancestry were constructively "white persons." Ozawa also asserted in this latter argument that the original intent of the citizenship statutes was to exclude African and Native Americans and not Asians. The Supreme Court rejected both defenses, holding that the act of 1906 only governed the procedure of naturalization and did not confer the privilege of citizenship on all aliens.

The Court also stated that the original intent of the naturalization acts from 1790 to 1870 was to include free white persons and to exclude all those who did not fit under the designation of "free white person." The only exception to this rule was the addition of those of African nativity and descent in 1870. In defining this designation, the Court held that "white person" was synonymous with a person of the Caucasian race. Given this definition, the Court affirmed the district court's opinion holding that Ozawa was effectively excluded from becoming a naturalized citizen of the United States. (JK)

BIBLIOGRAPHY

Barker, Lucius and Twiley W. Barker, Jr. *Civil Liberties and the Constitution: Cases and Commentaries.* Upper Saddle River, NJ: Prentice-Hall, 1999.

——. *Freedom, Courts, Politics: Studies in Civil Liberties.* Englewood Cliffs, NJ: Prentice-Hall, 1972.

Tamesa Minoru v. United States (1945)

Tamesa Minoru v. United States (1945) grew out of the protest of Tamesa Minoru, one of 63 defendants found guilty for violating a draft law. He protested the ruling of *Fujii v. United States*, 148 F. 2d 198, which found the 63 Japanese Americans guilty. An appeals court judge stated the defendants were not above the law and must carry out the service required of them as U.S. citizens. In *Tamesa Minoru v. United States,* 325 U.S. 868 (1945), the U.S. Supreme Court upheld the decision. **See also** Executive Order 9814.

BIBLIOGRAPHY

Chuman, Frank F. *The Bamboo People.* Del Mar, CA: Publisher's Inc., 1976.

Tang Tun v. Harry Edsell (1912)

Tang Tun was an American-born Chinese man. He lived in China between the ages of five and 18, and he returned to the United States in 1897. At the age of 26, he returned to China again, and married a Chinese woman. He then returned to the United States with his wife in 1906 but was denied admission at Port Sumas, Washington, by Harry Edsell, the immigration inspector. Tang Tun presented evidence of his birth in the United States, as well as the official permission to return signed by a U.S. immigration officer in 1905, but the secretary of commerce upheld Edsell's decision. The case was then heard in district court, which decided that Tang Tun had not been given an adequate hearing, and that he had proven his citizenship and should be allowed to remain in the United States. The circuit court then reversed this decision and stated that the action of the secretary of commerce was final. Finally, in *Tang Tun v. Harry Edsell,* 223 U.S. 673 (1912), the U.S. Supreme Court maintained this opinion as well and Tang Tun was denied admission to his own country.

BIBLIOGRAPHY

Konvitz, Milton R. *The Alien and the Asiatic in American Law.* Ithaca, NY: Cornell University Press, 1946.

Tape v. Hurley (1885)

Mamia Tape, a Chinese student at the Spring Valley School in San Francisco, was expelled by principal Jennie Hurley, who was acting under the authority and jurisdiction of superintendent of schools A.J. Moulder. Moulder had previously made orders excluding all Chinese students from participating in the district's schools, a decision that was ratified by the board of education on October 21, 1884.

At the municipal court level, it was found that such exclusions were unconstitutional because all children, regardless of their ancestral national origins, were guaranteed the right to a full education. Upon appeal, in *Tape v. Hurley* (1885), the Supreme Court of California affirmed this decision and ordered the school board to change its policies. However, instead of allowing Mamie Tape to continue to enroll at the Spring Valley School, the board of education created a separate, segregated institution (the Oriental Public School) for Tape to attend.

BIBLIOGRAPHY

McClain, Charles. *In Search of Equality.* Berkeley: University of California Press, 1994.

Wollenberg, Charles. *All Deliberate Speed: Segregation and Exclusion of California Schools, 1855–1975.* Berkeley: University of California Press, 1994.

Terrace et al. v. Thompson, Attorney General of Washington (1923)

Terrace et al. v. Thompson, Attorney General of Washington, 263 U.S. 197 (1923), was one of six cases reaching the U.S. Supreme Court that challenged the constitutionality of the **Alien Land Laws** of the Western states. In all six cases, the Court ruled that the land laws were constitutional. This case reached the Supreme Court as an appeal from the U.S. District Court for the Western District of Washington. Terrace argued that the Washington Alien Land Law of 1921 was in violation of the due process of law, the equal protection clause of the Fourteenth Amendment of the Constitution, and the 1911 treaty between the United States and Japan.

BIBLIOGRAPHY

Chuman, Frank F. *The Bamboo People: the Law and Japanese-Americans.* Del Mar, CA: Publisher's Inc., 1976.

Konvitz, Milton R., *The Alien and the Asiatic in American Law.* Ithaca, NY: Cornell University Press, 1946.

George Kiyoshi Togasaki (1895–)

George Togasoki was one of many Japanese, Chinese, and Korean children who, in the early years of the twentieth century, were sent to an exclusively Asian school, under a regulation enforced by the San Francisco School Board. When Togasaki returned from World War I, he joined a group of *nisei* (first-generation Japanese Americans) who were struggling to succeed in American society. The group, known as the **American Loyalty League**, was an early version of the **Japanese American Citizens League.** Togasaki later moved to Tokyo and eventually was named president of the Japan *Times.* He also served as chairman of the board of Japan Christian University.

BIBLIOGRAPHY

Daniels, Roger. *The Politics of Prejudice.* Berkeley: University of California Press, 1962.

Hosokawa, Bill. *Nisei.* New York: William Morrow, 1969.

Tolan Committee

On April 22, 1940, the U.S. House of Representatives called for the formation of a congressional committee, chaired by Congressman John Tolan (D-CA), to investigate the problems facing migrant farm workers. During the Great Depression, the number of farm jobs decreased drastically, creating labor surpluses and fierce competition. Through many interviews and hearings, the Tolan committee discovered that migrant workers often suffered exploitative practices and deplorable housing conditions because there were no government regulations to protect these workers. Committee members also discovered that many migrant workers were not eligible for federal assistance because of federal residency requirements. On April 3, 1941, the committee submitted a report to Congress in which they recommended that private employment agencies be engaged to regulate interstate commerce. They also recommended that the government establish Farm Security Act camps to improve the conditions of housing and sanitation of migrant laborers, and that a new category of public assistance be created under the Social Security Act to provide relief to farm workers.

BIBLIOGRAPHY

Girdner, Audrie and Anne Loftis. *The Great Betrayal: The Evacuation of the Japanese-Americans During World War II.* New York: Macmillan, 1969.

Hosokawa, Bill. *JACL in Quest of Justice.* New York: William Morrow, 1982.

Maeley L. Tom (1941–)

Born in San Francisco, Maeley Tom is the first minority person and the first woman to serve as chief administrative officer in the California Assembly and the chief of staff to the California Senate president pro tempore. She assisted in the creation of the First Asian Pacific Affairs Office in the California Legislature. She organized the first national Conference of Asian Pacific Democrats. Tom was the only Asian American executive committee member of the 1989 Democratic National Committee.

BIBLIOGRAPHY

Wei, William. *The Asian American Movement.* Philadelphia: Temple University Press, 1993.

Tom Hong v. United States (1903)

From 1891 to 1895, Tom Hong, Tom Dock, and Lee Kit owned and operated the Kwong Yen Ti Company. In this role, the men declared themselves legal merchants of the United States, even though they performed some duties (such as bookkeeping) that were beyond the normal definition of a merchant's duties. A few years later, the three men were brought to court on charges that they had violated the Chinese Exclusion Act **(Immigration Act of 1882)** because none of them had a certificate of residence.

Hong, Dock, and Kit argued to the court that a certificate of residence was not necessary; while the Chinese Exclusion Act called for such paperwork from Chinese laborers engaged in mining, fishing, peddling, laundry, and other related occupations, it did not hold jurisdiction over merchants like themselves. The court, however, disagreed with the men's pleas, stating that they did not meet the definition of a merchant as described by a 1893 amendment to the act. Furthermore, the court explained that the law dictated that all merchants have their names listed in their company's title, which Hong and the others had not done.

In *Tom Hong v. United States,* 193 U.S. 517 (1903), the U.S. Supreme Court disagreed with the lower court's findings against the three men. The Court held that provisions which require that a merchant's name be listed in the company's title were unnecessary, especially in partnership situations such as the one with Hong, Dock, and Kit. It also reversed the judgment in regards to certificate mandates, stating such requirements did not apply at the time of the company's creation.

BIBLIOGRAPHY

Gyory, Andrew. Closing the Gate. Chapel Hill: University of North Carolina 1988.

Tomoya Kawakita v. United States (1951)

Tomoya Kawakita v. United States, 190 F 2d (1951), involved a Japanese American, Kawakita Tomoya, who moved to Japan before the start of **World War II** and attended Meiji University. While in Japan, he continued to renew his U.S. passport; in 1945, when the war was over, he applied for a new passport. He swore that he had not perpetrated any acts against the United States, and he was issued a passport. He returned to the United States in 1946 and was reunited with his family. However, in 1947 Tomoya was recognized by an American veteran who had been a prisoner of war (POW) who reported Tomoya to the Federal Bureau of Investigation. Tomoya was arrested and tried in federal court on 15 counts of mistreatment of American POWs in Japan. It was established that Tomoya had worked as an interpreter for the Oeyama Nickel Company, which used POWs for forced labor in their mines and factories. Tomoya's defense was that by placing his name in a family registry in 1943, he had renounced his American citizenship and could not be tried as an American citizen; the court rejected this argument, convicted Tomoya of treason, and sentenced him to death. In 1953 his sentence was commuted to life imprisonment. President John F. Kennedy later pardoned Tomoya and sent him back to Japan, stipulating that he could never return to the United States.

BIBLIOGRAPHY

Chuman, Frank F. *The Bamboo People: The Law and Japanese-Americans.* Del Mar, CA: Publisher's Inc., 1976.

Kim, Hyung-Chan, ed. *Asian Americans and the Supreme Court: A Documentary History.* New York: Greenwood Press, 1992.

Treaty of Chemulp'o (1882)

The Treaty of Chemulp'o (1882) was also known as the Treaty of Amity and Commerce (and the Korean-American Treaty of 1882). It was the agreement that established diplomatic relations between Korea and the United States. The United States became the first Western nation to recognize Korea diplomatically. Korea hoped that the United States would help control Japan's advances into Korea. Article 5 of the treaty allowed Koreans to reside in the United States. (Chemulp'o is the old name for the city of Inchon.)

BIBLIOGRAPHY

Lee, Yur-Bok and Wayne Patterson. *One Hundred Years of Korean-American Relations, 1882–1982.* University, AL: University of Alabama Press, 1986.

Treaty of Edo (1858)

The Treaty of Edo (1858) was signed as the Treaty of Commerce and Navigation. It provided for the opening of more ports located on the shores of the United States for Japanese boats. It voided the Treaty of Karagawa (1854). The United States gave Japan's citizens the right to go to the United States and the Japanese allowed Americans to reside there.

BIBLIOGRAPHY

Dulles, Foster R. *Yankees and Samurai.* New York: Harper and Row, 1965.

Ichihashi, Yamato. *Japanese in the United States.* Stanford, CA: Stanford University Press, 1932.

Treaty of Paris (1898)

The Treaty of Paris was signed by the United States and Spain in 1898 following the conclusion of the **Spanish-American War.** In this treaty, provisions were made stating that the Philippine Islands would become an official territory of the United States, which meant that Filipinos would be considered U.S. nationals but be excluded from full U.S. citizenship. On December 10, 1898, the treaty was signed into practice and reparations were soon made to help expedite the transition of power. On February 6, 1899, the Treaty of Paris was ratified by the United States Congress. After that, Filipinos owed allegiance to the United States, a fact that helped them avoid restrictions placed on other aliens under the **Immigration Act of 1924,** as well as providing them with other benefits. Over the years, however, there was debate as to whether Filipinos should be provided the same rights as U.S. citizens.

BIBLIOGRAPHY

Musicant, Ivan. *Empire by Default.* New York: Henry Holt, 1998.

Tydings-McDuffie Act (1934)

In 1934 Manuel Quezon, president of the Philippine Senate, met with the U.S. Congress to negotiate an agreement that would lead to Filipino political independence. Quezon, an activist and leader, was the Filipino resident commissioner in Washington, D.C., from 1909 to 1916. He led the opposition to the **Hare-Hawes-Cutting Act,** which was passed in 1933 and which promised political independence to the Philippine Islands in 1943. In order to work out an alternative arrangement to the Hare-Hawes-Cutting Act, Quezon went to Washington in 1933 and met with President Franklin D. Roosevelt; Senator Millard Tydings, chairman of the Senate

Committee on Territories and Insular Affairs; and George Dern, the secretary of war. Together they worked on a new bill to establish the Commonwealth of the Philippines. The new bill (which established a Filipino export tax, among other things) was hammered out and the president signed the bill on March 24, 1934. **See also** Filipino Americans; Filipino Repatriation Act of 1935; Immigration Restriction Movement; Jones Act of 1916; Philippine Naturalization.

BIBLIOGRAPHY

Melendy, H. Brett. *Asians in America: Filipinos, Koreans, and East Indians.* Boston: Twayne Publishers, 1977.

Taylor, George E. *The Philippines and the United States: Problems of Partnership.* New York: Frederick A. Praeger, 1964.

United Chinese Society

The United Chinese Society was created as the Hawaiian chapter of the Chinese Benevolent Association. The goal of the organization was to fight discriminatory laws and to provide legal support for its members. The first **Consolidated Chinese Benevolent Association** was originally formed in California in 1882 to consolidate all of the existing Chinese organizations. From there, many sprung up around the country, including the United Chinese Society based in Hawaii. However, most of the chapters continued to regard the San Francisco office as the head office and looked to that office for guidance and policy.

BIBLIOGRAPHY

Glick, Clarence E. *Sojourners and Settlers.* Honolulu: University Press of Hawaii, 1980.

United Farm Workers Organizing Committee

The United Farm Workers Organizing Committee was a farm workers union in California, formed when the mostly Filipino **Agricultural Workers Organizing Committee** merged with the Latino-led National Farm Workers Association. After 1924, Filipino workers began immigrating to the United States; at the time, Asian immigration was banned and there was a labor shortage in the country. Many worked on farms in California and were called "pinoys." Unions tried to organize them but met with little success because of the power of the Associated Farmers of California. However, in 1940s Filipino workers began demanding better wages and improved working conditions, but they did not organize until Larry Dulay Itliong led the Agricultural Workers Organizing Committee in the Delano Grape strike in 1965. Cesar Chavez and the National Farm Workers Association joined the strike; when the strike was over, the two unions combined to form the United Farm Workers Organizing Committee.

BIBLIOGRAPHY

Fusco, Paul and George D. Horowitz. *La Causa, the California Grape Strike.* New York: Collier Books, 1970.

Meister, Dick and Ann Loftis. *A Long Time Coming.* New York: Macmillan, 1977.

United Korean Society

The United Korean Society was established in 1907 to represent the interests of Koreans in Hawaii. In 1909, the organization merged with the **Mutual Assistance Society** located on the mainland of the United States to become the **Korean National Association.**

BIBLIOGRAPHY

Choy, Bong-Youn. *Koreans in America.* Chicago: Nelson Hall, 1979.

United States v. Bhagat Singh Thind (1922)

In 1913, Bhagat Singh Thind migrated from his birthplace in India to the United States. After serving with the U.S. Army for six months during World War I, Thind went to district court to apply for U.S. citizenship, believing that his service proved his loyalty to the country. The Immigration and Naturalization Service of the United States Justice Department argued that such an appeal should be denied based on guidelines established in the **Immigration Act of 1917/Barred Zone Act of 1917.** This act, they stated, put restrictions on nonwhite South Asian immigrants to prevent naturalization. Both the district court and the court of appeals allowed for Thind's citizenship, categorizing him as white, thereby excluding him from the Barred Zone Act. As a result, the case went on to the United States Supreme Court.

In *United States v. Bhagat Singh Thind,* 261 U.S. 204 (1922),Thind's attorney argued that their client was allowed citizenship rights as a Caucasian member of the Aryan race, a distinction that separated him from restrictions against all nonwhites. The Court disagreed, however, stating the "Aryan Caucasians" were not the same as "whites." They furthered their statements on evidence showing that Asian Indians had greater difficulties blending into U.S. society than white immigrants like the English, French, Italians, and Germans, which thereby proved such ethnic discrepancies.

As a result, Thind was denied U.S. citizenship and the United States government began stripping citizenship from other Asian Indians. Many Indians, upset with the decision and other subsequent injustices, returned to their homeland of India. In all, around 3,000 immigrants left between 1920 and 1940, dropping the total U.S. Asian Indian population to under 2,400 people.

BIBLIOGRAPHY

Chandrushekhas, F., ed. *From India to America.* La Jolla: Population Review, 1982.

Konvitz, Milton R. *Civil Rights in Immigration. Ithaca:* Cornell University Press, 1953.

United States v. Ju Toy (1905)

Ju Toy was born in the United States to Chinese parents. After visiting China, he was denied reentry to the United States by the immigration department. He appealed the decision and was again denied reentry by the secretary of commerce and labor. The case then went before the district court, which decided that Ju Toy should be allowed to enter his own country. However, in *United States v. Ju Toy,* 198 U.S. 253 (1905), the Supreme Court decided against Ju Toy, stating that the decision of an executive officer, such as the secretary of commerce and labor, constituted due process, and that a person of Chinese descent did not have the right to a habeas corpus proceeding. **See also** Immigration Restriction Movement.

BIBLIOGRAPHY

Konvitz, Milton R. *The Alien and the Asiatic in American Law.* Ithaca, NY: Cornell University Press, 1946.

United States v. Jung Ah Lung (1888)

Jung Ah Lung, a Chinese laborer, was denied reentry to the United States in 1885 because he failed to produce the proper certificate of identity required under the Chinese Exclusion Act (**Immigration Act of 1882**). Jung Ah Lung maintained that he had obtained the permit when he left the United States in 1883, and that it had been stolen. The lower court upheld his right to reenter the United States. The federal government then appealed and the case was heard by the Supreme Court. In the decision *United States v. Jung Ah Lung,* 124 U.S. 621 (1888), the Court found that the law required Chinese laborers leaving the country to obtain a permit, but the law did not state that they must present it upon reentry. **See also** Immigration Restriction Movement.

BIBLIOGRAPHY

Chen, Jack. *The Chinese of America.* New York: Harper and Row, 1980.

Konvitz, Milton R. *The Alien and the Asiatic in American Law.* Ithaca, NY: Cornell University Press, 1946.

United States v. Sakharam Ganesh Pandit (1926)

After receiving his Ph.D. in India, Sakharam Ganesh Pandit came to the United States and petitioned to become a citizen. The government granted his request in 1914, and three years later he was admitted to the California bar. He was also appointed to the office of the notary public by the governor of California. In the 1920s the government tried to take away Pandit's citizenship, stating it had been unlawfully gained and that he could not become a citizen because he was an Asian American. He argued that the court had heard the government's opposition in 1914 and decided to grant him citizenship, and they could not oppose it again. The case was heard by the

district court, the court of appeals and the U.S. Supreme Court, and all three sided with Pandit.

BIBLIOGRAPHY

Chandrashekhar, S. *From India to America.* La Jolla, CA: Population Review, 1982.

United States v. Sing Tuck (1904)

United States v. Sing Tuck, 24, 194 U.S. 161 (1904), was a case involving five Chinese men who entered the United States through Canada. When stopped for questioning, they all alleged that they were U.S. citizens. The immigration authorities detained them for a period of time in deportation houses, which the Chinese men claimed was unlawful. The case was heard by the circuit court, which ruled that the immigration authorities had not acted unlawfully. The case went before the circuit court of appeals, which reversed the lower court's decision, but the U.S. Supreme Court heard the case in 1904 and decided against the five Chinese men.

BIBLIOGRAPHY

Konvitz, Milton R. *The Alien and the Asiatic in American Law.* Ithaca, NY: Cornell University Press, 1946.

United States v. Wong Kim Ark (1898)

United States v. Wong Kim Ark, 169 U.S. 649 (1898), was a case involving Wong Kim Ark, who was born in 1873 to Chinese parents living in San Francisco. In 1894, after a brief visit to China, he was denied reentry into the United States under the Chinese Exclusion Act (**Immigration Act of 1882**). His case was heard by the U.S. Supreme Court in 1898, which ruled that under the Fourteenth Amendment, Wong Kim Ark had the right to U.S. citizenship. This was a landmark case for Asian Americans, who were not permitted to become naturalized citizens of the United States. However, in affirming the rights of Asian-American children born in the United States, the Supreme Court also reiterated the constitutionality of the Chinese Exclusion Act, which prevented Chinese immigration.

BIBLIOGRAPHY

Konvitz, Milton R. *The Alien and the Asiatic in American Law.* Ithaca, NY: Cornell University Press, 1946.

Supreme Court Reporter. 169 U.S. 649 (1898): 456–488.

Edison Uno (1929–1976)

At the age of 12 (during **World War II**), Edison Uno was sent to an **internment camp** along with millions of other Americans of Japanese decent. Before his release, he spent time at four different camps. This event would shape Uno's future; at age 18 he became the president of the **Japanese American Citizens League (JACL)** local branch of East Los Angeles. Eventually, he became president of the national JACL and worked on a number of important initiatives, including the repeal of Title II of the Internal Security Act of 1950 and a pardon for **Iva Toguri D'Aquino** ("Tokyo Rose"). He was also the driving force behind the **redress movement** that sought compensation from the United Sates government for

Clifford Uyeda

its internment of Japanese Americans during World War II. However, he did not live to see the enacting of redress legislation. **See also** Civil Liberties Act of 1988.

BIBLIOGRAPHY
Zia, Helen and Susan B. Gall, eds. *Notable Asian Americans.* Detroit, MI: Gale, 1995.

Clifford Uyeda (1917–)

Unlike most young Japanese Americans on the West Coast, Clifford Uyeda was not interned in a camp during the war because he was at medical school at Tulane (in New Orleans)

at the time. From 1951 to 1953, he served in the United States Air Force as a medical officer. Active in the **Japanese American Citizens League (JACL),** he was elected its president in 1978 and served until 1980. Prior to his tenure at JACL, he helped form the **National Committee for Redress.** In 1984, he became president of the National Japanese American Historical Society and editor of *Nikkei Heritage*.

BIBLIOGRAPHY
Unterburger, Amy L. *Who's Who Among Asian Americans.* Detroit, MI: Gale, 1994.

David M. Valderrama (1933–)

David Valderrama is the first probate judge in the United States of Filipino ancestry. As a delegate to the Assembly of Maryland, he is also the first high-ranking Filipino elected official. Born in Manila, Philippines, Valderrama was elected as the vice-chairman of the Democratic Central Committee in 1982. His next major step was his appointment by the Maryland governor as judge of the Orphan's Court. He became the Maryland State Representative to the National College of Probate Judges and the Orphan's Court liaison judge from Prince George's County to the Maryland General Assembly. In 1993, Valderrama was appointed to represent the Maryland General Assembly on the board of directors of the Council of Governments.

BIBLIOGRAPHY

Greenberg, Rick. "Ambition: Here Comes De Judge." *Regardie's: The Business of Washington* (February 1988).

Francisco Varona (d. 1941)

Sent by Hawaii's governor-general Francis B. Harrison in 1920 to investigate the working conditions of Filipinos on Hawaii's sugar plantations, Francisco Varona produced a report that chronicled worker discrimination and resulted in mandates against the plantation owners. Varona also helped to implement improved transportation for the workers between their homes and the plantations. Varona was appointed assistant to the Philippine Resident Commissioner in 1939 in charge of mediating labor disputes. He also served as national division chief of the Philippine Resident's Office, where he served until his death in 1941.

BIBLIOGRAPHY

Melendy, H. Brett. *Asians in America*. Boston: Twayne, 1977.

Varsity Victory Volunteers

The Varsity Victory Volunteers was a group of *nisei* labor volunteers formed in Hawaii during **World War II** as a result of Japanese-American exclusion from the United States Army after the attack on **Pearl Harbor**. In February 1942, the group was organized, gathering former soldiers and other volunteers to work as an auxiliary to the 34th Combat Engineers Regiment. The Varsity Victory Volunteers worked tirelessly in the war effort, undertaking the difficult construction projects and war labor, performing other manual labor while also supporting Hawaiian bond drives. This visible sign of support and dedication to the U.S. war cause helped quiet fears and contributed to the eventual annulment of service bans on Japanese Americans. Because of this, the Varsity Victory Volunteers disbanded in January of 1943, having many of its members move on to join the all Japanese-American **442nd Regimental Combat Team.**

BIBLIOGRAPHY

Girdner, Audrie and Ann Loftis. *The Great Betrayal: The Evacuation of the Japanese-Americans During World War II*. New York: Macmillan, 1969.
tenBroek, Jacobus, Edward N. Barnhart, and Floyd W. Matson. *Prejudice, War and the Constitution*. Berkeley: University of California Press, 1970.

Venice Celery Strike of 1936

The Venice Celery Strike was a labor strike of 800 Mexicans, 200 Japanese, and a smaller number of Filipino celery pickers. They wanted better wages and collective bargaining rights from the celery growers in Venice, California. The California Farm Laborers Association allied with the Farm Workers of America for the protest. The growers received help from the police, the U.S. Immigration Service, and the Japanese consulate. The growers also received the support of the **Japanese American Citizens League.** The strike lasted from April 17 until June 8, when the workers compromised on wages and dropped the fight for collective bargaining.

BIBLIOGRAPHY

Iwata, Masakazu. *Planted in Good Soil*. New York: Lang, 1992.

Phillip Villamin Vera Cruz (1904–1994)

Phillip Vera Cruz is the longtime leader of the movement to unionize the United States farmworkers. Vera Cruz is the leader of the successful sit-down strike in the vineyards of Coachella, California, in 1965. The strike was organized through the **Agricultural Workers Organizing Committee** of the AFL-CIO. The strike led to the creation of the United Farmworkers of America. In 1989, Vera Cruz was rewarded the first Ninoy M. Aquino award for his lifelong service to the Filipino community in the United States.

BIBLIOGRAPHY

Cacas, Sam. "Filipino American Labor Leader Dies." *Asian Week*. (June 17, 1994): 14.

Vietnam War

In 1954, Vietnam defeated France at Dien Bien Phu and agreed to a partition of the country between north and south at the 17th parallel. North Vietnam was controlled by the Vietnamese communists who had fought France, while South Vietnam was controlled by Vietnamese who had sided with the French. The North Vietnamese never abandoned the goal of eventually unifying the country (under communist rule). In 1964, President Lyndon Johnson used the pretext of a brief naval engagement between American and Vietnamese ships to increase American involvement in the north–south conflict and assist the Republic of Vietnam (South Vietnam), but a massive commitment of ground troops did not come until 1965. Eventually, 500,000 troops were involved. By 1973, when American military forces withdrew from Vietnam in accordance with the Paris Accords, some 55,000 American troops had been killed, and serious questions had been raised about domestic and foreign policies formulated in Washington, D.C.

During the war, many observers noted that African Americans and Hispanics shared a disproportionately high share of the burden of fighting. The rise of the Black Power movement has been attributed in part to the rage among African Americans over their mistreatment during the war, both at home and abroad. Similarly, agitation to end racism emerged from the Hispanic community, especially from Mexican Americans in California and the southwestern states.

Asian Americans accounted for an extremely high percentage of those suffering from post-traumatic stress. They were often assigned to risky reconnaissance patrols, used in training to represent the enemy, and often fired upon in error; wounded Asian-American soldiers were occasionally left behind because they resembled the enemy. The Viet Cong (South Vietnamese communists) put high prices on their heads. Instances have also been reported of returning Caucasian veterans from the war who took out their aggression against civilian Asian-American "gooks." The Asian-American political movement emerged in part from frustrations over these circumstances.

In the aftermath of the war, approximately 1 million Indochinese refugees were admitted to the United States, eventually accounting for about 15 percent of all Asian Americans. Some American military personnel fathered children who were left behind, yet these Amerasians were ostracized within Vietnam. Accordingly, on December 22, 1987, Congress passed the Amerasian Homecoming Act, which enabled these children and their immediate families to migrate to the United States. (MH)

BIBLIOGRAPHY

Bass, Thomas A. *Vietnamerica: The War Comes Home*. New York: Soho Press, 1996.

Mullen, Robert W. *Blacks in America's Wars: The Shift in Attitudes from the Revolutionary War to Vietnam*. New York: Monad Press, 1973.

Santoli, Al. *To Bear Any Burden: The Vietnam War and Its Aftermath in the Words of American and Southeast Asians*. New York: Dutton, 1985.

Zaroulis, Nancy and Gerald Sullivan. *Who Spoke Up? American Protest and the War in Vietnam, 1963–1973*. Garden City, NY: Doubleday, 1984.

Visco v. Los Angeles County (1931)

Gavino C. Visco, a Filipino man, attempted to get a marriage license to wed his fiancee, Ruth M. Sales, who was a Mexican Indian. Both Visco and Sales foresaw potential conflicts because of their different ethnic backgrounds, worrying that sentiment against mixed race marriages would prevent their union and the issuance of a marriage license by the county clerk's office. However, in his decision for *Visco v. Los Angeles County* (1931), Judge Walter Guerin of the Los Angeles County Superior Court allowed the marriage license to be issued. Guerin stated in his ruling that current California law did not prevent marriages between Filipinos and Mexican-Indians. Furthermore, he added that marriage was always a legal union regardless of the participants' race or national origin, telling Visco he would have allowed the marriage even if his wife was white. As a result, Visco and Sales were allowed to wed, and the case established a precedent for future interracial marriage cases.

BIBLIOGRAPHY

Sickels, Robert J. *Race, Marriage, and the Law*. Albuquerque: University of New Mexico, 1972.

Donald Voorhees (1916–1989)

Donald Voorhees, born in Kansas, was appointed by President Richard Nixon to the federal district court in Seattle, Washington. Voorhees presided in the 1988 coram nobis rehearing of the **Gordon Hirabayashi** wartime internment and curfew case of 1943. There he ruled in favor of Hirabayashi. Another notable decision by Voorhees was the ordering of a busing plan to establish a racial balance in the Seattle school system. **See also** *Hirabayashi v. United States* (1943).

BIBLIOGRAPHY

Spickard, Paul R. *Japanese Americans: The Formation and Transformations of an Ethnic Group*. New York: Twayne Publishers, 1996.

John D. Waihee (1946–)

Born in Hawaii, John Waihee was the fourth elected governor of Hawaii and the first governor of Hawaiian ancestry. Under the rules of Hawaii, Waihee had to step down in 1994, because he could not occupy the office for more than two terms. He was elected to the State House of Representatives in 1980 and won the race for governor only two years later. During his tenure as governor, the levels of housing increased and Hawaii boasted one of the lowest unemployment rates in the nation.

BIBLIOGRAPHY

Cannon, Lou. "Years-Long Recovery for Kavai Seen; Island's Economy Virtually Wiped Out." *The Washington Post* (September 17, 1992): A3.

Cannon, Lou. "Waving (and Lowering) Flag in Hawaii; Pride, Anger Result as Governor Pushes Native People's Cause on Coup's Centennial." *The Washington Post* (January 17, 1993).

Ron Wakabayashi (1944–)

Ron Wakabayashi is the executive director of the Los Angeles City Human Relations Commission. Prior to his appointment, he served as national director of the **Japanese American Citizens League** and vice president of United Way of Greater Los Angeles. An activist who became involved in the Asian-American student movement in the 1960s, Wakabayashi has been commended for his ability to work with the diverse ethnic make-up of Los Angeles.

BIBLIOGRAPHY

Lee, Elisa. "Wakabayashi Tries to Forge Racial Harmony" *AsianWeek* (June 22, 1998): 11.

O'Brien, David J. and Stephen S. Fugita. *The Japanese American Experience.* Bloomington: Indiana University Press, 1991.

War Agency Liquidation Division

The War Agency Liquidation Division was established in 1946 to help Japanese Americans readjust to new environments once leaving the **internment camps.** The division operated under the Office of the Secretary of the Interior. It was formed in the anticipation of the dissolution of all camps by the **War Relocation Authority.**

BIBLIOGRAPHY

Girdner, Audrie and Anne Loftis. *The Great Betrayal: The Evacuation of the Japanese-Americans During World War II.* New York: Macmillan, 1969.

War Brides Act of 1945

After **World War II,** many spouses and children were left behind in Asia because they were denied permission to immigrate to the United States. The War Brides Act of 1945, originally put forth by Representative Samuel Dickstein (D-NY), gave almost 3,000 Asians nonquota resident status in the United States and permitted them to immigrate between 1945 and 1953. This applied to husbands, wives, and children of U.S. servicemen and women. **See also** Fiancees Act of 1946; Immigration Policy; Immigration Restriction Movement. **See** War Brides Act (1945) in Appendix 1.

BIBLIOGRAPHY

Bennett, Marion T. *American Immigration Policies: A History.* Washington, D.C.: Public Affairs Press, 1963.

Kung, S.E. *Chinese in American Life.* Seattle: University of Washington Press, 1962.

War Relocation Authority (WRA)

The War Relocation Authority (WRA) was the governing body during **World War II** that oversaw the evacuation and relocation of more than 110,000 Japanese Americans living on the West Coast. The agency was established in President Franklin D. Roosevelt's **Executive Order 9102** in 1942; Milton Eisenhower was director of the agency until June 1942, when Dillon Myer took over. The agency was responsible for setting up the 12 **assembly centers**, where evacuees convened before being transported to WRA **internment camps/relocation centers**. WRA was responsible for creating, maintaining, and regulating 10 camps, which were built and fully operational by November 3, 1942. WRA continued to oversee the operation of the camps until December 1944, when the U.S. Supreme Court ruled that it was unconstitutional to detain a U.S. citizen who proclaimed their loyalty to the United States. The WRA immediately announced that the camps would close, and by June 1944 the WRA had ceased all operations. **See also** Executive Order 9066; Japanese-American Evacuation and Settlement Study; War Agency Liquidation Division. **See** Executive Order 9066 in Appendix 1.

BIBLIOGRAPHY

Daniels, Roger. *Concentration Camps, U.S.: Japanese Americans and World War II.* New York: Holt Rinehart and Winston, 1971.

Myer, Dillon S. *Uprooted Americans.* Tucson: University of Arizona Press, 1971.

Wartime Civil Control Administration

The Wartime Civil Control Administration was created in 1942 as a part of the Western Defense Command. The group was established as an official United States Army unit focused on the control of civilian affairs, specifically the forced relocation and eventual incarceration of Japanese Americans in World War II **assembly centers.** The Wartime Civil Control Administration also supervised the movement of interned Japanese and Japanese Americans from assembly centers to **internment camps.** The administration often worked with the **War Relocation Authority** in these tasks and other matters designated under **Executive Order 9066. See also** World War II.

BIBLIOGRAPHY

Girdner, Audrie and Ann Loftis. *The Great Betrayal: The Evacuation of the Japanese-Americans During World War II.* New York: Macmillan, 1969.

tenBroek, Jacobus, Edward N. Barnhart, and Floyd W. Matson. *Prejudice, War and the Constitution.* Berkeley: University of California Press, 1970.

Watsonville Anti-Filipino Riot (1930)

In Watsonville, California, a riot began in January 1930 and lasted for four days. The targets of the riot were Filipinos, who were terrorized, chased from their homes, and had their property destroyed. The riot left one Filipino dead and many others scared enough to want to move. The riot was the eventual result of the Asiatic Exclusion Act of 1924; the act prohibited Asian laborers from working in the United States, thus causing a huge influx of Filipino workers (who, as citizens of a U.S. colony, were exempt from the prohibition). The Filipinos, considered U.S. nationals by the government, were still subject to racial prejudice. Several incidents of violence against Filipinos were reported in Washington state and California before the Watsonville riot. Leaders of the Watsonville incident were eventually brought to court; eight men were sentenced to two years in prison but were given probation. The man who murdered a Filipino worker in Watsonville during the riot was never brought to trial. **See also** Filipino-Americans; Exeter Riot of 1929.

BIBLIOGRAPHY

Hundley, Norris, ed. *The Asian American: The Historical Experience.* Santa Barbara, CA: ABC-Clio Press, 1976.

Quinsaat, Jesse. *Letters in Exile.* Berkeley: Regents of the University of California, 1976.

Webb v. O'Brien (1923)

J. O'Brien entered into a deal with Inouye in which they would both benefit from sowing and harvesting O'Brien's land. Inouye was Japanese and therefore unable to own land under the **California Alien Land Act of 1913**. The California attorney general Ulysse Webb pressed charges against the two men for entering into a deal that would give Inouye land rights, and O'Brien was informed that the state might seize his land. In *Webb v. O'Brien,* 263 U.S. 313 (1923), the Supreme Court ruled that O'Brien had wrongfully entered into an agreement with Inouye; the Court thus upheld the constitutionality of the Alien Land Act. **See** California Alien Land Act of 1920 in Appendix 1.

BIBLIOGRAPHY

Chuman, Frank F. *The Bamboo People: The Law and Japanese-Americans.* Del Mar, CA: Publisher's Inc., 1976.

Consulate-General of Japan. *Documentary History of Law Cases Affecting Japanese in the United States, 1916–1924.* vol. 2. San Francisco: Consulate-General of Japan, 1925.

Michiko Nishiura Weglyn (1926–)

Michiko Weglyn is one of the most prominent Japanese-American costume designers in the United States. Her most prestigious work as a designer came during her years on "The Perry Como Show" from 1956 to 1965. She was perhaps even better known for revealing new aspects of Asian-American history by writing *Years of Infamy: The Untold Story of America's Concentration Camps.* The book was about the **internment camps** for the Japanese in the United States during **World War II.** In 1977 she was awarded the Anis Field-Wolf Award in Race Relations for her book. She received the "Justice in Action Award" from the Asian American Legal Defense and Educational Fund in 1987.

BIBLIOGRAPHY

Perkins, Robert. "U.S. 'Infamy' Recalled." *The Springfield Union* (March 11, 1977).

Seko, Sachi. "Digging for Roots." *Pacific Citizen* (February 27, 1976): 4.

White v. Chin Fong (1920)

Chin Fong established residency in the United States for more than a year before leaving for China. Upon his return, he was denied reentry to the United States by Edward White, commissioner of immigration for the port of San Francisco, and detained pending deportation. The case was heard by the district court, which ruled against Chin, but the circuit court of appeals reversed the district court's decision. The case came before the U.S. Supreme Court; in *White v. Chin Fong,* 40 253 U.S. 90 (1920), the Court ruled on a technicality that Chin should be allowed to reenter. **See also** Immigration Restriction Movement.

BIBLIOGRAPHY

Konvitz, Milton R. *The Alien and the Asiatic in American Law.* Ithaca, NY: Cornell University Press, 1946.

Richard S.H. "Dickie" Wong (1933–)

"Dickie" Wong, born in Honolulu, was a Hawaiian state senator. He was also on the five-member board that controlled Princess Bernice Pauahi Bishop's $8 billion dollar estate. He served in the state legislature for 26 years, the longest in the Hawaiian state history. Wong won the election to the state house in 1966, and then the senate in 1974. He also served as senate president from 1979 to 1992. Wong was known for keeping close to the working-class values of the community.

BIBLIOGRAPHY

Wei, William. *The Asian American Movement.* Philadelphia: Temple University Press, 1993.

Wong Wing v. United States (1895)

In 1892, Wong Wing and three other Chinese immigrants were ordered by a Michigan federal court to be imprisoned at hard labor and later deported for attempting to illegally enter the United States. The court based this decision on recommendations by the customs inspector and provisions outlined in the **Geary Act of 1892.** The four Chinese men fought this ruling on a writ of habeus corpus, stating that they were being held unlawfully, and arguing that their Fifth and Sixth Amendment rights had been violated. In *Wong Wing v. United States,* 163 U.S. 288 (1895), the United States Supreme Court, agreed that the Geary Act unjustly burdened Fifth and Sixth Amendment constitutional rights, and that due process had not been followed. In ruling for the imprisoned Chinese men, the supreme Court cited two relevant cases, **Chae Chan Ping v. United States (1889)** and **Fong Yue Ting v. United States (1983),** as contributing to their decision. This case marked the first time that the U.S. Supreme Court had supported the rights of illegal Chinese immigrants already set for deportation.

BIBLIOGRAPHY

Konvitz, Milton R. *The Alien and the Asiatic in American Law.* Ithaca: Cornell University Press, 1946.

McClain, Charles J. *In Search of Equality.* Berkeley: University of California, 1994.

Michael Woo (1951–)

Michael Woo, a moderate Democrat, became the first Asian American to hold a seat on the Los Angeles City Council when he was elected in 1985. To win that election, he defeated a 14-year incumbent council member. Praised as a coalition builder, he has blocked attempts to further marginalize his constituents by redistricting him into a more heavily Latino district. Fighting back, he claimed that the white majority was trying to pit the two minority groups against each other. In 1987, *California Journal* named Woo one of the seven most promising young politicians in the state.

BIBLIOGRAPHY

Block, A.G. "Politicians on the Rise." *California Journal* (November 1987): 534–542.

Wei, William. *Asian American Movement.* Philadelphia: Temple University Press, 1994.

S.B. Woo (1937–)

Believing that more scientists were needed in government, physics professor Shien-Biau Woo ran for lieutenant governor of Delaware in 1984 and won. His election marked the highest statewide office ever held by an Asian American in the U.S. mainland prior to the victory of **Gary Locke** in 1996. (PL)

BIBLIOGRAPHY

Personal interview with S.B. Woo, April 27, 1996.

Workingmen's Party of California

In 1877 the Workingmen's Party of California was founded by Dennis Kearney, an Irish drayman. The organization's members, most of whom were recent immigrants from Ireland, expressed anti-Chinese sentiment because they believed that Chinese labor was replacing white workingmen. Between 1877 and 1881, the Workingmen's Party of California went from sandlot meetings to organized political actions. The organization rallied around the cry that "the Chinese must go" and argued for legislation that would prohibit California companies from hiring Chinese labor. **See also** Asiatic Exclusion League; Foreign Miners Tax; Immigration Convention of 1878; League of Deliverance. (FHM)

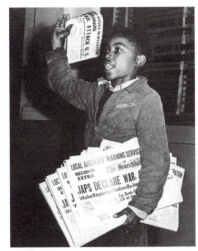

In December 1941, a newspaper boy in Redding, California, sells the latest edition describing the Japanese attack on Pearl Harbor and the American entry into World War II. *Library of Congress.*

BIBLIOGRAPHY

Shumsky, Neil Larry. *The Evolution of Political Protest and the Workingmen's Party of California.* Columbus: Ohio State University Press, 1991.

World War II (1939–1945)

World War II involved almost every country across the globe. The principal participants were Germany, Italy, and Japan (known as the Axis Powers), and the Allies: France, Great Britain, the United States, the Soviet Union, and to a lesser extent, China. In Asia, the foundation for the war began in 1932 when Japan established a puppet state in Manchuria. It was the first of a series of many encroachments upon Chinese territory that led to a formal outbreak of war.

On December 7, 1941, Japan attacked United States installations at **Pearl Harbor,** Hawaii, and in the Philippines. As a result of these attacks, the U.S. government interned Japanese Americans who lived on the West Coast in wartime **internment camps/relocation centers** away from the coast. Thousands of Japanese Americans were deported after renouncing their allegiance to the United States. In the war itself, the Japanese gained control of most of Southeast Asia, the East Indies, and the western Pacific before their advance was halted at the Battle of Midway (June 3–6, 1942).

The Chinese did not fair well during the war. In the end, they had lost millions of lives and about $31 billion in public and private property. The Chinese people rallied around the nationalist government, headed by Chiang Kai-Shek, during the war. The Chinese communists, however, were able to increase their party membership. In fact, they increased party membership by around 40,000 from 1937 to 1.2 million in 1945. This growth paved the way for a full-scale civil war after the war ended and for the eventual triumph of communism. The turnaround for China was the bombing of Pearl Harbor. It brought the United States into the war as part of the allied power. The Japanese navy was almost completely eliminated in the battle of Leyte Gulf battle in October 1944. By the middle of 1945, Japan was devastated by the massive bombings by the United States, including the destruction of Hiroshima (on August 6) and Nagasaki (on August 9) by atomic bombs. Japan formally surrendered on September 2, 1945.

The war brought many changes to Asian Americans in the United States. The end of the war brought thousands of Chinese and Filipino women to the United States, when they emigrated under the **War Brides Act** and **Fiancees Act.** The sociopolitical consequences of Japanese-American internment would lead to the **redress movement** that successfully culminated in the **Civil Liberties Act of 1988. See also** 100th Infantry Battalion; 442nd Regimental Combat Team; Displaced Persons Act of 1948; Executive Order 9066. **See** Civil Liberties Act (1988); Executive Order 9066; Public Law 503 (1942); and War Brides Act (1945) in Appendix 1.

BIBLIOGRAPHY

Boyle, John. *China and Japan at War, 1937 to 1945: The Politics of Collaboration.* Stanford, CA: Stanford University Press, 1972.

Iriye, Akira. *The Origins of the Second World War in Asia and the Pacific.* New York: Longman, 1987.

Yamashita Takui v. Hinkle (1922)

Yamashita Takui v. Hinkle, 43, 260, U.S. 199 (1922), was a case brought before the U.S. Supreme Court, involving a Japanese-born man, Yamashita Takui. The secretary of the state of Washington state had refused to incorporate Yamashita's Japanese real estate company on the grounds that Yamashita could not be a citizen and therefore could not incorporate a company. But Yamashita had been granted U.S. citizenship in 1906. The case was heard by the Washington Supreme Court, which decided in favor of Yamashita, but this ruling was overturned by the U.S. Supreme Court. The Court decided that because Yamashita had been born in Japan, he could not become a U.S. citizen, and the court that had granted him citizenship had done so in error.

BIBLIOGRAPHY

O'Brien, David J. and Stephen S. Fugita. *The Japanese American Experience.* Bloomington: Indiana University Press, 1991.

Yamataya Kaoru v. Thomas M. Fisher (1903)

Yamataya Kaoru arrived in Seattle, Washington, in 1901 but was forbidden to enter the United States. Thomas Fisher, an immigration inspector, decided that Yamataya had come to the United States without any financial support, which violated the act of March 3, 1891, and she should not be permitted to enter the United States. Acting on this information, the secretary of the treasury issued a warrant to arrest Yamataya and place her in jail until she could be deported. She appealed to the U.S. Supreme Court, which heard the case in 1903. In *Yamataya Kaoru v. Thomas M. Fisher,* 189 U.S. 86 (1903), the Court ruled that in arresting Yamataya until she could be deported, no treaty had been violated and that the immigration inspector had not acted unlawfully.

BIBLIOGRAPHY

O'Brien, David J. and Stephen S. Fugita. *The Japanese American Experience.* Bloomington: Indiana University Press, 1991.

Minoru Yasui

Minoru Yasui was born and raised in Portland, Oregon. He graduated from the University of Oregon and attended law school. He then went on to serve as second lieutenant of the U.S. Army Infantry Reserve. He worked briefly for the Japanese Consulate Office in Chicago. In 1942 after the bombing of **Pearl Harbor,** a military curfew was ordered on the West Coast, applying only to "enemy aliens." Yasui felt that this curfew was unconstitutional, and he violated it on purpose so that he could bring the case to court. The case was tried in federal court, and it was decided that **Public Proclamation No. 3,** which had imposed the curfew, had done so illegally and had violated the constitutional rights of U.S. citizens. However, the court decided that Yasui had given up his U.S. citizenship when he worked for the Japanese Consulate and he was sentenced to a year in prison for breaking the law. **See also** *Minoru Yasui v. United States.*

BIBLIOGRAPHY

Daniels, Roger. *Asian America.* Seattle: University of Washington Press, 1988.

Melinda Yee (1963–)

Melinda Yee serves in San Francisco as the special assistant to Democratic mayor Willie Brown. She has worked on behalf of Asian Americans from many sectors. In 1988, Yee was named the executive director of the Organization of Chinese Americans, a national, nonpartisan group. She has testified before Congress on pro-family immigration policies. She left in 1990 to serve as the director of constituencies for the Democratic National Committee. In 1991 she coordinated the first national Asian Pacific American Democratic Summit. In 1992 Yee was named the director of the Asian Pacific American Political Affairs. President Bill Clinton appointed Yee the special assistant in the Office of Presidential Personnel in the White House in 1993. Yee was then quickly appointed as special assistant to the secretary of commerce and senior advisor on the Pacific Rim. Yee became embroiled in controversy in 1996 when she threw away her hand-written notes about the Clinton foreign trade missions after a federal judge ordered to see them.

BIBLIOGRAPHY

Perkins, Joseph, "Donorgate Finally Has its 'Smoking Gun'," *The San Diego Union-Tribune* (June 12, 1998): B9, B13.

Yellow Peril

Yellow peril—a term that has been employed throughout U.S. history since the 1880s—is the belief that Japanese and Chinese pose a significant threat to Western culture. The term itself was most likely the work of Kaiser Wilhelm II, who commissioned the German artist H. Knackfuss to paint a picture as a gift to the Russian tsar. The picture showed the archangel Michael (Germany) protecting maidens (Russia, France, Britain, Austria, Spain, and Portugal) from the yellow peril.

In the United States, the term was applied to Japanese and Chinese immigrants because of the perceived lack of assimilation into U.S. culture and by the growing anti-Japanese and anti-Chinese propaganda of leading newspapers published by men like William Randolph Hearst, who frequently published anti-Japanese articles in his paper. The propaganda warned U.S. citizens, especially those in California, that there was a conspiracy to invade the United States. The theme became a popular one to exploit in movies and literature as well.

This fear of Asian invasion was deeply held by many Westerners and the events of **Pearl Harbor** in 1941 did not help the paranoia over Japanese Americans. Two additional military conflicts have involved the United States in wars in Asia (**Korea** and **Vietnam**); as a result, the fear of Asian Americans is still alive in many Americans.

While the actions of those spreading "yellow peril" propaganda have become more subtle in recent years, the residual effects of this myth still exist. Manufacturers and labor unions involved in the production of cars, steel, and electronics have often attacked Asian competitors as trying to dominate the U.S. market and control American access to products. Part of the appeal of these claims is to racial differences, which hearkens back to the idea of Asians as a threat to the West.

BIBLIOGRAPHY

Miller, Stuart C. *The Unwelcome Immigrant.* Berkeley: University of California Press, 1969.
Thompson, Richard A. *The Yellow Peril, 1890–1924.* New York: Arno Press, 1978.
Wu, William F. *The Yellow Peril.* Hamden, CT: Archon Books, 1982.

Yick Wo v. Hopkins (1886)

In 1880 San Francisco passed City Ordinance 1569, which stated that all laundries whose buildings were made of wood needed to adhere to specific requirements and that the laundry owners needed to obtain permission from the city to operate. Shortly thereafter, Yick Wo, a Chinese man who operated a laundry in San Francisco, was found guilty of violating the city ordinance. Wo appealed to the California Supreme Court, which upheld the verdict of the lower court. However, in *Yick Wo v. Hopkins*, 6, 118 U.S. 356 (1886), the U.S. Supreme Court reversed the decision, stating that the ordinance intended to deny equal protection under the law to a specific group, and that by targeting the life, liberty, and property of this group without due process, the ordinance was unconstitutional. **See also** Laundry Ordinances.

BIBLIOGRAPHY

"*Yick Wo v. Hopkins*; 118 U.S.. 356 (1886)." *Los Angeles Times* (January 25, 1987): 1.

Karl G. Yoneda (1906–)

In 1936, Karl Yoneda joined the International Longshoremen's and Warehousemen's Union and began a long career as a labor activist. During the 1930s, he was briefly jailed for his political activities on behalf of Japanese laborers in the United States. He was responsible for the formation of the Los Angeles Workingmen Organizing Committee and was editor of the newspaper *Rodo Shimbum* (Labor News). Late in his life, the pioneering Yoneda wrote a critical study of Japanese labor in the United States.

BIBLIOGRAPHY

Yoneda, Karl G. *Ganbette: Sixty-Year Struggle of a Kibei Worker.* Los Angeles: University of California Press, 1983.

Wendy Yoshimura (1943–)

Wendy Yoshimura, born during **World War II** in an **internment camp** for Japanese Americans, was arrested with Patty Hearst in San Francisco in 1975. Hearst, the daughter of the head of the Hearst Corporation, was abducted by the radical Symbionese Liberation Army (SLA). She became a member of SLA shortly after her abduction. Yoshimura was never charged of being a member of the SLA, but she was convicted of the possession of explosives and a machine gun. The weapons were confiscated in a 1972 garage raid in Berkeley. The material was part of an alleged plan to bomb the Navy Reserve Officers' Training Corps building on the University of California, Berkeley, campus.

BIBLIOGRAPHY

"7 Must Testify about SLA Role in '75 Bank Robbery, Murder." *The San Diego Union-Tribune* (September 7, 1990): A5.

Yu Cong Eng v. Trinidad (1925)

The case of *Yu Cong Eng v. Trinidad,* 271 U.S. 500 (1925), dealt with the legality of the Philippine Chinese Bookkeeping Act, which was approved on February 21, 1921. This act made it illegal for an individual or company doing business in the Philippines to keep account books in languages other than English, Spanish, or other local Filipino dialects. The provision assisted the collection of sales tax and income tax within the islands by overcoming any language barriers. According to the act, violators could have their property taken from them.

Yu Cong Eng, a Chinese wholesale lumber merchant, was found to be in violation of the Philippine Chinese Bookkeeping Act after it was discovered that he was keeping account records in Chinese, the only language he knew. After being found guilty by the district and supreme courts of the Philippine Islands, Yu Cong Eng appealed to the U.S. Supreme Court. The Court eventually found that the bookkeeping law was unconstitutional, because it denied Chinese workers due process and equal rights protection. The court also ruled that the act violated the Philippine Autonomy Act (**Jones Act of 1916**), which ensured that all people living on the islands, regardless of race, were provided equal protection of liberty and property.

BIBLIOGRAPHY

Kovitz, Milton R. *The Alien and Asiatic in American Law.* Ithaca, NY: Cornell University Press, 1946.

Yung Wing (1828–1912)

In 1854 Yung Wing became the first Chinese graduate of Yale College. He returned to the United States in 1872 as the chief commissioner of the Chinese Educational Mission to the United States. Yung's efforts allowed more than 100 Chinese students to receive higher education in the United States. (FHM)

BIBLIOGRAPHY

Yung, Wing. *My Life in China and America.* New York: Henry Holt and Company, 1909.

Z

Hoyt Zia (1953–)

In 1981, Hoyt Zia, a Chinese American, graduated from law school at the University of California at Los Angeles after first serving three years in the U.S. military. Zia proceeded to become president of the Asian American Bar Association of the Greater Bay Area, president of the Asian Pacific Bar of California, and chair of the California bar's Ethnic Minority Relations Committee. In 1989, Zia represented California at the American Bar Association in Honolulu, Hawaii, where he cofounded and became president of the National Asian Pacific American Bar Association. He currently serves in the Commerce Department supervising legal aspects of imports and exports of technology.

BIBLIOGRAPHY

Wu, Frank H. "Washington Journal: Coordinated Responses." *AsianWeek* (October 31, 1996): 11.

Appendixes

1

Documents

1. Burlingame Treaty (1868)

Article V

The United States of America and the Emperor of China cordially recognize the inherent and inalienable right of man to change his home and allegiance, and also the mutual advantage of the free migration and emigration of their citizens and subjects, respectively, from the one country to the other, for purposes of curiosity, of trade, or as permanent residents. The high contracting parties, therefore, join in reprobating any other than an entirely voluntary emigration for these purposes. They consequently agree to pass laws making it a penal offense for a citizen of the United States or Chinese subjects to take Chinese subjects either to the United States or to any other foreign country, or for a Chinese subject or citizen of the United States to take citizens of the United States to China or to any other foreign country, without their free and voluntary consent respectively.

Article VI

Citizens of the United States visiting or residing in China shall enjoy the same privilege, immunities, or exemption in respect to travel or residence as may there be enjoyed by the citizens or subjects of the most favored nation. And, reciprocally, Chinese subjects visiting or residing in the United States, shall enjoy the same privileges, immunities, and exemptions in respect to travel or residence as may there be enjoyed by the citizens or subjects of the most favored nation. But nothing herein contained shall be held to confer naturalization upon citizens of the United States in China, nor upon the subjects of China in the United States.

2. A Letter on Chinese Immigration by John Stuart Mill (1869)

Dear Sir:

The subject on which you have asked my opinion involved two of the most difficult and embarrassing questions of political morality—the extent and limits of the right of those who have first taken possession of an unoccupied portion of the earth's surface to exclude the remainder of mankind from inhabiting it, and the means which can be legitimately used by the more improved branches of the human species to protect themselves from being hurtfully incroached upon by those of a lower grade in civilization. The Chinese immigration to America raises both these questions. To furnish a general answer to either of them would be a most arduous undertaking.

Concerning the purely economical view of the subject, I entirely agree with you; and it could hardly be better stated and argued than it is in your article in the *New York Tribune*. That the Chinese immigration, if it attains great dimensions, must be economically injurious to the mass of the present population; that it must diminish their wages, and reduce them to a lower stage of physical comfort and well-being, I have no doubt. Nothing can be more fallacious than the attempts to make out that thus to lower wages is the way to raise them, or that there is any compensation, in an economical point of view, to those whose labor is displaced, or who are obliged to work for a greatly reduced remuneration. On general principles this state of things, were it sure to continue, would justify the exclusion of the immigrants, on the ground that, with their habits in respect to population, only a temporary good is done to the Chinese people by admitting part of their surplus numbers, while an permanent harm is done to a more civilized and improved portion of mankind.

But there is also much to be said on the other side. Is it justifiable to assume that the character and habits of the Chinese are unsusceptible of improvement? The institutions of the United States are the most potent means that have yet existed of spreading the most important elements of civilization down to the poorest and most ignorant of the laboring masses. If every Chinese child were compulsorily brought under your school system . . . and kept under it for a sufficient number of years, would not the Chinese population be in time raised to the level of American? I believe, indeed, that hitherto the number of Chinese born in America has not been very great; but so long as this is the case—so long (that is) as the Chinese do not come in families and settle, but those who come are mostly men, and return to their native country, the evil can hardly reach so great a magnitude as to require that it should be put a stop to by force.

One kind of restrictive measure seems to me not only desirable, but absolutely called for: the most stringent laws against introducing Chinese immigrants as coolies, i.e., under contracts binding them to the service of particular persons. All such obligations are a form of compulsory labor, that is, of slavery; and though I know that the legal invalidity of such contracts does not prevent them from being made, I cannot but think that if pains were taken to make it known to the immigrants that such engagements are not legally biding, and especially if it were made a penal offense to enter into them, that mode of immigration would receive a considerable check; and it does not seem probable that any other mode, among so poor a population as the Chinese, can attain such dimensions as to compete very injuriously with American labor. Short of that point, the opportunity given to numerous Chinese of becoming familiar with better and more civilized habits of like, is one of the best chances that can be opened up for the improvement of the Chinese in their own country, and one which it does not seem to me that it would be right to withhold from them. I am, dear sir,

Your very sincerely,
J.S. Mill

3. "Disgraceful Persecution of a Boy" by Mark Twain (1870)

In San Francisco, the other day, "A well-dressed boy, on his way to Sunday school, was arrested and thrown into the city prison for stoning Chinamen." What a commentary is this upon human justice! What sad prominence it gives to our human disposition to tyrannize over the weak! San Francisco has little right to take credit to herself for her treatment of this poor boy. What had the child's education been? How should he suppose it was wrong to stone a Chinaman? Before we side against him, along with outraged San Francisco, let us give him a chance—let us hear the testimony for the defense.

He was a "well-dressed" boy, and a Sunday-school scholar, and therefore, the chances are that his parents were intelligent, well-to-do people, with just enough natural villainy in their composition to make them yearn after the daily papers, and enjoy them; and so this boy had opportunities to learn all through the week how to do right, as well as on Sunday.

It was in this way that he found out that the great commonwealth of California imposes an unlawful mining-tax upon John the foreigner, and allows Patrick the foreigner to dig gold for nothing—probably because the degraded Mongol is at no expense for whisky, and the refined Celt cannot exist without it.

It was in this way that he found out that a respectable number of the tax-gatherers—it would be unkind to say all of them—collect the taxes twice, instead of once; and that, inasmuch as they do it solely to discourage Chinese immigration into the mines, it is a thing that is much applauded, and likewise regarded as singularly facetious.

It was in this way that he found out that when a white man robs a sluice box (by the term white man is meant Spaniards, Mexicans, Portuguese, Irish, Hondurans, Peruvians, Chileans, etc., etc.), they make him leave the camp; and when a Chinaman does that thing, they hang him.

It was in this way that he found out that in many districts of the vast Pacific coast, so strong is the wild free love of justice in the hearts of the people, that whenever any secret and mysterious crime is committed, they say, "Let justice be done, though the heavens fall," and go straightway and swing a Chinaman.

It was in this way that he found out that by studying one half of each day's "local items," it would appear that the police of San Francisco were either asleep or dead, and by studying the other half it would seem that the reporters were gone mad with admiration of the energy, the virtue, the high effectiveness, and the daredevil intrepidity of that very police-making exultant mention of how "the Argus-eyed officer So-an-so," captured a wretched knave of a Chinaman who was stealing chickens, and brought him gloriously to the city prison; and how "the gallant officer Such-and-such-a-one," quietly kept an eye on the movements of an "un-suspecting, almond-eyed son of Confucius" (your reporter is nothing if not facetious), following him around with that far-off look of vacancy and unconsciousness always so finely affected by that inscrutable being, the forty-dollar policeman, during a walking interval, and captured him at last in the very act of placing his hands in a suspicious manner upon a paper of tacks, left by the owner in an exposed situation; and how one officer performed this prodigious thing, and another officer that, and another the other—and pretty much every one of these performances having for a dazzling central incident a Chinaman guilty of a shilling's worth of crime, an unfortunate, whose misdemeanor must be hurrahed into something enormous in order to keep the public from noticing how many really important rascals went uncaptured in the meantime, and how overrated those glorified policemen actually are.

It was in this way that the boy found out that the legislature, being aware that the Constitution has made America an asylum for the poor and the oppressed of all nations, and that therefore the poor and oppressed who fly to our shelter must not be charged a disabling admission fee, made a law that every Chinaman, upon landing, must be *vaccinated* upon the wharf and pay to the State's appointed officer ten dollars for the service, when there are plenty of doctors in San Francisco who would be glad enough to do it for him for fifty cents.

It was in this way that the boy found out that a Chinaman had no rights that any man was bound to respect; that he had no sorrows that any man was bound to pity, that neither his life nor his liberty was worth the purchase of a penny when a white man needed a scapegoat; that nobody loved Chinamen, that nobody befriended them, nobody spared them suffering when it was convenient to inflict it; everybody, individuals, communities, the majesty of the State itself, joined in hating, abusing, and persecuting these humble strangers.

And, therefore, what could have been more natural than for this sunny-hearted boy, tripping along to Sunday school, with his mind teeming with freshly-learned incentives to high and virtuous action, to say to himself—"Ah, there goes a Chinaman! God will not love me if I do not stone him."

And for this he was arrested and put in the city jail.

Everything conspired to teach him that it was a high and holy thing to stone a Chinaman, and yet he no sooner attempts to do his duty than he is punished for it—he, poor chap, who has been aware all his life that one of the principal recreations of the police, out toward the Gold Refinery, is to look on with tranquil enjoyment while the butchers of Brennan Street set their dogs on unoffending Chinamen, and make them flee for their lives.

Keeping in mind the tuition in the humanities which the entire "Pacific coast" gives its youth, there is a very sublimity of incongruity in the virtuous flourish wit which the good city fathers of San Francisco proclaim (as they have lately done) that "The police are positively ordered to arrest all boys of every description and wherever found, who engage in assaulting Chinamen."

Still, let us be truly glad they have made the order, notwithstanding its inconsistency; and let us rest perfectly confident that the police are glad, too. Because there is no personal peril in arresting boys, provided they be of the small kind, and the reporters will have to laud their performances just as loyally as ever, or go without items.

The new form for local items in San Francisco will now be: "the ever vigilant and efficient officer So-and-so succeeded, yesterday afternoon, in arresting Master Tommy Jones, after a determined resistance," etc., etc., followed by the customary statistics and final hurrah, with its unconscious sarcasm: "We are happy in being able to state that this is the forty-seventh boy arrested by this gallant officer since the new ordinance went into effect. The most extraor-dinary activity prevails in the police department. Nothing like it has been seen since we can remember."

I have many such memories in my mind, but am thinking just at present of one particular one, where the Brennan Street butchers set their dogs on a Chinaman who was quietly passing with a basket of clothes on his head; and while the dogs mutilated his flesh, a butcher increased the hilarity of the occasion by knocking some the Chinaman's teeth down his throat with half a brick. This incident sticks in my memory with a more malevolent tenacity perhaps, on account of the fact that I was in the employ of a San Francisco journal at the time, and was not allowed to publish it because if might offend some of the peculiar element that subscribed for the paper. (M.T.)

4. Irwin Convention (1885)

Be it enacted by the Senate and House of Representatives of the United States of American in Congress assembled, That from and after the passage of this act it shall be unlawful for any person, company, partnership, or corporation, in any manner whatsoever, to repay the transportation, or in any way assist or encourage the importation or migration of any alien or aliens, any foreigner or foreigners, into the United States, its Territories, or the District of Columbia, under contract or agreement, parol or special, express or implied, made previous to the importation of migration of such alien or aliens, foreigner or foreigners, to perform labor or service of any kind in the United States, its Territories, or the District of Columbia.

Section 2

That all contracts or agreements, express or implied, parol, or special, which may hereafter be made by and between any personal company, partnership or corporation, and any foreigner or foreigners, alien or aliens, to perform labor or service or having reference to the performance of labor or service by any person in the United States, its Territories, or the district of Columbia previous to the migration or importation of the person or persons whose labor or service is contracted for into the United States, shall be utterly void and of no effect.

Section 3

That for every violation of any of the provisions of section one of this act the person, partnership, company, or corporation violating the same, by knowingly assisting, encouraging or soliciting the migration or importation of any alien or aliens, foreigner or foreigners, into the United States, its Territories, or the District of Columbia, to perform labor or service of any kind under contract or agreement, express or implied, parol or special, with such alien or aliens, foreigner or foreigners, previous to becoming residents or citizens of the United States, shall forfeit and pay for every offense the sum of one thousand dollars, which may be used for and recovered by the United States or by any person who shall first bring his action therefore including any such alien or foreigner who may be a party to any such contract or agreement, as debts of like amount are now recovered in the circuit courts of the United States; and separate suits may be brought for each alien or foreigner being a party to such contract or agreement aforesaid. And it shall be the duty of the district attorney of the proper district to prosecute every such suit at the expense of the United States.

Section 4

That the master of any vessel who shall knowingly bring within the United States any such vessel, and land, or permit to be landed, from any foreign port, or place, any alien laborer, mechanic, or artisan who, previous to embarkation on such vessel, had entered into contract or agreement, parol or special, express or implied, to perform labor or service in the United States, shall be deemed guilty of a misdemeanor, and on conviction thereof, shall be punished by a fine of not more than five hundred dollars for each and every such alien laborer, mechanic or artisan so brought as aforesaid, and may also be imprisoned for a term not exceeding six months.

Section 5

That nothing in this act shall be so construed as to prevent any citizen or subject of any foreign country temporarily residing in the United States, either in private or official capacity, from engaging, under contract or otherwise, persons not residents or citizens of the United States to act as private secretaries, servants, or domestics for such foreigner temporarily residing in the United States as aforesaid; nor shall this act be so construed as to prevent any person, or persons, partnership, or corporation from engaging under contract or agreement, skilled workman in foreign countries to perform labor in the United States in or upon any new industry not at present established in the United States; Provided, That skilled labor for the purpose cannot be otherwise obtained; nor shall the provisions of this act apply to professional actors, artists, lecturers, or singers, nor to persons employed strictly as personal or domestic servants; Provided, That nothing in this act shall be construed as prohibiting any individual from assisting any member of his family or any relative or personal friend, to migrate from any foreign country to the United States, for the purposes of settlement here.

Section 6

That all laws or parts of laws conflicting herewith be, and the same are hereby, repealed.

5. Chinese Equal Rights League (1892)

To the American People, Friends of Humanity:

We, the members of the Chinese Equal Rights League in the United States, who have adopted this country and its customs in the main, are at this moment engaged in a perilous struggle in which our dearest rights as men and residents are involved. Doubtless the reading public is acquainted with the fact that during the last session of the Fifty-second Congress, a Bill was passed, styled the "Geary Bill" or "Chinese Registration Act," in which the attempt is made to humiliate every Chinaman, regardless of his moral, intellectual and material standing in the community, neither his long residence in the country is considered. By this mean and unjust Act discriminating between foreign residents from different countries has traversed and contraversed the fundamental principles of common law.

As residents of the United States we claim a common manhood with all other nationalities, and believe we should have that manhood recognized according to the principles of common humanity and American freedom. This monstrous and inhuman measure is a blot upon the civilization of the Western World, and is destined to retard the progress already made by the good people of this country in the East in art, science, and commerce and religion.

We appeal to the humane, liberty-loving sentiment of the American people, who are lovers of equal rights and even-handed justice, a people from who sprung such illustrious characters as Washington, Jefferson, Clay, Sumner, lastly Lincoln, the citizen of the world, the friend of humanity and the champion of freedom: such illustrious warriors as Sherman, Sheridan, Logan and Grant, whose deeds of valor in the cause of freedom are to be seen in the grand march of American development—a development which merits the emulation of the nations of the earth. Must this growth be retarded simply on account of the doings of a misguided element who have suffered their feelings to control reason, encourage a prejudice fiendish in its nature and purpose against a class of people who are industrious, law-abiding and honest? Can there be found a more inoffensive class in the body politic? Not that we are cowards, but because we believe that mildness and simplicity should be the controlling element in the character of a great man as well as in a great race of people. We have and are still paying our portion of government taxation, thereby assisting in supporting the Government, and thereby sharing an equal part in the support of the nation.

We love and admire the Government, and look with joy to her instrumentality in promoting every good and just cause among men, to her unwavering love of human rights, to her glorious efforts for the advancement of human happiness.

We, therefore, appeal for an equal chance in the race of life in this our adopted home—a large number of us have spent almost our entire lives in this country and claim no other but this as ours. Our motto is *"Character and fitness should be the requirement of all who are desirous of becoming citizens of the American Republic."*

We feel keenly the disgrace unjustly and maliciously heaped upon us by a cruel Congress. That for the purpose of prohibiting Chinese immigration more than one hundred thousand honest and respectable Chinese residents should be made to wear the badge of disgrace as ticket-of-leave men in your penitentiaries; that they should be tagged and branded as a whole lot of cattle for the slaughter; that they should be seen upon your streets with tearful eyes and heavy hearts, objects of scorn and public ridicule. No! We do not believe it, that so great a people as the Americans would consent to so small a principle toward a mere handful of defenseless men.

Out interest is here, because our homes, our families and our all are here. America is our home through long residence. Why, then, should we not consider your welfare ours? Chinese immigration, as well as Irish, Italian and other immigration, cannot be stopped by the persecution of our law-abiding citizens in the United States.

Treat us as men, and we will do our duty as men, and will aid you to stop this obnoxious evil that threatens the welfare of this Republic. We do not want any more Chinese here than you do. The scarcer the Chinese here, the better would be our conditions among you.

6. California Alien Land Act (1920)

Section 1. All aliens eligible to citizenship under the laws of the United States may acquire, possess, enjoy, transmit and inherit real property, or any interest therein, in this state, in the same manner and to the same extent as citizens of the United States, except as otherwise provided by the laws of this state.

Section 2. All aliens other than those mentioned in section one of this act may acquire, possess, enjoy and transfer real property, or any interest therein, in this state, in the manner and to the extent and for the purpose prescribed by any treaty now existing between the government of the United States and the nation or country of which such alien is a citizen or subject, and not otherwise. . . .

Section 4. Hereafter no alien mentioned in section two hereof and no company, association or corporation . . . may be appointed guardian of that portion of the estate of a minor which consists of property which such alien or such company, association or corporation is inhibited from acquiring, possessing, enjoying or transferring by reason of the provisions of this act. The public administration of the proper county, or any other competent person or corporation, may be appointed guardian by the estate of a minor citizen whose parents are ineligible to appointment under the provisions of this section.

On such notice to the guardian as the court may require, the superior court may remove the guardian of such an estate whenever it appears to the satisfaction of the court:

(a) That the guardian has failed to file the report required by the provisions of section five hereof; or

(b) That the property of the ward has not been or is not being administered with due regard to the primary interest of the ward; or

(c) that facts exist which would make the guardian ineligible to appointment in the first instance; or

(d) that facts establishing any other legal ground for removal exist. . . .

Section 6. Whenever it appears to the court in any probate proceeding that by reason of the provisions of this act any heir or devisee cannot take real property of in this state or membership or shares of stock in a company, association or corporation which, but for said provisions, said heir or devisee would take as such, the court, instead of ordering a distribution of such property to such heir or devisee, shall order sale of said property to be made in the manner provided by law for probate sales of property and the proceeds of such sale shall be distributed to such heir or devisee in lieu of such property.

Section 7. Any real property hereafter acquired in fee in violation of the provisions of this act by alien mentioned in section two of this act, or by any company, association or corporation mentioned in section three of this act, shall escheat to, and become and remain the property of the state of California. The attorney general or district attorney of the proper county shall institute proceedings to have the escheat of such real property adjudged and enforced in the manner provided by section four hundred seventy-four of the Political Code and title eight, part three of the Code of Civil Procedure. Upon the entry of final judgment in such proceedings, the title of such real property shall pass to the State of California. The provisions of the section and of sections two and three of this act shall not apply to any real property hereafter acquired in the enforcement or in satisfaction of any lien now existing upon, or interest in such property, so long as such real property so acquired shall remain the property of the alien, company, association or corporation acquiring the same in such manner. No alien, company, association or corporation mentioned in section two or section three hereof shall hold for a longer period than two years the possession of any agricultural land acquired in the enforcement or in satisfaction of a mortgage or other lien hereafter made or acquired in good faith to secure a debt.

7. Public Law 503 (1942)

Be it enacted by the Senate and House of Representatives of the United States of America in Congress assembled, That whoever shall enter, remain in, leave, or commit any act in any military area or military zone prescribed, under the authority of an Executive Order of the President, by the Secretary of War, or by any military commander designated by the Secretary of War, contrary to the restrictions applicable to any such area or zone or contrary to the order of the Secretary of War or any such military commander, shall, if it appears that he knew or should have known of the existence and extent of the restrictions or order and that his act was in violation thereof, be guilty of a misdemeanor and upon conviction shall be liable to a fine of not to exceed $5,000 or to imprisonment for not more than one year, or both, for each offense.

8. Executive Order 9066 (1942)

Whereas, The successful prosecution of the war requires every possible protection against espionage and against sabotage to national-defense material, national-defense premises and national-defense utilities as defined in Section 4, Act of April 20, 1918, 40 Stat. 533, as amended by the Act of November 30, 1940, 54 Stat. 1220, and the Act of August 21, 1941, 55 Stat. 655 (U.S.C., Title 50, Sect. 104):

Now, therefore, By virtue of the authority vested in me as President of the United States, and Commander in Chief of the Army and Navy, I hereby authorize and direct the Secretary of War, and the Military Commanders whom he may from time to time designate, whenever he or any designated Commander deems such action necessary or desirable, to prescribe military areas in such places and of such extent as he or the appropriate Military Commander may determine, from which any or all persons may be excluded, and with respect to which, the right of any person to enter, remain in, or leave shall be subject to whatever restriction the Secretary of War or the appropriate Military Commander may impose in his discretion. The Secretary of War is hereby authorized to provide for residents of any such areas who are excluded therefrom, such transportation, food, shelter, and other accommodations as may be necessary, in the judgment of the Secretary of War or the said Military Commander, and until other arrangements are made, to accomplish the purpose of this order. The designation of military areas in any region or locality shall supersede designations of prohibited and restricted areas by the Attorney General under the Proclamations of December 7 and 8, 1941, and shall supersede the responsibility and authority of the Attorney General under the said proclamations in respect of such prohibited and restricted areas.

I hereby further authorize and direct the Secretary of War and the said Military Commanders to take such steps as he or the appropriate Military Commander may deem advisable to enforce compliance with the restrictions applicable to each Military area hereinabove authorized to be designated, including the use of Federal troops and other Federal Agencies, with authority to accept assistance of state and local agencies.

I hereby further authorize and direct all Executive Departments, independent establishments and other Federal Agencies, to assist the Secretary of War or the said Military Commanders in carrying out this Executive Order, including the furnishing of medical aid, hospitalizations, food, clothing, transportation, use of land, shelter, and other supplies, equipment, utilities, facilities, and services.

This order shall not be construed as modifying or limiting in any way the authority heretofore granted under Executive Order No. 8972, dated December 12, 1941, nor shall it be construed as limiting or modifying the duty and responsibility of the Federal Bureau of Investigation, with respect to the investigations of alleged acts of sabotage or the duty and responsibility of the Attorney General and the Department of Justice under the Proclamations of December 7 and 8, 1941, prescribing regulations for the conduct and control of alien enemies, except as such duty and responsibility is superseded by the designation of military areas hereunder.

9. War Brides Act (1945)

Be it enacted by the Senate and House of Representatives of the United States of America in Congress assembled, That notwithstanding any of the several clauses of section 3 of the Act of February 5, 1917, excluding physically and mentally defective aliens, and notwithstanding the documentary requirements of any of the immigration laws or regulations, Executive Orders, or Presidential proclamations issued thereunder, alien spouses or alien children of United States citizens serving in, or having an honorable discharge certificate from the armed forces of the United States during the Second World War shall, if otherwise admissible under the immigration laws and if application for admission is made within three years of the effective date of this Act, be admitted to the United States: Provided, That every alien of the foregoing description shall be medically examined at the time of arrival in accordance with the provisions of section 16 of the Act of February 5, 1917, and if found suffering from any disability which would be the basis for a ground of exclusion except for the provision of this Act, the Immigration and Naturalization Service shall forthwith notify the appropriate public medical officer of the local community to which the alien is destined: Provided further,

Section 2

That the provisions of this Act shall not affect the duties of the United States Public Health Service so far as they relate to quarantinable diseases.

Regardless of section 9 of the Immigration Act of 1924, any alien admitted under section 1 of this Act shall be deemed to be a nonquota immigrant as defined in section 4(a) of the Immigration Act of 1924.

Section 3

Any alien admitted under section 1 of this Act who at any time returns to the United States after temporary absence abroad shall not be excluded because of the disability or disabilities that existed at the time of that admission.

Section 4

No fine or penalty shall be imposed under the Act of February 5, 1917, except those arising under section 14, because of the transportation to the United States of any alien admitted under this Act.

Section 5

For the purposes of this Act, the Second World War shall be deemed to have commenced on December 7, 1941, and to have ceased upon the termination of hostilities as declared by the President or by joint resolution of Congress.

59 Statutes at Large 271

10. Civil Liberties Act (1988)

An Act to implement recommendations of the Commission on Wartime Relocation and Internment of Civilians.

Be it enacted by the Senate and House of Representatives of the United States of America in Congress assembled,

Section 1

The purposes of this Act are to—

(1) acknowledge the fundamental injustice of the evacuation, relocation, and internment of United States citizens and permanent resident aliens of Japanese ancestry during World War II;

(2) apologize on behalf of the people of the United States for the evacuation, relocation, and internment of such citizens and permanent resident aliens;

(3) provide for a public education fund to finance efforts to inform the public about the internment of such individuals so as to prevent the recurrence of any similar event;

(4) make restitution to those individuals of Japanese ancestry who were interned;

(5) make restitution to Aleut residents of the Pribilof Islands and the Aleutian Islands west of Unimak Island, in settlement of United States obligations in equity and at law for-

(A) injustices suffered and unreasonable hardships endured while those Aleut residents were under United States control during World War II;

(B)personal property taken or destroyed by the United States forces during World War II;

(C) community property, including community church property, taken or destroyed by United States forces during World War II; and

(D) traditional village lands on Attu Island not rehabilitated after World War II for Aleut occupation or other productive use;

(6) discourage the occurrence of similar injustices and violations of civil liberties in the future; and

(7) make more credible and sincere any declaration of concern by the United States over violations of human rights committed by other nations.

Section 2

(a) With Regard To Individuals Of Japanese Ancestry—The Congress recognizes that, as descried by the Commission on Wartime Relocation and Internment of Civilians, a grave injustice was done to both citizens and permanent resident aliens of Japanese ancestry by the evacuation, relocation, and internment of civilians during World War II. As the Commission documents, these actions were carried out without adequate security reasons and without any acts of espionage or sabotage documented by the Commission, and were motivated largely by racial prejudice, wartime hysteria, and a failure of political leadership. The excluded individuals of Japanese ancestry suffered enormous damages both material and intangible, and there were incalculable losses in education and job training, all of which resulted in significant human suffering for which appropriate compensation has not been made. For these fundamental violations of the basic civil liberties and constitutional rights of those individuals of Japanese ancestry, the Congress apologizes on behalf of the Nation.

(b) With Respect To The Aleuts—The Congress recognizes that, as described by the Commission on Wartime Relocation and Internment of Civilians, the Aleut civilian residents of the Pribilof Islands and the Aleutian Islands west of Unimak Island were relocated during World War II to temporary camps in isolated regions of southeast Alaska where they remained under United States control and in the care of the United States, until long after any potential danger to their home villages had passed. The United States failed to provide reasonable care for the Aleuts, and this resulted in widespread illness, disease, and death among the residents of the camps; and the United States further failed to protect Aleut personal and community property while such property was in its possession or under its control. The United States has not compensated the Aleuts adequately for the conversion or destruction of community property caused by the United States military occupation of Aleut villages during World War II. There is no remedy for injustices suffered by the Aleuts during World War II except an Act of Congress providing appropriate compensation for those losses which are attributable to the conduct of United States forces and other officials and employees of the United States.

11. Voting Rights Language Assistance Act (1992)

An Act To Amend the Voting Rights Act of 1965 with respect to bilingual election requirements.

Be enacted by the Senate and House of Representatives of the United States of America in Congress assembled,

Section 1

This act may be cited as the "Voting Rights Language Assistance Act of 1991."

Section 2

Subsection (b) of section 203 of the Voting Rights Act of 1965 (42 U.S.C. 1973aa-1a(b)) is amended to read as follows:

"(b) BILINGUAL VOTING MATERIALS REQUIREMENT.—

"(1) GENERALLY, —Before August 6, 2007, no covered State or political subdivision shall provide voting materials only in the English language.

"(2) COVERED STATES AND POLITICAL SUBDIVISIONS.—

"(A) GENERALLY.—A State or political subdivision is a covered State or political subdivision if the Director of the Census determines, based upon census data, that—

"(i)(I) more than 5 percent of the citizens of voting age of such State or political subdivision are members of a single language minority and are limited-English proficient;

"(II) more than 10,000 of the citizens of voting age of such political subdivision are members of a single language minority and are limited-English proficient; or

"(III) in the case of a political subdivision that contains all or any part of an Indian reservation, more than 5 percent of the American Indian or Alaska Native citizens of voting age, within the Indian reservation are members of a single language minority and are limited-English proficient; and

"(ii) the illiteracy rate of the citizens in the language minority as a group is higher than the national illiteracy rate.

"(B) EXCEPTION.—The prohibitions of this subsection do not apply in a political subdivision that has less than 5 percent voting age limited-English proficient citizens of each language minority which comprises over 5 percent of the statewide limited-English proficient population of voting age citizens, unless the political subdivision is a covered political subdivision independently of its State.

"(3) DEFINITIONS.—As used in this section—

"(A) the term 'voting materials' means registration or voting notices, forms, instructions, assistance, or other materials or information relating to the electoral process, including ballots;

"(B) the term 'limited-English proficient' means unable to speak or understand English adequately enough to participate in the electoral process;

"(C) the term 'Indian reservation' means any area that is an American Indian or Alaska Native area, as defined by the Census Bureau for the purposes of the 1990 decennial census;

"(D) the term 'citizens' means citizens of the United States; and

"(E) the term 'illiteracy' means the failure to complete the 5th primary grade.

"(4) SPECIAL RULE.—The determinations of the Director of the Census under this subsection shall be effective upon publication in the *Federal Register* and shall not be subject to review in any court."

Asian-American Organizations

American Citizens for Justice
P.O. Box 2735
Southfield, MI 48037-2735
(810) 352-1020
President: Annie Malayang

Founded in 1983 as an organization of Asian Pacifics and other concerned individuals. Seeks to overcome ethnic discrimination and racial intolerance. In doing so, focuses on the connection between civil rights and safety, mental health, and welfare. Also runs the Asian American Center for Justice, monitors relevant legislation and law enforcement issues, and supports Asian Pacific American culture, history, and heritage. Offers the publication *Justice Update*, a quarterly newsletter.

American Council for Free Asia
214 Massachusetts Avenue NE, Ste. 300
Washington, D.C. 20002
(202) 54-7150
Executive Director: Gina Jarmin

The American Council for Free Asia was founded in 1978. Goals of the group include encouraging U.S. diplomatic relations with noncommunist countries, lobbying Congress in favor of weapons deals with noncommunist Asia, and supporting American occupation within Asia.

American Immigration Lawyers Association
1400 I Street NW, Ste. 120
Washington, D.C. 20005
(202) 371-9377
(202) 463-6525 Fax
Web site: http://www.aila.org
Executive Director: Warren Leiden

The American Immigration Lawyers Association was founded in 1946 by lawyers specializing in immigration and nationality litigation. The organization works to promote justice within their field, as well as support individuals in legal issues concerning immigration and civil rights.

The Asia Foundation
P.O. Box 193223
San Francisco, CA 94119-3223
(415) 982-4640
(415) 392-8863 Fax
Web site: http://www.asiafoundation.com
President: William P. Fuller

Founded in 1954 with the support of U.S. government grants and private contributions. Goals include strengthening democracy in Asia and the Pacific Islands, promoting Asian-Pacific cooperation, and

maintaining educational programs. Also supports representative government, effective legal practices, successful economics, and a responsible media. Provides a number of special programs, including Books for Asia, the Center for Asian Pacific Affairs, Asian-American Exchange, and Partners for International Education and Training; these programs offer everything from U.S. job training to educational opportunities.

Asia Resource Center
P.O. Box 15275
Washington, D.C. 20003
(202) 547-1114
Director: Roger Rumpf

Founded in 1971, the Asia Resource Center was known previously as the Indochina Resource Center and the Southeast Asia Resource Center. Works to enact U.S. policies that support peace, justice, and disarmament in Asia. Also offers a speakers' bureau, Asian studies programs, and various publications.

Asian American Center for Justice of the American Citizens for Justice
P.O. Box 2735
Southfield, MI 48037-2730
(810) 352-1020
Executive Director: Nati Lim Jenks

Formed in 1983 under the guidance and direction of American Citizens for Justice. Works to eliminate discrimination and violence against Asian Americans by offering legal consultation and education, monitoring ethnic violence, and providing other services. Also offers a speakers' bureau, conducts research programs and civil rights education projects, and works with government offices to develop affirmative action plans geared towards recruiting Asian Pacific Americans.

Asian American Curriculum Project
P.O. Box 1587
234 Main Street
San Mateo, CA 94401
(415) 343-9408
(800) 874-2242
(415) 343-5711 Fax
General Manager: Florence M. Hongo

Founded in 1971, the Asian American Curriculum Project seeks to develop and distribute Asian-American studies information and curriculum materials to schools, libraries, and other institutions. Works toward furthering public understanding of Asian Americans. Sponsors demonstrations when appropriate.

Asian American Free Labor Institute
1925 K Street NW, Ste. 301
Washington, D.C. 20006
(202) 778-4500
(202) 778-4525 Fax
Executive Director: Kenneth P. Hutchison

The Asian American Free Labor Institute was formed in 1968. The organization seeks to provide free and effective trade unions in Asia, the Middle East, and the South Pacific. It also offers services in democratic trade, technical assistance, education, cooperatives, and related fields.

Asian American Legal Defense and Education Fund
99 Hudson Street
New York, NY 10013
(212) 966-5932
(212) 96604303 Fax
Executive Director: Margaret Fung

Founded in 1974. Seeks to attack problems plaguing the Asian-American community through legal and educational support. Offers bilingual legal counseling and representation for those in need, as well as working on litigation cases that affect Asian Americans. Focuses on immigration, employment, voting rights, racial violence, environmental issues, and Japanese-American redress. Also monitors and records legal events of interest to the group, provides legal training sessions, and offers a law student intern project.

Asian American Manufacturers Association
770 Menlo Avenue, Ste. 227
Menlo Park, CA 94025
(415) 321-2262
(415) 325-5499 Fax
E-mail: aama@3wc.com
Web site: http://www.3wc.com/aama/
Executive Director: Regina Lau

Founded in 1980, the Asian American Manufacturers Association seeks to enhance Asian-American business opportunities. The group provides educational programs in areas such as management and business operations. Publications by the organization include *AAMA News*, *Asian American Entrepreneurs and Executives of Public Companies in the High Tech Industry*, and other resources.

Asian and Pacific Islander American Health Forum
c/o Tessie Guillermo
116 New Montgomery, Ste. 531
San Francisco, CA 94105
(415) 512-2710
(415) 512-3881 Fax
E-mail: hforum@apiahf.org
Web site: http://www.apiahf.org/apiahf
Executive Director: Tessie Guillermo

Founded in 1986. Supports health policies, programs, and research as it relates to Asian and Pacific Americans. Focuses its efforts on infectious diseases, AIDS/HIV, diabetes, cancer, hypertension, substance abuse, and mental health disorders. Publications include *Confronting Critical Health Issues of Asian and Pacific Americans*.

Asian Benevolent Corps
2423 Pennsylvania Avenue NW, No. 100
Washington, D.C. 20037-1724
(202) 331-0192
Board Chairman: Dr. Dwan Tai

Founded in 1963, the Asian Benevolent Corps supports cultural, artistic, and educational activities. Also backs economic development and community service. Publishes *Asian Voice*.

Asian Business League of San Francisco
233 Sansome Street, Ste. 515
San Francisco, CA 94104
(415) 788-4664
(415) 788-4756 Fax
Executive Director: Forrest Gok

Founded in 1980, the Asian Business League of San Francisco seeks to promote local business and trade for Asians along the Pacific basin. Provides business development, networking, and personnel placement, along with a number of publications.

Asian Indian Chamber of Commerce
c/o Dr. Ahmed Kutty
3511 47th Avenue
Kearney, NE 68847-1666
President: Dr. Ahmed Kutty

Founded in 1983 as a division of the National Association of Americans of Asian Indian Descent. Provides communication networking among Asian-Indian American businesses, as well as management and technical assistance referrals. Offers information on federal and state assistance programs. Provides seminars and workshops.

Asian-Indian Women in America
RD 1 Box 98
Palisades, NY 10964
(914) 365-1066
(914) 425-5804 Fax
President: Ms. Uma Shah

Founded in 1980 to provide social, economic, and cultural services to American Asian-Indians. Focuses on issues such as spouse abuse, single-parent families, career development, and battered women. Offers counseling, financial assistance, and workshops. Monitors political developments, maintains a speakers' bureau, and offers a number of publications.

Asian/Pacific Islander Law Students Association
UCLA School of Law
405 Hilgard Avenue
Los Angeles, CA 90024-1476
(310) 825-1304

Formerly known as the Asian/Pacific Law Students Association, the Asian/Pacific Islander Law Students Association was formed in 1981. The group seeks to provide a communication network for Asian/Pacific law students and to support them in their endeavors. Also works to strengthen the tie and commitment between Asian/Pacific law students and their community, as well as improve the U.S. legal system.

Asian Political Scientists Group in USA
c/o Dr. Chun-Tu Hsueh
Huang Hsing Foundation
14017 Wagon Way
Silver Spring, MD 20906
Executive Officer: Dr. Chun-Tu Hsueh

Appendix 2: Asian-American Organizations

Founded in 1973 as a group of American political scientists of Asian descent seeking to promote professional and ethnic interests. Provides discussion groups, research studies, placement services, and publications such as *Asian Political Scientists in North America: Professional and Ethnic Problems.*

Asian Resources

2251 Florim Road, Ste. E
Sacramento, CA 95822
(916) 424-8960
(916) 424-3431 Fax
Executive Director: May O. Lee

Founded in 1980, Asian Resources offers information and employment assistance to unemployed and disadvantaged individuals, such as refugees. Also provides educational seminars, skilled-labor training sessions, and placement services.

Asian Watch Committee

1522 K Street NW, Ste. 910
Washington, D.C. 20005
(202) 371-6592
(202) 371-0124 Fax
Executive Director: Sidney Jones

Formed in 1985, the Asian Watch Committee monitors American human rights policies, especially as they pertain to Asian Americans and Asian countries. Also supports civil rights endeavors.

Association for Asian American Studies

c/o Anita Affeldt
Cornell University
425 Caldwell Hall
Ithaca, NY 14853-2602
(607) 255-3320
(607) 254-4996 Fax
President: Gail M. Nomura

Founded in 1979 with the goal of advancing research and education in Asian-American studies. Provides communication links with interested parties, offers various activities, events, and programs, and educates the public about Asian-American history. Publications include *Anthology* and *Occasional Papers.*

Association of Asian Indians in America

7 Heather Lane
Muttontown, NY 11753
(516) 938-4965
President: Dr. Marandis Kukar

Founded in 1967, the Association of Asian Indians in America was originally known as the Association of Indians in America. The group works to promote Asian-Indian citizenship rights for U.S. residents, foster Indian cultural activities, and support studies programs. Also backs Indo-American economic relations and tourism. Represents Asian Indians at Congressional and Senate hearings. Conducts charity and cultural programs.

Association of Asian/Pacific American Artists

10153 1/2 Riverside Drive, No. 199
Toluca Lake, CA 91602-2533
(213) 874-0786
(213) 874-4755 Fax
President: Ernest Harada

The Association of Asian/Pacific American Artists was founded in 1976. The organization supports equal opportunity employment practices within the entertainment business and fights for an end to media stereotyping. Offers seminars on the theater, motion pictures, and other forms of entertainment media, as well as a number of publications.

Association of Asian/Pacific Community Health Organizations

1212 Broadway, No. 730
Oakland, CA 94612
(510) 272-9536
Contact: Stephen P. Jiang

The Association of Asian/Pacific Community Health Organizations was founded in 1987. Seeks to improve access to and availability of culturally and linguistically appropriate health care for Asian Americans and Pacific Islanders. Also supports appropriate organization, agency, and committee endeavors. Resources include *Behind the Mask: AIDS . . . It Affects All of Us*, *Thalassemia Among Asians*, and similar publications.

Association of Immigration Attorneys

401 Broadway, Ste. 1802
New York, NY 10013
(212) 226-3913
(212) 335-0028 Fax
Legal Counsel: Peter Hirsch

The Association of Immigration Attorneys was founded in 1983 as an association of U.S. immigration law attorneys. Lobbies Congress on behalf of immigrants, works toward pro-alien legislation, and provides communication among legal professional with similar goals.

Association of Indian Muslims of America

11649 Masters Run
Ellicott City, MD 21042
(410) 730-5456
(410) 922-0665 Fax
President: Kaleem Kawaja

Founded in 1985 to support Muslim Indian living in the United States. Strives to initiate communication between Muslim Indians and government organizations, Islamic groups, and other Asian Indians in the United States. Focuses on cultural, economic, educational, and human rights; current events; educational assistance; and crisis relief funds.

Black, Indian, Hispanic, and Asian Women in Action

122 West Franklin Avenue, Ste. 306
Minneapolis, MN 55404
(612) 870-1193
(612) 870-0855 Fax
Executive Officer: Alice O. Lynch

Founded in 1983, Black, Indian, Hispanic, and Asian Women in Action seeks to provide educational support for the purpose of empowering women of color within the United States. Focuses on family violence, economics, education, substance abuse, and health issues. Also works for social change. Publishes *Unison*, a quarterly newsletter.

Campaign Against U.S. Military Bases in the Philippines

c/o Steve Shalom
135 Hadden Place
Montclair, NJ 07043
(201) 783-4778
Coordinator: Steve Shalom

Founded in 1979 to work toward the removal of American military bases from the Philippines. The group views these bases as an infringement upon Philippine sovereignty and a catalyst for potential unwanted nuclear altercations. Gains support from Filipino Americans, Philippine natives, and interested groups.

Catholic Interracial Council of New York

899 10th Avenue
New York, NY 10019
(212) 237-8255
Executive Director: Hubert Johnson

Founded in 1934. Works with government and church organizations to overcome discrimination and promote social justice. Promotes and provides community action programs, research, workshops, and educational activities.

Center for Constitutional Rights

666 Broadway, 7th Floor
New York, NY 10012
(212) 614-6464
(212) 614-6499 Fax
Executive Director: Miriam Thompson

Founded in 1967, the Center for Constitutional Rights was known formerly as the Civil Rights Defense Fund and later as the Law Center for Constitutional Rights. Focuses on issues such as civil liberties, racism, civil rights, voting, and affirmative action.

Chinese for Affirmative Action

17 Walter V. Lum Place
San Francisco, CA 94108
(415) 274-6750
(415) 397-8770 Fax
Web site: http://www.caasf.org
Executive Director: Henry Der

Chinese for Affirmative Action was founded in 1969. The group seeks equal opportunity and civil rights protection for Asian Americans. Works with community groups and government offices to ensure fair employment, Asian-American political and community participation, bilingual services availability, and the achievement of affirmative action goals. Provides speakers, library holdings, and counseling services.

Church Coalition for Human Rights in the Philippines

Box 70
110 Maryland Avenue NE, Ste. 210
Washington, D.C. 20002
(202) 543-1094
(202) 546-0090 Fax
Executive Director: Rev. Kathryn Johnson

Founded in 1986 with the intent of dealing with human rights and justice issues affecting people from the Philippines. Focuses on issues dealing with political prisoners, economic development, militarization, minorities' rights, and educational topics. Publications include *Philippine News Survey* and *Philippine Witness*.

Committee against Anti-Asian Violence

191 East 3rd Street
New York, NY 10009
(212) 473-6485
(212) 473-5569 Fax
Web site: http://home.dti.net/foil/resources/caaav.htm
Executive Director: Anannya Bhattacharjee

The Committee against Anti-Asian Violence was founded in 1986. The group seeks to combat racial violence and police brutality against Asian Americans. Provides discussion forums as well as assistance for racial violence victims. Works to uncover the political, economical, and misplaced cultural roots of racism. Offers a number of publications.

Committee for Restoration of Democracy in Burma

P.O. Box 39045
Washington, D.C. 20016
(703) 834-5670
President: Tin Muang Win

Founded in 1986 by Asian Americans seeking to return Burma to a democratic government. Works with other groups with similar interests to provide a united front. Also participates in and organizes worldwide demonstrations, as well as lobbying the U.S. government to help restore democracy to Burma.

Committee on Migration and Refugee Affairs

c/o Interaction
200 Park Avenue South
New York, NY 10003
(212) 777-8210
Contact: Cindy Suh

Founded in 1946, the Committee on Migration and Refugee Affairs provides refugee assistance, legal services, and protection. Also works on American refugee and immigration policies.

Committee on Women in Asian Studies

c/o Jyotsna Vard
Texas A&M University
Department of Psychology
College Station, TX 77843
(409) 845-2576
(409) 845-472 Fax
Chairperson: Sucheta Mazumdar

Founded in 1972 to focus on the social, economic, and political position of Asian women. Also concentrates on issues concerning sexual discrimination and division, education, and poverty. Provides workshops, research, and publications.

Department of Civil Rights, AFL-CIO

815 16th Street NW
Washington, C 20006
(202) 637-5270
Web site: http://www.aflcio.org
Director: Richard Womack

Founded in 1955. Functions as a liaison between women's and civil rights groups and government offices connected to equal opportunity issues. Assists in implementing state and federal equal opportunity laws, as well as developing affirmative action programs. Also provides information on civil rights, speakers for unions and other organizations, and helps resolve difficulties involving Title VII of the 1964 Civil Rights Act and Executive Order 11246.

Equal Rights Congress

4167 South Normandy Avenue
Los Angeles, CA 90037
(213) 291-1092
Executive Director: Nacho Gonzalez

The Equal Rights Congress was founded in 1976. Seeks to help those discriminated against because of religion, sex, nationality, or economic status. Provides educational programs, speakers, training, seminars, and technical assistance. Publications include *Equal Rights Advocate* and *Southern Advocate*.

Free Pacific Association

86 Riverside Drive
New York, NY 10024
(212) 787-6969
(212) 799-2600
President: Rev. Paul Chan

Founded in 1956 as a collection of Pacific Islanders dedicated to opposing communist imperialism and theory. Also provides educational services for the purpose of providing individuals within the Pacific islands the leadership skills needed to maintain the affairs of their own lands.

Friends of India Society International

103 Periwinkle Court
Greenbelt, MD 20770
(301) 345-6090
(301) 345-0559 Fax
Contact: R.S. Dwivedi

Founded in 1976 to support people of Indian origin living in the United States and other locations outside of India. Promotes cultural, social, economic, and political issues as they affect Asian Indians. Provides communication between Indians and their new countries of residence, and studies problems harming Asian-India American citizens and other Indians. Supports peace, civil rights and liberties, human rights, freedom of expression, and an end to stereotyping. Provides lectures and publications.

Honolulu Japanese Chamber of Commerce

2454 South Beretania Street
Honolulu, HI 96826
(808) 949-5534
Web site: http://www.hula.net/~cyber/hjcc.html
President: Ronald R. Ushijima

The Honolulu Japanese Chamber of Commerce was formed in 1900. The organization supports cultural, economic, social, and political development for Japanese and Hawaiian community groups. Publications include the monthly *Shoko Newsletter*.

India-America Chamber of Commerce

P.O. Box 2110
New York, NY 10185-2110
(212) 755-7181
(212) 424-8256
(212) 424-8500 Fax
President: Rajiv Khanna

Founded in 1934, the India-America Chamber of Commerce acts as a forum on economic development and commercial relations for Indo-American businesses. Focuses on economics, trade, and similar issues. Works with the U.S. Chamber of Commerce.

Indian American Forum for Political Education

700 Woodward Building
733 15th Street NW
Washington, D.C. 20005
(202) 347-9400
Contact: Abdul Shaikh, Ph.D.

The Indian American Forum for Political Education was found in 1982 to promote political and civic awareness among Indian Americans. Also helps the exchange of ideas between Indian Americans and U.S. political and public figures. Supports voter registration and the study of political issues. Offers study programs on civic and social responsibilities.

International Association of Official Human Rights

444 North Capitol Street, Ste. 634
Washington, D.C. 20001
(202) 624-5410
(202) 624-8588 Fax

Founded in 1949 as a compilation of government human rights agencies seeking to promote human rights. Works closely with federal agencies involved with civil rights enforcement, while also striving to provide state equal rights legislation. Provides training services on equal opportunity, civil rights-based curriculum, and other topics.

Jack and Jill of America Foundation

c/o Violet D. Greer
P.O. Drawer 3689
Chattanooga, TN 37404
(615) 624-6097
Board Secretary: Violet D. Greer

Founded in 1968. Works to improve educational, social, cultural, and civic opportunities for minority youths; also provides educational grant monies to community projects and monitors relevant legislative issues. Provides college-prep, preschool, and other programs.

Japanese American Citizens League

1765 Sutter Street
San Francisco, CA 94115
(415) 921-5228
(415) 931-4671 Fax
Web site: http://jacl.org/main.htm
National Director: William Yoshino

Founded in 1929, the Japanese American Citizens League focuses on educational, civil, and human rights. Works to preserve and maintain the cultural and ethnic heritage of Japanese Americans. Publications include the weekly *Pacific Citizen*.

Korean American Coalition

3421 W. 8th Street, 2nd Floor
Los Angeles, CA 90005
(213) 365-5999
(213) 380-7990 Fax
Web site: www.kac83.org/top.html
President: Jerry C. Lu

The Korean American Coalition was founded in 1983. Works to educate, empower, and assist Korean Americans, as well as educate other communities about Koreans culture. Provides educational programs, leadership development, and community networking. Also focuses on voter registration and Korean community issues.

Leadership Education for Asian Pacifics

327 East 2nd Street, Ste. 226
Los Angeles, CA 90012
(213) 485-1422
(213) 485-0050 Fax
Executive Director: J.D. Hokoyama
E-mail: leap90012@aol.com

Founded in 1983. Seeks to achieve full participation and equality for Asian Pacific Americans through leadership, empowerment, and policy. Also strives to utilize the talents and resources of the Asian Pacific community for the betterment of all. Provides policy research and workshops. Provides a number of publications, including *Beyond Asian American Poverty: Community Economic Development Policies and Strategies*, *Leap Connection*, *The State of Asian Pacific America: Policy Issues to the Year 2020*, *Reapportionment and Redistricting in Los Angeles: Implications for Asian Pacific Americans*, and *The State of Asian Pacific American: Economic Diversity, Issues, and Policies*.

Minorities International Network for Trade

P.O. Box 1483, Murray Hill Station
New York, NY 10156
(212) 725-3312
(212) 725-3312 Fax
Executive Officer: Peter J. Robinson, Jr.

The Minorities International Network for Trade was founded in 1987. The group provides networking and communication between government offices and businesses, especially on commercial, social, and cultural topics. Also focuses on trade and education.

National Advisory Council for South Asian Affairs

3105 Beaverwood Lane
Silver Spring, MD 20906
(301) 460-7090
Executive Director: Dr. Vasant G. Telang

Founded in 1979 to support people who immigrated to America from South Asian countries. Seeks to monitor and influence U.S. foreign policy issues for the purpose of assisting individuals from South Asian countries. Meets with the Bureau of Asian Affairs and the U.S. Department of State.

National Alliance against Racist and Political Repression

11 John Street, Room 702
New York, NY 10038
(212) 406-3330
(212) 406-3542
Executive Director: Charlene Mitchell

Founded in 1973. Strives to overcome human rights oppression. Focuses on persecution against political activists, prisoners' rights, labor rights, police crimes, and federal legislation. Opposes the death penalty, FBI and CIA involvement with social change organizations, suppression of antiracism military movements, and attacks on lawyers, war resisters, and others seeking civil rights.

National Asian Pacific Center on Aging

Melbourne Tower, Ste. 914
1511 3rd Avenue
Seattle, WA 98101
(206) 624-1221
(206) 624-1023 Fax
Executive Director: Don Watanabe

The National Asian Pacific Center on Aging was founded in 1979. The group seeks to gain better health services for the elderly, provide a better informational and technical base for community health services, and include Pacific Asians in organizational activities. Also provides training and technical assistance. Publications include the quarterly *Asian Pacific Affairs*, *Directory of Pacific/Asian Media Services*, *Pacific/Asian Elderly Bibliography*, and *Registry of Services for Pacific/Asian Elderly*.

National Association for Asian and Pacific American Education

c/o ARC Associates
1212 Broadway, Ste. 400
Oakland, CA 94612
(510) 834-9455
(510) 763-1490 Fax
E-mail: janet_Lu@arcoarland.org
President: Janet Y.H. Lu

Founded in 1977, the National Association for Asian and Pacific American Education seeks to unify Asian/Pacific American communities through educational opportunities. Also supports the inclusion of Asian and Pacific American culture within school curricula, more awareness and support for multicultural education, and research on related topics. Offers a number of publications, including *Contemporary Perspectives on Asian and Pacific American Education: A Resource Guide for Asian Pacific American Students*.

National Association for the Education and Advancement of Cambodian, Laotian, and Vietnamese Americans

Illinois Research Center
Des Plaines, IL 60018
(708) 803-3112
President: Ngoc Diep Nguyen

Founded in 1979 as the National Association for Vietnamese American Education. Works to provide equal rights and educational opportunities to Indochinese Americans, as well as promote their culture and society. Focuses on legislative needs in health, education, social services, and welfare. Offers speakers and workshops.

National Association of Americans of Asian Indian Descent

c/o Dr. Ahmed Kutty
3511 47th Avenue
Kearney, NE 68847-1666
President: Dr. Sridltart Kazil

Founded in 1980. Works to promote, protect, and foster the economic, social, political, and educational interests of Asian Indians living in the United States. Also strives to unite the Indian community and support Indian rights. Provides seminars, workshops, and referrals. Publications include *NAAAID Newsletter*, *Indian American Times*, and other brochures and materials.

National Association of Asian American Professionals

P.O. Box 772
New York, NY 10002
(917) 643-NAAP
Web site: http://www.mindspring.com/~tseng/naaap
President: Tiffany Woo

Founded in 1982 to increase cultural and educational awareness of Asian Americans. Known formerly as the National Association of Young Asian Pacifics, the group currently offers assistance, high school mentoring programs, professional networking, social programs, and other assistance focused towards the Asian American community.

National Association of Human Rights Workers

c/o Ronald McEldreath
Florida Commission on Human Relations
Building F, Ste. 240
325 John Knox Road
Tallahassee, FL 32303
(904) 488-7082

President: Ronald McEldreath

Formed in 1947 as the National Association of Intergroup Relations Officials. Membership consists of government and private organization employees of groups focusing on civil rights and liberties, interracial and inter-ethnic relations, and religious understanding. Provides communication for members and offers a united front on rights issues. Publications include the quarterly *Journal of Intergroup Relations*.

National Association of Medical Minority Educators

c/o Dr. Charles J. Alexander
Marquette University
Office of Multicultural Concerns
Milwaukee, WI 53233
(414) 288-5861
(414) 288-5788 Fax
President: Dr. Charles J. Alexander

Founded in 1975. Supports Asian Americans and other minority groups in the health care profession. Provides health profession programs, training, student development, recruitment fairs, and other educational opportunities. Strives for better health care for minorities, whether it be through private, public, or governmental avenues.

National Association of Minority Political Women

6120 Oregon Avenue NW
Washington, D.C. 20015
(202) 686-1216
President: Mary E. Ivey

Founded in 1983, the National Association of Minority Political Women consists of professional minority women seeking to gain knowledge on, access to, and greater participation in the political process. Provides research and educational programs.

National Center for Urban Ethnic Affairs

P.O. Box 20, Cardinal Station
Washington, D.C. 20064
(202) 319-5129
President: Dr. John A. Kromkowski

Founded in 1970. Provides community programs and policies based on ethnic cultural diversity, as well as assisting urban community organizations and congregations on interpreting policy issues. Creates partnerships among government agencies, community groups, and interested businesses to focus on topics such as human services, education, economics, housing, cultural well-being, and urban renewal. Provides workshops, training, publications, and technical support.

National Council for Families and Television

346 9th Street, 2nd Floor
San Francisco, CA 94103
(415) 863-0814
(415) 863-7428 Fax
Executive Director: Deann Borshay

Founded in 1980. Provides services in all broadcast media fields, including radio, film, television, and video. Strives to overcome Asian-American stereotyping in the media. Sponsors educational radio broadcasts, provides workshops and other special services, and maintains a speakers' bureau. Publications include *Asian American Network* and *Cross Current Media*.

National Federation of Asian-American United Methodists

330 Ellis Street, Room 508
San Francisco, CA 94102
(415) 776-7747
(415) 776-1154 Fax
Executive Director: Dr. Peter Sun

Founded in 1975. Seeks to meet the needs, concerns, and interests of Asian Americans before the Methodist Church and other relevant boards and agencies. Provides cultural interpretation of religion, leadership training, and a number of publications, including *Asian American News and Resources*.

National Federation of Indian American Associations

100 Briar Brae Road
Stamford, CT 06903
(516) 421-2699
(203) 329-8010
Web site: http://www.nfia.net
Chairman: Thomas Abraham

Formed in 1980, the National Federation of Indian American Associations was first known as the National Council of Asian Indian Organizations in North America and later as the National Federation of Asian Indian Organizations of America. Goals of the group include providing communication among Indian organizations, Indo-American communities, and Asian-Indian U.S. citizens, representing Indian interests, and promoting and preserving Indian heritage and culture. Also coordinates social, economic, cultural, educational, and community issues of relevance to people of Indian origin. Focuses on monitoring and influencing legislative activities, as well as political education.

National Immigration, Refugee, and Citizenship Forum

220 I Street NE, Ste. 220
Washington, D.C. 20002
(202) 544-0004
(202) 544-1905 Fax
Director: Frank Sharry

The National Immigration, Refugee, and Citizenship Forum was founded in 1982 as the National Forum on Immigration and Refugee Policy. Membership consists of American churches, state and local government agencies, refugee and immigration bureaus, and labor organizations. Examines and seeks to influence policies concerning immigration, refugees, and citizenship.

National Institute for Multicultural Education

844 Grecian NW
Albuquerque, NM 87107
(505) 344-6898
President: Dr. Tomas Villarreal, Jr.

Founded in 1975, the National Institute for Multicultural Education promotes equal opportunity education. It also competes for government grants and funding for ethnic school programs. The group offers programs on bilingual services, computer, special education, and youth advocacy.

National Rainbow Coalition

30 West Washington Street, Ste. 300
Chicago, IL 60602
(312) 855-3773
Web site: http://www.archive.org/pres96/dolesville/rainnbow.html
President: Jesse L. Jackson, Jr.

Founded in 1984. Seeks to end economic, racial, and sexual discrimination and violence. Works for tax reform, greater political and economic opportunity, an unpolluted environment, and peace-driven foreign policy. Also strives for greater voter participation and rights.

Organization of Chinese American Women

1300 North Street NW, Ste. 100
Washington, D.C. 20005
(202) 638-0330
(202) 638-2916 Fax
Web site: http://www2.ari.net/oca/
Executive Director: Pauline W. Tsui

Formed in 1977. Supports the needs of Chinese American women, as well as seeking to educate the public about their needs. Works to integrate Chinese American women into other women's programs, to overcome unequal employment issues, and to put an end to racial stereotypes and discrimination. Provides leadership training, access to policy-making positions, and assistance to poverty-stricken immigrants. Also offers networking, job placement services, and training opportunities.

Organization of Chinese Americans

10001 Connecticut Avenue NW, Ste. 707
Washington, D.C. 20036
(202) 223-5500
(202) 276-0540 Fax
Web site: http://www.ocanatl.org
Executive Director: Daphne Kwok

Founded in 1973 by Chinese-Americans seeking to foster the needs of their community. Goals include promotion of equal rights and opportunities, supporting cultural awareness, and upholding the U.S. Constitution and democracy. Also provides political, cultural, and educational seminars.

Overseas Indian Congress of North America

55 Canoe Brook Parkway
Summit, NJ 07901
(908) 273-5178
President: Dr. Shobha Singh

Founded in 1980 by Indian professionals living in the United States. Promotes religious harmony and understanding, minority rights, and democratic institutions. Also focuses on cultural, economic, and political situations in areas such as India, Pakistan, and Bangladesh. Offers a discussion forum, information services, and programs on political education and cultural exchange.

Pacific Islands Association

224 West 35th Street, Room 908
New York, NY 10001
(212) 695-7370
President: Lelei Lelulu

The Pacific Islands Association was founded in 1982. The group provides seminars on American-Pacific Island issues, as well as a speakers' bureau. Publications include *American-Pacific Trade Relations Marine Minerals and Energy Development in the Pacific*, *Investment Opportunities in the Pacific*, *Strategic Interests in the Pacific Island Nations*, and *Women in Development*.

Pacifica Foundation

3729 Cahuenga Blvd. West
North Hollywood, CA 91604
(818) 985-8800
Web site: http://www.igc.apc.org/pacifica
Executive Director: Patricia Scott

Founded in 1946, the Pacifica Foundation provides radio programming on public affairs, literature, drama, and music. The group seeks to assist in gaining international peace, promote study in the areas of economics, politics, religion, and philosophy, and provide news and information to the community. Also works to overcome racism. Provides radio archives of historic events and speeches; the foundation also offers several publications.

Society for the Protection of East Asians' Human Rights/USA

Columbia University
927 International Affairs Building
New York, NY 10027
(212) 865-3719
(212) 749-1497 Fax
E-mail: 1670044@MCI.com

Founded in 1977 to promote peace and human rights for all people of Asian origin. Provide information, research programs, and educational services.

Southeast Asia Center

1124-1128 West Ainslie
Chicago, IL 60640
(312) 989-6927
Executive Director: Peter R. Porr

Founded in 1979 as the Association of Chinese from Indochina. Seeks to help Laotian, Hmong, Cambodian, Vietnamese, and Chinese refugees and immigrants. Strives to sensitize people about and support non-English speaking individuals from Indochina. Provides social services, minority advocacy, and language classes. Organizes legislative lobbying and legal action.

United States Pan Asian American Chamber of Commerce

1329 18th Street NW
Washington, D.C. 20036
(202) 296-5221
(202) 296-5225 Fax
Web site: http://www.his.com/~uspaacc
President: Susan Au Allen

Founded in 1984 to promote Asian-American business interests. Provides educational and networking services, a speakers' bureau, and scholarship funding. Offers charity assistance, research, and a quarterly newsletter, *East-West Report*. Monitors social, political, and other issues relevant to the group and its cause.

U.S.-Asia Institute

232 East Capitol Street NE
Washington, D.C. 20003
(202) 544-3181
(202) 543-1748 Fax
President: Juli Konshima

The U.S.-Asia Institute was founded in 1979. Acknowledges, supports, and fosters the cultural, social, and economic role of Asian Americans within U.S. society. Utilizes the skills of Asian Americans to promote better economic policy, foreign policy, cultural exchange, and communication between the United States and Asia. Offers a number of publications, including *An Asian/Pacific American Perspective: Future Directions of U.S.*, *U.S.-Asia Institute—Policy Forum*, and other journals, reports, and newsletters on similar topics.

Women for Racial and Economic Equality
198 Broadway, Room 606
New York, NY 10038
(212) 385-1103
Chairperson: Rudean Leinaeng

Founded in 1975. Seeks to end race and sex discrimination in the areas of hiring, pay, and promotion, as well as other business civil freedoms. Also lobbies for equal employment, health issues, education, and child care. Supports quality public education, federally funded child care, and the Women's Bill of Rights, a set of legislative demands striving for social equality and economic independence.

3
Tables

Asian-American Members of the U.S. House of Representatives

Name	State	Party	Dates
Daniel Inuoye	Hawaii	Democrat	1959–63
Spark M. Matsunaga	Hawaii	Democrat	1963–77
Patsy Mink	Hawaii	Democrat	1965–77, 1990–
Norman Mineta	California	Democrat	1975–95
Daniel K. Akaka	Hawaii	Democrat	1977–90
Robert Matsui	California	Democrat	1978–
Patricia Saiki	Hawaii	Republican	1987–91
Eni Faleomavaega	American Samoa	Democrat	1989–
Robert A. Underwood	Guam	Democrat	1993–
David Wu	Oregon	Democrat	1999–

Asian-American Members of the U.S. Senate

Name	State	Party	Dates
Hiram Fong	Hawaii	Republican	1959–77
Daniel K. Inouye	Hawaii	Democrat	1963–
S.I. Hayakawa	California	Republican	1977–83
Spark M. Matsunaga	Hawaii	Democrat	1977–90
Daniel K. Akaka	Hawaii	Democrat	1990–

Timeline

Date	Blacks	Asian Americans	Latinos	Native Americans
1787	The United States Constitution is written; it contains the 3/5ths clause, which states that black slaves will be counted as 3/5ths of a person for purposes of representation and taxation.			The United States Congress passes the Northwest Ordinance, which establishes a mechanism for creating states out of the territories of the Upper Midwest, a region still largely under Native control.
1789	Delaware passes a law forbidding its citizens from participating in the slave trade.			The Indian Department becomes part of the U.S. Department of War.
1790	The U.S. government and the Creek Indians sign a treaty providing for the return of black fugitive slaves.			The first of the Trade and Intercourse Acts is enacted to establish uniform relations with Native tribes.
1791	Vermont enters the Union as a free state.			
1792	Virginia passes a law that punishes whites with six months in prison for marrying a black.			
1793	Congress passes the first Fugitive Slave Act, which calls for the return of runaway slaves.			Federal agents and representatives from 13 tribes meet, but they fail to resolve land disputes.
1794	Richard Allen founds the first AME Church in Philadelphia.			Little Turtle's War begins in the Indiana Territory.

Date	Blacks	Asian Americans	Latinos	Native Americans
1795			The Treaty of San Lorenzo (also known as Pinckney's Treaty) between Spain and the U.S. opens the Mississippi to American navigation.	
1796	Tennessee enters the Union as a slave state.			The Trading Houses Act establishes government-operated trading houses.
1797	Connecticut law emancipates slaves at age 21.		The American Lodge is founded to work for the independence of Spanish colonies in America.	
1798	Georgia abolishes the slave trade.		The Naturalization Act raises the number of years of residence for citizenship from 5 to 14. The Alien Act grants the president authority to expel any alien deemed dangerous.	
1799	Upon his death in December, George Washington frees his slaves.			Handsome Lake's religious movement begins among the Iroquois.
1800	South Carolina bars the entrance of free blacks into the state.			
1802	Governor William H. Harrison of the Indiana Territory seeks suspension of the Northwest Ordinance to allow slavery in the territory.			
1803	Ohio enters the Union as a free state, but disenfranchises blacks.		The United States buys the Louisiana Territory from France for $15 million, bringing areas of Hispanic settlement under U.S. control.	Through the Louisiana Purchase, the United States acquires 800,000 square miles of new territory inhabited by numerous Native tribes.
1804	New Jersey passes a law providing for the gradual emancipation of slaves.			Lewis and Clark begin their expedition of western exploration, making contact with many Native peoples.

Date	Blacks	Asian Americans	Latinos	Native Americans
1806	Virginia requires all freed slaves to leave the state within one year of gaining freedom.			
1807	Two boatloads of Africans in Charleston, South Carolina, starve themselves to death rather than become slaves.			
1808	Congress bars the importation of slaves.			
1809	New York passes a law recognizing marriages between blacks.			By the Treaty of Fort Wayne, the Delaware Tribe to relinquishes approximately 3 million acres. Tecumseh creates a multi-tribal alliance to resist U.S. incursions into Indian lands in the Midwest.
1810	In *Maryland v. Dolly Chapple*, the Court decides that slaves may testify in court when the victims are also slaves.			
1811	Delaware forbids free blacks from entering the state, and those who leave for more than six months lose their residency.		Congress adopts the "no-transfer" resolution to prevent Spanish Florida from passing to another European power.	William Henry Harrison engages Tecumseh's multi-tribal alliance at the Battle of Tippecanoe in the Indiana Territory.
1812	British forces encourage slaves to revolt during the War of 1812.			The British encourage Native Americans to attack American settlements during the War of 1812.
1813	New York State ends slavery.			The Red Stick war begins in the Southeast.
1814	Two black battalions serve at the Battle of New Orleans under the command of General Andrew Jackson.			

Date	Blacks	Asian Americans	Latinos	Native Americans
1815	The Underground Railroad for helping escaped slaves reach safety in the North and Canada is formally established.			To avoid white settlers from the East, Indians begin to migrate to Texas in large numbers.
1816	The American Colonization Society, which advocates resettlement of slaves in Africa, is founded.			
1817	Mississippi enters the Union as a slave state.			The First Seminole War begins in Florida.
1818	Connecticut is the only New England state that still officially disenfranchises blacks.			Delaware Treaty is adopted, in which the Delaware give up Indiana in exchange for land west of the Mississippi River.
1819	Alabama enters the Union as a slave state.		The United States buys Florida from Spain for $5 million as part of the Adams-Onis Treaty.	
1820	Congress adopts the Missouri Compromise, which establishes the boundary between slave and free states.	Arrival of the first Chinese in the United States.		John C. Calhoun argues for Indian guardianship.
1821	Maine outlaws interracial marriages and voids existing ones.			Sequoyah creates the Cherokee syllabary for writing Indian language.
1822	Denmark Vesey and his coconspirators are captured and punished for their planned slave revolt in Charleston, SC.			David Moncock becomes the first Native American to graduate from West Point.
1823	U.S. district court rules that slaves taken to free states become free.		The Monroe Doctrine, which tells European nations to remain out of the Americas, is adopted as U.S. policy.	In *Johnson v. McIntosh*, the U.S. Supreme Court rules that the Native American tribes have land rights. Office of Indian Affairs is created within the War Department.
1824	Dartmouth College opens admissions to blacks.			

Date	Blacks	Asian Americans	Latinos	Native Americans
1825				Tocqueville criticizes U.S. Indian policy and predicts that only the grave will give Indians rest.
1826	Free blacks allowed to own real estate in South Carolina.			The Treaty of Buffalo Creek is signed.
1827	The *Freedman's Journal* begins publication.			Cherokee Nation adopts a constitution.
1828				The *Cherokee Phoenix* begins publication.
1829	South Carolina governor Stephen Miller argues that slavery is a national benefit, not an evil.			William Apess, a Pequot, publishes his book *A Son of the Forest*.
1830	First National Negro Convention is held in Philadelphia.			The Indian Removal Act is passed. The Treaty of Dancing Rabbit Creek cedes to the U.S. more than 10 million acres of Indian land in Alabama and Mississippi.
1831	Nat Turner leads a slave revolt in Virginia.			In *Cherokee Nation v. Georgia*, the U.S. Supreme Court rules that Native American tribes are "domestic dependent nations."
1832	Abolitionist William Lloyd Garrison publishes *Thoughts on African Colonization*.			The Black Hawk War begins in the Midwest. In *Worcester v. Georgia*, the U.S. Supreme Court rules that the federal government has the right to regulate Indian affairs.
1833	The American Anti-Slavery Society, which is open to both blacks and whites, is founded.			
1834	A three-day anti-abolition riot erupts in Philadelphia.			Department of Indian Affairs is reorganized.
1835	President Andrew Jackson forbids the post office from delivering abolitionist literature in the South.			Texas Rangers begin raids against the Comanche. The Second Seminole War begins in Florida.

Date	Blacks	Asian Americans	Latinos	Native Americans
1836	A gag rule is adopted by Congress that forbids the discussion of slavery on the House floor.		The Treaty of Velasco officially marks the establishment of the Republic of Texas.	Creek Indians leave Alabama because of increasing white settlement.
1837	Michigan disenfranchises blacks.			Sioux Treaty calls for the Sioux to cede all lands east of the Mississippi River.
1838	Former President John Quincy Adams defends Africans who took command of the *Amistad* slave ship in American waters.			Forced removal of Cherokees from the Southeast to Indian Territory (Oklahoma) becomes a "Trail of Tears" marked by thousands of deaths.
1839	The Liberty Party, an anti-slavery third party, is founded.			
1840	U.S. House of Representatives votes to refuse abolitionist petitions.			The United States adopts a land policy establishing an Indian Territory in Kansas and Oklahoma.
1841	Frederick Douglass makes his first anti-slavery speech for the Massachusetts Anti-Slavery Society.		Republic of Texas President Mirabeau Lamar sends armed forces to foment revolution in New Mexico; the so-called Santa Fe Expedition is a failure.	
1842	In *Prigg v. Pennsylvania*, an antikidnapping law to prevent the return of slaves to the South is ruled unconstitutional.			
1843	Sojourner Truth begins her abolitionist work.			
1845	Texas enters the Union as a slave state and disenfranchises blacks.		The United States annexes Texas.	
1846	The Odd Fellows, a black fraternal organization, is founded.		Mexican-American War begins.	Navajos resist U.S. settlers in California and New Mexico.
1847	Frederick Douglass begins publication of *Northern Star.*			Last of the Mohicans monument is erected in Norwich, Connecticut.

Date	Blacks	Asian Americans	Latinos	Native Americans
1848	The Free Soil Party, which opposes the extension of slavery, is formed.	Gold rush at Sutter's Creek brings many Chinese to California.	The Treaty of Guadalupe Hildalgo ends the Mexican-American War.	California Gold Rush begins, initiating heavy white settlement.
1849	Harriet Tubman escapes to freedom and begins her work helping others to escape.			The Department of Interior is created and the Bureau of Indian Affairs is put under its jurisdiction.
1850	Congress adopts the Compromise of 1850, which brings California into the union as a free state and creates a stronger Fugitive Slave Act.	A monthly tax, known as the Foreign Miners' License Tax, is enacted in California.		Period of genocide against California Indians begins.
1851	Virginia law requires freed slaves to leave the state within one year or be reinslaved.	Chinese population in California goes from 4,000 to 25,000.	The California Land Act of 1851 is signed, facilitating legalization of land belonging to Californians prior to U.S. takeover.	Treaty of Fort Laramie protects the Mormon Trail against Indian depredations.
1852	Harriet Beecher Stowe's novel *Uncle Tom's Cabin* is published.	First group of Chinese contract laborers land in Hawaii.	Manuel Requema, a Hispanic American, is elected to the first Los Angeles Board of Supervisors.	
1853			With the Gadsden Purchase, the United States acquires 44,000 acres in the Southwest (now parts of Arizona and New Mexico).	California governor John McDougal asks for troops to put down Indian rebellions.
1854	The Kansas-Nebraska Act leaves the question of slavery up to the settlers of the Kansas and Nebraska territories themselves.	In *People v. Hall*, the California Supreme Court rules that Chinese cannot give testimony in court.	The United States offers $130 million to Spain for Cuba and threatens that if Spain does not sell, the United States may support independence for the island (Ostend Manifesto).	The Teton Dakota resist U.S. intrusions into their lands.
1855	Maine, Michigan, and Massachusetts forbid the enforcement of the federal Fugitive Slave Act of 1850.	California passes a law to discourage Chinese from entering the state.	The Anti-Vagrancy Act, known as "the greaser law," prohibits bear-baiting, cockfighting, and bullfights.	The Walla Walla Council negotiates a series of treaties with Native American tribes. The Third Seminole War begins in Florida.

Date	Blacks	Asian Americans	Latinos	Native Americans
1856	Widespread slave insurrections occur in several southern states, including Louisiana, Florida, Arkansas, Georgia, South Carolina, Virginia, Kentucky, and Tennessee.		For eleven days, Manuel Requena serves as mayor of Los Angeles.	When Indian agent Henry L. Dodge goes missing, U.S. troops attack the Apache.
1857	The U.S. Supreme Court rules in *Dred Scott v. Sandford*, denying that slaves can be citizens.			Pawnee Treaty trades Pawnee lands in Nebraska and Dakota for other lands in Dakota.
1858	John Brown leads a raid on a federal arsenal at Harper's Ferry, Virginia.	California legislature passes "An Act to Prevent the Further Immigration of Chinese or Mongolians to This State."		The Navajo War begins over grazing rights.
1859	In *Ableman v. Booth*, the Fugitive Slave Act of 1850 is upheld by the U.S. Supreme Court.	Chinese are excluded from public schools in San Francisco.	Juan Nepomuceno Cortina leads a guerrilla war against settlers in South Texas.	Salt River Reservation is established in Arizona.
1860	Abraham Lincoln is elected as the first Republican president on a platform opposing the extension of slavery in the territories and South Carolina secedes.	Nakahama Manjiro, the first Japanese person in the United States, arrives in San Francisco aboard the *Kanin Maru*.		Choctaw Constitutional Government is established.
1861	Civil War begins.			The Cherokees side with the Confederacy in the Civil War.
1862	Congress authorizes black enlistment.	California passes "An Act to Protect Free White Labor Against Competition with Chinese Coolie Labor and to Discourage the Immigration of the Chinese into the State of California."	Homestead Act is signed, allowing squatters in the West to settle and claim vacant lands.	Little Crow carries out a war of resistance, known as the Minnesota Uprising, against poor treatment by federal authorities.
1863	Emancipation Proclamation takes effect on January 1.	The California Police Tax is ruled unconstitutional by the decision in *Lin Sing v. Washburn*.		The Long Walk of the Navajo occurs.
1864	Fugitive Slave Act is repealed.			The Sand Creek Massacre occurs in Colorado.

Date	Blacks	Asian Americans	Latinos	Native Americans
1865	Thirteenth Amendment, which abolishes slavery, is ratified.	The Central Pacific Railroad recruits Chinese workers for the construction of the transcontinental railroad.		U.S. Army commissions Indian scouts.
1866	Congress overrides President Andrew Johnson's veto of the Civil Rights Act.			The Bozeman Trail wars occur, with Native Americans resisting the building of army forts on their lands.
1867	First Reconstruction Act is passed, which grants blacks voting rights in southern states.			U.S. government purchases Alaska. The Commission Act is signed, for negotiating peace treaties with Native American nations.
1868	Fourteenth Amendment, which guarantees citizenship, is ratified.	The Burlingame Treaty is signed, which allows for the emigration of Chinese to the United States.	U.S. Senate rejects treaty to annex the Dominican Republic.	The Second Treaty of Fort Laramie pledges the protection of Indian lands. U.S. Seventh Cavalry leads the Washita River Massacre.
1869	Ebenezer Don Carlos Bassett becomes the first African-American diplomat when he is appointed minister to Haiti.	The first group of Japanese immigrants comes to mainland United States, settles in Gold Hill (CA), and establishes the Wakamatsu Tea and Silk Farm Colony.	President Ulysses S. Grant announces the building of the Panama Canal.	Board of Indian Commission is formed.
1870	Ratification of the Fifteenth Amendment.	Colorado passes a resolution welcoming Chinese immigrants.		President Ulysses S. Grant adopts a peace policy toward the Indians.
1871	Congress passes the Ku Klux Klan Act to curb the activities of that group.	Anti-Chinese riot breaks out in Los Angeles.		Congress passes an act on March 3 that ends treaty negotiations with Native American nations. In *McKay v. Campbell*, the U.S. Supreme Court holds that Indian people born with "tribal allegiance" are not U.S. citizens.
1872	Black speakers address the Republican National Convention in Philadelphia.	The Chinese Education Mission is organized by Yung Wing.		Modoc War in northern California begins when Modoc Indians led by Captain Jack return from Oregon to reclaim ancestral lands.

Date	Blacks	Asian	Latinos	Native
1873	The Slaughterhouse Cases determine that the Fourteenth Amendment does not guarantee state rights.	The International Workingmen's Association adopts an official anti-coolie policy.		
1874	Joseph H. Rainey (R-SC) becomes the first black to preside over the U.S. House of Representatives.			The Red River War occurs in Texas and the Indian Territory of Oklahoma.
1875	Congress enacts the Civil Rights Act, which guarantees equal rights in public accommodations and jury duty.	U.S. Congress passes an immigration act—the Page Law—that prohibits Chinese, Japanese, and Mongolian convicts and prostitutes from coming to the United States.	The U.S. Supreme Court rules in *Hernandez v. New York* that the federal government has sole authority over immigration.	Camp Verde Reservation is revoked by presidential executive order.
1876	President Ulysses S. Grant sends federal troops into South Carolina to restore peace after race riots.			General Custer and part of his command are wiped out at the Battle of Little Big Horn in Montana.
1877	Reconstruction comes to an end.	Miyama Kanichi organizes the Japanese Gospel Society in San Francisco.	The Salt Wars erupt as Anglos attempt to take control of the salt mines near El Paso (TX).	The Nez Perce tribe is exiled from their homelands in the Northwest; they are then pursued by U.S. forces in an unsuccessful attempt to escape to Canada.
1878	Georgia establishes a poll tax as a method of disenfranchising blacks.	In the case In *re Ah Yup*, the U.S. Supreme Court rules that Chinese are not eligible for naturalized citizenship.		Bancock War erupts in northern Idaho.
1879		California adopts new state constitution that contains many discriminatory measures against Chinese immigrants.		The Carlisle Indian School is founded by Captain Richard H. Pratt.
1880	The U.S. Supreme Court rules in *Stauder v. West Virginia* that the exclusion of blacks from jury duty is unconstitutional.	U.S. government revises the Burlingame Treaty with China.	Immigration to the United States from other parts of the Americas is stimulated by the advent of the railroad.	The ghost dance is banned by the U.S. government.

Date	Blacks	Asian Americans	Latinos	Native Americans
1881	Booker T. Washington founds Tuskegee Institute in Tuskegee, Alabama.	Congress passes an act to suspend Chinese immigration for 20 years, but the act is vetoed by President Chester A. Arthur.		Helen Hunt Jackson publishes *A Century of Dishonor.*
1882		The law known as the Chinese Exclusion Act (Immigration Act of 1882), or "An Act to Execute Certain Treaty Stipulations Relating to Chinese," is signed into law.		The "Act to Civilize Pueblo Indians" is passed.
1883	The Supreme Court rules that the Civil Rights Act of 1875 is unconstitutional.			In *Ex Parte Crow Dog*, the U.S. Supreme Court rules that states have no jurisdiction over crimes committed on Indian reservations.
1884	John R. Lynch is elected as the first black chairman of the Republican National Committee.	Congress passes "An Act to Amend an Act Entitled an Act to Execute Certain Treaty Stipulations Relating to Chinese," which imposes more restrictions.		In *Elk v. Wilkins*, the U.S. Supreme Court rules that Indians who leave the reservations to live among white people are not citizens simply because they were born within the United States.
1885		An Anti-Chinese riot breaks out in Rock Springs, Wyoming.		Congress passes the Indian Major Crimes Act to overturn the impact of *Ex Parte Crow Dog* (1883).
1886	New Mexico Territory repeals its anti-interracial marriage law.	Japan legalizes the emigration of its people abroad. The U.S. Supreme Court rules in the case of *Yick Wo v. Hopkins*, establishing the principle that no state may deny any person of his or her life, liberty, or property without due process of the law.		In *U.S. v. Kagama*, the U.S. Supreme Court upholds the constitutionality of the Indian Major Crimes Act (1885).
1887	Georgia Supreme Court upholds the right of Amanda A. Dickson to inherit her white father's estate.	Japanese replace Chinese as a source of cheap labor after passage of the Exclusion Act.		The General Allotment Act (Dawes Severalty Act) divides reservation lands into individual parcels.

Date	Blacks	Asian Americans	Latinos	Native Americans
1888	Henry P. Cheatham (R-NC) is elected to the U.S. House of Representatives.	Scott Act voids 20,000 Chinese reentry certificates.		Congress passes the White Men and Indian Women Act.
1889	Frederick Douglass is appointed minister to Haiti.	*Chae Chan Ping v. U.S.* upholds the constitutionality of Chinese exclusionary laws.	The International Union of American Republics is founded in Washington, D.C. (forerunner of the Organization of American States).	Oklahoma is opened to white settlers.
1890	Mississippi imposes the understanding test to keep blacks from voting.		Felix Martinez, Jr. founds El Partido del Pueblo Unido, the first Hispanic American third party.	Wounded Knee Massacre occurs on the Pine Ridge Reservation.
1891		First Chinese-English newspaper, *The Chinese World,* begins publication in San Francisco.		The Indian Schools Act is passed.
1892	Ida B. Wells begins her antilynching crusade.	Geary Act prohibits Chinese immigration for another 10 years.		Intoxication in Indian Country Act prohibits the sale of liquor on reservations.
1893	George Murray (R-SC) is elected to the U.S. House of Representatives.	Japanese residents in San Francisco form their first trade association, the Japanese Shoemakers' League.		U.S. troops forcibly gather Hopi children for enforced education.
1894	U.S. Congress repeals the Enforcement Act, making it easier to disenfranchise blacks.	Japanese immigration to Hawaii under the Irwin Convention comes to an end.	Alianza Hispano Americans, a civil rights organization, is founded in Tucson, AZ.	Thomas Edison captures the Sioux Ghost Dance on kinescope.
1895	Booker T. Washington's Atlanta Compromise Address calls for a policy of gradualism and accommodation.	The Native Sons of the Golden State is organized under the leadership of Walter Lum, Joseph Lum, and Ng Gunn.		
1896	In *Plessy v. Ferguson*, the U.S. Supreme Court rules that separate but equal satisfies constitutional requirements.	Chinatown in Honolulu is burned down during a bubonic plague scare.	A revolutionary junta is formed in New York to lead the Puerto Rican independence movement.	
1897		Hawaii's Executive Council on Immigration bans Koreans from being brought into Hawaii as contract laborers.	Miguel A. Otero, Jr. is appointed governor of New Mexico by President William McKinley.	Education Appropriation Act mandates funding for Indian schools. Indian Liquor Act bans sale or distribution of liquor to Native Americans.

Date	Blacks	Asian Americans	Latinos	Native Americans
1898	Louisiana enacts a grandfather clause to prevent freed slaves from voting.	U.S. Supreme Court rules in *U.S. v. Wong Kim Ark* regarding citizenship with relation to parentage.	The USS *Maine* is destroyed in Havana Harbor; this ignites the Spanish-American War. Spain signs the Treaty of Paris transferring Puerto Rico, Guam, and the Philippines to the United States.	The Curtis Act allots the lands of the Cherokee, Choctaw, Chickasaw, Creek, and Seminole as well as abolishes their governments.
1899	Sutton Griggs's *Imperium and Imperio,* the first black power novel, is published.	The Filipino-American War starts. Congress makes Hawaii a territory of the United States.		In *Stephens v. Cherokee Nation*, the U.S. Supreme Court rules that Congress has plenary power over Indian tribes.
1900	W.E.B. Du Bois serves as secretary at the first Pan-African Conference.	Bubonic plague scare in San Francisco leads to quarantine of Chinatown.	The Foraker Act establishes citizenship for Puerto Ricans.	
1901		First Korean immigrant, Peter Ryu, arrives in Hawaii.	The Platt Amendment guarantees U.S. interests in Cuba and is made part of the Cuban Constitution.	Five Civilized Tribe Citizenship Act grants U.S. citizenship to members of the Five Civilized tribes.
1902		Chinese exclusion is extended for another 10 years.	Cuba declares its independence from all foreign countries, including the United States. The Reclamation Act is signed, which dispossesses many Hispanic Americans of their land.	Alex Posey writes his Fus Fixico Letters, which satirizes the Dawes Act.
1903	W.E.B. Du Bois's *The Souls of Black Folk* is published, it rejects the gradualism of Booker T. Washington.	The pensionado program—aimed at giving higher education to Filipino students—begins.	The Hay-Bunau-Virilla Treaty settles the issue of where to build the Panama Canal.	In *Lone Wolf v. Hitchcock*, the U.S. Supreme Court rules that Congress has authority to dispose of Native American lands.
1904	Boley, Oklahoma, an all-black town, is founded.	Japanese contract laborers strike for the first time in Hawaii.	President Theodore Roosevelt issues a corollary to the Monroe Doctrine that states that the United States will exercise police powers in the Western Hemisphere.	

Date	Blacks	Asian Americans	Latinos	Native Americans
1905	The Niagara Movement of African American intellectuals and activists begins under the leadership of W.E.B. Du Bois and William Monroe Trotter.	The Mutual Cooperation Federation is established among Koreans in San Francisco.		In *U.S. v. Winans*, the U.S. Supreme Court rules that treaties may reserve certain hunting and fishing rights off-reservation.
1906	Brownsville (TX) incident occurs in which black soldiers are wrongly court martialed for raiding the town.	San Francisco School Board creates an international incident by ordering children of Japanese and Korean residents to attend the segregated Oriental Public School.		The Burke Act is signed, amending the General Allotment Act. The Alaskan Allotment Act allows Alaska natives to file for 160-acre parcels.
1907	The U.S. Supreme Court determines that railroads may segregate passengers on interstate trains even within states that do not allow segregation.	Theodore Roosevelt signs an executive order banning Japanese immigrants from coming to the mainland from Hawaii, Mexico, or Canada.		Charles Curtis becomes the first Native American to be elected to the U.S. Senate.
1908	In *Berea College v. Kentucky*, the U.S. Supreme Court upholds a segregation requirement in private institutions.	The United States and Japan sign the Gentlemen's Agreement, which limits the number of Japanese laborers emigrating to the United States.		In *Winters v. U.S.*, the U.S. Supreme Court rules that Indians have the right to sufficient water for agricultural purposes.
1909	The National Association for the Advancement of Colored People (NAACP) is formed.	Japanese sugar plantation workers strike in Hawaii.		
1910	The first issue of W.E.B. Du Bois's magazine *Crisis* debuts.	California attempts to stop the immigration of Asian Indians to the state.		The Omnibus Act is signed, establishing procedures to determine Native American heirship of trust lands and other resources.
1911	Marcus Garvey founds the Universal Negro Improvement Association.	President William Howard Taft stops the California legislature from passing anti-Japanese laws.		The Society of the American Indian—a self-sufficiency, self-rule group—is established in Columbus, OH.
1912	James Weldon Johnson's *The Autobiography of an Ex-Colored Man* launches the Harlem Renaissance.			The Classification and Appraisal of Unallotted Indian Lands Act permits the secretary of the interior to reappraise and reclassify unalloted Indian lands.

Date	Blacks	Asian Americans	Latinos	Native Americans
1913	President Woodrow Wilson institutes a policy of government-wide segregation in federal offices, restrooms, and cafeterias.	California passes the alien land law, which prevents aliens ineligible for citizenship from owning or leasing land for more than three years.	Ladislas Lazaro becomes the first Latino congressman from Louisiana.	In *U.S. v. Sandoval,* the Supreme Court upholds the power of Congress to regulate the Pueblo Indians.
1915	In *Guinn and Beal v. U.S.,* the U.S. Supreme Court rules that grandfather clauses are unconstitutional.	The Japanese Chamber of Commerce is formed in southern California.	The Plan de San Diego uprising occurs.	
1916	*The Journal of Negro History* publishes its first volume.			In *U.S. v. Nice,* the U.S. Supreme Court rules that citizenship and guardianship are not incompatible.
1917	The U.S. Supreme Court overturns a Louisville, KY, ordinance that prevents blacks and whites from living in the same neighborhood.	Arizona adopts an alien land law.	The Jones Act is signed, extending U.S. citizenship to Puerto Ricans. The Immigration Act of 1917 passes, imposing a literacy test on all immigrants. Selective Service Act becomes law.	8,000 Native Americans serve in the armed forces.
1918	The African Black Brotherhood, a radical group, is formed.	Servicemen of Asian ancestry who had served in World War I are granted the right of naturalization.		The Native American Church, which uses peyote in its ceremonies, is established in Oklahoma.
1919	Marcus Garvey founds the Black Star Line.	The California Joint Immigration Committee is formed.		U.S. citizenship is granted to Native Americans who served in the armed forces during World War I.
1920		California passes the Alien Land Act to close loopholes in the original law.	The Order of the Sons of America, an early civil rights organization, is founded in Texas.	
1921	George Washington Carver addresses Congress on the peanut tariff.	President Warren Harding signs into law the Quota Immigration Act of 1921.	The Pan American Round Table, a Anglo-Latino organization, is formed to fight discrimination in San Antonio.	The Snyder Act allows for the federal government to make expenditures on behalf of Indians regardless of the amount of their Indian blood.

Date	Blacks	Asian Americans	Latinos	Native Americans
1922	An antilynching bill passes the U.S. House of Representatives but dies in the Senate.	The Cable Act declares that American female citizens who marry an alien ineligible for citizenship lose their citizenship.		
1923	Marcus Garvey is sentenced to five years for mail fraud.	In *U.S. v. Bhagat Singh Thind*, the U.S. Supreme Court rules that Asian Indians are not eligible for naturalized citizenship.	Soledad C. Chacon is the first Hispanic woman elected to state office in New Mexico as secretary of state.	Committee of 100 is appointed to study the condition of Native Americans.
1924		The Immigration Act of 1924 denies entry to almost all Asians.	Fighting breaks out in Argentine, KS, because whites want separate schools from Mexican Americans.	The General Citizenship Act is passed, allowing some Native Americans citizenship.
1925	A. Philip Randolph organizes the Brotherhood of Sleeping Car Porters.	The Filipino Federation of America is founded.	The Border Patrol is created by Congress.	Zane Grey's *The Vanishing Americans* is serialized.
1926	Violette N. Anderson becomes the first black women to argue before the U.S. Supreme Court.		La Sociedad de Madres Mexicanas, the first female civil rights organization, is formed.	The National Council of American Indians is founded by Gertrude Bonnin.
1927	Marcus Garvey's sentence is commuted by President Calvin Coolidge.	The AFL passes a resolution calling on Congress to ban Filipino immigration.		
1928		House Bill 13,900 is introduced to exclude Filipinos from the United States.	New Mexico's Octaviano Larrazolo becomes the first Latino U.S. Senator.	Charles Curtis serves as vice president in the Hoover administration.
1929		The Japanese American Citizens League is formed.	League of United Latin American Citizens (LULAC) is founded in Texas.	
1930	W.D. Fard founds the Temple of Islam.	Anti-Filipino riot in Watsonville, CA, kills Fermin Tober.		U.S. Senate investigates the kidnapping of Navajo children.
1931	Nine African Americans are convicted of raping two white women. These so-called Scottsboro (AL) Boys win a new trial on appeal.	The Cable Act is amended to allow women to retain citizenship even though they are married to aliens ineligible for U.S. citizenship.		

Date	Blacks	Asian Americans	Latinos	Native Americans
1932	Sterling Brown's *Southern Road,* social protest poetry, is published.	Hare-Hawes-Cutting Act makes Filipinos ineligible for citizenship.	The first significant youth civil rights organization, the Mexican American Movement, is formed in Los Angeles.	The Leavitt Act forbids the assessment of Indian lands for construction funds.
1933	President Franklin D. Roosevelt forms an unofficial black cabinet.	The Filipino Labor Union is formed in response to growing anti-Filipino sentiment.	The Roosevelt administration reverses the policy of English as the official language in Puerto Rico. Mexican farm workers strike the Central Valley cotton industry in California.	The Indian New Deal is led by John Collier.
1934	W.D. Fard disappears and Elijah Muhammad takes control of the Nation of Islam.	Tydings-McDuffie Act establishes a plan for Philippine independence and reduces Filipino immigration to 50 persons a year.	Platt Amendment is annulled.	The Indian Reorganization Act is signed. Johnson-O'Malley Act replaces the General Allotment Act.
1935	Mary McLeod Bethune founds the National Council of Negro Women.	The Filipino Repatriation Act provides funds to aid Filipinos to return to the Philippines.	Dennis Chavez is the first Latino elected to the U.S. Senate.	The U.S. government must compensate the Creek Nation for 5,000 acres it took more than 100 years ago, according to the U.S. Supreme Court in *U.S. v. Creek Nation.*
1936	Mary McLeod Bethune is appointed head of the Office of Minority Affairs.	The Cable Act of 1922 is repealed.		The Oklahoma Indian Welfare Act is enacted.
1937	William H. Hastie is appointed the first black federal judge.	A Korean resident, Haan Kil-soo, testifies at a hearing in Hawaii that the Japanese government is trying to organize Asians in Hawaii against whites.		
1938	The decision in the case *Missouri ex rel Gaines* requires equal education facilities.	The first Filipino National Conference is held in California.	Pecan shellers strike in San Antonio.	In *U.S. v. Shoshoni,* the U.S. Supreme Court rules that tribal rights include mineral and natural resources.
1939	Senator Theodore Bilbo (D-MS) introduces a Back to Africa Bill.		El Congreso Nacional del Pueblo de Habla Hispana is founded. The organization seeks to unite all Spanish-speaking ethnic groups.	

Date	Blacks	Asian Americans	Latinos	Native Americans
1940	Benjamin B. Davis, Sr. becomes the first African-American general.	The American Federation of Labor charters the Filipino Federated Agricultural Laborers Association.		Native Americans register for the draft.
1941	Four days of race rioting in East St. Louis, Illinois.	The United States abrogates the treaty of commerce and friendship with Japan and freezes the assets of Japanese nationals in the United States. Japan attacks Pearl Harbor in December.	The Fair Employment Practices Act eliminates discrimination in employment.	Felix Cohen's *Handbook of Federal Indian Law* is published.
1942	Committee on Racial Equality is founded.	President Roosevelt signs Executive Orders 9066 and 9102.		In *Seminole Nation v. U.S.*, the U.S. Supreme Court rules that the U.S. government has the highest responsibility for Indian trust funds.
1943	Blacks riot in Detroit to protest their exclusion from civilian defense jobs; federal troops are used to end the protests.	Tule Lake becomes an internment camp for relocated Japanese Americans.	"Braceros," Mexican agricultural workers, are used during World War II labor shortages. The "Zoot Suit" riots occur in southern California.	
1944	In *Smith v. Allwright*, the U.S. Supreme Court rules that blacks must be permitted to vote in primaries.	U.S. Supreme Court rules in *Korematsu v. U.S.* that the government cannot hold loyal citizens of the United States in detention against their will.	Operation Bootstrap, a program of the Puerto Rican government to meet U.S. labor demands, stimulates migration of workers.	The National Congress of American Indians is founded to guard Native American rights.
1945	Mary McLeod Bethune is sent to San Francisco as part of the U.S. delegation to the United Nations charter meetings.	War Brides Act of 1945 allows U.S. servicemen who marry Chinese women to bring them home as citizens.	In *Mendez et al. v. Westminster School District et al.*, the U.S. Supreme Court rules that the school district may not segregate Mexican Americans.	Iroquois Six Nations seek United Nations membership.
1946	The Committee of Civil Rights is formed by presidential executive order to investigate racial injustice and make recommendations.	Luce-Cellar Act grants naturalization rights to Asian Indians and Filipinos.	Jesus T. Pinero is appointed the first Puerto Rican governor by President Harry Truman.	The Indian Claims Commission Act is signed, providing a legal forum for tribes to sue the federal government for the loss of lands.
1947	Ralph J. Bunche is appointed to the United Nations' Palestine Commission.	President Harry Truman pardons the 267 Japanese Americans who ignore the draft.	The American G.I. Forum is organized by Mexican American veterans.	U.S. Army discontinues its use of Indian scouts.

Date	Blacks	Asian Americans	Latinos	Native Americans
1948	In *Shelley v. Kraemer*, the U.S. Supreme Court rules that segregated housing covenants cannot be enforced.	Displaced Persons Act gives permanent resident status to 3,500 Chinese caught in the United States because of the Chinese Civil War.		Sculptor Korczak Ziolkowski begins work on the Crazy Horse monument in South Dakota.
1949		The United States grants refugee status to 5,000 Chinese after China becomes communist.	Luis Muñoz Marin becomes the first native governor of Puerto Rico.	The Hoover Commission argues that Native Americans need to be integrated into U.S. society.
1950	Ralph Bunche wins Nobel Peace Prize.	Korean War begins.	U.S. Congress upgrades Puerto Rico's political status to commonwealth on July 3.	Dillon S. Meyer, new commissioner of Indian affairs, advocates termination policy.
1951	Douglas MacArthur refuses to desegregate U.S. troops.	Chinese Americans are banned from sending money to relatives in China.	The Bracero Program is revived, bringing an annual average of 350,000 Mexican workers to the United States until 1964.	Public Law 280 is signed, allowing greater state jurisdiction over criminal cases involving Native Americans.
1952		McCarran-Walter Act grants right of naturalization to Japanese.	Congress passes the Immigration and Nationality Act of 1952, known as the McCarran-Walter Act.	
1953	James Baldwin's *Go Tell It on the Mountain* is published.	The Refugee Relief Act allows Chinese political refugees to come to the United States. The armistice ending the Korean War is signed.		The Termination Resolution is initiated by Congress to sever the federal government's relationship with Native American nations.
1954	The U.S. Supreme Court rules in the landmark case *Brown v. Board of Education* that separate but equal is unconstitutional.		Landmark case of *Hernandez v. Texas* acknowledges that Hispanic Americans are not being treated as "whites"; the decision paves the way for legal attacks on discrimination.	Congress enacts numerous termination acts with various tribes.
1955	The Montgomery bus boycott follows the refusal of Rosa Parks to give up her bus seat to a white person.			The Indian Health Service is transferred from the Department of the Interior to the Department of Health, Education, and Welfare.
1956	Southern Manifesto is signed by 101 southern members of Congress calling on states to resist the Brown decision.	California repeals its alien land laws.	Henry B. Gonzalez becomes the first Mexican American elected to the Texas senate.	

Date	Blacks	Asian Americans	Latinos	Native Americans
1957	The Southern Christian Leadership Conference (SCLC) is founded by Martin Luther King, Jr.	The Korean Foundation is organized.	Raymond Telles is elected mayor of El Paso, Texas.	The League of Native American Indians is formed.
1958				In *Williams v. Lee*, the U.S. Supreme Court rules that in some cases tribal governments have exclusive jurisdiction.
1959		Hawaii becomes the 50th state of the Union.	The Mexican American Political Association is founded by Edward Roybal.	Attempts are made to form an organization called United Indian Nations.
1960	Student Nonviolent Coordinating Committee is started.		The Chicano Movement begins.	
1961	Whitney M. Young, Jr. becomes executive director of the National Urban League.		ASPIRA is founded to promote education of Hispanic youth.	W.W. Keeler heads the Task Force on Indian Affairs, which downplays termination.
1962		Daniel K. Inouye is elected a U.S. senator and Spark Matsunaga is elected to Congress.	The United Farm Workers Organizing Committee in California begins as an independent organization, led by Cesar Chavez.	The Indian Economic Report is issued, which finds the average Indian living in abject poverty.
1963	During the March on Washington, Martin Luther King delivers his "I Have a Dream" speech.		In Crystal City, Texas, Mexican Americans oust five white city council members and replace them with Mexican Americans.	The State of Washington rules against Native American fishing rights.
1964	The Twenty-fourth Amendment outlaws poll taxes.	Patsy Takemoto Mink becomes the first Asian American woman to serve in Congress.	Congress enacts the Civil Rights Act of 1964. Title VII establishes the Equal Employment Opportunity Commission (EEOC) to monitor discrimination.	American Indian Historical Society is founded to research and teach about Native Americans.
1965	Malcolm X is assassinated.	President Lyndon Johnson signs into law a new immigration policy to enable large numbers of immigrants from Asian countries to come to the United States.	United Farm Workers organize successful Delano grape strike.	The U.S. Supreme Court rules in *Warren Trading Post v. Arizona Tax Commission* that the state of Arizona cannot tax trading posts on Indian territory because they are regulated by the federal government.

Date	Blacks	Asian Americans	Latinos	Native Americans
1966	Robert Weaver, secretary of Housing and Urban Development, becomes the first black cabinet secretary.	March Fong Eu is elected to the California legislature, becoming the first Asian American woman to serve there.	United Farm Workers become part of the AFL-CIO. Cubans are airlifted to the United States.	Robert LaFollette Bennett becomes only the second Native American to head the BIA.
1967	U.S. Supreme Court unanimously overturns a Virginia law that prohibits interracial marriage.		Hector Perez Garcia is appointed alternative delegate to the United Nations by President Lyndon Johnson.	President Lyndon Johnson, in a special message on Indian affairs, calls for more self-help initiatives.
1968	Martin Luther King, Jr. is assassinated.	Students strike at San Francisco State University demanding the establishment of ethnic studies programs.	La Raza Unida Party is formed in Texas to obtain control of community governments where Chicanos are the majority.	The American Indian Civil Rights Act guarantees reservation residents many civil liberties. The American Indian Movement (AIM) is founded in Minneapolis.
1969	The federal government adopts the Philadelphia Plan, by which contracts valued at more than $500,000 must have a certain number of minority members employed in fulfilling them.	The Japanese American Curriculum Project is founded by Florence M. Hongo.	The First National Chicano Youth Liberation Conference is held in Denver, CO.	Occupation of Alcatraz Island by Native American people begins.
1970	The Congressional Black Caucus is formed.	The Japanese American Citizens League national convention discusses a resolution on redress.	A Chicano Moratorium on the Vietnam War is organized in Los Angeles, where journalist Ruben Salazar is accidentally killed by police.	Native Americans occupy Fort Lawton, hoping to have the federal government donate the closing military base to them for a cultural center.
1971	In *Swann v. Charlotte-Mecklenberg*, the U.S. Supreme Court rules that busing is constitutional.	Herbert Choy, a Korean American, becomes the first Asian American to serve on the federal bench.	La Raza Unida Party wins the city elections in Crystal City, Texas.	Alaska Native Claims Settlement Act is signed.
1972	Angela Davis is acquitted of all charges against her.	The Asian Law Caucus is founded by Dale Minami.	Romana Acosta Banuelos becomes the first Hispanic treasurer of the United States.	The Trail of Broken Treaties Caravan proceeds to Washington, D.C., to protest treaty violations.
1973	Tom Bradley is elected mayor of Los Angeles.		The Labor Council of Latin American Advancement (LCLAA) is formed.	Wounded Knee II seeks to highlight the plight of Native Americans.

Date	Blacks	Asian Americans	Latinos	Native Americans
1974	Maynard Jackson is elected mayor of Atlanta.	The U.S. Supreme Court rules in *Lau v. Nichols* that children who speak little English must be provided with bilingual instruction.	Equal Educational Opportunity Act is enacted.	The Navajo-Hopi Land Settlement Act facilitates negotiations.
1975	William T. Coleman is appointed secretary of the Treasury by President Gerald Ford.	More than 130,000 refugees from Vietnam, Kampuchea, and Laos enter the United States as those countries fall to the communists.	Voting Rights Act Amendments of 1975 ban literacy tests.	Indian Self-Determination and Education Assistance Act expands tribal control over tribal governments and education.
1976	Barbara Jordan is the keynote speaker at the Democratic National Convention.	President Gerald Ford officially rescinds Executive Order 9066.	Vilma Martinez wins the Jefferson Award for public service for her work as director of the Mexican American Legal Defense and Education Fund (MALDEF).	President Gerald Ford announces Native American Awareness Week (October 10).
1977	Clifford Alexander, Jr. becomes the first black secretary of the army.	President Ford pardons Iva D'Aquino, "Tokyo Rose."	Congressional Hispanic Caucus is founded with private funds.	The American Indian Policy Review Commission Report by Congress recommends that Native American nations be considered sovereign political bodies.
1978	Benjamin Hooks becomes head of the NAACP, succeeding Roy Wilkins.	The Japanese American Citizens League adopts resolution calling for redress and reparations for the internment of Japanese Americans during World War II.	United Nations recognizes Puerto Rico as a colony of the United States.	The American Indian Freedom of Religion Act protects the rights of Native Americans to follow traditional religious practices. The Federal Acknowledgment Program is initiated. Indian Child Welfare Act is recognized. The Longest Walk occurs.
1979		John Ta-Chuan Fang starts Asian Week.	Puerto Rican Nationalists accused of shootings in 1954 are released.	2,000 Indian activists protest the mining of uranium in the Black Hills of South Dakota.
1980	The U.S. Supreme Court rules in *City of Mobile v. Bolden* that plaintiffs must show intentional discrimination to have local elections invalidated.	The Orderly Departure Program is established by the UN High Commission on Refugees and the Vietnamese government for the emigration of Vietnamese.	Refugee Act of 1980 removes definition of refugee as one who flees from communist regime.	In *U.S. v. Sioux Nation*, the U.S. Supreme Court upholds a judgment against the federal government's illegal taking of the Black Hills.

Date	Blacks	Asian Americans	Latinos	Native Americans
1981	100,000 march on Washington, D.C., seeking the creation of a federal holiday to honor Martin Luther King, Jr.	Commission on Wartime Relocation and Internment of Civilians concludes that Executive Order 9066 resulted from race prejudice, war hysteria, and a failure of political leadership.	Henry G. Cisneros is elected mayor of San Antonio.	The U.S. Civil Rights Commission issues a report that says U.S. government Indian policies have been marked by inaction and missed opportunities.
1982	Congress extends the provisions of the Voting Rights Act of 1965.	Vincent Chin is beaten to death by two white Americans.	Dorothy Comstock Riley becomes the first Latina to serve on a state supreme court when she is appointed to the Michigan high court.	The Indian Claims Limitations Act limits the time period in which claims can be filed.
1983	Harold Washington becomes first black mayor of Chicago.	The report of the Commission on Wartime Relocation and Internment of Civilians is released.	Federico Pena is elected mayor of Denver.	President Ronald Reagan issues the first Native American policy statement since 1975, in which he commits the U.S. government to dealing with Native American tribes government-to-government.
1984	Wilson Goode is the first black mayor of Philadelphia.	Filipino World War II veterans are denied U.S. citizenship.		Senate Select Committee on Indian Affairs becomes a permanent standing committee.
1985	Reuben V. Anderson becomes the first black to serve on the Mississippi supreme court.	Federal district court overturns Minoru Yasui's conviction for violating curfew orders during World War II.	Xavier Suarez, a Cuban-born citizen, is elected mayor of Miami.	In *Dann v. U.S.*, the U.S. Supreme Court rules that because the Shoshoni tribe kept proceeds from a settlement in an interest-bearing account, the tribe's continued claim on the land was voided.
1986		Federal district court overturns Gordon Hirabayashi's 1942 conviction.	Congress enacts the Immigration Reform and Control Act (IRCA), creating an alien legalization program.	Ben Nighthorse Campbell of Colorado becomes the second Native American to serve in the U.S. House of Representatives.
1987	Kurt Schmoke is elected mayor of Baltimore.	Patricia Saiki becomes the first Republican to represent Hawaii in Congress.	Bob Martinez is the first Hispanic governor of Florida.	

Date	Blacks	Asian Americans	Latinos	Native Americans
1988	Jesse Jackson becomes contender for Democratic presidential nomination.	Civil Liberties Act of 1988 is signed into law by President Ronald Reagan.	President Ronald Reagan appoints the first Hispanic secretary of education, Dr. Lauro F. Cavazos.	Indian Gaming Regulatory Act officially legalizes certain types of gambling on reservations and establishes the National Indian Gaming Commission.
1989	Louis Sullivan is appointed secretary of Health and Human Services by President George Bush.	Elaine L. Chao is appointed deputy secretary of the Department of Transportation.	Ileana Ros-Lehtinen is the first Cuban American elected to Congress.	U.S. Congress approves construction of the National Museum of the American Indian to be part of the Smithsonian Institution. Violence erupts on St. Regis Mohawk Reservation over gambling.
1990	Democrat L. Douglas Wilder becomes the first black governor of Virginia.	President George Bush proclaims May 1990 Asian/Pacific American Heritage Month.	President George Bush appoints the first Hispanic woman surgeon general, Antonia C. Novello.	In *Duro v. Reina*, the U.S. Supreme Court rules that tribes cannot have criminal jurisdiction over non-Indians on reservation lands.
1991	Clarence Thomas is appointed to U.S. Supreme Court.	Patricia Saiki is appointed the head of the Small Business Administration.	The proposed North American Free Trade Agreement expands the maquiladora concept, offering greater tax abatements for U.S. businesses.	Navajo leader Peter MacDonald is convicted of conspiracy, fraud, and extortion; he is sentenced to six years in federal prison and fined $11,000.
1992	The Rodney King riots occur in California.	Korean businesses are looted as a result of the riots in Los Angeles.	Henry Bonilla is elected as the first Republican Hispanic American to serve in Congress from Texas.	Ben Nighthorse Campbell of Colorado is elected as a Democrat to the U.S. Senate.
1993	Democrat Carol Moseley-Braun of Illinois becomes the first black woman senator.		Norma Contu is appointed assistant secretary for civil rights in the Department of Education.	The International Year of Indigenous People is proclaimed. Ada Deer becomes first Native American woman to serve as assistant secretary of Indian affairs.
1994		March Fong Eu is appointed ambassador to Micronesia.	California's Proposition 187 bars undocumented immigrants from receiving public education, welfare, and Medicaid.	The Walk for Justice is staged to draw attention to Native American issues.

Date	Blacks	Asian Americans	Latinos	Native Americans
1995				Wilma Mankiller, chief of the Cherokee Nation of Oklahoma since 1985, resigns her post citing health concerns.
1996	Alexis Herman is nominated as secretary of labor in the second Clinton administration.	The Clinton reelection campaign is tied to illegal Chinese money.	The Hispanic Walk for Justice has 100,000 marchers calling for immigration reform, affirmative action, welfare, and other programs.	
1997	David Satcher is nominated by President Bill Clinton for the post of surgeon general.	Bill Lan Lee is appointed on an acting basis to head the Justice Department's Division of Civil Rights.	Loretta Sanchez becomes the first Mexican American congresswoman from California.	Ada Deer, assistant secretary for Indian affairs, resigns her post.
1998	Anthony Williams is elected mayor of Washington, D.C.	Matt Fong, son of March Fong Eu, is unsuccessful in his bid for the U.S. Senate in California.	Republican Governor George W. Bush of Texas is reelected with widespread support from Hispanic voters.	

Index

by Virgil Diodato

Note: This is the index to both volumes of the *Encyclopedia*. Pages 1–398 are found in Volume 1, and pages 399–774 are found in Volume 2. Boldface page references refer to major entries. Illustrations are indicated by "illus."

AIRFA. *See* American Indian Religious Freedom Act

Aiso, John, **241**

Akaka, Daniel K., **241–42,** 302

Akwesasne Notes (periodical), **581,** 657

Alabama Christian Movement for Human Rights (ACMHR), 30

Alabama Democratic Conference (ADC), **23**

Al-Amin, Jamil Abdullah, 35. *See also* Brown, H. "Rap"

Alamo, **416,** 416 (illus.), 519, 547–48

Alarcon, Arthur L., **416**

Alaska Allotment Act of 1906, **581–82**

Alaska Coalition, 733

Alaska Federation of Natives (AFN), **582,** 629, 733

Alaska Native Brotherhood (ANB), **582**

Alaska Native Claims Settlement Act of 1971 (ANCSA), 576, **582**

Alaska Native Reorganization Act of 1936, **582–83**

Alaska Native Sisterhood (ANS), 582

Alaska natives. *See* Native Alaskans

Alatorre, Richard, **416**

Albany Plan, **583**

Albermarle Paper Co. v. Moody, **23**

Albert, Carl, 295

Albizu Campos, Pedro, **416–17,** 451

Albuquerque walkout, **417**

Alcatraz Island occupation, **583,** 665, 679, 705, 707

Alcea Band. See United States v. Alcea Band of Tillamooks

Alcoholism, **583–84,** 636, 640

Aleuts, 77. *See also* Native Alaskans

Alexander, Clifford L., Jr., **23**

Alexander, Raymond Pace, **23–24**

Alexander, Robert, 144

Alexander, Sadie Tanner Mossell, 23, **24**

Alexander v. Holmes County Board of Education, **24**

Alexander VI (pope), 573

Ali, Muhammad, 145, 177

Alianza Federal de Mercedes, 478, 500, 519

Alianza Federal de Pueblos Libres, **417,** 451, 478, 500, 519

Alianza Hispano-Americana, **417,** 435, 492

Alien Land Act of 1920, **242,** 273, 303, 307, 326, 334–35, 360–61. *See also* California Alien Land Act of 1913

Alien land laws, **242,** 339

Alinsky, Saul, **417,** 435

ALL. *See* American Loyalty League

All-African Peoples Revolutionary Party, 39

All-American Girl (television sitcom), 261

All Chinatown Anti-Japanese Patriotic Organization, 258

"All deliberate speed," **24**

All Indian Pueblo Council, 733

Allegiance, Declaration of, 608–9

Allegiance questionnaire, **304–5,** 316, 328

Allen, Elise, **585**

Allen, Richard, **24,** 76, 125, 143

Allen v. Board of Elections, **25**

Allen v. NAACP. See NAACP v. Allen

Allen, William Barclay, **24**

Allende, Salvador, 523

Alliance for Progress, 461, 523

Alliance of Asian Pacific Labor (AAPL), **242**

Alliance of Minority Women for Business and Political Development, 209

Allotment, **585,** 608, 616, 637, 714. *See also* Alaska Allotment Act of 1906; Dawes Act of 1887

Allwright. See Smith v. Allwright

Alpha Suffrage Club (ASC), **25**

Alu Like, 314

Alurista, 493

Alvarez, Everett, Jr., **418**

Alvarez-Martinez, Luz, **418**

AMA. *See* American Missionary Association

Amalgamated Clothing Workers of America, 455, 456

Amathla, Charley, 667

AME Church. *See* African Methodist Episcopal Church

Amendment of 1884, **242**

Amerasian Homecoming Act of 1987, **242–43,** 346

AmerAsian League, 313

America Is in the Heart (book), 254

American Anti-Slavery Society, **25,** 25 (illus.)

American Association for Affirmative Action, 209

American Association of Blacks in Energy, 209

American Association of Retired Persons (AARP), 185

American Baptist Black Caucus, 209–10

American Citizens for Justice, **243,** 364

American Civic Association, 210

American Civil Liberties Union (ACLU), 77, 122, 210, 427, 604

American Civil Liberties Union Foundation, 210

American Colonization Society, **25,** 54, 79, 91, 146, 170

American Coordinating Council on Political Education, **418,** 435

American Council for Free Asia, 364

American Council of Spanish-Speaking People, **418**

American Federation of Teachers (AFT), 431

American Friends Service Committee, 733

American G.I. Forum of the United States, **418,** 441, 444–45, 460, 482, 526, 558

American G.I. Forum Women, 558

American Horse, **585,** 585 (illus.)

American Immigration Lawyers Association, 364

American Independent Party (AIP), **25–26,** 165

American Indian Affairs Association Education Conference, **585–86**

"American Indian," as name, semantics of, 572–73

American Indian Chicago Conference (AICC), **586,** 655

American Indian Culture Research Center, 733

American Indian Defense Association (AIDA), **586,** 592, 600

American Indian Development Centers, 111

American Indian Graduate Center, 733

American Indian Health Care Association, 733

American Indian Heritage Foundation, 733–34

American Indian Higher Education Consortium, 734

American Indian Institute, 734

American Indian Law Center, 734

American Indian Liberation Crusade, 734

American Indian Movement (AIM), 570, **586,** 606, 613, 629, 679, 734. *See also* Red Power

noted individuals in, 572, 586, 590, 592, 655, 669, 690, 705

protests by, 583, 586, 651, 673, 698, 716

American Indian National Bank, 666

American Indian Opportunities Industrialization Centers, 592

American Indian Policy Review Commission, **586–87**

American Indian Press Association, 715

American Indian Religious Freedom Act (AIRFA), 575, **587,** 651, 667, 679. *See also* Religious freedom

American Indian Ritual Object Reparation Foundation, 734

American Indians. *See* Native Americans

American Institute for Economic Development, 210

American Legion, 303

American Loyalty League (ALL), **243,** 339. *See also* Japanese American Citizens League

American Missionary Association (AMA), **26**

American Missionary (periodical), 26

American Muslim Mission, 145. *See also* Nation of Islam

American Negro Academy, **26,** 54

American Party, 26. *See also* American Independent Party

American Political Science Association, 37

American Revolution

African Americans, 27, 77, 154

Native Americans, **587–88,** 593, 619, 620, 628, 634, 658, 678, 701–02

American Tobacco Company v. Patterson, **26**

Americanization. *See also* Assimilation; Citizenship

Hispanic Americans, 408–9, 453–54, 475, 506

Native Americans, 592

Americans Betrayed (book), 230, 291

Americans for Indian Opportunity, 628, 690, 734

Americans with Disabilities Act, 63, 240

Americas, the, and Native Americans, 572

Amherst, Jeffrey, 674

Amistad case, 26

Amos. See Hadnot et al. v. Amos

Anaya, Tony, **418–19**

ANB. *See* Alaska Native Brotherhood

ANCSA. *See* Alaska Native Claims Settlement Act of 1971
Anderson, Owanah, **588**
Anderson, Reuben V., **26**
Anderson, Wallace "Mad Bear," 705
Angel Island, **243,** 243 (illus.), 301
Angell, James B., 243
Angell Treaty of 1880, **243**
Anglo-Saxonism, 6–7
Anguiano, Lupe, **419**
Annexation of Hawaii, 241–42, **244,** 261, 291, 301, 303, 318
ANS. *See* Alaska Native Sisterhood
Anthony, Susan B., 169
Anti-Asian Committee, 303
Anti-Chinese Union, 244
Anti-Coolie clubs, **244**
Anti-Coolie League, 263
Antidraft movement, 269
Anti-lynching crusade, 90
Anti-lynching legislation, 10, **26,** 93
Antimiscegenation laws, 104, **244–45.** *See also* Interracial marriage
Anti-Semitism, 62, 73, 99, 154
Anti-slavery movement. *See* Abolitionist movement
Anti-Vagrancy Act, **426–27**
Antoine v. Washington, 631
Antonio Maceo Brigade, 429
Aoki, Daniel T., **245**
Apache Wars, 597
APALA. *See* Asian Pacific American Labor Alliance
Apartheid, 155. *See also* South Africa
Apess, William, **588,** 691
Apodaca, Jerry, **419**
Apologies
    for enslavement of blacks, 147
    for internment of Japanese, 260, 292
    for overthrow of Hawaiian monarchy, 260, 292
Appeal to the Colored Citizens of the World, An (pamphlet), 8, 180
Application of Andy (court case), 675
Apportionment. *See* Reapportionment; Redistricting
Appropriation Act of 1799, **588**
Aquash, Anna Mae Pictou, **588**
Aquino, Benigno, 231
Aquino, Ninoy M., 345
Aragon, Manuel, **419**
Aramaki, Reverend, 278
Arbens, Jacobo, 523
Archaeological Resources Protection Act of 1979 (ARPA), **588.** *See also* Burial sites
Archer, Dennis, **26**
Archuleta, Diego, **419**
Argall, Samuel, 672
Argentina, 524
Arguelles, John A., **419**
Arias, Oscar, 524
Arikaree, Battle of the, 683
Aristotle, 22, 672
Ariyoshi, George, 229, **245**
Arizona v. California, **588–89,** 600

Armigo, Manuel, **419**
Arnold. See Rice v. Arnold
Aronson, Arnold, 100
ARPA. *See* Archaeological Resources Protection Act of 1979
Arrow (Americans for Restitution and Righting of Old Wrongs), 734
Arthur, Claudeen Bates, **589**
Articles of Confederation, **589,** 609, 700
Artifacts, protection needed for, 575, 606, 649, 680
Asakura v. City of Seattle et al., **245**
ASC. *See* Alpha Suffrage Club
Asia Foundation, The, 364
Asia Resource Center, 364
Asian American Center for Justice of the American Citizens for Justice, 364
Asian American Curriculum Project, 278, 364
Asian American Free Labor Institute, 365
Asian American Legal Defense and Education Fund, 313, 365
Asian American Manufacturers Association, 365
Asian American movement, **245–46**
Asian American Political Coalition, **246**
Asian American Professional Women, 315
Asian American Voters Coalition, 248
Asian Americans, 229–373
    growth and diversity, 229, 231–33, 323
    homeland issues, 230, 231, 234
    intergroup relations, 142, **246–50,** 304
    trends, 233–35
Asian Americans for Community Involvement, **250**
Asian Americans for Equal Employment, 250
Asian Americans for Equality (AAFE), **250,** 258
Asian and Pacific Islander American Health Forum, 365
Asian Business League of San Francisco, 365
Asian Indian Americans, 231, 232, 234. *See also* Asian Americans
    Asiatic Exclusion League, 251–52
    Barred Zone Act of 1917, 342
    Indian Immigration Act of 1946, 305
Asian Indian Chamber of Commerce, 365
Asian Indian Women in America, 365
Asian Law Alliance, **250**
Asian Law Caucus, **251,** 276, 280, 308
Asian Lesbians of the East Coast, 256. *See also* Gay Asian Pacific Alliance; Homosexual rights
Asian Pacific American Labor Alliance (APALA), **251**
Asian Pacific American Legal Center of Southern California, **251**
Asian Pacific American Policy Institute, 300
Asian Pacific American Political Affairs, 351
Asian Pacific Democratic Club, **251**
Asian/Pacific Islander Law Students Association, 365
Asian Pacific Legal Center of Southern California, 234
Asian/Pacific Women's Network, **251**

Asian Political Scientists Group in USA, 365–66
Asian Resources, 366
Asian Watch Committee, 366
Asian Women United, **251**
Asian Women's Shelter, 306
Asiatic Exclusion Act of 1924, 348
Asiatic Exclusion League, **251–52,** 253, 333
Asociacion Nacional Pro Personas Mayores, 558
ASPIRA, **419–20,** 429, 499, 558
Assembly centers, **252,** 260, 264, 267, 268, 275, 297, 347. *See also* Internment camps/relocation centers
Assembly of First Nations National Indian Brotherhood, 734
Assimilation. *See also* Acculturation; Cultural nationalism; Termination policy
    African Americans, 156, 157
    Hispanic Americans, 402, **420,** 432, 441, 450, 454, 475, 480, 506
    integration as, 156, 157
    Native Americans, 572, 577, 585, 589, 602, 603, 608, 610, 613, 620–21, 626, 713
Assimilationist policy, **589,** 631
Associated Farmers of California, 241, 342
Association for Asian American Studies, 366
Association for Multicultural Counseling and Development, 210
Association for the Study of Afro American Life and History, 210
Association for the Study of Negro Life and History, 29
Association of African American People's Legal Council, 210
Association of American Indian Affairs, 735
Association of Asian Indians in America, 366
Association of Asian/Pacific American Artists, 366
Association of Asian/Pacific Community Health Organizations, 366
Association of Black Catholics Against Abortion, 210
Association of Community Organizations for Reform Now (ACORN), 176
Association of Community Tribal Schools, 735
Association of Hispanic Arts, 558
Association of Immigration Attorneys, 366
Association of Indian Muslims of America, 366
Association of Indians in America, **252**
Association of Korean Political Studies in North America, **252**
Association of Urban Universities, 210
At-large districts, **27**
At-large voting systems, 27, 40, 61, 75–76, 129, 526
"Atlanta Compromise Address," **27,** 49
Atlanta Enquirer (newspaper), 87
Atlanta Negro Voters League, 39
Attucks, Crispus, **27**
Austin, Moses, 519

private discrimination, 142
procedural due process, 161
public accommodations, 80, 108, 127
reapportionment, 158
voting, 28, 34, 83, 104, 160
Fourth Amendment, 632
Fourth World, The (book), 654
FPC. *See* Fair Play Committee
France, 346, 523, 621–22, 645, 646, 651
Frank, Billy, Jr., **621**
Frank McNiel et al. v. Springfield Park District, **75–76**
Frankfurter, Felix, 508
Franklin, Benjamin, 285, 570, 669
Franklin, John Hope, 116
Franks, Gary A., 50, **76**
Fraternal Council of Negro Churches, 144
Frazier, E. Franklin, 30
Frazier, Johnnie, 76
Frazier v. North Carolina, **76**
Frederick Douglass's Paper (newspaper), 64, 121
Free Africa Society, 24, **76,** 94
Free African Liberation Organization African Liberation Movement, 214
Free exercise clause, 667, 679
Free Federation of Puerto Rican Workers, 469
Free Hindustan, 264
Free Pacific Association, 368
Free South Africa movement, 168
Free Speech (newspaper), 186
Freedmen's Aid Society, **76**
Freedmen's Bureau, 26, **76,** 141, 156, 170
"Freedom from Want" (essay), 254
Freedom riders, 44, 49, 101, 163
Freedom's Journal (newspaper), 52, **76–77,** 152, 194–95
Freeman, Jo, 132, 133
Freeman v. Pitts, **77**
Fremont, John C., 489
French and Indian War, 583, **621–22**
Freneau, Philip, 711
Frick, Raymond L., 272
Frick v. Webb, **272**
Friends of India Society International, 368
Friends of the Indian, **622**
Frye, Henry E., **77**
Fugitive Slave Act (1793), 8, **77**
Fugitive Slave Act (1850), 9, **77**
Fugitive slave clause, 9
Fujii Sei v. State of California, **272,** 307
Fujii v. United States, 338
Fukuyama, Francis, **272**
Fulani, Lenora, **77**
Full Employment and Balanced Growth Act of 1978, 85, **88**
Fullilove v. Klutznick, **77**
Furman v. Georgia, **77–78**
"Fus Fixico" letters, 674
Fuste, Jose Antonio, **458**
Fuster, Jamie B., **458**

Gadsden, James, 459, 623
Gadsden Purchase, **623**
Gadsden Treaty, **459,** 548–50

Gaines, Lloyd, 111
Galarza, Ernesto, **459,** 481
Gall, **623,** 623 (illus.)
Gallegos, Jose Manuel, **459,** 497
Gambia, 51
Game theory, 47
Gaming, 570–71, **623–25,** 634
court cases, 596, 623, 624, 681, 688
legislation, 598, 623–24
Gamson, William, 47
Gandhi, Mohandas K., 98, 190
Gang Prevention and Youth Recreation Act, 182
Gangs, 182, **459–60,** 533
Gantt, Harvey, **79**
GAPA. *See* Gay Asian Pacific Alliance
Garcia, Chris, 422, 444
Garcia, Hector, **460,** 526
Garcia, Hippolito Frank, **460**
Garcia, Jesus G., **460**
Garcia, Robert, 69, **460–61,** 515
Garfield, James R., 601
Garner, Edward, 165
Garner Standard, 165
Garner, William, 173
Garnet, Henry Highland, **79,** 119
Garrison, William Lloyd, 25, 103
Garvey, Marcus, 31, 32, **79,** 91, 117, 125, 144, 157, 174
Garza, Ben, Jr., **461,** 479
Garza, Emilio M., **461**
Garza, Reynaldo, **461**
Garza v. County of Los Angeles, 530
Gaston County, North Carolina v. United States, **80**
Gates, Merrill E., 647
Gay Asian Pacific Alliance (GAPA), 307. *See also* Asian Lesbians of the East Coast
Gay rights, 24, 598
Gayanashagowa, 723–24
Gayle v. Browder, **80**
Geary Act of 1892, 271, **273,** 280, 308, 349
General Allotment Act. *See* Dawes Act of 1887
General Citizenship Act of 1924, 614, 621, **625,** 638
General Deficiency Appropriation Account Act of 1904, **273**
Gentlemen's Agreement, 255, **273–74,** 280, 281, 285, 292
George III (king), 5
Georgia v. United States, **80**
Gephard, Richard, 425
Germ warfare, 674
Germany, 534
Geronimo, 597, 598, **625,** 711
Gerry, Elbridge, 137, 508
Gerrymandering, 508, 529. *See also* Racial gerrymandering
Gesta de Jayuya, 417
Ghadar Revolutionary Party, **274**
Ghana, 32, 65, 188
Ghent, Treaty of, 633, **700,** 701
Ghettos, 11, 132, 176

Ghost Dance movement, 592, 605, **625–26,** 630, 671, 678, 689, 716, 717
GI Bill of Rights, 460
G.I. Forum, American. *See* American G.I. Forum of the United States
Giago, Tim, **626**
Gibson, Kenneth Allen, **80**
Gibson, William F., **80**
Gideon v. Wainwright, 132
Gierbolini, Gilberto, **461**
Gil, Federico, 523
Gilbert, Madonna, 715
Gillespie, Arlene F., **461**
Gingles. See Thornburg v. Gingles
Gladstone Realtors v. Village of Bellwood, **80**
Glass ceiling, 63, 246, 247
Glass Ceiling Commission, 63
Glazer, Nathan, 311
Gold rush, **626**
Goldwater, Barry, 129, 148, 149
Gomez, Rudolph, 420
Gompers, Samuel, 469
Gong Lum et al. v. Rice et al., **274**
Gonzales, Rodolfo "Corky," 417, 432, 440, 441, 451, **461,** 477, 493, 504
Gonzales, Stephanie, **462**
Gonzalez, Charles A., 462
Gonzalez, Henry Babosa, 462 (illus.), **462,** 502
Gonzalez Parsons, Lucia, 499
Good Cause, 80
Good Fight, The (book), 40
Good Neighbor policy, 523
Goode, W. Wilson, **80–81**
Government contracts. *See* Contracts, government
Goyahkla, 625. *See also* Geronimo
Gradual Civilization Act of 1857, **626**
Graham v. Richardson, **462**
Gramm, Phil, 274
Gramm, Wendy Lee, **274**
Grand Council of Hispanic Societies in Public Service, 559
Grandfather clauses, 10, **81,** 82, 100, 104, 528
Granger, Lester B., **81**
Grant, Ulysses S., 76, 593, 626, 668, 679, 686, 713
Grant's Peace Policy, **626–27**
Grape boycott, **462–63**
Grape pickers strike, 430, 462
Grave sites. *See* Burial sites
Gray et al. v. Board of Trustees of the University of Tennessee et al., **81**
Gray, William H., III, **81**
Great Binding Law, 723–24
Great Britain, 651, 670, 674, 683, 695
American Revolution, 620, 634, 657–58, 690
Anglo-Saxonism, 6, 7
France and, in North America, 621–22, 645–46, 677
Jay's Treaty, 641
War of 1812, 700, 701, 712
Great Depression, 58, 132, 147, 148, 184, 285, 308, 339, 519

Murray, George Washington, **115**
Murray, Hugh Campbell, 321
Musgrove, Mary, **659**
Muslim Mosque, Inc., 106
Muslims, Black. *See* Black Muslims
Mutual aid societies, 422, 435, **492**
Mutual Assistance Society, 295, 296, **312,** 342
My Bondage and My Freedom, 64
Myer, Dillon S., 267, 347
Myers, Polly Anne, 104

Naachid ceremony, 663
NAACP Legal Defense and Education Fund,
    Inc. (LDF), 23, 36, 43, 51, 66, 94, 107,
    116, 215
NAACP v. Alabama ex. Rel. Flowers, 113
NAACP v. Allen, **116**
Nabrit, James Madison, Jr., **116,** 158 (illus.)
NACCS. *See* National Association for
    Chicana and Chicano Studies
NACW. *See* National Association of Colored
    Women
NAFTA. *See* North American Free Trade
    Agreement
Nagle, John D., 256
NAGPRA. *See* Native American Graves Pro-
    tection and Repatriation Act of 1990
Naim Ham Say, 313
NAIM: North American Indian Ministries,
    737
Naim, Ruby Elaine, 313
Naim v. Naim, **313**
Nakai, Raymond, **660**
Nakanishi, Don, 308
NALEO. *See* National Association of Latino
    Elected and Appointed Officials
NAPALC. *See* National Asian Pacific Ameri-
    can Legal Consortium
Napoleon, 649
Narbona, 654, 663
NARF. *See* Native American Rights Fund
Narragansett massacre, 575
Narrative of Frederick Douglass, 64
Nash, Diane, 101
Nash, Gary, 8
Nash, Philip Tajitsu, **313**
Nashville Student movement, 101
Natal, colony of, 146
Natchez Revolt, **660**
Nation of Islam, 32, 72, 73, 106, 111, 114,
    116–17, 145, 146, 157, 205–07
National Advisory Council for South Asian
    Affairs, 369
National African American Summit, 39
National Afro-American Council, 75
National Afro-American League, 75
National Alliance against Racist and Political
    Repression, 369
National Alliance of Black Organizations, 215
National Alliance of Black School Educators,
    215
National Alliance of Spanish-Speaking People
    for Equality, 561
National American Indian Court Clerks Asso-
    ciation, 738

National American Indian Housing Council,
    738
National Asian Pacific American Association,
    277
National Asian Pacific American Bar Associa-
    tion, **313,** 354
National Asian Pacific American Law Stu-
    dents Association, 313
National Asian Pacific American Legal Con-
    sortium (NAPALC), **313**
National Asian Pacific Center on Aging, 369
National Asian Women's Network, 277
National Association for Asian and Pacific
    American Education, 369
National Association for Black Veterans, 215
National Association for Chicana and Chicano
    Studies (NACCS), 491, **493,** 516, 561
National Association for Chicano Studies, 493
National Association for Equal Opportunity in
    Higher Education, 216
National Association for Native American
    Children of Alcoholics, 738
National Association for the Advancement of
    Black Americans in Vocational Educa-
    tion, 216
National Association for the Advancement of
    Colored People (NAACP), 78, 82, 113,
    117, 135, 216, 661
  anti-lynching legislation and, 26
  noted individuals in, 39, 65, 70, 72, 80, 84,
    88, 93, 94, 95, 110, 121, 160, 165,
    182, 183, 186, 187, 188
  publication of, 54
  school desegregation cases, 11, 24, 36, 43,
    157
National Association for the Education and
    Advancement of Cambodian, Laotian,
    and Vietnamese Americans, 369
National Association for the Hispanic Elderly,
    477
National Association of Americans of Asian
    Indian Descent, 369
National Association of Asian American Pro-
    fessionals, 369
National Association of Black County Offi-
    cials, 216
National Association of Black Women Attor-
    neys, 216
National Association of Blacks in Criminal
    Justice, 216
National Association of Blacks within Gov-
    ernment, 216
National Association of Colored Women
    (NACW), 29, 90, **117,** 118, 165
National Association of Cuban-American
    Women, **493**
National Association of Hispanic Federal Ex-
    ecutives, 561
National Association of Human Rights Work-
    ers, 369–70
National Association of Latino Elected and
    Appointed Officials (NALEO), 408, 416,
    452, **493,** 561
National Association of Medical Minority
    Educators, 370

National Association of Minority Political
    Women, 370
National Association of Negro Business and
    Professional Women's Clubs, 216
National Association of Puerto Rican His-
    panic Social Workers, 562
National Association of State Universities and
    Land Grant Colleges, 216
National Baptist Convention, 50, 144
National Black Caucus of Local Elected Offi-
    cials, 216–17
National Black Caucus of State Legislators,
    217
National Black Child Development Institute,
    217
National Black Election Study (NBES), **117**
National Black Law Student Association, 217
National Black Leadership Roundtable, 217
National Black on Black Love Campaign, 217
National Black Republican Council, 217
National Black Sisters' Conference, 217
National Black Survival Fund, 217
National Black United Front, 32, 217
National Black United Fund, 218
National Black Women's Consciousness Rais-
    ing Association, 218
National Black Women's Political Leadership
    Caucus, 218
National Black Youth Leadership, 218
National Business League, 218
National Caucus and Center on Black Aged,
    218
National Center for American Indian and
    Alaskan Native Health Research, 738
National Center for American Indian Enter-
    prise Development, 738
National Center for Urban Environmental
    Studies, 218
National Center for Urban Ethnic Affairs, 370
National Chicano Moratorium Committee,
    431, 432
National Chicano Youth Liberation Confer-
    ence, 481, **493–94**
National Chinese Welfare Council, **314**
National Coalition for Indian Education, 738
National Coalition for Quality Integrated Edu-
    cation, 218
National Coalition for Redress and Repara-
    tions, 317
National Coalition of Blacks for Reparations
    in America (N'COBRA), 147, 218–19
National Coalition of Hispanic Health and
    Human Services, 444
National Coalition on Black Voter Participa-
    tion, 32, **117–18,** 123, 219
National Coalition to End Racism in
    America's Child Care System, 219
National Committee for Redress, **314,** 317,
    329, 344
National Concilio of America, 562
National Conference of Black Christians,
    144–45
National Conference of Black Lawyers, 219
National Conference of Black Mayors, 219

Index